Qualitative approaches to research on plurilingual education

Enfocaments qualitatius per a la recerca en educació plurilingüe

Enfoques cualitativos para la investigación en educación plurilingüe

Editors / Editores / Editoras

Emilee Moore, Melinda Dooly

Published by Research-publishing.net, not-for-profit association
Dublin, Ireland; Voillans, France, info@research-publishing.net

© 2017 by Editors (collective work)
© 2017 by Authors (individual work)

Qualitative approaches to research on plurilingual education (English)
Enfocaments qualitatius per a la recerca en educació plurilingüe (Catalan)
Enfoques cualitativos para la investigación en educación plurilingüe (Spanish)

Edited by Emilee Moore and Melinda Dooly

Rights: This volume is published under the Attribution-NonCommercial-NoDerivatives (CC BY-NC-ND) licence; individual articles may have a different licence. Under the CC BY-NC-ND licence, the volume is freely available online (https://doi.org/10.14705/rpnet.2017.emmd2016.9781908416476) for anybody to read, download, copy, and redistribute provided that the author(s), editorial team, and publisher are properly cited. Commercial use and derivative works are, however, not permitted.

Disclaimer: Research-publishing.net does not take any responsibility for the content of the pages written by the authors of this book. The authors have recognised that the work described was not published before, or that it was not under consideration for publication elsewhere. While the information in this book are believed to be true and accurate on the date of its going to press, neither the editorial team, nor the publisher can accept any legal responsibility for any errors or omissions that may be made. The publisher makes no warranty, expressed or implied, with respect to the material contained herein. While Research-publishing.net is committed to publishing works of integrity, the words are the authors' alone.

Trademark notice: product or corporate names may be trademarks or registered trademarks, and are used only for identification and explanation without intent to infringe.

Copyrighted material: every effort has been made by the editorial team to trace copyright holders and to obtain their permission for the use of copyrighted material in this book. In the event of errors or omissions, please notify the publisher of any corrections that will need to be incorporated in future editions of this book.

Typeset by Research-publishing.net
Cover design and cover photos by © Raphaël Savina (raphael@savina.net)

ISBN13: 978-1-908416-46-9 (Paperback - Print on demand, black and white)
Print on demand technology is a high-quality, innovative and ecological printing method; with which the book is never 'out of stock' or 'out of print'.
ISBN13: 978-1-908416-47-6 (Ebook, PDF, colour)
ISBN13: 978-1-908416-48-3 (Ebook, EPUB, colour)

Legal deposit, Ireland: The National Library of Ireland, The Library of Trinity College, The Library of the University of Limerick, The Library of Dublin City University, The Library of NUI Cork, The Library of NUI Maynooth, The Library of University College Dublin, The Library of NUI Galway.
Legal deposit, United Kingdom: The British Library.
British Library Cataloguing-in-Publication Data.
A cataloguing record for this book is available from the British Library.
Legal deposit, France: Bibliothèque Nationale de France - Dépôt légal: March 2017.

Table of contents
Índex de continguts
Índice de contenidos

vi   Collaborators
        Col·laboradores i col·laboradors
        Colaboradoras y colaboradores

xiv   Prólogo
xviii   Prologue
        Amparo Tusón Valls

1   Introduction: qualitative approaches to research on plurilingual education
11   Introducció: enfocaments qualitatius per a la recerca en educació plurilingüe
        Melinda Dooly, Emilee Moore

Section 1 - Secció 1 - Sección 1

23   Investigar con docentes
46   Doing research with teachers
        Luci Nussbaum

69   Investigar las propias prácticas docentes a través de la investigación-acción
88   Investigating one's own teaching practices using action research
        Xavier Pascual

107   Producir conocimiento sobre el plurilingüismo junto a jóvenes estudiantes: un reto para la etnografía en colaboración
129   Producing knowledge about plurilingualism with young students: a challenge for collaborative ethnography
        Virginia Unamuno, Adriana Patiño

Table of contents, Índex de continguts, Índice de contenidos

151 Un acercamiento etnográfico al estudio de las variedades lingüísticas de jóvenes latinoamericanos en Barcelona
170 An ethnographic approach to the study of linguistic varieties used by young Latin Americans in Barcelona
Víctor Corona

189 A Mediated Discourse Analysis (MDA) approach to multimodal data
212 Una aproximació a dades multimodals amb l'anàlisi del discurs mediat
Melinda Dooly

237 Educational ethnography in blended learning environments
264 Etnografia educativa en contextos d'aprenentatge mixt
Victoria Antoniadou, Melinda Dooly

293 L'anàlisi de la conversa al servei de la recerca en el camp de l'adquisició de segones llengües (CA-for-SLA)
321 Conversation analysis at the service of research in the field of second language acquisition (CA-for-SLA)
Dolors Masats

Section 2 - Secció 2 - Sección 2

351 Research ethics
363 Ética de la investigación
Melinda Dooly, Emilee Moore, Claudia Vallejo

377 Instruments per a la recollida de dades
390 Instruments for gathering data
Laia Canals

403 Collecting, transcribing, analyzing and presenting plurilingual interactional data
418 Recoger, transcribir, analizar y presentar datos interaccionales plurilingües
Emilee Moore, Júlia Llompart

435 Collecting, organizing and analyzing multimodal data sets: the contributions of CAQDAS
451 Recoger, organizar y analizar corpus de datos multimodales: las contribuciones de los CAQDAS
Victoria Antoniadou

469 Com s'escriu un text de recerca?
483 How to write a research paper
Eulàlia Borràs

497 Epíleg
501 Epilogue
Artur Noguerol

505 Author index
Índex d'autores i autors
Índice de autoras y autores

Collaborators
Col·laboradores i col·laboradors
Colaboradoras y colaboradores

Editors / Editores / Editoras

Melinda Dooly holds a Serra Húnter fellowship as researcher and senior lecturer in the Department of Language, Literature and Social Science Education at the Universitat Autònoma de Barcelona. She teaches English as a Foreign Language Methodology (TEFL) and research methods courses, focusing on telecollaboration in education at both undergraduate and graduate levels. She has taught on short-term stays in different countries worldwide, including an honorary lectureship at the Institute of Education University College London. Her principal research addresses technology-enhanced project-based language learning and 21st century competences in teacher education. She has published widely in international journals and authored chapters and books in this area of study. She is co-editor of the book series Telecollaboration in Education (Peter Lang). Her current research interest is in project-based telecollaborative language learning and very young learners. She currently leads the GREIP research group.

Emilee Moore holds a Serra Húnter fellowship as researcher and lecturer in the Department of Language, Literature and Social Science Education at the Universitat Autònoma de Barcelona. She was visiting postdoctoral researcher in the School of Education as part of the Beatriu Pinós program (Generalitat de Catalunya) and tutor in the School of Languages, Cultures and Societies at the University of Leeds from 2015 to 2017. Most of her teaching has contributed to the development of teachers for plurilingual preschool, primary, secondary and tertiary education. She studies meaning-making practices in multilingual and multicultural, formal and non-formal educational contexts, integrating approaches from linguistic ethnography, the study of interaction and sociocultural learning theories. She has participated in several large, Spanish, UK and European research projects, and a number of smaller teaching innovation and socio-educational projects and published widely in international journals and books.

Collaborators, col·laboradores i col·laboradors, colaboradoras y colaboradores

Authors / Autores i autors / Autoras y autores

Victoria Antoniadou is a Ph.D. graduate from the Department of Language, Literature and Social Science Education at the Universitat Autònoma de Barcelona. Her research and publications focus on the use of telecollaboration in Initial Teacher Education and ethnographic methods for tracing teacher learning in multi-sited, multimodal learning environments. She is interested in the pedagogical uses of computer-mediated communication and the ways they can potentiate cross-border, collaborative and learning-laden interactions. She has participated in EU-funded projects. She has taught English as a foreign language to dentistry students at the Universitat Internacional de Catalunya, as well as methods for teaching English to young learners at the European University of Cyprus. She currently teaches English as a foreign language to young learners and adults in Cyprus, and provides interpreting and teaching coordination services to the University of Nicosia Medical School implementing the St. George's Problem-Based Learning program. She also collaborates with healthcare organizations in Cyprus on the introduction of telecollaboration in patient-centered care.

Eulàlia Borràs és doctora pel Departament de Didàctica de la Llengua i la Literatura, i de les Ciències Socials de la Universitat Autònoma de Barcelona. Exerceix com a professora a l'Escola d'Enginyeria d'Igualada (UPC), on imparteix classes de comunicació oral i escrita per a enginyers. La seva recerca explora la gestió de la classe multilingüe i les relacions entre les polítiques universitàries i els usos lingüístics a la universitat. La seva tesi doctoral aborda, des d'un punt de vista etnogràfic i etnometodològic, la introducció de l'aprenentatge integrat de continguts i llengua estrangera (AICLE) a la universitat en matèries de ciències i d'enginyeria. Actualment s'interessa pel treball en grups plurilingües en l'àmbit educatiu i en el laboral, així com per la gestió de la multimodalitat i la interculturalitat en aquests entorns multilingües.

Laia Canals és professora associada del Departament de Didàctica de la Llengua i la Literatura, i de les Ciències Socials de la Universitat Autònoma de Barcelona. Dóna classes de didàctica de la llengua i acollida lingüística en el Grau d'Educació Primària de la UAB i coordina cursos avançats de llengua

Collaborators, col·laboradores i col·laboradors, colaboradoras y colaboradores

anglesa a la Universitat Oberta de Catalunya. Les seves línies d'investigació inclouen l'adquisició de segones llengües per part d'estudiants d'origen estranger, l'ensenyament i aprenentatge d'idiomes assistits per ordinador o mitjançant l'ús de les TIC i la formació de professorat per desenvolupar les seves pràctiques docents en els contextos esmentats.

Víctor Corona obtuvo un doctorado en Didáctica de la Lengua y la Literatura en la Universitat Autònoma de Barcelona en 2012, donde también impartió cursos de metodología etnográfica, sociolingüística y educación plurilingüe. Después, realizó una estancia de 7 meses en el Instituto de Investigación y Desarrollo Educativo (Baja California, México) en el 2014 como investigador invitado. Se incorporó como investigador postdoctoral al laboratorio ICAR de la Escuela Normal Superior de Lyon (Francia) en enero de 2015. Ha impartido clases de sociolingüística en la Universidad Lyon 2 y en Paris V Descartes, La Sorbonne. Su investigación actual se interesa en las prácticas lingüísticas de estudiantes de formación profesional en escuelas de mecánica automotriz. Su interés de investigación se relaciona con la lingüística de la interacción, el contacto de lenguas, y la construcción identitaria de los jóvenes en relación con las estilizaciones lingüísticas y discursos sociales.

Júlia Llompart és doctora pel Departament de Didàctica de la Llengua i la Literatura, i de les Ciències Socials de la Universitat Autònoma de Barcelona. Va defensar la seva tesi doctoral en l'àmbit de la didàctica de les llengües i la sociolingüística educativa. És llicenciada en Traducció i Interpretació (català, anglès i àrab), però, va encaminar la seva formació posterior cap a la didàctica de les llengües. Ha participat en diversos projectes nacionals i internacionals. D'altra banda, ha estat professora a primària, secundària i a l'ensenyament superior. Va ser directora de la unitat de Catalan Studies i professora lectora de llengua i cultura catalanes (2009-2011) i professora lectora d'espanyol (2012-2013) a la Universitat de Massachusetts, Amherst, EUA. Actualment compagina la tasca docent a la UAB amb l'activitat investigadora.

Dolors Masats is a teacher trainer and researcher at the Universitat Autònoma de Barcelona. She got a BA in English Language and Literature and a Ph.D. in

Collaborators, col·laboradores i col·laboradors, colaboradoras y colaboradores

Educational Sciences from the same university. She is actively involved in various national and international research projects, which give her the opportunity to go into depth in the field of discourse analysis applied to language learning, to reflect upon how to incorporate methodological proposals to deal with language and cultural diversity in the foreign language class, to explore the benefit of the use of video and ICT in language learning and to design, implement and evaluate task- and content-based materials for language learners.

Artur Noguerol, professor de Didàctica de la Llengua i la Literatura de la Facultat de Ciències de l'Educació de la UAB, ha estat mestre en tots els nivells de l'ensenyament i ha estat redactor i coordinador de diferents col·leccions de llibres per a l'ensenyament de llengües en l'Educació Primària i Secundària. També ha participat com a redactor i coordinador dels programes per a l'ensenyament de llengües en l'Educació Obligatòria i Postobligatòria, elaborats per la Generalitat de Catalunya. Així mateix ha estat redactor i coordinador en la redacció i implementació dels programes de Segona Ensenyança del Govern d'Andorra dels anys 90, i actualment també coordina la revisió i renovació dels programes de les quatre llengües per a la Primera i Segona Ensenyança, i el Batxillerat. Igualment ha col·laborat en molts cursos de formació permanent del professorat, dintre i fora del país, tant els organitzats per la UAB o altres universitats del país, com els organitzats per l'Associació de Mestres Rosa Sensat. Ha participat en diversos projectes d'investigació educativa europeus com EVLANG, JALING i CARAP del CELV de Graz i en altres de l'Estat Espanyol i de la Generalitat de Catalunya com a membre del GREIP, havent participat en la publicació de diferents llibres i articles sobre les temàtiques dels projectes en què ha participat.

Luci Nussbaum és professora jubilada del Departament de Didàctica de la Llengua i la Literatura, i de les Ciències Socials de la Universitat Autònoma de Barcelona i ha estat coordinadora de l'equip d'investigació GREIP des de la seva creació fins al 2014. S'interessa per la didàctica del plurilingüisme, entès com a un camp de creació i avaluació de dispositius d'ensenyament i aprenentatge en què s'articulen recursos i experiències disponibles per adquirir noves competències lingüístiques, socials i acadèmiques en llengües segones i estrangeres. És especialista en l'estudi de la interacció verbal en situacions de multilingüisme escolar i social des de les perspectives de la sociolingüística interaccional i de l'anàlisi de la conversa.

Xavier Pascual és professor associat del Departament de Didàctica de la Llengua i la Literatura, i de les Ciències Socials de la Universitat Autònoma de Barcelona. Dóna classes de didàctica de la llengua al Màster de Formació de Professorat d'Educació Secundària Obligatòria i Batxillerat, Formació Professional i Ensenyament d'Idiomes i és tutor de diversos treballs de fi de grau i de fi de màster en altres graus de la Facultat de Ciències de l'Educació. És professor titular de francès de l'Escola Oficial d'Idiomes de Barcelona Drassanes i ha participat com a expert en diferents projectes d'innovació educativa al Centre Europeu de Llengües Modernes del Consell d'Europa. Coordina un projecte Erasmus+ sobre aprenentatge de llengües en contextos específics. Les seves línies d'investigació inclouen l'adquisició de la competència intercultural en l'ensenyament de llengües i la formació de professorat per desenvolupar les seves pràctiques docents.

Adriana Patiño lectures in the Department of Modern Languages at the University of Southampton. She is interested in how multilinguals use the linguistic repertoires they have at their disposal in order to communicate and construct identities in daily practices. Schools have been, for her, apposite sites to observe the ways in which speakers give value and negotiate their language uses across the different practices and routines of the institution. Language socialization processes as well as storytelling co-produced in linguistic ethnography have been the focus of her more recent research. Her work has been published in peer-reviewed journals such as *Linguistics and Education* (2014), *International Journal of Multilingualism* (2014), *Journal of Language, Identity, and Education* (2011 and 2013), and *AILA Review* (2016) amongst others.

Amparo Tusón Valls es catedrática de escuela universitaria de Lengua Española (Departamento de Filología Española) de la Universitat Autònoma de Barcelona. Ejerce su docencia en la Facultad de Ciencias de la Educación y en la Facultad de Letras. Inició su investigación analizando los fenómenos de

Collaborators, col·laboradores i col·laborador, colaboradoras y colaboradores

contacto de lenguas (catalán-español) y sus efectos en la vida de las aulas (este fue el tema de su tesis doctoral, realizada bajo la dirección del Dr. J. J. Gumperz, y presentada en el año 1985). Se ha dedicado a la formación inicial y permanente del profesorado y al estudio de los procesos de aprendizaje del español como lengua primera, segunda y extranjera, desde una perspectiva discursiva. De forma específica, ha analizado los fenómenos relacionados con el desarrollo de la competencia discursiva oral en las aulas, desde un enfoque etnográfico. Ha publicado diferentes artículos y libros entre los que cabe destacar Análisis de la conversación; Ciencias del lenguaje, competencia comunicativa y enseñanza de la lengua (con Carlos Lomas y Andrés Osoro); Las cosas del decir: Manual de Análisis del discurso (con Helena Calsamiglia) y Enseñanza del lenguaje, emancipación comunicativa y educación crítica. El aprendizaje de competencias comunicativas en el aula (con Carlos Lomas). También ha sido codirectora de la revista Textos de Didáctica de la Lengua y de la Literatura. Actualmente forma parte de consejo asesor.

Virginia Unamuno es investigadora independiente del Consejo Nacional de Ciencia y Técnica (CONICET) de Argentina y profesora de sociolingüística en la Universidad Nacional de San Martín. Interesada en los estudios del multilingüismo desde perspectivas interaccionales y etnográficas, actualmente dirige un proyecto de investigación sobre los nuevos usos y nuevos modos de transmisión de las lenguas indígenas en el Chaco, Corrientes y Santiago del Estero. Es autora de *Lenguas, escuela y diversidad sociocultural* (Graó) y *Lenguaje y educación* (UNQUI), así como de numerosos artículos en revistas especializadas.

Claudia Vallejo es estudiante doctoral, profesora asociada e investigadora en el Departamento de Didáctica de la Lengua y la Literatura, y de las Ciencias Sociales de la Universidad Autónoma de Barcelona, donde imparte asignaturas sobre plurilingüismo y tutorías de prácticas en el grado de Educación Primaria. Ha participado y participa en diversos proyectos locales e internacionales y en actividades de formación sobre educación en contextos multilingües, sobre infancia y ciudadanía y sobre desigualdades sociales en educación. Su tesis doctoral en curso analiza prácticas plurilingües e interculturales en un programa extraescolar para estudiantes 'en riesgo' de fracaso escolar y su potencial para desarrollar espacios transformadores, inclusivos e igualitarios.

Reviews / Revisions / Revisiones

All of the chapters in this volume have undergone an internal process of peer review by other authors. They have also been reviewed by graduate students in the Official Master's Degree in Research in Education at the Universitat Autònoma de Barcelona.

Tots els capítols d'aquest volum han estat sotmesos a un procés intern de revisió per part d'altres autores i autors. També han estat revisats pels estudiants del Màster Oficial en Recerca en Educació de la Universitat Autònoma de Barcelona.

Todos los capítulos de este volumen han sido sometidos a un proceso interno de revisión por parte de otras autoras y autores. También han sido revisados por los estudiantes del Máster Oficial en Investigación en Educación de la Universitat Autònoma de Barcelona.

Translations and corrections / Traduccions i correccions / Traducciones y correcciones

We would like to acknowledge the following organizations for their contribution to the translations and revisions of the chapters in this handbook:

Ens agradaria agrair a les següents organitzacions la seva contribució a les traduccions i revisions dels capítols d'aquest volum:

Queremos agradecer a las siguientes organizaciones su contribución a las traducciones y revisiones de los capítulos de este volumen:

- Kis Communications

Collaborators, col·laboradores i col·laboradors, colaboradoras y colaboradores

- UAB Servei de Llengües

Acknowledgements / Agraïments / Agradecimientos

We wish to thank Amparo Tuson and Artur Noguerol for the insightful words that open and close this handbook. This project has been financed by the Research Group on Plurilingual Interaction and Teaching (GREIP, 2014 SGR 595), of which the editors and authors are all members.

Volem agrair a Amparo Tuson i Artur Noguerol les seves paraules d'inspiració que obren i tanquen aquest volum. Aquest projecte ha estat finançat pel Grup de recerca en ensenyament i interacció plurilingües (GREIP, 2014 SGR 595), del qual tots els contribuents a aquest volum són membres.

Queremos agradecer a Amparo Tusón y Artur Noguerol sus palabras de inspiración que abren y cierran este volumen. Este proyecto ha sido financiado por el Grupo de investigación en enseñanza e interacción plurilingües (GREIP, 2014 SGR 595), del cual todos los contribuyentes a este volumen son miembros.

Prólogo

Amparo Tusón Valls[1]

Cuando alguien inicia una aventura, se supone que lo hace porque siente ilusión, curiosidad ante algo que desea conocer y que ha planificado tanto como ha podido o sabido, pero, a la vez, se encuentra ante toda una serie de interrogantes, sabe que en el trayecto aparecerán desafíos, obstáculos que superar, descubrimientos reconfortantes y dificultades imprevistas, personas interesantes y amables que le ayudarán y tal vez otras que le pondrán dificultades. Habrá procurado leer lo que se ha escrito sobre ese camino y esos parajes que quiere descubrir. Con suerte, conocerá a alguien que le podrá aconsejar porque ha pasado por experiencias similares, aunque cada aventura es única y singular. Y será más difícil si se ha de adentrar en esos terrenos desconocidos a solas, con poco equipaje y sin saber si aquello que ha metido en la mochila será lo adecuado para manejarse por los diferentes territorios que irán apareciendo en el camino que le llevará al final de la aventura.

Pues bien, investigar es algo muy parecido a una aventura, especialmente si se trata de una investigación cualitativa y que además implica observar, describir y analizar el comportamiento de grupos humanos. De ahí el interés de este libro, porque presenta experiencias valiosísimas de personas que ya han transitado e investigado un terreno concreto que, en este caso, es el de la educación en entornos escolares plurilingües.

La perspectiva antropológica que propone la etnografía es un punto de partida para enfocar la mirada de quien investiga hacia las formas de comportamiento de grupos de personas, en este caso en diferentes tipos de aulas, con el fin de entender sus valores, sus normas, descubrir cómo construyen sus identidades individuales y colectivas a través de la manera en que utilizan los recursos comunicativos que tienen a su disposición (verbales y no verbales), y encontrar

---

1. Universitat Autònoma de Barcelona, Bellaterra, Cataluña/España; amparo.tuson@uab.cat

Para citar: Tusón Valls, A. (2017). Prólogo. En E. Moore y M. Dooly (Eds), *Enfoques cualitativos para la investigación en educación plurilingüe* (pp. xiv-xvii). Research-publishing.net. https://doi.org/10.14705/rpnet.2017.emmd2016.616

las formas en que categorizan esos recursos –que normalmente incluyen varias lenguas y variedades lingüísticas– y a quienes los utilizan.

Este tipo de enfoque cualitativo tiene implicaciones importantes. Quien investiga debe ser consciente de su propias creencias y valores para evitar al máximo que influyan en sus observaciones y análisis. A través de la observación participante, tiene que implicarse en las actividades cotidianas de las personas a las que estudia, porque solo así podrá llegar a acceder y poner en cuestión sus apreciaciones evitando actuar con prejuicios, por lo que también sus actuaciones deben formar parte del análisis.

Llevar a cabo la observación participante en un aula quiere decir colaborar, cooperar con el profesor o la profesora en todo momento. No se trata, como bien se manifiesta desde la introducción de este volumen, de ir al aula, grabar, hacer unas cuantas anotaciones, tal vez alguna entrevista y llevarse esos 'datos' al despacho de la universidad para allí analizarlos. Se trata, por el contrario, de llevar a cabo un proyecto de investigación-acción junto con el profesorado del aula.

Metodológicamente, se ha de partir de un interrogante, de algo que queremos saber cómo funciona; a partir de ahí, se debe establecer un plan, que ha de ser flexible para cambiarlo si es necesario de acuerdo con las observaciones que se vayan realizando. Una parte central del trabajo consiste en recoger datos 'naturales' a través de grabaciones en audio o en video, transcribirlas, analizarlas, contrastar con otras investigaciones similares y con la profesora o el profesor los avances que se van haciendo para, con sus observaciones, preguntas y críticas, enriquecer los propios análisis. Se pueden también ampliar, si se cree conveniente, las observaciones a otros agentes educativos (entrevistas con la dirección del centro, por ejemplo) o de la comunidad (entrevistas con algún padre o alguna madre, por ejemplo) e incluir esos datos en el análisis.

Se trata, también, y esto es muy importante, de que los resultados que se van obteniendo sirvan para introducir cambios y mejoras en la realidad que se analiza, para hacer propuestas educativas innovadoras y empoderar tanto al

Prólogo

alumnado como al profesorado para que den más sentido a sus tareas cotidianas, de manera que la investigación se convierta en un instrumento para contribuir a 'cambiar el mundo', desde esas comunidades, esos microcosmos que son las aulas, donde se crean y se recrean, pero también se pueden transformar las relaciones sociales de la comunidad de la que forman parte. Porque en el aula se dan relaciones de solidaridad, de amistad, de respeto, pero también puede haber abusos de poder, antipatías, malentendidos y conflictos de muchos tipos que hay que saber gestionar y solucionar.

Además, se deben hacer públicos los resultados. Presentarlos, exponerlos, explicarlos en reuniones del claustro de la escuela, en reuniones de padres y madres, en seminarios, en jornadas de estudio o congresos donde se pueden contrastar los resultados con los de colegas que trabajan en estudios semejantes. Publicar artículos en revistas compartiendo autoría, siempre que sea posible, con el profesor o la profesora con quien se ha trabajado codo con codo.

Pues bien, todos estos aspectos forman parte de las diferentes contribuciones que componen este manual y que se detallan en la introducción. Dedicado a aquellas personas que se inician en la investigación cualitativa en ámbitos educativos, estos trabajos constituyen una preciosa guía de ese viaje, de esa aventura, como decía al principio, que debe ser la investigación. Los autores y las autoras de los diferentes textos han sabido componer, cada cual a partir de su propia experiencia investigadora, un mosaico que, a modo de mapa, servirá sin duda de orientación y compañía para quienes se propongan abordar y responder nuevas preguntas, nuevos problemas, ya que en este volumen encontrarán instrumentos teóricos, metodológicos y técnicos que les permitirán llevar a cabo con éxito sus propias investigaciones.

Es para mí un gran placer poder presentar con este prólogo los trabajos de componentes del grupo de investigación GREIP, al que tengo el honor de pertenecer, ya que he seguido de cerca la evolución y el crecimiento de estas personas, a las que admiro y respeto por su capacidad, no solo para investigar con una actitud ética irreprochable, sino también y de manera especial, por su disposición continua para compartir con toda generosidad sus hallazgos y sus dificultades y para colaborar entre unos y otras en la tarea de promover actitudes críticas que puedan producir cambios y transformaciones en las prácticas educativas.

Prologue

Amparo Tuson Valls[1]

When someone starts out on an adventure, it is assumed that they are excited, curious about something, and have planned as much as possible. At the same time, they are facing a series of questions, know that they will encounter challenges along the way, obstacles to overcome, comforting discoveries and unforeseen difficulties, as well as interesting and kind people who will help and perhaps others who will make things difficult. They will have tried to read what has been written about the journey and places they want to discover. With a bit of luck, they will meet someone who can advise them based on similar experiences, although each adventure is unique and individual. Entering unknown terrain alone, with little luggage and without knowing whether the equipment being carried will be sufficient for the adventure, is challenging indeed.

Researching is quite like an adventure, especially if we are talking about qualitative research that implies observation, description and analysis of the behavior of human groups. Hence the relevance of this handbook, which presents valuable experiences by people who have already traveled and researched in a specific field, that of plurilingual education.

The anthropological perspective proposed by ethnography is a starting point to focus researchers' views on the behavior of groups of people, including in different types of classrooms. It allows researchers to understand values and norms, to discover how participants construct their individual and collective identities through the way they use the communicative resources available to them (verbal and non-verbal), and to uncover the ways in which participants categorize those resources – which normally include several languages and language varieties – and their users.

---

1. Universitat Autònoma de Barcelona, Bellaterra, Catalonia/Spain; amparo.tuson@uab.cat

How to cite: Tuson Valls, A. (2017). Prologue. In E. Moore & M. Dooly (Eds), *Qualitative approaches to research on plurilingual education* (pp. xviii-xx). Research-publishing.net. https://doi.org/10.14705/rpnet.2017.emmd2016.617

This type of qualitative approach has important implications. Researchers must be aware of their own beliefs and values in order to avoid influences on their observations and analysis as much as possible. Through participant observation, researchers must be involved in the daily activities of the people they study, because that is the only way to access and question different understandings and to avoid acting with prejudice. Researchers' actions must also form part of the analysis.

Conducting participant observation in educational settings such as classrooms means collaborating and cooperating with teachers at all times. It is not a question, as is made clear in the chapters in this volume, of going into educational spaces, recording, taking a few notes and maybe conducting some interviews, and of taking those 'data' to the university office for analysis. Researching in educational settings is, on the contrary, about carrying out projects aimed at action together with participants, especially with teachers.

Methodologically, we must start with a question, something that we want to know. From there, we establish a plan, which must be flexible enough to change if necessary according to the observations made. A central part of the research will consist in collecting 'natural' data through audio or video recordings, transcribing, analyzing, and contrasting with other similar studies and sharing the ongoing research with participants in order to enrich the findings with their own observations, questions and criticisms. Observations with other educational agents (e.g. interviews with school management) or from the community (e.g. interviews with mothers and fathers) can also be conducted to expand the scope of the study and for inclusion in the analysis.

It is very important that the results that are obtained serve to introduce changes and improvements in the reality that is analyzed, to make innovative educational proposals and to empower both students and teachers to make their daily activities more significant. Research thus becomes an instrument that contributes to 'changing the world', from within those educational communities, those classroom microcosms, where social relations are created and recreated, but can also be transformed. Contexts such as classrooms are ones in which

Prologue

relationships of solidarity, friendship and respect are present, at the same time as power abuses, antipathies, misunderstandings and conflicts of many types need to be managed and resolved.

The results of research should be made public. They ought to be presented, explained, shared in teachers' meetings, parents' meetings, in seminars, study groups or at conferences amongst colleagues working on similar projects. Texts for publication should include joint authorship by teachers and researchers who have worked side by side on the research whenever possible.

All of these aspects are included in the different contributions that make up this handbook and are detailed in the introduction. Dedicated to those who are starting out on qualitative research in educational contexts, these chapters constitute a precious guide for that journey, that adventure, as I said at the beginning, that research should be. The authors of the different texts have composed, each from their own research experience, a mosaic that will undoubtedly serve as a map, guide and companion for those who intend to address and answer new questions and explore new problems. In this volume, readers will find theoretical, methodological and technical instruments that will allow them to carry out their own research successfully.

It is a great pleasure for me to be able to present the work of GREIP members with this prologue, a research group that I have the honor to belong to and that I have been able to follow the evolution and growth of. The authors are people whom I admire and respect for their ability not only to investigate with an irreproachable ethical attitude, but especially for their continuous disposition to share their research findings and challenges with generosity, and to collaborate in the task of promoting critical attitudes that can produce changes and transformations in educational practices.

1 Introduction: qualitative approaches to research on plurilingual education

Melinda Dooly[1] and Emilee Moore[2]

1. Introduction

This handbook has been conceived as a guide for young researchers embarking on the exciting journey of investigating different aspects of plurilingual education. The text can also serve to review ideas previously encountered, and perhaps as a means of interrogating research methodologies in plurilingual contexts for those who already have ample experience under their belt. The idea of carrying out research can seem daunting at the beginning for those who are not immersed in the world of investigation. This handbook hopes to calm some of those qualms by offering descriptions of different methodologies together with case studies that exemplify those methodologies, as well as chapters that provide practical tips to help the researcher in the compilation, organization and analysis of research data.

The notion of plurilingualism is central to the research described in this handbook, and is a term we use to refer to the entire "repertoire of resources" (Lüdi & Py, 2009, p. 159) that speakers and hearers have at their disposal for accomplishing different goals, including communicating and learning (Nussbaum, 2013). Our use of the term plurilingualism is similar to how other researchers use the term multilingualism (e.g. Conteh & Meier, 2014) or dynamic bilingualism (e.g. García, 2009). It encompasses more recently coined notions that describe particular plurilingual practices, such as translanguaging (García & Wei, 2014). It is testimony to several decades of research carried out by members of the

---

1. Universitat Autònoma de Barcelona, Bellaterra, Catalonia/Spain; melindaann.dooly@uab.cat

2. Universitat Autònoma de Barcelona, Bellaterra, Catalonia/Spain; emilee.moore@uab.cat

How to cite this chapter: Dooly, M., & Moore, E. (2017). Introduction: qualitative approaches to research on plurilingual education. In E. Moore & M. Dooly (Eds), *Qualitative approaches to research on plurilingual education* (pp. 1-10). Research-publishing.net. https://doi.org/10.14705/rpnet.2017.emmd2016.618

Chapter 1

Research Group on Plurilingual Interaction and Teaching (GREIP), many of whom are authors of the chapters that make up this handbook, as well as by researchers in other linguistically diverse regions of the world.

Plurilingual educational contexts are those in which whole repertoires are available to educators and learners as part, or in spite of, an explicit language policy. Qualitative research in plurilingual educational contexts has allowed for an array of hidden and often stigmatized ways of communication, often from members of linguistic minority groups, to be brought to the forefront of theory. It has also helped open up spaces of freedom and possibility for teachers, learners and their communicative repertoires, in particular through collaborative engagements by researchers, teachers and students. In this way, it has helped shape approaches to language education that are appropriate to the social reality of linguistic diversity and inclusive of all students.

Undertaking investigations in plurilingual educational environments can present unique challenges for researchers. These include the need for constant reflexion of one's own emerging ideologies in relation to language and language education, and the plurilingual competences required for establishing rapport with participants and for handling research data in different languages. The authors of this handbook present some of the ways in which they have navigated through the challenges that their particular research in plurilingual educational contexts entailed.

Our understanding of research is quite wide; we do not restrict our definition of the word to the strictest definitions of 'scientific method'. We hold with an idea of educational research as a systematic inquiry into one or more aspects related to our education world – systematic not because the inquiry is based on a positivist[3] framework or methodology, but because the inquiry, stemming from whatever

---

3. As Thomson (1995) explains, positivism is an approach to research that is based on a belief in universal laws and always aims to be objective and neutral. This implies that the researcher usually has a pre-established hypothesis before beginning the study, based on assumptions of universality. A possible problem with this approach is that this may limit the researcher to interpreting the social world as objective or absolute, whereas a qualitative approach opens the researcher to other interpretations that emerge from the context and the participants themselves. It also does not assume that research can be entirely neutral as the researcher is inevitably a participant in the interaction being studied and will have an impact in some way (small or large).

method that is chosen, follows specific and meaningful steps in the research design, data collection and analysis. Research is viewed as an inquiry because it departs from an interrogation of a specific phenomena or phenomenon (in our case related to teaching and/or learning languages in plurilingual contexts) that we, as educators-investigators want to know more about. This does not mean that we will always find a definitive answer to our questions, but the inquiry begins with a need to know more. Research in education quite often deals with seeking results that are applicable to educational practice, although the focus of the study can cover many diverse sites – both formal and informal contexts.

Many new researchers wonder if there is a particular methodology they should apply to their study. However, qualitative research is not limited to only one approach. Because qualitative research is principally interpretive (and flexible to the context and the needs of the study), it can draw from many different approaches such as ethnography, phenomenology, discursive psychology, participant observations, case studies, conversation analysis or grounded theory (to name a few). The best method for a study is, therefore, the approach that will help the researcher answer their research question.

The methodologies presented in this textbook fall within the framework of qualitative research, entailing an interpretive, naturalistic approach towards the object of study. Qualitative researchers study things in their natural settings – this immersion in the setting can help researchers produce a thick description (Geertz, 1973). Researchers then attempt to make sense of observed phenomena through the meanings people bring to them. A qualitative approach aims to 'interpret' how the social world is experienced and understood by individuals within their social context.

> "Data analysis is a systematic search for meaning. It is a way to process qualitative data so that what has been learned can be communicated to others. Analysis means organizing and interrogating data in ways that allow researchers to see patterns, identify themes, discover relationships, develop explanations, make interpretations, mount critiques, or generate theories. It often involves synthesis, evaluation,

interpretation, categorization, hypothesizing, comparison, and pattern finding. It always involves what H. F. Wolcott calls 'mindwork'. [...] Researchers always engage their own intellectual capacities to make sense of qualitative data" (Hatch, 2002, p. 148).

These mental processes also imply that data generation methods will be flexible and sensitive to the social context in which they are compiled and that the data will not be dealt with in a decontextualized manner (e.g. data will not be produced in laboratory settings). Because qualitative research often includes a complex and large data corpus, it is not always easy to know how to begin the analysis. Creswell (2009) proposes this general outline of procedures to help guide the new researcher. First, carefully organize and prepare the data for analysis (e.g. saving videos into files and labeling them by dates or participants, creating folders of multimodal data collected such as homework assignments, etc.). Next, go through all the data completely in order to get the big picture of what is happening and to draw some first impressions of the meaning-making taking place in the interaction. Next, approach the data through the theoretical approach that you have decided, for instance, someone following a 'nexus approach' (Scollon & Scollon, 2007; see Dooly, this volume) would begin to look for examples of intersection of data to create coded sub-sections. Eventually this will lead to visible connections that will help the researcher find and argue for a more holistic vision of what is occurring in the interaction.

Interpretation of qualitative data implies that the researchers seek to make connections between events, perceptions and actions through holistic and contextualized analysis. That said, it is important to bear in mind that there are multiple possible frameworks within the paradigm of qualitative research and may employ many diverse tools. Indeed, because so many terms have been used to define qualitative research, it can be quite confusing for new researchers to understand exactly what it is or how it is applicable to the study site. In 1990, Tesch found that 46 different terms have been applied to qualitative research.

With such a wide panorama of what constitutes qualitative research, someone new to investigating contextualized data may easily be overwhelmed. Creswell

(2009, pp. 175-176) provides a useful overview of what can be considered some key features of good practice in qualitative research. Summarizing these points, the most significant is that qualitative research should include fieldwork – there should be interaction between the researcher and the participants in the study. Accordingly, the data will be gathered *in situ*, and that the data collected is natural – the interactions take place where they would naturally occur, and they are not re-constructed (as in laboratory conditions) or taken out of context. This implies that most data is collected through observation of the participants' behavior. This may include close and direct interaction with the participants – for instance when the researcher is also the teacher in the study or in cases of collaborative or participatory research (see chapters by Nussbaum, this volume, and Unamuno & Patiño, this volume; also Bergold & Thomas, 2012).

Also, collected data often consist of multiple sources (e.g. several video recordings of different classes, focus groups or interviews, and perhaps even collected output from the interactions such as essays or posters). This underscores an important aim of qualitative data, which is to describe, reflect and provide insight into the complexity of human behavior (Creswell, 2009).

As discussed earlier, qualitative research does not usually begin with pre-established notions or hypotheses of what will be found in the data, including pre-conceived ideas about what constitutes 'language'. Researchers take an 'emic' approach; that is, methods are used to try to provide insights from the perspective of participants, to see things as their informants do (Harris, 1976). This has particular implications for data transcription and analysis in plurilingual settings as the researchers must be aware of their own language ideologies and how this may have an impact on the study (see Moore & Llompart, this volume).

This brings us to another point made by Creswell (2009). Qualitative researchers must be fully aware of the impact they may have on both the collection and interpretation of the data. The study does not take place in a vacuum and the researcher brings their own baggage to the investigation, which may have an effect on how they perceive what is taking place during the observed interaction (including, as stated above, language ideologies).

So what should a qualitative researcher bear in mind? The investigator should ensure that the research design is clearly linked to the research questions and to the methodological approaches used for collecting the data. These are, in turn, plainly integrated into the analysis as well as the delineated purposes of the research. The research design should take into account the context in which the data is collected while maintaining sufficient flexibility to adapt to situational changes – changes which often lead to unexpected but highly relevant new issues and lines of inquiry. Flexibility is needed because human beings do not always act logically or predictably; our social world is not orderly or systematic. This also implies that qualitative methodology is not completely precise but does not mean that the researcher should not proceed in a well-structured and systematic way.

The qualitative researchers should always be aware of their role in the research process and how this may have an impact on the study. This requires constant, critical self-reflexive scrutiny. Qualitative researchers need to make sure that the chosen approach, tools, and analytical framework are appropriate to the aim of the object of inquiry. Above all, qualitative research should be conducted as an ethical practice (see Dooly, Moore, & Vallejo, this volume). In contexts of plurilingual education, such ethical practice may involve activism, including working towards alternative models of language education together with teachers and students in the face of emerging linguistic inequalities and injustices (Piller, 2016).

It is often argued that qualitative research lacks the 'rigor' or reliability of quantitative research, often based on the argument that the data extracts are 'cherry-picked' (selected to show the 'best' results) and that there is no statistical or numerical supporting data. But this is not necessarily true. In qualitative research, reliability is ensured through an examination of the consistency of responses. Reliability stems from a thorough documentation of all procedures, checking and re-checking of transcripts for errors, avoiding 'drift' in the coding (for instance, more than one coder going through the data), working with a team of researchers (e.g. data sessions) in order to cross-check the transcriptions, the code-checking and comparing results and interpretation of the data (Creswell, 2009, p. 191).

2. What is included in this handbook?

We have endeavored to cover all of the aspects of qualitative research that can 'entangle' the newly initiated researcher, specifically focusing on plurilingual contexts of language teaching and learning. Thus, we include here ethnographic studies, studies that use interviews, action-research studies, studies based on conversation analysis and studies within school and digital environments. The foci are also diverse: plurilingual student interaction, teacher collaboration and development, and task- and project-based learning. We also include more practical chapters that discuss how to write up your research, deal with ethic issues that emerge from conducting educational investigations, describe processes of collecting, organizing and analyzing plurilingual and multimodal corpora, and give ideas about how to elicit data through interviews, surveys, tasks and other instruments.

The first section of the handbook aims to give the researcher examples of research in the field of plurilingual education, as it has been undertaken by members of the GREIP research group. The chapter by **Nussbaum** (Chapter 2) provides the researcher with an overview of the complexities of carrying out research in a school, especially when the focus endeavors to include plurilingual resources in learning process in classrooms. The author gives a brief overview of the main features of action research before showing how this framework can be used for collaborative research between teacher and researcher, using ethnography and conversational analysis as tools for gathering and analyzing data. Next, **Pascual** (Chapter 3) offers a different angle on action research. This author describes the ways in which the action research framework can be applied to data gathered during a teaching intervention, in a situation in which the researcher is also simultaneously the teacher, in order to 'interrogate' whether proposed outcomes were achieved or not. In this case, the outcomes are related to integrating intercultural dimensions in foreign language teaching. **Unamuno and Patiño** (Chapter 4) present research in a secondary school setting, which aimed to describe how teenagers categorized their language practices at school and beyond. The authors describe a collaborative and interdisciplinary research process as it emerged, discussing approaches such as linguistic ethnography, language socialization and linguistic landscapes that were central to the study. The chapter shows how the youths became researchers of their own realities through the project design and presents an analysis of visual data collected by them. This is followed by **Corona**'s (Chapter 5) longitudinal ethnographic work, involving secondary school students in both school and non-school environments. The study aimed at understanding youth's identity construction as discerned through their use of language varieties and other aspects of their repertoires. The author presents a fine-grained analysis of data from a focus group discussion that helps illuminate his findings. Also including interactional analyses in her chapter, **Dooly** (Chapter 6) outlines the application of Mediated Discourse Analysis (MDA) to data gathered through 'blended learning' environments (interaction carried out in both the classroom and online), giving a short case study to illustrate the principal features of this approach. The following chapter by **Antoniadou and Dooly** (Chapter 7) places special emphasis on the particularities of collecting and managing multimodal data taken from digital, educational environments, based on a study in teacher-education. Finally, **Masats** (Chapter 8) presents a research project conducted in a primary school that involved task-based language learning, in order to introduce some basic notions of conversation analysis.

The second section of this book provides the researcher with practical resources and knowledge needed for efficiently setting up and carrying out studies in language education. The first chapter in this section, by **Dooly, Moore, and Vallejo** (Chapter 9), summarizes ethical points that all researchers should bear in mind, and provides practical ideas for anticipating and dealing with ethical and legal issues that might arise. **Canals**' chapter (10) gives the researcher a detailed synopsis of some of the issues to bear in mind when designing a data collection framework, including (but not limited to) tips on how to know what kind of data is appropriate for the anticipated study, as well as different means of eliciting that data. Next, **Moore and Lompart** (Chapter 11), outline the process of recording, transcribing, analyzing and presenting interactional data, referring to different software to aid in the process, and in particular to CLAN and ELAN. Chapter 12, by **Antoniadou**, discusses the practicalities involved in collecting and analysing multimodal data and offers guidelines for working with the Transana, Atlas.ti, and NVIVO software packages. Finally, to wrap up this section, **Borràs** (Chapter 13) describes the intricate process of writing up, adequately and professionally, the research report.

Each chapter has been conceived to stand on its own, providing sufficient background for the reader to follow the argument without referring to other chapters (although references to other chapters are made). Thus researchers can selectively choose those chapters that are most relevant to their current research or issues they may be dealing with. The chapters also include recommendations for further readings and links to resources that may assist in the research process. It is our hope that this handbook will serve as a practical, empirically-informed guide that can help researchers in contexts of plurilingual education plan, implement and write quality research.

Works cited

Bergold, J., & Thomas, S. (2012). Participatory research methods: a methodological approach in motion. *Forum Qualitative Sozialforschung / Forum: Qualitative Social Research, 13*(1), Art. 30. http://nbn-resolving.de/urn:nbn:de:0114-fqs1201302

Conteh, J., & Meier, G. (2014). *The multilingual turn in languages education: opportunities and challenges*. Bristol: Multilingual Matters.

Creswell, J. W. (2009). *Research design: qualitative, quantitative, and mixed methods approaches* (3rd ed.). Los Angeles: Sage Publications.

Dooly, M. (2017). A Mediated Discourse Analysis (MDA) approach to multimodal data. In E. Moore & M. Dooly (Eds), *Qualitative approaches to research on plurilingual education* (pp. 189-211). Research-publishing.net. https://doi.org/10.14705/rpnet.2017.emmd2016.628

Dooly, M., Moore, E., & Vallejo, C. (2017). Research ethics. In E. Moore & M. Dooly (Eds), *Qualitative approaches to research on plurilingual education* (pp. 351-362). Research-publishing.net. https://doi.org/10.14705/rpnet.2017.emmd2016.634

García, O. (2009). *Bilingual education in the 21st century: a global perspective*. Oxford, UK: Wiley-Blackwell.

García, O., & Wei, L. (2014). *Translanguaging: language, bilingualism and education*. New York, NY: Palgrave Macmillan. https://doi.org/10.1057/9781137385765

Geertz, C. (1973). *The interpretation of cultures*. New York: Basic Books.

Harris, M. (1976). History and significance of the emic/etic distinction. *Annual Review of Anthropology, 5*, 329-350. https://doi.org/10.1146/annurev.an.05.100176.001553

Hatch, J. A. (2002). *Doing qualitative research in education settings*. Albany: SUNY Press.

Lüdi, G., & Py, B. (2009). To be or not to be ... a plurilingual speaker. *International Journal of Multilingualism, 6*(2), 154-167. https://doi.org/10.1080/14790710902846715

Moore, E., & Llompart, J. (2017). Collecting, transcribing, analyzing and presenting plurilingual interactional data. In E. Moore & M. Dooly (Eds), *Qualitative approaches to research on plurilingual education* (pp. 403-417). Research-publishing.net. https://doi.org/10.14705/rpnet.2017.emmd2016.638

Nussbaum, L. (2013). De las lenguas en contacto al habla plurilingüe. In A. Maldonado & V. Unamuno (Eds), *Prácticas y repertorios plurilingües en Argentina* (pp. 273-283). Bellaterra: GREIP-UAB.

Nussbaum, L. (2017). Doing research with teachers. In E. Moore & M. Dooly (Eds), *Qualitative approaches to research on plurilingual education* (pp. 46-67). Research-publishing.net. https://doi.org/10.14705/rpnet.2017.emmd2016.621

Piller, I. (2016). *Linguistic diversity and social justice: an introduction to applied sociolinguistics*. Oxford: Oxford University Press. https://doi.org/10.1093/acprof:oso/9780199937240.001.0001

Scollon, R., & Scollon, S. W. (2007). Nexus analysis: refocusing ethnography on action. *Journal of Sociolinguistics, 11*(5), 608-625. https://doi.org/10.1111/j.1467-9841.2007.00342.x

Tesch, R. (1990). *Qualitative research: analysis types and software tools*. New York: Falmer.

Thompson, N. (1995). *Theory and practice in health and social care*. Milton Keynes: Open University Press.

Unamuno, V., & Patiño, A. (2017). Producing knowledge about plurilingualism with young students: a challenge for collaborative ethnography. In E. Moore & M. Dooly (Eds), *Qualitative approaches to research on plurilingual education* (pp. 129-149). Research-publishing.net. https://doi.org/10.14705/rpnet.2017.emmd2016.625

1 Introducció: enfocaments qualitatius per a la recerca en educació plurilingüe

Melinda Dooly[1] i Emilee Moore[2]

1. Introducció

Aquest manual s'ha concebut com una guia per a joves investigadors i investigadores que s'embarquen en l'emocionant viatge de la investigació de diferents aspectes de l'educació plurilingüe. El text també pot servir per revisar idees que s'han trobat anteriorment, i potser, com a una forma de qüestionar les metodologies d'investigació en contextos plurilingües per a les persones que ja tenen una àmplia experiència. La idea de dur a terme una investigació pot semblar inicialment descoratjadora per a aquelles persones que no estan immersos en el món de la recerca. Aquest manual pretén fer més fàcils algunes d'aquestes dificultats oferint descripcions de diferents metodologies, juntament amb estudis que les exemplifiquen, així com capítols que proporcionen consells pràctics per ajudar a investigadors i investigadores en la recopilació, organització i anàlisi de dades de la recerca.

El concepte del plurilingüisme és fonamental per a la recerca que es descriu en aquest manual i és un terme que fem servir per referir-nos a tot el repertori de recursos (Lüdi i Py, 2009, p. 159) que els parlants i oients tenen a la seva disposició per aconseguir diferents objectius, que inclouen la comunicació i l'aprenentatge (Nussbaum, 2013). Aquí, fem servir el terme plurilingüisme de forma similar a la que altres investigadors usen multilingüisme (per exemple, Conteh i Meier, 2014) o bilingüisme dinàmic (per exemple, García, 2009). Abasta les nocions que s'han encunyat més recentment per descriure determinades pràctiques

---

1. Universitat Autònoma de Barcelona, Bellaterra, Catalunya/Espanya; melindaann.dooly@uab.cat

2. Universitat Autònoma de Barcelona, Bellaterra, Catalunya/Espanya; emilee.moore@uab.cat

Per citar aquest capítol: Dooly, M., i Moore, E. (2017). Introducció: enfocaments qualitatius per a la recerca en educació plurilingüe. A E. Moore i M. Dooly (Eds), *Enfocaments qualitatius per a la recerca en educació plurilingüe* (p. 11-20). Research-publishing.net. https://doi.org/10.14705/rpnet.2017.emmd2016.619

plurilingües, com el *translanguaging* (García i Wei, 2014). Aquest manual és un testimoni de la recerca, realitzada durant diverses dècades, dels membres del Grup de Recerca en Ensenyament i Interacció Plurilingüe (GREIP), molts dels quals són autors i autores dels capítols que el componen.

Els contextos educatius plurilingües són aquells en què docents i estudiants tenen a la seva disposició repertoris lingüístics amplis, gràcies a una política lingüística explícita, o malgrat aquesta. La recerca qualitativa en contextos educatius plurilingües ha permès centrar l'atenció en una gran varietat de formes de comunicació ocultes i de vegades estigmatitzades, sovint dels membres de minories lingüístiques. També ha ajudat a obrir espais de llibertat i possibilitat per als docents, estudiants i els seus repertoris comunicatius, especialment a través de compromisos col·laboratius entre equips investigadors, professorat i alumnat. D'aquesta manera, ha ajudat a donar forma a enfocaments de l'ensenyament de llengües apropiats per a la realitat social de la diversitat lingüística i que són inclusius per a tot l'alumnat.

Dur a terme investigacions en entorns educatius plurilingües pot presentar reptes únics per als equips investigadors. Per exemple, la necessitat costant de reflexionar sobre les pròpies ideologies emergents en relació amb la llengua i l'ensenyament de llengua, i les competències plurilingües necessàries per establir una bona relació amb les persones participants i per al maneig de dades d'investigació en diferents idiomes. Les persones que han contribuït a escriure aquest manual presenten algunes de les maneres en què han afrontat els desafiaments de la seva investigació, especialment en contextos educatius plurilingües.

Entenem la investigació de forma molt àmplia; no restringim la nostra definició de la paraula al 'mètode científic'. Per a nosaltres, la investigació educativa ha de ser sistemàtica, no perquè es basi en un marc o una metodologia 'positivista'[3], sinó perquè es deriva de qualsevol mètode que es triï i segueix passos específics i significatius en el seu disseny, i en la recopilació i l'anàlisi de dades. La

---

3. Segons Thompson (1995), el positivisme és una aproximació a la ciència que es basa en la creença en lleis universals i la insistència en l'objectivitat i la neutralitat. Sovint s'estableix una hipòtesi abans de començar la recerca. Un dels problemes de l'aproximació positivista és que les persones investigadores poden veure les seves perspectives del món social com a objectives o absolutes sense considerar possibles interpretacions subjectives 'quotidianes' o el context de la investigació.

investigació s'entén com una indagació, ja que parteix de la interrogació d'un fenomen o fenòmens específics (en el nostre cas relacionat amb l'ensenyament i l'aprenentatge de llengües en contextos plurilingües) que nosaltres, com a docents-investigadors volem conèixer en més profunditat. Això no vol dir que sempre trobem una resposta definitiva a les nostres preguntes, però la investigació s'inicia amb una necessitat de saber-ne més. La investigació en educació sovint s'ocupa de buscar resultats que es poden aplicar a la pràctica educativa tot i que el focus de l'estudi pot cobrir contextos molts diversos –tant formals com informals.

Moltes persones es pregunten si existeix una metodologia concreta que hagin d'aplicar al seu estudi. No obstant això, la investigació qualitativa no és una sola aproximació. Atès que la investigació qualitativa és principalment interpretativa (i flexible segons el context i les necessitats de l'estudi), es pot extreure de molts enfocaments diferents, com ara l'etnografia, la fenomenologia, la psicologia discursiva, l'observació participant, els estudis de cas, l'anàlisi de la conversa o el mostreig teòric (per dir-ne unes quantes). El millor mètode per a un estudi és, per tant, el que ajudi a respondre la pregunta d'investigació.

Les metodologies presentades en aquest manual s'inclouen en el marc de la investigació qualitativa, el que implica un enfocament interpretatiu, naturalista envers l'objecte d'estudi. Quan fem recerca qualitativa, estudiem les coses en el seu entorn natural –aquesta immersió en l'entorn pot ajudar-nos a produir una descripció completa (Geertz, 1973). Després, intentem atorgar sentit als fenòmens observats a través dels significats que els donen les persones. Una aproximació qualitativa vol dir interpretar com els individus dins del seu context social experimenten i entenen el món social.

> "Data analysis is a systematic search for meaning. It is a way to process qualitative data so that what has been learned can be communicated to others. Analysis means organizing and interrogating data in ways that allow researchers to see patterns, identify themes, discover relationships, develop explanations, make interpretations, mount critiques, or generate theories. It often involves synthesis, evaluation,

interpretation, categorization, hypothesizing, comparison, and pattern finding. It always involves what H. F. Wolcott calls 'mindwork'. [...] Researchers always engage their own intellectual capacities to make sense of qualitative data"[4] (Hatch, 2002, p. 148).

Aquests processos mentals també impliquen que els mètodes per generar dades seran flexibles i sensibles al context social en què es compilen, i que les dades no es tractaran de manera descontextualitzada (per exemple, les dades no es produiran en escenaris de 'laboratori'). Com que la investigació qualitativa sovint inclou un corpus de dades complex i ampli, no sempre és fàcil saber com començar l'anàlisi. Creswell (2009) proposa un esquema general dels procediments per ajudar a guiar els nous investigadors i investigadores. En primer lloc, cal organitzar i preparar acuradament les dades per a l'anàlisi. Després, s'han de conèixer totes les dades per tal d'obtenir una idea general de la interacció i del significat global possible. A continuació, arriba l'aplicació de l'enfocament teòric escollit; per exemple, si es fa una 'anàlisi de nexe' (Scollon i Scollon, 2007; vegeu Dooly, en aquest volum) s'ha de codificar, classificar i organitzar les dades, buscant-hi interconnexions. Finalment, s'ha d'intentar interpretar les dades en un sentit holístic, per entendre-les en la seva globalitat.

La interpretació de les dades qualitatives implica que les persones investigadores intenten establir connexions entre els esdeveniments, les percepcions i les accions a través d'una anàlisi integral i contextualitzada. Dit això, és important tenir en compte que hi ha diversos marcs possibles dins el paradigma de la investigació qualitativa i que es poden fer servir moltes eines diferents. De fet, com que s'han utilitzat molts termes per definir la investigació qualitativa, pot ser complicat entendre exactament què és o com es pot fer. El 1990, Tesch va destacar que s'han aplicat 46 termes per designar la investigació qualitativa.

---

4. "L'anàlisi de dades és una cerca sistemàtica de significat. És una manera de processar les dades qualitatives de manera que es pot comunicar als altres el que s'ha après. Analitzar significa organitzar i interrogar les dades en formes que permeten que la persona investigadora vegi patrons, identifiqui temes, descobreixi relacions, desenvolupi explicacions, faci interpretacions, aporti crítiques o generi teories. Sovint implica la síntesi, l'avaluació, la interpretació, la categorització, la formulació d'hipòtesis, la comparació, i la cerca de patrons. Sempre implica el que H. F. Wolcott diu 'mindwork' (feina mental). [...] Les persones investigadores sempre involucren les seves pròpies capacitats intel·lectuals per donar sentit a les dades qualitatives" (Hatch, 2002, p. 148).

És útil tenir en compte la descripció de Creswell (2009, p. 175-176) de les característiques generals comunes de bones pràctiques en la investigació qualitativa. La investigació qualitativa normalment es du a terme in situ (o sigui, que hi ha treball de camp) i inclou la interacció directa amb les persones participants en el seu context natural. Les investigacions col·laboratives i participatives són un bon exemple d'aquesta interacció (vegeu els capítols de Nussbaum, en aquest volum, i Unamuno i Patiño, en aquest volum; també Bergold i Thomas, 2012).

Es recopilen dades de fonts diverses (per exemple, l'observació a l'aula, per mitjà d'entrevistes o discussions en grup, o les respostes d'activitats de classe). La investigació qualitativa intenta reflectir la complexitat de la conducta humana mitjançant la descripció, la identificació i l'explicació de les múltiples perspectives i factors que hi intervenen (Creswell, 2009).

La investigació qualitativa no sol començar amb nocions o categories del que es trobarà les dades, la qual cosa inclou les idees preconcebudes sobre què constitueix 'llengua'. S'opta per un enfocament 'emic', és a dir, la perspectiva de les persones participants (Harris, 1976). Això té implicacions particulars per a la transcripció i l'anàlisi de dades en entorns plurilingües (vegeu Moore i Llompart, en aquest volum).

Finalment, cal ser conscient de l'impacte que els antecedents i les idees prèvies poden tenir en la interpretació de les dades, incloent-hi les ideologies lingüístiques de la persona investigadora (vegeu Creswell, 2009).

Llavors, què haurien de tenir en compte els investigadors i investigadores novells? Han d'assegurar-se que el disseny de la investigació està clarament relacionat amb les preguntes de recerca i els enfocaments metodològics utilitzats per recollir dades. Alhora, aquests han d'estar clarament integrats en l'anàlisi i els propòsits marcats de la investigació. El disseny de la investigació ha de tenir en compte el context en què es recullen les dades, i ha de ser prou flexible per adaptar-se als canvis de situació –canvis que sovint condueixen a nous temes i línies d'investigació, inesperats però de gran rellevància. La flexibilitat és necessària perquè els éssers humans no sempre actuen de manera lògica o predictible; el nostre món social no és ordenat o sistemàtic. Això no vol dir que les persones investigadores no hagin de procedir de manera ben estructurada i sistemàtica.

Cal ser conscient del nostre paper en el procés de la investigació i com pot influir en l'estudi. Això requereix un escrutini constant, crític i d'autoreflexió. Ens hem d'assegurar que l'enfocament, les eines i el marc d'anàlisi triats són adequats per a l'objectiu de la investigació. Per sobre de tot, la investigació qualitativa s'ha de dur a terme com una pràctica ètica (vegeu Dooly, Moore, i Vallejo, en aquest volum). En contextos d'educació plurilingüe, aquesta pràctica ètica pot implicar activisme, en el sentit de treballar cap a models alternatius d'ensenyament de llengües, juntament amb docents i estudiants, enfront de les noves desigualtats i injustícies lingüístiques (Piller, 2016).

Sovint s'argumenta que la investigació qualitativa no té el 'rigor' o la fiabilitat de la investigació quantitativa, moltes vegades per la idea que els extractes de dades es 'manipulen' (se seleccionen per mostrar els 'millors' resultats), o perquè no hi ha cap estadística o dades numèriques que donin suport als resultats. Però això no és necessàriament cert. En la investigació qualitativa, la fiabilitat es garanteix mitjançant una anàlisi de la coherència de les respostes de les persones participants. Deriva de documentar-se de forma exhaustiva de tots els procediments, de verificar i tornar a verificar les transcripcions buscant errors, d'evitar incoherències en les codificacions (per exemple, que més d'un codificador revisi les dades), de treballar amb un equip d'investigadors (per exemple, en sessions de dades) per tal de comparar les transcripcions, revisar les codificacions i comparar els resultats i la interpretació de les dades (Creswell, 2009, p. 191).

2. Contingut del manual

Ens hem esforçat per cobrir tots els aspectes de la investigació qualitativa que poden confondre investigadors i investigadores novells que se centren específicament en contextos educatius plurilingües. Per tant, incloem estudis etnogràfics, estudis que utilitzen entrevistes, estudis d'investigació-acció, estudis basats en l'anàlisi de la conversa i estudis en entorns escolars i digitals. Els focus també són diversos: la interacció entre estudiants plurilingüe; la col·laboració entre docents, alumnat i investigadors; i l'aprenentatge basat en tasques i projectes. També incloem capítols més pràctics que tracten sobre com escriure una investigació; com fer front als problemes ètics que sorgeixen durant les investigacions educatives; com iniciar-se en la recopilació, organització i anàlisi de dades; i com obtenir dades a través d'entrevistes, enquestes, tasques i altres instruments.

La primera secció del manual té com a objectiu oferir exemples de recerques concretes que han dut a terme els membres del grup de recerca GREIP. El capítol de **Nussbaum** (Capítol 2) proporciona una visió general de les complexitats de fer recerca en una escola, especialment quan l'objectiu pretén incloure recursos plurilingües en el procés d'aprenentatge a les aules. L'autora descriu breument les característiques principals de la investigació-acció abans de mostrar com es pot utilitzar aquest marc per a la investigació col·laborativa entre docents i investigadors, fent servir l'etnografia i l'anàlisi de la conversa com a eines per a la recopilació i l'anàlisi de dades. A continuació, **Pascual** (Capítol 3) ofereix un punt de vista diferent de la investigació-acció. Aquest autor descriu les formes en què es pot aplicar la investigació-acció a una situació en què l'investigador és alhora el professor. En aquest cas, l'estudi està relacionat amb la integració de la dimensió intercultural en l'ensenyament de llengües estrangeres. **Unamuno i Patiño** (Capítol 4) presenten una investigació en un institut, que té per objecte descriure com els adolescents classifiquen les seves pràctiques lingüístiques a l'escola i a fora. Les autores descriuen el procés de recerca col·laborativa i interdisciplinària tal com va anar la seva experiència, i discuteixen enfocaments com ara l'etnografia lingüística, la socialització lingüística i l'anàlisi dels paisatges lingüístics, que van ser centrals en l'estudi. El capítol mostra com els estudiants es van convertir en investigadors i investigadores de la seva pròpia realitat a través del disseny del projecte i presenta una anàlisi de dades visuals. Tot seguit, es presenta l'estudi etnogràfic longitudinal de **Corona** (Capítol 5), que comptava amb la participació d'estudiants de secundària en entorns escolars i no escolars. L'estudi es proposa entendre la construcció de la identitat dels joves a través de l'ús de les varietats lingüístiques i altres aspectes dels seus repertoris. L'autor presenta una anàlisi detallada de les dades a partir d'una discussió de grup. Un altre capítol que també inclou anàlisis d'interacció és el de **Dooly** (Capítol 6). Descriu l'aplicació de l'anàlisi del discurs mediat (*mediated discourse analysis*, MDA, en anglès) a les dades recollides en entorns d'aprenentatge mixt (interacció que es du a terme tant a l'aula com en línia). En el següent capítol, d'**Antoniadou i Dooly** (Capítol 7), es posa especial èmfasi en les particularitats de la recollida i gestió de dades multimodals d'entorns educatius digitals, i es basa en un estudi de formació de professorat. Finalment, **Masats** (Capítol 8) presenta un projecte de recerca dut a terme en una escola primària que es va centrar en l'aprenentatge de llengües basat en tasques. El capítol introdueix algunes nocions bàsiques de l'anàlisi de la conversa.

La segona secció d'aquest llibre proporciona recursos pràctics i coneixements útils per configurar estudis en l'ensenyament i aprenentatge de llengües de manera eficient i dur-los a terme. El primer capítol d'aquesta secció, de **Dooly, Moore, i Vallejo** (Capítol 9), resumeix els punts ètics que s'han de tenir en compte, i ofereix idees pràctiques per anticipar i tractar les qüestions ètiques i legals que poden sorgir. El capítol de **Canals** (Capítol 10) ofereix una sinopsi detallada d'algunes de les qüestions que cal considerar a l'hora de dissenyar la recopilació de dades, que inclou consells sobre com saber quin tipus de dades són apropiades per a l'estudi que es vol fer, així com diferents mitjans per obtenir les dades. A continuació, **Moore i Lompart** (Capítol 11) descriuen el procés de gravació, transcripció, anàlisi i presentació de dades d'interacció, fent referència a diferents programes informàtics per ajudar en el procés, especialment CLAN i ELAN. El capítol 12, d'**Antoniadou**, analitza els aspectes pràctics involucrats en la recol·lecció i anàlisi de dades multimodals, i ofereix pautes per treballar amb Transana, Atlas.ti i NVIVO. Finalment, per concloure aquesta secció, **Borràs** (Capítol 13) descriu l'intricat procés de redacció de l'informe d'investigació.

Cada capítol s'ha concebut per sostenir-se per ell mateix, proporcionant una base suficient perquè el destinatari pugui seguir l'argument sense haver de consultar altres capítols (encara que es fan referències creuades). Els capítols també inclouen recomanacions de noves lectures i enllaços a recursos que poden ajudar en el procés d'investigació. Esperem que aquest manual serveixi com una guia pràctica, informada empíricament, que ajudi a planificar, executar i escriure investigacions de qualitat en contextos de l'educació plurilingüe.

Obres citades

Bergold, J., i Thomas, S. (2012). Participatory research methods: a methodological approach in motion. *Forum Qualitative Sozialforschung / Forum: Qualitative Social Research, 13*(1), Art. 30. http://nbn-resolving.de/urn:nbn:de:0114-fqs1201302

Conteh, J., i Meier, G. (2014). *The multilingual turn in languages education: opportunities and challenges.* Bristol: Multilingual Matters.

Creswell, J. W. (2009). *Research design: qualitative, quantitative, and mixed methods approaches* (3a edició). Los Angeles: Sage Publications.

Dooly, M. (2017). Una aproximació a dades multimodals amb l'anàlisi del discurs mediat. A E. Moore i M. Dooly (Eds), *Enfocaments qualitatius per a la recerca en educació plurilingüe* (p. 212-235). Research-publishing.net. https://doi.org/10.14705/rpnet.2017.emmd2016.629

Dooly, M., Moore, E., i Vallejo, C. (2017). Ética de la investigación. A E. Moore i M. Dooly (Eds), *Enfoques cualitativos para la investigación en educación plurilingüe* (p. 363-375). Research-publishing.net. https://doi.org/10.14705/rpnet.2017.emmd2016.635

García, O. (2009). *Bilingual education in the 21st century: a global perspective.* Oxford, UK: Wiley-Blackwell.

García, O., i Wei, L. (2014). *Translanguaging: language, bilingualism and education.* Nova York, NY: Palgrave Macmillan. https://doi.org/10.1057/9781137385765

Geertz, C. (1973). *The interpretation of cultures.* Nova York: Basic Books.

Harris, M. (1976). History and significance of the emic/etic distinction. *Annual Review of Anthropology, 5*, 329-350. https://doi.org/10.1146/annurev.an.05.100176.001553

Hatch, J. A. (2002). *Doing qualitative research in education settings.* Albany: SUNY Press.

Lüdi, G., i Py, B. (2009). To be or not to be ... a plurilingual speaker. *International Journal of Multilingualism, 6*(2), 154-167. https://doi.org/10.1080/14790710902846715

Moore, E., i Llompart, J. (2017). Recoger, transcribir, analizar y presentar datos interaccionales plurilingües. A E. Moore i M. Dooly (Eds), *Enfoques cualitativos para la investigación en educación plurilingüe* (p. 418-433). Research-publishing.net. https://doi.org/10.14705/rpnet.2017.emmd2016.639

Nussbaum, L. (2013). De las lenguas en contacto al habla plurilingüe. A A. Maldonado i V. Unamuno (Eds), *Prácticas y repertorios plurilingües en Argentina* (p. 273-283). Bellaterra: GREIP-UAB.

Nussbaum, L. (2017). Investigar con docentes. A E. Moore i M. Dooly (Eds), *Enfoques cualitativos para la investigación en educación plurilingüe* (p. 23-45). Research-publishing.net. https://doi.org/10.14705/rpnet.2017.emmd2016.620

Piller, I. (2016). *Linguistic diversity and social justice: an introduction to applied sociolinguistics*. Oxford: Oxford University Press. https://doi.org/10.1093/acprof:oso/9780199937240.001.0001

Scollon, R., i Scollon, S. W. (2007). Nexus analysis: refocusing ethnography on action. *Journal of Sociolinguistics, 11*(5), 608-625. https://doi.org/10.1111/j.1467-9841.2007.00342.x

Tesch, R. (1990). *Qualitative research: analysis types and software tools*. Nova York: Falmer.

Thompson, N. (1995). *Theory and practice in health and social care*. Milton Keynes: Open University Press.

Unamuno, V., i Patiño, A. (2017). Producir conocimiento sobre el plurilingüismo junto a jóvenes estudiantes: un reto para la etnografía en colaboración. A E. Moore i M. Dooly (Eds), *Enfoques cualitativos para la investigación en educación plurilingüe* (p. 107-128). Research-publishing.net. https://doi.org/10.14705/rpnet.2017.emmd2016.624

Section 1

Secció 1

Sección 1

2 Investigar con docentes

Luci Nussbaum[1]

Conceptos clave: investigación-acción, investigación colaborativa, etnografía, etnometodología, análisis de la conversación, secuencias didácticas plurilingües.

1. Introducción

La institución educativa es un lugar idóneo para la investigación en ciencias sociales, no solo por la relevancia de su misión (formar a futuras generaciones) sino también porque centrifuga los cambios de la sociedad, los conflictos y las tensiones. Por ello, la escuela sirve de terreno tanto para la investigación en enseñanza y aprendizaje, como para un amplio abanico de disciplinas (sociología, antropología, psicología social y análisis del discurso, entre otras). En nuestro caso, nos ha interesado en su dimensión de observatorio sociolingüístico, de espacio de aprendizaje de lenguas y de construcción de competencias plurilingües. En este sentido, la escuela ofrece la ventaja de reunir, en un solo edificio, a los actores cuyas prácticas comunicativas y de aprendizaje se desea investigar; es también un lugar de actualización de las políticas lingüísticas, de socialización y de observación de la evolución de planteamientos didácticos sobre educación lingüística.

La entrada de personas investigadoras en los centros educativos es compleja puesto que los equipos docentes desconfían a veces de sus propósitos (Unamuno, 2004). En efecto, la actividad investigadora puede suponer un ejercicio de poder al interpretar realidades sociales y legitimarlas a través de la divulgación (Heller, 2002). Asimismo, en muchos casos, los resultados de la investigación

---

1. Universitat Autònoma de Barcelona, Bellaterra, Cataluña/España; luci.nussbaum@uab.cat

Para citar este capítulo: Nussbaum, L. (2017). Investigar con docentes. En E. Moore y M. Dooly (Eds), *Enfoques cualitativos para la investigación en educación plurilingüe* (pp. 23-45). Research-publishing.net. https://doi.org/10.14705/rpnet.2017.emmd2016.620

no son útiles para los centros educativos y, en cambio, constituyen una fuente de beneficios simbólicos para quien investiga, además de acrecentar su currículum y proporcionale prestigio profesional. Por ello, los equipos docentes recelan a menudo de quien llama a sus puertas para investigar y ocultan a veces a la observación externa ciertos espacios y ciertas prácticas.

La investigación en la escuela supone, pues, un largo camino de reconocimiento, de confianza mutua entre personas investigadoras y equipos docentes, y de negociación de equilibrios. Según nuestra experiencia, la compensación más efectiva para ambas partes es llevar a cabo un proyecto común, en el que personas investigadoras y docentes se sitúen en espacios complementarios –y no asimétricos– para construir en colaboración conocimientos didácticos. Esta opción es, para los equipos de investigación externos a la escuela, una excelente ocasión para adquirir experiencia educativa y para contrastar teoría y práctica, además constituye una fuente de inspiración para futuras pesquisas. Para los equipos docentes supone la oportunidad de compartir las inquietudes del trabajo de aula con colegas que ayudan a reflexionar, además de la compensación de ser copartícipe de la construcción de saberes didácticos y de divulgarlos conjuntamente.

Este capítulo se propone reconstruir los procesos de algunas de nuestras experiencias, que pueden resultar útiles para estudiantes de maestría y doctorado que pretendan emprender estudios en centros educativos sobre las diferentes facetas de la educación en diversas lenguas. En la segunda sección de este texto, se esbozarán algunos aspectos de la investigación colaborativa entre docentes e investigadoras universitarias, indicando diferencias y confluencias entre investigación-acción, etnografía y enfoques conversacionales para analizar datos, e investigación colaborativa entre equipos docentes y de investigación. En la tercera sección, se presentará un enfoque de didáctica del plurilingüismo, que responde a nuestra concepción de la educación en diversas lenguas y se discutirá un modelo de intervención didáctica que se ha desarrollado de manera fructífera en el GREIP y que ha permitido recoger un número de datos importantes para entender el desarrollo de los aprendizajes plurilingües. En la cuarta sección, se propondrá un ejemplo de investigación colaborativa. Finalmente, se concluirá con algunas consideraciones de carácter general.

2. Investigar innovando

La investigación colaborativa se sitúa en el ámbito de lo que se denomina la investigación-acción, modalidad de trabajo definida por Kurt Lewin (1946) como lugar de confluencia entre los estudios en ciencias sociales y los programas de acción social. El objetivo principal de la propuesta de Lewin es lograr, al mismo tiempo, avances teóricos y cambios sociales, borrando las tradicionales fronteras entre producción de conocimiento y su aplicación a ámbitos sociales. En el campo educativo, se entiende la investigación-acción como un procedimiento de reflexión sobre los procesos de enseñanza y de aprendizaje para intervenir en ellos a fin de mejorarlos (Burns, 1999; Elliot, 1991/1993; Stenhouse, 1985/1987; van Lier, 1988).

A menudo, en las publicaciones educativas se establecen distinciones entre investigación-acción, investigación etnográfica e investigación colaborativa, atendiendo a quienes sean actores o ejecutores del proceso y a sus intereses. Según estas visiones, la investigación-acción sería la tarea propia del docente, mientras que la investigación etnográfica sería el terreno de investigaciones –ajenas a las inquietudes docentes–, interesadas en construir explicaciones sobre prácticas sociales en las instituciones educativas. La investigación colaborativa, en cambio, sería el terreno común tanto de investigadores como de docentes. En este sentido, cabe destacar que, en la investigación llevada a cabo en el GREIP, se ha promovido la divulgación de resultados mediante la producción conjunta de textos escritos cooperativamente entre investigadoras, docentes y estudiantes en formación.

La investigación colaborativa se nutre de los principios de la investigación-acción, puesto que se pretende mejorar la práctica docente, pero necesita de los instrumentos que proporciona la etnografía, campo en el que los procesos de investigación colaborativa cobran cada vez más relevancia. Por lo tanto, en nuestra experiencia, las tres propuestas se hallan íntimamente relacionadas y pueden conjugarse. En esta sección, hablaremos, en primer lugar, de investigación-acción, a continuación enumeraremos los procedimientos etnográficos que ayudan a llevarla a cabo y presentaremos nuestra opción para el análisis de los datos. Terminaremos esta sección refiriéndonos a la investigación colaborativa.

Capítulo 2

2.1. La investigación-acción

La investigación-acción (véase también Pascual, en este volumen) es un procedimiento que sistematiza la reflexión que todo docente realiza, de manera informal, sobre su práctica cotidiana (Nussbaum, 2016). En efecto, al salir del aula, los docentes suelen hacer un balance sobre cómo ha funcionado la clase y, a partir de ahí, piensan en ajustes para preparar sesiones posteriores. Para ello, tienen en cuenta las experiencias acumuladas, las orientaciones extraídas de sus lecturas, de la asistencia a jornadas de formación o de las reflexiones realizadas con colegas. Pero estas acciones no son suficientes. Si se quiere innovar asentando las acciones en la realidad educativa, es preciso observar de manera sistemática lo que ocurre en el aula e interpretar los fenómenos atendiendo a todas las circunstancias que constituyen la vida de la clase. Los docentes que innovan son personas que recogen información de manera ordenada, la analizan y la contrastan con la investigación sobre prácticas didácticas exitosas, plantean intervenciones, las evalúan y las divulgan. Las fases de la investigación-acción se reflejan en el siguiente esquema (Figura 1).

Figura 1. Fases de la investigación-acción

La investigación-acción puede abarcar todo un programa de trabajo o un aspecto simple, como por ejemplo, ir adecuando progresivamente las actividades de aula para un estudiante con dificultades de aprendizaje. En cualquier caso, el problema habrá sido definido a partir de la observación formalizada (fases 1 y 2), que deberá dotarse de instrumentos para recoger datos y poder analizarlos. Ello conduce a buscar respuestas al problema (o problemas) planteado (fase 3) que orienten la modificación de las prácticas precedentes para mejorar la intervención didáctica. Estas propuestas surgirán de la lectura reflexiva de artículos especializados que recojan problemáticas semejantes y soluciones a las mismas, o bien de la discusión con otros colegas. Las fases 4 y 5 implican no solo programar y llevar a cabo la intervención diseñada, sino también dotarse de instrumentos para recoger informaciones cuyo análisis (fase 6) permita evaluar los resultados de la intervención (fase 7) y preparar la divulgación (fase 8) de la experiencia entre colegas próximos o entre la comunidad de didáctica de las lenguas a partir de publicaciones y encuentros. Compartir los resultados de la investigación es un procedimiento esencial para fomentar el diálogo entre docentes e investigadores y para la construcción del ámbito de la didáctica de las lenguas (Camps, 2003). La evaluación de la intervención planteará nuevos problemas (fase 9), que conducirán a reiniciar el proceso.

Es difícil –aunque no imposible– realizar una investigación-acción en solitario, puesto que el proceso requiere tareas complejas. Por ello, defendemos su realización en colaboración con otras personas. En cualquier caso, parece oportuno recurrir a los procedimientos etnográficos y de exploración, que resumiremos a continuación.

2.2. Procedimientos etnográficos

La etnografía –disciplina que, desde sus inicios, se vincula a la tradición de estudios en antropología y, más tarde, a los trabajos en antropología lingüística y en sociolingüística (véanse, también, las contribuciones de Antoniadou y Dooly, en este volumen; Corona, en este volumen; Unamuno y Patiño, en este volumen)– persigue, en contextos educativos, una descripción densa, es decir, completa y pluridimensional, de la vida escolar para dar cuenta de su complejidad. Ello comporta, como se verá, recoger datos de índole diversa para contrastarlos e interpretarlos, tal como lo hacen los propios actores sociales implicados

–alumnado, docentes, etc.–, aplicando miradas emic, es decir, sin proyectar interpretaciones externas (a estas nos referimos como miradas etic), para captar la manera en que los participantes en eventos comunicativos entienden y construyen sus acciones (para una discusión sobre miradas investigadoras emic vs. etic, véanse Headland, Pike, y Harris, 1990).

Erickson (1984) señala dos principios básicos de la etnografía en contextos educativos: (1) *making the familiar strange* (contemplar como extraño lo familiar), es decir, buscar el sentido profundo a lo que parece regular, habitual, para el grupo que se estudia (normas, rituales, uso de tal o tal lengua para tal o tal actividad, etc), y (2) *stating researchable questions* (formular cuestiones investigables), es decir, plantearse preguntas a las que se pueda responder con la observación de la vida cotidiana del grupo objeto de estudio.

Los procedimientos propiamente etnográficos comprenden trabajar durante períodos extensos, de manera que se adquiera el estatus de miembro del grupo en que se desarrolla la investigación y se pueda desarrollar lo que se denomina observación participante, no solo en el sentido de ser admitido como miembro del grupo, sino sobre todo en el sentido de comprometerse activamente en los acontecimientos que se desarrollan en su seno (Rappaport, 2008). En nuestro caso, hemos podido realizar dicho tipo de investigación porque nos hemos integrado en las clases regulares y nos hemos incorporado como docentes o ayudantes del equipo docente en las actividades habituales de aula. Ello ha permitido recoger datos naturales mediante el registro audiovisual o auditivo de las actividades del grupo.

Además de estos datos centrales, la etnografía se sirve de diarios de campo, entrevistas, conversaciones informales, grupos de discusión y, por supuesto, del análisis de documentos escritos. La etnografía propone también triangular los datos, es decir, hacer dialogar entre ellas a las diversas fuentes de información. Así, por ejemplo, los usos verbales de los docentes (recogidos mediante registros) pueden responder a determinadas políticas lingüísticas (estipuladas en documentos oficiales), mientras que los del alumnado pueden reflejar su resistencia a dichas políticas mediante determinados usos verbales (también registrados en interacciones en el aula). Los procesos de triangulación son necesarios, tanto para el diálogo entre los datos, como para el regreso, una y otra vez, al análisis de las transcripciones realizadas por diferentes miembros del grupo. Además, el procedimiento etnográfico permite captar el impacto del dispositivo de investigación en los datos obtenidos.

2.3. Incorporar el dispositivo de investigación al análisis

En los procesos de recolección y análisis de datos (véanse Moore y Llompart, en este volumen), Mondada (2003) plantea tres principios que toda investigación debe contemplar (véase también Masats, en este volumen).

- Principio de observabilidad: los fenómenos que interesa analizar son descritos por los propios hablantes mediante su actividad. Así, por ejemplo, solo podremos decir que un estudiante usa una lengua dada si vemos claramente que se orienta hacia el empleo de dicha lengua, estén o no sus enunciados acordes con la norma establecida por las gramáticas o los diccionarios.

- Principio de disponibilidad: la manera de recoger datos y de tratarlos permite, o no, hacer visibles los fenómenos que se pretende estudiar. Este principio implica que si queremos, por ejemplo, estudiar la participación del alumnado, tendremos que dotarnos de dispositivos que permitan captar sus acciones durante la clase (las anotaciones que realiza en el cuaderno, la manipulación de objetos, las interacciones con compañeros, las miradas, la posición del cuerpo, etc.). De otra forma, solo tendremos una visión parcial de su participación.

- Principio de simetría: el dispositivo de investigación debe ser incluido en el análisis de los datos. A menudo, se dice que los procedimientos de investigación (presencia de la persona observadora, cámaras, etc.) modifican la realidad. Sin embargo, según dicho principio, no se da tal modificación, puesto que no existe una realidad esencial que preexista al momento en que se recogen los datos. Por ello, un análisis riguroso de los datos obliga a incorporar el dispositivo de investigación (presencia de quien investiga, cámara, etc.) en el análisis de los mismos, considerando el dispositivo como parte constitutiva de la construcción de los datos.

Veamos un ejemplo. Se trata del registro audiovisual de una actividad de grupo en la que participan tres niñas y un niño de quinto grado de primaria y su maestra, en una clase de ciencias en que se emplea el francés como lengua vehicular. En el proyecto docente se pretendía documentar los procedimientos de integración de aprendizajes científicos y lingüísticos. El grupo se halla frente a un ordenador, en cuya pantalla se muestra un esquema de la respiración y la alimentación de las plantas escrito en catalán. La maestra pretende que este alumnado conceptualice los procesos de la vida de las plantas, reconozca los conceptos en catalán –dado que se trata de un contenido del currículo general de ciencias– y pueda después explicar los fenómenos al resto de la clase en francés[2].

La Figura 2 muestra la disposición del grupo; la maestra está detrás, fuera del alcance de la cámara, que está a su lado.

Figura 2.   Colocación de la cámara

---

[2]. Estos datos fueron recogidos por I. Camacho y transcritos por L. Nussbaum.

El registro audiovisual permite transcribir las intervenciones orales de la maestra y de las niñas y el niño y analizar las acciones verbales de integración de contenidos curriculares y lenguas (principio de observabilidad), pero no totalmente, porque en la recogida de datos, la cámara no captó lo que estaba escrito en la pantalla ni los movimientos corporales o visuales de la maestra, de manera que el principio de disponibilidad no se pudo cumplir en su totalidad. Finalmente, el análisis pudo recoger los movimientos y miradas del alumnado, que se orientan hacia la cámara, hacia el ordenador, hacia la maestra o hacia los demás participantes (principio de simetría).

Incorporar el dispositivo de investigación al estudio de los datos implica, desde nuestro punto de vista, analizarlos de manera afinada aplicando los procedimientos que propone el análisis conversacional.

2.4. Analizar datos desde el análisis conversacional

En nuestra tarea, hemos hecho compatibles perspectivas etnográficas para recoger datos en el aula (y fuera de ella, como se verá al final de este capítulo) y perspectivas del análisis conversacional de orientación etnometodológica para el análisis de los mismos (véase también Masats, en este volumen). El recurso a un enfoque conversacional se revela particularmente fructífero para recuperar la interpretación que realizan los actores (alumnado y docentes) respecto de las políticas lingüísticas institucionales –la perspectiva emic a la que se ha aludido–, para entender los regímenes de interacción y para establecer nexos con otras observaciones realizadas en el seno de los centros educativos. Al mismo tiempo, el análisis conversacional permite rastrear los aprendizajes disciplinares (Moore y Nussbaum, 2011) y las actividades que realizan los aprendices como *plurilingües emergentes* (García, 2009).

La etnometodología se propone analizar los *métodos* que utilizan las personas para dar sentido a sus actividades con otras personas. Ello supone explorar la construcción e interpretación del sentido en la interacción social, en las actividades socialmente situadas y cómo las personas eligen, entre las múltiples posibilidades de interpretación, lo que es relevante en la acción en curso, mediante sus intervenciones en la conversación. El estudio de las interacciones deberá observar las orientaciones de las personas, adoptando su perspectiva, en el seno de las propias interacciones (perspectiva emic) y sin proyectar una mirada externa. El análisis conversacional sostiene que la participación de los hablantes está anclada en el contexto de la interacción, entendido este no solamente como el marco situacional sino principalmente como el entorno secuencial, en el turno de habla precedente y en el posterior. Las contribuciones de los hablantes crean así el contexto en cada secuencia de la interacción, manteniéndolo o renovándolo. Se trata de un enfoque que preconiza que no hay que atribuir a lo que hacen las personas influencias externas, a no ser que los individuos las hagan relevantes.

Los enfoques conversacionales son relativamente recientes en los estudios sobre aprendizaje de lenguas. No obstante, algunas publicaciones en los últimos años muestran que esta es una perspectiva en alza (véanse en este sentido las revisiones de Hall, 2004; Markee, 2015; Seedhouse, 2005; también Masats, en este volumen).

El análisis conversacional es escrupuloso con las la transcripciones consignando no solo los datos lingüísticos, sino también todos los aspectos multimodales (posición del cuerpo, movimientos, miradas, uso de objetos, etc.) que contribuyen al desarrollo de la interacción (Moore y Nussbaum, 2011). Ello se basa en considerar que la transcripción forma parte de una primera etapa de análisis de los datos y tiene, por lo tanto, consecuencias importantes en la interpretación de del habla-en-interacción (Duranti,1997/2000; Nussbaum, 2006; véanse también Moore y Llompart, en este volumen). En este sentido, uno de los procedimientos altamente fructíferos que ha adoptado el GREIP (siguiendo las propuestas de otros equipos de investigación) es estudiar las transcripciones colectivamente, en actividades denominadas sesiones de análisis datos, en las que se someten los registros y las transcripciones a examen colectivo, con lo cual es posible llegar a transcripciones más justas y evitar interpretaciones subjetivas.

El trabajo sistemático mediante los procedimientos mencionados permite entender los beneficios de la acción cooperativa en el proceso de recogida de datos. Además, cuando la investigación-acción se realiza de manera colaborativa con colegas interesados en la innovación didáctica, la tarea es más eficaz porque se suman esfuerzos para construir conocimientos didácticos, a la vez que se atiende a ellos desde intereses profesionales específicos. En el epígrafe siguiente, trataremos de esta forma de investigación-acción.

3. La investigación colaborativa

Desde hace años, nuestro grupo de investigación ha llevado a cabo estudios sobre educación plurilingüe en centros educativos de Cataluña implicando en ellos a docentes en ejercicio, a futuros docentes en formación y a jóvenes investigadores e investigadoras de nuestro grupo, que han realizado sus trabajos de maestría o de doctorado en este marco.

Nuestra opción por la investigación colaborativa se basa en un conjunto de reflexiones que se esbozan a continuación (véanse también Nussbaum y Unamuno, 2006; Unamuno, 2004). Los productos finales de la investigación en ámbitos educativos están frecuentemente influenciados por el punto de vista teórico adoptado por quien investiga, que, frecuentemente, ignora el de las personas investigadas (docentes y alumnado). Ello puede generar intranquilidad en las escuelas, que se sienten observadas sin obtener un retorno útil sobre dicha observación. Este escollo puede ser salvado si los equipos de investigación (o los individuos que investigan) adquieren compromisos con los centros docentes, con las familias y con el alumnado (Carr, 1995/1996), para responder a sus necesidades elaborando proyectos de investigación compartidos, que permitan el diálogo entre los agentes y las diversas concepciones sobre la educación (Cazden, 1986/1989). La investigación para y en la acción (Elliot, 1991/1993; Stenhouse, 1985/1987) con una orientación cooperativa permite equilibrar los desajustes entre quien investiga y quien es investigado y acercar a los equipos y a los sujetos de investigación y acortar las distancias entre teoría y práctica.

Nuestro objetivo es experimentar, junto con docentes y estudiantes, nuevas fórmulas para enseñar lenguas locales (catalán y castellano) y lenguas extranjeras, de manera integrada (González et al., 2008; Nussbaum, 2008; Nussbaum y

Rocha, 2008) y, a la vez, construir saberes didácticos situados en un contexto de gran heterogeneidad de aprendices, en centros que escolarizan en catalán, y cuya misión es enseñar también castellano y una o dos lenguas extranjeras, y formar a personas plurilingües sensibles a la diversidad lingüística del entorno y del mundo. La Figura 3 ilustra esta relación colaborativa.

Figura 3. Investigación colaborativa

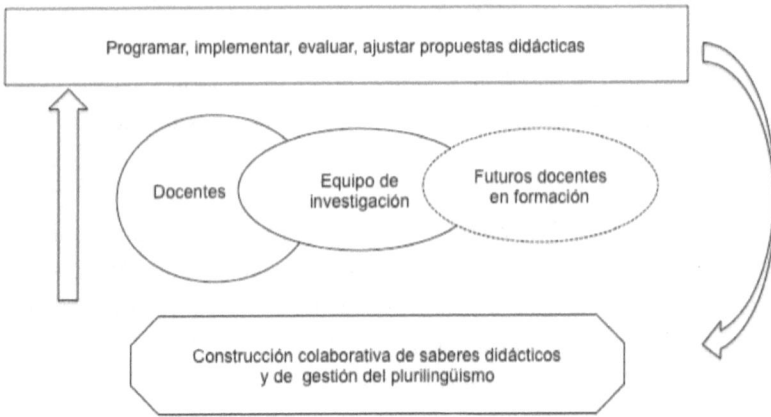

A continuación, esbozaremos algunas de las líneas de trabajo desarrolladas en dichas acciones colaborativas.

4. Los proyectos plurilingües

Históricamente, las lenguas se han enseñado de manera separada, con el argumento de proporcionar un contacto más intenso con la lengua en cuestión y evitar posibles mezclas entre sistemas lingüísticos. La base de este lugar común es la prevalencia de una visión monolingüe de los aprendizajes plurilingües, entendidos como compartimentos estancos (Creese y Blackledge, 2010; Cummins, 2005; entre otros). Sin embargo, la existencia de usos plurilingües, en clase y fuera de ella, para llevar a cabo actividades comunicativas (lectura, intercambios mediados por las tecnologías, etc.) parece anular la regla *una lengua para cada aula*; por otro lado, los recursos híbridos, lejos de ser un obstáculo para el aprendizaje de nuevas habilidades, constituyen un andamiaje útil para participar en prácticas de aprendizaje complejas, que conducen precisamente a la adquisición de competencias para actuar en modo unilingüe, es decir, empleando una sola lengua cuando las circunstancias lo exigen (Moore y Nussbaum, 2011; Nussbaum, 2014).

En este sentido, Duverger (2007), refiriéndose a la enseñanza integrada de contenidos curriculares y lenguas, habla de didactizar el plurilingüismo en la escuela. El autor distingue tres tipos de regímenes de plurilingüismo: macro, meso y micro. El primer tipo se refiere a la programación de enseñanzas en lenguas diferentes para materias y períodos de tiempo, como suele establecerse en los proyectos lingüísticos de centro. Así, por ejemplo, es posible programar la enseñanza de las matemáticas en inglés o de las ciencias en francés. El segundo tipo, el régimen meso, se refiere a programar el uso de lenguas determinadas para actividades específicas, por ejemplo, si se está trabajando en geografía, es posible consultar mapas u otros documentos en inglés o en castellano, aunque la secuencia didáctica se lleve a término en catalán. Finalmente, el tercer tipo se refiere a los usos plurilingües no planificados, que tienen lugar en las escuelas situadas en ámbitos multilingües (Nussbaum, 2014). Los regímenes meso, que consisten en elegir lenguas distintas para momentos precisos de una secuencia didáctica, inspiran una parte de nuestro trabajo colaborativo en los centros (véanse los apartados siguientes).

Concebimos el aprendizaje como una práctica social situada, lo que significa presentar el conocimiento en contexto e involucrar al alumnado en la realización de actividades prácticas y socialmente significativas mediante la realización de proyectos educativos. El trabajo por proyectos (véanse, para una fundamentación teórica, Camps, 2003; Perrenoud, 1999) se muestra aquí como una herramienta útil, en el sentido que considera al alumnado como un equipo investigador (Lambert, 2012), que sigue un recorrido para llegar a crear un producto final (o diversos), concebido para ser transferido a otras personas a fin de comunicar conocimiento más allá del aula.

Capítulo 2

Un proyecto integra de forma natural el aprendizaje de disciplinas y las actividades lingüísticas necesarias para acceder al conocimiento: utilización de recursos tecnológicos para buscar información, lectura de textos escritos y documentos multimodales; prácticas sociales dentro y fuera del aula de clases y, por supuesto, el uso de diferentes recursos lingüísticos. El enfoque por proyectos permite adoptar diferentes lenguas (regímenes meso, en términos de Duverger), según la fase de desarrollo de la secuencia didáctica. Así, una entrevista puede ser preparada en castellano, un texto en Internet se puede leer en inglés y un reportaje, como producto final, puede ser diseñado en catalán y contener secuencias en varias lenguas. Esta flexibilidad organizativa se adecúa a una concepción de la clase como una comunidad de práctica (Lave y Wenger, 1991), en la que los estudiantes pueden participar de diversas maneras, según sus capacidades, para adquirir las competencias expertas que permiten actuar en contextos diversos (Hall Cheng, y Carlson, 2006).

La Figura 4 esquematiza una secuencia didáctica. Las actividades centrales pueden ser realizadas de manera natural en modos plurilingües, puesto que plurilingüe es el entorno en que estas tienen lugar. El producto final, en cambio, puede ser realizado en modo unilingüe, para atender así a las competencias académicas exigidas en el currículo.

Nuestro enfoque, resultado del análisis de datos y de la reflexión cooperativa con docentes, estudiantes en prácticas e investigadores en formación, reposa en la observación y la discusión previa de las competencias de partida del alumnado, de sus prácticas sociales habituales y del papel de la escuela en su educación plurilingüe. Nuestro punto de partida es la inclusión de modos plurilingües flexibles, especialmente para el tratamiento de los saberes escolares a partir de la interacción en el aula, que se desarrolla en diferentes formatos (docente-alumnado, alumnado-alumnado). También desarrollamos, en cada secuencia didáctica, un trabajo profundo de diversos géneros discursivos –en función del producto final acordado–, a partir de la lectura de textos en papel o en línea y de producciones parciales del alumnado. Estas etapas conducen a la construcción de un producto final unilingüe, que debe cumplir con la formalidad inherente al discurso académico. La Figura 5 ilustra el proceso.

Figura 4. Esquema de secuencia didáctica

Figura 5. De los modos plurilingües al discurso académico unilingüe

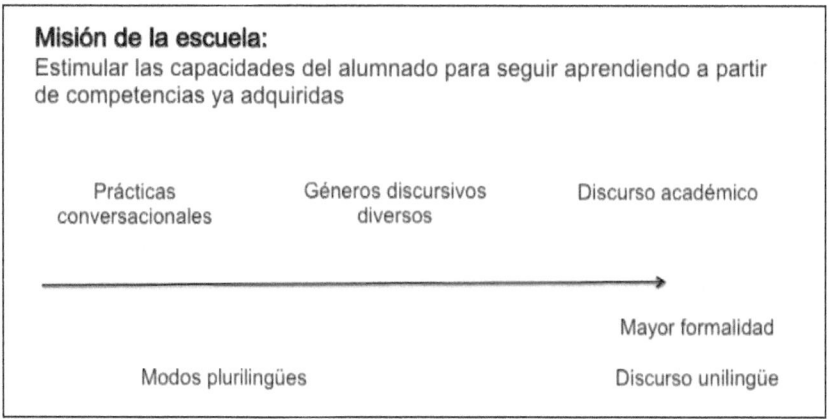

Este enfoque radicalmente plurilingüe persigue aprovechar todos los recursos disponibles para crear vínculos entre usos sociales de las lenguas y prácticas escolares.

5. Un ejemplo de investigación colaborativa

Ilustraremos nuestro trabajo[3], llevado a cabo en una escuela de Barcelona, situada en un entorno con gran presencia de personas de orígenes geográficos y sociolingüísticos muy diversos. El centro acoge a más de un 90 % de niñas y niños de dichos orígenes. La lengua de enseñanza en la escuela es el catalán, pero el alumnado emplea el castellano como lengua de comunicación entre pares y como lengua de relación con las personas del barrio, con quienes no comparten las mismas lenguas de origen, hecho muy frecuente en zonas metropolitanas de Cataluña (Nussbaum y Unamuno, 2006). Esta circunstancia sociolingüística provoca que los niños y las niñas perciban el aprendizaje del catalán como una exigencia escolar poco *útil* para la vida cotidiana. Además, el centro escolariza a alumnado con competencias muy diversas: un porcentaje elevado se ha incorporado tardíamente al centro y, por ello, no posee las mismas competencias que el resto del alumnado.

Al inicio del proyecto[4], dirigido a un grupo de quinto grado de primaria, el equipo se formuló un conjunto de retos que parten de las circunstancias arriba enunciadas:

- hacer descubrir al alumnado que el catalán es una lengua de uso habitual en otros contextos geográficos y sociales;

- promover usos orales y escritos significativos.

Ambos retos condujeron a la necesidad de abrir las puertas de la clase, para observar usos sociales del catalán en otros contextos, en los que el alumnado pudiera participar empleando sus recursos lingüísticos y observando maneras de actuar en entornos distintos al de la escuela. Asimismo, nos planteamos tomar en cuenta la diversidad de competencias del alumnado para que

---

[3]. Las personas interesadas en el tipo de propuesta que aquí se describe pueden consultar: http://grupsderecerca.uab.cat/greip/es/content/materiales

[4]. Diseñaron el proyecto: Montserrat Colet, Víctor Corona, Violeta García, Luci Nussbaum, Adriana Patiño, Pepa Rocha, con la asesoría de Montserrat Oller y Àngels Prat.

la totalidad de niños y niñas pudieran involucrarse en la realización de un proyecto significativo.

A partir de un contenido curricular central (las comarcas de Cataluña), el proyecto se propuso integrar otros contenidos curriculares referidos al territorio (geografía, historia, recursos naturales, economía, población, ocupaciones de sus habitantes, medios de comunicación, manifestaciones culturales), al uso de procedimientos diversos para obtener información (entrevistas a otros escolares y a personas adultas, consultas a Internet, registros de vídeo y de audio, etc.), y a la utilización de distintas formas de representación (mapas, gráficos, etc.). Al final del recorrido de aprendizaje, el alumnado tenía que hacer un reportaje para la radio de la escuela, con la finalidad de divulgar su experiencia entre otros escolares del centro o de otras escuelas.

El proyecto se estructuró en cuatro etapas (véanse Corona, Nussbaum, y Rocha, 2008). Con ellas se perseguía el aprendizaje de formas de trabajo extrapolables a otras situaciones, además de dar protagonismo al alumnado como agente investigador de la realidad física y social. En este sentido, cabe destacar, por un lado, la fase en que el alumnado contactó con estudiantes de otros dos centros a través de un foro virtual, para recabar información sobre los territorios objeto de estudio y, por otro lado, los viajes que se realizaron a dichos centros para conocer en persona a los escolares con quienes habían interactuado virtualmente y para recoger nuevas informaciones.

Con todo este conjunto de actividades se consiguió que chicos y chicas constataran que el uso del catalán es un hecho habitual en ciertos lugares y que pudieran emplear dicha lengua para propósitos prácticos, además de construir un producto final utilizando un registro escolar del catalán. No obstante, el uso de otras lenguas se incluyó en el proceso como un hecho natural, de la misma manera que ocurre en la vida escolar, cuando es preciso consultar documentos para recoger información, y en las interacciones cotidianas improvisadas fuera del ámbito escolar.

El desarrollo de la secuencia, que duró varias semanas, permitió recoger un conjunto de datos altamente relevantes para el equipo docente y el equipo investigador: grabaciones de las discusiones del equipo, del trabajo en el aula, durante el proceso y durante el registro del producto final; grabaciones de entrevistas con personas en la calle y con niños y niñas de las escuelas visitadas; documentos escritos por el alumnado, etc. Esta recogida de datos se hizo de manera etnográfica y gracias a la observación participante en todo el proceso.

Este corpus fue explotado más tarde, tanto para las discusiones del equipo (evaluación de la propuesta didáctica, discusión de aspectos mejorables) como para reconstruir conjuntamente saberes didácticos con otras personas del GREIP interesadas en descubrir cómo se construyen y reconstruyen las competencias lingüísticas y comunicativas en contextos de alta diversidad sociolingüística. En este análisis de los datos, se emplearon procedimientos del análisis de la conversación.

Los resultados de los análisis realizados fueron divulgados en diversos encuentros con otros docentes e investigadores y sirvieron, en gran medida, para argumentar la eficacia de los enfoques plurilingües para aumentar las competencias unilingües necesarias en la participación de determinados encuentros sociales.

6. A modo de conclusión

El proyecto global del GREIP consiste en documentar los usos y los aprendizajes plurilingües de escolares en contextos de gran diversidad lingüística. La aproximación al terreno –el conocimiento de los centros, de las aulas, de las prácticas comunicativas en la escuela, de las visiones del alumnado respecto de los usos lingüísticos, etc.– constituye una condición necesaria para poder realizar, junto con los equipos docentes, propuestas de enseñanza significativas para el alumnado.

Entendemos el aprendizaje de lenguas como una actividad social que se realiza fundamentalmente en interacción con otras personas (docentes, pares, familiares, etc.) y con documentos escritos, en entornos escolares y fuera de ellos, y también mediados por las tecnologías. Por ello, en nuestras investigaciones, damos un peso muy relevante a los datos obtenidos en las interacciones, puesto que son dichos datos los que permiten reconstruir los procesos cognitivos situados.

En este texto, hemos tratado de articular el trabajo colaborativo del equipo de investigación con los equipos docentes en los centros, con el interés de contribuir a la didáctica de las lenguas, que entendemos anclada en realidades educativas concretas. Este trabajo colaborativo, enmarcado en la investigación-acción, se sirve de la etnografía, cuyas propuestas permiten acercarse a la vida cotidiana de las aulas y entender, desde dentro, las prácticas lingüísticas entre los sujetos objeto de estudio, cuyas competencias se quieren aumentar mediante propuestas didácticas eficaces. El estudio de los procesos generados por la intervención didáctica, mediante el análisis minucioso de las interacciones que en ellos ocurren, nos permite proyectar una mirada crítica sobre nuestra actuación didáctica y plantearnos nuevos desafíos.

Obras citadas

Antoniadou, V., y Dooly, M. (2017). Etnografia educativa en contextos d'aprenentatge mixt. En E. Moore y M. Dooly (Eds), *Enfoques cualitativos para la investigación en educación plurilingüe* (pp. 264-292). Research-publishing.net. https://doi.org/10.14705/rpnet.2017.emmd2016.631

Burns, A. (1999). *Collaborative action research for English language teachers*. Cambridge: Cambridge University Press.

Camps, A. (Ed.). (2003). *Secuencias didácticas para aprender a escribir.* Barcelona: Editorial Graó.Carr, W. (1995/1996). *Una teoría para la educación. Hacia una investigación educativa crítica.* Madrid: Morata.

Cazden, C. (1986/1999). El discurso en el aula. En M. Wittroc (Ed.), *La investigación en la enseñanza, vol III: Métodos cualitativos y de observación* (pp. 627-719). Barcelona: Paidós.

Corona, V. (2017). Un acercamiento etnográfico al estudio de las variedades lingüísticas de jóvenes latinoamericanos en Barcelona. En E. Moore y M. Dooly (Eds), *Enfoques cualitativos para la investigación en educación plurilingüe* (pp. 151-169). Research-publishing.net. https://doi.org/10.14705/rpnet.2017.emmd2016.626

Corona, V., Nussbaum, L., y Rocha, P. (2008). El castellano que usan los escolares de Cataluña. *Cuadernos de Pedagogía, 378*, 27-30.

Creese, A., y Blackledge, A. (2010). Translanguaging in the bilingual classroom: a pedagogy for learning and teaching? *The Modern Language Journal, 94*(1), 103-115. https://doi.org/10.1111/j.1540-4781.2009.00986.x

Cummins, J. (2005). A proposal for action: strategies 354 for recognizing heritage language competence as a learning resource within the mainstream classroom. *Modern Language Journal, 89*(4), 585-592.

Duranti, A. (1997/2000). *Antropología lingüística*. Madrid: Cambridge University Press. https://doi.org/10.1017/CBO9780511810190

Duverger, J. (2007). Didactiser l'alternance des langues en cours de DNL. *Tréma, 28*. https://doi.org/10.4000/trema.302

Elliot, J. (1991/1993). *El cambio educativo desde la investigación-acción*. Madrid: Morata.

Erickson, F. (1984). What makes school ethnography 'ethnographic'? *Anthropology and Education Quarterly, 15*(1), 51-66. https://doi.org/10.1525/aeq.1984.15.1.05x1472p

García, O. (2009). *Bilingual education in the 21st century: a global perspective*. Oxford: Wiley-Blackwell.

González, P, Llobet, L., Masats, D., Nussbaum, L., y Unamuno, V. (2008). Tres en uno: inclusión de alumnado diverso, integración de contenidos y formación de profesorado. En J. L. Barrio (Coord.), *El proceso de enseñar lenguas. Investigaciones en didáctica de la lengua* (pp. 107-133). Madrid: Ed. La Muralla.

Hall, J. K. (2004). Language learning as an interactional achievement. *The Modern Language Journal, 88*(4), 607-612.

Hall, J. K., Cheng, A., y Carlson, M. T. (2006). Reconceptualizing multicompetence as a theory of language knowledge. *Applied Linguistics, 27*(2), 220-240. https://doi.org/10.1093/applin/aml013

Headland, T. N., Pike, K. L., y Harris, M. (Eds). (1990). *Emics and etics: the insider/outsider debate*. Newbury Park, California: Sage Publications.

Heller, M. (2002). *Éléments d'une sociolinguistique critique*. Paris: Didier.

Lambert, P. (2012). Identifier la pluralité des ressources des élèves en contexte monolingue et normatif. Une enquête ethnographique auprès de lycéennes. En M. Dreyfus y J. Prieurs (Eds), *Hétérogénéité et variation. Perspectives socolinguistiques, didactiques et anthropologiques* (pp. 182-195). París: Michel Houdiard.

Lave, J., y Wenger, E. (1991). *Situated learning: legitimate peripherical participation*. Nueva York: Cambridge University Press. https://doi.org/10.1017/CBO9780511815355

Lewin, K. (1946). Action research and minority problems. *Journal of Social Issues, 2*(4), 34-46. https://doi.org/10.1111/j.1540-4560.1946.tb02295.x

Markee, N. (2015). Introduction: classroom discourse and interaction research. En N. Markee (Ed.), *Handbook of classroom discourse and interaction* (pp. 3-19). Boston, MA: Wiley.

Masats, D. (2017). L'anàlisi de la conversa al servei de la recerca en el camp de l'adquisició de segones llengües (CA-for-SLA). En E. Moore y M. Dooly (Eds), *Enfoques cualitativos para la investigación en educación plurilingüe* (pp. 293-320). Research-publishing.net. https://doi.org/10.14705/rpnet.2017.emmd2016.632

Mondada, L. (2003). Observer les activités de classe dans leur diversité: choix méthodologiques et enjeux théoriques. En J. Perera, L. Nussbaum, y M. Milian (Eds), *L'educació lingüística en situacions multiculturals i multilingües* (pp. 49-70). Barcelona: Universitat de Barcelona.

Moore, E., y Llompart, J. (2017). Recoger, transcribir, analizar y presentar datos interaccionales plurilingües. En E. Moore y M. Dooly (Eds), *Enfoques cualitativos para la investigación en educación plurilingüe* (pp. 418-433). Research-publishing.net. https://doi.org/10.14705/rpnet.2017.emmd2016.639

Moore, E., y Nussbaum, L. (2011). Què aporta l'anàlisi conversacional a la comprensió de les situacions d'AICLE. En C. Escobar y L. Nussbaum (Eds), *Aprendre en una Altra llengua / Learning through another language / Aprender en otra lengua* (pp. 93-118). Bellaterra: Servei de publicacions de la UAB.

Nussbaum, L. (2006). La transcripción de la interacción en contextos de contacto y de aprendizaje de lenguas. En Y. Bürki y E. de Steffani (Eds), *Transcribir la lengua: de la filología al análisis de la conversación* (pp. 195-218). Berna: Peter Lang.

Nussbaum, L. (2008). Construire le plurilinguisme à l'école: de la recherche à l'intervention et de l'intervention à la recherche. En M. Candelier, G. Ioannitou, D. Omer, y M. T. Vasseur (Eds), *Conscience du plurilinguisme. Pratiques, représentations et interventions* (pp. 125-144). Rennes: Presses Universitaires de Rennes.

Nussbaum, L. (2014). Una didàctica del plurilingüisme. *Bellaterra Journal of Teaching & Learning Language & Literature, 7*(3), 1-13.

Nussbaum, L. (2016). Estudio de la interacción en el aula de lengua extranjera. En D. Masats y L. Nussbaum (Eds), *Enseñanza y aprendizaje de las lenguas extranjeras en educación secundaria obligatoria* (pp.113-142). Madrid: Síntesis.

Nussbaum, L., y Rocha, P. (2008). L'organisation sociale de l'apprentissage dans une approche par projet. *Babylonia, 3*, 52-55.

Nussbaum, L., y Unamuno, V. (2006). Les competències comunicatives multilingües. En L. Nussbaum y V. Unamuno (Eds), *Usos i competències multilingües entre escolars d'origen immigrant* (pp. 41-62). Bellaterra: Servei de publicacions de la UAB.

Pascual, X. (2017). Investigar las propias prácticas docentes a través de la investigación-acción. En E. Moore y M. Dooly (Eds), *Enfoques cualitativos para la investigación en educación plurilingüe* (pp. 69-87). Research-publishing.net. https://doi.org/10.14705/rpnet.2017.emmd2016.622

Perrenoud, P. (1999). *Apprendre à l'école à travers des projets: pourquoi? comment?* Faculté de psychologie et des sciences de l'éducation Université de Genève. http://www.unige.ch/fapse/SSE/teachers/perrenoud/php_main/php_1999/1999_17.htlm

Rappaport, J. (2008). Beyond participant observation. Collaborative ethnography as theoretical innovation. *Collaborative Anthropologies, 1*, 1-31. https://doi.org/10.1353/cla.0.0014

Seedhouse, P. (2005). Conversation analysis and language learning. *Language Teaching, 38*(4), 1-23. https://doi.org/10.1017/s0261444805003010

Stenhouse, L. (1985/1987). *La investigación como base de la enseñanza*. Madrid. Morata.

Unamuno, V. (2004). Dilemas metodológicos, preguntas de investigación. *Estudios de Sociolingüística, 5*(2), 219-230.

Unamuno, V., y Patiño, A. (2017). Producir conocimiento sobre el plurilingüismo junto a jóvenes estudiantes: un reto para la etnografía en colaboración. En E. Moore y M. Dooly (Eds), *Enfoques cualitativos para la investigación en educación plurilingüe* (pp. 107-128). Research-publishing.net. https://doi.org/10.14705/rpnet.2017.emmd2016.624

Van Lier, L. (1988). *The classroom and the language learner: ethnography and second language classroom research*. Londres, Nueva York: Longman.

Lecturas recomendadas

Camps, A., Rios, I., y Cambra, M. (Coords.). (2000). *Recerca i formació en didàctica de la llengua*. Barcelona: Graó.

Green, J. L., Castanheira, M. L., Skukauskaite, A., y Hammond, J. W. (2015). Developing a multifaceted research process: an ethnographic perspective for reading across traditions. En N. Markee (Coord.), *The handbook of classroom discourse and interaction* (pp. 26-43). Malden: Wiley & Sons.

Harklau, L. (2005). Ethnography and ethnographic research on second language teaching and learning. En E. Hinkel (Coord.), *Handbook of research in second language learning* (pp. 179-194). Mahwah, NJ: Lawrence Erlbaum.

Madrid, D. (2001). Introducción a la investigación en el aula de lengua extranjera. En M. E. García Sánchez y M. S Salaberri (Coords.), *Metodología de investigación en el área de filología inglesa* (pp. 11-45). Universidad de Almería: Secretariado de Publicaciones.

Moore, E., y Nussbaum, L. (2013). La lingüística interaccional y la comunicación en las aulas. *Textos de Didáctica de la Lengua y de la Literatura, 63*, 43-50.

Noffke, S. E., y Somekh, B. (Coords.). (2009). *The Sage handbook of educational action research.* London: Sage. https://doi.org/10.4135/9780857021021

Nussbaum, L. (2007). Análisis interaccional para el estudio del plurilingüismo escolar. *EMIGRA Working Papers, 108.* https://ddd.uab.cat/pub/emigrawp/emigrawp_a2007n108/emigrawp_a2007n108p1.pdf

Nussbaum, L., Escobar, C., y Unamuno, V. (2006). Una lingüística interactivista de la enseñanza y el aprendizaje de lenguas. En A. Camps (Ed.), *Diálogo e investigación en las aulas. Investigaciones en Didáctica de la Lengua y la Literatura* (pp. 183-204). Barcelona: Graó.

Nussbaum L., y Masats, D. (2012). Socialisation langagière en Catalogne: le mutilinguisme comme étayage de pratiques monolingues. En A M. Dreyfus y J. M. Prieurs (Eds), *Hétérogénéité et variation. Perspectives socolinguistiques, didactiques et anthropologiques* (pp. 155-167). París: Michel Houdiard.

Páginas web con recursos mencionados

Materiales didácticos

Materiales producidos por el GREIP en colaboración con docentes: http://grupsderecerca.uab.cat/greip/es/content/materiales

2 Doing research with teachers

Luci Nussbaum[1]

Key concepts: action research, collaborative research, ethnography, ethnomethodology, conversation analysis, plurilingual didactic sequences.

---

1. Introduction

Educational institutions are the ideal place for conducting research in the social sciences, due both to the relevance of their mission (educating future generations) and because they centrifuge changes in society, conflicts and tensions. Consequently, schools serve as a scenario for both research in teaching and learning and for a broad spectrum of disciplines (sociology, anthropology, social psychology and discourse analysis, for example). In our case, we were interested in their dimension as a sociolinguistic observatory, as a space for learning languages and for building plurilingual skills. In this respect, schools offer the advantage of bringing together, in a single building, all the actors whose communicative and learning practices we want to investigate; they are also a place for updating language policies, for socialization and for observation of the development of didactic approaches to language education.

The presence of researchers in schools is complex, given that faculty is often wary of their intentions (Unamuno, 2004). Indeed, research activities may represent an exercise of power by interpreting social realities and by legitimizing them through dissemination (Heller, 2002). Furthermore, in many

---

1. Universitat Autònoma de Barcelona, Bellaterra, Catalonia/Spain; luci.nussbaum@uab.cat

How to cite this chapter: Nussbaum, L. (2017). Doing research with teachers. In E. Moore & M. Dooly (Eds), *Qualitative approaches to research on plurilingual education* (pp. 46-67). Research-publishing.net. https://doi.org/10.14705/rpnet.2017.emmd2016.621

cases the results of the research are of no use to the educational institutions themselves, and yet represent a source of symbolic benefits for the researcher, boosting their curriculum and bringing them professional prestige. For this reason, teaching staff are often wary of those who knock on their doors to conduct research, and sometimes hide certain spaces and practices from outside observation.

Research in schools thus entails a long journey of mutual recognition and trust between the researchers and the teaching staff, and a negotiation of give-and-take. In our experience, the most effective reward for both parties is engaging in a mutually satisfying project in which both the researchers and the teachers occupy complementary spaces – rather than asymmetrical ones – to collaboratively build educational knowledge. For external research teams working in a school, this option represents an excellent opportunity to acquire educational experience, to compare theory and practice, and as a source of inspiration for future investigations. For teachers, it offers a chance to share their professional concerns with colleagues who can help them to reflect upon them, as well as the reward of being a collaborative participant in building didactic knowledge and disseminating it jointly.

This chapter aims to construe the process of some of our experiences, which may be useful for developing teachers and doctoral students who intend to undertake studies in educational institutions on the different facets of language teaching. The second section of the article outlines certain aspects of the collaborative research process between teachers and university researchers, pointing out the differences and similarities between action research, ethnography and conversational approaches to analyzing data, and collaborative research involving teaching and research teams. The third section presents a didactic approach to plurilingualism that addresses our conception of linguistically diverse education, and discusses a model of educational intervention that has been successfully developed by the GREIP group and has enabled us to gather a body of important data for understanding the process of plurilingual learning. The fourth section puts forward an example of collaborative research. Finally, the chapter concludes with some general considerations.

Chapter 2

2. Innovation through research

Collaborative research falls under what is known as action research, a working methodology coined by Kurt Lewin (1946) as being the convergence between social sciences studies and social action programs. The main objective of Lewin's proposition is to achieve theoretical advances and social changes in parallel, blurring the conventional boundaries between the production of knowledge and its implementation in social environments. In the field of education, action research is understood to be a process of reflection on teaching and learning in order to intervene in them and hence bring improvement (Burns, 1999; Elliot, 1991/1993; Stenhouse, 1985/1987; van Lier, 1988).

Educational publications often establish distinctions between action research, ethnographic research and collaborative research, depending on the actors or executors of the process and their interests. According to these viewpoints, action research should be the task of the teacher, while ethnographic research would be the work of researchers – at a distance from teaching concerns – interested in constructing explanations about social practices in educational institutions. Collaborative research, meanwhile, would be the common ground of both researchers and teachers. In this respect, it is worth noting that the research undertaken by the GREIP group encourages the dissemination of findings through the joint production of texts written collaboratively by researchers, teachers and trainee teachers.

Collaborative research is nourished by the principles of action research, given that its aim is to improve teaching practice, but it needs the instruments provided by ethnography, a field in which collaborative research processes are becoming more and more important. Consequently, in our experience, the three options are very closely related, and can be combined. In this section we will firstly discuss action research before enumerating the ethnographic procedures that help to implement it and presenting our views on data analysis. We will conclude this section with a reference to collaborative research.

2.1. Action research

Action research (see also Pascual, this volume) is a procedure that systematizes the considerations that all teachers make informally on their everyday practices (Nussbaum, 2016). Indeed, when leaving the classroom, the teacher tends to carry out a mental review of how the lesson went, on which they base any considerations of adjustments in future classes. In doing so, they take into consideration the experiences they have amassed, guidance from their reading, attendance of training seminars or discussions with colleagues, but these actions are not enough. If one wishes to innovate by implementing actions in an educational situation, it is necessary to systematically observe what goes on in the classroom and interpret these phenomena in view of all the circumstances that make up life in the classroom. The innovative teacher is one who gathers information systematically, analyzes it and compares it with research on successful educational practices, plans his or her interventions, evaluates them and disseminates them. The stages of action research are shown in the following diagram (Figure 1).

Figure 1. The phases of action research

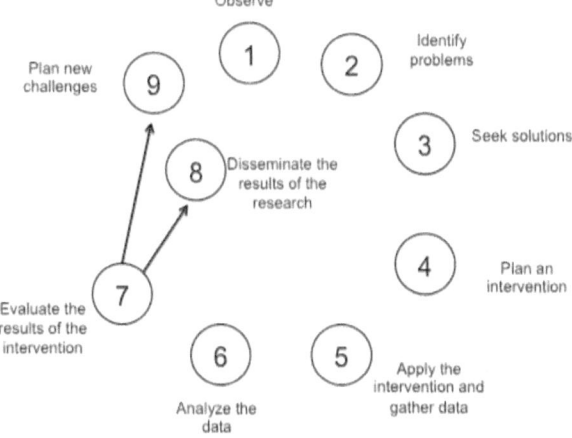

Action research can encompass a whole working program or a small aspect of it, such as progressively adjusting lesson activities for a student with learning difficulties. In any event, the problem will have been defined based on formalized observation (Phases 1 and 2), for which instruments to gather and analyze data should be provided. This will lead to the search for solutions to the problem (or problems), in Phase 3, to guide any modifications to previous practices to improve the educational intervention. These proposals will emerge from a considered perusal of specialist articles that reflect similar problems and the solutions to them, or discussions with other colleagues. Phases 4 and 5 entail not only planning and implementing the intervention but also amassing the instruments to gather information whose analysis (Phase 6) will enable the results of the intervention to be assessed (Phase 7) and to prepare the information to disseminate the experience, in Phase 8, to immediate colleagues and to the language teaching community by means of publications and meetings. Sharing the results of research is an essential process to encourage dialogue among teachers and researchers and to amplify the sphere of language teaching (Camps, 2003). An assessment of the intervention is likely to throw up new challenges (Phase 9) that will lead to the resumption of the process.

It is difficult, though not impossible, to conduct action research alone, given that the process entails complex tasks. This is why we believe it should be conducted with other people. Whatever the case, it seems opportune to revisit the ethnographic and exploratory procedures, which are summed up below.

2.2. Ethnographic procedures

Ethnography – the discipline which, since its inception, has been associated with the tradition of anthropology and, later on, linguistic anthropology and sociolinguistics (see also the contributions to this handbook by Antoniadou & Dooly, this volume; Corona, this volume; Unamuno & Patiño, this volume) – pursues, in educational contexts, a thick description of school life. In other words, it seeks a comprehensive and multidimensional description, in order to render the complexity of educational institutions. As we shall see, this entails gathering various types of data to compare and interpret them, as the stakeholders involved themselves do – students, teachers, etc. – by applying an emic approach; in other words, without projecting external interpretations (which would be an etic approach), to capture the way in which participants in communicative events understand and construe their actions (for a discussion on emic versus etic approaches, see Headland, Pike, & Harris, 1990).

Erickson (1984) notes two basic principles of ethnography in educational contexts: (1) making the familiar strange, or seeking the deeper meaning of what might seem ordinary and habitual, for the study group (behavioral norms, rituals, the use of a certain language for a certain activity, etc.); and (2) stating researchable questions, or asking questions that can be answered by observing the daily life of the study group.

Ethnographic procedures per se entail working for long periods of time to acquire the status of a member of the group that is being studied, and being able to engage in what is known as participant observation, not only in the sense of being accepted as a member of the group but, most importantly, in the sense of getting actively involved in the events that take place within the group (Rappaport, 2008). In our case, we have been able to engage in this type of research because we have integrated in regular classes and joined in as teachers or teaching assistants in classroom activities. This has enabled us to gather natural data through audio and visual recordings of the group's activities.

In addition to these core data, ethnography uses field diaries, interviews, informal conversations, discussion groups and, of course, the analysis of written documents. Ethnography also proposes the triangulation of data; in other words, generating a dialogue between the different sources of information. For example, the verbal usage of teachers (gathered by recordings) may respond to certain language policies (stipulated in official documents), while those of the students might reflect their resistance to these policies (also recorded from classroom interactions). Triangulation processes are necessary not only for generating a dialogue between data but also for returning, time and again, to the analysis of the transcripts made by the different members of the group. Furthermore, ethnographic procedures allow one to capture the impact of the research protocol on the data obtained.

2.3. Incorporating the research device in the analysis

In the processes of gathering and analyzing data (see Moore & Llompart, this volume), Mondada (2003) suggests three principles that all researchers should abide by (see also Masats, this volume).

- The principle of observability: the phenomena of interest to be analyzed are described by the speakers themselves through their activity. For example, we can only say that a student uses a particular language if we can clearly see that he/she orients towards the use of that language, whether or not his/her statements abide by the rules laid down by grammar or dictionaries.

- The principle of availability: the manner in which data are gathered and processed reveals or hides the phenomena to be studied. This principle implies that if, for example, we want to study student participation, we will need to equip ourselves with the instruments to capture their actions during the class (the notes they make in their notebooks, the way they handle objects, their interactions with fellow students, their glances, body language, etc.). Otherwise, we would only have a partial overview of their participation.

- The principle of symmetry: the research set-up should be accounted for in the data analysis. It is often said that research procedures (the presence of the observer, cameras, etc.) modify reality. However, according to this principle there is no such change, given that there is no essential reality that pre-exists at the time the data are gathered. For this reason, a thorough analysis of the data makes the inclusion of the research set-up (the presence of the researcher, camera, etc.) essential in the analysis, considering it as a constituent part of the construction of the data.

Let us take, by way of example, an audiovisual recording of a group activity involving three girls and one boy in the fifth year of primary school, and their teacher, in a science lesson in which French is used as the vehicular language. The aim of the teaching project was to document the procedures of integrating science and language learning. The group is facing a computer, whose screen displays a diagram of the respiration and nutritional process of plants, written in Catalan. The teacher wants the students to conceptualize the life processes of the plants, recognize their names in Catalan – given that the content forms part of the general science curriculum – and later explain the phenomena to the rest of the class in French[2].

Figure 2 shows the positions of the group: the teacher is behind, out of the camera's range, which is at her side.

Figure 2. Position of the camera

This audiovisual recording lets us transcribe the oral interventions of the teacher and the children and analyze the verbal actions of integrating curricular and language content (the principle of observability). However, we cannot do

---

2. These data were gathered by I. Camacho and transcribed by L. Nussbaum.

this entirely because, in collecting the data, the camera did not capture what is written on the screen or the body or eye movements of the teacher. So, the principle of availability is not completely fulfilled. The analysis was able to capture the movements and glances of the students, who were facing the camera, the computer, the teacher and the other students (the principle of symmetry).

Taking into account the research set-up in studying data implies, from our point of view, analyzing the data exhaustively by applying the procedures of conversation analysis.

2.4. Analyzing data using conversation analysis

In our research, we see ethnographic perspectives for gathering data in the classroom (and outside it, as will be seen at the end of this chapter) as being compatible with the analytical perspectives of conversation analysis with an ethnomethodological orientation (see also Masats, this volume). The use of a conversational approach proves to be particularly successful for recovering the interpretation of actors (students and teachers) with regard to institutional language policies – the emic perspective referred to above – for understanding systems of interaction, and for establishing connections with other observations undertaken in the schools. At the same time, conversation analysis allows us to examine curricular learning (Moore & Nussbaum, 2011) and the activities undertaken by learners as 'emergent plurilinguals' (García, 2009).

The purpose of ethnomethodology is to explain the principles that govern social actions based on a study of the 'methods' that people use to make their everyday activities congruous. This task entails studying how meaning is constructed interactively, how people interpret the activity they are engaged in, how they choose what is relevant, and document it through their conversational moves. A study of these interactions should observe towards which logic people are orienting, adopting their perspective, from within their system (an emic perspective) and not from outside. Conversation analysis suggests that the contributions of speakers are anchored in the interactional context, this being understood not just as the situational framework, but primarily as a sequential environment in terms of the turns of the preceding and the next speakers. The contributions of speakers thus create the context in each sequence of interaction, maintaining it or refreshing it. This is thus an approach in which one should not seek influences from the situation on what the speakers are doing, unless the individuals concerned orient towards a specific aspect, making it relevant.

Until quite recently, conversational approaches have been little used in studies on language learning. However, some publications in the last few years have shown that this is a perspective that is becoming increasingly relevant (see, in this respect, the reviews by Hall, 2004; Markee, 2015; Seedhouse, 2005; also Masats, this volume).

Conversation analysis calls for a thorough examination of all the data in the transcription; not only linguistic data, but all the multimodal aspects (body position, movements, glances, use of objects, etc.) that contribute to the progress of interaction (Moore & Nussbaum, 2011). This is justified by the principle whereby transcription is already the first phase of the analysis, and therefore has clear implications for the interpretation of verbal activity (Duranti, 1997/2000; Nussbaum, 2006; see also Moore & Llompart, this volume). In this respect, one of the extremely productive procedures adopted by the GREIP group (following the proposals of other research teams) is to study transcriptions collectively in data analysis sessions. Recordings and transcripts are examined as a group, making it possible to achieve more accurate transcriptions and avoid subjective interpretations.

Systematic work using the abovementioned procedures gives an understanding of the benefits of cooperative action in the data collection process. Furthermore, when action research is done collaboratively with colleagues who are also interested in educational innovation, the task is much more efficient because efforts are united to construct didactic knowledge, while at the same time addressing it from the perspective of specific professional interests. In the following section we will deal with this form of action research.

3. Collaborative research

For some years now, our research group has been undertaking studies on plurilingual education in educational institutions in Catalonia, with the involvement of active teachers, trainee teachers and young researchers in our group whose master's or PhD projects were in this field.

Our choice to do collaborative research is based on a series of considerations, which are detailed below (see also Nussbaum & Unamuno, 2006; Unamuno, 2004). Investigations in educational contexts often only consider the researchers' perspectives and ignore those of the participants (teachers and students). The unease that can be felt in classrooms when under observation can only be overcome by active and committed participation of research groups with schools, students and families (Carr, 1995/1996) in order to articulate their needs through joint endeavors. The aim is thus to design research projects that allow a dialogue between different agents, theories and conceptions of education (Cazden, 1986/1989). Research for and in action (Elliot, 1991/1993, Stenhouse, 1985/1987), with a cooperative orientation, helps to overcome the tension between the researcher and the object of the research, by considering that the person doing the research is also a subject of it, thus reducing the gap between research teams and their subjects, and between theory and practice. This involves a gradual process of fine-tuning which can sometimes be frustrating for everyone involved, but often successful.

Our objective is to experiment, along with teachers and students, with new forms of teaching local languages (Catalan and Spanish) and foreign languages in an integrated way (González et al., 2008; Nussbaum, 2008; Nussbaum & Rocha, 2008). At the same time, we aim to construct situated didactic knowledge in contexts of learner heterogeneity, in schools that teach in Catalan, Spanish and one or two foreign languages, and to educate plurilingual people on the linguistic diversity of their milieu and the world. Figure 3 illustrates this collaborative relationship.

Figure 3. Collaborative research

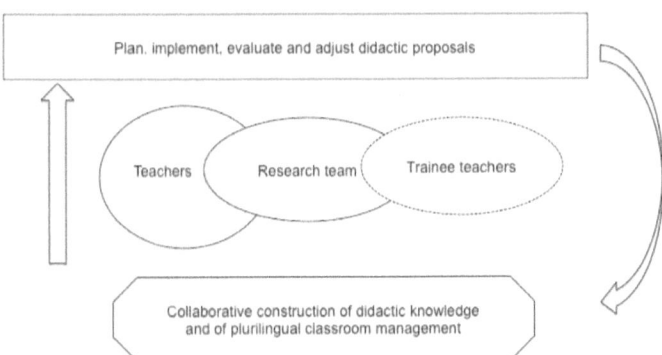

Detailed below are some of the lines of work undertaken in these collaborative actions.

4. Plurilingual projects

Historically, languages have been taught separately, the argument being that this provides more intensive contact with the language in question and avoids any possible cross-contamination between linguistic systems. The basis for this common stance is the prevalence of a monolingual vision of multilingual learning, with languages being understood as separate compartments of knowledge (Creese & Blackledge, 2010; Cummins, 2005; amongst others). However, the existence of plurilingual usage both in and outside the classroom in communicative activities (reading, exchanges mediated by technology, etc.) would seem to obviate the rule of 'one language for each classroom'. And yet, hybrid resources, far from being an obstacle to learning new skills, constitute a useful structural base for taking part in complex learning practices which, in fact, lead to the acquisition of competences for acting unilingually, i.e. using a single language when the circumstances so require (Moore & Nussbaum, 2011; Nussbaum, 2014).

In this respect, Duverger (2007), when referring to the integrated teaching of curricular content and languages, talks about the didactization of plurilingualism in schools. The author distinguishes three types of plurilingual regimes: macro-level, meso-level and micro-level. The first refers to the planning of teaching in different languages in terms of subjects and time periods, which tends to be defined in the school's language curriculum. Thus, for example, it is possible to plan the teaching of mathematics in English or science in French. The second type, the meso-level regime, refers to planning the use of certain languages for specific activities. For example, if the subject is geography, it is possible to refer to maps or other documents in either English or Spanish, although the didactic sequence would be taught in Catalan. Finally, the micro-level refers to the unplanned plurilingual usage that takes place in schools in multilingual areas (Nussbaum, 2014). The meso-level regime, which consists of choosing different languages for specific moments of a learning unit, has been the inspiration for part of our collaborative work in schools (see the following sections).

We view learning as a situated social practice, which means presenting knowledge in a context and involving the students in practical and socially significant activities by engaging in educational projects. Project-based work (see, for a theoretical foundation, Camps, 2003; Perrenoud, 1999) is considered a useful tool, in the sense that it positions the students as part of a research team (Lambert, 2012) who follow a path to attain an end product (or several products), with the idea of it being presented to other people to spread this knowledge beyond the classroom.

A project naturally integrates subject learning and the linguistic activities necessary to access the knowledge in question: the use of technological resources to search for information, the reading of written texts and multimodal documents; social practices in and outside the classroom, and, of course, the use of different language resources. A project-based approach allows different languages to be adopted (the meso-level regime, according to Duverger, 2007) depending on the phase of the project. Thus an interview might be prepared in Spanish; a text on the internet could be read in English; and a report, as a final product, might be drafted in Catalan and contain sections in different languages.

This organizational flexibility reflects the concept of the class as a community of practice (Lave & Wenger, 1991) in which the students participate in different ways, according to their abilities, to acquire the expert skills that will enable them to act in different contexts (Hall, Cheng, & Carlson, 2006).

Figure 4 shows a diagram of a project sequence. The core activities can be done naturally in plurilingual modes, given that the environment in which they take place is plurilingual. The final product, however, can be done in a single language to demonstrate the academic skills required by the curriculum.

Figure 4. Diagram of an educational sequence

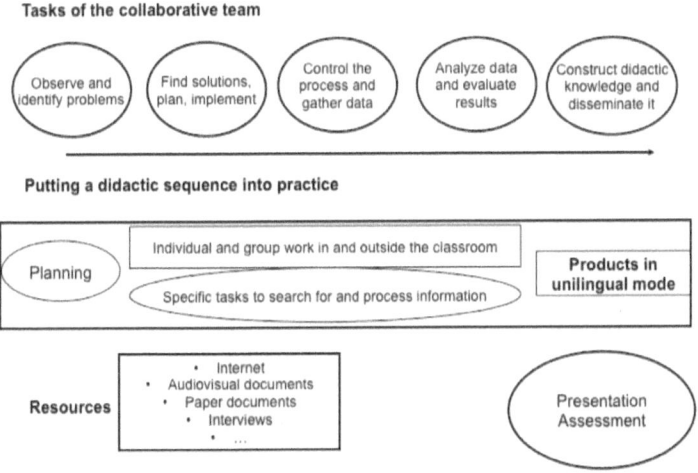

Our approach, the result of data analysis and collaborative reflection with teachers, trainee teachers and research interns, lies in the prior observation of and discussion about the initial competences of the students, their regular social practices, and the role of the school in their plurilingual education. Our starting point is the inclusion of flexible plurilingual modes, especially for the treatment of educational knowledge in classroom interactions taking various different formats (teacher-student, student-student). In each didactic sequence we also undertake an in-depth examination of different discursive genres encountered

Chapter 2

– depending on the agreed final product – through the use of texts either in hard copy or online, and in the different outputs of students. These stages lead to the construction of a final unilingual product which should fulfill the formal educational requirements of academic discourse. Figure 5 illustrates the process.

Figure 5. From plurilingual modes to unilingual academic discourse

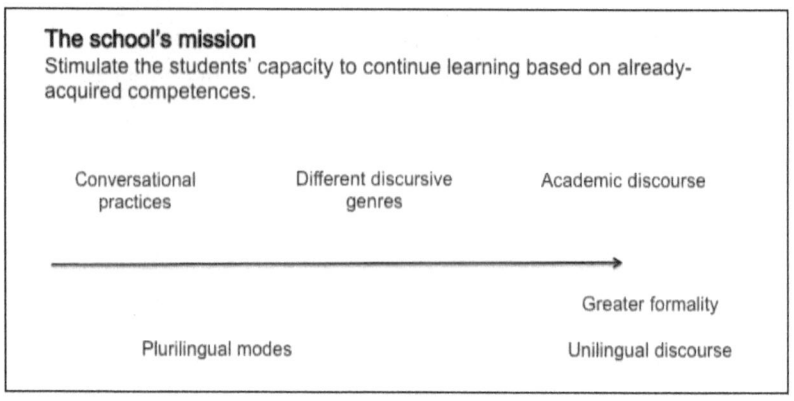

This radically plurilingual approach seeks to take advantage of every possible resource to create bonds between the social use of language and school-based practices.

5. An example of collaborative research

Our work is illustrated[3] with the case of a school in Barcelona, located in a neighborhood with a significant percentage of people from very different geographic and sociolinguistic backgrounds. More than 90% of the children at this school have family trajectories of immigration. Although the vehicular language of the school is Catalan, students use Spanish to communicate with their peers and it is also used in personal relations between adults in the neighborhood who do not share the same native language, a very common

---

3. Those interested in the collaborative teaching proposals described herein can refer to http://grupsderecerca.uab.cat/greip/en/content/materials

situation in the metropolitan areas of Catalonia (Nussbaum & Unamuno, 2006). This sociolinguistic situation means that children perceive the learning of Catalan as an educational requirement that is not very useful in their everyday lives. Furthermore, the school also has to teach students with a very wide range of skills: a high percentage of them enroll at a late stage and hence do not have the same skills as the children who have received regular schooling.

At the start of the project[4], aimed at a group of fifth-grade primary school students, the team formulated two main goals based on the circumstances described above:

- making the students aware that Catalan is a language that is used regularly in other geographical and social contexts;

- promoting significant oral and written use of the language.

Both goals led to the need to open up the classroom to observe the social uses of Catalan in other contexts in which students might take part, using their linguistic resources and observing the ways they act in different environments from the school one. We also planned to take into account the students' very diverse skillsets so that all of them could get involved in putting together a significant project.

Based on the curricular content (the counties of Catalonia), the project proposed to integrate a range of curricular objectives: the exploration of the region (its geography, history, natural resources, economy, population, professions of its inhabitants, media and cultural manifestations); the use of different procedures to obtain and store information (interviews with other students and adults, internet research, the use of video and audio recordings, etc.), and the use of different forms of representing information (maps, graphs, etc.). At the end of the process, students would need to produce a radio report for the school radio in order to disseminate their experience to other students at the school and to other schools.

---

4. The project was designed by: Montserrat Colet, Víctor Corona, Violeta García, Luci Nussbaum, Adriana Patiño and Pepa Rocha, with the advice of Montserrat Oller and Àngels Prat.

The project was structured over four phases (see Corona, Nussbaum, & Rocha, 2008). The aim was to enable students to learn working methods that could be extrapolated to other situations, as well as putting them in an active role as researchers of physical and social situations. In one of the phases, students made contact by means of a virtual forum with students at the same grade from two schools in different geographical regions to gather information on the counties of their counterparts. In another, students met up with their virtual counterparts to gather more information.

Through the project, the students were able to see that the use of Catalan was a regular part of everyday life in some places, and they were able to use the language for practical purposes, including to construct a final product using standard spoken Catalan. Having said that, the use of other languages was integrated naturally in communicative and learning practices for collecting information and in spontaneous interactions with other people outside of the classroom.

The implementation of the sequence, which lasted several weeks, allowed us to gather data that were very important for both the teaching team and the research group: recordings of team discussions; of the class work, during the process and during the recording of the final product; recordings of interviews with the general public and with other children at the schools visited; documents written by the students, etc. The collection of data was done ethnographically, thanks to participant observation during the whole process.

This body of work was used later on in team discussions (evaluation of the educational proposition, discussions of aspects that could be improved upon, etc.) to jointly construct didactic knowledge with other people from the GREIP group with an interest in finding out how language and communication skills are built and rebuilt in highly diverse sociolinguistic contexts. In analyzing these data, conversation analysis procedures were used. The results of the analyses were disclosed at various meetings with other teachers and researchers and served to a large extent to provide arguments in support of the efficacy of plurilingual approaches to increase the unilingual skills necessary to take part in certain social encounters.

6. Concluding words

The overall aim of the GREIP group is to document the plurilingual uses and learning of students in contexts of significant language diversity. A fieldwork approach – knowledge of the schools, the classrooms, the communication practices used in the school, the opinions of the students with regard to language usage, etc. – constitutes a necessary condition to be able to undertake, in conjunction with the teaching staff, significant teaching proposals for the students.

We view language learning as a social activity that is essentially carried out by interacting with other people (teachers, parents, family members, etc.) and with texts, within and outside the educational environment, as well as through the mediation of technology. For this reason, in our research we put a very high priority on the data obtained from interactions, given that it is these data that enable us to reconstruct situated cognitive processes.

In this text we have tried to articulate the collaborative work of the research team and the teaching staff in the schools in the interest of contributing to language education anchored in specific educational contexts. This collaborative work, enshrined in action research, makes use of ethnography, which allows a closer perspective on the everyday life of classrooms and helps understand, from within, the linguistic practices among the subjects of the study, as well as promoting the development of their competences through efficient teaching proposals. The study of the processes generated by didactic interventions, by means of a meticulous analysis of the interactions that take place in them, allows us to take a critical view on teaching approaches and plan for new challenges.

Works cited

Antoniadou, V., & Dooly, M. (2017). Educational ethnography in blended learning environments. In E. Moore & M. Dooly (Eds), *Qualitative approaches to research on plurilingual education* (pp. 237-263). Research-publishing.net. https://doi.org/10.14705/rpnet.2017.emmd2016.630

Burns, A. (1999). *Collaborative action research for English language teachers*. Cambridge: Cambridge University Press.

Camps, A. (Ed.). (2003). *Secuencias didácticas para aprender a escribir.* Barcelona: Editorial Graó.

Corona, V. (2017). An ethnographic approach to the study of linguistic varieties used by young Latin Americans in Barcelona. In E. Moore & M. Dooly (Eds), *Qualitative approaches to research on plurilingual education* (pp. 170-188). Research-publishing.net. https://doi.org/10.14705/rpnet.2017.emmd2016.627

Carr, W. (1995/1996). *For Education: Towards Critical Educational Inquiry*. Madrid: Morata.

Cazden, C. (1986/1999). El discurso en el aula. In M. Wittroc (Ed.), *La investigación en la enseñanza, vol III: Métodos cualitativos y de observación* (pp. 627-719). Barcelona: Paidós.

Corona, V., Nussbaum, L., & Rocha, P. (2008). El castellano que usan los escolares de Cataluña. *Cuadernos de Pedagogía, 378*, 27-30.

Creese, A., & Blackledge, A. (2010). Translanguaging in the bilingual classroom: a pedagogy for learning and teaching? *The Modern Language Journal, 94*(1), 103-115. https://doi.org/10.1111/j.1540-4781.2009.00986.x

Cummins, J. (2005). A proposal for action: strategies 354 for recognizing heritage language competence as a learning resource within the mainstream classroom. *Modern Language Journal, 89*(4), 585-592.

Duranti, A. (1997/2000). *Antropología lingüística*. Madrid: Cambridge University Press. https://doi.org/10.1017/CBO9780511810190

Duverger, J. (2007). Didactiser l'alternance des langues en cours de DNL. *Tréma, 28*. https://doi.org/10.4000/trema.302

Elliot, J. (1991/1993). *Action research for educational change*. Madrid: Morata.

Erickson, F. (1984). What makes school ethnography 'ethnographic'? *Anthropology and Education Quarterly, 15*(1), 51-66. https://doi.org/10.1525/aeq.1984.15.1.05x1472p

García, O. (2009). *Bilingual education in the 21st century: a global perspective*. Oxford: Wiley-Blackwell.

González, P, Llobet, L., Masats, D., Nussbaum, L., & Unamuno, V. (2008). Tres en uno: inclusión de alumnado diverso, integración de contenidos y formación de profesorado. In J. L. Barrio (Ed.), *El proceso de enseñar lenguas. Investigaciones en didáctica de la lengua* (pp. 107-133). Madrid: Ed. La Muralla.

Hall, J. K. (2004). Language learning as an interactional achievement. *The Modern Language Journal, 88*(4), 607-612.

Hall, J. K., Cheng, A., & Carlson, M. T. (2006). Reconceptualizing multicompetence as a theory of language knowledge. *Applied Linguistics, 27*(2), 220-240. https://doi.org/10.1093/applin/aml013

Headland, T. N., Pike, K. L., & Harris, M. (Eds). (1990). *Emics and etics: the insider/outsider debate*. Newbury Park, California: Sage Publications.

Heller, M. (2002). *Éléments d'une sociolinguistique critique*. Paris: Didier.

Lambert, P. (2012). Identifier la pluralité des ressources des élèves en contexte monolingue et normatif. Une enquête ethnographique auprès de lycéennes. In M. Dreyfus & J. Prieurs (Eds), *Hétérogénéité et variation. Perspectives socolinguistiques, didactiques et anthropologiques* (pp. 182-195). Paris: Michel Houdiard.

Lave, J., & Wenger, E. (1991). *Situated learning: legitimate peripherical participation*. New York: Cambridge University Press. https://doi.org/10.1017/CBO9780511815355

Lewin, K. (1946). Action research and minority problems. *Journal of Social Issues, 2*(4), 34-46. https://doi.org/10.1111/j.1540-4560.1946.tb02295.x

Markee, N. (2015). Introduction: classroom discourse and interaction research. In N. Markee (Ed.), *Handbook of classroom discourse and interaction* (pp. 3-19). Boston, MA: Wiley.

Masats, D. (2017). Conversation analysis at the service of research in the field of second language acquisition (CA-for-SLA). In E. Moore & M. Dooly (Eds), *Qualitative approaches to research on plurilingual education* (pp. 321-347). Research-publishing.net. https://doi.org/10.14705/rpnet.2017.emmd2016.633

Mondada, L. (2003). Observer les activités de classe dans leur diversité: choix méthodologiques et enjeux théoriques. In J. Perera, L. Nussbaum, & M. Milian (Eds), *L'educació lingüística en situacions multiculturals i multilingües* (pp. 49-70). Barcelona: University of Barcelona.

Moore, E., & Llompart, J. (2017). Collecting, transcribing, analyzing and presenting plurilingual interactional data. In E. Moore & M. Dooly (Eds), *Qualitative approaches to research on plurilingual education* (pp. 403-417). Research-publishing.net. https://doi.org/10.14705/rpnet.2017.emmd2016.638

Moore, E., & Nussbaum, L. (2011). Què aporta l'anàlisi conversacional a la comprensió de les situacions d'AICLE. In C. Escobar & L. Nussbaum (Eds), *Aprendre en una Altra llengua / Learning through another language / Aprender en otra lengua* (pp. 93-118). Bellaterra: UAB publication service.

Nussbaum, L. (2006). La transcripción de la interacción en contextos de contacto y de aprendizaje de lenguas. In Y. Bürki & E. de Steffani (Eds), *Transcribir la lengua: de la filología al análisis de la conversación* (pp. 195-218). Bern: Peter Lang.

Nussbaum, L. (2008). Construire le plurilinguisme à l'école: de la recherche à l'intervention et de l'intervention à la recherche. In M. Candelier, G. Ioannitou, D. Omer, & M. T. Vasseur (Eds), *Conscience du plurilinguisme. Pratiques, représentations et interventions* (pp. 125-144). Rennes: Presses Universitaires de Rennes.

Nussbaum, L. (2014). Una didàctica del plurilingüisme. *Bellaterra Journal of Teaching & Learning Language & Literature, 7*(3), 1-13.

Nussbaum, L. (2016). Estudio de la interacción en el aula de lengua extranjera. In D. Masats & L. Nussbaum (Eds), *Enseñanza y aprendizaje de las lenguas extranjeras en educación secundaria obligatoria* (pp. 113-142). Madrid: Síntesis.

Nussbaum, L., & Rocha, P. (2008). L'organisation sociale de l'apprentissage dans une approche par projet. *Babylonia, 3*, 52-55.

Nussbaum, L., & Unamuno, V. (2006). Les competències comunicatives multilingües. In L. Nussbaum & V. Unamuno (Eds), *Usos i competències multilingües entre escolars d'origen immigrant* (pp. 41-62). Bellaterra: UAB publication service.

Pascual, X. (2017). Investigating one's own teaching practices using action research. In E. Moore & M. Dooly (Eds), *Qualitative approaches to research on plurilingual education* (pp. 88-105). Research-publishing.net. https://doi.org/10.14705/rpnet.2017.emmd2016.623

Perrenoud, P. (1999). *Apprendre à l'école à travers des projets: pourquoi ? comment ?* Faculty of Psychology and Education Sciences, University of Geneva. http://www.unige.ch/fapse/SSE/teachers/perrenoud/php_main/php_1999/1999_17.html

Rappaport, J. (2008). Beyond participant observation. Collaborative ethnography as theoretical innovation. *Collaborative Anthropologies, 1*, 1-31. https://doi.org/10.1353/cla.0.0014

Seedhouse, P. (2005). Conversation analysis and language learning. *Language Teaching, 38*(4), 1-23. https://doi.org/10.1017/s0261444805003010

Stenhouse, L. (1985/1987). *La investigación como base de la enseñanza*. Madrid. Morata.

Unamuno, V. (2004). Dilemas metodológicos, preguntas de investigación. *Estudios de Sociolingüística, 5*(2), 219-230.

Unamuno, V., & Patiño, A. (2017). Producing knowledge about plurilingualism with young students: a challenge for collaborative ethnography. In E. Moore & M. Dooly (Eds), *Qualitative approaches to research on plurilingual education* (pp. 129-149). Research-publishing.net. https://doi.org/10.14705/rpnet.2017.emmd2016.625

Van Lier, L. (1988). *The classroom and the language learner: ethnography and second language classroom research*. London, New York: Longman.

Recommended reading

Camps, A., Rios, I., & Cambra, M. (Eds). (2000). *Recerca i formació en didàctica de la llengua*. Barcelona: Graó.

Green, J. L., Castanheira, M. L., Skukauskaite, A., & Hammond, J. W. (2015). Developing a multifaceted research process: an ethnographic perspective for reading across traditions. In N. Markee (Ed.), *The handbook of classroom discourse and interaction*. Malden: Wiley & Sons.

Harklau, L. (2005). Ethnography and ethnographic research on second language teaching and learning. In E. Hinkel (Ed.), *Handbook of research in second language learning* (pp. 179-194). Mahwah, NJ: Lawrence Erlbaum.

Madrid, D. (2001). Introducción a la investigación en el aula de lengua extranjera. In M. E. García Sánchez & M. S Salaberri (Eds), *Metodología de investigación en el área de filología inglesa* (pp. 11-45). Almería: Universidad de Almería, Secretariado de Publicaciones.

Moore, E., & Nussbaum, L. (2013). La lingüística interaccional y la comunicación en las aulas. *Textos de Didáctica de la Lengua y de la Literatura, 63*, 43-50.

Noffke, S. E., & Somekh, B. (Eds). (2009). *The Sage handbook of educational action research*. London: Sage. https://doi.org/10.4135/9780857021021

Nussbaum, L. (2007). Análisis interaccional para el estudio del plurilingüismo escolar. *EMIGRA Working Papers, 108*. https://ddd.uab.cat/pub/emigrawp/emigrawp_a2007n108/emigrawp_a2007n108p1.pdf

Nussbaum, L., Escobar, C., & Unamuno, V. (2006). Una lingüística interactivista de la enseñanza y el aprendizaje de llenguas. In A. Camps (Ed.), *Diálogo e investigación en las aulas. Investigaciones en Didáctica de la Lengua y la Literatura* (pp. 183-204). Barcelona: Graó.

Nussbaum L., & Masats, D. (2012). Socialisation langagière en Catalogne : le mutilinguisme comme étayage de pratiques monolingües. In M. Dreyfus & J. M. Prieurs (Eds), *Hétérogénéité et variation. Perspectives socolinguistiques, didactiques et anthropologiques* (pp. 155-167). Paris: Michel Houdiard.

Websites with resources mentioned

Educational material

Material produced by the GREIP group in collaboration with teachers: http://grupsderecerca.uab.cat/greip/en/content/materials

3 Investigar las propias prácticas docentes a través de la investigación-acción

Xavier Pascual[1]

Conceptos clave: investigación-acción, prácticas docentes, métodos mixtos, observación de aula, cuestionarios.

---

1. Introducción

La investigación que se explica en adelante y que ejemplifica la investigación-acción pretendió aportar a las nuevas definiciones curriculares y profesionales, a partir del análisis sistemático de las posibilidades y límites que se presentan al trabajar, la dimensión intercultural en las aulas de lengua extranjera con adultos.

La metodología de la investigación-acción se ha definido de muchas maneras (cf. Bizquerra Alzina, 2009; Cohen y Manion, 1990; Kemmis y McTaggart, 1988; Latorre, 2007; van Lier, 2001). Goyette y Lessard-Hébert (1988) señalan diversas diferencias epistemológicas que

> "convergen en torno a tres elementos básicos: a) desde el punto de vista del objeto (el qué); b) desde el punto de vista de la metodología (el cómo) y c) desde el punto de vista del investigador (el quién)" (Rizo y Romeu, 2008, s.p.).

Tanto Suárez Pazos (2002) como Latorre (2007) avisan de que el concepto que constituye la investigación-acción ha sido durante décadas muy distorsionado en su aplicación.

---

1. Universitat Autònoma de Barcelona, Bellaterra, Cataluña/España; xavier.pascual@uab.cat

Para citar este capítulo: Pascual, X. (2017). Investigar las propias prácticas docentes a través de la investigación-acción. En E. Moore y M. Dooly (Eds), *Enfoques cualitativos para la investigación en educación plurilingüe* (pp. 69-87). Research-publishing.net. https://doi.org/10.14705/rpnet.2017.emmd2016.622

"Atentos a las distorsiones más usuales, situaremos en primer lugar lo que no es la [investigación-acción...]. (a) No es lo que habitualmente hace un profesor cuando reflexiona sobre lo que acontece en su trabajo; como investigación, se trata de tareas sistemáticas basadas en evidencias; (b) no es una simple resolución de problemas, implica también mejorar, comprender; (c) no se trata de una investigación sobre otras personas, sino sobre uno mismo, en colaboración con otros implicados y colaboradores; y (d) no es la aplicación del método científico a la enseñanza, es una modalidad diferente que se interesa por el punto de vista de los implicados, cambiando tanto al investigador como a la situación investigada" (Suárez Pazos, 2002, p. 43).

Se pueden destacar algunos rasgos comunes entre todas las definiciones: (1) es un método de investigación (normalmente) cualitativa; (2) se sitúa el centro de atención en lo que ocurre en la actividad docente cotidiana (en la educación, principalmente en interacciones en el aula); (3) tiene como principal objetivo detectar qué aspectos deben ser mejorados y cómo cambiarlos (véase Nussbaum, en este volumen).

En resumen, se puede decir que la propuesta de una investigación-acción se basa en la necesidad de integrar el trabajo investigador y la práctica docente, de tal forma que se puedan obtener datos y resultados que puedan servir para su transformación (Bisquerra Alzina, 2009; van Lier, 2001). La investigación-acción se orienta hacia el análisis de acciones y situaciones sociales susceptibles de ser problematizadas y que están abiertas a cambios. Si bien parte de una descripción inicial (estado inicial), se trata de una disciplina de intervención orientada hacia la modificación (estado final).

En general, se atribuye la introducción al concepto de investigación-acción a Kurt Lewin, que lo introdujo en los años 50 (Lewin, 1973) pero hasta los años 70 no hubo un movimiento que recogiera el concepto como un acercamiento sistemático de investigación cualitativa hacia las prácticas docentes. Encabezada por Lawrence Stenhouse (1984) y John Elliott (1993) en Gran Bretaña, empezó a ser aceptada la propuesta de que los docentes son las personas más apropiadas para investigar y mejorar sus propias acciones. Posteriormente, en los años 80, Stephen Kemmis, junto con Wilfred Carr (Carr y Kemmis, 1988) ofrecieron la visión de que la investigación-acción no es solamente un proceso de cambio de las prácticas individuales de los docentes, sino un proceso de transformación social que se lleva a cabo colaborativamente con las personas participantes y otras personas interesadas de los contextos (alumnado, otros docentes, equipos de investigación y la comunidad más cercana; véanse Nussbaum, en este volumen; Unamuno y Patiño, en este volumen).

Este tipo de investigaciones se basan en una fase diagnóstica de la que se deriva el diseño de la intervención, cuyo seguimiento da lugar a la interpretación de las transformaciones. La investigación-acción implica para sus participantes la autorreflexión sobre su propia actuación y la de los demás, poniendo en un lugar central el diálogo entre la teoría, el sujeto investigador y la situación investigada.

Se trata de un proceso en espiral, en el que los momentos de problematización, diagnóstico, diseño de una propuesta de intervención, aplicación, evaluación, etc. vuelven a iniciarse en una nueva versión del circuito.

El diseño de este tipo de investigaciones comporta considerar los siguientes pasos, característicos de la investigación-acción:

- *Problematización*: se trata de establecer un campo problemático definido por cierta molestia social derivada de alguna o de todas las personas participantes, de dificultades o limitaciones para la actuación, de acuerdo con los objetivos individuales o institucionales.

- *Diagnóstico*: tras la problematización y el establecimiento del foco del proceso de investigación, se hace necesario realizar un diagnóstico claro de la situación. Para ello, es importante obtener información, organizarla y analizarla para comprender la situación inicial o punto de partida de la investigación.

- *Diseño de una propuesta de intervención*: tras la identificación del objeto-problema y el análisis de la situación inicial, se diseñan la intervención y las herramientas de seguimiento.

- *Aplicación de la intervención*: se considera aquí el proceso que involucra la realización y observación de la intervención.

- *Evaluación*: las evidencias que se han registrado sobre los resultados de la intervención se recogen y sistematizan en este momento del proceso. La evaluación es también la instancia de redefinición del problema, a partir de la información que proporciona el análisis.

Todos estos pasos implican la triangulación de datos, es decir, la recogida, análisis y contraste de diversos tipos de datos (videos, transcripciones, productos de los estudiantes, documentos oficiales del centro, etc.). En la recogida y análisis de datos en este estudio, se emplearon tanto métodos cualitativos como cuantitativos. Siguiendo la terminología de Morse (2010), se emplearon métodos mixtos con un diseño cualitativo y cuantitativo. El estudio se basó, en gran parte, en la observación sistemática de las interacciones en el aula y en otros datos cualitativos. Sin embargo, también se utilizaron métodos cuantitativos, por ejemplo, los cuestionarios, como se explicará a continuación.

En la sociedad actual, se ejerce cada vez más presión sobre los docentes para que sean innovadores, sobre todo frente a los avances científicos y tecnológicos y los nuevos paisajes demográficos. Existe una sensación generalizada de cambios vertiginosos y, como consecuencia, un incremento en las exigencias a dar respuestas a desafíos sociales a través de la educación. Las viejas concepciones sobre el papel de las instituciones educativas y sobre los procesos de enseñanza y aprendizaje están cambiando (véase Dooly, en este volumen). En este sentido, hay muchos autores que consideran la investigación-acción como la metodología más idónea para enfrentar estos retos.

"La complejidad de la práctica educativa hace necesario que el profesorado asuma el papel de investigador; que esté atento a las contingencias del contexto; que se cuestione las situaciones problemáticas de la práctica; que dé respuesta a las necesidades del alumnado y trate de buscar nuevos enfoques. La enseñanza es un proceso donde tienen lugar simultáneamente múltiples elementos en interacción, lo que hace difícil su indagación y conocimiento" (Latorre, 2007, p. 12).

En este sentido, este capítulo parte de un estudio del contexto educativo que no solo sirve para comprender el lugar en el que se inserta la investigación que se explica, sino que también ofrece datos importantes para el análisis de la situación inicial y compleja de la que se partía. Se trata de un trabajo de diagnosis que permitió definir de manera más clara y objetiva la problemática inicial y las necesidades de transformación.

2. El estudio: el desarrollo de la competencia intercultural en aulas de lenguas extranjeras

Hace décadas que las políticas oficiales sobre la didáctica de las lenguas defienden una enseñanza más integrada de lengua y cultura (Council of Europe, 2001). Esta concepción de la enseñanza de lenguas implica una crítica a los enfoques que, a partir de una concepción instrumental de la lengua –centrada exclusivamente en la adquisición de competencias lingüísticas–, han marginado las dimensiones culturales e interculturales en muchos centros. Este fue el caso en el contexto del estudio presentado aquí: una Escuela Oficial de Idiomas (E.O.I.) en Barcelona.

Los expertos en didáctica de la lengua extranjera señalan, desde hace ya unas décadas, que los estudiantes no solo necesitan desarrollar una competencia gramatical, sino también una competencia comunicativa que les permita emplear las lenguas de manera apropiada social y culturalmente (Council of Europe, 2001). Es en este sentido que el aprendizaje de las lenguas no puede ser concebido como un proceso independiente al desarrollo de la competencia intercultural, necesaria para participar de manera efectiva en contextos culturalmente significativos para los usuarios.

La incorporación de una dimensión intercultural en la enseñanza de lenguas hace replantear el perfil del estudiante. Si el docente puede ser concebido como mediador de lenguas y culturas, el estudiante empieza a concebirse como un locutor que se convierte en plurilingüe, por una parte, y en intercultural, por la otra. Este nuevo perfil de estudiante comporta una redefinición radical de las propuestas de enseñanza-aprendizaje.

Para aportar en las nuevas definiciones curriculares y profesionales, a partir del análisis sistemático de las posibilidades y límites que se presentan al trabajar la dimensión intercultural en las aulas de lengua extranjera con adultos, se optó por una investigación sobre la propia práctica del investigador-docente y sobre el contexto. Se enmarcó el estudio en la investigación-acción, considerando que partía de una problemática relevante para el investigador, para el colectivo de docentes de lenguas extranjeras en general, y para los estudiantes, y que los resultados podrían ser aplicados para la transformación de las prácticas y los contextos analizados.

3. Objetivos del estudio

Como introducción a esta investigación, se propuso explorar, en primer lugar, la especificidad de las nociones de competencia comunicativa, competencia intercultural, conciencia intercultural y dimensión intercultural del proceso de enseñanza-aprendizaje de lenguas. Se consideró que la definición de estos conceptos y su racionalización para la intervención pedagógica eran importantes tanto para la investigación como para la práctica.

Se partía de la base de que el estudio del desarrollo de la competencia intercultural y de la dimensión intercultural del proceso de enseñanza y aprendizaje de lenguas comporta el análisis sistemático del contexto. Como ya se ha dicho, no se trata simplemente de una descripción del lugar en donde se inserta la práctica docente e investigadora, sino más bien de un análisis de variables que se articulan en la definición de la problemática inicial de la que partía mi investigación.

En coherencia con el planteamiento general de esta investigación, el primer objetivo de la misma era explorar y describir las dimensiones institucional, docente y del alumnado del contexto de inscripción. Concretamente:

Objetivo 1. Describir las dimensiones institucional, docente y del alumnado del contexto socioeducativo, considerando:

- los elementos culturales e interculturales del currículo vigente de francés en las E.O.I. de Cataluña;

- las categorías relativas a la sensibilidad intercultural;

- las prácticas interculturales declaradas por el profesorado.

Siguiendo a van Lier (2001), la investigación-acción comporta incluir en el estudio el diseño y la evaluación de materiales específicamente creados para incidir en la competencia lingüística e intercultural del estudiante. Este era justamente el segundo objetivo de la investigación.

Objetivo 2. Analizar la dimensión intercultural del proceso de enseñanza y aprendizaje de lenguas, a partir de la aplicación de una intervención didáctica orientada al desarrollo conjunto de la competencia intercultural y las competencias lingüísticas previstas en el currículo de cuarto nivel de las E.O.I. (uso de la lengua, expresión oral y escrita, comprensión oral y escrita).

- Observar la interrelación entre materiales, actividades y práctica docente.

- Observar la actuación del alumnado en el proceso de enseñanza-aprendizaje, atendiendo específicamente a su dimensión intercultural.

- Analizar las relaciones entre las competencias intercultural y lingüística en dicho proceso.

Si bien los indicadores utilizados para la evaluación de la competencia lingüística eran los que se aplicaban de forma institucional en las E.O.I, no existían indicadores relativos a la competencia intercultural estandarizados. Por ello, y a partir del análisis de diferentes propuestas derivadas de numerosas investigaciones precedentes (por ejemplo, Byram, 1992; Byram, Gribkova, y Starkey, 2002; Candillier, 2007; Meyer, 1994), me propuse también desarrollar una propuesta propia en función de los resultados del contexto de investigación en el que se trabajaba. Así, el objetivo 3 de esta investigación fue:

Objetivo 3. A partir del análisis crítico de las diferentes propuestas disponibles para la evaluación de la competencia intercultural en clase de lenguas extranjeras, elaborar un conjunto de indicadores aplicables para el aula de francés con adultos y aplicarlos para medir su pertinencia y funcionalidad.

- Comparar y analizar diferentes propuestas para la evaluación de la competencia intercultural en lengua extranjera.

- Elaborar un conjunto de indicadores que pudieran ser operativos en la evaluación del desarrollo de la competencia intercultural en clase de lenguas extranjeras con adultos.

- Medir su eficacia y funcionalidad a través de la aplicación a datos concretos extraídos de dinámicas naturales de intervención socioeducativas.

A la elaboración de estos indicadores le siguió su aplicación concreta. Por ello, el objetivo 4 se centró en el análisis del impacto de la intervención didáctica en el desarrollo de la competencia intercultural según los indicadores elaborados. Concretamente:

Objetivo 4. Medir el impacto de una intervención didáctica orientada a la dimensión intercultural del proceso de enseñanza-aprendizaje de lenguas en el desarrollo de la competencia intercultural.

- Desarrollar una propuesta de indicadores con la finalidad de evaluar los aspectos más relevantes de la competencia intercultural desarrollada en clase de lengua.

- Comparar los resultados relativos a las competencias interculturales y lingüísticas de dos actividades equiparables, desarrolladas por el mismo alumnado, en dos momentos del proceso de enseñanza-aprendizaje.

- Contrastar los resultados obtenidos a partir de dichas actividades por el grupo-meta (participante de la intervención didáctica) y el grupo-control (no expuesto a dicha intervención).

4. Recogida de datos: recursos diversos para triangular los resultados

El análisis de la dimensión institucional hizo necesario el desarrollo de instrumentos de investigación dirigidos a determinar la presencia de contenidos culturales e interculturales en el currículo, en el temario de acceso al cargo docente y en los libros de texto. Para poder, en primer lugar, obtener numerosos datos en un tiempo limitado, se optó por el uso de cuestionarios y por comparar dos grupos (grupo-meta y grupo-control), para medir el perfil intercultural inicial de las personas participantes. Esta diagnosis inicial también sirvió para medir, de forma más precisa, el impacto de la intervención didáctica en el desarrollo de la competencia intercultural, objeto de la investigación. Posteriormente, se diseñó y observó la intervención didáctica para un análisis cualitativo más profundo. Se explica cada fase en detalle más abajo.

4.1. Cuestionarios

La dimensión docente (véase el objetivo 1) fue explorada a través de dos cuestionarios dirigidos a obtener, por una parte, información general sobre categorías relacionadas con la sensibilización de los agentes educativos respecto a la dimensión intercultural de las prácticas pedagógicas y, por otra parte, descripciones de los propios docentes sobre dichas prácticas. Para acercarse a la dimensión del alumnado, desarrollamos un cuestionario abierto con el objetivo de recoger descripciones individuales de sus experiencias lingüísticas e interculturales, y un test de estereotipos culturales. Estos instrumentos también fueron utilizados en esta investigación para recoger datos sobre el desarrollo y el impacto de la intervención didáctica propuesta.

Las preguntas fueron medidas con una escala Likert de 5 puntos, con valores comprendidos entre 1, equivalente a totalmente en desacuerdo, y 5, equivalente a totalmente de acuerdo. Hubo un total de 30 preguntas, estimadas suficientes para conseguir una noción global de actitudes del profesorado y del alumnado relativas a la didáctica de las competencias interculturales, sin que llegara a ser un cuestionario demasiado engorroso y largo de responder (véase Canals, en este volumen, para más información sobre cuestionarios). He aquí algunas de las afirmaciones que aparecían en el cuestionario:

- El aprendizaje de lenguas extranjeras me ha ayudado a cambiar mis actitudes y creencias hacia otras comunidades y culturas.

- Las actividades interculturales pueden ayudar a mejorar la competencia comunicativa del alumnado.

- Conocer la civilización y la lengua convierte a los estudiantes en locutores interculturales.

- Es importante que los estudiantes reflexionen sobre su propia cultura y que la analicen desde una perspectiva externa para poder comprender mejor a los demás.

4.2. Test de estereotipos culturales

Se realizó el test con el grupo-control y el grupo-meta antes y después de la aplicación de la intervención didáctica. He aquí un ejemplo (Tabla 1).

Tabla 1. Ejemplo del test de estereotipos culturales

Utilícese la siguiente escala de valores para indicar si estos adjetivos describen con mayor precisión a personas de tu misma nacionalidad (columna A) o a nativos de la lengua francesa (columna B).		
Escala: 1 = nunca; 2 = rara vez; 3 = a veces; 4 = con frecuencia; 5 = muy a menudo.		
Adjetivos	**A**	**B**
Emocional		
Arrogante		
Serio		
Amable		
Seguro de sí mismo		
Lógico		
Generoso		
Tranquilo		
Perezoso		
Eficiente		
Impaciente		
Testarudo		
Honrado		
Competente		
Alegre		
Tímido		
Trabajador		
Ruidoso		
Tolerante		

4.3. Intervención didáctica

El análisis del contexto fue acompañado por una etapa de intervención, que tuvo como objetivo diseñar, aplicar y evaluar una intervención didáctica orientada a los aspectos de la competencia intercultural.

La intervención docente fue enmarcada por una serie de materiales desarrollados específicamente para trabajar la dimensión intercultural de la enseñanza de la lengua. Partiendo del supuesto de que la dimensión intercultural es una dimensión imbricada en los saberes lingüísticos, tanto el diseño como el análisis del impacto de la intervención didáctica se realizaron desde un punto de vista en el que confluían los aspectos interculturales y lingüísticos. Se puede considerar que si el docente de lenguas extranjeras tiene un rol en el desarrollo de las dimensiones interculturales de las competencias en lengua de sus estudiantes, este no puede ser separado del que implica su guía en el desarrollo integral de la competencia comunicativa.

Para la elaboración de materiales de educación intercultural, se contemplaron temas que involucraban la vida cotidiana de los estudiantes y sus conocimientos previos. Las actividades eran diversas, incluían simulaciones, debates, comentarios críticos sobre diferentes documentos de prensa, etc. Estos materiales habían sido previamente empleados y validados por el grupo de trabajo Aplicación y Evaluación de Materiales de Educación Global, coordinado por la ONG Intercultura y constituido al amparo del convenio suscrito entre dicha ONG y el Ministerio de Educación, Cultura y Deporte, y privilegiaron, sobre todo, las competencias relativas a la comprensión lectora y la expresión oral.

El seguimiento de la intervención en el aula se hizo a través de la observación sistemática, apoyada por una pauta de observación dirigida a la rápida descripción de algunos elementos contextuales importantes, como son, entre otros, la distribución física de las personas participantes, la organización de la participación en clase y el ambiente general durante la actividad (véase, también, Canals, en este volumen). La observación sistemática de las clases se hizo con la ayuda de una observadora externa. A través de la pauta de observación se registraron aspectos del comportamiento de los estudiantes en su trabajo con los materiales, observando especialmente los constantes y los cambios. La Tabla 2 muestra un fragmento de la pauta de observación enfocada a las relaciones pedagógicas en cuanto a la didáctica de la lengua extranjera y las competencias culturales de manera integrada.

Las observaciones se realizaron en un período de dos meses y medio y, simultáneamente, se grabó en formato video el trabajo de cada grupo en el aula durante varias actividades. Estas grabaciones fueron transcritas (véanse Moore y Llompart, en este volumen). Para poder comparar momentos iniciales y finales de las competencias en lenguas del alumnado involucrado en la investigación, optamos por dos estrategias metodológicas: por un lado, realizamos una comparación entre dos actividades orales y escritas de clase equiparables, una previa y otra posterior a la intervención objeto de análisis, y, por otro lado, se contrastaron estas actividades con las llevadas a cabo con un grupo-clase con el que no se había desarrollado la intervención didáctica citada. También se obtuvieron datos a través de autoevaluaciones de los estudiantes al acabar la intervención didáctica.

Tabla 2. Fragmento de la pauta de observación

Observación	Siempre	A veces	Nunca
El docente hace preguntas que apelan a experiencias y conocimientos previos de los estudiantes (referidas a situaciones de aprendizaje intercultural vividas o a la vida cotidiana).			
Organiza e indica cómo trabajar en grupo.			
Recorre los grupos y da instrucciones.			
Amplía el tema de la actividad, entregando más información.			
Cuenta experiencias o ideas propias que influyen en la opinión de los estudiantes.			
Favorece la relación entre el alumnado y la libre expresión de sus ideas.			

Las transcripciones sirvieron para indagar más sobre las interacciones observadas en los videos y para comparar y contrastar las respuestas obtenidas durante la encuesta inicial. Para hacerlo, los fragmentos transcritos fueron categorizados según unidades temáticas que correspondían a temas destacables de las observaciones y de los perfiles interculturales iniciales recogidos en los cuestionarios. Posteriormente, estas categorías de unidades temáticas fueron contrastadas con descriptores de diferentes etapas de la interculturalidad, desde la etapa monocultural (perfil mínimo), hasta la etapa transcultural (perfil elevado). Se muestra un ejemplo de estas categorizaciones en la Tabla 3.

Tabla 3. Ejemplo de datos según la etapa intercultural – perfil medio

III. Es flexible en cuanto a su posición en un conflicto intercultural
ou ça dépend, c'est compliqué … il faut voir chaque cas, mais c'est vrai que c'est une situation chaque fois plus habituelle … je veux dire que le monde est destiné à se métisser (AOF-SO)
il y a plusieurs solutions … il pourrait se convertir à l'Islam et puis à la maison faire ce qu'on veut (AOF-CG)

5. Resultados

Uno de los aspectos más importantes de esta investigación fue el análisis de los datos obtenidos antes, durante y después de la intervención didáctica. El análisis del conjunto de los datos obtenidos nos permitió llegar a conclusiones respecto a los cambios que había propiciado la intervención didáctica en la competencia lingüística e intercultural de los estudiantes. Tal como se ha explicado, la propuesta era integradora, es decir, pretendía, de manera paralela, desarrollar la competencia intercultural de los estudiantes y cumplir con los objetivos lingüísticos del programa de cuarto nivel de la E.O.I. Esta doble meta nos llevó a preocuparnos no solo por los cambios en el perfil y competencia interculturales, sino especialmente por las relaciones entre estos elementos y los lingüísticos. Esto responde al hecho de que, como docente de francés en una E.O.I., se debe responder a un contenido y a que los estudiantes deben de ser evaluados como los demás.

Por ello, el análisis de la intervención didáctica que diseñamos para esta investigación debía considerar si esta fue exitosa al permitir trabajar ambos aspectos (lingüísticos e interculturales) de manera integrada. También fue importante tener en cuenta los datos obtenidos en las autoevaluaciones de los estudiantes al acabar la intervención didáctica: si percibieron, o no, esta integración como novedosa para ellos. El análisis tuvo el objetivo, por un lado, de describir el impacto de la intervención didáctica en los cambios de perfiles y competencias lingüísticas e interculturales, a través de la comparación con el otro grupo de cuarto nivel, que no siguió la intervención didáctica (denominado grupo control para esta investigación). Por otro lado, el análisis pretendía valorar también la percepción de los estudiantes sobre la intervención, especialmente sobre qué habían aprendido, teniendo en cuenta las relaciones entre competencias en lengua y competencias interculturales.

De los datos de esta investigación se desprende que el desarrollo de la competencia intercultural resulta un proceso singularmente complejo, extremadamente difícil y largo, pero, al mismo tiempo, necesario e ineludible. Un elemento que apareció de manera clara era que el desarrollo de la competencia intercultural no se produce en clase de lengua, pero esta puede constituirse como un espacio favorable para dicho desarrollo.

Para que esto sea posible, es necesario revisar profundamente la visión tradicional sobre la relación entre lengua y cultura, orientada hacia la creación y reproducción de estereotipos. La presente investigación demostró que esta visión sobre la lengua y la cultura suele estar vigente en las E.O.I., a pesar de la entrada en circulación del Marco Común Europeo de Referencia (MCER), que instituye la competencia intercultural como parte de las competencias que deben desarrollarse en la enseñanza de lenguas.

El análisis de las encuestas aplicadas a docentes de las E.O.I. arrojó que, si bien estos reconocen la importancia de incluir aspectos relativos al hecho intercultural en su práctica docente, presentan una visión de la cultura como producto, es decir, como conjunto de productos individuales o colectivos legitimados por un estado. En el caso de la enseñanza y aprendizaje del francés, la cultura se presenta como equivalente a la tradicional noción de civilización, es decir, el conocimiento de las instituciones, horarios y producciones culturales y artísticas más destacables de la cultura meta.

Esto es coherente con las selecciones que realizan los manuales de texto que empleaban los docentes encuestados, en los que las actividades relativas a la cultura se limitaban a enseñar productos culturales y descripciones de colectivos asociados a Francia o, en menor grado, a territorios de la francofonía, que se presentan en general como homogéneos. La escasa referencia a otros colectivos o grupos culturales se limitaba a Europa. Estos contenidos, junto con las prácticas docentes descritas por los docentes, contribuyen a la reproducción de estereotipos y a su consolidación en el imaginario colectivo de los estudiantes.

Según el relato de los docentes, sus prácticas docentes se limitan a aspectos relativos a lo que tradicionalmente se llama civilización francesa, sin incluir actividades en las que se reflexione en torno a la cultura del alumnado o a la diversidad cultural de la clase. Se excluye así uno de los aspectos fundamentales del desarrollo de la competencia intercultural, que a las etapas de conocimiento, reconocimiento y aceptación de la identidad cultural del otro, se suma la aceptación de la propia identidad cultural.

El estudio aportó también información sobre qué tipo de actividades pueden incidir en el desarrollo de lo que hemos definido como competencia intercultural, y sobre las posibilidades de integración de este tipo de actividades en las clases de lengua extranjera. No obstante, las pautas didácticas que se extraen deben ser consideradas como parte de una propuesta susceptible de ser modificada a tenor de otros contextos.

6. A modo de conclusión

La dificultad de medir la transformación de la competencia intercultural de las personas es uno de los grandes obstáculos de investigaciones como la que se ha descrito en este capítulo. Así, por ejemplo, aunque las respuestas obtenidas a través de cuestionarios anónimos merecen atención, hay que contemplar la posibilidad de que, por muchos motivos, no siempre sean fiables. Esta posibilidad nos llevó, en este estudio, a desarrollar un conjunto de indicadores e instrumentos para recoger diferentes datos que pudieran ayudar a objetivar los cambios observados y a triangular los resultados. La estrategia de adoptar métodos mixtos, con un por diseño cualitativo y cuantitativo, fue de utilidad para contrastar los datos de los cuestionarios, las observaciones propias y externas realizadas a lo largo de la intervención, y otros datos recogidos.

Si bien las conclusiones extraídas no tienen carácter definitivo, puesto que el análisis realizado es limitado, estas resultan orientativas y esclarecedoras, principalmente respecto al desarrollo de la competencia intercultural en clase de lengua extranjera, y a la potencialidad que ofrece la bifocalización sobre la lengua y sobre la interculturalidad en la programación de la enseñanza-aprendizaje de la lengua extranjera.

Obras citadas

Bizquerra Alzina, R. (Coord.). (2009). *Metodología de la investigación educativa* (2a ed.). Madrid: La Muralla.

Byram, M. (1992). *Culture et éducation en langue étrangère*. París: Hatier.

Byram, M., Gribkova, B., y Starkey, H. (2002). *Developing the intercultural dimension in language teaching: a practical introduction for teachers*. Bruselas: Council of Europe.

Canals, L. (2017). Instruments per a la recollida de dades. En E. Moore y M. Dooly (Eds), *Enfoques cualitativos para la investigación en educación plurilingüe* (pp. 377-389). Research-publishing.net. https://doi.org/10.14705/rpnet.2017.emmd2016.636

Candillier, M. (Ed.). (2007). *Across languages and cultures*. Graz: European Centre for Modern Languages. http://archive.ecml.at/mtp2/publications/C4_report_ALC_E.pdf

Carr, W., y Kemmis, S. (1988). *Teoría crítica de la enseñanza. La investigación-acción en la formación del profesorado*. Barcelona: Martínez Roca.

Cohen, L., y Manion, L. (1990). *Métodos de investigación educativa*. Madrid: La Muralla.

Council of Europe. (2001). *Common European framework of reference for languages: learning, teaching and assessment*. Cambridge: Cambridge University Press.

Dooly, M. (2017). Una aproximació a dades multimodals amb l'anàlisi del discurs mediat. En E. Moore y M. Dooly (Eds), *Enfoques cualitativos para la investigación en educación plurilingüe* (pp. 212-235). Research-publishing.net. https://doi.org/10.14705/rpnet.2017.emmd2016.629

Elliott, J. (1993). *El cambio educativo desde la investigación-acción*. Madrid: Morata.

Goyette, G., y Lessard-Hébert, M. (1988). *La investigación-acción. Funciones, fundamentos e instrumentación*. Barcelona: Laertes.

Kemmis, K., y McTaggart, R. (1988). *Cómo planificar la investigación-acción*. Barcelona: Laertes.

Latorre, A. (2007). *La investigación-acción. Conocer y cambiar la práctica educativa* (4a ed.). Barcelona: Graó.

Lewin, K. (Ed.). (1973). *Resolving social conflicts: Selected papers on group dynamics.* Londres: Souvenir Press.

Meyer, M. (1994). Developing intercultural competence: Case studies of advanced language learners. En R. Genesee (Coord.), *Educating second language children: the whole child, the whole curriculum, the whole community* (pp. 159-182). Nueva York: Cambridge University Press.

Moore, E., y Llompart, J. (2017). Recoger, transcribir, analizar y presentar datos interaccionales plurilingües. En E. Moore y M. Dooly (Eds), *Enfoques cualitativos para la investigación en educación plurilingüe* (pp. 418-433). Research-publishing.net. https://doi.org/10.14705/rpnet.2017.emmd2016.639

Morse, J. M. (2010). Practice and procedures for mixed method design: maintaining control, rigor and complexity. En A. Tassakkori, y C. Teddlie (Eds), *Handbook of mixed method design* (2nd edn) (pp. 339-352). Thousand Oaks, CA: Sage.

Nussbaum, L. (2017). Investigar con docentes. En E. Moore y M. Dooly (Eds), *Enfoques cualitativos para la investigación en educación plurilingüe* (pp. 23-45). Research-publishing.net. https://doi.org/10.14705/rpnet.2017.emmd2016.620

Rizo, M., y Romeu, V. (2008). Investigación-acción-participativa y comunicación intercultural. Relato de una experiencia de investigación con estudiantes de dos universidades de la Ciudad de México. *Razón y Palabra*, 65. http://www.razonypalabra.org.mx/N/n65/index65.html

Stenhouse, K. (1984). *Investigación y desarrollo del currículo.* Madrid: Morata.

Suárez Pazos, M. (2002). Algunas reflexiones sobre la investigación-acción colaboradora en la educación. *Revista Electrónica de Enseñanza de las Ciencias, 1*(1), 40-56.

Unamuno, V., y Patiño, A. (2017). Producir conocimiento sobre el plurilingüismo junto a jóvenes estudiantes: un reto para la etnografía en colaboración. En E. Moore y M. Dooly (Eds), *Enfoques cualitativos para la investigación en educación plurilingüe* (pp. 107-128). Research-publishing.net. https://doi.org/10.14705/rpnet.2017.emmd2016.624

Lecturas recomendadas

Aguado, T. (2005). La educación intercultural en la práctica escolar: investigación en el ámbito español. *Revista de Educación, 21*(7), 43-52.

Byram, M., Nichols, A., y Stevens, D. (2001). *Developing intercultural competence in practice*. Clevedon: Multilingual Matters.

Isisag, K. U. (2010). The acceptance and recognition of cultural diversity in foreign language teaching. *Academik Bakis, 4*(7), 251-260.

Lund, R. E. (2008). Intercultural competence –an aim for the teaching of English in Norway? *Acta Didactica Norge, 2*(1), 1-16.

Oliveras, A. (2000). *Hacia la competencia intercultural en el aprendizaje de una lengua extranjera. Estudio del choque cultural y los malentendidos*. Madrid: Edinumen.

Paricio, M. S. (2011). Contribución de las lenguas extranjeras al desarrollo de actitudes de tolerancia y respeto hacia el 'otro'. *Linguarum Arena, 2,* 79-89.

Tassakkori, A., y Teddlie, C. (2010). (Eds), *Handbook of mixed method design* (2a edn). Thousand Oaks, CA: Sage.

3 Investigating one's own teaching practices using action research

Xavier Pascual[1]

Key concepts: action research, teaching practices, mixed methods, classroom observation, questionnaires.

---

1. Introduction

The aim of the research described below, which is an example of action research, was to contribute to new curricular and professional definitions based on a systematic analysis of the possibilities and limitations that arise when working with the intercultural dimension of foreign language classes for adults.

The action research method has been defined in many ways (cf. Bizquerra Alzina, 2009; Cohen & Manion, 1990; Kemmis & McTaggart, 1988; Latorre, 2007; van Lier, 2001). Goyette and Lessard-Hébert (1988) point out various epistemological differences that

> "convergen en torno a tres elementos básicos: a) desde el punto de vista del objeto (el qué); b) desde el punto de vista de la metodología (el cómo) y c) desde el punto de vista del investigador (el quién)" (Rizo & Romeu, 2008, n.p.)[2].

Both Suárez Pazos (2002) and Latorre (2007) warn that for decades the concept behind action research has been greatly distorted in its application.

---

1. Universitat Autònoma de Barcelona, Bellaterra, Catalonia/Spain; xavier.pascual@uab.cat

2. "converge around three basic elements: a) from the point of view of the object (the what); b) from the point of view of the methodology (the how); and c) from the point of view of the researcher (the who)" (Rizo & Romeu, 2008, n/p).

How to cite this chapter: Pascual, X. (2017). Investigating one's own teaching practices using action research. In E. Moore & M. Dooly (Eds), *Qualitative approaches to research on plurilingual education* (pp. 88-105). Research-publishing.net. https://doi.org/10.14705/rpnet.2017.emmd2016.623

"Atentos a las distorsiones más usuales, situaremos en primer lugar lo que no es la [investigación-acción...]. (a) No es lo que habitualmente hace un profesor cuando reflexiona sobre lo que acontece en su trabajo; como investigación, se trata de tareas sistemáticas basadas en evidencias; (b) no es una simple resolución de problemas, implica también mejorar, comprender; (c) no se trata de una investigación sobre otras personas, sino sobre uno mismo, en colaboración con otros implicados y colaboradores; y (d) no es la aplicación del método científico a la enseñanza, es una modalidad diferente que se interesa por el punto de vista de los implicados, cambiando tanto al investigador como a la situación investigada" (Suárez Pazos, 2002, p. 43)[3].

It is possible to pick out some common features among all the definitions: (1) it is (usually) a qualitative research method; (2) it focuses on what happens during everyday teaching activities (in education, mainly with regard to classroom interactions); and (3) its main objective is to identify which aspects need to be improved and how to change them (see Nussbaum, this volume).

To summarize, it can be said that the proposition of action research is based on the need to integrate research with the job of teaching in order to gather data and results that can be used to transform it (Bisquerra Alzina, 2009; van Lier, 2001). Action research is aimed at analyzing actions and social situations susceptible to becoming problematic and which are open to change. Although it starts out with an initial description (initial state), it is an intervention discipline directed towards modification (final state).

Generally speaking, the introduction of the concept of action research was attributed to Kurt Lewin, beginning in the 1950's (Lewin, 1973), but up until the 1970's no movement adopted the concept as a systematic approach

---

3. "In considering the most common distortions, we firstly detail what [action research] is not [...]. (a) It is not what teachers would normally do when reflecting upon what happens in their work; as research, it is about systematic tasks based on evidence; (b) it is not the simple resolution of problems; it also implies improvement, and understanding; (c) it is not about research into other people but into oneself, in cooperation with others involved and collaborators; and (d) it is not the application of scientific methods to teaching, it is a different approach that takes an interest in the opinions of those involved, changing both the researcher and the situation being investigated" (Suárez Pazos, 2002, p. 43).

to qualitative research into teaching practices. Led by Lawrence Stenhouse (1984) and John Elliott (1993) in Great Britain, the idea began to become accepted that teachers themselves are the most appropriate people to conduct research and improve their own performance. Later, in the 1980's, Stephen Kemmis, together with Wilfred Carr (Carr & Kemmis, 1988) put forward the view that action research is not only a process for changing the way individual teachers act, but rather a process of social transformation to be carried out collaboratively with participants and stakeholders in these contexts (students, other teachers, researchers and the immediate community; see Nussbaum, this volume; Unamuno & Patiño, this volume).

This type of research is based on a diagnostic phase that shapes the design of the intervention, the monitoring of which results in the interpretation of the transformations. For those taking part, action research implies reflecting on their own performance and that of others, giving a central role to the dialogue between the theory, the researcher and the situation being investigated.

It is a spiral process, in which the periods of problematization, diagnosis, the design of an intervention proposal, its application, assessment, etc. all start over again in a new version of the circuit.

The design of this type of research involves taking into account the following steps that are characteristic of action research:

- *Problematization*: this involves establishing a problematic area defined by a certain level of 'social disturbance' deriving from some or all of the participants in terms of difficulties or limitations in acting in compliance with individual or institutional objectives.

- *Diagnosis*: following the problematization and the definition of the focus of the research process, a clear diagnosis of the situation becomes necessary. To do this, it is important to obtain information, organize it and analyze it in order to understand the initial situation or the starting point for the research.

- *Drawing up an intervention proposal*: after identifying the problem in question and analyzing the starting point, the intervention and its monitoring tools are designed.

- *Applying the intervention*: here consideration is given to the process involved in executing and observing the intervention.

- *Assessment*: the information gathered from recording the results of the intervention is collected and systemized at this point in the process. The assessment also provides a means of redefining the problem, based on the information provided by the analysis.

All these steps involve data triangulation; i.e. collecting, analyzing and comparing different types of data (videos, transcripts, student output, official documents from the educational center, etc.). Both qualitative and quantitative methods have been used in the collection and analysis of data in this study. Following the terminology used by Morse (2010), mixed methods were used with a QUAL+quant design (qualitative and quantitative). To a large extent, the study is based on the systematic observation of classroom interactions and on other qualitative data. Nevertheless, quantitative methods were also used, such as questionnaires, which will be explained further on.

In today's society, there is increasing pressure on teachers to be innovators, especially in response to scientific and technological advances and new demographic landscapes. There is a general sense of dramatic change and consequently an increase in demands for social challenges to be met through education. Old conceptions about the role of educational institutions and the processes of teaching and learning are changing (see Dooly, this volume). In this respect, there are many authors who regard action research as the most appropriate methodology for tackling these challenges.

> "La complejidad de la práctica educativa hace necesario que el profesorado asuma el papel de investigador; que esté atento a las contingencias del contexto; que se cuestione las situaciones problemáticas

de la práctica; que dé respuesta a las necesidades del alumnado y trate de buscar nuevos enfoques. La enseñanza es un proceso donde tienen lugar simultáneamente múltiples elementos en interacción, lo que hace difícil su indagación y conocimiento" (Latorre, 2007, p. 12)[4].

Accordingly, this chapter begins with a study of the educational context that not only serves to understand the place in which the research described was applied but also provides important data for the analysis of the complex initial situation from which it began. It is a diagnostic study that permits a clearer and more objective definition of the initial problem and the requirements for transformation.

2. The study: the development of intercultural competence in foreign language classrooms

For decades, official policies on language teaching have advocated greater integration of language learning with culture (Council of Europe, 2001). This concept of language teaching implies a criticism of approaches which, based on an instrumental conception of language – concentrating exclusively on acquiring linguistic skills – have marginalized the cultural and intercultural aspects of many centers. This was the case in the context of the study described here: an Official Language School (Escola Oficial d'Idiomes or EOIs) in Barcelona.

For decades now, experts in teaching foreign languages have been pointing out that students need not only to develop grammatical competence, but also communication skills that will enable them to use language in a socially and culturally appropriate way (Council of Europe, 2001). It is in this respect that language learning cannot be conceived as a separate process from the

---

[4]. "The complexity of educational practice obliges teaching staff to take on the role of researchers; to be aware of the eventualities that can arise in this context; to question problematic situations in the practice of teaching; to respond to the needs of the students and to seek out new approaches. Teaching is a process by which multiple elements of interaction come together simultaneously, making it difficult to investigate and understand" (Latorre, 2007, p. 12).

development of the necessary intercultural competence for users to participate effectively in culturally meaningful contexts.

Incorporating an intercultural dimension in language teaching implies a reassessment of the profile of the student. If the teacher can be viewed as an intermediary for access to languages and cultures, students begin to see themselves as speakers who, on the one hand become plurilingual and on the other, intercultural. This new student profile entails a radical redefinition of teaching-learning concepts.

In order to contribute to new curricular and professional definitions based on the systematic analysis of the possibilities and limitations presented when working with the intercultural dimension in adult foreign language classrooms, it was decided to conduct an investigation of the researcher's own practice of being a teacher and of the context. The study qualified as action research given that it originated in a problem relevant to the researcher, to foreign language teachers in general, and to students, and that the results could be used to transform the practices and contexts analyzed.

3. Objectives of the study

As an introduction to this research, we firstly proposed exploring the specificity of notions of communicative competence, intercultural competence, intercultural awareness and the intercultural dimension of the process of teaching and learning languages. It was felt that defining and rationalizing these concepts for pedagogical intervention were equally important in both research and practice.

We began from the basis that studying the development of intercultural competence and the intercultural dimension of the process of teaching and learning languages entails a systematic analysis of the context. As already mentioned, it is not simply a matter of describing the place where the practice of teaching and research is introduced, but rather an analysis of the variables articulated in the definition of the initial problem on which my research was based.

Consistent with the general approach of this research, the first objective was to explore and describe the institutional, teaching and student aspects of the context. Specifically:

Objective 1. Describe the institutional, teaching and student aspects of the socio-educational context, taking into consideration:

- the cultural and intercultural elements of the current French curriculum in the EOIs (Official Language Schools) of Catalonia;
- the categories that relate to intercultural sensitivity; and
- intercultural practices declared by the teaching staff.

In line with van Lier (2001), action research involves including in the study the design and assessment of material specifically created to impact on students' linguistic and intercultural competence. This was precisely the second objective of this study.

Objective 2. Analyze the intercultural dimension of the process of teaching and learning languages, based on a didactic intervention aimed at jointly developing the intercultural and linguistic competences anticipated in the fourth level of the EOIs (use of language, oral and written expression, oral and written comprehension).

- Observe the interrelationship between materials, activities and teaching practices.
- Observe how students perform in the teaching-learning process, paying specific attention to its intercultural dimension.

- Analyze the relationships between intercultural and linguistic competences in this process.

Although the indicators used to assess linguistic competence were those applied institutionally by the EOIs, no standard indicators existed for intercultural competence. Therefore, based on an analysis of different proposals from numerous previous investigations (for example, Byram, 1992; Byram, Gribkova, & Starkey, 2002; Candillier, 2007; Meyer, 1994), I also decided to develop my own proposal based on the results of the research context I was working on. Thus, Objective 3 of this investigation was:

Objective 3. Based on a critical analysis of the different proposals available, to evaluate intercultural competence in foreign language classes, to develop a set of indicators applicable to a French class for adults, and to apply them in order to measure their relevance and functionality.

- Compare and analyze different proposals for assessing intercultural competence in a foreign language.

- Prepare a set of indicators that could be used to assess the development of intercultural competence in a foreign language class with adults.

- Measure their efficacy and functionality by applying concrete data extracted from the natural dynamics of socio-educative intervention.

Once these indicators were prepared, they were put into specific action. To do this, Objective 4 concentrated on analyzing the impact of the didactic intervention in developing intercultural competence according to the indicators established. Specifically:

Objective 4. Measure the impact of a didactic intervention directed at the intercultural dimension of the teaching-learning process of languages in the development of intercultural competence.

- Develop a proposal of indicators designed to assess the most relevant aspects of intercultural competence developed in a language class.

- Compare the results relative to the intercultural and linguistic competences of two comparable activities, developed by the same student body at two points in the teaching-learning process.

- Verify the results obtained based on these activities using a target group (participant in the didactic intervention) and a control group (not exposed to the aforesaid intervention).

4. Data collection: a variety of resources to triangulate the results

Conducting an analysis of the institutional dimension made it necessary to develop research tools to determine the presence of cultural and intercultural content in the curriculum, in the syllabus of teacher training courses, and in textbooks. Firstly, in order to obtain numerous data in a limited time, it was decided to use questionnaires and to compare two groups (a target group and a control group) to measure 'the initial intercultural profile' of the participants. This initial diagnosis also served to measure the objective of the research more accurately, i.e. the impact of the didactic intervention on developing intercultural competence. Next, the didactic intervention was designed and observed for a more in-depth qualitative analysis. Each phase is explained in more detail below.

4.1. Questionnaires

The teaching dimension (see Objective 1) was explored using two questionnaires designed to obtain, on the one hand, general information on categories related to raising awareness of the agents involved in education with regard to the intercultural dimension of pedagogical practices and, on the other, descriptions of these practices by the teachers themselves. Our approach to the student dimension was based on developing an open questionnaire aimed at collecting individual descriptions of their linguistic and intercultural experiences, and a cultural stereotype test. These tools were also used in this research to collect data on the development and impact of the didactic intervention proposed.

The questions were measured using a 5-point Likert scale giving a value of one equivalent to strongly disagree and five to strongly agree. There were 30 questions in total, which felt to be sufficient to achieve an overview of the attitudes of teaching staff and the student body towards the teaching of intercultural competences without it becoming too cumbersome and lengthy to respond to (see Canals, this volume, for more information on questionnaires). Some examples of the statements include:

- Learning foreign languages has helped me change my attitudes and beliefs about other communities and cultures.

- Intercultural activities can help improve a student's ability to communicate.

- Learning about civilization and language enables students to become intercultural spokespeople.

- It is important for students to reflect on their own culture and to analyze it from an external perspective in order to better understand others.

4.2. Test for cultural stereotypes

A test was conducted with the control group and target group before and after the didactic intervention. An example of this follows (Table 1).

Chapter 3

Table 1. Example of cultural stereotype test

Use the following scale of values to indicate if these adjectives describe more accurately people of your own nationality (Column A) or native French speakers (Column B). Scale: 1 = never; 2 = rarely; 3 = occasionally; 4 = frequently; 5 = very often.		
Adjectives	**A**	**B**
Emotional		
Arrogant		
Serious		
Friendly		
Self-confident		
Logical		
Generous		
Calm		
Lazy		
Efficient		
Impatient		
Stubborn		
Honorable		
Competent		
Cheerful		
Timid		
Hardworking		
Noisy		
Tolerant		

4.3. Didactic intervention

The analysis of the context was accompanied by a period of intervention, the objective of which was to design, apply and assess a didactic intervention directed at aspects of intercultural competence.

The teaching intervention was contained within a series of materials specifically developed to work on the intercultural dimension of language teaching. Based on the assumption that the intercultural dimension is interwoven with linguistic knowledge, both the design and the analysis of the impact of the didactic intervention were undertaken from a perspective in which intercultural and linguistic aspects came together. It could be argued that if foreign language teachers are to have a role in developing intercultural aspects as part of teaching language skills, this cannot be separated from what is implicit in their role in guiding the all-round development of communication skills.

The preparation of intercultural teaching materials took into account elements that form part of students' everyday lives and their previous knowledge. The activities were diverse, including simulations, debates, critical analyses of a variety of press articles, etc. These materials had previously been used and ratified by the working group Aplicación y Evaluación de Materiales de Educación Global (Application and Assessment of Global Education Materials) coordinated by the NGO Intercultura, set up as part of the agreement between this NGO and the Spanish Ministry of Education, Culture and Sport and concentrating particularly on skills related to reading comprehension and oral expression.

Monitoring classroom intervention was done by systematic observation, supported by an observation template for making a rapid description of some important contextual elements, including the physical distribution of those taking part, how classroom participation was organized, and the general ambience during the activity (also see Canals, this volume). The systematic observation of classes was undertaken with the assistance of an external observer. Using the observation template, various aspects of student behavior were recorded as they worked with the material, paying particular attention to the constants and the changes. Table 2 shows an extract from the observation template focused on pedagogical relationships in terms of teaching a foreign language and cultural competences in an integrated way.

Table 2. Extract from the observation template

Observation	Always	Sometimes	Never
The teacher asks questions that call on the students' previous knowledge and experiences (with reference to intercultural situations encountered or to everyday life).			
Organizes students and shows them how to work as a group.			

Chapter 3

Goes around the groups and gives instructions.			
Broadens the scope of the activity, providing more information.			
Relates their own experiences or ideas that influence the opinions of the students.			
Encourages students to relate to each other and freely express their ideas.			

Observations were made over a period of two-and-a-half months, during which time the classroom work of each group was simultaneously recorded on video throughout a variety of activities. These recordings were then transcribed (see Moore & Llompart, this volume). In order to compare moments from the initial and final periods of the language skills acquired by students involved in the research, we opted for two methodological strategies: on the one hand, we made a comparison between two comparable oral and written activities, one before and one after the intervention that was the subject of the analysis, and on the other we compared these activities against those carried out with a group/class with which the aforementioned didactic intervention had not been undertaken. Data were also obtained from student self-assessments at the end of the didactic intervention.

The transcripts were useful for further investigation into the interactions observed in the videos and to compare and contrast the answers given during the initial survey. To achieve this, the transcribed fragments were categorized according to themed topics that corresponded to the most noteworthy observations, and intercultural profiles were collected from the initial questionnaires. Next, these categories of themed units were checked against descriptors of different stages of interculturality from the monocultural stage (minimum profile), up to the transcultural stage (high profile). Table 3 shows an example of these categorizations.

Table 3. Example of data according to the intercultural stage – average profile

III. Is your position flexible in a situation of intercultural conflict?
oh that depends, it's complicated… you have to look at each case, but it's true that it's an increasingly common situation… what I mean is that the world is destined to become a melting pot (AOF-SO)
there are several solutions… one could convert to Islam and then do whatever one likes at home (AOF-CG)

5. Results

One of the most important aspects of this research was analyzing the data obtained before, during and after the didactic intervention. Analyzing the data as a whole allowed us to draw conclusions on the changes facilitated by the didactic intervention in the students' linguistic and intercultural competences. As explained, this was an integrative proposal, which means that it had the parallel objective of developing students' intercultural competence as well as fulfilling the linguistic objectives of the fourth EOI course. This double goal meant that we were not only concerned with changes in profiles and intercultural competences, but also particularly with the relationships between these elements and linguistic factors. This fulfils the requirement that, as a French teacher in an EOI, there is certain content that must be complied with and students must be assessed in the same way as all the others.

Therefore, the analysis of the didactic intervention that we designed for this research needed to consider if this intervention was successful in allowing both aspects to be worked on (linguistic and intercultural) in an integrated way. It was also important to take into account the data obtained from the students' self-assessments upon completing the didactic intervention: if they saw this integration as something new to them or not. The objective of the analysis was, on the one hand, to describe the impact of the didactic intervention on changes in profiles and linguistic and intercultural competences through comparison with the other fourth level group who did not follow the didactic intervention (known as the control group in this research); and on the other, it also sought to evaluate the students' perception of the intervention, especially in terms of what they had learnt, taking into account the relationships between language skills and intercultural skills.

From the data stemming from this research it can be deduced that developing intercultural competence is a singularly complex process, extremely difficult and lengthy, but at the same time necessary and unavoidable. One factor that emerged clearly was that developing intercultural competence does not typically take place in language classes, but classes could still be considered as a favorable setting for such development to take place.

Chapter 3

For this to become possible, it is necessary to thoroughly review traditional attitudes to the relationship between language and culture, which are aimed at creating and perpetuating stereotypes. This research shows that these attitudes towards language and culture persist in EOIs despite the introduction of the Common European Framework of Reference for Languages (CEFRL), which establishes intercultural competence as one of the skills that must be developed in the teaching of languages.

The analysis of questionnaires applied to EOI teachers reveals that, while they recognize the importance of including intercultural aspects in their teaching methods, what they present is a vision of culture as a product; that is, as a collection of individual or collective products legitimized by a state. In the case of teaching and learning French, culture is presented as equivalent to the traditional concept of 'civilization', i.e. knowledge of the institutions, times and the most notable cultural and artistic output of the target culture.

This is consistent with the selections made by the textbooks used by the teachers surveyed, in which activities relating to culture were limited to teaching about cultural products and to descriptions of groups associated with France or, to a lesser degree, to French-speaking countries, which are generally presented as a homogeneous group. The few references to other collectives or cultural groups were limited to Europe. This content, along with the manner in which teachers present it, contributes to perpetuating stereotypes and consolidating them in the collective imagination of students.

According to the teachers' accounts, their teaching methods are limited to aspects of what is traditionally referred to as 'French civilization', without including activities in which consideration is given to the culture of the student body or the cultural diversity of the class. Thus, one of the fundamental aspects for developing intercultural competence is excluded, which is to add acceptance of one's own cultural identity to the knowledge, recognition and acceptance of someone else's.

The study also provided information on what type of activities may have an impact on the development of what we have defined as intercultural competence, and the possibilities of integrating such activities into foreign language classes. Nevertheless, the teaching guidelines extracted must be considered as part of a proposal that is open to modification in terms of other contexts.

6. Concluding words

The difficulty of measuring the transformation of people's intercultural competence is one of the great obstacles to investigations such as the one described in this chapter. For example, although the answers obtained from anonymous questionnaires merit attention, the possibility should be considered that, for many reasons, they are not always reliable. This possibility led us, in this study, to develop a set of indicators and instruments to collect different data that could assist in making the changes observed more objective and triangulate the results. The strategy of adopting mixed methods, with a QUAL+quant design, was useful for comparing data from the questionnaires, observations made both internally and externally throughout the process, and other data collected.

While it is true that the conclusions drawn are not definitive given the limited nature of the analysis, they remain illustrative and illuminating mainly with regard to developing intercultural competence in language teaching classes, and to the potential offered by adopting a bifocal approach to language and interculturality in programming the teaching-learning of foreign languages.

Works cited

Bizquerra Alzina, R. (Ed.). (2009). *Metodología de la investigación educativa* (2nd ed.). Madrid: La Muralla.

Byram, M. (1992). *Culture et éducation en langue étrangère*. Paris: Hatier.

Byram, M., Gribkova, B., & Starkey, H. (2002). *Developing the intercultural dimension in language teaching: a practical introduction for teachers*. Brussels: Council of Europe.

Canals, L. (2017). Instruments for gathering data. In E. Moore & M. Dooly (Eds), *Qualitative approaches to research on plurilingual education* (pp. 390-401). Research-publishing.net. https://doi.org/10.14705/rpnet.2017.emmd2016.637

Candillier, M. (Ed.). (2007). *Across languages and cultures*. Graz: European Centre for Modern Languages. http://archive.ecml.at/mtp2/publications/C4_report_ALC_E.pdf

Carr, W., & Kemmis, S. (1988). *Teoría crítica de la enseñanza. La investigación-acción en la formación del profesorado*. Barcelona: Martínez Roca.

Cohen, L., & Manion, L. (1990). *Métodos de investigación educativa*. Madrid: La Muralla.

Council of Europe. (2001). *Common European framework of reference for languages: learning, teaching and assessment*. Cambridge: Cambridge University Press.

Dooly, M. (2017). A Mediated Discourse Analysis (MDA) approach to multimodal data. In E. Moore & M. Dooly (Eds), *Qualitative approaches to research on plurilingual education* (pp. 189-211). Research-publishing.net. https://doi.org/10.14705/rpnet.2017.emmd2016.628

Elliott, J. (1993). *El cambio educativo desde la investigación-acción*. Madrid: Morata.

Goyette, G., & Lessard-Hébert, M. (1988). *La investigación-acción. Funciones, fundamentos e instrumentación*. Barcelona: Laertes.

Kemmis, K., & McTaggart, R. (1988). *Cómo planificar la investigación-acción*. Barcelona: Laertes.

Latorre, A. (2007). *La investigación-acción. Conocer y cambiar la práctica educativa* (4th ed.). Barcelona: Graó.

Lewin, K. (Ed.). (1973). *Resolving social conflicts: selected papers on group dynamics*. London: Souvenir Press.

Meyer, M. (1994). Developing intercultural competence: case studies of advanced language learners. In R. Genesee (Ed.), *Educating second language children: the whole child, the whole curriculum, the whole community* (pp. 159-182). New York: Cambridge University Press.

Moore, E., & Llompart, J. (2017). Collecting, transcribing, analyzing and presenting plurilingual interactional data. In E. Moore & M. Dooly (Eds), *Qualitative approaches to research on plurilingual education* (pp. 403-417). Research-publishing.net. https://doi.org/10.14705/rpnet.2017.emmd2016.638

Morse, J. M. (2010). Practice and procedures for mixed method design: maintaining control, rigor and complexity. In A. Tassakkori, & C. Teddlie (Eds.), *Handbook of mixed method design* (2nd ed.) (pp. 339-352). Thousand Oaks, CA: Sage.

Nussbaum, L. (2017). Doing research with teachers. In E. Moore & M. Dooly (Eds), *Qualitative approaches to research on plurilingual education* (pp. 46-67). Research-publishing.net. https://doi.org/10.14705/rpnet.2017.emmd2016.621

Rizo, M., & Romeu, V. (2008). Investigación-acción-participativa y comunicación intercultural. Relato de una experiencia de investigación con estudiantes de dos universidades de la Ciudad de México. *Razón y Palabra*, 65. http://www.razonypalabra.org.mx/N/n65/index65.html

Stenhouse, K. (1984). *Investigación y desarrollo del currículo*. Madrid: Morata.

Suárez Pazos, M. (2002). Algunas reflexiones sobre la investigación-acción colaboradora en la educación. *Revista Electrónica de Enseñanza de las Ciencias, 1*(1), 40-56.

Unamuno, V., & Patiño, A. (2017). Producing knowledge about plurilingualism with young students: a challenge for collaborative ethnography. In E. Moore & M. Dooly (Eds), *Qualitative approaches to research on plurilingual education* (pp. 129-149). Research-publishing.net. https://doi.org/10.14705/rpnet.2017.emmd2016.625

Van Lier, L. (2001). La investigación-acción. *Textos de Didáctica de la Lengua y la Literatura, 27*, 81-88.

Recommended reading

Aguado, T. (2005). La educación intercultural en la práctica escolar: investigación en el ámbito español. *Revista de Educación, 21*(7), 43-52.

Byram, M., Nichols, A., & Stevens, D. (2001). *Developing intercultural competence in practice*. Clevedon: Multilingual Matters.

Isisag, K. U. (2010). The acceptance and recognition of cultural diversity in foreign language teaching. *Academik Bakis, 4*(7), 251-260.

Lund, R. E. (2008). Intercultural competence – an aim for the teaching of English in Norway? *Acta Didactica Norge, 2*(1), 1-16.

Oliveras, A. (2000). *Hacia la intercultural competence en el aprendizaje de una lengua extranjera. Estudio del choque cultural y los malentendidos*. Madrid: Edinumen.

Paricio, M. S. (2011). Contribución de las lenguas extranjeras al desarrollo de actitudes de tolerancia y respeto hacia el 'otro'. *Linguarum Arena, 2*, 79-89.

Tassakkori, A., & Teddlie, C. (2010). (Eds), *Handbook of mixed method design* (2nd ed.). Thousand Oaks, CA: Sage.

4 Producir conocimiento sobre el plurilingüismo junto a jóvenes estudiantes: un reto para la etnografía en colaboración

Virginia Unamuno[1] y Adriana Patiño[2]

Conceptos clave: etnografía, investigación colaborativa, socialización lingüística, paisaje lingüístico, secuencias didácticas plurilingües, estudiantes como investigadores.

1. Introducción

Una de las preocupaciones centrales de las investigaciones del GREIP ha sido el desarrollo de una aproximación interdisciplinaria al plurilingüismo que pudiera resultar útil a la educación. Tal aproximación se fue construyendo sobre la base de considerar, de manera situada y a partir del estudio de datos interaccionales, las competencias que hacen posible la adquisición de los conocimientos, las orientaciones y las prácticas que permiten participar efectivamente en las interacciones cotidianas en contextos educativos y sociales diversos (Codó, Nussbaum, y Unamuno, 2007; Nussbaum y Unamuno, 2006).

Dar cuenta de cómo se gestiona el plurilingüismo y, más específicamente, las competencias plurilingües en las aulas, se erige así en un objeto de investigación vinculado fuertemente a la necesidad de comprender situaciones de enseñanza-aprendizaje complejas, pues, por un lado, se ponen en juego repertorios comunicativos diversos y, por otro, participan personas con diferentes saberes, categorizadas institucionalmente de forma desigual. La descripción de dicha

---

1. CONICET-Centro de Estudios del Lenguaje en Sociedad (CELES)-UNSAM, Buenos Aires, Argentina; vunamuno@conicet.gov.ar

2. University of Southampton, Southampton, Reino Unido; a.patino@soton.co.uk

Para citar este capítulo: Unamuno, V., y Patiño, A. (2017). Producir conocimiento sobre el plurilingüismo junto a jóvenes estudiantes: un reto para la etnografía en colaboración. En E. Moore y M. Dooly (Eds), *Enfoques cualitativos para la investigación en educación plurilingüe* (pp. 107-128). Research-publishing.net. https://doi.org/10.14705/rpnet.2017.emmd2016.624

gestión conlleva el estudio de las competencias plurilingües de forma situada, de manera que se puedan ofrecer herramientas a los diferentes actores del proceso escolar para promover las intervenciones socioeducativas acordes a situaciones particulares, plantear acciones escolares inclusivas, prevenir la conformación y reproducción de prejuicios, así como dar pistas para evitar la exclusión social de las minorías.

En el contexto educativo catalán, el interés por investigar en pos de una educación inclusiva tiene una larga historia. En parte, puede relacionarse con la investigación desarrollada desde el final de la dictadura franquista, para acompañar el proyecto dirigido a construir una escuela que incluyera a diferentes sectores sociales, caracterizados por ser usuarios de lenguas diferentes. Desde nuestro punto de vista, este proceso fundacional de la relación entre investigación y enseñanza marcó profundamente la manera de trabajar del grupo GREIP, para el que es importante dar cuenta de procesos escolares, pero también construir una relación estrecha entre la universidad y la escuela, creando así una manera particular de investigar.

El interés científico por el plurilingüismo, la enseñanza socialmente adecuada de lenguas y la inclusión social están presentes en diversos proyectos del GREIP relacionados con el estudio de procesos de enseñanza-aprendizaje de lenguas primeras, segundas y extranjeras en contextos de diversidad lingüística. Sin embargo, estos intereses fueron cambiando en relación con los cambios sociales: a la complejidad inicial del sistema escolar catalán, marcado por modelos de educación bilingüe en los que la lengua de la escuela y la de la familia se definían como recursos disponibles para la escolarización, se sumaron nuevas condiciones educativas relacionadas con un cambio importante, iniciado a comienzos del siglo XXI entre la población estudiantil de Cataluña. Nos referimos a la escolarización de alumnado de origen inmigrante en el sistema escolar catalán, que marcó una transformación de la composición de la población escolar y creó un nuevo contexto de enseñanza-aprendizaje, caracterizado por profundas desigualdades, relacionadas, principalmente, con el acceso a las lenguas de escolarización y a los contenidos curriculares vehiculizados por estas. En este marco de transformaciones, el GREIP se preocupó no solo por investigar qué estaba pasando en las escuelas, sino por acompañar a sus actores en la búsqueda de estrategias metodológicas y en la creación de recursos para hacer frente a los nuevos retos que tales cambios planteaban.

La inquietud despertada por el plurilingüismo en las aulas de Cataluña llevó al GREIP a un intenso debate con diferentes agentes educativos, y a la necesidad de investigar, entre otras cosas, las formas y estrategias de:

- mejorar las formas de comunicación entre participantes alóctonos y autóctonos dentro del espacio escolar;

- hacer visibles las competencias lingüísticas de las que disponen todos los sujetos, más allá de aquellas que las instituciones educativas consideran curricularmente;

- reflexionar sobre el modelo de lengua para ser enseñada y las formas de comunicación y actuación verbal categorizadas como *aceptables*.

Entre los años 2003 y 2007 trabajamos con diferentes escuelas de nivel primario (véanse Nussbaum y Unamuno, 2006). En esos estudios constatamos que, a lo largo de la escolarización, los niños y niñas migrados aprendían la lengua catalana, vehicular de la enseñanza, pero solo algunos se la apropiaban como lengua de comunicación. Constatamos también que en las escuelas había una inquietud particular por el hecho de que el alumnado, a medida que avanzaba en los cursos, dejaba de emplear públicamente esta lengua.

De alguna forma, nos interesamos por continuar en esta línea de trabajo. Sin embargo, consideramos que no podíamos quedarnos solo con investigar lo que ocurría en los centros educativos. Debíamos ir más allá: incluir prácticas lingüísticas del entorno e incluir la mirada de los propios estudiantes sobre los usos lingüísticos propios y ajenos. Así, pensamos que una manera de hacerlo podía ser diseñar un proyecto que incluyera a los jóvenes como investigadores.

Como en otras investigaciones del GREIP, recurrimos entonces a un diseño metodológico basado en la investigación en colaboración. Para ello, propusimos diseñar el proyecto junto con los docentes de dos centros de secundaria. Tal como lo explica Nussbaum (en este volumen), se entiende que este tipo de investigación es innovadora y se sitúa metodológicamente un punto más allá de la investigación participativa, pues permite trabajar en equipo con todos los participantes en el diseño y discusión de métodos y técnicas, así como en el intercambio de intereses, objetivos y beneficios.

En este marco de reflexiones, propusimos el proyecto *La competencia multilingüe de los jóvenes: continuidades y discontinuidades entre las prácticas escolares y las prácticas de entorno* (DECOMASAI), realizado entre 2007 y 2010 por varios miembros del GREIP[3]. Su objetivo fue el estudio de las prácticas comunicativas dentro y fuera del ámbito escolar, considerando tales prácticas como instancias de socialización lingüística. Partimos de un diseño metodológico en colaboración, de perfil etnográfico y foco interaccional, centrado en dos estudios de caso (los resultados se pueden encontrar en Codó y Patiño-Santos, 2014; Corona, Nussbaum, y Unamuno, 2013).

El presente capítulo se centra especialmente en los aspectos metodológicos del citado proyecto. Nuestro objeto es indagar en la trama de colaboración que se fue articulando a lo largo del mismo, movilizando a los diferentes actores que participaron en el proyecto. Consideramos que estas relaciones son las que nos permiten ir identificando y describiendo las formas en que los jóvenes categorizan las prácticas lingüísticas escolares y de entorno, y dan sentido al contexto sociolingüístico que enmarca su socialización lingüística.

2. El proyecto DECOMASAI

El proyecto DECOMASAI se inició a comienzos del año escolar 2007-2008. Contactamos y comenzamos a trabajar junto con los docentes de lengua

---

[3]. Virginia Unamuno (IP entre 2007 y 2009) y Dolors Masats (IP entre 2009 y 2010). Otros miembros: Eva Codó, Víctor Corona, Luci Nussbaum, Amparo Tusón, Adriana Patiño, Cristina Escobar y Artur Noguerol.

castellana y catalana de dos centros públicos de educación secundaria situados en el área metropolitana de Barcelona. Nos referimos a los centros como *El Turó del Vent*[4] (TV), localizado en el área de la Sagrera, al norte de Barcelona (distrito de Sant Andreu) y *Els Quatre Gats* (QG), localizado en Badalona. Los dos institutos nos ofrecían contextos importantes para el estudio de la gestión de los diferentes repertorios plurilingües del alumnado.

El TV, localizado en una zona industrial, no presentaba un número alto de alumnado de origen inmigrante. Así, durante el curso 2006/07, de 485 estudiantes, 93 procedían de fuera de España. Quizás por esto, en el momento de realizar la investigación, la diversidad cultural no ocupaba un lugar importante dentro de las actividades curriculares o extracurriculares del proyecto educativo del centro. A pesar de la poca presencia de alumnado alóctono, este se concentraba en lo que los docentes denominaban *grupos adaptados*. Fueron precisamente los estudiantes de dos grupos adaptados de 2°A y 3°A quienes participaron en el proyecto.

El QG, por el contrario, presentaba un 90 % de alumnado de origen, en su mayoría, latinoamericano. Este centro, acostumbrado a albergar alumnado alóctono, había implementado la diversidad cultural como uno de los contenidos transversales del currículo desde hacía varios años. Algunos de los docentes estaban acostumbrados a organizar actividades extraescolares para promover proyectos interculturales, como teatro, escritura creativa o cuentería en varias lenguas. El grupo con el que se trabajó fue 4° de la ESO, pues la mayoría de los estudiantes poseía una experiencia previa de utilización del vídeo durante las actividades extraescolares.

La propuesta consensuada con los dos institutos consistió en seleccionar, entre los contenidos curriculares de cada ciclo escolar de la Educación Secundaria Obligatoria (ESO), aquellos que podrían tratarse a través de una propuesta de innovación que involucrara la observación y el registro, por parte del alumnado, de las prácticas comunicativas dentro y fuera del entorno escolar.

---

4. Atendiendo a los principios de la investigación etnográfica, se utilizan seudónimos para proteger la identidad de los informantes y los lugares en los que se llevó a cabo la intervención.

Capítulo 4

Cada grupo (2º y 3º en TV y 4 º en QG) se dividió en 4 equipos de expertos en algunos de los temas contenidos en el currículo propio de las asignaturas de lengua:

- multilingüismo;

- variedades lingüísticas (del catalán y del castellano);

- comunicación gráfica;

- comunicación no verbal.

Figura 1.   Resumen de la secuencia didáctica

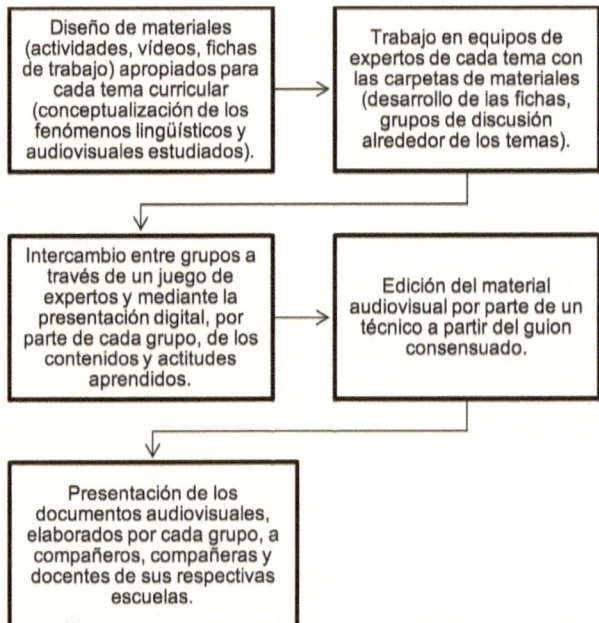

En coherencia con las investigaciones colaborativas anteriores del GREIP, la propuesta de intervención didáctica se basó en el trabajo por proyectos (véase

Nussbaum, en este volumen). Al ligar esta intervención con las tareas escolares, se intentaba crear situaciones que permitieran observar la forma en la que los participantes actuaban en la vida cotidiana, de manera que se pudo ver a los estudiantes trabajar en contextos espontáneos, sin atención del docente, y en contextos formales, presentando su trabajo a toda la clase. En el siguiente gráfico (Figura 1) se muestran las fases más importantes de la intervención didáctica.

3. Los estudiantes como investigadores

Como ya se ha señalado, el diseño del proyecto se basó en una investigación colaborativa entre diferentes tipos de actores: docentes-investigadores universitarios, docentes de secundaria y estudiantes. Mientras que los docentes de secundaria trabajaron activamente con el equipo universitario en el diseño de los materiales didácticos, la planificación de las intervenciones y su ejecución, los jóvenes tuvieron a su cargo el trabajo de terreno. Como muestra el gráfico anterior, para ello, los estudiantes tuvieron dos instancias de formación.

En primer lugar, en el marco de las asignaturas curriculares, los jóvenes participaron en talleres sobre los temas del currículo que se habían seleccionado. La propuesta didáctica fue trabajar en grupos de expertos. Cada grupo tendría a su cargo la investigación de uno de estos temas, tanto a partir de materiales teóricos como a través de la reflexión empírica.

En segundo lugar, los jóvenes se formaron en el manejo de técnicas audiovisuales, que les permitirían recoger datos y obtener insumos para realizar un breve documental, cuyo objetivo sería explicar al resto de la clase el tema o fenómeno que iban a investigar. Este documento audiovisual serviría, también, como material didáctico en los centros escolares. En el marco de este proyecto, los jóvenes también participaron en un taller sobre guion audiovisual y fueron entrenados para la realización de entrevistas.

Con estas herramientas, investigadores, docentes y estudiantes salieron de las aulas a producir paisajes lingüísticos (véase el apartado siguiente), tomando en cuenta diversos aspectos verbales y no verbales presentes tanto en el centro educativo como en su entorno.

4. Construir el marco teórico-metodológico

Una de las cuestiones complejas de este proyecto fue encontrar un marco teórico-metodológico de referencia para llevar a cabo nuestros propósitos. Algunos de nosotros habíamos sido formados en el análisis del discurso (véanse Antoniadou y Dooly, en este volumen), mientras que otros proveníamos de la sociolingüística interaccional y del análisis de la conversación (véanse Masats, en este volumen; Nussbaumen, este volumen). Por ello, a lo largo del proyecto, se vio que era posible explorar diversos enfoques para poder conceptualizar las complejidades del mismo e intentar conciliar al menos tres aspectos: lo que queríamos ver (nuestras metas u objetivos); lo que surgía a lo largo del trabajo colectivo con docentes y estudiantes, y lo que finalmente pudimos registrar a lo largo del mismo.

Fuimos, así, revisando y dialogando con diversas disciplinas. Aquí nos referiremos particularmente a dos: a los estudios de socialización lingüística (Bailey y Schecter, 2003; Baquedano-López y Kattan, 2008; Duff, 2003; Schieffelin y Ochs, 1986) y a los estudios del paisaje lingüístico (Shohamy, Ben-Rafael, y Barni, 2010).

En el primer caso, los estudios de socialización lingüística se mostraron pertinentes, especialmente respecto a nuestros objetivos. Esta rama de la antropología lingüística se preocupa por estudiar los procesos a través de los cuales "a child or other novice acquires the knowledge, orientations and practices that enable him or her to participate effectively and appropriately in the social life of a particular community" (Garret y Baquedano-López, 2002, p. 339)[5]. Consideramos que nuestra meta de aproximarnos a las prácticas comunicativas de jóvenes provenientes de otros lugares del mundo, en el marco de su escolarización en Cataluña, se asociaba directamente a tal objetivo.

---
5. "un niño o recién llegado adquiere el conocimiento, las orientaciones y las prácticas que le permiten participar efectiva y adecuadamente en la vida social de una comunidad" (Garret y Baquedano-López, 2002, p. 339).

Además, el marco de la socialización lingüística articula muy bien con los estudios interaccionales que lleva a cabo el GREIP. En ambas aproximaciones se considera que es en la interacción verbal en donde se aprenden los patrones comunicativos de una comunidad. De hecho, se entiende que, a lo largo de nuestra vida, las personas nos socializamos a través del lenguaje y para usar el lenguaje, pues es a través de nuestras interacciones cotidianas y dentro de los diferentes contextos en los que participamos, que aprendemos a comunicarnos no solo verbalmente sino a expresar emociones (afecto, alegría, enfado, acuerdo, desacuerdo, etc.).

Al establecer que el aprendizaje (lingüístico y cultural) no es un hecho puntual que se lleva a cabo en la escuela, sino que se trata de un proceso continuo que ocurre a lo largo de la vida en la interacción con los demás, los estudios de socialización lingüística nos ofrecían, además, un marco interesante para analizar las relaciones entre los contextos y las prácticas de socialización lingüística en las instituciones educativas y fuera de ellas. Por lo tanto, sus estrategias metodológicas se nos presentaban como pertinentes en la comprensión de las diferencias, similitudes y rupturas entre diferentes tipos de prácticas (escolares y no escolares) en las que participaban los jóvenes migrantes con los que interactuábamos.

En el segundo caso, nos interesaron los estudios sobre paisaje lingüístico. Tales estudios se proponen investigar "the way linguistic signs mark the public space" (Shohamy et al., 2010, p. xiv)[6], es decir, *leer* en usos lingüísticos públicos de un momento y de una comunidad dados relaciones entre ideologías lingüísticas, identidades individuales y colectivas, y prácticas sociales y políticas. Además, consideramos que como este tipo de estudios se preocupa por producir, mediante técnicas cualitativas de investigación, una *fotografía* de los repertorios lingüísticos públicos, sus estrategias analíticas podían servirnos para explicar los usos lingüísticos que recogerían los estudiantes en sus producciones audiovisuales.

---

6. "cómo los objetos lingüísticos marcan los espacios públicos" (Shohamy et al., 2010, p. xiv).

Como ya han señalado diversos autores (p.ej. Mondada, 2000; Scollon y Scollon, 2003), la noción de paisaje lingüístico está vinculada a la relación entre lengua, acción y territorio, y utilizarla teóricamente puede ser útil para comprender el modo en que los actores sociales se apropian o responden a tales usos, interactuando con ellos en tanto que *voces* de identidades colectivas presentes en el espacio público. En este sentido, nos pareció interesante observar no solo las elecciones y los recortes que los estudiantes hacían de los usos lingüísticos en los espacios públicos, sino también los modos en que respondían a estos a través de sus prácticas narrativas audiovisuales.

Los estudios cualitativos de perfil etnográfico se caracterizan por ir construyendo, a lo largo del trabajo de investigación, el entramado conceptual necesario para dar cuenta de lo que se observa y se analiza. Es parte de los resultados de este tipo de estudios producir nuevas conceptualizaciones. A diferencia de otro tipo de estudios que pretenden la generalización de resultados, los estudios que se enmarcan en los estudios de caso y en la etnografía pretenden producir conceptualizaciones que puedan ser útiles a nuevos casos y contextos.

5. Resultados: ¿con qué datos contamos?

Uno de los aspectos más importantes de este proyecto radica en su diseño innovador y en su propuesta colaborativa no solo con docentes, sino también con estudiantes. Sin embargo, se trata de un proyecto complejo, con muchas capas, muchos juegos de miradas, muchas personas que miran y muchas que son miradas. En este sentido, cabe preguntarse por lo que se definió como dato: ¿qué, de todo lo que sucedió en el campo, son los *datos* del proyecto? ¿Cuáles fueron las circunstancias que llevaron a que estos resultados surgieran de esta manera y con esta forma (discursiva, audiovisual, etc.)?

Quizá sirva en esta instancia hablar de la organización del equipo investigador y de su relación con los tipos de datos que se produjeron a lo largo del mismo. Así, también, convendría distinguir entre registros y datos, para poder entender las dinámicas analíticas.

El equipo se organizó alrededor de diversas tareas de investigación: (1) registro etnográfico a través de notas en el cuaderno de campo de los centros escolares y de su entorno; (2) observación participante, grabación y filmación de las actividades didácticas (clases y talleres de formación de los jóvenes investigadores), y (3) observación-participante y filmación de las salidas de campo que realizaron los jóvenes con los docentes.

Al final del proyecto, el equipo contaba con los siguientes registros y materiales (Tabla 1).

Tabla 1. Resumen de los datos recogidos y los materiales utilizados

Registros/Grabaciones	Materiales de clase
a. Registros en audio producidos mediante grabadoras que los estudiantes manipulaban durante las actividades de grupo.	a. El material elaborado durante las sesiones de trabajo de grupo.
b. Registros audiovisuales (filmaciones) grabados por el equipo investigador durante las sesiones de trabajo en el aula y fuera de ella.	b. Guiones documentales y de entrevistas elaborados para la realización de los documentos audiovisuales.
c. Registros audiovisuales realizados por los estudiantes en la búsqueda de imágenes, momentos, historias que querían incluir en su propia producción audiovisual.	c. Las presentaciones digitales finales elaboradas por cada equipo de trabajo, en las que los estudiantes explicaban lo que se había trabajado de cada grupo (en relación con diferentes temas del currículo escolar) a sus compañeros y compañeras.
d. Registro audiovisual de una sesión del claustro de docentes de lengua catalana, donde la profesora que participó en el proyecto presenta este a sus compañeros y compañeras, así como lo realizado en cada una de las sesiones, sus resultados y su propia evaluación de la propuesta didáctica y de investigación en colaboración.	
e. Entrevista realizada por un miembro del equipo investigador a dos docentes del centro TV, donde exponen su perspectiva sobre lo que hicieron.	
f. Registros en cuaderno de campo de todo el proceso.	

Capítulo 4

Desde el punto de vista de la investigación etnográfica, existe una diferencia entre los registros y otros materiales empíricos, por un lado, y los datos, por otro. Los primeros se consideran ligados a la experiencia empírica inmediata e insumos en el proceso interpretativo que enmarca la producción de datos. Los datos en sí se entienden relacionados con procesos analíticos.

En el proyecto que presentamos esto es de suma importancia. La gran cantidad y la diversidad de tipos de registros no hicieron posible un tratamiento sistemático ni un análisis minucioso de los mismos. Sin embargo, restaron a disposición, en tanto que insumos a los que se vuelve una y otra vez durante todo el proceso interpretativo. Esto comporta, en la práctica, que no todos los registros en audio o en video fueron transcritos: permanecieron disponibles para el equipo investigador para volver a ellos cada vez que las preguntas de investigación fueron formulándose durante la experiencia de campo o después de ella.

Un ejemplo puede servir para aclarar este punto. Durante la experiencia de trabajo de campo, filmamos, grabamos, observamos, etc., en muchas y diversas instancias. Como ya se ha señalado, los jóvenes estudiantes participaron en el proceso investigador teniendo a cargo tareas de investigación. Pero, además, debido al hecho de que estas tareas se dirigían a la producción de un material audiovisual para ser compartido, estos jóvenes tomaron decisiones respecto al material recogido, conservando partes y descartando otras. En estas decisiones, contextualizadas por todo el proceso etnográfico en que participamos colectivamente, emergen datos que vale la pena considerar.

6. Leyendo recortes, descartes y decisiones: las huellas de la actuación de los estudiantes como investigadores

Uno de los datos que nos pareció interesante analizar se refiere a la manera en que los estudiantes hicieron el puente entre los aprendizajes escolares, situados especialmente en los talleres de lengua, y su mirada sobre el mundo que los rodea. Como ya hemos señalado, uno de los grupos trató el tema de la comunicación gráfica. En su trabajo de investigación, los estudiantes produjeron un paisaje lingüístico que ponía en relación (y en tensión) a la comunicación institucional con la comunicación privada. El cuadernillo con el que trabajamos en los talleres incluía algunas definiciones (sacadas del libro de texto utilizado por el profesorado) sobre comunicación, así como ejemplos. En cuanto a las actividades, se les propuso buscar en Internet, a partir de una propuesta guiada, otros ejemplos. Una vez conceptualizado el tema, el alumnado, entrenado para usar las herramientas audiovisuales, elaboró un guion y salió a filmar, tanto fuera del aula como de la institución escolar. La idea era observar y comparar prácticas de comunicación, registrando diferencias respecto a los artefactos, géneros y lenguas presentes en los entornos habituales de los jóvenes.

En el material que finalmente seleccionaron para su documental, los estudiantes hicieron patente cierta tensión entre una voz, la institucional, que hablaba normalmente en la lengua oficial de la escuela, el catalán, y otras voces, que seleccionaban otras lenguas y otros géneros discursivos. Estas voces quedaron retratadas, por ejemplo, en los carteles informativos para los padres y en los carteles de la asociación de padres y madres (AMPA). Pero también, las selecciones que realizaron los estudiantes entre todo el material registrado mostraron la manera en que las prácticas discursivas institucionales se limitaban al contexto escolar, mientras que las otras, multilingües y transgresoras en cuanto a la normativa escrita convencional, atravesaban los muros simbólicos que separaban el centro escolar de su entorno. Los registros de pequeñas notas, escritos marginales, comentarios al margen, etc. iban y venían desde el centro educativo al entorno, y lo hacían en lenguas y formatos múltiples y diversos.

Los siguientes fotogramas, por ejemplo, muestran algunos de estos hechos de comunicación, registrados por el alumnado en el seno de la escuela: un cartel en castellano en el que se invita a los compañeros a felicitar a una chica por su aniversario (Figura 2, derecha) o las inscripciones en la puerta de un lavabo (Figura 2, izquierda). A través de su registro y selección, estas prácticas, que podían ser consideradas marginales desde el punto de vista adulto e institucional, se señalaron como relevantes desde el punto de vista de los jóvenes.

Figura 2. Izquierda: inscripciones en los lavabos; derecha: anuncios sociales en los pasillos

Como ya se ha explicado anteriormente, otro de los grupos trabajó en torno a la comunicación no verbal. Las sesiones de taller con los grupos, las carpetas de actividades, las páginas web visitadas y los materiales audiovisuales trabajados en clase focalizaban la relevancia de la gestualidad, la mímica facial y la distancia interpersonal en la interpretación de los hechos verbales.

Sin embargo, en uno de los dos centros, una vez dada la consigna al grupo encargado de documentar la comunicación no verbal dentro y fuera de la escuela, los estudiantes tomaron una decisión interesante que sorprendió al resto del equipo. Los estudiantes eligieron registrar calzados, con todas sus formas, marcas, colores y aspectos (Figura 3). Los calzados, según se desprende de los registros, se erigían en materialidades decisivas de comunicación no verbal para su comunidad (la de los jóvenes de Barcelona). Esta manera de conceptualizar el tema de la comunicación no verbal por parte de los jóvenes y su relación (o más bien distancia) con los materiales de clase muestran formas de apropiación de los discursos escolares y producen datos interesantes sobre los recursos semióticos que los jóvenes utilizan en la vida cotidiana, relacionados, según explican, con las categorizaciones y las identidades colectivas de los jóvenes. En este caso, el paisaje lingüístico producido (en su amplio sentido) pone en evidencia clasificaciones nativas sobre el mundo social en que participan y que tiene un sentido clave en sus formas de socialización. Raramente estas relaciones semióticas son consideradas en las instituciones escolares.

Figura 3. Temas de interés para los estudiantes

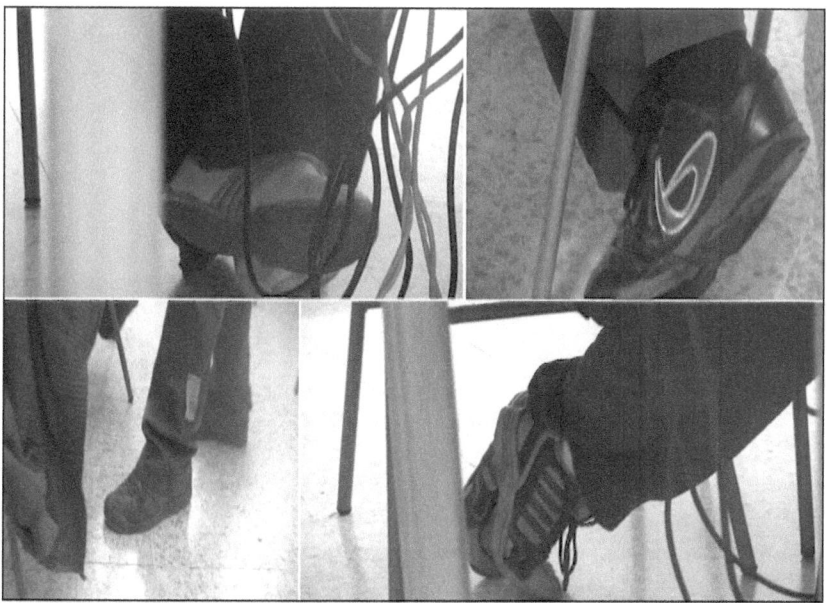

Otro de los grupos se dedicó a investigar la diversidad lingüística y el plurilingüismo. El reto de documentar un fenómeno relativo al lenguaje (objeto de sus clases de lengua) y el hecho de querer considerar en tal documentación tanto el entorno escolar como el no escolar hizo que los estudiantes tuvieran que mirar lo que les rodeaba de otro modo. Buscaron información, imágenes y testimonios que representaran lo que querían explicar sobre la diversidad lingüística y el plurilingüismo, poniendo en juego diversas miradas y estrategias (Figura 4).

Con estos propósitos, los estudiantes salieron a la calle, recorrieron el barrio, conversaron con conocidos y familiares, en ámbitos donde habitualmente pareciera que lo que se enseña en la escuela nada tiene que ver. Así, por ejemplo, entrevistaron al abuelo de uno de los estudiantes, para que explicara los cambios sociolingüísticos (entre otros) que había observado a lo largo de los últimos veinte años; también entrevistaron a tenderos de diferentes establecimientos del barrio para que hablaran de las lenguas que ellos y sus clientes usaban habitualmente. Pero también, exploraron su propio centro educativo y entrevistaron a sus docentes, venidos de otros lugares de los Países Catalanes, para que dieran testimonio de las diferencias dialectales que presenta la lengua catalana a lo largo de los mismos, y ejemplificaran casos de discriminación por razones de habla.

Figura 4.   El plurilingüismo en la calle

Los registros de estos testimonios fueron, posteriormente, procesados de tal manera que quedaron equiparados en los documentales que realizaron. Este trabajo sobre los registros pone en evidencia, creemos, la intención del alumnado de mostrar que la diversidad lingüística no puede considerarse solo un fenómeno del barrio ni de las migraciones, sino algo transversal a los grupos, a los contextos, situado en su dimensión histórico-social. El paisaje lingüístico producido en este caso hacía énfasis en su relación con los diferentes momentos e historias de Cataluña, en la que todos somos diversos. De algún modo, la mirada de los estudiantes, perceptible en la manera de tratar el tema de la diversidad lingüística, y las formas en que se produjeron colectivamente los documentales minimizaron las distancias escuela-entorno que docentes, e incluso investigadores, subrayaban en sus prácticas pedagógicas y en sus discursos cotidianos. Produjeron, también, un paisaje lingüístico contestatario de aquellos que producen los discursos oficiales que clasifican entre *nosotros* y *ellos*, los diversos.

7. A modo de conclusión

El propósito de este capítulo era presentar un ejemplo de cómo se hace ciencia social en el GREIP. Se refiere, específicamente, al hecho de que las propuestas de investigación del grupo, de carácter colaborativo y bajo el marco de la etnografía, afrontan un primer reto complejo que tiene que ver con observar, interpretar y reflexionar colectivamente sobre cómo producen conocimiento, y poder explorar, además, cómo este se modifica.

Este reto puede resumirse en dos instancias: por un lado, proponerse investigar junto con otros actores, no universitarios, de manera simétrica, creando situaciones de colaboración; por otro lado, plantear una investigación que se combina y se nutre con la intervención educativa, de manera que, al mismo tiempo que observamos fenómenos relativos a la enseñanza y el aprendizaje de lenguas, construimos junto a otros actores –estudiantes y docentes– maneras diferentes de enseñar y de aprender.

La manera de hacer y entender la ciencia del GREIP afronta, asimismo, un segundo reto de tipo metodológico, que tiene que ver con la búsqueda constante de cómo recoger datos naturales sin alterar en alto grado las realidades de las aulas estudiadas. Entendemos que el estudio de las prácticas es el que permite dar cuenta de las maneras en las que los actores sociales comprenden su realidad, acercándonos a las formas locales en que los participantes describen y categorizan el plurilingüismo. A partir de los registros naturales que hacemos junto con otros, producimos datos que ponen en evidencia los procesos de adquisición de los saberes lingüísticos y culturales de los novicios o recién llegados, así como de su grado de participación en nuevos contextos, es decir, damos cuenta de los aprendizajes entendidos como instancias de socialización lingüística.

La consideración de las formas locales de clasificación e interpretación social se ha puesto de relevancia a lo largo de este capítulo. Como ya hemos mencionado, la opción del proyecto DECOMASAI de incorporar a los jóvenes como investigadores nos ha permitido construir nuevos saberes sobre la diversidad lingüística y comunicativa que caracteriza a los centros educativos contemporáneos. Esta producción de saberes ha sido posible por haber considerado, en diálogo con otras, la perspectiva de los jóvenes sobre los objetos sociales que investigamos.

Pero, a la vez, el proyecto se ha constituido en sí mismo en un marco interesante para probar maneras alternativas de enseñar. Tal y como se ha intentado mostrar, poner la diversidad lingüística y comunicativa en el centro de la propuesta escolar, haciendo de los estudiantes actores en su investigación, ha resultado una estrategia productiva en relación con nuevos aprendizajes y en relación con nuevas actitudes lingüísticas. Los jóvenes que participaron en este proyecto se mostraron más interesados, atentos y comprensivos hacia la diversidad de lenguas, pero también hacia las diferentes personas y los diferentes grupos con los que interactuaron. Sin embargo, a lo largo del proyecto, los estudiantes con los que trabajamos, pero también los docentes, tomaron mayor conciencia sobre el funcionamiento interno y social de las lenguas que investigaron, y desarrollaron mejores capacidades para su análisis. Con ello, se evidencian indicios de sus mutuos procesos de socialización lingüística. No solo los recién llegados transforman sus disposiciones e ideologías lingüísticas, sino que los autóctonos se dan cuenta de su nueva realidad y aprenden a enfrentarla de manera creativa.

Nuestros datos muestran, también, que los jóvenes han podido establecer relaciones productivas entre los contenidos teóricos de los talleres y los hechos observados en la escuela y su entorno, elaborando guiones que permiten recuperar maneras particulares de describir estos hechos sociales. Han podido producir continuidades entre prácticas comunicativas y lingüísticas que no estaban previstas, así como focalizar rupturas entre las prácticas comunicativas observadas en los diferentes entornos, explorados por ellos de manera novedosa para nosotros. Han podido, también, categorizar los saberes lingüísticos de sus pares, y explicar contenidos curriculares a través de categorías propias, distantes, a veces, de las empleadas por los docentes y de las utilizadas en los materiales que habíamos diseñado a lo largo de la propuesta de enseñanza.

En cuanto a los retos, limitaciones y potenciales de la investigación en colaboración, en primer lugar, se puede señalar que, a diferencia de otros diseños de investigación, proponerse llevar a cabo una investigación que comparta el rol investigador con otros actores comporta estar dispuesto a negociar con ellos (docentes y estudiantes, en nuestro caso) los objetivos de la investigación, sus tiempos y sus condiciones. Esto implica estar dispuesto a rediseñar constantemente los instrumentos y el plan de trabajo desarrollado en función de los intereses, tiempos y agenda de aquellos con quienes investigamos, que no están inmersos en la lógica universitaria ni académica. Investigar con quienes se sitúan en otros terrenos implica también negociar sentidos sobre los objetos que investigamos y sobre la manera de hacerlo. Pero también trae aparejado entender que el mismo proceso de investigación es negociable y abierto.

En segundo lugar, hacer etnografía comporta disponer de tiempo y predisposición para pasar largas sesiones en los lugares en los que investigamos y con las personas que participan. Muchas veces este tipo de investigaciones implican estar en condiciones de dejar de hacer otras cosas, y esto no es siempre fácil.

En tercer lugar, este tipo de diseño de investigación implica no tener muy claro en el inicio lo que se busca, sino estar abierto a lo que uno va a encontrar (cfr. método inductivo, investigación cualitativa; véase la introducción de Dooly y Moore, en este volumen). Este grado de atención flotante que exige, al menos inicialmente, el trabajo de investigación etnográfica, es difícil y quienes investigan suelen preguntarse continuamente si lo que están haciendo es investigar o perder el tiempo. Sin embargo, si durante este proceso, quienes investigan se dejan atravesar por lo cotidiano pueden llegar a ese punto en el que algo de lo que pasa, de lo que se observa, de la situación en que se participa es suficientemente interesante, sorprendente o inquietante para ser narrado: ahí el trabajo etnográfico entra en otra etapa.

Para concluir, quizá cabe decir que muchas veces, como equipo, nos preguntábamos si no sería más fácil, más barato y más eficaz, diseñar y ejecutar investigaciones de tipo experimental, usar encuestas, pasar test, etc., Pero hay algo maravilloso de la investigación cualitativa que es ese momento en el que lo cotidiano se transforma en extraño, lo que no sorprende se vuelve absolutamente raro, porque ha ido transformándose al cambiar la mirada con la que la persona que investiga se acerca y explora lo de todos los días y porque se ha conseguido, o al menos intentado, poner en diálogo la mirada de quien investiga sobre la realidad que se explora y la mirada de los otros sobre dicha realidad: en ese cruce de miradas, aparece lo que investigamos, y se convierte en algo fascinante.

Obras citadas

Antoniadou, V., y Dooly, M. (2017). Etnografia educativa en contextos d'aprenentatge mixt. En E. Moore y M. Dooly (Eds), *Enfoques cualitativos para la investigación en educación plurilingüe* (pp. 264-292). Research-publishing.net. https://doi.org/10.14705/rpnet.2017.emmd2016.631

Baquedano-López, P., y Kattan, S. (2008). Language socialization in schools. En P. Duff y N. Hornberger (Eds), *Encyclopedia of language and education, Volume 8: Language socialization* (pp. 161-173). Boston, MA: Springer. https://doi.org/10.1007/978-0-387-30424-3_204

Bayley, R., y S. R. Schecter (Eds). (2003). *Language socialization in bilingual and multilingual societies*. Bristol: Multilingual Matters.

Codó, E., Nussbaum, L., y Unamuno, V. (2007). La noció de competència plurilingüe en el terreny de l'acollida lingüística. En O. Guasch y L. Nussbaum (Eds), *Aproximacions a la noció de competència plurilingüe* (pp. 47-60). Bellaterra: Publicacions de la UAB.

Codó, E., y Patiño-Santos, A. (2014). Beyond language: class, social categorization and academic achievement in a Catalan high school. *Linguistics and Education, 25*, 51-63. https://doi.org/10.1016/j.linged.2013.08.002

Corona, V., Nussbaum, L., y Unamuno, V. (2013). The emergence of new linguistic repertoires among Barcelona's youth of Latin American Origin. *International Journal of Bilingual Education and Bilingualism, 16*(2), 182-194. https://doi.org/10.1080/13670050.2012.720668

Dooly, M., y Moore, E. (2017). Introducció: enfocaments qualitatius per a la recerca en educació plurilingüe. En E. Moore y M. Dooly (Eds), *Enfoques cualitativos para la investigación en educación plurilingüe* (pp. 11-20). Research-publishing.net. https://doi.org/10.14705/rpnet.2017.emmd2016.619

Duff, P. (2003). New directions in second language socialization research. *Korean Journal of English Language and Linguistics, 3*, 309-339.

Garrett, P. B., y Baquedano-López, P. (2002). Language socialization: reproduction and continuity, transformation and change. *Annual Review of Anthropology, 31*, 339-361. https://doi.org/10.1146/annurev.anthro.31.040402.085352

Masats, D. (2017). L'anàlisi de la conversa al servei de la recerca en el camp de l'adquisició de segones llengües (CA-for-SLA). En E. Moore y M. Dooly (Eds), *Enfocaments qualitatius per a la recerca en educació plurilingüe* (pp. 293-320). Research-publishing.net. https://doi.org/10.14705/rpnet.2017.emmd2016.632

Mondada, L. (2000). *Décrire la ville*. Paris: Édition Payot et Rivages.

Nussbaum, L. (2017). Investigar con docentes. En E. Moore y M. Dooly (Eds), *Enfoques cualitativos para la investigación en educación plurilingüe* (pp. 23-45). Research-publishing.net. https://doi.org/10.14705/rpnet.2017.emmd2016.620

Nussbaum, L., y Unamuno, V. (Eds). (2006). *Usos i competències multilingües entre escolars d'origen immigrant*. Bellaterra: Servei de Publicacions de la UAB.

Schieffelin, B. B., y Ochs, E. (1986). *Language socialization across cultures*. Cambridge: Cambridge University Press.

Scollon, R., y Scollon, S. B. K. (2003). *Discourses in place: language in the material world*. Londres/Nueva York: Routledge. https://doi.org/10.4324/9780203422724

Shohamy, E., Ben-Rafael, E., y Barni, M. (2010). *Linguistic landscapes in the city*. Bristol: Multilingual Matters.

Lecturas recomendadas

Clark, J. (2004). Participatory research with children and young people: philosophy, possibilities and perils. *Action Research Expeditions, 4*(11), 1-18.

Codó E., Patiño Santos, A., y Unamuno, V. (2012). La sociolingüística con perspectiva etnográfica en el mundo hispano. Nuevos contextos, nuevas aproximaciones. Volumen especial de *Spanish in Context, 9*(2). Amsterdam: John Benjamins.

Duff, P. (2008). Language socialization, higher education, and work. En P. Duff y N. Hornberger (Eds), *Encyclopedia of language and education. Volume 8: language socialization* (pp. 257-270). Nueva York: Springer.

Ochs, E., y Schieffelin, B. (2011). The theory of language socialization. En A. Duranti, E. Ochs, y B. Schieffelin (Eds), *The handbook of language socialization* (pp. 1-21). Malden, MA: Wiley-Blackwell.

Patiño-Santos, A. (2016). Etnografía y sociolingüística. En J. Gutiérrez-Rexach (Ed.), *Enciclopedia de Lingüística Hispánica* (pp. 53-63). Abingdon, Reino Unido: Routledge.

Shohamy, E., Ben-Rafael, E., y Barni, M. (2010). *Linguistic landscapes in the city*. Bristol: Multilingual Matters.

Unamuno, V. (2011). Entre iguales: notas sobre la socialización lingüística del alumnado inmigrado en Barcelona. *Sociolinguistic Studies, 5*(2), 321-346.

Páginas web con recursos mencionados

Materiales didácticos del proyecto DECOMASAI: http://pagines.uab.cat/decomasai/

4 Producing knowledge about plurilingualism with young students: a challenge for collaborative ethnography

Virginia Unamuno[1] and Adriana Patiño[2]

Key concepts: ethnography, collaborative research, language socialization, linguistic landscape, plurilingual teaching sequences, students as researchers.

1. Introduction

One of the core concerns of the research undertaken by GREIP has been to develop an interdisciplinary approach to plurilingualism that could be useful in education. This approach was established by taking into consideration, in a situated manner and based on the study of interactional data, the competences that make it possible to acquire the knowledge, orientations and practices that allow effective participation in a variety of everyday interactions in educational and social contexts (Codó, Nussbaum, & Unamuno, 2007; Nussbaum & Unamuno, 2006).

Giving an account of how plurilingualism and, more specifically, plurilingual competences should be managed in the classroom thus becomes a research subject strongly connected with the need to understand complex teaching-learning situations. On the one hand, different communicative repertoires are brought into play and, on the other, they involve people with different sets of knowledge, categorized unequally on an institution level. Describing this form of classroom management entails: studying plurilingual competences in a situated manner

---

1. CONICET-Centro de Estudios del Lenguaje en Sociedad (CELES)-UNSAM, Buenos Aires, Argentina; vunamuno@conicet.gov.ar

2. University of Southampton, Southampton, United Kingdom; a.patino@soton.ac.uk

How to cite this chapter: Unamuno, V., & Patiño, A. (2017). Producing knowledge about plurilingualism with young students: a challenge for collaborative ethnography. In E. Moore & M. Dooly (Eds), *Qualitative approaches to research on plurilingual education* (pp. 129-149). Research-publishing.net. https://doi.org/10.14705/rpnet.2017.emmd2016.625

so that tools can be provided for the different actors involved in the schooling process in order to promote socio-educational interventions according to a particular situation; putting forward inclusive schooling initiatives; preventing prejudice from forming and reproducing; and providing guidelines to prevent the social exclusion of minorities.

In the context of education in Catalonia, there is a long history of interest in research undertaken in pursuit of inclusive education. This can linked partly to research carried out from the end of the Franco dictatorship to support the building of an educational system that would include different social sectors, characterized by being speakers of different languages. From our point of view, this foundational process of relating research and teaching had a profound effect on the way in which the GREIP group works insofar as it places importance on giving attention to school processes, but also to building a close relationship between universities and schools, thus creating a particular way of undertaking research.

Scientific interest in plurilingualism, the socially appropriate teaching of languages, and social inclusion are all present in the various projects of the GREIP group in relation to the study of teaching-language processes of first, second and foreign languages in contexts of linguistic diversity. Nevertheless, these interests kept shifting in response to social changes. Added to the initial complexity of the Catalan educational system, characterized by bilingual education models in which the language used at school and the one used at home were defined as resources available for schooling, new educational conditions came into play with the significant change in the student population of Catalonia that began at the start of the 21st century. We are referring here to students of immigrant origin entering the Catalan school system, something that marked a transformation in the composition of the school population and created a new teaching-learning context characterized by profound inequalities, mainly with regard to access to the languages used for teaching and to the curricular content. Within this context of transformations, the GREIP group was concerned not just with investigating what was happening in schools, but rather with supporting its agents in the search for methodological strategies and creating resources to face the new challenges that these changes presented.

The disquiet aroused by plurilingualism in Catalan classrooms led the GREIP group into an intensive debate with a variety of educational agents, and the need to investigate, amongst other things, the means and strategies to:

- improve the ways in which recently arrived and autochthonous participants communicate within the school environment;

- make visible the linguistic competences of all students, above and beyond those that educational institutions offer in their curriculum;

- reflect on the language model to use in teaching and the forms of communication and verbal actions categorized as 'acceptable'.

Between 2003 and 2007 we worked with different primary schools (see Nussbaum & Unamuno, 2006). In these studies we were able to verify that throughout their schooling, immigrant children learnt Catalan as a vehicular language for teaching but only a few appropriated it as their language of communication. We also found that there was a specific concern in the schools due to the fact that, as students progressed through academic years, they stopped using Catalan in public.

To a certain extent, we were interested in continuing with this line of work. However, we did not feel we could limit ourselves only to what was happening in educational institutions. We needed to go further: to include linguistic practices in non-school environments and the views of the students themselves on their own and others' language uses. We thought, therefore, that one way of doing this could be to design a project that included young people as researchers.

Thus, as with other GREIP group investigations, we resorted to a methodological design based on collaborative research. To do so, we proposed designing the project jointly with the teachers of two secondary schools. As Nussbaum (this volume) explains, this type of research is viewed as innovative and in methodological terms it goes one step beyond participative research as it facilitates teamwork with all the participants in the design and discussion of methods and techniques, as well as the exchange of interests, objectives and benefits.

Taking into account these considerations, we put forward the project 'Multilingual competences of secondary school students: continuities and discontinuities between educational and non-educational practices' (DECOMASAI), which was carried out between 2007 and 2010 by various members of the GREIP[3] group. Its objective was to study communicative practices in both school and non-school environments, viewing such practices as examples of language socialization. We started out from a collaborative methodological design with an ethnographic profile and an interactional focus, based on two case studies (the results can be found in Codó & Patiño-Santos, 2014; Corona, Nussbaum, & Unamuno, 2013).

This chapter concentrates primarily on the methodological aspects of the project in question. Our goal is to explore the network of collaboration that was built up throughout the life of the project, mobilizing the various agents who took part in it. We believe that it is these relationships that allowed us to make progress in identifying and describing the ways that young people categorize school and non-school linguistic practices and give meaning to the sociolinguistic context that frames their language socialization.

2. The DECOMASAI project

The DECOMASAI project began at the start of the 2007/2008 academic year. We contacted and started to work together with teachers of Spanish and Catalan in two state secondary schools in the metropolitan area of Barcelona: *El Turó del Vent*[4] (TV) situated in the Sagrera area in the north of Barcelona (district of Sant Andreu) and *Els Quatre Gats* (QG), in Badalona. The two schools provided

---

3. Virginia Unamuno (PI between 2007 and 2009) and Dolors Masats (PI from 2009 to 2010). Other members: Eva Codó, Víctor Corona, Luci Nussbaum, Amparo Tuson, Adriana Patiño, Cristina Escobar and Artur Noguerol.

4. In accordance with the principles of ethnographic research, pseudonyms are used to protect the identity of the sources and the places where the activity was carried out.

important contexts for studying the way in which the different plurilingual repertoires of the student body were managed.

The TV school, located in an industrial zone, did not have a high number of students of immigrant origin. During the 2006/07 academic year, of 485 students, 93 came from outside Spain. Perhaps this was the reason why, at the time of the investigation, cultural diversity did not play a major role in the curricular and extracurricular activities that formed part of the school's educational project. In spite of there only being a minor presence of recently arrived students, these were concentrated in what the teachers called 'adapted groups'. Specifically, it was students from two adapted groups of Compulsory Secondary Education (*Educación Secundaria Obligatoria*, ESO), 2nd grade A and 3rd grade A, who took part in the project.

Conversely, 90% of QG's students were mainly from Latin America. This school, being used to taking in recently arrived students, had introduced cultural diversity some years previously as one of the cross-cutting factors in its curricular content. Some of the teachers were already accustomed to organizing extracurricular activities to promote intercultural projects such as theatre, creative writing or storytelling in different languages. The group worked with was the 4th grade of ESO, given that most of the students had previous experience of using video in their extracurricular activities.

The proposal agreed with the two schools consisted of selecting curricular content from each cycle of the ESO course that was suitable for being approached in an innovative way. This would involve the students observing and noting down communicative practices in both school and non-school environments.

Each group (2nd and 3rd graders at TV and 4th graders at QG) was divided into four teams of experts in some of the topics included in the language subjects:

- multilingualism;

- linguistic varieties (of Catalan and Spanish);

- graphic communication;

- non-verbal communication.

In line with previous GREIP collaborative investigations, the proposed didactic intervention was based on project work (see Nussbaum, this volume). When linking this intervention with school tasks, an attempt was made to create situations that allowed participants to be observed behaving as they do in everyday life, so that students could be seen acting in spontaneous situations without the formal supervision of teachers, and in formal situations, presenting their work to the entire class. The following flowchart (Figure 1) shows the most important phases of the didactic intervention.

Figure 1. Summary of the didactic sequence

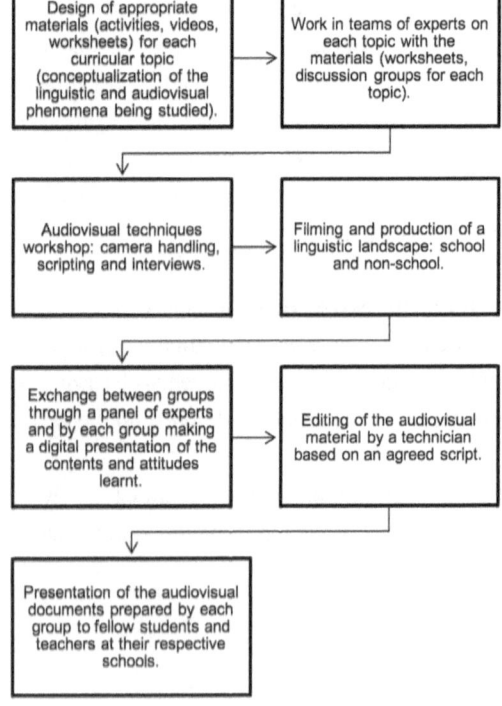

3. Students as researchers

As mentioned above, the design of the project was based on collaborative research involving different types of actors: university teacher-researchers, secondary school teachers, and students. While the secondary school teachers worked actively with the university team in the design of the teaching materials, the planning of the interventions and their execution, the students were responsible for the fieldwork. As the above flowchart shows, the youngsters had two stages of training.

First, within the framework of their curricular courses, they took part in workshops on topics that had been selected from the curriculum. The teaching proposition was to work in expert groups. Each group would be responsible for researching one of those topics, based on both theoretical material and empirical reflection.

Second, the students were trained in managing audiovisual techniques that allowed them to collect data and obtain material for making a brief documentary, the objective of which would be to explain to their other classmates the topic or phenomenon they investigated. This audiovisual document would also be useful as teaching material at other schools. As part of this workshop, the youngsters also took part in a session on audiovisual scripting and were trained to conduct interviews.

With these tools, researchers, teachers and students set out from the classroom to produce linguistic landscapes (see the following section), taking into account various verbal and non-verbal aspects present in both school and non-school environments.

4. Constructing the theoretical-methodological framework

One of complex questions for this project was finding a theoretical-methodological frame of reference within which to carry out the work proposed. Some researchers had been trained in discourse analysis (see Antoniadou & Dooly, this volume), while others of us had a background in interactional sociolinguistics and conversation analysis (see Masats, this volume; Nussbaum, this volume). Because of this, it became evident during the project that it was possible to explore different approaches to conceptualize the complexities and try to reconcile at least three aspects: what we wanted to look at (our goals or objectives); what emerged during the group work with teachers and students; and what we were finally able to take note of along the way.

Our progress was, therefore, one of revision and dialogue with a number of disciplines. Here we refer to two in particular: studies on language socialization (Bayley & Schecter, 2003; Baquedano-López & Kattan, 2008, Duff, 2003; Schieffelin & Ochs, 1986) and studies on linguistic landscapes (Shohamy, Ben-Rafael, & Barni, 2010).

In the first case, language socialization studies proved to be particularly relevant to our objectives. This branch of linguistic anthropology is concerned with studying the processes by which "a child or other novice acquires the knowledge, orientations and practices that enable him or her to participate effectively and appropriately in the social life of a particular community" (Garrett & Baquedano-López, 2002, p. 339). We believed that our goal of approaching the communicative practices of young people coming from other parts of the world within the framework of their schooling in Catalonia was directly associated with such an objective.

In addition, the framework of language socialization dovetails very well with the interactional studies undertaken by the GREIP group. Both approaches believe that the communicative patterns of a community are learnt through verbal interaction. In fact, it is accepted that, throughout our lives, we become socialized through language and it is through our use of language in the course of our everyday interactions and the different contexts we are engaged in that we learn not only to communicate verbally but also to express emotions (affection, joy, anger, agreement, disagreement, etc.).

Once it is established that learning (linguistic and cultural) is not a once-off event that takes place at school, but rather a continuous process lasting a lifetime that occurs through interaction with others, language socialization studies also provide an interesting framework for analyzing the relationships between the contexts and practices of language socialization both inside and outside educational institutions. Therefore, its methodological strategies appeared relevant to us in understanding the differences, similarities and ruptures between the different types of practices (school and non-school) involving the young people we were interacting with.

In the second case we were interested in studies on the linguistic landscape. These studies propose examining "the way linguistic signs mark the public space" (Shohamy et al., 2010, p. xiv). This implies 'reading into' public linguistic usage belonging to a particular moment and to a community, given the relationships between language ideologies, individual and collective identities, and social and political practices. Additionally, as this type of study is interested in using qualitative research techniques to produce a 'snapshot' of public linguistic repertoires, we believed its analytical strategies could be of use to us in explaining the linguistic uses that the students would collect in their audiovisual productions.

As several authors have indicated (e.g. Mondada, 2000; Scollon & Scollon, 2003), the concept of linguistic landscape is linked to the relationship between language, action and territory, and using it theoretically can be useful for understanding the way in which social actors appropriate or respond to such uses, interacting with them as 'voices' of collective identities present in the public space. In this respect we felt it interesting to observe not only which linguistic uses in public spaces the students chose to include or leave out, but also the ways in which they responded to these choices through their audiovisual narratives.

Ethnographically-based qualitative studies are characterized by constructing the conceptual framework necessary to account for what is being observed and analyzed throughout the course of the research. Part of the role of the results from this type of study is to produce new conceptualizations. Unlike other types of study that seek to generalize results, studies based on case studies and ethnography aim to come up with conceptualizations that can be of use in new cases and contexts.

5. Results: what data are available?

One of the most important aspects of this project lies in its innovative design and collaborative nature, not only with teachers but also with students. It is, however, a complex, multi-layered project with a great deal of interplay of perspectives, many people observing and many being observed. In this respect, it is worth asking oneself what can be defined as data. What, out of everything that took place in the field, are the 'data' of the project? What were the circumstances that led these data to emerge in this way and in this format (discursive, audiovisual, etc.)?

Perhaps, in this case, it would be helpful to talk about the organization of the research team and its relationship with the type of data produced over the course of the study. It would also be worthwhile to distinguish between records and data in order to understand the analytical dynamics.

The team was organized around various research tasks: (1) ethnographical records in the form of fieldnotes from both school and non-school environments; (2) participant observation, recording and filming of teaching activities (classes and training workshops with the young researchers); and (3) participant observation and filming of the field trips undertaken by the youngsters and their teachers.

At the end of the project, the team had gathered the following records and materials (Table 1).

From the point of view of ethnographic research, there is a difference between records and other empirical material on the one hand, and data on the other. The former are considered to be linked to immediate empirical experience and embedded in the interpretative process within which the production of data is framed. The data themselves are understood to be related to analytical processes.

Table 1. Summary of the data collected and the materials used

Records/Recordings	Class materials
a. Audio records taken by recorders managed by the students during group activities.	a. Material produced during group work sessions.
b. Audiovisual recordings filmed by researchers from our team during work sessions inside and outside the classroom.	b. Documentary and interview scripts prepared in order to produce audiovisual documentation.
c. Audiovisual recordings produced by students looking for images, moments and stories they wanted to include in their own audiovisual production.	c. Final digital presentations prepared by each work team, in which the students explain what each group has worked on (relative to different topics in the school curriculum) to their classmates.
d. Audiovisual recording of a Catalan teachers' staff meeting, during which the teacher taking part in the project made a presentation to her colleagues, explaining what had been done in each session, the results and her own assessment of the didactic proposal and collaborative research.	
e. Interview conducted by a member of the research team with two teachers from the TV school, in which they explained their views of the activities.	
f. Fieldnotes of the entire process.	

This is of prime importance to the project that we are presenting. The enormous quantity and variety of records made it impossible to carry out a systematic treatment or detailed analysis of all of them. Nevertheless, they remained available, as input that came up time and again during the interpretative process. This means that, in practice, not all of the audio or video recordings were transcribed: they remained available for researchers to return to them whenever research questions cropped up during or after the field experience.

An example may serve to clarify this point. While carrying out fieldwork we filmed, recorded, observed, etc. in many and varied situations. As mentioned, the students took part in the research process by taking responsibility for certain tasks. Additionally, however, due to the fact that these tasks were aimed at producing audiovisual material to be shared, the students made decisions with regard to the material collected, keeping some of it and discarding others. It is from these decisions, contextualized by the whole ethnological process in which we were collectively participating, that data emerged that was worthy of consideration.

6. Reading clips, discarding material and making decisions: the hallmarks of the student's performance as researchers

One of the data that seemed interesting to analyze concerned the way students made a connection between school learning, particularly with reference to language workshops, and their view of the world around them. As indicated, one of the groups addressed the subject of graphic communication. Their work generated a linguistic landscape that compared the relationship (and tension) between institutional and private communication. The booklet we were using in the workshops included some definitions of communication (taken from the textbook used by the teachers) to use as examples. In terms of the activities, students were invited, based on a guided proposal, to look for further examples on the internet. Once they had the concept of the subject clear and had been trained in how to use audiovisual tools, the students produced a script and went out to film both outside the classroom and outside the school altogether. The idea was to observe and compare communication practices, noting the differences in terms of mechanisms, types and languages present in the young people's habitual environment.

In the material finally selected for their documentary, the students clearly displayed a certain level of tension between one voice, the institutional one, which was normally Catalan, the official language of the school, and other voices that were selected from other languages and other discursive types. These voices were portrayed, for example, in the information posters for parents and on the posters for the Parents' Association. Yet also the selections made by the students from all the material logged showed the way in which institutional discursive practices were confined to the school context, while the others, multilingual and rule-breaking in terms of the conventional written norm, broke through the symbolic walls separating the school from its setting. Records of short notes, minor annotations, comments in the margin, etc., came and went from the school to the surrounding area in a great many varied formats and languages.

The following photographs, for example, show some of the communications recorded by the students within the school setting: a poster in Spanish inviting classmates to congratulate a girl on her birthday (Figure 2, right) or graffiti on a lavatory door (Figure 2, left). The fact that practices were noted and selected which, from an adult and institutional perspective could be considered as marginal, shows that they were relevant from the standpoint of the young people.

Figure 2. Left: graffiti in the toilets; right: social announcements in the corridors

As explained earlier, another of the groups worked on non-verbal communication. The group workshop sessions, worksheets, websites visited and audiovisual material worked on in class focused on the importance of body language, facial expressions and interpersonal distance in the interpretation of verbal events.

Chapter 4

Nevertheless, in one of the two schools, once the group responsible had been assigned the task of documenting non-verbal communication inside and outside the school, the students took an interesting decision that surprised the rest of the team. The students chose to record footwear in all of its forms, brands, colors and appearances (Figure 3). According to their records, shoes were a highly significant means of non-verbal communication in their community (the youth of Barcelona). This way of conceptualizing the subject of non-verbal communication by young people and their relationship with (or maybe distance from) class materials, demonstrates ways to appropriate school discourses and produce interesting data on the semiotic resources used by young people in their everyday lives related, as they explain, to the categorizations and collective identities of youth. In this case, the resulting linguistic landscape (in its broadest sense) reveals native classifications of the social world in which young people are involved that have a key meaning for the ways in which they socialize. These semiotic relationships are rarely considered in educational institutions.

Figure 3. Topics of interest for students

Another of the groups focused on researching linguistic diversity and plurilingualism. The challenge of having to document a phenomenon related to language (the subject of their language classes), and the fact of wanting this documentation to consider environments both inside and outside school, meant that the students had to view what surrounded them in a different way. They looked for information, images and statements that represented what they wanted to explain about linguistic diversity and plurilingualism, bringing into play a variety of viewpoints and strategies (Figure 4).

It was with these intentions that the students took to the streets, toured the neighborhood and spoke to acquaintances and relatives in milieus that normally have 'nothing to do' with what is taught at school. For example, one of their grandfathers was interviewed so that he could explain the sociolinguistic changes (amongst others) he had noted over the course of the last twenty years. Others interviewed shopkeepers from different neighborhood establishments to talk about the languages they and their customers use on a regular basis. But they also researched their own school and interviewed teachers who had come from different parts of Catalonia so they could comment on the dialectal differences present in the Catalan language throughout its regions and give examples of cases of speech discrimination.

The records of these statements were later processed in such a way that those pertaining to both school and non-school environments could be compared. We believe that this work on the records shows the students' intention to demonstrate that linguistic diversity cannot be viewed only as a phenomenon relating to the neighborhood or immigration, but rather as something that cuts across groups and contexts located in their historical-social dimension. The linguistic landscape produced in this case places an emphasis on the different moments and stories of Catalonia, in which all of us are diverse. In a way, the students' point of view as perceived in their approach to the subject of linguistic diversity and the way they produced their documentaries collectively minimized the distance between in-school and outside school environments that teachers and even researchers have been reinforcing in their teaching methods and everyday discourse. They also produced a linguistic landscape

Chapter 4

that goes against the one promoted by the official discourses that classify between 'us' and 'them', the latter being diverse.

Figure 4. Plurilingualism in the street

7. Concluding words

The purpose of this chapter was to present an example of the way we do social science in GREIP. In particular, it discussed how research of a collaborative nature and within the framework of ethnography involves the complex task of observing, interpreting and collectively reflecting on how knowledge is yielded, and furthermore of exploring how this knowledge might be modified.

This task can be resolved in two ways: on the one hand, by proposing research together with other non-university actors in a symmetrical way, creating collaborative situations; and on the other, by suggesting research that is combined and sustained within an educational intervention, so that at the same time as observing phenomena related to the teaching and learning of languages, we construct different ways of teaching and learning along with students and teachers.

The way in which GREIP does and understands science also faces a second challenge of a methodological nature, which relates to the constant search for how to gather natural data without greatly altering the realities of the classrooms under study. We believe that the study of practices is what enables us to give an account of the ways in which social actors view their reality, closing in on the localized ways in which the participants describe and categorize plurilingualism.

The way we produce data that reveal the processes by which novices or new arrivals acquire linguistic and cultural knowledge, as well as their degree of participation in new contexts, is based on natural records that we collect together with others. This means that we take into account learning understood as instances of language socialization.

The importance of considering local forms of social classification and interpretation has been evident throughout this chapter. As we mentioned, the option offered by the DECOMASAI project to include young people as researchers allowed us to amass new knowledge about the linguistic and communicative diversity that characterizes our educational institutions. The production of this knowledge was made possible by taking into consideration, in dialogue with others, the perspective of young people on the social subjects we were researching.

Yet, at the same time, the project established itself as an interesting framework for trying out alternative teaching methods. As we have tried to demonstrate, placing linguistic and communicative diversity at the center of the curriculum and turning students into actors in its research proved to be a productive strategy with regard to new learning and new linguistic attitudes. The young people who took part in this project turned out to be more interested, attentive and understanding towards the diversity of languages, but also towards the different people and groups with which they interacted. Throughout the course of the project, both the students and the teachers we worked with became more aware of the internal and social function of the languages they were researching, and developed better skills with which to analyze them. With this, signs of their mutual processes of language socialization became evident. Newcomers are not the only ones who transform their linguistic aptitudes and ideologies; the native population also becomes aware of this new reality and learns to deal with it in a creative way.

Our data also show that young people were able to establish productive relationships between the theoretical content of the workshops and the situations observed inside and outside school, preparing scripts that accounted for specific ways in which to describe these social situations. They were able to come up with unforeseen continuities between communicative and linguistic practices, as well as to focus on ruptures in the communicative practices observed within the different environments they explored in what was, for us, an original way. They were also able to categorize the linguistic knowledge of their peers and explain curricular content according to their own categories which, at times, were very distant from those used by the teachers and from the materials we had designed over the course of the teaching proposal.

With regard to the challenges, limitations and potential of collaborative research, the first thing to point out is that, unlike other research designs, attempting to carry out research that shares the role of researcher with other actors entails being willing to negotiate the research objectives with them (teachers and students in our case) as well as timings and conditions. This implies being willing to constantly redesign the instruments and the working plan developed according to the interests, timings and agenda of our fellow researchers, who are not immersed in university or academic rationales. Undertaking research alongside people from other fields also involves negotiating the focus of the objectives being investigated and the ways of going about it. But it also brings with it an understanding that the process of research itself is negotiable and open.

Secondly, ethnography involves having the time and inclination to spend long periods in the places being researched and with the people taking part. This type of research often involves being in a position to leave other things to one side, which is not always easy.

Thirdly, this type of research design implies not being very clear at the outset about what is being sought, but rather being open to what might be discovered (cf. inductive method, qualitative research; refer to the introduction by Dooly & Moore, this volume). This level of floating attention that ethnographic research work demands, at least initially, is challenging, and researchers usually find they are constantly asking themselves if what they are doing is research or wasting time. Nevertheless, if during this process researchers allow the everyday to wash over them, they can get to that point at which something that happens or something they observe in the situation under study is sufficiently interesting, surprising or disturbing to be narrated: it is at this point that ethnographical work enters a different phase.

To conclude, perhaps it is worth mentioning that on many occasions, as a team, we asked ourselves if it would not have been easier, less expensive and more efficient to design and execute experimental research, use surveys, run tests, etc. But there is something marvelous about qualitative research, which is that moment when the everyday becomes extraordinary and that which does not surprise becomes an absolute rarity. It is the fact that the research transforms itself according to the viewpoint from which the researcher approaches and explores everyday realities. It is having achieved, or at least attempted, a dialogue between the view of the researcher about the situation being explored and the views of others about that same situation. What we are researching appears in this crossover of viewpoints, and this is what makes it so fascinating.

Works cited

Antoniadou, V., & Dooly, M. (2017). Educational ethnography in blended learning environments. In E. Moore & M. Dooly (Eds), *Qualitative approaches to research on plurilingual education* (pp. 237-263). Research-publishing.net. https://doi.org/10.14705/rpnet.2017.emmd2016.630

Baquedano-López, P., & Kattan, S. (2008). Language socialization in schools. In P. Duff & N. Hornberger (Eds), *Encyclopedia of language and education, Volume 8: Language socialization* (pp. 161-173). Boston, MA: Springer. https://doi.org/10.1007/978-0-387-30424-3_204

Bayley, R., & S. R. Schecter (Eds). (2003). *Language socialization in bilingual and multilingual societies*. Bristol: Multilingual Matters.

Codó, E., Nussbaum, L., & Unamuno, V. (2007). La noció de competència plurilingual en el terreny de l'acollida lingüistic. In O. Guasch & L. Nussbaum (Eds), *Aproximacions a la noció de competència plurilingual* (pp. 47-60). Bellaterra: UAB publications.

Codó, E., & Patiño-Santos, A. (2014). Beyond language: class, social categorization and academic achievement in a Catalan high school. *Linguistics and Education, 25*, 51-63. https://doi.org/10.1016/j.linged.2013.08.002

Corona, V., Nussbaum, L., & Unamuno, V. (2013). The emergence of new linguistic repertoires among Barcelona's youth of Latin American Origin. *International Journal of Bilingual Education and Bilingualism, 16*(2), 182-194. https://doi.org/10.1080/13670050.2012.720668

Dooly, M., & Moore, E. (2017). Introduction: qualitative approaches to research on plurilingual education. In E. Moore & M. Dooly (Eds), *Qualitative approaches to research on plurilingual education* (pp. 1-10). Research-publishing.net. https://doi.org/10.14705/rpnet.2017.emmd2016.618

Duff, P. (2003). New directions in second language socialization research. *Korean Journal of English Language and Linguistics, 3*, 309-339.

Garrett, P. B., & Baquedano-López, P. (2002). Language socialization: reproduction and continuity, transformation and change. *Annual Review of Anthropology, 31*, 339-361. https://doi.org/10.1146/annurev.anthro.31.040402.085352

Masats, D. (2017). Conversation analysis at the service of research in the field of second language acquisition (CA-for-SLA). In E. Moore & M. Dooly (Eds), *Qualitative approaches to research on plurilingual education* (pp. 321-347). Research-publishing.net. https://doi.org/10.14705/rpnet.2017.emmd2016.633

Mondada, L. (2000). *Décrire la ville*. Paris: Édition Payot et Rivages.

Nussbaum, L. (2017). Doing research with teachers. In E. Moore & M. Dooly (Eds), *Qualitative approaches to research on plurilingual education* (pp. 46-67). Research-publishing.net. https://doi.org/10.14705/rpnet.2017.emmd2016.621

Nussbaum, L., & Unamuno, V. (Eds). (2006). *Usos i competències multilingües entre escolars d'origen immigrant*. Bellaterra: UAB Publications Service.

Schieffelin, B. B., & Ochs, E. (1986). *Language socialization across cultures*. Cambridge: Cambridge University Press.

Scollon, R., & Scollon, S. B. K. (2003). *Discourses in place: language in the material world*. London/New York: Routledge. https://doi.org/10.4324/9780203422724

Shohamy, E., Ben-Rafael, E., & Barni, M. (2010). *Linguistic landscapes in the city*. Bristol: Multilingual Matters.

Recommended reading

Clark, J. (2004). Participatory research with children and young people: philosophy, possibilities and perils. *Action Research Expeditions, 4*(11), 1-18.

Codó E., Patiño Santos, A., & Unamuno, V. (2012). La sociolinguistic con perspectiva ethnographic en el mundo hispano. Nuevos contexts, nuevas aproximaciones. Special edition of *Spanish in Context, 9*(2). Amsterdam: John Benjamins.

Duff, P. (2008). Language socialization, higher education, and work. In P. Duff & N. Hornberger (Eds), *Encyclopedia of language and education. Volume 8: Language Socialization* (pp. 257-270). New York: Springer. https://doi.org/10.1007/978-0-387-30424-3_211

Ochs, E., & Schieffelin, B. (2011). The theory of language socialization. In A. Duranti, E. Ochs, & B. Schieffelin (Eds), *The handbook of language socialization* (pp. 1-21). Malden, MA: Wiley-Blackwell. https://doi.org/10.1002/9781444342901.ch1

Patiño-Santos, A. (2016). Etnografía y sociolingüística. In J. Gutiérrez-Rexach (Ed.), *Enciclopedia de Lingüística Hispánica* (pp. 53-63). Abingdon, UK: Routledge.

Shohamy, E., Ben-Rafael, E., & Barni, M. (2010). *Linguistic landscapes in the city*. Bristol: Multilingual Matters.

Unamuno, V. (2011). Entre iguales: notas sobre la linguistic socialization del alumnado inmigrado en Barcelona. *Sociolinguistic Studies, 5*(2): 321-346.

Websites with resources mentioned

Teaching materials from the DECOMASAI project: http://pagines.uab.cat/decomasai/

# 5 Un acercamiento etnográfico al estudio de las variedades lingüísticas de jóvenes latinoamericanos en Barcelona

Víctor Corona[1]

Conceptos clave: etnografía, sociolingüística interaccional, longitudinalidad, grupos de discusión, entrevistas, análisis de interacción.

---

1. Introducción

Este capítulo explica parte de un estudio más amplio. Se basa, concretamente, en la investigación que he venido realizando en la ciudad de Barcelona, alrededor de lo que significa *ser latino* en el contexto juvenil y escolar desde el año 2005 hasta el día de hoy. Se trata de un trabajo inspirado, fundamentalmente, en la etnografía de la comunicación y en las técnicas que le son propias, como la observación-participante y la recogida de diferentes datos cualitativos.

A finales del 2005 y principios del 2006, inicié un estudio etnográfico en un barrio de Barcelona que había recibido un importante número de inmigrantes de América Latina. El asesinato de un chico latinoamericano en el 2004 y otros incidentes violentos que involucraban a los jóvenes de este origen comenzaron a levantar ciertas alarmas sociales que, de hecho, propiciaron que organismos gubernamentales como el Ayuntamiento de Barcelona crearan programas para atender, de forma concreta, a los jóvenes latinoamericanos. Estos programas contaron con la colaboración de trabajadores sociales, mediadores culturales y sociólogos expertos en la, al parecer, particular forma de socializar de los jóvenes latinoamericanos. Corría el año 2008 y *les émeutes de la banlieue* de algunas

---

1. ICAR, Université Lyon 2, Lyon, Francia; victor.corona@ens-lyon.fr

Para citar este capítulo: Corona, V. (2017). Un acercamiento etnográfico al estudio de las variedades lingüísticas de jóvenes latinoamericanos en Barcelona. En E. Moore y M. Dooly (Eds), *Enfoques cualitativos para la investigación en educación plurilingüe* (pp. 151-168). Research-publishing.net. https://doi.org/10.14705/rpnet.2017.emmd2016.626

© 2017 Víctor Corona (CC BY) 151

Capítulo 5

ciudades francesas eran utilizadas, sobre todo por los medios de comunicación, como una de las posibles consecuencias si no se atendía a estos jóvenes.

Comencé a preguntarme cómo se construye *lo latino*, y las consecuencias que este fenómeno puede cobrar en los diferentes procesos de desigualdad social, en la escuela y fuera de la escuela. Hay distintas posibilidades teóricas, metodológicas, e incluso ideológicas, de acercarse a *lo latino*. Uno tiene la posibilidad de hacerlo asumiendo categorías sociales dadas o ponerlas en cuestionamiento a través del trabajo de campo. Uno puede sostener el discurso hegemónico de los medios masivos de comunicación y, en parte, de las instituciones políticas y educativas, o puede intentar refutarlo, contestarle. Toda investigación conlleva un conjunto de decisiones que no solo afectan al modo en que se restringe y se limita el tema de investigación, sino también a la postura que se tomará para acercarse a los fenómenos que se desean investigar. Preguntas, decisiones y perspectivas nos acompañan durante todo el proceso, sin que sean necesariamente coherentes entre sí. Es el bagaje de quien investiga, lo que le acompaña durante el trabajo de campo aparece sigilosamente en las preguntas que hace durante las entrevistas, se inmiscuye en las formas en que se anotan las observaciones, en la manera en que se fragmenta una filmación o en las decisiones que continuamente se toman respecto a lo que es relevante o no para contar lo que queremos contar. Sobre estas preguntas, perspectivas y decisiones versa el presente capítulo.

¿Cuáles eran los objetivos de mi investigación?

El objetivo general de esta investigación era realizar una descripción profunda sobre el papel de las lenguas, de los repertorios lingüísticos, en la construcción de identidades en el contexto juvenil de Barcelona. Para esto, me centré en un grupo de jóvenes latinoamericanos que habían abandonado los estudios, o estaban a punto de abandonarlos. Este objetivo general se desglosó en los siguientes objetivos específicos:

- Describir las prácticas comunicativas y rituales verbales que diferentes participantes sociales categorizan como *latinos*, atendiendo a sus dimensiones escolares y no escolares.

- Investigar los diferentes recursos a partir de los cuales se construye *lo latino*, prestando especial atención a los elementos lingüísticos.

- Hacer una comparación entre lo que dicen los manuales de dialectología sobre las variedades del español y la forma de hablar de algunos chicos latinoamericanos en el contexto de estudio.

- Estudiar la relevancia que tienen géneros discursivos diferentes a la conversación, como el *hip-hop* y el reguetón, en la construcción de lo latino.

- Analizar los procesos de desigualdad escolar en que participan jóvenes que se identifican como miembros de *lo latino*.

Cabe señalar que este estudio se basa en el análisis de datos, en los que participaban, principalmente, chicos de origen latinoamericano. Esto se justifica por el hecho de que lo latino se construye como una identidad inminentemente masculina. Esta emergencia de lo latino responde a la construcción de la masculinidad en contextos educativos y conecta con otros fenómenos descritos por Willis (1977), Hewitt (1986), Tetreault (2008) o Fagyal (2010). Durante el trabajo de campo, pude recoger diversos datos en los que participaban chicas latinoamericanas, pero por razones prácticas no siempre las pude incluir en los puntos que discuto en el presente capítulo. Estos datos dejan ver, y es un tema que puede ser abordado en estudios posteriores, que las chicas pueden presentar otras formas de participación en el mundo de lo latino.

2. Tomar postura: apuntes sobre la metodología elegida

Heller (2002) considera que el trabajo de investigación nunca es neutro. Los temas de interés, las preguntas que nos hacemos, los instrumentos de investigación y las lecturas teóricas responden a intereses subjetivos, motivados, en gran medida, por nuestra propia trayectoria como individuos y nuestra posición social. En palabras de Heller (2002), es necesario aceptar el conocimiento, incluido el producido por la investigación, como subjetivo, parcial, socialmente situado e interesado. Mi investigación se enmarca en esta percepción, pues se encuentra lejos de una concepción neutra y objetiva. Tampoco pretende llegar a conclusiones y verdades absolutas. Se trata de un intento de dar respuesta a ciertos fenómenos que involucran a las lenguas y las identidades, pero que, especialmente, involucran a personas.

Sin duda, las características de cada investigador e investigadora contribuye y tiene una resonancia en el producto de investigación. Como menciona Heller (2002):

> "[j]e crois qu'en bout de ligne, tout(e) chercheur(e) a explicitement ou implicitement une prise de position. Une bonne socialisation de nouveaux spécialistes doit donc en tenir compte. Je présenterai ici la mienne, non parce que je la trouve la meilleure que autres pour tout le monde, mais parce qu'elle fonctionne pour moi, et que je compte, en présentant mes propres démarches faciliter à mes lectrices et lecteurs la formulation de leur propre prise de position et les démarches qui en en découleront" (p. 22)[2].

Mi investigación no pretende ser interpretada como una verdad absoluta, si acaso, como un relato en el que se busca dar respuesta, entre otras cosas, al discurso hegemónico que circulaba (y sigue circulando) alrededor de los jóvenes de origen latinoamericano en el contexto de Barcelona.

3. Haciendo etnografía

El trabajo que desarrollé se basó en una etnografía. En su momento, consideré

---

[2]. "Creo que, en última instancia, cualquier persona investigadora explícita o implícitamente tiene tomada una posición. Una buena socialización de especialista debe tomarlo en cuenta. Voy a presentar aquí mi postura, no porque la encuentre mejor que otras para todo el mundo, sino porque funciona para mí, y cuento con que, presentando mis propios procedimientos, pueda facilitar la formulación de la toma de posición y de los procedimientos que de ésta se deriven por parte de mis lectores y lectoras" (Heller, 2002, p. 22).

que las características de este tipo de investigación podrían ayudarme a entender la complejidad en la que se construían estos discursos y el papel que tenían los propios participantes sociales. La etnografía ha demostrado ser una herramienta de gran utilidad no solamente para los trabajos antropológicos o sociológicos, sino también para investigaciones con intereses sociolingüísticos, como en este caso. Las etnografías de tipo sociolingüístico tienen como característica general la constante reflexión, tanto sobre los datos como sobre el propio proceso de análisis y reflexión. Se señala la importancia de las preguntas planteadas, del papel de la persona investigadora, sus ideas, sus motivaciones y cómo en conjunto todo esto representa una toma de posición respecto al tema de interés. Esta reflexión sobre la metodología es la que la hace reconocerse como crítica, puesto que intenta ser reflexiva, no solamente con el tema de interés, sino con los mismos mecanismos de interpretación.

4. La etnografía sociolingüística

Autores como Heller (2002) o Coupland (2007) mencionan que el análisis de la etnografía sociolingüística no se centra en la lengua en sí, sino en la lengua como práctica social. Esto se traduce en que la atención en los datos no se basa únicamente en las formas o estructuras lingüísticas, como podría hacerse desde un estudio lingüístico más normativo, sino en el papel que estas prácticas cobran en la interacción, según los participantes sociales que intervienen.

La etnografía sociolingüística tiene como uno de sus objetivos relacionar la descripción y el análisis de las prácticas y procesos sociales. Según Heller (2002), la interpretación que hagamos del análisis de los datos etnográficos debería tener en cuenta las dinámicas sociales que acontecen a mayor escala, tanto en el espacio como en el tiempo. Así, por ejemplo, algunos de los chicos que aparecen en este trabajo se refieren a la *degradación* que han sufrido sus variedades del castellano después de haber inmigrado a Barcelona. Es decir, su forma de hablar en Guayaquil era considerada *educada*, pero al llegar aquí, y al estar en contacto con otras formas de hablar, pasó a ser considerada como *inferior*.

Capítulo 5

En este análisis, como apunta Blommaert (2010), podemos identificar cómo un proceso tan global como el de la migración repercute también en los valores de las prácticas lingüísticas cotidianas. Siguiendo a este autor, este ejemplo reflejaría cómo estos fenómenos migratorios llevan implícitos ciertos movimientos (del centro a la periferia) en los que los hablantes se ven trasladados de una esfera social a otra, no por la *calidad lingüística* de sus variedades, sino por el rol social que tienen en un contexto determinado. En este caso, puede ser que una forma concreta del español de Guayaquil, considerada como *educada* en un contexto ecuatoriano, al llegar a Barcelona reciba valoraciones diferentes, relativas a la identificación de sus usuarios en tanto que inmigrantes de clase social baja.

La etnografía sociolingüística intenta, así, descubrir cómo se construyen este tipo de diferencias y desigualdades sociales, y su correspondencia con las diferencias y jerarquías de formas lingüísticas. Autores como Heller (1999, 2003), Heller y Martin-Jones (2001), Rampton (1995, 2006), Pujolar (1997, 2000), Martín-Rojo (2010) y Unamuno (1999, 2003) han insistido, mediante sus respectivos trabajos, en que esta perspectiva de la sociolingüística crítica puede ayudarnos a comprender, además, el funcionamiento de las instituciones sociales en la construcción de categorías que derivan en la producción y la reproducción de estas desigualdades sociales. Otro de los aspectos a destacar de la investigación sociolingüística etnográfica es su preocupación por el impacto que esta puede tener en la comunidad en la que se desarrolla. En el terreno de la educación, con investigaciones que se llevan a cabo en el seno de la comunidad escolar, pueden surgir cambios en las dinámicas de los participantes sociales, y esto se considera parte del proceso, reflexionando sobre ello. Probablemente, no se trate de cambios a gran escala o que involucren a todo un centro educativo, pero sí de pequeñas modificaciones en algunas actitudes o percepciones en relación con los usos lingüísticos, las identidades y las situaciones de desigualdad que pueden generarse.

En el caso de la investigación que se presenta en este capítulo, para citar un ejemplo, a partir del trabajo desarrollado en las escuelas, algunos docentes manifestaron un cambio de actitud hacia las diferentes variedades lingüísticas del castellano, e incluso hacia las prácticas lingüísticas híbridas, evaluadas, normalmente, como prácticas deficientes. Heller (2002) señala respecto a este punto:

> "[t]oute recherche en sciences sociales est une forme d'action sociale, sous la forme spécifique de la construction du savoir. La sociolinguistique est particulièrement bien placée pour reconnaître cette caractéristique, puisque la construction sociale du savoir passe par la communication et l'interaction, qui forment l'objet de base de la recherche sociolinguistique. Cette action sociale, cette construction du savoir, est traversée par la nécessité d'un certain degré de réflexibilité, c'est-à-dire par le besoin de devenir conscient de la façon dont l'action de la recherche est reliée au savoir qu'elle construit et de rendre ce processus explicite, tout en tenant compte de ses conséquences sociales. Je cherche à explorer les possibilités d'une sociolinguistique que je qualificarais d'engagé, de critique, de réflexive, et surtout de voir comment une telle chose pourrait être réalisée concrètement" (p. 22)[3].

En resumen, se podría decir que la sociolingüística de perspectiva etnográfica es una disciplina que postula la necesidad de un constante ejercicio de reflexión metodológica y que entiende que los datos obtenidos en la interacción social y las categorías empleadas por quien investiga nunca son neutrales (Heller y Martin-Jones, 2001; Rampton, 2006). De hecho, hay quien afirma que la discusión y la reflexión sobre los datos en la sociolingüística constituye uno de los elementos que han contribuido a la mejora de esta práctica investigadora (Pérez-Milans, 2011) de la disciplina.

---

3. "Cualquier investigación en ciencias sociales es una forma de acción social, en la forma específica de la construcción del conocimiento. La sociolingüística se encuentra particularmente bien situada para reconocer esta característica, ya que la construcción social del conocimiento ocurre a través de la comunicación y de la interacción, que forman el objeto base de la investigación sociolingüística. Esta acción social, esta construcción del saber, se halla atravesada por la necesidad de un cierto grado de reflexividad, es decir, por la necesidad de tomar conciencia de la forma en que la acción de la investigación se halla vinculada al saber que construye y de dar cuenta explícita de este proceso, tomando en consideración sus consecuencias sociales. Trato de explorar las posibilidades de una sociolingüística que yo calificaría como comprometida, crítica, reflexiva, y sobre todo de ver cómo ello podría llevarse a cabo en concreto" (Heller, 2002, p. 22).

Capítulo 5

Para este trabajo, han sido también fundamentales los aportes del llamado enfoque etnometodológico (Atkinson, 1988; Coulon, 1998; Garfinkel, 1967; véanse los capítulos de Masats, en este volumen, y Nussbaum, en este volumen), especialmente su consideración de que la investigación social exige incluir en el análisis también a quien investiga. Es decir, el trabajo para dar cuenta de la realidad social exige mostrar el rol que las personas investigadoras juegan en la obtención y en el análisis posterior de los datos a través de entrevistas, grupos de discusión, grabaciones de clases, conversaciones espontáneas, etc. (Mondada, 1999). Este principio, que también recupera la sociolingüística interaccional (Heller y Martin-Jones, 2001; Rampton, 1995, 2006), permite considerar a quien investiga como participante e incluir en el proceso de investigación reflexiones sobre la figura de la persona investigadora y su papel como agente que, junto con los otros participantes, construye la realidad social estudiada.

5. El estudio: las variedades lingüísticas de jóvenes latinoamericanos en Barcelona

El corpus de la investigación lo recogí durante un largo proceso de trabajo etnográfico (2005-2009). Se ha realizado, principalmente, en un Instituto de Educación Secundaria (y en sus alrededores) ubicado en la zona norte de la ciudad de Barcelona. Los participantes que intervienen en este trabajo no fueron seleccionados siguiendo pautas establecidas. Durante la labor de observador-participante, algunos jóvenes expresaron la intención de involucrarse en la investigación y, siguiendo la dinámica natural de la socialización, un participante fue llamando a otro y así, sucesivamente, se fue constituyendo el corpus que he recabado.

El corpus total se conforma de 21 entrevistas, 12 grupos de discusión y 4 horas de grabación en diferentes clases, todas registradas en audio y video. También cuenta con redacciones de los estudiantes y otro tipo de documentos, como canciones escritas por los estudiantes o las anotaciones del diario de campo. El corpus abarca también otros espacios fuera del colegio, como parques, bares y plazas. También las voces de padres, madres y docentes.

5.1. Tipología y recogida de los datos

Básicamente, los datos recogidos se clasificaron de la siguiente manera:

- Archivos de audio de entrevistas y grupos de discusión.
- Archivos de audio y video de aula en clases de lengua.
- Archivos de video en espacios de interacción en los centros escolares.
- Fragmentos de música, redacciones y otros documentos.
- Registro del diario de campo.

El corpus de este trabajo de investigación fue compuesto por decenas de personas que, a través de entrevistas, grupos de discusión o conversaciones, dentro y fuera del aula, expresaron ideas, se posicionaron frente a otros, se presentaron a los demás, etc. La complejidad de hacer que estos diferentes discursos puedan ser estudiados de manera conjunta, creando así una gran red de voces que se entrelazan para dar paso a la creación de realidades diversas, es latente.

5.2. Tratamiento y análisis

Para transcribir utilicé principalmente Transana. También utilicé ELAN para fragmentos en los que me interesaba describir con más detalle las interacciones, regularmente más breves (véanse los capítulos de Antoniadou, en este volumen, y Moore y Llompart, en este volumen). La gran mayoría de las entrevistas y los grupos de discusión fueron transcritos en su totalidad. Los datos de aula, sobre todo los registrados en video, fueron transcritos parcialmente.

Para el análisis tomé en cuenta diferentes aportaciones de la sociolingüística interaccional (Blommaert, 1995; Gumperz, 1976; Pujolar, 2000; Rampton, 1995). En este sentido, el tratamiento de los datos intentó atender los aportes de

Capítulo 5

la tradición etnometodológica y los trabajos de los analistas de la conversación (véanse los capítulos de Masats, en este volumen; Nussbaum, en este volumen).

6. Un ejemplo de análisis interaccional: el descubrimiento de un hablar latino

En este apartado, mostraré un ejemplo de análisis para dar una idea de cómo procesé el corpus recogido en el estudio. La forma de hablar latina emerge como una especie de variedad híbrida, difícil de reconocer como propia de una zona dialectal concreta. Se trata de una mezcla que se mueve dentro del repertorio lingüístico que conforma el panorama sociolingüístico en el que se desenvolvían estos chicos. Evidentemente, las variedades locales, incluidas las lenguas catalana y castellana peninsular, a las que podríamos considerar dominantes en sentidos diversos y complejos, forman parte de este repertorio sobre la base del que se articula la variedad *latina*.

Para aclarar lo que acabo de decir, creo que vale la pena recurrir a los datos grabados. Se trata de un fragmento que forma parte de los datos recogidos durante el primer periodo de la etnografía (2006), en el que conversa un grupo de seis adolescentes de primer año de la educación secundaria (es decir, un grupo de discusión, véase Canals, en este volumen). El origen de los chicos es diverso: tres son ecuatorianos de Guayaquil (Ignacio, Raúl y Pedro), uno de un pueblo cercano a Quito (Néstor), un chico boliviano (Oscar) y Alex, peruano de Chiclayo. Es evidente, por la numeración de los turnos de habla del fragmento que se ha extraído de una conversación mucho más larga. La simbología de la transcripción usada (véanse Moore y Llompart, en este volumen) se encuentra en el anejo.

Fragmento 1

377.	INV.	de:e así de:el_ pues de:el-| bueno lo que ustedes llaman racismo_ o diferencia [+**diferensia**+] de trato\\|
378.	IGN.	yo sé que aquí en cuarto\\| hay de una:a\\| una de ra_ una chica de_
379.	PDR:	PDR: de segundo_ el jaime *tío*\\|

380.	OSC:	XXXX
381.	PDR:	va diciendo [+disiendo+] indio de mierda|
382.	VCR:	cómo/|
383.	PDR:	que le pegaron\\| ayer-|
384.	VCR:	qué pasó/|
385.	ALX:	al jaime_ qué jaime/|
386.	PDR:	al gordo_ *tío* u:un_
387.	ALX:	al que_ un bajo\\|
388.	PDR:	no\\| el que tiene aquí morado\\| al que le pegó el agustín-|
389.	VCR:	por qué/|
390.	ALX:	porque va diciendo [+disiendo+] negro de mierda a todo el mundo_ *tío*\\| y al final lo callas así\\| (F) pua_ le metes un quiño y le dejas el ojo morado_así\\|
391.	PDR:	el agustín le estaba <u>dando puñetes así_ le dieron un puñete</u>
392.	RAL:	qué pone aquí/|
393.	PDR:	y:y-| *le denunciaron*[+**denunsiaron**+] _*tío*\\|
<u>Variedada peninsular</u>		
<u>Variedad latina</u>		
Corpus 2006-2007 Grup de Reforç		
Participantes: Víctor, Pedro, Raúl, Oscar, Alex, Ignacioio		

Este breve fragmento puede servir para hablar de hibridización y para problematizarla. También servirá para mostrar que interpretar datos interaccionales quiere decir analizarlos turno por turno, de manera detallada, no simplemente presentarlos o parafrasearlos (Antaki, Billig, Edwards, y Potter, 2003).

En el turno 377, el investigador propone el tema del racismo, que luego reformula como "diferencia de trato". Los chicos construyeron a partir de ahí un relato de forma colaborativa, para describir así lo que entendían por racismo. Ignacio, con la intención de responder a la pregunta del investigador, hacía referencia a una chica, pero Pedro, en el turno 379, toma la palabra y propone otro relato. En su caso, Alex habla de un chico al que un compañero latinoamericano le había pegado por "ir diciendo indio de mierda a todo el mundo".

El color <u>verde</u> señala las palabras o expresiones que se asignan a variedades del castellano americano y el *rojo*, aquellas que pueden identificarse como parte del

Capítulo 5

español peninsular, es decir, no propias de ninguna de las variedades americanas del español. En negrita he marcado el rasgo *seseante*.

Así, una observación externa sobre el fragmento permite constatar, por ejemplo, la utilización de "tío" como apelación de uso coloquial, significado que recoge la Real Academia Española (RAE, 2002). El uso de "tío" en este sentido está muy extendido en diferentes esferas sociales de España y no es exclusivo de los jóvenes o de las zonas castellano-hablantes. De hecho, Pujolar (1997), en su estudio sobre el habla y las identidades de los jóvenes en Barcelona, ya mencionaba la extensión de esta forma entre los jóvenes, independientemente de las lenguas en las que se expresan cotidianamente (catalán, castellano, o ambas, en este caso). Una mirada sobre la variedad latina ligada a las prácticas locales y a las identidades permite afirmar que el uso de "tío" forma también parte de dicha variedad. Esto es así, independientemente del hecho que el uso de la expresión "tío", en el sentido que los chicos la usan aquí, no forme parte del léxico de las diferentes variedades del español americano de estos jóvenes. "Tío" en América solo recoge el significado respecto a una persona, hermano o hermana de su padre o madre (RAE, 2002).

Pedro y Alex usaban "tío" en su relato sin que esto causara ningún tipo de reacción que permitiera inferir que esta palabra era extraña para los otros participantes. No vemos procedimientos que la *extranjericen* en el sentido de Mondada (1999). Por el contrario, la palabra era una más en el discurso y obtenía allí un rol clave en la construcción del relato. Es un apelativo que situaba la conversación como interacción entre pares jóvenes, describiendo la actividad como claramente informal.

Pero no solo "tío" merece un comentario en este sentido. Así, por ejemplo, en el turno 390 Alex utiliza la expresión "le metes un quiño" (le das un golpe) refiriéndose a la forma de reaccionar frente a un incidente que considera racista. La palabra "quiño" aparece en el diccionario de la RAE como una expresión coloquial de Ecuador, que proviene del quechua *k'iñay* que significa golpear.

Si bien podría sospecharse que Alex usa la palabra "quiñar" como parte de su variedad de origen, esto no es así. Alex no es ecuatoriano, sino peruano. Si bien es difícil saber si esta palabra aparece o no en las diferentes variedades del español peruano –lo que podría esperarse, debido a la proximidad geográfica y al sustrato quechua también en las hablas castellanas del Perú–, lo que me interesa destacar es la falta de correspondencia mecánica entre las formas que se usan en el relato y los lugares de origen de los chicos. Esta falta de correspondencia, creo, otorga a "tío" o a "quiño" un valor aún más especial: son empleadas por Alex para construir un relato en el que la voz latina es protagonista y en el que, el *bricolage* es clave para construir la autenticidad en el relato.

En este mismo sentido, puede interpretarse el turno 391, donde Pedro introduce la frase "dar puñetes". Si seguimos tomando como referencia el diccionario de la RAE, encontramos esta expresión definida como "dar golpes con la mano cerrada". Si bien no se especifica el origen, puede suponerse que no es peninsular, ya que no está recogida en otros diccionarios de esta zona, como por ejemplo, en el Diccionario de Uso del Español, de María Moliner (2007).

El carácter composicional o de *bricolage* que estoy comentando no solo afecta al léxico sino también a aspectos interesantes de la sintaxis. En el turno 393, Pedro concluye el incidente diciendo: "le denunciaron tío", utilizando una forma *leísta* que, según la RAE, es característica de los dialectos del centro de la península Ibérica y que es considerada vulgar en otras zonas. En América Latina, el uso del pronombre dativo con verbos como *denunciar*, no solo no es frecuente sino que es considerado un error y corregido sistemáticamente. Si bien hay estudios que consideran que existen algunos casos de leísmo en América Latina, inducidos por el contacto con lenguas aborígenes, esto no es generalizado.

Además de este uso particular del *le* que he señalado, lo que quiero remarcar especialmente es que se trata de un uso que, como pasa con los otros rasgos que he marcado, aparecía en el relato sin provocar ninguna reacción que permitiera entender que se trata de una marca que los participantes consideran parte de una variedad ajena o no auténtica de sus hablantes. Por el contrario, para estos

Capítulo 5

chicos, no parecía ser un indicio que sugiera que la forma de hablar que emplean es o no latina. Más bien, como intento mostrar, se trataba de una variedad que los demás reconocían como adecuada a la actividad en que participaban.

Entre los aspectos fonológicos, son dos los elementos que destacaron en los datos. Por un lado, fue notable el *seseo* que, al menos en Barcelona, es un rasgo marcado, porque no forma parte del castellano que se escucha habitualmente en la ciudad ni tampoco el que actúa de modelo en las prácticas escolares. Por otro lado, y en relación con el *seseo*, creo que determinados usos del fonema *s* y su alternancia con otros fonemas en contextos específicos también adquieren una significación particular. Así, por ejemplo, en el fragmento anterior, todos los hablantes, incluido el investigador, utilizan una variedad *seseante* del castellano.

Más allá de la diferencia que existe entre los fonemas disponibles en la lengua, las variedades americanas se caracterizan, además, por el uso de un conjunto de alófonos para el fonema [s] que no se corresponden con los peninsulares, y que varían de la forma ápico-alveolar sorda prototípica del norte de España. En América Latina, la *s* es extremadamente variable, y tiende a asimilarse a otros fenómenos adyacentes e incluso a alternar con la aspiración o con la elisión total delante de algunas consonantes. Esta *s*, que muchos reconocen como típica americana, no es homogénea en los dialectos, aunque sí lo es en contraposición a la *s* del norte peninsular. Según los datos que pude recoger, los chicos *latinos* también presentan una variabilidad importante en cuanto al uso de la *s*. Lo que sí parece invariable, y los jóvenes lo señalan en su discurso, es el seseo.

El segundo fenómeno se refiere a la prosodia, es decir, a los rasgos que atañen a la frecuencia, la duración, la intensidad y el ritmo de los sonidos del habla. Como señalan diferentes autores (Hayward, 2000; Llisterri, 1991), la prosodia es polisémica y cumple muchas funciones en la oralidad, además, tiene un valor semántico-pragmático evidente. Pero lo que nos interesa aquí, es que, según los lingüistas, tiene un papel fundamental en la asignación de valores sociolingüísticos, como origen geográfico, social, de género, etc.

7. A modo de conclusión

En este capítulo, se ha intentado mostrar cómo el acercamiento etnográfico puede ser de gran utilidad para conocer cómo las comunidades entienden sus identidades y el rol que las lenguas tienen en este proceso. He mostrado cuáles eran las preguntas de investigación y, en consecuencia, la metodología elegida, así como el tratamiento de los datos.

En los datos interaccionales que he puesto como ejemplo, hemos visto también cómo ciertos elementos sociolingüísticos de algunos de los jóvenes latinoamericanos se interpretan como un estilo o una variedad emergente, ligada a una identidad social concreta: *lo latino*. La dialectología tradicional es poco útil para describir estos fenómenos, puesto que no es posible identificar las formas de habla con espacios geográficos concretos. Se trata de discurso polifónico en el que participan rasgos que pueden asociarse a variedades del español de ambos continentes. A modo de *bricolage*, estos recursos se concatenan en una variedad múltiple, que es identificada por sus usuarios y por otras personas, como parte de *lo latino*.

La etnografía, sin embargo, tiene ciertas limitaciones. Personalmente, una de las más difíciles a las que me enfrenté durante mi trabajo fue establecer una distancia con los participantes. El contacto y trabajo continuo con los chicos, y la empatía creada, en ocasiones se giraba en mi contra para hallar una visión crítica de las observaciones. Otra de las dificultades que tuve fue la organización y categorización del corpus de datos. La naturaleza de mi investigación tuvo como consecuencia una producción enorme de datos (véanse también Unamuno y Patiño, en este volumen). En ocasiones, esta recopilación no fue lo sistemática que debía haber sido, lo que me ocasionó problemas a la hora de relacionar, por ejemplo, las entrevistas y el diario de campo con las preguntas de investigación. En este sentido, pueden servir de ayuda los capítulos de Antoniadou (en este volumen) y de Moore y Llompart (en este volumen), en los que se ofrecen estrategias para la organización de los datos etnográficos.

Capítulo 5

Agradecimientos

Victor Corona agradece al proyecto ASLAN (ANR-10-LABX-0081) de la Universidad de Lyon por el apoyo financiero de su investigación en curso dentro del programa 'Investissements d'Avenir' (ANR-11 - IDEX - 0007). El proyecto ASLAN está financiado por el gobierno francés, a través del Instituto Nacional de Investigación (ANR).

Obras citadas

Antaki, C., Billig, M., Edwards, D., y Potter, J. (2003). Discourse analysis means doing analysis: a critique of six analytic shortcomings. *Discourse Analysis Online*. http://extra.shu.ac.uk/daol/articles/v1/n1/a1/antaki2002002-paper.html

Antoniadou, V. (2017). Recoger, organizar y analizar corpus de datos multimodales: las contribuciones de los CAQDAS. En E. Moore y M. Dooly (Eds), *Enfoques cualitativos para la investigación en educación plurilingüe* (pp. 451-467). Research-publishing.net. https://doi.org/10.14705/rpnet.2017.emmd2016.641

Atkinson, P. (1988). Ethnomethodology: a critical review. *Annual Review of Sociology, 14*, 441-465. https://doi.org/10.1146/annurev.so.14.080188.002301

Blommaert, J. (1995). *Handbook of pragmatics*. Amsterdam: John Benjamins.

Blommaert, J. (2010). *The sociolinguistics of globalization*. Cambridge: Cambridge University Press. https://doi.org/10.1017/CBO9780511845307

Canals, L. (2017). Instruments per a la recollida de dades. *Enfoques cualitativos para la investigación en educación plurilingüe* (pp. 377-389). Research-publishing.net. https://doi.org/10.14705/rpnet.2017.emmd2016.636

Coulon, A. (1998). *La etnometodología*. Madrid: Cátedra.

Coupland, N. (2007). *Style: language variation and identity*. Cambridge: Cambridge University Press. https://doi.org/10.1017/CBO9780511755064

Fagyal, Z. (2010). *Accents de banlieue : aspects prosodiques du français populaire en contact avec les langues de l'immigration*. París: L'Harmattan.

Garfinkel, H. (1967). *Studies in ethnomethodology*. Nueva Jersey: Prentice Hall.

Gumperz, J. (1976). Language, communication and public negotiation. En P. Sanday (Ed.), *Anthropology and the public interest: fieldwork and theory*. Nueva York: Academic Press.

Hayward, K. (2000). *Experimental phonetics*. Harlow: Longman.

Heller, M. (1999). *Linguistic minorities and modernity: a sociolinguistic ethnography*. Londres: Longman.

Heller, M. (2002) *Éléments d'une sociolinguistique critique*. París: Didier.

Heller, M. (2003). Globalization, the new economy, and the commodification of language and identity. *Journal of Sociolinguistics, 7*(4), 473-492. https://doi.org/10.1111/j.1467-9841.2003.00238.x

Heller, M., y Martin-Jones, M. (2001). *Voices of authority: education and linguistic difference*. Westport, Conn: Ablex Pub.

Hewitt, R. (1986). *White talk black talk: inter-racial friendship and communication amongst adolescents*. Cambridge: Cambridge University Press.

Llisterri, J. (1991). *Introducción a la fonética: el método experimental*. Barcelona: Anthropos.

Martín-Rojo, L. (2010). *Constructing inequality in multilingual classrooms*. Berlin: De Gruyter Mouton.

Masats, D. (2017). L'anàlisi de la conversa al servei de la recerca en el camp de l'adquisició de segones llengües (CA-for-SLA). En E. Moore y M. Dooly (Eds), *Enfoques cualitativos para la investigación en educación plurilingüe* (pp. 293-320). Research-publishing.net. https://doi.org/10.14705/rpnet.2017.emmd2016.632

Moliner, M. (2007). *Diccionario de uso del español (3ª edición)*. Madrid: Gredos.

Mondada, L. (1999). L'accomplissement de «l'étrangéité» dans et par l'interaction : procédures de catégorisation des locuteurs. *Langages, 33*(134), 20-34. https://doi.org/10.3406/lgge.1999.2190

Moore, E., y Llompart, J. (2017). Recoger, transcribir, analizar y presentar datos interaccionales plurilingües. En E. Moore y M. Dooly (Eds), *Enfoques cualitativos para la investigación en educación plurilingüe* (pp. 418-433). Research-publishing.net. https://doi.org/10.14705/rpnet.2017.emmd2016.639

Nussbaum, L. (2017). Investigar con docentes. En E. Moore y M. Dooly (Eds), *Enfoques cualitativos para la investigación en educación plurilingüe* (pp. 23-45). Research-publishing.net. https://doi.org/10.14705/rpnet.2017.emmd2016.620

Pérez-Milans, M. (2011). Being a Chinese newcomer in Madrid compulsory education: ideological constructions in language education practice. *Journal of Pragmatics, 43*(4), 1005-1022. https://doi.org/10.1016/j.pragma.2010.10.003

Pujolar, J. (1997). *De què vas, tio?* Barcelona: Empúries.

Pujolar, J. (2000). *Gender, heteroglossia and power: a sociolinguistic study of youth culture.* Berlin: Walter de Gruyter.

Rampton, B. (1995). *Crossing: language and ethnicity among adolescents.* Londres: Longman.

Rampton, B. (2006). *Language in late modernity: interaction in an urban school.* Cambridge University Press. https://doi.org/10.1017/cbo9780511486722

Real Academia Española. (2002). *Diccionario de la lengua española* (22ª ed.). Madrid: Espasa.

Tetreault, C. (2008). La Racaille: figuring gender, generation, and stigmatized space in a French cité. *Gender and Language, 2*(2), 141-170. https://doi.org/10.1558/genl.v2i2.141

Unamuno, V. (1999). *Lenguas, escuela y diversidad sociocultural. Etnografía de la acción comunicativa.* Barcelona: Publicacions de la Universitat de Barcelona.

Unamuno, V. (2003). *Lengua, escuela y diversidad sociocultural. Hacia una educación lingüística crítica.* Barcelona: Editorial Graó.

Unamuno, V., y Patiño, A. (2017). Producir conocimiento sobre el plurilingüismo junto a jóvenes estudiantes: un reto para la etnografía en colaboración. En E. Moore y M. Dooly (Eds), *Enfoques cualitativos para la investigación en educación plurilingüe* (pp. 107-128). Research-publishing.net. https://doi.org/10.14705/rpnet.2017.emmd2016.624

Willis, P. (1977). *Learning to labour: how working class kids get working class jobs.* Nueva York: Colombia University.

Lecturas recomendadas

Gumperz, J. (1976). Language, communication and public negotiation. En P. Sanday (Ed.), *Anthropology and the public interest: fieldwork and theory.* Nueva York: Academic Press.

Heller, M. (2002). *Éléments d'une sociolinguistique critique.* París: Didier.

Martín-Rojo, L. (2010). *Constructing inequality in multilingual classrooms.* Berlin: De Gruyter Mouton.

Pujolar, J. (2000). *Gender, heteroglossia and power: a sociolinguistic study of youth culture.* Berlin: Walter de Gruyter.

Rampton, B. (1999). Styling the other: introduction. *Journal of Sociolinguistics, 3*(4), 421-427. https://doi.org/10.1111/1467-9481.00088

Willis, P. (1977). *Learning to labour: how working class kids get working class jobs.* Nueva York: Colombia University.

Anejo

Adaptación de la simbología de transcripción GREIP (véanse Moore y Llompart, en este volumen):

Secuencias tonales:
    descendente \
    ascendente /
Pausas:
    corta |
    mediana ||
    larga <número de segundos>
Alargamiento silábico (según la duración): · ·· ···
Encabalgamientos: =texto hablanteA= =texto hablanteB=
Interrupciones: Texto_
Intensidad:
    piano {(P) texto}
    pianissimo {(PP) texto}
    forte {(F) text}
    fortissimo {(FF) texto}
Tono:
    alto {(A)texto}
    bajo {(B)texto}
Tiempo:
    acelerado {(AC) texto}
    desacelerado {(DC)
Enunciados acompañados de risa: {(@) texto}
Comentarios: [comentario]
Fragmentos incomprensibles (según duración): XXX | XXX XXX | XXX XXX XXX
Fragmentos dudosos: {(?) texto}

5. An ethnographic approach to the study of linguistic varieties used by young Latin Americans in Barcelona

Víctor Corona[1]

> Key concepts: ethnography, interactional sociolinguistics, longitudinal studies, discussion groups, interviews, analysis of interaction.

1. Introduction

This chapter explains part of a broader study. To be specific, it is based on the research I have been conducting in the city of Barcelona from 2005 through to the present day on what it means to *be Latino* in a youth- and school-based context. The work was essentially inspired by the ethnography of communication and the techniques inherent in it, such as participant observation and gathering different qualitative data.

In late 2005 and early 2006, I embarked on an ethnographic study in a neighborhood of Barcelona where a large number of immigrants from Latin America had settled. The murder of a Latin American boy in 2004 and other violent incidents involving young people of similar origin sparked a certain amount of social alarm which motivated government bodies such as Barcelona City Council to create programs specifically targeted at young Latin Americans. These programs relied on the collaboration of social workers, cultural mediators and sociologists who were experts in the – apparently – particular way of socializing of young Latin Americans. This was around 2008, and the suburban riots in some French cities were used, especially by the media, as one of the potential consequences of not addressing the issue of these young people.

---

1. ICAR, Université Lyon 2, Lyon, France; victor.corona@ens-lyon.fr

How to cite this chapter: Corona, V. (2017). An ethnographic approach to the study of linguistic varieties used by young Latin Americans in Barcelona. In E. Moore & M. Dooly (Eds), *Qualitative approaches to research on plurilingual education* (pp. 170-188). Research-publishing.net. https://doi.org/10.14705/rpnet.2017.emmd2016.627

I started wondering about the production of *Latino-ness* and the consequences that this phenomenon might accrue in processes of social inequality within and outside of schools. There are different theoretical, methodological and even ideological ways of approaching Latino-ness. There is the possibility of assuming certain social categories, or putting them to the test through fieldwork. One might sustain the hegemonic discourse of the mass media and, to some extent, political and educational institutions, or try to refute and address them. All research entails a series of decisions that not only affect the way in which the subject matter of the research is restricted or limited but also the stance that will be taken to approach the phenomena that one wishes to investigate. Questions, decisions and perspectives crop up during the entire process, without necessarily being consistent with each other. This is the baggage of the researcher, which accompanies us during fieldwork, emerges surreptitiously in the questions we ask during interviews, inveigles itself in the way we note down our observations, edit a filmed recording, or encroaches on the decisions we constantly have to make with regard to what is relevant, or not, in relating what we wish to relate. This chapter deals with these questions, perspectives and decisions.

What were the objectives of my research?

The main objective of this research was to produce a thick description of the role of languages, of linguistic repertoires, in building the social identities of a particular group of young people in Barcelona. I focused on a group of Latin American youths who had already dropped out of school or were in the process of doing so. This general objective can be broken down into the following specific objectives:

- Describe the communicative practices and verbal rituals that different social participants categorize as Latino both in and outside the school.

- Investigate the different resources based upon which Latino-ness is built, paying particular attention to linguistic elements.

Chapter 5

- Make a comparison between what dialectology manuals say about varieties of Spanish and the way certain Latin American youths talk in the context of the study.

- Study the importance of different discursive genres in conversation, such as hip-hop and reggaeton, in building Latino-ness.

- Analyze processes of inequalities at school involving young people who would classify themselves as Latinos.

It is worth mentioning that this study is based on an analysis of data in which boys of Latin American origin were the main participants. This is justified by the fact that Latino-ness is constructed as an eminently masculine identity. This emergence of Latino-ness in relation to the construction of masculinity in educational contexts is connected to other phenomena described by Willis (1977), Hewitt (1986), Tetreault (2008) and Fagyal (2010). During the fieldwork, I was able to gather a corpus of data involving Latin American girls, but for practical reasons I could not always include them in the parts of the study discussed in this chapter. This data made it evident, and this is a subject that could be pursued in subsequent studies, that girls may have other ways of participating in the Latino world.

2. Taking a stance: some notes on the methodology used

Heller (2002) advocated that research is never neutral. The subjects of interest, the questions we ask ourselves, the research instruments and theoretical readings all relate to subjective interests, motivated to a large extent by our own backgrounds as individuals and our social position. According to Heller (2002), it is necessary to accept knowledge, including that produced by research, as subjective, partisan, socially situated and self-serving. My research is enshrined in this notion, as it is far from being neutral and objective. Nor does it aim to reach absolute conclusions and truths. It is an attempt to come up with a response to certain phenomena that involve languages and identities, but most particularly involve people.

There is no doubt that the characteristics that each researcher brings along contribute to and resonate in the end product of a research project. As Heller (2002) said,

> "[j]e crois qu'en bout de ligne, tout(e) chercheur(e) a explicitement ou implicitement une prise de position. Une bonne socialisation de nouveaux spécialistes doit donc en tenir compte. Je présenterai ici la mienne, non parce que je la trouve la meilleure que autres pour tout le monde, mais parce qu'elle fonctionne pour moi, et que je compte, en présentant mes propres démarches faciliter à mes lectrices et lecteurs la formulation de leur propre prise de position et les démarches qui en en découleront" (p. 22)².

My research does not aspire to be interpreted as an absolute truth, but rather as a narrative that seeks to provide an answer, amongst other things, to the hegemonic discourse that surrounded (and continues to surround) young men of Latin American origin in the context of Barcelona.

3. Creating ethnography

The work I undertook was based on ethnography. At that time, I believed that the characteristics of this type of research could help me to understand the complexity of what was behind these discourses, and the role that different social participants played in them. Ethnography has proved to be an extremely useful tool not only in anthropological and sociological studies but also for research with sociolinguistic interests, as in this case. Sociolinguistic-type ethnographies share the general characteristic of constant reflection about not only the data

---

2. "I believe that, ultimately, every researcher has to take a stance, whether explicitly or implicitly. A good socialization of new specialists should therefore take this into account. I will present my position here, not because I find it better than anyone else's, but because it works for me, and that I believe, that by presenting my own procedures, I can facilitate the formulation of a positioning and of the procedures that derive from it by my readers" (Heller, 2002, p. 22).

per se but also the actual process of analysis and reflection. It emphasizes the importance of the questions asked, the role of the researcher, their ideas, their motivations and how, as a whole, all of this represents taking a stance with regard to the topic of interest. This reflection on the methodology is what defines ethnographical research as critical, as it aims to be reflexive not only in terms of the subject of interest but also the mechanisms of interpretation themselves.

4. Sociolinguistic ethnography

Authors such as Heller (2002) and Coupland (2007) mention that analyses in sociolinguistic ethnography do not focus on language itself but on language as a social practice. This means that the attention given to data is not based solely on linguistic forms or structures, as might be the case in a more conventional linguistic study, but on the role that these practices take on in interactions, depending on the social participants involved in them.

One of the objectives of sociolinguistic ethnography is to associate the description and analysis of social practices and processes. According to Heller (2002), the interpretation we make of the analysis of ethnographic data should consider the social dynamics that happen on a broader scale, in terms of both space and time. For example, some of the youths who appear in this work mention the 'deterioration' that their varieties of Spanish have experienced since migrating to Barcelona. In other words, the way they used to speak in Guayaquil was regarded as 'educated', but on arriving here, and coming into contact with other linguistic forms, they believe it has become 'inferior'.

In this analysis, as noted by Blommaert (2010), we can identify how a process as universal as migration can also impact on the values of everyday linguistic practices. According to this author, this example would reflect how these migratory phenomena inherently involve certain movements (from the center to the outskirts) in which the speakers are transferred from one social sphere to another, not because of the 'linguistic quality' of their varieties but because of the social role they have in a particular context. In this case, it may be that the specific form of Spanish that in Guayaquil is regarded as 'educated', in the Ecuadorian context, is viewed differently when they come to Barcelona in relation to the identity of its users, who might be perceived as immigrants of a lower social class.

Sociolinguistic ethnography thus attempts to discover how these kinds of social differences and inequalities come about, and their correspondence with the differences and hierarchies of linguistic forms. Authors such as Heller (1999, 2003), Heller and Martin-Jones (2001), Rampton (1995, 2006), Pujolar (1997, 2000), Martín-Rojo (2010) and Unamuno (1999, 2003) have insisted, through their respective studies, that this perspective of critical sociolinguistics can also help us to understand the workings of social institutions in the construction of categories deriving from the production and reproduction of these social inequalities. Another of the aspects worth highlighting of ethnographic sociolinguistic research is its concern for the impact that this can have in the community in which it occurs. In the field of education, with research that takes place at the heart of the school's community, changes can arise in the dynamics of the social participants and this is considered part of the process, sparking further reflection. These are unlikely to be major changes or involve the whole educational center, but they *are* small changes in certain attitudes or perceptions in relation to the language uses, identities and situations of inequality that might be generated.

In the case of the research presented in this chapter, to give an example, based on the work carried out in schools, some teachers evinced a change of attitude towards the different linguistic varieties of Spanish, and even towards hybrid linguistic practices, normally evaluated as deficient practices. Heller (2002) notes with regard to this point:

> "[t]oute recherche en sciences sociales est une forme d'action sociale, sous la forme spécifique de la construction du savoir. La sociolinguistique est particulièrement bien placée pour reconnaître cette caractéristique, puisque la construction sociale du savoir passe par la communication et l'interaction, qui forment l'objet de base de la

recherche sociolinguistique. Cette action sociale, cette construction du savoir, est traversée par la nécessité d'un certain degré de réflexibilité, c'est-à-dire par le besoin de devenir conscient de la façon dont l'action de la recherche est reliée au savoir qu'elle construit et de rendre ce processus explicite, tout en tenant compte de ses conséquences sociales. Je cherche à explorer les possibilités d'une sociolinguistique que je qualificarais d'engagé, de critique, de réflexive, et surtout de voir comment une telle chose pourrait être réalisée concrètement" (p. 22)[3].

To sum up, one could say that sociolinguistics with an ethnographic perspective is a discipline that postulates the need for constant engagement in methodological consideration, and which understands that the data obtained from social interaction and the categories used by the researcher are never neutral (Heller & Martin-Jones, 2001; Rampton, 2006). Indeed, some say that discussions and reflections on data in sociolinguistics is one of the elements that have made the most useful contribution to improving this research practice in the discipline (Pérez-Milans, 2011).

Another fundamental contribution to this work was the so-called ethnomethodological approach (Atkinson, 1988; Coulon, 1998; Garfinkel, 1967; see the chapters by Nussbaum, this volume and Masats, this volume), especially its consideration that social research demands that the researcher is also included in the analysis. In other words, giving an account of the social reality calls for showing the role that the researchers play in gathering and subsequently analyzing information from interviews, discussion groups, lesson recordings, spontaneous conversations, etc. (Mondada, 1999). This principle, which is also taken up in interactional sociolinguistics (Heller & Martin-Jones, 2001; Rampton, 1995, 2006), allows the researcher to be considered as a participant and includes him or her. In the research process, reflections

---

[3]. "All research in social sciences is a form of social action, in the specific form of the construction of knowledge. Sociolinguistics is particularly well placed to recognize this characteristic, since the social construction of knowledge entails communication and interaction, which form the basic purpose of sociolinguistic research. This social action, this construction of knowledge, is riven by the need for a certain degree of 'reflexibility'; in other words, by the need to become aware of the way in which the action of research is connected to the knowledge it builds and renders this process explicit, taking into account its social consequences. I try to explore the possibilities of a sociolinguistic approach that I would describe as engaged, critical and reflexive and, above all, to see how such a concept could be realized specifically" (Heller, 2002, p. 22).

are embedded about the figure of the researcher and their role as an agent who, along with the other participants, is involved in building the social reality under study.

5. The study: the linguistic varieties of young Latin Americans in Barcelona

The data making up the corpus of the research described in this chapter were gathered during a long process of ethnographic work from 2005 to 2009. It was mainly conducted at a secondary education school (and the surrounding area) in the northern part of the city of Barcelona. The participants in this project were not selected following the usual guidelines. During the participant-observation process, some of the youngsters expressed a wish to get involved in the research, and following the natural dynamics of socialization, one participant called another one and so on and so forth until the corpus of data that I collated was constituted.

The total corpus consists of 21 interviews, 12 discussion groups and four hours of different classes, all recorded on audio or video. It also contains documents written by the students and other texts, such as songs written by the students or notes in the fieldwork diary. The corpus covered different spaces outside of the school, including parks, bars and squares, and also included the voices of mothers, fathers and teachers.

5.1. Type and collection of data

Essentially, the collected data were classified as follows:

- Audio recordings of interviews and discussion groups.

- Audio and video recordings of language lessons in the classroom.

- Video recordings of interactional spaces in schools.

Chapter 5

- Collection of music, pieces of writing and other documents.

- Notes in the fieldwork diary.

The corpus of this research was composed by dozens of people who, through interviews, discussion groups and conversations in and outside the classroom, expressed their ideas, explained their stances as opposed to other people's, introduced themselves to other people, etc. The complexity of making all these different discourses manageable to be studied as a whole, thus creating a giant network of interwoven voices leading to the creation of different realities, is patently obvious.

5.2. Processing and analysis

The data was transcribed with different programs: primarily, I used Transana, while I also used ELAN for shorter fragments that I wanted to analyze in depth (see the chapters by Antoniadou, this volume, and Moore & Llompart, this volume). Most of the interviews and discussion groups were transcribed in full. The classroom data, especially the video recordings, were only transcribed partially.

To analyze the data I considered different contributions on interactional sociolinguistics (Blommaert, 1995; Gumperz, 1976; Pujolar, 2000; Rampton, 1995). In this respect, the data processing tried to address the contributions of the ethnomethodology tradition and the work of conversational analysts (see Masats, this volume; Nussbaum, this volume).

6. An example of interactional analysis: the discovery of Latino speech

This section shows an example of an analysis to give an idea of how I processed the corpus of data gathered in the study. The Latino way of speaking emerged as a kind of hybrid variety that is difficult to recognize as inherent to a specific dialectal zone. It is a mixture that moves within a linguistic repertoire formed by the sociolinguistic scenario in which these young people live. Obviously local varieties, including Catalan and peninsular Castilian, which might be considered dominant in various different and complex senses, form part of this repertoire on which the Latino variety is structured.

To clarify what I have just said above, I believe it is worth taking a look at some of the recorded data. This is an excerpt that forms part of the data gathered during the first period of the ethnographic study (2006), featuring a conversation between a group of six teenagers in their first year of secondary education (i.e. a discussion group; see Canals, this volume). The boys were of various different origins: three of them were Ecuadorians from Guayaquil (Ignacio, Raúl and Pedro), one was from a village near Quito (Néstor), one was Bolivian (Oscar) and one a Peruvian boy from Chiclayo (Alex). It is obvious from the numbers of the utterances in this excerpt that this has been extracted from a much longer conversation. The transcript symbols used (see Moore & Llompart, this volume) can be found in the Appendix.

Fragment 1

377.	INV.	de:e así de:el_ pues de:el-| bueno lo que ustedes llaman racismo_ o diferencia [+**diferensia**+] de trato|
378.	IGN.	yo sé que aquí en cuarto| hay de una:a| una de ra_ una chica de_
379.	PDR:	de segundo_ el jaime *tío*|
380.	OSC:	XXXX
381.	PDR:	va diciendo [+**disiendo**+] indio de mierda|
382.	VCR:	cómo/|
383.	PDR:	que le pegaron| ayer-|
384.	VCR:	qué pasó/|
385.	ALX:	al jaime_ qué jaime/|
386.	PDR:	al gordo_ *tío* u:un_
387.	ALX:	al que_ un bajo|
388.	PDR:	no| el que tiene aquí morado| al que le pegó el agustín-|
389.	VCR:	por qué/|
390.	ALX:	porque va diciendo [+**disiendo**+] negro de mierda a todo el mundo_ *tío*| y al final lo callas así| (F) pua_ le metes un quiño y le dejas el ojo morado_así|

Chapter 5

391.	PDR:	el agustín le estaba <u>dando puñetes así</u> <u>le dieron un puñete</u>
392.	RAL:	qué pone aquí/|
393.	PDR:	y:y-| *le denunciaron*[+**denunsiaron**+] _*tío*|
Peninsular Castilian variety <u>Latino variety</u>		
Corpus 2006-2007 Support group **Participants: Víctor, Pedro, Raúl, Oscar, Alex, Ignacio**		

This short excerpt can be used to talk about hybridization and also problematize it. It also serves to demonstrate that interpreting interactional data means analyzing it utterance by utterance in a detailed way, not simply presenting or paraphrasing them (Antaki, Billig, Edwards, & Potter, 2003).

In utterance 377, the researcher puts forward the topic of racism, which is later reformulated as "different treatment". Based on this, the boys band together to describe what they understand by racism. Ignacio, intending to answer the researcher's question, refers to a girl but Pedro, in utterance 379, pushes in to put forward another story. Meanwhile, Alex talks about a boy who a Latin American friend of his had hit for "going round telling everyone he was an *indio de mierda* (shitty Indian)".

<u>Green</u> is used to highlight the words or expressions assigned to varieties of American Spanish, and *red* to highlight those that can be identified as part of Peninsular Spanish; in other words, not typical of any of the American varieties of Spanish. The *seseo* trait[4] is highlighted in bold.

Thus an external observation of the excerpt shows us, for example, the use of the word "*tío*" (mate) as a colloquially-used epithet, a definition given by the Royal Spanish Academy, the Real Academia Española (RAE, 2002). The use of "*tío*" in this sense is very widespread in every social sphere in Spain and is not exclusive to young people or Spanish-speaking areas. Indeed, Pujolar (1997), in his study on the speech and identities of young people in Barcelona, mentioned the widespread use of this term among youth, regardless of the language they used on an everyday basis (Catalan, Spanish or both, in this

---

4. Pronunciation of the letter c and z as /s/ rather than /θ/, the latter being typical of some Peninsular varieties.

case). A look at the Latino variety, linked to local practices and identities, confirms that the use of "*tío*" is also part of this variety. This is the case regardless of the fact that the use of the expression "*tío*", in the sense that the boys are using it here, does not form part of the lexicon of the different varieties of American Spanish of these youths. The only meaning of "*tío*" in Latin America is uncle, or aunt in the feminine version; i.e. the brother or sister of a parent (RAE, 2002).

Pedro and Alex used "*tío*" in their stories without this causing any kind of reaction that would have us infer that this word was unusual to the other participants. We do not witness any procedures that 'foreignize' it in the sense of Mondada (1999). Quite the contrary; the word was just one more in the conversation and occupied a key role in the construction of the story. It is an epithet that positions the conversation as one between young peers, denoting the activity as a clearly informal one.

But "*tío*" is not the only word that warrants a comment in this sense. For example, in turn 390, Alex uses the expression "*le metes un quiño*" (you smack him one), referring to the way in which someone reacted to an incident they considered racist. The word "*quiño*" appears in the RAE dictionary as a colloquial Ecuadorian expression that stems from the Quechuan word *k'iñay*, meaning to hit.

While one might suspect that Alex used the word "*quiñar*" as part of his variety of origin, this is not the case. Alex is not Ecuadorian, but Peruvian. While it is difficult to establish whether or not this word appears in one of the different varieties of Peruvian Spanish – which would not be surprising, given the geographical proximity and the Quechuan background to Castilian speech in Peru, what *is* interesting is the lack of a mechanical correspondence between the forms used in the story and the countries of origin of the boys. This lack of correspondence, I believe, gives the words "*tío*" and "*quiño*" an even more special value: they are used by Alex to construct a story in which the Latino voice is the protagonist, and in which *bricolage* is key to giving the story authenticity.

Chapter 5

Turn 391 can also be interpreted in this sense, where Pedro introduces the phrase "*dar puñetes*". If we continue to use the RAE as a reference, this expression is defined as 'administering blows with a closed fist'. While it does not specify the origin, one might assume that it is not peninsular, as it does not appear in other dictionaries for this area, such as the *Diccionario de Uso del Español* by María Moliner (2007).

The compositional nature or *bricolage* I am commenting on not only affects the lexicon but also interesting aspects of syntax. In turn 393, Pedro concludes the incident by saying: "*le denunciaron tío*" (they reported him, mate), using a *leísta* form[5] which, according to the RAE, is characteristic of the dialects of the central Iberian Peninsula and considered to be vulgar in other areas. In Latin America the use of the indirect object pronoun with verbs such as *denunciar* (report) is not only uncommon but is considered to be a mistake and is systematically corrected. While there are studies that claim there are certain cases of *leísmo* in Latin America as a result of contact with aboriginal languages, this is not generalized.

In addition to this specific use of the pronoun "*le*" mentioned above, something I would particularly like to point out is that this is a use which, like the other traits I have highlighted, appeared in the conversation without causing any kind of reaction that might lead one to understand that it was something that the participants regarded as part of a non-local or unauthentic variety of the speakers. Quite the contrary; for these youths it did not seem to be an indication that would suggest that the way they speak is Latino or not. Rather, as I am trying to demonstrate, it was a variety that the others recognized as appropriate for the activity in which they were participating.

Among phonological aspects, two of them stood out in the data. Firstly, there was notable use of *seseo* which, at least in Barcelona, is a pronounced trait because it does not form part of the Spanish that is customarily heard in the city, nor is it used as a model in schools. Secondly, and related to this, I believe that certain uses of the phoneme [s] and its alternation with other phonemes in specific contexts

---

5. Use of the indirect object pronoun le rather than the direct object pronoun lo.

also acquires a particular significance. For example, in the above excerpt all the speakers, including the researcher, used the *seseante* variety of Spanish.

Above and beyond the difference between the phonemes available in the language, the Latin American varieties are also characterized by the use of a set of allophones for the phoneme [s] that do not correspond to the ones used in Peninsular Spanish, and are different from the voiceless alveolar fricatives typical of northern Spain. In Latin America, the 's' is extremely variable, and tends to be assimilated with other adjacent phonemes and even alternates with aspiration or with total elision in front of certain consonants. This 's', which many people recognize as typically American, is not homogenous in dialects, although it is in contraposition to the 's' of the northern Peninsula. According to my data, Latinos also present significant variability with regard to the use of the 's'. What does appear to be invariable, and this was expressed by the youths in their conversation, is the *seseo*.

The second phenomenon refers to prosody; in other words, the traits that concern the frequency, duration, intensity and rhythm of speech sounds. As noted by several authors (Hayward, 2000; Llisterri, 1991), prosody is polysemic and fulfills many functions in orality, and has an evident semantic-pragmatic value. But what is of interest here is that, according to linguists, it plays a fundamental role in assigning sociolinguistic values, such as geographical origin, social status, gender, etc.

7. Concluding words

In this chapter I have tried to show how the ethnographic approach can be of great use in appreciating how communities understand their identities and the role that languages play in this process. I have outlined the research questions and consequently the methodology chosen and the way data were processed.

In the interactional data I have provided as an example, we have also seen how certain sociolinguistic characteristics of some of the Latin American youths can be interpreted as a style or an emerging variety, associated with a specific social identity: Latino. Traditional dialectology would be inadequate, as it is not possible to relate the variety used by these youths with a particular geographical origin. Rather, the excerpt reflects a polyphonic discourse which features traits that could be associated with varieties of Spanish from both continents. As a kind of *bricolage*, these resources are concatenated in a multiple variety which is identified by its users and by other people as Latino.

Ethnography, however, has certain limitations. Personally, one of the biggest difficulties I came across during my research was establishing a distance from the participants. Continual contact and work with the youths and the empathy this led to sometimes turned against me when trying to form a critical perspective of my observations. Another difficulty I experienced was the organization and classification of the corpus of data. The nature of my research resulted in a vast amount of data (see also Unamuno & Patiño, this volume). Sometimes, this compilation was not as systematic as it should have been, which caused problems when it came to relating the interviews and the fieldnotes with the research questions. In this respect, the chapters by Antoniadou (this volume), and Moore and Llompart (this volume) may be of assistance, in which they offer strategies for organizing ethnographic data.

Acknowledgments

Victor Corona is grateful to the ASLAN project (ANR-10-LABX-0081) of the Université de Lyon for its financial support of his ongoing research within the program 'Investissements d'Avenir' (ANR-11-IDEX-0007). The ASLAN project is funded by the French government, via the National Research Agency (ANR).

Works cited

Antaki, C., Billig, M., Edwards, D., & Potter, J. (2003). Discourse analysis means doing analysis: a critique of six analytic shortcomings. *Discourse Analysis Online*. http://extra.shu.ac.uk/daol/articles/v1/n1/a1/antaki2002002-paper.html

Antoniadou, V. (2017). Collecting, organizing and analyzing multimodal data sets: the contributions of CAQDAS. In E. Moore & M. Dooly (Eds), *Qualitative approaches to research on plurilingual education* (pp. 435-450). Research-publishing.net. https://doi.org/10.14705/rpnet.2017.emmd2016.640

Atkinson, P. (1988). Ethnomethodology: a critical review. *Annual Review of Sociology, 14*, 441-465. https://doi.org/10.1146/annurev.so.14.080188.002301

Blommaert, J. (1995). *Handbook of pragmatics*. Amsterdam: John Benjamins.

Blommaert, J. (2010). *The sociolinguistics of globalization*. Cambridge: Cambridge University Press. https://doi.org/10.1017/CBO9780511845307

Canals, L. (2017). Instruments for gathering data. In E. Moore & M. Dooly (Eds), *Qualitative approaches to research on plurilingual education* (pp. 390-401). Research-publishing.net. https://doi.org/10.14705/rpnet.2017.emmd2016.637

Coulon, A. (1998). *Ethnometodolgy*. Madrid: Cátedra.

Coupland, N. (2007). *Style: language variation and identity*. Cambridge: Cambridge University Press. https://doi.org/10.1017/CBO9780511755064

Fagyal, Z. (2010). *Accents de banlieue : aspects prosodiques du français populaire en contact avec les langues de l'immigration*. Paris: L'Harmattan.

Garfinkel, H. (1967). *Studies in ethnomethodology*. New Jersey: Prentice Hall.

Gumperz, J. (1976). Language, communication and public negotiation. In P. Sanday (Ed.), *Anthropology and the public interest: fieldwork and theory*. New York: Academic Press.

Hayward, K. (2000). *Experimental phonetics*. Harlow: Longman.

Heller, M. (1999). *Linguistic minorities and modernity: a sociolinguistic ethnography*. London: Longman.

Heller, M. (2002). *Éléments d'une sociolinguiste critique*. Paris: Didier.

Heller, M. (2003). Globalization, the new economy, and the commodification of language and identity. *Journal of Sociolinguistics, 7*(4), 473-492. https://doi.org/10.1111/j.1467-9841.2003.00238.x

Heller, M., & Martin-Jones, M. (2001). *Voices of authority: education and linguistic difference*. Westport, Conn: Ablex Pub.

Hewitt, R. (1986). *White talk black talk: inter-racial friendship and communication amongst adolescents*. Cambridge: Cambridge University Press.

Llisterri, J. (1991). *Introducción a la fonética: el método experimental*. Barcelona: Anthropos.

Martín-Rojo, L. (2010). *Constructing inequality in multilingual classrooms*. Berlin: De Gruyter Mouton. https://doi.org/10.1515/9783110226645

Masats, D. (2017). Conversation analysis at the service of research in the field of second language acquisition (CA-for-SLA). In E. Moore & M. Dooly (Eds), *Qualitative approaches to research on plurilingual education* (pp. 321-347). Research-publishing. net. https://doi.org/10.14705/rpnet.2017.emmd2016.633

Moliner, M. (2007). *Diccionario de uso del español (3rd edition)*. Madrid: Gredos.

Mondada, L. (1999). L'accomplissement de «l'étrangéité» dans et par l'interaction : procédures de catégorisation des locuteurs. *Langages, 33*(134), 20-34. https://doi.org/10.3406/lgge.1999.2190

Moore, E., & and Llompart, J. (2017). Collecting, transcribing, analyzing and presenting plurilingual interactional data. In E. Moore & M. Dooly (Eds), *Qualitative approaches to research on plurilingual education* (pp. 403-417). Research-publishing.net. https://doi.org/10.14705/rpnet.2017.emmd2016.638

Nussbaum, L. (2017). Doing research with teachers. In E. Moore & M. Dooly (Eds), *Qualitative approaches to research on plurilingual education* (pp. 46-67). Research-publishing.net. https://doi.org/10.14705/rpnet.2017.emmd2016.621

Pérez-Milans, M. (2011). Being a Chinese newcomer in Madrid compulsory education: ideological constructions in language education practice. *Journal of Pragmatics, 43*(4), 1005-1022. https://doi.org/10.1016/j.pragma.2010.10.003

Pujolar, J. (1997). *De què vas, tio?* Barcelona: Empúries.

Pujolar, J. (2000). *Gender, heteroglossia and power: a sociolinguistic study of youth culture.* Berlin: Walter de Gruyter.

Rampton, B. (1995). *Crossing: language and ethnicity among adolescents*. London: Longman.

Rampton, B. (2006). *Language in late modernity: interaction in an urban school*. Cambridge University Press. https://doi.org/10.1017/cbo9780511486722

Real Academia Española. (2002). *Diccionario de la lengua española* (22nd ed.). Madrid: Espasa.

Tetreault, C. (2008). La racaille: figuring gender, generation, and stigmatized space in a French cité. *Gender and Language, 2*(2), 141-170. https://doi.org/10.1558/genl.v2i2.141

Unamuno, V. (1999). *Lenguas, escuela y diversidad sociocultural. Etnografía de la acción comunicativa*. Barcelona: University of Barcelona Publications.

Unamuno, V. (2003). *Lengua, escuela y diversidad sociocultural. Hacia una educación lingüística crítica*. Barcelona: Editorial Graó.

Unamuno, V., & Patiño, A. (2017). Producing knowledge about plurilingualism with young students: a challenge for collaborative ethnography. In E. Moore & M. Dooly (Eds), *Qualitative approaches to research on plurilingual education* (pp. 129-149). Research-publishing.net. https://doi.org/10.14705/rpnet.2017.emmd2016.625

Willis, P. (1977). *Learning to labour: how working class kids get working class jobs.* New York: Colombia University.

Recommended reading

Gumperz, J. (1976). Language, communication and public negotiation. In P. Sanday (Ed.), *Anthropology and the public interest: fieldwork and theory.* New York: Academic Press.
Heller, M. (2002). *Éléments d'une sociolinguistique critique.* Paris: Didier.
Martín-Rojo, L. (2010). *Constructing inequality in multilingual classrooms.* Berlin: De Gruyter Mouton.
Pujolar, J. (2000). *Gender, heteroglossia and power: a sociolinguistic study of youth culture.* Berlin: Walter de Gruyter.
Rampton, B. (1999). Styling the other: introduction. *Journal of Sociolinguistics, 3*(4), 421-427. https://doi.org/10.1111/1467-9481.00088
Willis, P. (1977). *Learning to labour: how working class kids get working class jobs.* New York: Colombia University.

Appendix

Adapted from GREIP transcription symbols (see Moore & Llompart, this volume):

Tonal sequences:
    Descending \
    Ascending /
Pauses:
    Short |
    Medium ||
    Long <number of seconds>
Syllabic lengthening (according to duration): · ·· ···
Overlaps: =spokentextA= =spokentextB=
Interruptions: Text_
Intensity:
    Piano {(P) text}
    Pianissimo {(PP) text}

Chapter 5

        Forte {(F) text}
        Fortissimo {(FF) text}
Tone:
        High {(A) text}
        Low {(B) text}
Tempo:
        Fast {(AC) text}
        Slow {(DC)
Utterances accompanied by laughter: {(@) texto}
Comments: [comments]
Incomprehensible fragments (according to duration): XXX | XXX XXX | XXX XXX XXX
Uncertain fragment: {(?) text}

6 A Mediated Discourse Analysis (MDA) approach to multimodal data

Melinda Dooly[1]

Key concepts: multimodality, mediated discourse analysis, MDA, nexus analysis, computer mediated communication, CMC, analysis of interaction.

1. Introduction

Just as research in language learning is moving beyond the four walls of the classroom, there is a growing awareness that language use (and simultaneous learning) takes place in increasingly complex and interconnected ways, in particular through the use of technology. "In the globalized era, transnational connections are thus increasingly 'taken to new levels' and 'shaped in new forms'" (Tarrow, 2005, p. xiii). As the catchphrase of 'global citizen' becomes entrenched in *vox populi*, there is now more recognition of the need for engaged and informed individuals who are not only traditionally literate, but adept in a new, systemic literacy (Seely Brown, 2008, p. xi). This is also what Kramsch (2006, p. 251) has called "symbolic competence" appropriate for today's "knowledge society" (see the so-called 'Paris Declaration', 2014, by the coalition GAPMIL). Kramsch (2006) uses the term symbolic competence to refer to a rather sophisticated ability to manipulate symbolic systems, including the many variants of discursive modalities (spoken, written, gestural, visual, electronic and so forth). However, as Blackledge, Creese, and Kaur Takhi (2013) point out, there is a need to move beyond simply harnessing multiple competences and repertoires of plurilingual learners. Teachers (and researchers) should strive to make visible the social, individual and cultural tensions and creativity that arise from their belonging to multiple communities. This affords them a space

---

[1]. Universitat Autònoma de Barcelona, Bellaterra, Catalonia/Spain; melindaann.dooly@uab.cat

How to cite this chapter: Dooly, M. (2017). A Mediated Discourse Analysis (MDA) approach to multimodal data. In E. Moore & M. Dooly (Eds), *Qualitative approaches to research on plurilingual education* (pp. 189-211). Research-publishing.net. https://doi.org/10.14705/rpnet.2017.emmd2016.628

where plurilingual learners can command and 'ventriloquate' the many different 'voices' that populate the multiple, plurilingual communities of which they are members.

This new understanding of 'being literate' foregrounds the issue of modality in questions of communicative competence (which is the baseline of most language teaching approaches in the EU; Council of Europe, 2001). This, in turn, implies that multimodality holds a substantial role in language teaching and learning research. Moreover, the increased ubiquity of embedded multimedia and access to the Internet in language classrooms has contributed significantly to scholarly interest in the multiple semiotic complexities of the representations in discursive exchanges that take place in blended learning (in-class lessons combined with online exchanges with geographically-distributed peers) as well as non-traditional (informal) language learning environments.

Concretely, multimodality research in education seeks to shed light on how learners make meaning while drawing on various communicative forms – language, image, music, sound, gesture, touch and smell – all of which (apart from touch and smell) are increasingly present in online and blended learning interactions. Inevitably, dealing with the plethora of data that stems from diverse media can be challenging for the researcher since they must find a coherent means of examining complex data, all of which may be compiled in vastly different formats and yet, at the same time, are all interrelated in the learning process. The data may also have been collected at different times and in diverse spatial orientations (in-class, online, screenshots of blended learning environments, etc.). In other words, the researcher must find a means of cogently discussing and analyzing a complex data corpus made up of different media and possibly diverse output. For instance, the corpus may consist of audio and video interactions of learners who are physically present in the classroom while they are interacting (through audio and video) with other learners who are not physically present (captured through a screencast and an in-class camera), thus triplicating or even quadruplicating the data collection. These data may then be combined with other data mediums (handouts completed during an online negotiation of a task, for instance) to contribute to an even more complex corpus.

Of course, multimodality is and always has been part of meaning making, as humans have always used more than written or spoken words to communicate. However, within Western society, especially in the context of education, there has been a "dominance of writing as the means of communication and representation" (Kress, 1998, p. 58), at least until recently. This has been changing over the past decades, especially as the use of computers and the Internet has gained ground. In a large part, the shift from books to screens has contributed to this development, moving us "from print to post-print text cultures" (Lankshear, 1997, p. 1), thus shepherding in what has been called the 'new communicative order' (Kress & van Leeuwen, 1996; Lankshear, 1997). Likewise, in the world of education, language professionals are now beginning to integrate the concept of the 'new communicative order' into their teaching, recognizing that words, images, sound, touch and other salient features of communication are all part of a wide spectrum of communicative practices and competences. Teachers now recognize that their learners must not only be knowledgeable of these practices, they must master them in order to be able to engage in the so-called 'knowledge society'.

Along these lines, this chapter summarizes an investigation into multimodal communicative competences in an online telecollaborative environment in which student-teachers (pupils studying to become foreign language teachers) interacted through diverse social media. The study was first published in Dooly and Sadler (2013) and permission has been granted to reprint sections for this handbook. In this case the student-teachers are plurilingual speakers. Their interaction is carried out through English, which is not the primary language of all the users. They are what Canagarajah (2007) has termed users of Lingua Franca English (LFE) and their use of LFE is intersubjectively and mutually negotiated in their communities.

> "Both LFE speakers and [native speakers] have competence in their respective varieties, though there is no limit to the development of their proficiency through experience and time. The competence of LFE speakers is of course distinct. This competence for cross-language contact and hybrid codes derives from their plurilingual life.

> Because of the diversity at the heart of this communicative medium, LFE is intersubjectively constructed in each specific context of interaction. The form of this English is negotiated by each set of speakers for their purposes" (Canagarajah, 2007, p. 925).

The study approach into the way in which the LFE is co-constructed and negotiated in their online interaction is based on Mediated Discourse Analysis (MDA), a research methodology that stems from Nexus Analysis (Scollon & Scollon, 2004, 2007). The use of MDA allowed the researcher to include different data resources (online text-based resources such as wikis or forums which may be seen as more static products stemming from a process) with diverse interactional data in order to trace the social actions that link online and offline learning processes.

2. Mediated discourse analysis

MDA (R. Scollon, 2001; S. Scollon, 2005) is based on the premise that actors are socialized in diverse forms and to varying extent through the discourse systems in which they participate and that each system is differentiated from the other by its embedded practices (Scollon & Scollon, 2004). This type of analysis offers a strategy for combining ethnography, conversation analysis (see Masats, this volume; Nussbaum, this volume) and discourse analysis (see Antoniadou & Dooly, this volume) and provides a theoretical account of how participants, context, discourses and objects (artifacts) facilitate action and social change reciprocally. MDA (as mentioned previously, it is sometimes called Nexus Analysis, Scollon & Scollon, 2004; Wohlwend, 2013) offers a means of exploring how multiple aspects of complex social action interrelate through varying discursive interactions instead of focusing analysis on only one discourse component in isolation.

MDA employs 'methodological interdiscursivity' (Scollon, 2000); that is it integrates multiple approaches for data gathering and data analysis (linguistic landscaping, multimodal analysis, discourse analysis, ethnographic observations, sociolinguistics interviews, etc.) in order to strengthen any potential weaknesses of the methodologies in use. The MDA approach highlights the way in which individual actions are afforded and made intelligible through participants' context, including individual histories, along with the sociohistorical discourses, and interactional organizations in which the action takes place. As part of the approach, 'nexus' can be understood as a 'site of engagement' where social action is facilitated by a set of social processes, such as discourses in place (discourses that participants will be familiar with), observable historical actions (personal and collective experiences that can be documented, e.g. previous class content), and interaction order (social practices of interaction such as teacher-pupil configurations). This is reflected in Figure 1. In other words, MDA allows the researcher to weave together an informed analysis of a particular site of engagement that takes into consideration background social processes that are relevant to the interaction (e.g. online text chat) or product (e.g. wiki) that is being analyzed.

Figure 1. Site of engagement (social action), based on Scollon and Scollon (2004)

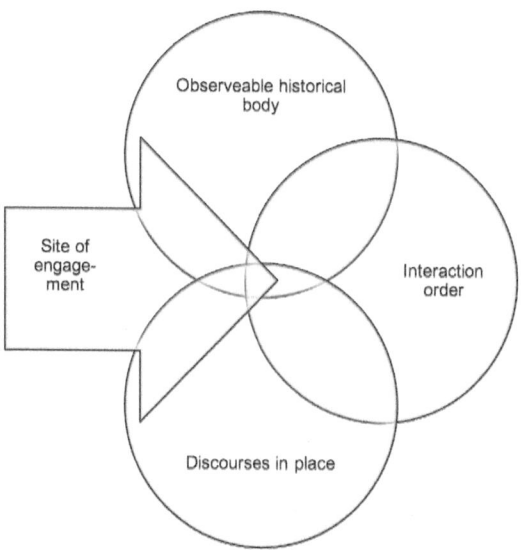

Chapter 6

This analytical sequencing of activities over an extended period of time allows researchers to identify significant mediated action against a background of discourses that are germane to the study (cycles of discourse: dominant discourses which may be overt or backgrounded, or internalized as practice, etc.). It also allows insight into interactional moments where participants' historical trajectories 'coincide' in an instance of social action and whose historical trajectories are altered by this social action.

MDA (also called Nexus Analysis) is attributed principally to two American linguistic ethnographers: Ron and Suzie Scollon. These two academics began examining the semiotic cycles of people, objects and discourse while carrying out research in Alaska in the early 1980's; looking at emergent use of the Internet for educational purposes as early as 1981. According to Jones and Norris (2005), the approach investigates the role texts (oral or written) may play in actions undertaken by social actors on the one hand and how these same texts arise as the outcomes of social interactive processes of production on the other hand. The approach is based on Ron Scollon's personal observations of the influence news media had on individuals around him (in particular, concerning escalating violence in the Vietnam War), followed by the two academics' interest in the intersections of different discursive practices on individual trajectories.

This approach allows for the tracing of discourses across disparate discursive genres in order to have a better understanding of the interrelationship of language(s) and other social semiotic data. As it has developed over time, researchers have incorporated various frameworks. Examples can be found that use interactional sociolinguistics, conversation analysis, anthropological linguistics or the ethnography of communication, critical discourse analysis, mediated action and activity theory, social semiotics, multimodal discourse analysis, and the New Literacy Studies. The flexibility of the approach is based on the notion that dealing with complex, longitudinal social issues (such as effective language teaching) calls for equally complex approaches; a simple one-dimensional approach will not suffice to illuminate the nexus between actor and social practices.

3. The study: developing teacher repertoires in sites of engagement

3.1. Data collection

Beginning from an educational ethnographic perspective, data sets were compiled in order to explore teacher development during a year-long telecollaborative exchange between student-teachers located in Catalonia and in the U.S. (see chapter by Antoniadou & Dooly, this volume for similar multimodal research). The same activities were repeated twice over a period of two years. In both years, in the first semester, student-teachers worked in small online groups to provide feedback and constructive criticism to group members' individual Teaching Sequence (TS) for implementation in their practicum schools; each collaborative group of three to four students included members from both universities. The activities in the first semester included:

- An ice breaking activity that consisted of a short personal introduction through the online presentation platform Voicethread, which was then commented on by the other students.

- Brainstorming of ideas (in an online forum) for their teaching sequences in order to form smaller online groups based on common interests and/or contexts from the brainstorming activities.

- Posting of first drafts of teaching sequences in a wiki (Zoho was used).

- Online discussions in small groups for feedback and suggestions on the TSs.

- Subsequent meetings and feedback for similar discussions, resulting in drafts 2, 3 and final draft.

- Posting of reflections of changes to the TS design and rationale for changes.

Chapter 6

For the online meetings, the modality – text or audio chat – and timetable were left up to each group to decide since one of the implicit goals was to get the students to practice with as many technological tools as possible. Therefore, the student-teachers were introduced, in face-to-face (f2f) workshops, to a number of Computer Mediated Communication (CMC) platforms (e.g. Skype, Google Hangouts), but the students themselves decided which best suited their needs. Student-teachers were asked to keep records of their meetings (text transcripts or audio files) which eventually became a component of their final teacher reflection portfolio (and part of the data corpus).

In the second semester, the student-teachers were asked to work together to design and develop podcasts and accompanying teaching activities. Working in groups, the student-teachers were provided with virtual spaces and tools for meetings, this time in a virtual world (Second Life). The groups worked together to create a podcast and related teaching (pre-, during and post-) activities, although there were different leaders for the varying tasks, depending on individual expertise (technological, pedagogical, etc.). The activities in the second semester included:

- A 'scavenger hunt' in Second Life virtual world to help student-teachers become familiar with the environment (the scavenger hunt also served as a way for the new groups to get to know each other).

- Introduction to the Second Life 'meeting rooms' where the members were encouraged to gather to work on their podcasts (not compulsory).

- Prescreening of podcast drafts in Second Life 'outdoor' cinema (drop-by schedule, individuals left observations in Second Life post box).

- Presentations of the final podcasts in Second Life cinema (whole group session).

- Implementation of podcast teaching activities (Catalan students only).

- Discussion and reflection on podcast development and implementation in Second Life group arena (followed by 'farewell party' in Second Life).

Data sets were comprised of online products (wikis used as a digital reflection report, screenshots from virtual world group interactions, and forum posts: shared documents of student-teachers' planned teaching sequences) and interactional data (recordings and transcripts of f2f classes, email exchanges between partnered students, recorded and transcribed text and audio chats between partnered students and groups in Second Life) along with complementary products of students' personal learning objectives (scanned from handouts), self-evaluation sheets (scanned), and class programs from both teachers and observers' field notes.

The data corpora includes different transcript formats due to the different communication media available to the participants. For instance, audio/video chats may have only been recorded as audio (the students decided how they documented their interactions), in which case a transcription of the audio recording was made by the researcher. The choice of narrow or broad transcription depended upon the research objective. In the case of text chats, the transcriptions were not altered beyond adding turn numbers (if the transcript did not provide them as was the case in Second Life text chat) and changing the names of the participants. The rendering of transcripts is described in more detail for each fragment below.

3.2. Summary of approach

In this study the social action consisted of practices designed to promote novice teachers' process of professionalization through technology-enhanced education courses. This social action interrelates with discourses and procedures that may either limit or facilitate action. Note that the study focused only on the discourse relevant to teacher professionalization and that which was made relevant and observable by the participants, such as specific referencing of teacher resources, teacher know-how or the use of what could be called 'teacher repertoire'. The 'sites of engagement' which were studied are also interconnected to interactional order (how the participants organize themselves in an online chat, for instance). In this way, the analysis could include the way in which the persons involved organized the social event (for instance, taking on the role of 'expert' in the chat).

Analysis of the social interaction that takes place in a 'site of engagement' (Figure 2) allowed the researcher to find traces of what Scollon and Scollon (2004) call 'historical bodies' (personal and collective discursive experiences that the participants make relevant in the social interaction such as classroom discussions) as well as 'discourses in place' (that is, discursive practices that will be familiar to them such as 'teacher talk'), along with the interactional order that the participants organize amongst themselves (e.g. taking on the role of collaborator or teacher).

Figure 2. Visualization of sites of engagement

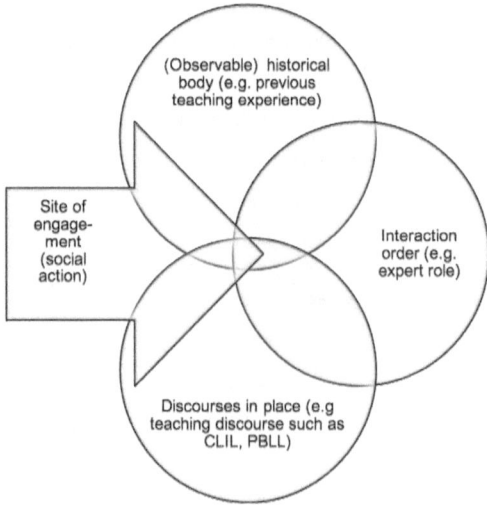

The research examined how discourse practices create 'teacher discourse' within teachers' Communities of Practice (CoP, Wenger, 1998) and how the student-teachers remediate this discourse in their knowledge construction during the process of becoming full-fledged members of this professional community. Because the order of interaction in the online products was not immediately observable (e.g. the actual performance of typing and posting in a forum), MDA allowed these actions to be considered as traces or artifacts (e.g. the forum threads of topic initiation and replies) which are left, thus showing traces of "communication and community through permalinked posts, comments, and references" (Efimova, Hendrick, & Anjewierden, 2005, p. 24).

3.3. Interaction order and discourses in place: talking like a teacher

The design of the activities fomented intensive, online discussion about individual teaching sequences, as seen in the transcript below where Clara (from Catalonia) is giving feedback to her partner Lynn (in the U.S.). The students used the Voice Over Internet Protocol (VOIP) program called Skype during which they recorded their exchanges.

In the following transcript (reproduced here with explicit written permission by the participants) it is possible to see how the student-teachers made the discourses they had been exposed to during their courses on language teaching methodology relevant in their social interaction. In other words, they ventriloquate the many different voices that can be found in the multiple, plurilingual communities of which they are members (Blackledge et al., 2013), including the 'professional teacher' community. The 'historical body' of previous teacher-learning experiences forms a nexus with the 'discourses in place' (teacher repertoire of specific language teaching approaches) within the 'site of engagement' of the VOIP feedback session: the discourse is part of the mediated discourse for the participants' feedback.

In particular, Clara brings up concepts of competences and Content Language and Integrated Learning (CLIL); she points out the need to provide clearly defined objectives and finally, the idea of project-based online interaction as a final output is proposed. All of these notions (competence-based learning, derivatives of communicative language teaching such as CLIL and project-based language learning, the importance of clear objectives for continuous, competence-based assessment) were key topics that had been extensively discussed and developed throughout the year in the f2f courses while the exchange was taking place online (NB: observation based on class programs and field notes).

The students were asked to record their online meetings but were given an option to erase any of the data they were not comfortable with (e.g. personal conversations that they preferred not to deliver to the researchers). Due to software limitations at the time, no visual recording of their interaction was possible; only audio (MP3 format) data were available for analysis. All raw data were anonymized before beginning the analysis. Different from other discourse approaches in this volume, the transcription uses only a few conventions of conversation analysis protocols (see Appendix for transcription key). A generally broad transcription was used in order to give information primarily on the words spoken, the transitional quality of the turn-taking and noticeable pauses (Sawyer, 2006; see also Moore & Llompart, this volume).

Fragment 1

1.	Clara:	ok [1] ok great (.) so i wrote that i thought about give you some feedback about your draft and i had three main ideas that i would like to comment with you
2.	Lynn:	ah that's XXX
3.	Clara:	it's that you can pras- practice reading comprehension and at the same time to: to work with certain learning i mean to learn something else (.) i mean to connect here in spain we've got uhm curriculum competences [2] yes here in spain we are working with competences and (.) and we can connect the english language with another subject for instance science
4.	Clara:	[and]
5.	Lynn:	[Ah I see]
6.	Clara:	it's i i thought that you could work the reading comprehension related with another subject (.) for instance history (.) and so on (.) to be more connected with them
7.	Lynn:	mmmm
8.	Lynn:	yeah yeah i see
(…)		
25.	Clara:	ok nice

26.	Lynn:	yeah that's a great idea thank you
27.	Clara:	(laughs) you're welcome (.) another thing that i thought that you could explain them what they are going to learn during these sequences because in your draft in the in the interaction i didn't see that you you wrote about how to to explain what the students will be able to do or what they are going to do during these teaching sequences so i thought that it could be a good idea for them to explain what they are going to achieve during these session (.) or not?
(…)		
35.	Clara:	the objectives (.) i mean do you have you seen my dropbox
36.	Lynn:	yeah i i saw yours
37.	Clara:	ah you tell me to think about your objectives no (1)
38.	Lynn:	ahm ahm i mean do you have any suggestion for my draft as for objectives?
39.	Clara:	objectives i mean so students will be able to (.) to umpreh comprehend different reading texts
40.	Lynn:	ah: i see ok yeah that would be great
41.	Clara:	Students will be able to (.) i don't know
42.	Lynn:	((laughs)) ok that sounds yeah oh good fine
43.	Clara:	((laughs)) what else what else you could prepare this ah also in your final i don't know session i thought that it could be a good a great idea if you could prepare a unit to collaborate on a project with another school from for example spain (.) and these schools would have to deal a reading text about a topic they could do it in pairs and then each pair will have a a peer assigned for the other i don't know how to (.) i'm reading i mean in this sess- the last session i mean all your teaching sequences will be focused like to building a project with another school and to share information
44.	Lynn:	i know what you mean when you say another school another school abroad
45.	Clara:	yeah
46.	Lynn:	ah i see: (.) just like us
Online Chat: Online Partner Feedback on Teaching Sequences		

In this fragment, as in the next one (Fragment 2; text chat), MDA underscores the participants' remediation of the 'discourses in place'. For instance, the 'SWBAT' term can be traced through several of the 'sites of engagement'. SWBAT is an acronym that stands for 'Students Will Be Able To' and was first introduced into nexus discourse by the U.S. teacher in f2f sessions at the beginning of the year. His student-teachers appropriated the term and then taught the term to the Catalan student-teachers in their online exchange (evidence of this was found in several of the online transcripts but for the sake of brevity are not included here). In the above fragment, in turn 39, Clara (the student-teacher from Catalonia) makes use of the term SWBAT to point out that her peer has not clearly described the TS learning objectives, "objectives I mean so students will be able to (.) to umpreh comprehend different reading texts". She returns to the term in turn 41.

In the next fragment, as in the oral chat, the students were responsible for saving the transcripts from their text chats and sending the text documents to the teachers as evidence of their online activities. The students' preferred means of doing so was to copy the entire chat session and paste it in a word document. In this fragment, Jazz (from the U.S.) and Sara (from Catalonia) are also discussing objectives, although in this case they are looking at the planning for their podcast they are collaborating on together and the term SWBAT comes up in turn 20 (Fragment 2). The two students are in Second Life but Sara was having problems with her audio chat so they had switched to text chat (also available in Second Life). In the fragment analyzed below, Sara elaborates further on the connection between the SWBAT and the different sections of the activity in turn 24, and finally, in turn 26 she indicates the direct connection between objectives and the post-activities they are designing for the podcast.

MDA also highlights the way in which the participants (in this case Jazz and Sara) organize themselves for social interaction during their podcast planning in Second Life. Both participants clearly identify themselves with the simulated 'activity groups' (they are aligned with the task), and both interactants call into play 'teacher talk' (e.g. objectives, topic, pre-activity, intro and related activities, age-related activities, etc.); all of which is very similar to the previous excerpt of the TS feedback session. In the case of the text chat transcripts, the researcher did not make any modifications except to add turn numbers and to change the chat usernames.

Fragment 2

| 1. | [12:10] Jazz: | We can use the pod cast as a pre activity |
| 2. | [12:10] Sara: | yes yes |

3.	[12:10] Jazz:	I mean we can do it for children. If we are going to use English
4.	[12:11] Sara:	I think the podcast should be like an intro and then we can do activities related to it
5.	[12:11] Jazz:	I can find native speakers of english easily
6.	[12:11] Janet:	yes
7.	[12:11] Sara:	yes children but what age???
8.	[12:12] Jazz:	Yes, I was thinking that it could be use for introduce vocabulary.
9.	[12:12] Jazz:	The age that works for use.
10.	(…)	
11.	[12:20] Jazz:	We can introduce some words with pictures. Put them voice and text.
12.	[12:20] Sara:	ok
13.	[12:20] Jazz:	Then do a short conversation example of using those words
14.	[12:20] Sara:	and the teacher goals are...
15.	[12:21] Sara:	Are the teacher goals and the objectives the same?
16.	[12:21] Jazz:	Prepared the students with the vocabulary necessary in order to complete the classroom activities.
17.	[12:21] Janet:	u mean the objectives?
18.	[12:21] Janet:	ok
19.	[12:22] Jazz:	With this vocabulary you can teach past tense, present tense or future.
20.	[12:22] Sara:	goals refers to what the T expects? and objectives is related to the SWBAT's?
21.	(…)	
22.	[12:42] Sara:	then the objectives (what we expect children to do by watching and listening to the podcast) could be the following
23.	[12:42] Jazz:	About the second one, is going to depend of how we design the posd cast
24.	[12:43] Sara:	SWBAT: 1)comprehension; 2) repdroduction (imitation) and finally 3) production
25.	[12:43] Jazz:	Thank you Sara
26.	[12:43] Sara:	the objectives go according to the postactivities

Brainstorming the podcast topic and content in a text chat in Second Life

The participants' mediated discourse included a shared teacher culture (or 'cycles of discourse') as demonstrated by similar jargon, topics, etc. which are made relevant by the participants during their virtual world interaction. The traits that are made relevant by the student-teachers in their online discourse

Chapter 6

are based on commonalities that they seem to attribute to the whole group, for instance, 'teacher-identity'. This 'shared' identity of 'teacher' in the virtual community allowed them to form a cohesion that was more important than other possible identities (for instance, exchange student, Korean, mother, wife, sister, etc.). This is clear in the way in which the majority of their online discourse aligns with 'teacher-talk', including their appropriation of SWBAT as part of the 'discourses in place'. This seems to indicate a gradual internalization of nexus of practice as the participants aligned themselves with the community of teaching practitioners (Wenger, 1998).

In the following Fragment 3, the term is made particularly relevant by the participants as they apply meta-reflection to not only extract its definition (in linguistic terms) but to also co-construct a fuller understanding of its meaning as it applies to their teacher knowledge. As in Fragment 2, the researcher changed the chat usernames. The timeframe is part of the original text chat transcript.

Fragment 3

[8:03] Lan@! dice:	and what will you assess while they're doing their presentation? will you do the posters in a cardboard format or it's better to use ICT (powerpoint presentation, for example)?
[8:03] Evelyn dice:	Lana, I really like your SWBAT as a list of activities, but the idea behind SWBAT is more to talk about what students will be able to do linguistically and this is how you can assess them
[8:04] Chu dice:	you can make assessing standard for exmaple, content, how clear...
[8:04] Lan@! dice:	that's another interesting point I've borrowed from you (SWABTS)
[8:04] Imogene dice:	you're welcome
[8:04] Lan@! dice:	so poster format?
[8:04] Evelyn dice:	But SWBAT is more like, "students will be able to use key english phrases in presenting a poster about their favorite sport." the language use is the key part of SWBAT
[8:05] Lan@! dice:	Thanks for the clarification! is good to have USA peers
Lan@!, Evelyn and Chu (participants) give TS feedback in text chat	

Following from the previous 'sites of engagement', the next 'artifact' (part of a students' self-evaluation of competences gained through the online experience) demonstrates an especially intriguing example of gradual internalization of discourse pertaining to the nexus of practice and the way in which the 'virtual' community of practice contributed to socially distributed cognition of the new participants (Figure 3). The term SWBAT is explicitly listed as one of the competences which was assimilated through the supportive environment of the telecollaborative exchange.

Figure 3. Student-teacher evaluation of assimilated competences

> 2. Your online experience with your UIUC peers?
>
> • Assessment = SWBAT's methodoly of phrasing objectives
> • My peers have helped me a lot, they gave me ideas & suggestions → it was up to me to take them or leave them.

Figure 4. Tracing discourse across disparate genres

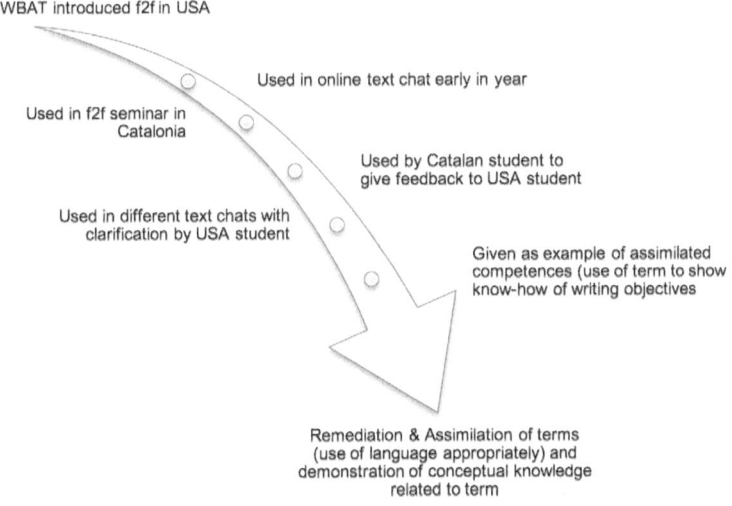

Chapter 6

This brief case study exemplifies how MDA can be applied to multimodal data sets through a focus on the nexus of practice not only of discourses and people, but also of concepts and artifacts. This allows the researcher to trace discourses across disparate genres in order to have a better understanding of the interrelationship of language(s) and other social semiotic data; as in this case wherein teachers become 'socialized' into the profession through different 'discourses in place' (Figure 4). We can see how the student-teachers are exposed to and participate in 'discourses in place' (in this case, specific educational jargon linked to conceptual knowledge necessary for language teachers to plan and design effective teaching sequences). Applying MDA afforded the opportunity of exploiting the linkages across events in multiple sites of engagement rather than simply looking at disparate data sets as disparate and isolated events.

4. Concluding words

MDA provides a useful approach for tracking the complexity of multiple literacies in overlapping contexts, including blended learning and online environments, while providing a fruitful means of analyzing a range of embodied discourses as they converge in sites of engagement. The approach can serve as a means of 'teasing out' traces of embedded discourses that intersect with participants in moments of the learning process in order to better identify specific instances of literacy acquisition that occur across diverse modalities.

The use of MDA highlights an understanding of literacy as a social practice (Barton & Hamilton, 2000; Street, 2000) as well as allowing for the intricate tension between the nexus of learner (agent) and discourse practices as mediational means (Wertsch, 1991, 1998) by taking into consideration the relationship between language and action: MDA sees language use as an action (not just a product) which is related to other forms of human action and other discursive practices. Thus, the researcher can see how related chains of mediated actions and interactional events across contexts are related to social practices within a wider nexus of practice.

When working with data from the Internet (e.g. looking at CoPs created through forums, wikis, text and audio chats, etc.), MDA proposes that it is as important to look at the social actions that are behind the production of Internet output, and not just to analyse the products. Analysing the 'sites of engagement', once transferred out of their 'environment' (e.g. screenshots of blog posts) inevitably renders the data much more 'static' than its original format. This can lead the researcher to focus on less dynamic aspects of the data rather than on the process of its production and the way in which different semiotic resources came into play in that process. MDA conceives of the Internet as "a cyberspace" that consists of "a collection of multiple overlapping spaces, virtual, geographical and physical, which accommodate multiple 'forms of life' and communicative possibilities" (Jones, 2008, p. 436). It is important that the researcher be aware that they are not simply looking at diverse visible spaces on users' screens; they are, in fact, linked social practices in both physical and virtual worlds.

Due to the complexity of multimodal data and its analysis, the researcher should strive to make their analysis 'trail' as detailed and auditable as possible. When considering the best way to collect and present data, researchers should bear in mind that sampling does not necessarily need to be sequential – it can be random. However, a clear rationale for the choice of inclusion must be provided, along with an explanation of choice of data collection and a minimum effort to be representative of as many linked sites as possible is preferable. Transparency of data collection and management are also vital: how were data stored and then used for analysis? For example, which data were transcribed and why? Which modalities were captured? (see chapters by Antoniadou, this volume, and Moore & Llompart, this volume). The research should be clearly contextualized and all the relevant information which might affect the results obtained should be put forth. As the complexity of learning environments is becoming a more acknowledged aspect of research, MDA can help provide the researcher with a framework that attempts "to explain how discourse (with a small d), along with meditational means, reproduces and transforms *Discourses*; and how *Discourses* create, reproduce and transform the actions that individual social actors (or groups) can take at any given moment" (Jones & Norris, 2005, p. 10).

Chapter 6

Works cited

Antoniadou, V. (2017). Collecting, organizing and analyzing multimodal data sets: the contributions of CAQDAS. In E. Moore & M. Dooly (Eds), *Qualitative approaches to research on plurilingual education* (pp. 435-450). Research-publishing.net. https://doi.org/10.14705/rpnet.2017.emmd2016.640

Antoniadou, V., & Dooly, M. (2017). Educational ethnography in blended learning environments. In E. Moore & M. Dooly (Eds), *Qualitative approaches to research on plurilingual education* (pp. 237-263). Research-publishing.net. https://doi.org/10.14705/rpnet.2017.emmd2016.630

Barton, D., & Hamilton, M. (2000). Literacy practices. In D. Barton, M. Hamilton, & R. Ivanic (Eds), *Situated literacies: reading and writing in context* (pp. 7-16). London: Routledge.

Blackledge, A., Creese, A., & Kaur Takhi, J. (2013). Language, superdiversity and education. In I. Saint-Georges & J.-J. Weber (Eds), *Multilingualism and multimodality. Current challenges for educational studies* (pp. 59-80). Rotterdam/Boston/Taipei: Sense Publishers. https://doi.org/10.1007/978-94-6209-266-2_4

Canagarajah, S. (2007). Lingua franca English, multilingual communities, and language acquisition. *The Modern Language Journal, 91*(1), 923-939. https://doi.org/10.1111/j.1540-4781.2007.00678.x

Council of Europe. (2001). *Common European framework of reference for languages: learning, teaching and assessment*. Cambridge: Cambridge University Press.

Dooly, M., & Sadler, R. (2013). Filling in the gaps: linking theory and practice through telecollaboration in teacher education. *ReCALL, 25*(1), 4-29. https://doi.org/10.1017/S0958344012000237

Efimova, L., Hendrick, S., & Anjewierden, A. (2005). Finding 'the life between buildings': an approach for defining a weblog community. Paper presented at *Internet Research 6.0: Internet Generations*. Chicago. http://blog.mathemagenic.com/2005/10/07/aoir-finding-the-life-between-buildings-an-approach-for-defining-a-weblog-community/

GAPMIL (Global Alliance for Partnerships on Media and Information Literacy). (2014). *Paris declaration media and information literacy in the digital era*. Paris: UNESCO.

Jones, R. H. (2008). Technology, democracy and participation in space. In R. Wodak & V. Koller (Eds), *Handbook of communication in the public sphere* (pp. 429-446). Berlin: Mouton de Gruyter.

Jones, R. H., & Norris S. (2005). Discourse as action/discourse in action. In S. Norris & R. H. Jones (Eds), *Discourse in action: introduction to mediated discourse analysis* (pp. 3-14). London: Routledge.

Kramsch, C. (2006). From communicative competence to symbolic competence. *The Modern Language Journal, 90*(2), 249-252. https://doi.org/10.1111/j.1540-4781.2006.00395_3.x

Kress, G. (1998). Visual and verbal modes of representation in electronically mediated communication: the potentials of new forms of text. In I. Snyder (Ed.), *Page to screen: taking literacy into the electronic era* (pp. 53-79). London: Routledge. https://doi.org/10.4324/9780203201220_chapter_3

Kress, G., & van Leeuwen, T. (1996). *Reading images: the grammar of visual design*. New York: Routledge.

Lankshear, C. (1997). *Changing literacies*. Buckingham: Open University Press.

Masats, D. (2017). Conversation analysis at the service of research in the field of second language acquisition (CA-for-SLA). In E. Moore & M. Dooly (Eds), *Qualitative approaches to research on plurilingual education* (pp. 321-347). Research-publishing.net. https://doi.org/10.14705/rpnet.2017.emmd2016.633

Moore, E., & Llompart, J. (2017). Collecting, transcribing, analyzing and presenting plurilingual interactional data. In E. Moore & M. Dooly (Eds), *Qualitative approaches to research on plurilingual education* (pp. 403-417). Research-publishing.net. https://doi.org/10.14705/rpnet.2017.emmd2016.638

Nussbaum, L. (2017). Doing research with teachers. In E. Moore & M. Dooly (Eds), *Qualitative approaches to research on plurilingual education* (pp. 46-67). Research-publishing.net. https://doi.org/10.14705/rpnet.2017.emmd2016.621

Sawyer, R. K. (Ed.). (2006). *The Cambridge handbook of the learning sciences*. Cambridge: Cambridge University Press.

Scollon, R. (2000). Methodological interdiscursivity: an ethnographic understanding of unfinalisability. In S. Sarangi & M. Coulthard (Eds), *Discourse and social life* (pp. 138-154). London: Pearson Education Limited.

Scollon, R. (2001). *Mediated discourse: the nexus of practice*. London: Routledge. https://doi.org/10.4324/9780203420065

Scollon, S. (2005). Agency distributed through time, space and tools: Bentham, Babbage and the census. In S. Norris & R. H. Jones (Eds), *Discourse in action: introduction to mediated discourse analysis* (pp. 172-182). London: Routledge.

Scollon, R., & Scollon, S. W. (2004). *Nexus analysis: discourse and the emerging internet.* New York: Routledge.

Scollon, R., & Scollon, S. W. (2007). Nexus analysis: refocusing ethnography on action. *Journal of Sociolinguistics, 11*(5), 608-625. https://doi.org/10.1111/j.1467-9841.2007.00342.x

Seely Brown, J. (2008). Foreword: creating a culture of learning. In T. Iiyoshi & M. S. Vijay Kumar (Eds), *Opening up education. The collective advancement of education through open technology, open content, and open knowledge* (pp. xi-xvii). Cambridge, MA: MIT Press.

Street, B. V. (2000). Literacy events and literacy practices: theory and practice in the new literacy studies. In M. Martin-Jones & K. Jones (Eds), *Multilingual literacies: comparative perspectives on research and practice* (pp. 17-29). Amsterdam: John Benjamin.

Tarrow, S. (2005). *The new transnational activism.* Cambridge: Cambridge University Press. https://doi.org/10.1017/CBO9780511791055

Wenger, E. (1998). *Communities of practice: learning, meaning, and identity.* Cambridge: Cambridge University Press. https://doi.org/10.1017/CBO9780511803932

Wertsch, J. V. (1991). *Voices of the mind: a sociocultural approach to mediated action.* Cambridge, MA: Harvard University Press.

Wertsch, J. V. (1998). *Mind as action.* New York: Oxford University.

Wohlwend, K. (2013). Mediated discourse analysis: tracking discourse in action. In P. Albers, T. Holbrook, & A. Seely Flint (Eds), *New methods of literacy research* (pp. 56-69). Abingdon: Routledge.

Recommended reading

Norris, S., & Jones, R. H. (Eds.). (2005). *Discourse in action: introducing mediated discourse analysis.* London: Routledge.

Scollon, R. (2001). *Mediated discourse: the nexus of practice.* London: Routledge. https://doi.org/10.4324/9780203420065

Scollon, R., & Scollon, S. W. (2003). *Discourses in place: language in the material world.* London: Routledge. https://doi.org/10.4324/9780203422724

Appendix

Adapted from CA conventions (see Moore & Llompart, this volume):

(.) short pause
[1] approximately 1 second pause
[2] approximately 2 second pause
: elongation of sound
- cut-off word
WOrd emphasize on syllable or word
[word]
[word] overlapping
XXX unintelligible
(…) part of transcript left out
((WORD)) transcriber notes

6 Una aproximació a dades multimodals amb l'anàlisi del discurs mediat

Melinda Dooly[1]

Conceptes clau: multimodalitat, anàlisis del discurs mediat, anàlisi de nexe, comunicació mediada per ordinador, anàlisi d'interacció.

---

1. Introducció

Al mateix temps que la investigació en l'aprenentatge de llengües s'està traslladant més enllà de les quatre parets de l'aula, està creixent la consciència que l'ús del llenguatge (i l'aprenentatge) es dóna d'una manera cada vegada més complexa i interconnectada, especialment mitjançant l'ús de la tecnologia. "In the globalized era, transnational connections are thus increasingly 'taken to new levels' and 'shaped in new forms'"[2] (Tarrow, 2005, p. xiii). A mesura que l'eslògan del 'ciutadà global' esdevé més popular, hi ha un major reconeixement de la necessitat que les persones participatives i informades no només estiguin alfabetitzades tradicionalment, sinó que siguin adeptes d'una nova alfabetització sistèmica (Seely Brown, 2008, p. xi). Això és, també, el que Kramsch (2006, p. 251) ha anomenat "competència simbòlica" apropiada per a la "societat del coneixement" actual (vegeu la 'Declaració de Paris', del 2014, de la coalició GAPMIL). Kramsch (2006) utilitza el terme de competència simbòlica per referir-se a una capacitat bastant sofisticada de manipular els sistemes simbòlics, que inclouen moltes variants de les modalitats discursives (parlada, escrita, gestual, visual, electrònica, etc.). No obstant això, tal com assenyalen Blackledge, Creese, i Kaur Takhi (2013), hi ha una necessitat d'anar més

---

1. Universitat Autònoma de Barcelona, Bellaterra, Catalunya/Espanya; melindaann.dooly@uab.cat

2. "En l'era de la globalització, les connexions transnacionals es porten cada vegada a 'nous nivells' i adopten 'noves formes'" (Tarrow, 2005, p. xiii).

Per citar aquest capítol: Dooly, M. (2017). Una aproximació a dades multimodals amb l'anàlisi del discurs mediat. A E. Moore i M. Dooly (Eds), *Enfocaments qualitatius per a la recerca en educació plurilingüe* (p. 212-235). Research-publishing.net. https://doi.org/10.14705/rpnet.2017.emmd2016.629

enllà de l'aprofitament de les múltiples competències i els repertoris complexos dels estudiants plurilingües. Els docents (i les persones investigadores) han d'esforçar-se per fer visibles les tensions socials, individuals i culturals, i la creativitat que es deriven de la pertinença a múltiples comunitats. Això els proporciona un espai on els estudiants plurilingües poden fer servir les diverses veus que formen part de les múltiples comunitats de les quals són membres.

Aquesta nova manera d'entendre el fet d'estar alfabetitzat posa en primer pla el tema de la modalitat en qüestions de competència comunicativa (que és la base de la majoria dels enfocaments d'ensenyament de llengües a la UE; Consell d'Europa, 2001). Això, al seu torn, implica que la multimodalitat ha de tenir un paper substancial en la investigació sobre l'ensenyament i l'aprenentatge de llengües. A més, l'augment de la ubiqüitat de la multimèdia integrada i l'accés a Internet a les classes de llengua han contribuït de manera significativa a fer créixer l'interès acadèmic en les diverses complexitats semiòtiques de les representacions en els intercanvis discursius que tenen lloc en l'aprenentatge mixt (classes a l'aula combinades amb intercanvis en línia amb companys distribuïts geogràficament), així com en entorns d'aprenentatge de llengües no tradicionals (informals).

En concret, la investigació multimodal en l'educació se centra en com els estudiants construeixen el significat a partir de diverses formes de comunicació –la llengua, la imatge, la música, el so, el gest, el tacte i l'olor–, que són cada cop més presents (excepte el tacte i l'olfacte) a les interaccions d'aprenentatge en línia i mixt. Inevitablement, en aquest tipus d'investigació cal tractar amb una gran quantitat de dades que es deriva dels diversos recursos, cosa que pot ser un repte, ja que s'ha de trobar una manera coherent d'examinar dades complexes, que poden haver-se recollit amb formats molt diferents, però, que, al mateix temps, estan totes relacionades entre si en el procés d'aprenentatge. Les dades també poden haver-se recopilat en moments diferents i en orientacions espacials diverses (a l'aula, en línia, captures de pantalla dels entorns d'aprenentatge mixt, etc.). En altres paraules, s'ha de trobar una manera convincent de discutir i analitzar un corpus de dades complex, format per diferents materials i amb resultats possiblement diversos. Per exemple, el corpus pot consistir en les

Capítol 6

interaccions d'àudio i vídeo dels estudiants que es troben físicament a l'aula, mentre interactuen (a través d'àudio i vídeo) amb altres estudiants que no hi estan físicament presents (capturats a través d'un *screencast* i una càmera a la seva aula), per tant, la recollida de dades es pot triplicar o fins i tot quadruplicar. Llavors, aquestes dades es poden combinar amb dades en altres suports (impresos completats durant la negociació en línia d'una tasca, per exemple) per contribuir a un corpus encara més complex.

Evidentment, la multimodalitat és, i sempre ha estat, part de la creació de sentit, ja que els éssers humans sempre han utilitzat més que paraules escrites o parlades per comunicar-se. No obstant això, en la societat occidental, especialment en el context de l'educació, hi ha hagut un "dominance of writing as the means of communication and representation" (Kress, 1998, p. 58)[3], almenys fins fa poc. Això ha anat canviant en les últimes dècades, especialment a mesura que ha guanyat terreny l'ús dels ordinadors i Internet. En gran part, el canvi dels llibres a les pantalles ha contribuït a aquest desenvolupament, que ens ha portat "from print to post-print text cultures" (Lankshear, 1997, p. 1)[4], el que s'ha anomenat 'nou ordre comunicatiu' (Kress i van Leeuwen, 1996; Lankshear, 1997). De la mateixa manera, en el món de l'educació, els professionals de la llengua estan començant a integrar el concepte del 'nou ordre comunicatiu' en el seu ensenyament, reconeixent que les paraules, les imatges, el so, el tacte i altres característiques destacades de la comunicació són part d'un ampli espectre de les pràctiques i les competències comunicatives. Els docents reconeixen que els seus estudiants no només han d'estar ben informats d'aquestes pràctiques, sinó que han de dominar-les, per tal de poder participar en la societat del coneixement.

En aquest sentit, aquest capítol resumeix una investigació sobre les competències comunicatives en un entorn multimodal telecol·laboratiu, en què docents en formació van interactuar a través de diversos mitjans socials. L'estudi va ser publicat prèviament en Dooly i Sadler (2013) i s'ha concedit permís de l'editorial

---

3. "predomini de l'escriptura com a mitjà de comunicació i representació" (Kress, 1998, p. 58)

4. "d'una cultura d'impressió de text a una de post-impressió" (Lankshear, 1997, p. 1)

de la revista per utilitzar algunes de les seccions en aquest capítol. En aquest cas, els estudiants-docents són parlants plurilingües. La interacció es porta a terme en anglès, que no és la primera llengua de tots els usuaris. Una part dels participants són el que Canagarajah (2007) ha anomenat usuaris de l'anglès com a llengua franca (en anglès *Lingua Franca English*, LFE) i el seu ús de LFE i es negocia mútuament en les seves comunitats.

> "Both LFE speakers and [native speakers] have competence in their respective varieties, though there is no limit to the development of their proficiency through experience and time. The competence of LFE speakers is of course distinct. This competence for cross-language contact and hybrid codes derives from their multilingual life.
>
> Because of the diversity at the heart of this communicative medium, LFE is intersubjectively constructed in each specific context of interaction. The form of this English is negotiated by each set of speakers for their purposes" (Canagarajah, 2007, p. 925) [5].

L'enfocament de l'estudi en la forma en què es construeix i negocia l'anglès com a llengua franca en la interacció en línia, es basa en l'anàlisi del discurs mediat (ADM, *Mediated Discourse Analysis* o MDA en anglès), una metodologia d'investigació que deriva de l'anàlisi de nexe (*nexus analysis*, en anglès) (Scollon i Scollon, 2004, 2007). L'ús de l'ADM permet incloure diferents fonts de dades (recursos basats en text en línia, com ara wikis o fòrums, que es poden considerar com a productes més estàtics derivats d'un procés) amb diverses dades d'interacció, per fer un seguiment de les accions socials que enllacen els processos d'aprenentatge en línia i fora de línia.

---

5. "Tant els parlants d'anglès com a llengua franca com els parlants nadius tenen competència en les seves varietats respectives, encara que no hi ha límit per desenvolupar la seva competència a través de l'experiència i el temps. La competència dels parlants d'anglès com a llengua franca és, evidentment, diferent. Aquesta competència de contacte interlingüístic i codis híbrids deriva de la seva vida plurilingüe.

A causa de la diversitat en el si d'aquest mitjà comunicatiu, l'anglès com a llengua franca es construeix intersubjectivament en cada context específic d'interacció. Cada conjunt de parlants negocia la forma d'aquest anglès per als seus propòsits" (Canagarajah, 2007, p. 925).

2. L'anàlisi del discurs mediat

L'anàlisi del discurs mediat (R. Scollon, 2001; S. Scollon, 2005) es basa en la premissa que els actors es socialitzen de maneres diverses i en diferent mesura a través dels sistemes de discurs en què participen, i que cada sistema es diferencia de l'altre per les seves pràctiques incorporades (Scollon i Scollon, 2004). Aquest tipus d'anàlisi ofereix una estratègia per combinar l'etnografia, l'anàlisi de la conversa (vegeu Masats, en aquest volum, i Nussbaum, en aquest volum) i l'anàlisi del discurs (vegeu Antoniadou i Dooly, en aquest volum), i proporciona una explicació teòrica de com els participants, el context, els discursos i els objectes (artefactes) faciliten l'acció i el canvi social de forma recíproca. L'ADM (com s'ha dit anteriorment, de vegades es diu anàlisi de nexe, Scollon i Scollon, 2004; Wohlwend, 2013) ofereix una manera per explorar com es relacionen múltiples aspectes de l'acció social complexa entre si a través de la variació d'interaccions discursives, en lloc de centrar l'anàlisi en un sol component del discurs aïllat.

L'ADM utilitza la 'interdiscursivitat metodològica' (Scollon, 2000); és a dir, que integra múltiples enfocaments per recollir i analitzar les dades (paisatgisme lingüístic, anàlisi multimodal, anàlisi del discurs, observacions etnogràfiques, entrevistes sociolingüístiques, etc.) per tal d'enfortir els possibles punts dèbils de les metodologies que s'usen. L'enfocament ADM destaca la forma en què es permeten les accions individuals i com es fan intel·ligibles mitjançant el context dels participants, que inclou les històries individuals, juntament amb els discursos sociohistòrics i l'organització de la interacció en què es produeix l'acció. Com a part de l'enfocament, el 'nexe' pot entendre's com un 'espai de compromís', on l'acció social es veu facilitada per un conjunt de processos socials, com ara discursos situats (discursos amb què els participants estaran familiaritzats), accions històriques observables (experiències personals i col·lectives que poden documentar-se, per exemple, el contingut de la classe anterior), i l'ordre de la interacció (pràctiques socials d'interacció, com les configuracions de professor-estudiant). Això es reflecteix en la Figura 1. En altres paraules, l'ADM permet que l'investigador teixeixi una anàlisi informada d'un espai de compromís concret que pren en consideració els processos socials del context que són rellevants per a la interacció (per exemple, un text d'un xat en línia) o el producte (per exemple, wiki) que s'està analitzant.

Figura 1. Espai de compromís (acció social), basat en Scollon i Scollon (2004)

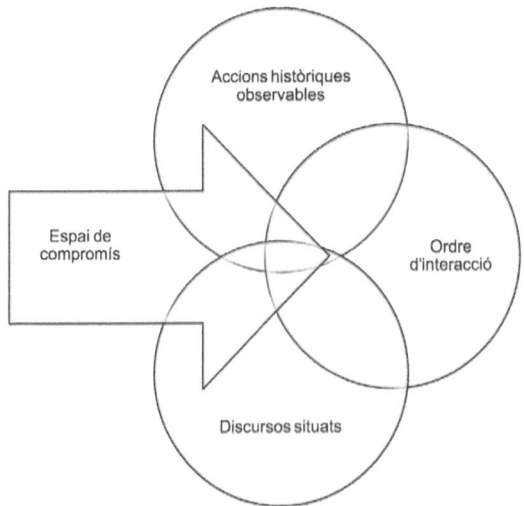

Aquesta seqüenciació analítica de les activitats durant un període prolongat de temps permet identificar una acció significativa transmesa en un context de discursos que són pertinents per a l'estudi (cicles de discurs, discursos dominants que poden ser oberts o en segon pla, o interioritzats com a pràctiques, etc.). També permet accedir als moments d'interacció, quan les trajectòries històriques dels participants 'coincideixen' en una instància de l'acció social i aquesta acció social altera les trajectòries històriques.

L'ADM (també anomenat anàlisi de nexe) s'atribueix principalment a dos etnògrafs lingüístics americans: Ron i Suzie Scollon. Aquests dos acadèmics van començar a examinar els cicles semiòtics de persones, objectes i discursos, mentre duien a terme una investigació a Alaska a principis dels vuitanta del segle passat; ja el 1981 observaven l'ús emergent d'Internet amb finalitats educatives. D'acord amb Jones i Norris (2005), aquest enfocament investiga el rol que poden exercir els textos (orals o escrits) en les accions que emprenen els actors socials, d'una banda, i com aquests mateixos textos apareixen com els resultats dels processos d'interacció social, per l'altra banda. L'enfocament es basa en observacions personals de Ron Scollon sobre la influència dels mitjans de comunicació en les persones del seu voltant (especialment, en relació amb l'augment de la violència a la guerra del Vietnam), que va ser seguida per l'interès dels dos acadèmics en les interseccions de les diferents pràctiques discursives en les trajectòries individuals.

Aquest enfocament permet seguir els discursos a través de gèneres discursius diversos per tal de comprendre millor la interrelació de la llengua (o les llengües), i altres dades semiòtiques i socials. A mesura que s'ha anat desenvolupant, els investigadors han incorporat diversos marcs. Es poden trobar exemples que utilitzen la sociolingüística interaccional, l'anàlisi de la conversa, la lingüística antropològica o l'etnografia de la comunicació, l'anàlisi crítica del discurs, la teoria de l'acció i l'activitat mediada, la semiòtica social, l'anàlisi del discurs multimodal, i els nous estudis de literacitat. La flexibilitat de l'enfocament es basa en la idea que tractar temes socials, longitudinals i complexos (com l'ensenyament de llengües) exigeix enfocaments igual de complexos; un enfocament unidimensional simple no és suficient per destacar el nexe entre l'actor i pràctiques socials.

3. L'estudi: desenvolupant el repertori del professorat en espais de compromís

3.1. Recollida de dades

Partint d'una perspectiva de l'etnogràfica educativa, es van recollir dades per tal d'explorar el desenvolupament docent durant un intercanvi telecol·laboratiu que va durar un any entre estudiants-docents ubicats a Espanya i als EUA (vegeu el capítol d'Antoniadou i Dooly, en aquest volum sobre una investigació multimodal similar). Es van repetir les mateixes activitats dues vegades al llarg d'un període de dos anys. En tots dos anys, en el primer semestre, els estudiants-docents van treballar en grups petits en línia per proporcionar retroalimentació i crítica constructiva a una Seqüència Didàctica (SD) individual dels membres del grup perquè la poguessin implementar durant les pràctiques a les escoles; cada grup de col·laboració de 3-4 estudiants incloïa membres de totes dues universitats. Les activitats en el primer semestre van incloure:

- Una activitat per trencar el gel, que consistia en una presentació personal breu a través de la plataforma de presentació en línia Voicethread, que els altres estudiants havien de comentar.

- Una pluja d'idees (en un fòrum en línia) per a les seqüències didàctiques amb la finalitat de formar grups en línia més petits, basats en interessos i/o contextos comuns de les activitats d'intercanvi d'idees.

- Un wiki en què es van compartir els primers esborranys de les seqüències didàctiques (es va utilitzar Zoho).

- Discussions en línia en grups petits per fer comentaris i suggeriments a la SD.

- Reunions per fer discussions similars i retroalimentació, que van tenir com a resultat els esborranys 2 i 3, i el projecte final.

- Reflexions compartides sobre els canvis en el disseny de la SD i la justificació dels canvis.

Per a les reunions en línia, cada grup podia decidir la modalitat –xat amb text o àudio– i el calendari, ja que un dels objectius implícits era aconseguir que els estudiants practiquessin amb tantes eines tecnològiques com fos possible. Per tant, els estudiants-docents van poder treballar amb els tallers cara a cara, una sèrie de plataformes de comunicació mediada per ordinador (per exemple, Skype, Google Hangouts), però els mateixos estudiants van decidir què era el que s'adaptava millor a les seves necessitats. Es va demanar als estudiants-docents que mantinguessin un registre de les seves reunions (transcripcions de text o arxius d'àudio), que va acabar sent en un component del portafolis docent final (i part del corpus de dades).

En el segon semestre, es va demanar als estudiants-docents que treballessin junts per dissenyar i desenvolupar podcasts i altres activitats educatives. Treballant en grups, es va proporcionar als estudiants-docents espais virtuals i eines per fer reunions, aquest cop en un món virtual (Second Life). Els grups van treballar junts per crear un podcast i activitats educatives que hi estaven relacionades (per fer abans, durant i després), tot i que hi havia diferents líders segons les tasques, depenent de l'experiència individual (tecnològica, pedagògica, etc.). Durant el segon semestre es van incloure les activitats següents:

- Una 'gimcana' al món virtual Second Life perquè els estudiants-docents es familiaritzessin amb l'entorn (també va servir perquè els nous grups es coneguessin els uns als altres).

- Introducció a les 'sales de reunions' de Second Life, que és on es va recomanar als membres que es reunissin per treballar en els podcasts (no era obligatori).

- Preselecció d'esborranys de podcast al cinema 'a l'aire lliure' de Second Life (durant un període determinat, els individus podien passar i deixar les seves observacions a la bústia de Second Life).

- Presentacions dels podcasts finals al cinema de Second Life (sessió de grup sencer).

- Aplicació de les activitats docents del podcast (només estudiants catalans).

- Debat i reflexió sobre el desenvolupament i l'aplicació del podcast a la zona de grup de Second Life (seguits per una 'festa de comiat' a Second Life).

El corpus de dades es compon de productes en línia (wikis utilitzats com un informe de la reflexió digital, captures de pantalla de les interaccions de grup al món virtual, missatges al fòrum, documents compartits de seqüències didàctiques programades pels estudiants-docents) i dades d'interacció (gravacions i transcripcions de les classes cara a cara, intercanvi de correus electrònics entre els estudiants agrupats, text gravat i transcrit dels xats d'àudio i per escrit entre els estudiants i els grups a Second Life), juntament amb productes complementaris dels objectius personals d'aprenentatge dels estudiants (escanejats), fulls d'autoavaluació (escanejats), programes de classe i notes de camp.

El corpus de dades inclou diferents formats de transcripció a causa dels diferents mitjans que els participants tenien a la seva disposició. Per exemple, els xats d'àudio/vídeo poden haver-se enregistrat només com a àudios (els estudiants van decidir com documentaven les seves interaccions). En aquest cas, la investigadora va fer una transcripció de l'enregistrament d'àudio. L'elecció de fer una transcripció estreta o ampla depenia de l'objectiu de la investigació. En el cas dels xats de text, les transcripcions només es van alterar per introduir el nombre de torn (si la transcripció no els proporcionava com era el cas del xat de text de Second Life) i per canviar els noms dels participants. L'entrega de les transcripcions es descriu en més detall per a cada fragment a continuació.

3.2. Resum de l'enfocament

En aquest estudi, l'acció social va consistir en pràctiques dissenyades per promoure el procés de professionalització de docents novells a través de cursos d'educació mitjançant noves tecnologies. Aquesta acció social s'interrelaciona amb discursos i procediments que poden limitar o facilitar l'acció. Cal tenir en compte que l'estudi es va centrar només en el discurs rellevant per a la professionalització docent i que els participants van fer rellevant i observable; per exemple, amb referències específiques a recursos docents, coneixement específic docent o l'ús del què es podria anomenar 'repertori docent'. Els 'espais de compromís' que es van estudiar també estan interconnectats amb l'ordre d'interacció (com els participants s'organitzen en un xat en línia, per exemple). D'aquesta manera, l'anàlisi podria incloure la forma en què les persones implicades van organitzar l'esdeveniment social (per exemple, assumir el paper d'expert al xat).

L'anàlisi de la interacció social que es porta a terme en un 'espai de compromís' (Figura 2) va permetre que la investigadora trobés rastres del que Scollon i Scollon (2004) anomenen 'cossos històrics' (experiències discursives personals i col·lectives que els participants converteixen en rellevants en la interacció social, com els debats a classe), així com 'discursos situats' (és a dir, pràctiques discursives que són familiars, com la 'parla del docent'), juntament amb l'ordre d'interacció en què els participants s'organitzen (per exemple, prenent el paper de persona col·laboradora o docent).

Figura 2. Visualització dels espais de compromís

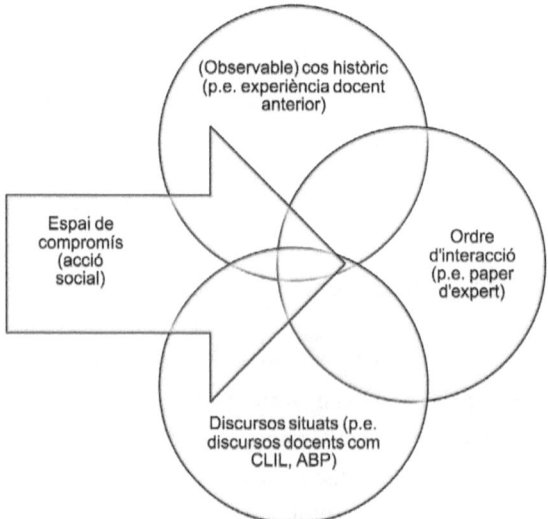

La investigació examina la manera en què les pràctiques del discurs creen 'discurs docent' a les Comunitats de Pràctica (CP, Wenger, 1998) dels docents i com els estudiants-docents retransmeten aquest discurs en la seva construcció del coneixement durant el procés de convertir-se en membres de ple dret d'aquesta comunitat professional. Com que l'ordre d'interacció dels productes en línia no era observable de forma immediata (per exemple, l'acció real d'escriure i contestar en un fòrum), l'ADM va permetre que aquestes accions es consideressin com a traces o artefactes (per exemple, la iniciació dels fils de conversa o les respostes al fòrum) que es deixen, i que, per tant, mostren les traces de "communication and community through permalinked posts, comments, and reference" (Efimova, Hendrick, i Anjewierden, 2005, p. 24)[6].

3.3. Ordre d'interacció i discursos situats: parlar com un professor

El disseny de les activitats intensives va fomentar la discussió en línia sobre les seqüències didàctiques individuals, com es veu en la transcripció de més avall, on la Clara (de Catalunya) fa comentaris a la seva parella Lynn (als EUA). Els estudiants utilitzen un programa de VoIP (Voice over Internet Protocol; veu sobre protocol d'internet), anomenat Skype, en el qual van gravar els seus intercanvis.

En la transcripció següent (que es reprodueix aquí amb el permís explícit i per escrit dels participants), es pot veure com els estudiants-docents van fer rellevants en la seva interacció social els discursos als quals havien estat exposats durant els seus cursos sobre metodologia de l'ensenyament de llengua. En altres paraules, fan circular les diverses veus que es troben en les múltiples comunitats plurilingües, de les quals són membres (Blackledge et al., 2013), i que inclouen la comunitat professional docent. El 'cos històric' d'experiències anteriors docent-estudiant forma un nexe amb els 'discursos situats' (repertori docent d'enfocaments d'ensenyament de llengües específics) dins l'"espai de compromís' de la sessió de retroalimentació VoIP: el discurs és part del discurs mediat per a la retroalimentació dels participants.

En particular, la Clara fa referència a conceptes de competències i a l'Aprenentatge Integrat de Continguts i Llengües Estrangeres (AICLE); assenyala la necessitat de proporcionar uns objectius definits clarament i, per acabar, comparteix la idea de la interacció en línia basada en projectes com

---

6. "la comunicació i la comunitat a través de missatges permalinked, comentaris i referències" (Efimova et al., 2005, p. 24).

a resultat final. Totes aquestes nocions (aprenentatge basat en competències; derivats d'ensenyament de llengües comunicatiu, com AICLE i l'aprenentatge de llengües basat en projectes; la importància dels objectius clars per a l'avaluació contínua i basada en competències) van ser els temes clau que s'havien tractat i desenvolupat al llarg de l'any, en els cursos cara a cara, mentre que l'intercanvi es va dur a terme en línia (segons els programes de classes i notes de camp).

Els mateixos estudiants van enregistrar les dades durant les reunions en línia i, després, van decidir quines dades estaven disposats a presentar (podien esborrar les dades que volguessin). Les limitacions del programari en el moment de gravació només van permetre enregistrar en format àudio (format mp3), però, encara que només estava disponible per a l'anàlisi la interacció d'àudio, els participants van tenir accés visual a les seves parelles, com es veu a la pantalla a través de la finestra del programari de Skype. Els estudiants van presentar les dades que van seleccionar a la investigadora en arxius d'àudio a través d'una carpeta en núvol. Totes les dades en brut van anonimitzar-se abans de començar l'anàlisi. A diferència d'altres plantejaments del discurs d'aquest volum, la transcripció utilitza només algunes convencions de l'anàlisi de la conversa (vegeu l'annex per a la llegenda de la transcripció). En general, es va utilitzar una transcripció àmplia per tal de donar informació, sobretot, de les paraules parlades, la qualitat de transició dels torns de paula i les pauses notables (Sawyer, 2006; vegeu també Moore i Llompart, en aquest volum).

Fragment 1

1.	Clara:	ok [1] ok great (.) so i wrote that i thought about give you some feedback about your draft and i had three main ideas that i would like to comment with you
2.	Lynn:	ah that's XXX
3.	Clara:	it's that you can pras- practice reading comprehension and at the same time to: to work with certain learning i mean to learn something else (.) i mean to connect here in spain we've got uhm curriculum competences [2] yes here in spain we are working with competences and (.) and we can connect the english language with another subject for instance science
4.	Clara:	[and]

5.	Lynn:	[Ah I see]
6.	Clara:	it's i i thought that you could work the reading comprehension related with another subject (.) for instance history (.) and so on (.) to be more connected with them
7.	Lynn:	mmmm
8.	Lynn:	yeah yeah i see
(…)		
25.	Clara:	ok nice
26.	Lynn:	yeah that's a great idea thank you
27.	Clara:	(laughs) you're welcome (.) another thing that i thought that you could explain them what they are going to learn during these sequences because in your draft in the in the interaction i didn't see that you you wrote about how to to explain what the students will be able to do or what they are going to do during these teaching sequences so i thought that it could be a good idea for them to explain what they are going to achieve during these session (.) or not?
(…)		
35.	Clara:	the objectives (.) i mean do you have you seen my dropbox
36.	Lynn:	yeah i i saw yours
37.	Clara:	ah you tell me to think about your objectives no (1)
38.	Lynn:	ahm ahm i mean do you have any suggestion for my draft as for objectives?
39.	Clara:	objectives i mean so students will be able to (.) to umpreh comprehend different reading texts
40.	Lynn:	ah: i see ok yeah that would be great
41.	Clara:	Students will be able to (.) i don't know
42.	Lynn:	((laughs)) ok that sounds yeah oh good fine
43.	Clara:	((laughs)) what else what else you could prepare this ah also in your final i don't know session i thought that it could be a good a great idea if you could prepare a unit to collaborate on a project with another school from for example spain (.) and these schools would have to deal a reading text about a topic they could do it in pairs and then each pair will have a a peer assigned for the other i don't know how to (.) i'm reading i mean in this sess- the last session i mean all your teaching sequences will be focused like to building a project with another school and to share information
44.	Lynn:	i know what you mean when you say another school another school abroad
45.	Clara:	yeah
46.	Lynn:	ah i see: (.) just like us
Xat en línia: Comentaris en línia dels companys sobre les seqüències didàctiques		

En aquest fragment, igual que en el següent (fragment 2; xat de text), l'ADM subratlla la 'retransmissió' dels participants dels 'discursos situats'. Per exemple, en tots els espais de compromís que s'inclouen, s'ha trobat el terme 'SWBAT'. SWBAT és un acrònim que significa *students will be able to* (els estudiants seran capaços de) i el va introduir per primera vegada al discurs de nexe el professor dels EUA a les sessions cara a cara a començaments d'any. Els seus estudiants-docents es van apropiar del terme i el van ensenyar als estudiants-docents catalans en el seu intercanvi en línia (es va trobar evidència d'això en diverses de les transcripcions en línia, però per qüestions de brevetat no s'inclouen aquí). En el fragment anterior, al torn 39, la Clara (l'estudiant-docent de Catalunya) usa el terme SWBAT per assenyalar que el seu company no ha descrit amb claredat els objectius d'aprenentatge de la SD, "objectives I mean so students will be able to (.) to umpreh comprehend different reading texts". Torna a fer servir el terme al torn 41.

Al fragment següent, igual que al xat oral, els estudiants eren responsables de desar les transcripcions de les seves converses de text i enviar els documents de text als docents com a evidència de les activitats en línia. La manera més habitual dels estudiants de fer-ho era copiant tota la sessió de xat i enganxant-la en un document de Word. En aquest fragment, el Jazz (dels EUA) i la Sara (d'Espanya) debaten, també, els objectius, encara que en aquest cas ho fan en relació amb la planificació del seu podcast que fan col·laborativament, i el terme SWBAT apareix al torn 20 (fragment 2). Els dos estudiants es troben a Second Life, però la Sara tenia problemes amb el seu xat d'àudio de manera que havien passat a fer servir el xat de text (també disponible a SL). En el fragment analitzat a continuació, la Sara dóna més detalls sobre la relació entre SWBAT i les diferents parts de l'activitat al torn 24 i, finalment, al torn 26 indica la connexió directa entre els objectius i les activitats posteriors que estan dissenyant per al podcast.

L'ADM també posa en relleu com s'organitzen els participants (en aquest cas, el Jazz, dels EUA, i la Sara, de Catalunya) per a la interacció social durant la planificació del podcast a Second Life. Tots dos participants s'identifiquen clarament amb els 'grups d'activitats' simulats (estan d'acord amb la tasca), i tots dos posen en joc la 'parla docent' (per exemple, els objectius, el tema, l'activitat anterior, la introducció i les activitats relacionades, les activitats segons l'edat, etc.); la qual cosa és molt similar a l'extracte anterior de la sessió de retroalimentació de la SD. En el cas de les transcripcions de converses de text, la investigadora no va fer cap modificació, excepte per afegir números de torn i canviar els noms d'usuari del xat.

Fragment 2

1.	[12:10] Jazz:	We can use the pod cast as a pre activity
2.	[12:10] Sara:	yes yes
3.	[12:10] Jazz:	I mean we can do it for children. If we are going to use English
4.	[12:11] Sara:	I think the podcast should be like an intro and then we can do activities related to it
5.	[12:11] Jazz:	I can find native speakers of english easily
6.	[12:11] Janet:	yes
7.	[12:11] Sara:	yes children but what age???
8.	[12:12] Jazz:	Yes, I was thinking that it could be use for introduce vocabulary.
9.	[12:12] Jazz:	The age that works for use.
10.	(...)	
11.	[12:20] Jazz:	We can introduce some words with pictures. Put them voice and text.
12.	[12:20] Sara:	ok
13.	[12:20] Jazz:	Then do a short conversation example of using those words
14.	[12:20] Sara:	and the teacher goals are...
15.	[12:21] Sara:	Are the teacher goals and the objectives the same?
16.	[12:21] Jazz:	Prepared the students with the vocabulary necessary in order to complete the classroom activities.
17.	[12:21] Janet:	u mean the objectives?
18.	[12:21] Janet:	ok
19.	[12:22] Jazz:	With this vocabulary you can teach past tense, present tense or future.
20.	[12:22] Sara:	goals refers to what the T expects? and objectives is related to the SWBAT's?
21.	(...)	
22.	[12:42] Sara:	then the objectives (what we expect children to do by watching and listening to the podcast) could be the following
23.	[12:42] Jazz:	About the second one, is going to depend of how we design the posd cast

24.	[12:43] Sara:	SWBAT: 1)comprehension; 2) repdroduction (imitation) and finally 3) production
25.	[12:43] Jazz:	Thank you Sara
26.	[12:43] Sara:	the objectives go according to the postactivities
Pluja d'idees sobre el tema i el contingut del podcast en un xat per escrit a Second Life		

El discurs transmès dels participants incloïa una cultura docent compartida (o 'cicles del discurs'), com demostra l'argot similar, els temes, etc., que els participants van destacar durant la seva interacció al món virtual. Els trets que destaquen els estudiants-docents en el seu discurs en línia es basen en els aspectes comuns que semblen atribuir a tot el grup, per exemple, la 'identitat docent'. Aquesta identitat 'compartida' de 'docent' a la comunitat virtual els va permetre formar una cohesió, ja que era més important que les altres identitats possibles (per exemple, estudiant d'intercanvi, coreà, mare, esposa, germana, etc.). Això és evident en la forma en què la major part del seu discurs en línia s'alinea amb la 'parla docent', fins i tot l'apropiació de SWBAT com a part dels 'discursos situats'. Això sembla indicar una internalització gradual de nexe de la pràctica a mesura que els participants s'alineen amb la comunitat de professionals docents (Wenger, 1998).

En el fragment següent (3) els participants fan que el terme sigui particularment rellevant quan apliquen la metareflexió per extreure'n la seva definició (en termes lingüístics) i, també, per construir conjuntament una comprensió més completa del significat, tal com s'aplica al seu coneixement del professor. (Igual que al fragment 2, l'investigador ha canviat els noms dels usuaris del xat. El marc temporal és part de la transcripció original del text del xat).

Fragment 3

[8:03] Lan@! dice:	and what will you assess while they're doing their presentation? will you do the posters in a cardboard format or it's better to use ICT (powerpoint presentation, for example)?
[8:03] Evelyn dice:	Lana, I really like your SWBAT as a list of activities, but the idea behind SWBAT is more to talk about what students will be able to do linguistically and this is how you can assess them

[8:04] Chu dice:	you can make assessing standard for exmaple, content, how clear...
[8:04] Lan@! dice:	that's another interesting point I've borrowed from you (SWABTS)
[8:04] Imogene dice:	you're welcome
[8:04] Lan@! dice:	so poster format?
[8:04] Evelyn dice:	But SWBAT is more like, "students will be able to use key english phrases in presenting a poster about their favorite sport." the language use is the key part of SWBAT
[8:05] Lan@! dice:	Thanks for the clarification! is good to have USA peers
Lan@!, Evelyn i Chu (participants) comenten la SD al xat en text	

Arran dels 'espais de compromís' anteriors, el següent artefacte (part de l'autoavaluació dels estudiants sobre les competències adquirides a través de l'experiència en línia) és un exemple especialment interessant de la internalització gradual del discurs que pertany al nexe de pràctica i la forma en què la comunitat de pràctica virtual va contribuir a la cognició socialment distribuïda dels nous participants (Figura 3). El terme SWBAT apareix explícitament com una de les competències assimilades a través de l'entorn de suport de l'intercanvi telecol·laboratiu.

Figura 3. Avaluació de les competències assimilades de l'estudiant-docent

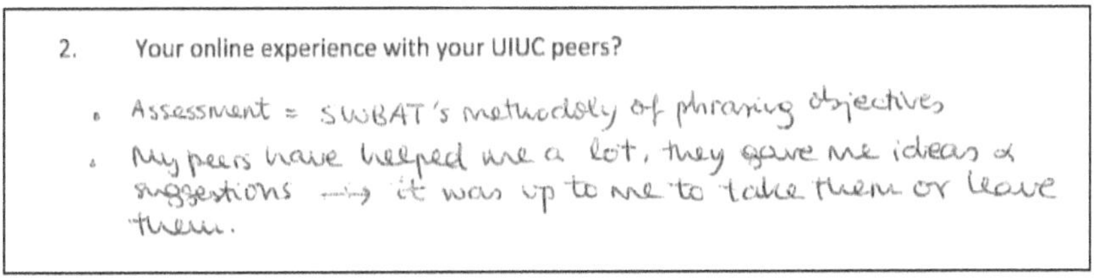

> 2. Your online experience with your UIUC peers?
> - Assessment = SWBAT's methodoly of phrasing objectives
> - My peers have helped me a lot, they gave me ideas of suggestions → it was up to me to take them or leave them.

Aquest capítol és un exemple de com es pot aplicar l'ADM a corpus de dades multimodals amb un enfocament en el nexe de pràctica, no només dels discursos i les persones, sinó també dels conceptes i artefactes. Això permet que la persona investigadora rastregi els discursos a través de gèneres diversos per tal d'entendre millor la interrelació de la llengua (o llengües) i altres dades de la semiòtica social; com en aquest cas en què els docents se socialitzen cap a la seva professió a través de diferents discursos situats (Figura 4). Podem veure com els estudiants-docents estan exposats a discursos situats i hi participen (en aquest cas, l'argot educatiu específic lligat al coneixement conceptual necessari per a docents de llengües per planificar i dissenyar seqüències didàctiques eficaces). L'aplicació de l'ADM ofereix l'oportunitat d'explotar els vincles entre els esdeveniments a múltiples espais de compromís en comptes de mirar conjunts de dades dispars com a esdeveniments dispars i aïllades.

Figura 4. Seguiment del discurs a través de gèneres diversos

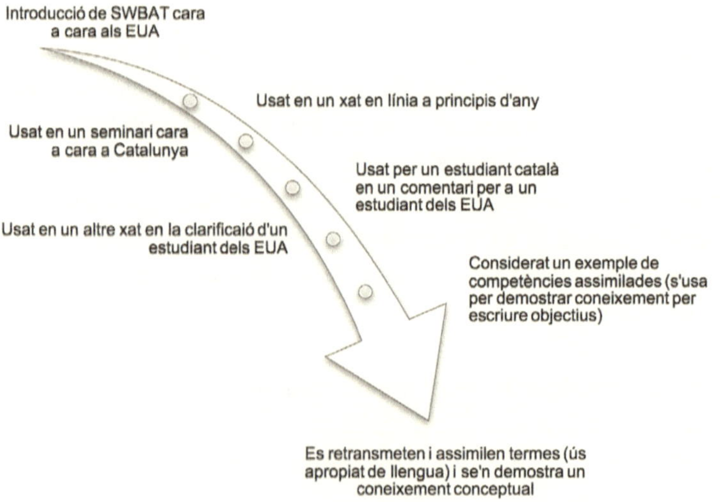

4. Conclusions

L'anàlisi del discurs mediat proporciona un enfocament útil per al seguiment de la complexitat de literacitats múltiples en contextos superposats, que inclouen l'aprenentatge mixt i un entorn en línia, alhora que proporciona una bona manera d'analitzar una sèrie de discursos quan convergeixen en espais de compromís. L'enfocament pot servir com un mitjà d'extreure les traces de discursos integrats que es creuen amb els participants en els moments del procés d'aprenentatge per tal d'identificar millor dels casos concrets de literacitat que es produeixen a través de diverses modalitats.

L'ús de l'ADM destaca una comprensió de la literacitat com una pràctica social (Barton i Hamilton, 2000; Street, 2000) i, al mateix temps, permet una tensió intricada entre el nexe de l'estudiant (agent) i les pràctiques discursives com a instruments de transmissió (Wertsch, 1991, 1998), tenint en compte la relació entre la llengua i l'acció: l'ADM entén l'ús del llenguatge com una acció (no només com un producte) que es relaciona amb altres formes d'acció humana i altres pràctiques discursives. Per tant, l'investigador pot veure com es relacionen les cadenes lligades a accions transmeses i esdeveniments d'interacció a través de contextos amb les pràctiques socials dins d'un nexe de pràctica més ampli.

Quan es treballa amb dades d'Internet (per exemple, mirant a les comunitats de pràctica creades a través de fòrums, wikis, xats de text i àudio, etc.), l'ADM proposa que és molt important tenir en compte les accions socials que hi ha darrere de la producció dels *outputs*, no només analitzar els productes. L'anàlisi dels espais de compromís, un cop transferits fora del seu 'entorn' (per exemple, captures de pantalles de les entrades del bloc), inevitablement, converteixen les dades en molt més estàtiques del que eren en el seu format original. Això pot fer que l'investigador se centri en els aspectes menys dinàmics de les dades en lloc d'en el procés de la seva producció i la forma en què entren en joc diferents recursos semiòtics en aquest procés. L'ADM concep Internet com un ciberespai que consisteix en "a collection of multiple overlapping spaces, virtual, geographical and physical, which accommodate multiple 'forms of life' and communicative possibilities" (Jones, 2008, p. 436)[7]. És important que l'investigador tingui en compte que no només està buscant en diversos espais visibles a la pantalla dels usuaris, sinó que, de fet, són pràctiques socials vinculades al món físic i virtual.

---

7. "una col·lecció d'espais múltiples superposats, virtuals, geogràfics i físics, que s'adapten a múltiples 'formes de vida' i a les possibilitats comunicatives" (Jones, 2008, p. 436).

Capítol 6

A causa de la complexitat de les dades multimodals i la seva anàlisi, la persona investigadora ha d'intentar fer que la seva anàlisi es pugui seguir de forma detallada i que es pugui inspeccionar tan fàcilment com sigui possible. Quan es considera la millor manera de recollir i presentar les dades, s'ha de tenir en compte que el mostreig no necessàriament ha de ser seqüencial –pot ser aleatori. No obstant això, s'ha d'oferir una justificació clara sobre l'elecció, juntament amb una explicació de la recollida de dades, i és preferible que es faci un mínim esforç perquè sigui representativa de la major quantitat d'espais vinculats com sigui possible. La transparència de la recollida i la gestió de dades també són vitals: com es van emmagatzemar les dades i com es van utilitzar per a l'anàlisi? Quines dades es van transcriure i per què? Quines modalitats es van capturar? (Vegeu els capítols d'Antoniadou, en aquest volum, i Moore i Llompart, en aquest volum). La investigació s'ha de contextualitzar clarament i s'ha d'oferir tota la informació rellevant que pugui afectar els resultats. A mesura que la complexitat dels entorns d'aprenentatge s'està convertint en un aspecte més reconegut de la investigació, l'ADM pot ajudar a proporcionar a les persones investigadores un marc que intenta "to explain how discourse (with a small d), along with meditational means, reproduces and transforms *Discourses*; and how *Discourses* create, reproduce and transform the actions that individual social actors (or groups) can take at any given moment" (Jones i Norris, 2005, p. 10)[8].

Obres citades

Antoniadou, V. (2017). Recoger, organizar y analizar corpus de datos multimodales: las contribuciones de los CAQDAS. A E. Moore i M. Dooly (Eds), *Enfocaments qualitatius per a la recerca en educació plurilingüe* (p. 451-467). Research-publishing.net. https://doi.org/10.14705/rpnet.2017.emmd2016.641

Antoniadou, V., i Dooly, M. (2017). Etnografia educativa en contextos d'aprenentatge mixt. A E. Moore i M. Dooly (Eds), *Enfocaments qualitatius per a la recerca en educació plurilingüe* (p. 264-292). Research-publishing.net. https://doi.org/10.14705/rpnet.2017.emmd2016.631

---

8. "explicar com el discurs (amb d minúscula), juntament amb els mitjans de transmissió, es reprodueix i transforma els Discursos, i com els Discursos creen, reprodueixen i transformen les accions que els actors socials individuals (o grups) poden prendre en un moment donat" (Jones i Norris, 2005, p. 10).

Barton, D., i Hamilton, M. (2000). Literacy practices. A D. Barton, M. Hamilton, i R. Ivanic (Eds), *Situated literacies: reading and writing in context* (p. 7-16). Londres: Routledge.

Blackledge, A., Creese, A., i Kaur Takhi, J. (2013). Language, superdiversity and education. A I. Saint-Georges i J.-J. Weber (Eds), *Multilingualism and multimodality. Current challenges for educational studies* (p. 59-80). Rotterdam/Boston/Taipei: Sense Publishers.

Canagarajah, S. (2007). Lingua franca English, multilingual communities, and language acquisition. *The Modern Language Journal, 91*(1), 923-939. https://doi.org/10.1111/j.1540-4781.2007.00678.x

Council of Europe. (2001). *Common European framework of reference for languages: learning, teaching and assessment.* Cambridge: Cambridge University Press.

Dooly, M., i Sadler, R. (2013). Filling in the gaps: linking theory and practice through telecollaboration in teacher education. *ReCALL, 25*(1), 4-29. https://doi.org/10.1017/S0958344012000237

Efimova, L., Hendrick, S., i Anjewierden, A. (2005). Finding 'the life between buildings': an approach for defining a weblog community. Comunicació presentada a *Internet Research 6.0: Internet Generations.* Chicago. http://blog.mathemagenic.com/2005/10/07/aoir-finding-the-life-between-buildings-an-approach-for-defining-a-weblog-community/

GAPMIL (Global Alliance for Partnerships on Media and Information Literacy). (2014). *Paris declaration media and information literacy in the digital era.* París: UNESCO.

Jones, R. H. (2008). Technology, democracy and participation in space. A R. Wodak i V. Koller (Eds), *Handbook of communication in the public sphere* (p. 429-446). Berlín: Mouton de Gruyter.

Jones, R. H., i Norris S. (2005). Discourse as action/discourse in action. Dins S. Norris i R. H. Jones (Eds), *Discourse in action: introduction to mediated discourse analysis* (p. 3-14). Londres: Routledge.

Kramsch, C. (2006). From communicative competence to symbolic competence. *The Modern Language Journal, 90*(2), 249-252. https://doi.org/10.1111/j.1540-4781.2006.00395_3.x

Kress, G. (1998). Visual and verbal modes of representation in electronically mediated communication: the potentials of new forms of text. A I. Snyder (Ed.), *Page to screen: taking literacy into the electronic era* (p. 53-79). Londres: Routledge.

Kress, G., i van Leeuwen, T. (1996). *Reading images: the grammar of visual design.* Nova York: Routledge.

Lankshear, C. (1997). *Changing literacies.* Buckingham: Open University Press.

Masats, D. (2017). L'anàlisi de la conversa al servei de la recerca en el camp de l'adquisició de segones llengües (CA-for-SLA). A E. Moore i M. Dooly (Eds), *Enfocaments qualitatius per a la recerca en educació plurilingüe* (p. 293-320). Research-publishing.net. https://doi.org/10.14705/rpnet.2017.emmd2016.632

Moore, E., i Llompart, J. (2017). Recoger, transcribir, analizar y presentar datos interaccionales plurilingües. A E. Moore i M. Dooly (Eds), *Enfocaments qualitatius per a la recerca en educació plurilingüe* (p. 418-433). Research-publishing.net. https://doi.org/10.14705/rpnet.2017.emmd2016.639

Nussbaum, L, (2017). Investigar con docentes. A E. Moore i M. Dooly (Eds), *Enfocaments qualitatius per a la recerca en educació plurilingüe* (p. 23-45). Research-publishing.net. https://doi.org/10.14705/rpnet.2017.emmd2016.620

Sawyer, R. K. (Ed.). (2006). *The Cambridge handbook of the learning sciences.* Cambridge: Cambridge University Press.

Scollon, R. (2000). Methodological interdiscursivity: an ethnographic understanding of unfinalisability. A S. Sarangi i M. Coulthard (Eds), *Discourse and social life* (p. 138-154). Londres: Pearson Education Limited.

Scollon, R. (2001). *Mediated discourse: the nexus of practice.* Londres: Routledge. https://doi.org/10.4324/9780203420065

Scollon, S. (2005). Agency distributed through time, space and tools: Bentham, Babbage and the census. A S. Norris i R. H. Jones (Eds), *Discourse in action: introduction to mediated discourse analysis* (p. 172-182). Londres: Routledge.

Scollon, R., i Scollon, S. W. (2004). *Nexus analysis: discourse and the emerging internet.* Nova York: Routledge.

Scollon, R., i Scollon, S. W. (2007). Nexus analysis: refocusing ethnography on action. *Journal of Sociolinguistics, 11*(5), 608-625. https://doi.org/10.1111/j.1467-9841.2007.00342.x

Seely Brown, J. (2008). Foreword: creating a culture of learning. A T. Iiyoshi i M. S. Vijay Kumar (Eds), *Opening up education. The collective advancement of education through open technology, open content, and open knowledge* (p. xi-xvii). Cambridge, MA: MIT Press.

Street, B. V. (2000). Literacy events and literacy practices: theory and practice in the new literacy studies. A M. Martin-Jones i K. Jones (Eds), *Multilingual literacies: comparative perspectives on research and practice* (p. 17-29). Àmsterdam: John Benjamin.

Tarrow, S. (2005). *The new transnational activism.* Cambridge: Cambridge University Press. https://doi.org/10.1017/CBO9780511791055

Wenger, E. (1998). *Communities of practice: Learning, meaning, and identity.* Cambridge: Cambridge University Press. https://doi.org/10.1017/CBO9780511803932

Wertsch, J. V. (1991). *Voices of the mind: a sociocultural approach to mediated action.* Cambridge, MA: Harvard University Press.

Wertsch, J. V. (1998). *Mind as action.* Nova York: Oxford University.

Wohlwend, K. (2013). Mediated discourse analysis: tracking discourse in action. A P. Albers, T. Holbrook, i A. Seely Flint (Eds), *New methods of literacy research* (p. 56-69). Abingdon: Routledge.

Lectures recomanades

Norris, S., i Jones, R. H. (Eds). (2005). *Discourse in action: introducing mediated discourse analysis.* Londres: Routledge.

Scollon, R. (2001). *Mediated discourse: the nexus of practice.* Londres: Routledge. https://doi.org/10.4324/9780203420065

Scollon, R., i Scollon, S. W. (2003). *Discourses in place: language in the material world.* Londres: Routledge. https://doi.org/10.4324/9780203422724

Annex

Adaptació de les convencions de l'anàlisi de la conversa (vegeu Moore i Llompart, en aquest volum):

(.) pausa curta
[1] pausa aproximada d'1 segon
[2] pausa aproximada de dos segons
: allargament del so
- paraula tallada
WOrd èmfasi en una síl·laba o paraula
[word]
[word] superposició
XXX inintel·ligible
(…) part de la transcripció no inclosa
((WORD)) notes del transcriptor

7 Educational ethnography in blended learning environments

Victoria Antoniadou[1] and Melinda Dooly[2]

Key concepts: ethnography, virtual ethnography, multiple case study, grounded theory, discourse analysis, CAQDAS.

---

1. Introduction

Digital ethnography, online ethnography, Virtual Ethnography (herein VE), or netnography, is a modern, expanded face of ethnographic research and a post positivist research approach (see the introduction by Dooly & Moore, this volume). It consists of adapted versions of more traditional ethnographic methods (see chapters by Corona, this volume; Nussbaum, this volume; Unamuno & Patiño, this volume) that aim to investigate the construction of communities, cultures, learning and teaching processes as they take place/are created through Computer-Mediated Communication (CMC), and increasingly, in digital or mobile mediated communication. This approach has been recently applied successfully to different educational arenas, including language teacher communities (Kulavuz-Onal & Vásquez, 2013) and plurilingual speakers' practices in online communities (Androutsopoulos, 2008). However, applications of this approach to formal educational environments are scarce, principally because it is limited to online data collection.

At the same time, it is an inarguable fact that there has been an educational transformation in many current language teaching practices as teachers learn to

---

1. Independent scholar, Nicosia, Cyprus; vicky.antoniadou@gmail.com

2. Universitat Autònoma de Barcelona, Bellaterra, Catalonia/Spain; melindaann.dooly@uab.cat

How to cite this chapter: Antoniadou, V., & Dooly, M. (2017). Educational ethnography in blended learning environments. In E. Moore & M. Dooly (Eds), *Qualitative approaches to research on plurilingual education* (pp. 237-263). Research-publishing.net. https://doi.org/10.14705/rpnet.2017.emmd2016.630

integrate the use of CMC technology into their lessons (see also the chapter by Dooly, this volume). Most of these online practices are based on the premise that people learn by interacting with the social and material environment and by receiving support or 'scaffolding' (Bruner, 1986; Vygotsky, 1978) from more knowledgeable others. In blended learning environments, especially where the language learning integrates telecollaborative interaction, these teaching approaches emphasize the fundamental role of language in mediating human social and cognitive (intellectual) development and the potential of CMC for promoting authentic interaction (Dooly, 2013). This seems almost inevitable given today's interconnectedness on a global scale so that social interaction has, nowadays, acquired much larger dimensions than simply talking with a fellow student in a seat across the aisle.

Additionally, there is a growing realization that technology can have an important role in sensitive pedagogical approaches for ethno-linguistically diverse student profiles (Darling, 2005; Hefflin, 2002; Johnson, 2005). "New technological tools can help promote a learning environment that not only accommodates to, but makes use of learners' differences" (Dooly, 2010, p. 7). This includes "the means of presenting information in manifold formats and multiple media; giving students varied ways to express and demonstrate what they have learned and providing multifarious entry points to engage student interest and motivate learning (Dooly, 2010, p. 7). However, there is a need for much more research into technology-enhanced language learning, in particular when working within plurilingual environments. "Unfortunately, these theories and practices are not widely understood nor implemented by teachers working with minority language students" (Dooly, 2010, p. 8).

> "The use of technology should be looked at holistically, not as a separate component of teaching. The aforementioned aim of fomenting research and wide-spread publication of innovative teaching approaches for minority language groups can also have an effect on local teaching practices as well. Most teachers are well-intentioned but at times their best efforts may be thwarted by lack of knowledge on how to achieve theoretically sound goals" (Dooly, 2010, p. 8).

This is where digital ethnography can play an important role. Traditionally, as other chapters in this volume show, ethnographic research is an approach that facilitates holistic analyses of interactional phenomena. This approach endeavors to investigate focal phenomena as part of a complete system created via the interaction between its constitutive individual parts in specific circumstances and conditions, leading to a unique and context-bound understanding of what is happening (Noblit, 1984; see also Taylor & Bogdan, 2000). In this sense, ethnographic research offers an in-depth understanding of the lived experience of a population in order to devise appropriate courses of action about a phenomenon (Beckmann & Langer, 2005; Elliot & Jankel-Elliott, 2002). Along these lines, immersive fieldwork in classrooms has been referred to as 'school' or 'educational' ethnography (Erickson, 1973; see also Nussbaum, this volume; Unamuno & Patiño, this volume).

For researchers interested in understanding the complexity of blended learning environments (language teaching environments that combine face-to-face lessons with CMC interactional activities), the abovementioned changes bring up new questions. For instance, in an era of multimodal education, where the field of study moves beyond the physical classroom, how can traditional ethnographic methods (i.e. prolonged engagement and deep immersion) be pursued and applied in online settings in order to enable an in-depth understanding of learners' subjective experiences across both physical and virtual settings? How can the researcher optimally combine in-class and online data taken from blended learning environments? How should the researcher collect and categorize data that are so different in nature (visual, textual, imagery, etc.)?

This chapter aims to answer some of the questions that emerge when carrying out educational ethnography in a blended learning environment. We will first outline how VE has been developed and applied by other researchers. Then, to better illustrate the approach, we will describe a doctoral research project that implemented VE, combined with Grounded Theory case studies, to trace learning in teacher education across classroom and online environments (i.e. through telecollaboration with U.S.-based peers; see also Dooly, this volume). The student-teachers, all of whom were plurilingual, were using English as a lingua franca to

Chapter 7

carry out the exchanges. In particular, the chapter links the research questions with the methods that were used to collect multimodal data, as well as the data sampling schemes employed. It discusses the challenges met, their solutions, and the contributions of the NVIVO program to the accomplishment of the research (see chapter by Antoniadou, this volume, for more details about the use of NVIVO).

2. A brief overview of the development of virtual ethnography

Green, Skukauskaite, and Baker (2012, p. 310) state that "in education, ethnographers enter a classroom, school, family group or community setting to identify insider knowledge by asking questions" that relate to what is taking place, by whom, what counts as knowledge and knowledge construction, what roles and relationships are discernible, what contextual factors have an impact on how knowledge is constructed, and how do individual and group actions promote or constrain "ways of knowing, being and doing" (Green et al., 2012, p. 310) of the members? These authors argue that ethnography should be regarded not as a method but as a "logic-in-use" approach, based on the premise that ethnography is applied as a "non-linear system, guided by an iterative, recursive and abductive logic" (Green et al., 2012, p. 309). This means that educational ethnographers do not have predefined steps or fieldwork methods. This is especially important to bear in mind when dealing with complex environments like blended learning contexts. Educational ethnography can be especially useful for researchers who are interested in an emic (see Dooly & Moore, this volume; Nussbaum, this volume), data-driven approach that helps explain precise details of the language learning process. In recent years, transferral of this approach to online and mobile interaction in learning environments has become more commonplace.

The methodological approach of virtual ethnography has been broadened and reformulated through new proposals such as digital ethnography, ethnography on/of/through the Internet, connective ethnography, networked ethnography, cyberethnography, etc. Each of these maintains its own dialogue with the established tradition of ethnography and formulates its relation to this tradition in different ways. (Domínguez Figaredo et al., 2007, para. 1).

A key aspect of understanding what VE implies is the recognition that this type of study is "potentially global in its geographical extent" (Greschke, 2007, para. 1) while at the same time endeavors to uncover, describe and understand what is constituted in the relationships at local (and 'glocal') levels, facilitated through virtual (or digital) dimensions. This implies that online research should move beyond merely capturing single-source onscreen data (e.g. textchat transcripts, blogs or forum posts, email exchanges), which, till now, has made up a large part of the online corpora in most studies on CMC in order to understand interrelated communicative patterns between different sites (both online and offline). As Androutsopoulos (2008) has pointed out, trying to understand interactants' discourse practices by relying exclusively on single-source onscreen log data does not really provide the researcher much perspective into the discursive bridging practices that individuals might use, not only between on and offline interaction but between different online sites and within multiple virtual communities.

This same author has identified two emergent types of VE. The first identified type of VE focuses on the integration (and penetration) of communication technologies in everyday life and the impact this may have on social and cultural practices. This type of VE is considered to be 'blended ethnography' as it combines data derived from both on and offline ethnography. This type of VE is exemplified in the case study included in this chapter. The second type of VE identified by Androutsopoulos (2008) consists of understanding emergent communication patterns across various CMC sites, thereby consisting only of online ethnography, or as the author explains, it is concerned with the "systematic observation [of] the dynamics of communication and semiotic production within web environments" (para. 10).

Indeed, the VE approach has been around long enough for a general framework to emerge (Hines, 2000). In this framework, four of the main aspects that constitute VE are:

Chapter 7

- VE provides a means of understanding the ways in which CMC becomes socially meaningful in everyday life and in learning processes.

- VE looks at field connections, not just field sites.

- There are no clear-cut boundaries between what is 'virtual' and what is 'real'.

- In VE, social media is understood as both sociocultural practices and sociocultural artifacts.

This framework also highlights aspects that pertain to the VE researcher, such as:

- VE researchers may need to be sufficiently adaptable to gather data both 'virtually' and 'physically'.

- Due to the way in which participants engage with the virtual communities, data collection will probably be intermittent, rather than long term immersion.

- Virtual engagement adds a reflexive dimension to data and analysis (the online site is both a place of continuing activity and fixed, already existent information).

Given that the 'work fields' or potential sites of VE research are 'pluri-local' and expansive (in particular through the reproduction of resources through linking to other sites), some important questions for the researcher emerge:

- How does the researcher determine the boundaries of the fieldwork?

- How does the researcher establish the parameters of exponential links (how many links between sites must a researcher observe and map)?

- What is the rationale for selection of what is included or excluded?

- What does it mean for the virtual ethnographer to 'be there' and be part of the community?

- Can the virtual ethnographer say they know enough about the community by only participating 'virtually'?

- How much of the behavior in the community is available to the researcher and how much that is available is actually monitored? (This refers back to the framework of intermittent participation and the merge between on and offline participation).

- Linked to the point above, should the 'physically-grounded' aspects of the subjects' lives be taken into account (Greschke, 2007)? If yes, how can this be managed?

Inevitably, there are also some emergent ethical issues to be considered when carrying out VE (see Dooly, Moore, & Vallejo, this volume, on research ethics) which are pertinent to online or digital data collection. The question of whether 'publicly' displayed resources require participants' permission to be used as data (and how to obtain this permission in a global virtual community) is still under debate in the VE community. Even more divisive is the question of whether it is ethical to become a member of a community in order to gather data (known as 'lurking' online), especially when dealing with more 'sensitive' virtual communities (for instance, a LGBTQ+ community or teenager sex education communities). Nonetheless, some general guidelines have been created by the Association of Internet Researchers (AoIR)[3]. In particular, it is suggested that anyone engaging in VE should make their purpose visible and transparent from the beginning (e.g. a post in the forum, an information card in virtual worlds) that not only states that the researcher is gathering data but also provides a link so that other members of the virtual community can find out more about the study and, ideally, provide their consent. Admittedly this is not a foolproof system, but it does indicate a willingness to be upfront with the rest of the community members.

---

3. See http://aoir.org

Anonymizing data is another rather thorny issue with VE. Different from data gathered in face-to-face environments (which is generally based on oral communication), changing the name of the participants does not easily erase the 'traces' of their interactions online, as is evidenced by the ease in which search engines can locate entire texts based on partial phrases pertaining to them. Some VE researchers prefer to paraphrase participants' interactions in order to avoid this possibility, although this inevitably blurs the lines even further between 'authentic' data and data which have been 're-interpreted' by the VE researcher.

Despite these issues and questions which are still under debate, the authors of this chapter fully endorse this type of research, especially as language learning processes increasingly move from offline to online environments (including blended learning environments as in the case presented below). As with any field of research, technology advances require the researcher to re-think current investigative practices. In VE, this is especially pertinent and brings an added dimension of reflexivity to such studies, along with exciting innovative research practices.

3. An ethnographic multiple-case study tracing teacher learning across classroom and online activity

Empirically illustrating the above, the following sections describe one example of VE application that was used to achieve a holistic understanding of the learning processes and outcomes in a blended learning environment. This study used telecollaboration alongside university instruction and school placement aiming at creating enhanced opportunities for student-teachers of English as a foreign language in primary education to develop: (1) domain knowledge and reflective skills, (2) collaborative learning, and (3) an experiential understanding of CMC for language education. The student-teachers' exchanges involved English as a lingua franca.

The virtual exchange took place across two semesters. In the first semester, the student-teachers in Catalonia had to design a seven-session teaching sequence in telecollaboration with seven classroom and 14 U.S.-based peers (with whom they were paired outside classroom hours). In the second semester, the same student-teachers had to collaboratively create a one-session podcast-based unit around a linguistic phenomenon of their choice. In the first semester, the interaction took place via synchronous MSN and Skype, and asynchronous email communication. In the second semester, the interaction took place via synchronous Second Life and MSN communication, offering the student-teachers knowledge and practice of different communication modalities and their affordances and shortcomings. Alongside university and virtual collaborations, the student-teachers in Catalonia were doing their placements in primary schools, where they observed and worked with experienced school teachers. At these same schools, the Catalonia-based student-teachers had to implement the teaching plans that they had collaboratively created with their virtual and classroom peers and tutors and reflect on the process and outcomes in wiki journals.

The overall research objective was to understand the ways in which task-based telecollaboration interacted with face-to-face collaboration and school placements, and discern the ways in which integrated telecollaboration can be used to enhance the learning output of conventional face-to-face Initial Teacher Education courses.

Looking to optimize data collection and research output, we integrated and framed the main methods of VE, i.e. prolonged engagement, deep immersion and participant observation within the wider scope and practice of multiple-case study research (Yin, 2003), with the analytical richness of data-driven Grounded Theory (GT) methods (Charmaz, 2006; Glaser & Strauss, 1967).

4. At the nexus of multiple-case study, ethnographic and grounded theory methods

Case study research aims at providing "an up-close and in-depth empirical investigation of a particular contemporary phenomenon within its real life context, using multiple sources of evidence" (Robson, 1993, p. 146; also Yin,

2003). There are different instantiations of case study research: (1) individual or single case studies, and (2) set of individual or multiple-case studies (Robson, 1993; Yin, 2003). Multiple-case studies usually involve three to five cases, allowing comparison and contrast between cases, i.e. different presentations/ manifestations of a phenomenon, and are said to produce better understandings and more robust interpretations than single case studies. Overall, the case study method provides tools for a holistic approach to phenomena, such as documents, quantitative and qualitative measurements in the form of open-ended questionnaires and interviews, archival records and physical artifacts (Yin, 2003). Single or multiple-case studies can be descriptive, responding to a 'what is happening' question; and exploratory and/or explanatory, providing answers to 'how/why did it happen' types of questions.

The methodological bricolage described herein was based on common philosophical assumptions between the research approaches, abiding to the interpretive paradigm (Halaweh, Fidler, & McRobb, 2008), and aiming at grounded theory-building (Eisenhardt, 1989) on teacher learning in blended environments. That is, we sought to understand learning processes and outcomes by interpreting the underlying meaning-making processes (Halaweh et al., 2008) and through the eyes of the participants. We approached the task not with pre-determined ideas of what constitutes learning, which is characteristic of positivist paradigms using quantitative measurements to confirm or reject theories (theory-testing). We sought to unravel the characteristics of the learning trajectories and outcomes of three out of the seven student-teachers, as they themselves experienced their learning process, and analyze various other related phenomena.

Case study research shares scope and techniques with ethnography, including fieldwork (direct and participant-observation), interviews and questionnaires, allowing the researcher to build a holistic account of an event, process, subject or practice; ethnography may often be classified as a type of descriptive case study research method. However, ethnography's defining feature is prolonged participant observation and the social relationship that is developed between participant and observer. This approach to data collection may or may not be complemented with interviews or other qualitative data, and findings cannot be generalized to other contexts. Through this type of prolonged and deep immersion into the research context, the researcher collects 'naturalistic unstructured data' (Flick, 2002), which are later coded in order to reveal the underlying components that make up human behavior and culture. The researcher him/herself becomes an instrument in the process of interpreting data, not without allowing possibilities for bias (Cohen & Manion, 1989).

Similar to ethnography, the GT method presents a set of techniques and strategies for compiling and analyzing data to understand significant aspects of the phenomenon under investigation (Charmaz, 2006; Strauss & Corbin, 1998). In GT, the researcher is participant-observer of the phenomenon in its naturalistic environment. S/he collects naturalistic 'unstructured' data, which s/he analyses as the collection process progresses, isolating themes and continuously verifying their importance with more data from participants. As an essentially data-driven method, GT does not develop from preconceived hypotheses but from the data itself, in which the participants indicate what is important for understanding the phenomenon. As its name suggests, the goal of GT is to develop middle-range theory to explain human behavior and processes (Charmaz, 2006). The researcher engages in extensive coding to represent the phenomenon being researched. While coding and categorizing, the researcher keeps memos and notes to explicate and complete coded categories. In turn, this memo-taking links the processes of coding data and writing first drafts of papers (Charmaz, 2006). GT aims at generating theory grounded on data. To do so, the researcher selects coded events from the larger corpus that help him/her develop theoretical concepts and accounts of the phenomenon s/he is researching (Strauss & Corbin, 1998). This process is called theoretical sampling or sampling for theory construction. A characteristic of the GT approach to qualitative research is that the researcher delays the literature review in order to maintain as clear a mind as possible while reading the data. This also marks an important difference with positivistic studies, where literature review is the first step in designing the research and serves as the basis for setting research objectives and methodologies for reaching them.

5. Discourse analysis

Discourse Analysis (DA) is a general approach to analyzing written and verbal 'texts', looking to make connections between these texts and their meanings (Lemke, 2012). Taking language-in-use or talk-in-interaction as the fundamental symbolic tool in the development of cognition, we were particularly interested in unraveling the relations between discourse/language-in-use and developing cognition over time, and across people and tools. To this end, we used a DA approach from Linguistic Anthropology of Education (Agha & Wortham, 2005; Wortham, 2006) that took into account the temporal and spatial dimension of the interaction (face-to-face and online modes) in order to conceptualize and identify the linguistic and conceptual resources that student-teachers explored, transferred and used across the different sites they were working in over the course of the academic year, as well as the different positioning associated with each use (Wortham, 2006). This approach recasts a type of frame analysis (Tannen, 1993) approach, which was adapted to the needs of our research context and coding process, and was driven by the following questions:

- What are the student-teachers doing in this interaction and in what spatial arrangements? What knowledge/skill are they working on?

- How far along the learning process are they doing this?

- What resources are they using from other sites, e.g. classroom content, school experience?

- Do these interactions relate to the gains that the student teachers report at the end of the year?

Coding along these lines allowed us to trace professional learning, i.e. development of teacher discourse and thinking across online and face-to-face sites over time. We will now move on to describe the multiple sources of evidence that we used for interpretation and triangulation purposes, as well as the data collection and analytical procedures used for capturing 'learning in the making'.

6. Multimodal data collection: methods used and types of data collected

6.1. Questionnaires and focal group interviews

Focal group interviews with the participants (see Canals, this volume) took place face-to-face at the very beginning of the research project in order to encourage a first meeting between the participants (student-teachers based in Catalonia) and enable them to share learning experiences and concerns regarding the online collaboration. The group interviews allowed the student-teachers to recall, reflect, and synthesize past learning experiences, clarify weaknesses, goals and set expectations from the course. These group interviews were recorded, transcribed and included in the analysis (see chapter by Moore & Llompart, this volume). Research-wise, they were used as focal process-oriented data, marking the beginning stage of development and serving as baseline for comparison with end-of-year learning gains. Open-ended questionnaires (see Canals, this volume) were used to document goals and expectations from this course. Student-teachers were also asked to rank their teaching competences on a summarized version of the European Portfolio of Student-Teacher of Languages (Newby et al., 2007).

6.2. Participant observation in the classroom and online

6.2.1. Classroom observation

All the face-to-face sessions at the university, in the first and second semesters, were video and audio-recorded on a weekly basis. In this research, participant-observation as it took place in the classroom can be described as including a moderate level of participation, concerned with maintaining a balance between 'insider' and 'outsider' roles, and allowing a good combination of involvement and necessary detachment in order to remain objective (DeWalt & DeWalt, 2002; Schwartz & Schwartz, 1955). It was made clear to the participants that the researcher was not participating in their assessment of the course. Therefore, she was able to observe the process as it was constructed naturally between the university tutor and student-teachers. Over time and through daily interaction, a

Chapter 7

relationship of trust was developed between the researcher and the participants. It is particularly important to develop a relationship of trust with the participants, especially in educational contexts. Given the workload that the participants have in these settings, it is important to respect the ethical issues involved and join participants in their interests and pursuits. In this setting, the shared interest was a genuine effort towards learning and improving teaching practice, even beyond academic achievement.

6.2.2. Online observation

In the first semester, the participants carried out the online exchange in out-of-class time, mainly at home. Participant observation could not be carried out without intruding on the participants' privacy. Recalling the definition of VE as adaptation of traditional ethnographic methods, student-teachers were asked to save and email their online interactions with their U.S.-based partners to their tutor and to the researcher. These transcripts were taken as 'natural protocols' of students' efforts in making sense of and structuring their physical and social environment (Roth, 1996).

Online observation took place during the initial Second Life meetings (platform used for telecollaboration in the second semester). Since this platform/tool was an entirely new 'locality' for the student-teachers, online observation provided the researcher with insights into the students' emotional state and familiarity with various aspects of technology, which were in turn useful for tracing digital development at the end of the course (this was relevant to the research objectives). The researcher, also present in Second Life, documented important aspects of this process in fieldnotes. The participants also documented their perspective of important aspects of this process in narrative form (described below).

6.3. Semi-structured interviews

Once themes began to emerge from reading the classroom and online data, the researcher followed up with semi-structured interviews with participants, seeking to corroborate the value of and further investigate these themes (in line with the GT methodology, as described above).

6.4. Narratives

The participants were asked to write online wiki narratives, later downloaded by the researcher. This data type facilitated a reconstruction of events by the participants themselves and helped the researcher establish a deeper understanding of the topics of interest, as well as triangulate findings (Jangu, 2012). Other types of self-reporting resources included:

- Minutes of the tutorial sessions documenting main occurrences and relevance to their learning process. These notes were contrasted with the researcher's own fieldnotes, and were used as triangulation data offering further insight into the student-teachers' own perceptions of experience.

- School journals. Student-teachers kept a diary of their placement experiences at the primary schools, throughout the placement. These documentations provided data about the student-teachers' interaction with the school environment and the ways they associated this practical teaching experience (co-teaching with expert teachers, observing them teach) with what they were learning at the university and online.

- Self-reflections and evaluations. These were several wiki texts consisting of: (1) self-reflections on the student-teachers' own teaching practice, implementing the materials they had collaboratively created with classroom and virtual peers and tutors; (2) students' evaluations of their learning experience (for this latter, the student-teachers had to reflect on the contributions of online chats and university sessions to their teacher education); and (3) reflections on development of teaching competence, based on the same summarized version of the European Portfolio of Student-Teacher of Languages, given at the beginning of the course. The student-teachers were writing these wiki texts from the beginning to the end of the year.

7. Data sampling

Quality ethnographic multiple-case study research is also a matter of selecting good and information-rich cases, otherwise referred to as information-oriented data-sampling (Yin, 2003; see also Dörnyei, 2007). Literature suggests choosing subjects that offer rich insights into unique or exemplary, unusual or particularly revealing sets of circumstances (Fenno, 1986), and not focusing on typical cases representing the phenomenon at hand. In this research project, we chose to focus on the learning trajectory of three out of the seven student-teachers who participated in the course. The three had very different profiles as learners (explained in more detail below). With this selection, we wanted to understand how a significant number of agents with different motivations in regards to teaching and CMC perceived the learning affordances of the task and learning environment and used them to construct knowledge. Such polarity between cases permits analytic generalization (Yin, 2003) about the learning affordances of this hybrid environment, since it provides evidence on the ways this environment can benefit subjects of various competency levels and motivations. For these three student-teachers, we had full data to reveal and triangulate their learning trajectory and output, and thus reliably carry out the research objectives.

In this research project, the key case was a student-teacher who presented exemplary performance and consistency throughout the course, responding to the tutor's intentions and objectives. We wanted thus to study the circumstances surrounding this performance in order to draw conclusions about aspects of effective telecollaboration for teacher learning. Our second case was considered critical because of this student-teacher's language barrier. She was considered a weak student, with compromised proficiency in the target language, yet she was tech-savvy, and increasingly motivated by the constant support she was receiving in this learning environment. Her performance across sites illustrated unique learning processes, developing professional identity and skill through imitation of the tutor's discourse and the learning practices she came across in the classroom and online. The third case was particularly revelatory of how engagement in this type of hybrid learning environment can work in odd circumstances. This student-teacher had a limited-level of digital proficiency, mainly because of personal aversion towards technology. In combination with a compromised English language proficiency, she initially felt very uncomfortable about engaging in online collaboration.

Apart from selecting cases, data sampling also involved distinguishing focal from triangulation data. Triangulation meant using data collected from different 'overlapping' sources and methods (Guba & Lincoln, 1994), and contrasting them with the findings from the focal data in order to determine their validity. Figure 1 below illustrates the progression and constant accumulation of data across multimodal settings. As this figure shows, each stage of data collection gradually generated more information, which facilitated a sequential understanding of the teacher learning process.

Figure 1. Representation of the data collection process and outcomes

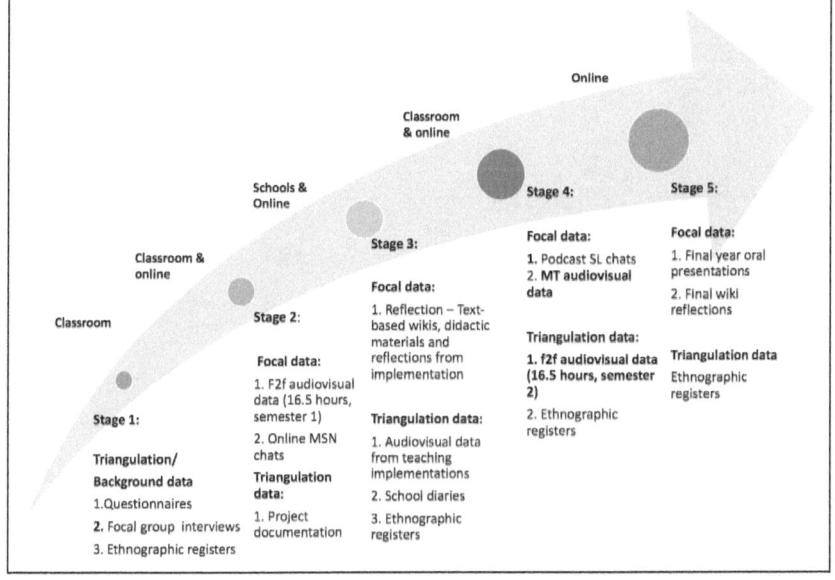

8. Data analysis: NVIVO8-assisted data management, coding and interpretation of findings

All data, focal and triangulation, were stored in the 'Internals' folder of NVIVO8 (Figure 2). Literature, which we used to theoretically substantiate this research, was linked, pasted or summarized in the 'Externals' folder. The original files were either physically stored on the computer's 'documents' folder, or available via websites outside NVIVO. In the case of small-sized articles, these were imported as PDFs in the 'Internals' folder (Figure 2).

Figure 2.   Storing data in NVIVO8

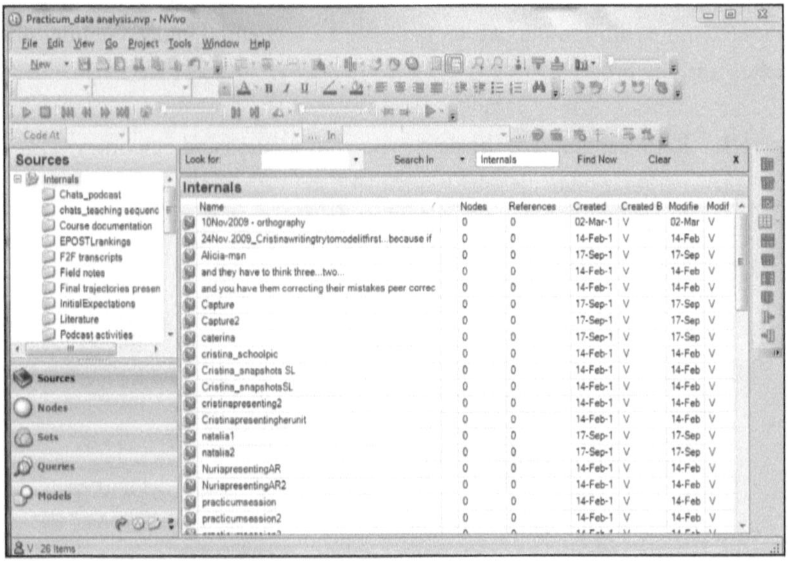

8.1.   Data analysis

With the research questions on the side as a reminder of research objectives/questions, the researcher began the data analysis process by coding the focal data, e.g. classroom and online interactions, and text reflections. Coding is the analytical process that facilitates categorization of large amounts of "raw/

unstructured data" into good coding schemes aiming to provide the analyst with a 'storyline' that allows him/her to answer his/her research questions (Strauss & Corbin, 1998). In this research, coding helped reveal the relationships between learning activity at university, online and school, and outcomes reported by the student-teachers at the end of the course.

Our coding was topic-oriented and aimed at tracing all interactions around the same topic (e.g. lesson planning, assessment). Also, the researcher was coding interactions that took place at different temporal and spatial arrangements. Pointing that out in our codes was important to our research objectives. To do so, the researcher used the -ing suffix to denote process and the -ed suffix for outcomes to signify outcome. One example of coded outcome is 'Learned terminology for setting linguistic objectives', and an example of coded process is 'Designing realistic objectives for four year-olds'. This coding method allowed emphasis on the temporal relationships between different data extracts, and also traced temporal and topic relationships between codes in order to establish a network of interactional episodes from which the student-teachers discernibly drew on to construct meaning around the topic/skill learned (Barab, Hay, & Yagamata-Lynch, 2001; Roth, 1996).

Following the coding stages of GT methodology, data analysis consisted of three cycles of coding; namely open, axial and theoretical. These coding stages aim at gradually focusing the analysis on relevant chunks of data for answering the research questions. Open codes result from an initial reading of the data, where the researcher reads and re-reads the data and isolates interesting aspects or verbatim participants' words (Figure 3).

Axial coding is the second stage of data codes, which picks up relationships between codes, and reduces the number of open codes by merging similar codes.

Alongside coding, a note-taking scheme was also devised and implemented, documenting the researcher's thoughts while coding as an answer to the whats and whys of codification and categorization, and helping to shed light on the relationships between codes during the axial coding stage (Figure 4).

Chapter 7

Figure 3. Free nodes – open coding stage

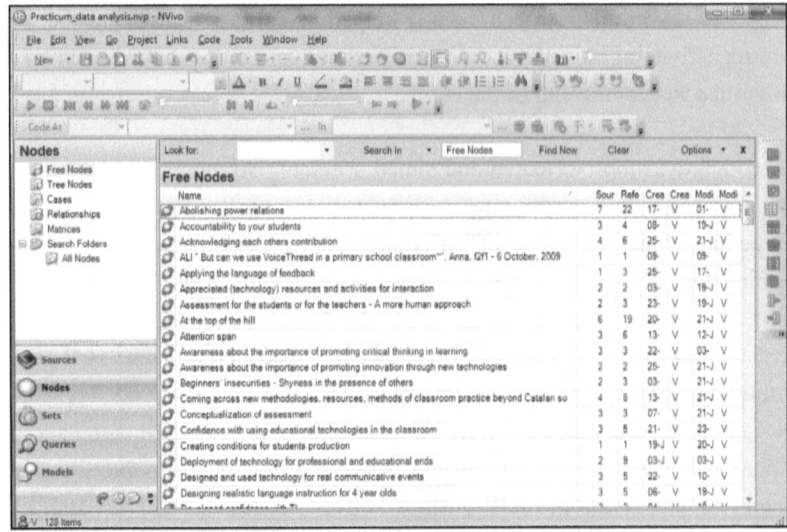

Figure 4. Tree nodes – axial coding stage

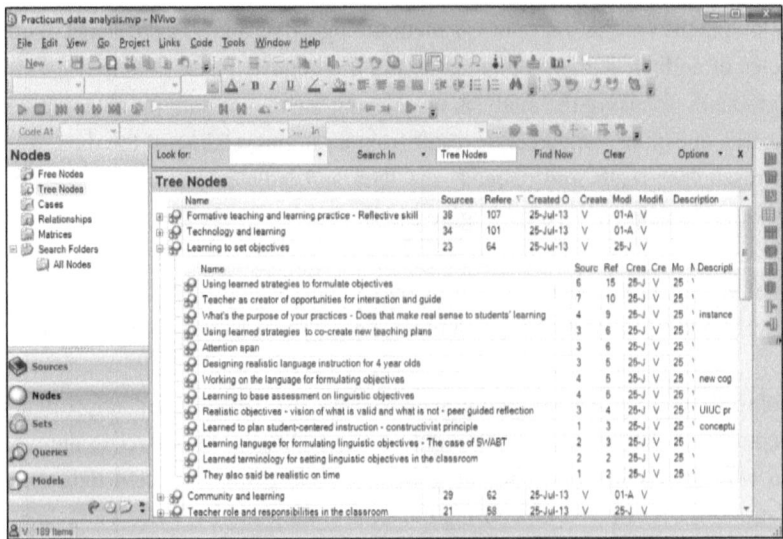

For the third coding stage, the researcher reviewed the literature for relevant theoretical background to explain and/or interpret his/her findings from the two previous coding stages. In this stage, the researcher creates larger categories that link data/codes with theory. This is the last building block in theory-building. The third and final analytical stage consisted in the eight categories illustrated in Figure 5 indicating learning outcomes, i.e., knowledge, skill and ability in different areas of teaching, e.g. formative teaching and learning practice, technology and learning, and learning to set objectives (lesson planning). These final categories were supported and reformulated along theoretical premises found in the literature.

Figure 5. Final categorizations in NVIVO – indicators of salience

Tree Nodes		
Name	Sources	Referen
Formative teaching and learning practice - Reflective skill	38	107
Technology and learning	34	101
Learning to set objectives	23	64
Community and learning	29	62
Teacher role and responsibilities in the classroom	21	58
Developed confidence	15	44
Materializing CLT through concrete examples of classroom practice	20	40
Lifelong learning	7	9

9. Data interpretation and formal output

We chose to focus on the three most salient categories (based on the quantitative measurements provided by NVIVO8) in order to preserve analytical rigor. The findings were finally presented as a storyline of 'learning in the making' culminating to specific knowledge, skill and competence that the focal students reported having learned at the end of the practicum.

In-depth discourse analysis, as described in the introductory section of the methodology above, informed the interpretation of sequential learning events that took place across universities and online and school environments at different points in time, and explained how symmetrical and asymmetrical interaction

Chapter 7

with virtual peers and tutors respectively as well as experiential learning from school practice and teaching implementation afforded teacher learning, within the formal parameters of contemporary teacher education (Antoniadou, 2013). Taken sequentially, these episodes depict how student-teachers use and combine the resources made available to them through interaction to construct new knowledge and reach qualitatively new cognitive outcomes in regards to strategic instructional planning, collaborative and digital knowledge and skills (Antoniadou, 2011, 2013; Dooly, 2011, 2013).

10. Concluding words

In this chapter, we have described a VE study. We have illustrated the types and processes of data collection in the VE. We have detailed how the analysis was carried out across multiple educational sites. We have explained how we used this data to carry out our research objectives, hoping to provide a practical how-to for future researchers interested in taking on ethnographic endeavors in computer-mediated learning environments. With this approach, we examined learning as a process, were able to discern critical episodes of interaction across instructional sites, and illustrated sequential meaning-making processes in regards to learning to teach.

The research described in this chapter verifies that there is no one typology of VE procedures for VE; rather VE implementation necessarily depends on and is informed by the contextual contingencies and relevancies of each particular site (Domínguez Figaredo et al., 2007). Institutional specifics and local challenges will necessarily influence the ways of investigation and impose adjustments to traditional ethnographic research.

Works cited

Agha, A., & Wortham, S. (2005). Discourse across speech-events: intertextuality and interdiscursivity in social life. *Journal of Linguistic Anthropology, 15*(1), special issue.

Androutsopoulos, J. (2008). Potentials and limitations of discourse-centred online ethnography. *Language@internet, 5.* http://www.languageatinternet.org/articles/2008/1610

Antoniadou, V. (2011). Virtual collaboration, 'perezhivanie' and teacher learning: a socio-cultural-historical perspective. *Bellaterra Journal of Teaching & Learning Language & Literature, 4*(3), 53-70.

Antoniadou, V. (2013). *Expanding the socio-material spaces of teacher education programmes: A qualitative trace of teacher professionalization through blended pedagogy in Catalonia.* Unpublished PhD dissertation. Universitat Autonoma de Barcelona.

Antoniadou, V. (2017). Collecting, organizing and analyzing multimodal data sets: the contributions of CAQDAS. In E. Moore & M. Dooly (Eds), *Qualitative approaches to research on plurilingual education* (pp. 435-450). Research-publishing.net. https://doi.org/10.14705/rpnet.2017.emmd2016.640

Barab, S. A, Hay, K. E., & Yagamata-Lynch, L. C. (2001). Constructing networks of action relevant episodes: an in-situ research methodology. *The Journal of the Learning Sciences, 10*(1&2), 63-112. https://doi.org/10.1207/S15327809JLS10-1-2_5

Beckmann, S., & Langer, R. (2005). Netnography: rich insights from online research. *Insights@ CBS, 14*(6). https://stosowana.files.wordpress.com/2010/10/670005_beckmann_langer_full_version.pdf

Bruner, J. S. (1986). *Actual minds, possible worlds.* Boston: Harvard University Press.

Canals, L. (2017). Instruments for gathering data. In E. Moore & M. Dooly (Eds), *Qualitative approaches to research on plurilingual education* (pp. 390-401). Research-publishing.net. https://doi.org/10.14705/rpnet.2017.emmd2016.637

Charmaz, K. (2006). *Constructing grounded theory: a practical guide through qualitative analysis.* London: Sage.

Cohen, L., & Manion, L. (1989). *Research methods in education* (3rd ed). London: Routledge.

Corona, V. (2017). An ethnographic approach to the study of linguistic varieties used by young Latin Americans in Barcelona. In E. Moore & M. Dooly (Eds), *Qualitative approaches to research on plurilingual education* (pp. 170-188). Research-publishing.net. https://doi.org/10.14705/rpnet.2017.emmd2016.627

Darling, D. (2005). Improving minority student achievement by making cultural connections. *Middle Ground, 36*(5), 46-50. https://doi.org/10.1080/00940771.2005.11461505

DeWalt, K. M., & DeWalt, B. R. (2002). *Participant observation: a guide for fieldworkers.* Walnut Creek, CA: AltaMira Press.

Domínguez Figaredo, D., Beaulieu, A., Estalella, A., Gómez, E., Schnettler, B., & Read, R. (2007). Virtual ethnography. *FQS Forum: Qualitative Social Research, 8*(3). http://www.qualitative-research.net/index.php/fqs/article/view/274

Dooly, M. (2010). Empowering language minorities through technology: which way to Go? *eLearning Papers, 19*, 1-12. https://www.openeducationeuropa.eu/sites/default/files/legacy_files/old/6_1272021672.pdf

Dooly, M. (2011). Divergent perceptions of telecollaborative language learning tasks: task-as-workplan vs. task-as-process. *Language Learning & Technology, 15*(2), 69-91.

Dooly, M. (2013). Focusing on the social: research into the distributed knowledge of novice teachers in online exchange. In C. Meskill (Ed.), *Online teaching and learning: sociocultural perspectives. Advances in digital language learning and teachng* (pp. 1-30). London/New York: Bloomsbury Academic.

Dooly, M. (2017). A Mediated Discourse Analysis (MDA) approach to multimodal data. In E. Moore & M. Dooly (Eds), *Qualitative approaches to research on plurilingual education* (pp. 189-211). Research-publishing.net. https://doi.org/10.14705/rpnet.2017.emmd2016.628

Dooly, M., & Moore, E. (2017). Introduction: qualitative approaches to research on plurilingual education. In E. Moore & M. Dooly (Eds), *Qualitative approaches to research on plurilingual education* (pp. 1-10). Research-publishing.net. https://doi.org/10.14705/rpnet.2017.emmd2016.618

Dooly, M., Moore, E., & Vallejo, C. (2017). (2017). Research ethics. In E. Moore & M. Dooly (Eds), *Qualitative approaches to research on plurilingual education* (pp. 351-362). Research-publishing.net. https://doi.org/10.14705/rpnet.2017.emmd2016.634

Dörnyei, Z. (2007). *Research methods in applied linguistics: quantitative, qualitative and mixed methodologies*. Oxford: Oxford University Press.

Eisenhardt, K. M. (1989). Building theories from case study research. *Academy of Management Review, 14*(4), 532–550.

Elliot, R., & Jankel-Elliott, N. (2002). Using ethnography in strategic consumer research. *Qualitative Market Research: an International Journal, 6*(5), 215-223.

Erickson, F. (1973). What makes school ethnography 'ethnographic'? *Council on Anthropology and Education Newsletter, 4*(2), 10-19. https://doi.org/10.1525/aeq.1973.4.2.05x0129y

Fenno, R. (1986). Observation, context, and sequence in the study of politics. *American Political Science Review, 80*(1), 3-15. https://doi.org/10.2307/1957081

Flick, U. (2002). *An introduction to qualitative research.* (2n ed.). Thousand Oaks/London: Sage Publications.

Glaser, B. G., & Strauss, A. L. (1967). *The discovery of grounded theory: strategies for qualitative research.* Chicago: Aldine.

Green, J. L., Skukauskaite, A., & Baker, W. D. (2012). Ethnography as epistemology. In J. Arthur, M. Waring, R. Coe, & L.V. Hedges (Eds), *Research methods and nethodologies in education* (pp. 309-321). London: Sage.

Greschke, H. M. (2007). Logging into the field—Methodological reflections on ethnographic research in a pluri-local and computer-mediated field. *FQS Forum: Qualitative Social Research, 8*(3). http://www.qualitative-research.net/index.php/fqs/article/view/279

Guba, E. G., & Lincoln, Y. S. (1994). Competing paradigms in qualitative research. In N. Denzin & Y. Lincoln (Eds), *Handbook of qualitative research* (pp. 105-117). London: Sage.

Halaweh, M., Fidler, C., & McRobb, S. (2008). Integrating the grounded theory method and case study research methodology within IS Research: a possible 'road map'. *ICIS 2008 Proceedings.* Paper 165. http://aisel.aisnet.org/icis2008/165

Hefflin, B. R. (2002). Learning to develop culturally relevant pedagogy: a lesson about cornrowed lives. *Urban Review, 33*(2), 131-149.

Hines, C. (2000). *Virtual ethnography.* London/New Delhi: Sage. https://doi.org/10.4135/9780857020277

Jangu, W. I. (2012). *Understanding the basics of qualitative research.* https://www.academia.edu/2321683/UNDERSTANDING_THE_BASICS_OF_QUALITATIVE_RESEARCH

Johnson, C. C. (2005). Making instruction relevant to language minority students at the middle level. *Middle School Journal, 37*(2), 10-14. https://doi.org/10.1080/00940771.2005.11461521

Kulavuz-Onal, D., & Vásquez, C. (2013). Reconceptualising fieldwork in a netnography of an online community of English language teachers. *Ethnography and Education, 8*(2), 224-238. https://doi.org/10.1080/17457823.2013.792511

Lemke, J. L. (2012). Multimedia and discourse analysis. In J. P. Gee & M. Handford (Eds), *Routledge handbook of discourse analysis* (pp. 79-89). New York: Routledge.

Moore, E., & Llompart, J. (2017). Collecting, transcribing, analyzing and presenting plurilingual interactional data. In E. Moore & M. Dooly (Eds), *Qualitative approaches to research on plurilingual education* (pp. 403-417). Research-publishing.net. https://doi.org/10.14705/rpnet.2017.emmd2016.638

Newby, D., Allan, R., Fenner, A-B., Jones, B., Komorowska, H., & Soghikyan, K. (2007). *European portfolio for student teachers of languages. A reflection tool for language teacher education.* Graz: European Centre for Modern Languages.

Noblit, G. (1984). The prospects of an applied ethnography for education: a sociology of knowledge interpretation. *Educational Evaluation and Policy Analysis, 5*(1), 95-101. https://doi.org/10.3102/01623737006001095

Nussbaum, L. (2017). Doing research with teachers. In E. Moore & M. Dooly (Eds), *Qualitative approaches to research on plurilingual education* (pp. 46-67). Research-publishing.net. https://doi.org/10.14705/rpnet.2017.emmd2016.621

Robson, C. (1993). *Real world research: a resource for social scientists and practitioners-researchers.* Oxford: Blackwell.

Roth, W. M. (1996). Knowledge diffusion in a grade 4-5 classroom during a unit on civil engineering : an analysis of a classroom community in terms of its changing resources and practices. *Cognition and Instruction, 14*(2), 179-220. https://doi.org/10.1207/s1532690xci1402_2

Schwartz, M. S., & Schwartz, C. G. (1955). Problems in participant observation. *American Journal of Sociology, 60*(4), 343-353. https://doi.org/10.1086/221566

Strauss, A., & Corbin, J. (1998). *Basics of qualitative research: techniques and procedures for developing grounded theory.* London: SAGE.

Tannen, D. (Ed.). (1993). *Framing in discourse.* Oxford: Oxford University Press.

Taylor, S. J., & Bogdan, R. (2000). *Introducción a los métodos cualitativos* (3rd ed.). Barcelona: Paidós.

Unamuno, V., & Patiño, A. (2017). Producing knowledge about plurilingualism with young students: a challenge for collaborative ethnography. In E. Moore & M. Dooly (Eds), *Qualitative approaches to research on plurilingual education* (pp. 129-149). Research-publishing.net. https://doi.org/10.14705/rpnet.2017.emmd2016.625

Vygotsky, L. S. (1978). *Mind in society: the development of higher psychological processes.* Boston: Harvard University Press.

Wortham, S. (2006). *Learning identity: the joint emergence of social identification and academic learning.* Cambridge: Cambridge University Press.

Yin, R. K. (2003). *Case study research: design and methods* (3rd ed.). Thousand Oaks/London/New Delhi: Sage.

Recommended Reading

Falzon, M-A. (Ed.). (2009). *Multi-sited ethnography: theory, praxis and locality in contemporary research*. Surrey: Ashgate.

Herring, S. C. (2004). Computer-mediated discourse analysis: an approach to researching online behavior. In S. A. Barab, R. Kling, & J. Gray (Eds), *Designing for virtual communities in the service of learning* (pp. 338-376). Cambridge/New York: Cambridge University Press. https://doi.org/10.1017/CBO9780511805080.016

7 Etnografia educativa en contextos d'aprenentatge mixt

Victoria Antoniadou[1] i Melinda Dooly[2]

Conceptes clau: etnografia, etnografia virtual, estudi de cas múltiple, mostreig teòric, anàlisi del discurs, CAQDAS.

1. Introducció

L'etnografia digital, l'etnografia en línia, l'Etnografia Virtual (en endavant EV) o la netnografia és una cara moderna, ampliada de la investigació etnogràfica i un enfocament d'investigació postpositivista (vegeu la introducció de Dooly i Moore, en aquest volum). Consisteix en versions adaptades dels mètodes etnogràfics més tradicionals (vegeu els capítols de Corona, en aquest volum; Nussbaum, en aquest volum; Unamuno i Patiño, en aquest volum) que tenen com a objectiu investigar la construcció de comunitats, les cultures i els processos d'aprenentatge i ensenyament que tenen lloc o que es creen a partir de la Comunicació Mediada per Ordinador (CMO), i cada vegada més, en la comunicació digital o mòbil. Darrerament, aquest enfocament s'ha aplicat amb èxit a diferents àmbits educatius, entre els quals hi havia les comunitats de docents de llengües (Kulavuz-Onal i Vásquez, 2013) i comunitats multilingües en línia (Androutsopoulos, 2008). No obstant això, aquest enfocament s'ha aplicat poques vegades a entorns educatius formals, principalment perquè es limita a recollir dades en línia.

És un fet indiscutible que hi ha hagut una transformació educativa en moltes de les pràctiques actuals d'ensenyament de llengües a mesura que els docents

---

1. Investigadora independent, Nicòsia, Xipre; vicky.antoniadou@gmail.com

2. Universitat Autònoma de Barcelona, Bellaterra, Catalunya/Espanya; melindaann.dooly@uab.cat

Per citar aquest capítol: Antoniadou, V., i Dooly, M. (2017). Etnografia educativa en contextos d'aprenentatge mixt. A E. Moore i M. Dooly (Eds), *Enfocaments qualitatius per a la recerca en educació plurilingüe* (p. 264-292). Research-publishing.net. https://doi.org/10.14705/rpnet.2017.emmd2016.631

han després a integrar la tecnologia de CMO a les seves classes (vegeu també el capítol de Dooly, en aquest volum). La majoria d'aquestes pràctiques en línia es basen en la premissa que les persones aprenen mitjançant la interacció amb l'entorn social i material, i quan reben suport o andamiatge (Bruner, 1986; Vygotsky, 1978) de persones amb més coneixement. En entorns d'aprenentatge mixt, especialment quan l'aprenentatge de llengües integra la interacció telecol·laborativa, aquests enfocaments d'ensenyament se centren en el paper fonamental de la llengua a l'hora de mediar el desenvolupament humà social i cognitiu (intel·lectual) i el potencial de la CMO per promoure interacció autèntica (Dooly, 2013). Això sembla gairebé inevitable, donada la interconnexió actual a escala global, de manera que la interacció social, avui dia, ha adquirit dimensions molt més grans que simplement parlar amb un company d'estudis que seu al pupitre del costat.

A més, està creixent la idea que la tecnologia pot tenir un paper important en aproximacions pedagògiques sensibles per a perfils d'estudiants diversos des del punt de vista de l'etnolingüística (Darling, 2005; Hefflin, 2002; Johnson, 2005). "New technological tools can help promote a learning environment that not only accommodates to, but makes use of learner's differences" (Dooly, 2010, p. 7)[3]. Això inclou "the means of presenting information in manifold formats and multiple media; giving students varied ways to express and demonstrate what they have learned and providing multifarious entry points to engage student interest and motivate learning" (Dooly, 2010, p. 7)[4]. No obstant això, hi ha la necessitat d'investigar més sobre l'aprenentatge de llengües amb noves tecnologies, especialment, quan es treballa en entorns plurilingües. "Unfortunately, these theories and practices are not widely understood nor implemented by teachers working with minority language students" (Dooly, 2010, p. 8)[5].

---

3. "Les noves eines tecnològiques poden ajudar a promoure un ambient d'aprenentatge que no només s'adapta a les diferècncies d'aprenentatge, sinó que les utilitza" (Dooly, 2010, p. 7).

4. "les maneres de presentar la informació en diferents formats i maneres, donant als estudiants diverses formes d'expressar i demostrar el que han après i proporcionant-los múltiples punts d'entrada per captar l'interès dels estudiants i motivar el seu aprenentatge" (Dooly, 2010, p. 7).

5. "Malauradament, els docents que treballen amb estudiants de llengües minoritària, generalment, no entenen ni implementen aquestes teories i pràctiques" (Dooly, 2010, p. 8).

> "The use of technology should be looked at holistically, not as a separate component of teaching. The aforementioned aim of fomenting research and wide-spread publication of innovative teaching approaches for minority language groups can also have an effect on local teaching practices as well. Most teachers are well-intentioned but at times their best efforts may be thwarted by lack of knowledge on how to achieve theoretically sound goals" (Dooly, 2010, p. 8)[6].

Aquí és on l'etnografia digital pot tenir un paper important. Tradicionalment, com mostren altres capítols d'aquest volum, la investigació etnogràfica ha estat un enfocament que facilita l'anàlisi holística de fenòmens d'interacció. Aquest enfocament pretén investigar els fenòmens focals com a part d'un sistema complet creat a través de la interacció entre les seves parts individuals constitutives en circumstàncies i condicions específiques, cosa que proporciona una comprensió única lligada al context en què està tenint lloc (Noblit, 1984; vegeu també Taylor i Bogdan, 2000). En aquest sentit, la investigació etnogràfica ofereix una comprensió en profunditat de l'experiència viscuda d'una població per tal d'idear formes d'actuació per un fenomen (Beckmann i Langer, 2005; Elliot i Jankel-Elliott, 2002). En aquest sentit, el treball de camp d'immersió en els centres educatius es coneix com a etnografia 'd'escola' o 'educativa' (Erickson, 1973; vegeu també Nussbaum, en aquest volum; Unamuno i Patiño, en aquest volum).

Per als investigadors interessats a comprendre la complexitat dels entorns d'aprenentatge mixt (entorns d'ensenyament de llengües que combinen les lliçons cara a cara amb les activitats d'interacció de CMO), els canvis que hem explicat generen noves preguntes. Per exemple, a l'era de l'educació multimodal, en què el camp d'estudi va més enllà de l'aula física, com es pot continuar amb els mètodes etnogràfics tradicionals (és a dir, el compromís profund i la immersió prolongada) i aplicar-los en els escenaris en línia per tal d'arribar a una

---

6. "L'ús de la tecnologia s'ha d'entendre de manera integral, no com un component separat de l'ensenyament. Aquest objectiu de fomentar la investigació i la publicació d'enfocaments d'ensenyament innovadors per als grups lingüístics minoritaris també pot tenir un efecte sobre les pràctiques d'ensenyament locals. La majoria dels professors tenen bona predisposició, però de vegades els millors esforços poden veure's frustrats per la falta de coneixement sobre com assolir els objectius teòrics sòlids" (Dooly, 2010, p. 8).

comprensió en profunditat de les experiències subjectives dels estudiants als dos entorns, el físic i el virtual? Com es poden combinar de manera òptima les dades extretes de la classe i les dades en línia recollides dels entorns d'aprenentatge mixt? Com s'han de recollir i classificar dades de naturalesa tan diferent (visual, textual, imatges, etc.)?

En aquest capítol es pretén donar resposta a algunes de les preguntes que sorgeixen quan s'aplica l'etnografia educativa en un entorn d'aprenentatge mixt. Primer, explicarem breument com altres investigadors han desenvolupat i aplicat l'EV. A continuació, per il·lustrar millor l'enfocament, descriurem un projecte de recerca doctoral que implementa l'EV per fer un seguiment de l'aprenentatge en la formació del professorat a l'aula i als entorns en línia (és a dir, a través de la telecol·laboració amb companys que eren físicament als EUA, vegeu també Dooly, en aquest volum). Els estudiants-docents, que eren tots plurilingües, utilitzaven l'anglès com a llengua franca per dur a terme els intercanvis. En particular, el capítol vincula les preguntes de recerca amb els mètodes que es van utilitzar per recopilar dades multimodals, així com els sistemes de mostreig de dades utilitzades. S'analitzen els problemes que es van trobar, les solucions i les contribucions del programa NVivo per realitzar la investigació (vegeu el capítol d'Antoniadou, en aquest volum, per a més detalls sobre l'ús del programa NVivo).

2. Una visió general breu del desenvolupament de l'etnografia virtual

Green, Skukauskaite, i Baker (2012) afirmen que "in education, ethnographers enter a classroom, school, family group or community setting to identify insider knowledge by asking qüestions" (p. 310)[7]. Aquestes preguntes es relacionen amb el que està passant, qui fa què, què compta com a coneixement i construcció del coneixement, quins rols i relacions es poden discernir, quins factors contextuals afecten la construcció del coneixement, i com es promouen o limiten les

---

7. "en l'educació, els etnògrafs entren en una aula, una escola, un context amb grup familiar o una comunitat per identificar el coneixement dels de dintre fent preguntes" (Green et al., 2012, p. 310).

formes de saber, ser i fer (Green et al., 2012, p. 310) dels membres les accions individuals i grupals. Aquests autors argumenten que l'etnografia no s'ha de considerar com un mètode, sinó com un enfocament de lògica-en-ús, basat en la premissa que l'etnografia s'aplica com un "non-linear system, guided by an iterative, recursive and abductive logic"[8] (Green et al, 2012, p. 309). És a dir, que els etnògrafs educatius no tenen passos o mètodes de treball de camp predefinits. Això és especialment rellevant quan es tracta d'entorns complexos com els contextos d'aprenentatge mixt. L'etnografia educativa pot ser especialment útil per les persones investigadores que estan interessades en un enfocament emic (vegeu Dooly i Moore, en aquest volum; Nussbaum, en aquest volum), definit per les dades que ajudi a explicar els detalls exactes del procés d'aprenentatge de llengües. En els últims anys, la transferència d'aquest enfocament en la interacció en línia i en mòbils en entorns d'aprenentatge ha esdevingut un tema més habitual.

The methodological approach of virtual ethnography has been broadened and reformulated through new proposals such as digital ethnography, ethnography on/of/through the Internet, connective ethnography, networked ethnography, cyberethnography, etc. Each of these maintains its own dialogue with the established tradition of ethnography and formulates its relation to this tradition in different ways (Domínguez Figaredo et al., 2007, par. 1)[9].

Un punt clau per entendre el que implica l'EV és reconèixer que aquest tipus d'estudi és potencialment global en el seu abast geogràfic (Greschke, 2007, par. 1), mentre que, al mateix temps, pretén descobrir, descriure i entendre el que es constitueix en les relacions a nivell local (i 'glocal'), facilitades a través de dimensions virtuals (o digitals). Això implica que la investigació en línia ha d'anar més enllà d'una simple captura de dades de la pantalla procedents d'una única font (per exemple, transcripcions de xats, entrades d'un blog o d'un fòrum, intercanvis de correus electrònics), que, fins ara, ha compost una

---

8. "un sistema no lineal, guiat per una lògica iterativa, recursiva i abductiva" (Green et al., 2012, p. 309).

9. "L'enfocament metodològic de l'etnografia virtual s'ha ampliat i reformulat a través de noves propostes, com l'etnografia digital, l'etnografia a/a través/d'Internet, l'etnografia connectiva, l'etnografia en xarxa, la ciberetnografia, etc. Cadascuna defensa el seu propi diàleg amb la tradició establerta per l'etnografia i formula la seva relació amb aquesta tradició de maneres diferents" (Domínguez Figaredo et al., 2007, par. 1).

gran part del corpus dels estudis sobre la comunicació mediada per ordinador, per tal de comprendre els patrons comunicatius interrelacionats entre diferents espais (tant en línia com fora de línia). Com assenyala Androutsopoulos (2008), intentar comprendre les pràctiques discursives dels interactuants fixant-se exclusivament en una sola font de dades en pantalla, en realitat, no proporciona gaire perspectiva a sobre les pràctiques discursives connectades que utilitzen els individus, no només entre espais en i fora de línia, també en interaccions entre diferents espais en línia i dins de múltiples comunitats virtuals.

Aquest mateix autor ha identificat dos tipus emergents d'EV. El primer tipus se centra en la integració (i la penetració) de tecnologies de comunicació en la vida quotidiana i l'impacte que poden tenir sobre les pràctiques socials i culturals. Aquest tipus d'EV es considera que és 'etnografia mixta', ja que combina les dades derivades de l'etnografia en línia i fora de línia. És un exemple d'aquest tipus d'EV l'estudi inclòs en aquest capítol. El segon tipus d'EV identificat per Androutsopoulos (2008) consisteix a entendre els patrons de comunicació emergents de diversos llocs de CMO, per tant, es tracta només d'etnografia en línia o, com explica l'autor, s'ocupa de la "systematic observation [of] the dynamics of communication and semiotic production within web environments"[10] (par. 10).

De fet, l'enfocament de l'EV ha existit prou temps perquè hagi aparegut un marc general (Hines, 2000). En aquest marc, hi ha quatre aspectes principals que constitueixen l'EV, que són els següents:

- L'EV proporciona un mitjà per comprendre les formes en què la CMO passa a ser socialment significativa en la vida quotidiana i en els processos d'aprenentatge.

- L'EV observa les connexions entre espais.

- No hi ha límits clars entre el que és 'virtual' i el que és 'real'.

---
10. "observació sistemàtica [de] la dinàmica de la comunicació i la producció semiòtica dins els entorns web" (Androutsopoulos, 2008, p. 10)

Capítol 7

- En l'EV, els mitjans de comunicació social s'entenen com a pràctiques socioculturals i artefactes socioculturals.

Aquest marc també posa de relleu els aspectes que afecten la persona investigadora, com es pot veure a continuació:

- Les persones investigadores hauran de ser capaços d'adaptar-se per recollir dades 'virtualment' i 'físicament'.

- A causa de la forma en què els participants s'involucren amb les comunitats virtuals, la recopilació de dades probablement serà intermitent, en comptes de ser una immersió a llarg termini.

- La participació virtual afegeix una dimensió reflexiva a les dades i a l'anàlisi (l'espai en línia és alhora un lloc d'activitat contínua i informació fixa ja existent).

Tenint en compte que els 'espais de treball' o els llocs potencials per a la investigació etnogràfica virtual són 'plurilocals' i expansius (especialment amb la reproducció dels recursos a través d'enllaços a altres llocs), sorgeixen algunes preguntes importants per a la persona investigadora:

- Com es determinen els límits del treball de camp?

- De quina manera s'estableixen els paràmetres d'enllaços exponencials (quants enllaços entre llocs s'han d'observar i analitzar)?

- Quin és el fonament per seleccionar el que s'inclou? I el que s'exclou?

- Què significa per als etnògrafs virtuals 'ser' i 'formar part' de la comunitat?

- Els etnògrafs virtuals poden determinar quan saben prou sobre la comunitat només participant-hi 'virtualment'?

- Quina part de la conducta en la comunitat està disponible per a les persones investigadores i, de la que està disponible, quina part realment es monitoritza? (Això es refereix al marc de la participació intermitent i la fusió entre la participació en línia i fora de línia.)

- En relació amb el punt anterior, s'han de tenir en compte els aspectes 'físics' de la vida dels subjectes (Greschke, 2007). Si és així, com pot gestionar-se?

Inevitablement, també s'han de considerar algunes qüestions ètiques, quan es du a terme EV (vegeu el capítol Dooly, Moore, i Vallejo, en aquest volum, sobre l'ètica de la investigació), que són pertinents per a la recol·lecció de dades en línia o digital. La qüestió de si els recursos que es mostren 'públicament' requereixen el permís dels participants per poder-se utilitzar com a dades (i com obtenir aquest permís en una comunitat virtual mundial) segueix sent objecte de debat a la comunitat d'EV. Encara hi ha més discussió sobre si és ètic fer-se membre d'una comunitat per tal de recopilar dades (conegut com *lurking* en anglès, 'estar a l'aguait'), especialment quan es tracta de comunitats virtuals més 'sensibles' (per exemple, una comunitat LGBTQ+ o d'educació sexual d'adolescents). No obstant això, l'Association of Internet Researchers (AoIR) ha creat algunes pautes generals[11]. Més concretament, se suggereix que qualsevol persona que exerceixi EV ha de fer visible i transparent el seu objectiu des del principi (per exemple, compartir-ho en un fòrum, fer una targeta d'informació als mons virtuals); no només ha d'explicar que està recollint dades, sinó que també ha de proporcionar un enllaç perquè altres membres de la comunitat virtual puguin trobar més informació sobre l'estudi i, si és possible, donar el seu consentiment. És cert que això no és un sistema a prova d'error, però sí que indica una disposició a ser transparent amb la resta dels membres de la comunitat.

Fer anònimes les dades és un altre tema bastant complicat amb l'EV. Com que són diferents de les dades recollides en ambients cara a cara (que generalment es basen en la comunicació oral), canviar el nom dels participants no esborra fàcilment les 'marques' de les seves interaccions en línia, com és evident tenint en

---

[11]. Vegeu http://aoir.org

compte la facilitat amb què els motors de cerca poden localitzar textos complets basant-se en frases parcials que en formen part. Algunes persones prefereixen parafrasejar les interaccions dels participants per tal d'evitar aquesta possibilitat, encara que això inevitablement desdibuixa les línies encara més entre les dades 'autèntiques' i les dades 'reinterpretades'.

Malgrat aquests problemes i preguntes que encara estan en debat, les autores d'aquest capítol donem suport absolut a aquest tipus d'investigació, especialment a mesura que els processos d'aprenentatge de llengües passen cada cop més a entorns virtuals (que inclouen entorns d'aprenentatge mixt, com en el cas que es presenta a continuació). Igual que amb qualsevol camp d'investigació, els avenços tecnològics requereixen un replantejament de les pràctiques d'investigació actuals. En EV, això és especialment pertinent i aporta una nova dimensió de la reflexivitat als estudis, juntament amb pràctiques d'investigació innovadores i interessants.

3. Un estudi etnogràfic de casos múltiples que rastreja l'aprenentatge docent a l'aula i l'activitat en línia

Per tal d'il·lustrar empíricament el que s'ha explicat anteriorment, les seccions següents descriuen un exemple d'una aplicació de l'EV que es va utilitzar per aconseguir una comprensió holística dels processos d'aprenentatge i els resultats en un entorn d'aprenentatge mixt. En aquest estudi, es va fer servir la telecol·laboració juntament amb l'ensenyament universitari i les pràctiques a una escola amb l'objectiu de crear més oportunitats per a estudiants-docents d'anglès com a llengua estrangera en l'ensenyament primari per desenvolupar (1) el coneixement del domini i l'habilitat reflexiva, (2) l'aprenentatge col·laboratiu i (3) la comprensió de l'experiència de la CMO per a l'ensenyament de llengües. Als intercanvis, els estudiants-docents usaven l'anglès com a llengua franca.

L'intercanvi virtual es va dur a terme durant dos semestres. En el primer semestre, els estudiants-docents a Catalunya van haver de dissenyar una seqüència didàctica de set sessions en telecol·laboració amb 7 estudiants locals i 14 estudiants que eren als EUA (amb els quals es van aparellar fora de les hores de classe). Al segon semestre, els mateixos estudiants-docents havien de crear una unitat col·laborativa d'una sessió basada en un podcast sobre el fenomen lingüístic que escollissin. En el primer semestre, la interacció es va dur a terme amb MSN i Skype, de forma sincrònica, i amb el correu electrònic per a la comunicació asíncrona. En el segon semestre la interacció sincrònica es va dur a terme a través de Second Life i MSN, per ensenyar als estudiants-docents diferents vies de comunicació i perquè poguessin practicar, per observar els avantatges i inconvenients de cada una. A part de les col·laboracions virtuals i a la universitat, els estudiants-docents de Catalunya estaven fent pràctiques a centres d'educació primària, on van observar i treballar amb docents experimentats de les escoles. En aquests centres, els estudiants-docents basats a Catalunya havien de posar en pràctica les sessions didàctiques que havien creat en col·laboració amb els seus companys virtuals i de classe, i tutors, i reflexionar sobre el procés i els resultats en un wiki en forma de diari.

L'objectiu general de la investigació era entendre les formes en què la telecol·laboració basada en tasques interactuava amb la col·laboració cara a cara i les pràctiques a l'escola, i discernir les formes en què es pot utilitzar la telecol·laboració integrada per millorar els resultats d'aprenentatge de cursos d'iniciació a la formació del professorat convencionals cara a cara. Per optimitzar la recollida de dades i els resultats de la recerca, vam integrar i utilitzar els principals mètodes de l'EV; és a dir, el compromís prolongat, la immersió en profunditat i l'observació participant en l'àmbit més ampli i la pràctica de la investigació d'estudis de cas múltiples (Yin, 2003), i la riquesa analítica del Mostreig Teòric (MT, *grounded theory*, en anglès) (Charmaz, 2006; Glaser i Strauss, 1967).

4. Al punt de trobada de mètodes d'estudi de cas múltiple, etnogràfics i el mostreig teòric

L'estudi de cas té com a objectiu proporcionar "an up-close and in-depth empirical investigation of a particular contemporary phenomenon within its real life context, using multiple sources of evidence" (Robson, 1993, p. 146; vegeu també Yin, 2003)[12]. Hi ha diferents exemples d'investigacions d'estudi de cas: (1) estudis de cas individuals o únics, i (2) un conjunt d'estudis de cas individuals o estudis de cas múltiples (Robson, 1993; Yin, 2003). Els estudis de cas múltiples normalment inclouen 3-5 casos, cosa que permet comparar-los i contrastar-los; és a dir, comprovar les diferents presentacions/manifestacions d'un fenomen. Es considera que els estudis de cas múltiples proporcionen una millor comprensió i interpretacions més sòlides que els estudis de cas únic. En general, el mètode d'estudi de cas proporciona eines per a un enfocament holístic dels fenòmens, com ara documents, els mesuraments quantitatius i qualitatius en forma de qüestionaris de tipus obert i entrevistes, registres d'arxius i objectes físics (Yin, 2003). Els estudis individuals o diversos dels casos poden ser descriptius, poden respondre a la pregunta del 'què està passant', o exploratoris i/o explicatius si proporcionen respostes a preguntes del tipus 'com/per què va passar'.

El bricolatge metodològic descrit en aquest document es basa en suposicions filosòfiques comunes entre els enfocaments d'investigació, respectant el paradigma interpretatiu (Halaweh, Fidler, i McRobb, 2008), i destinades a crear una teoria fonamentada (Eisenhardt, 1989) sobre l'aprenentatge dels docents en entorns mixtos. És a dir, hem intentat entendre els processos i els resultats d'aprenentatge interpretant els processos de construcció de significats subjacents (Halaweh et al., 2008) i a través dels ulls dels participants. Ens vam acostar a la tasca sense idees predeterminades del que constitueix l'aprenentatge, a diferència dels paradigmes positivistes que utilitzen mètodes quantitatius per confirmar o rebutjar les teories (provar la teoria). Hem intentat desxifrar les característiques de les trajectòries i els resultats d'aprenentatge de tres dels set estudiants-docents, de la mateixa manera que ells mateixos els van experimentar, i analitzem altres fenòmens relacionats.

La investigació d'estudi de cas comparteix abast i tècniques amb l'etnografia, com el treball de camp (l'observació directa i participant), les entrevistes i els qüestionaris, el que permet construir una explicació global d'un esdeveniment,

---

12. "una investigació empírica de prop i en profunditat d'un fenomen contemporani concret dins del seu context de real, utilitzant múltiples fonts d'evidència" (Robson, 1993, p. 146).

procés, objecte o pràctica. Sovint l'etnografia es pot classificar com un tipus de mètode d'investigació per a estudis de cas descriptius. No obstant això, la característica definitòria de l'etnografia és l'observació participant de llarga durada i la relació social que es desenvolupa entre les persones participants i observadores. Aquest enfocament de la recol·lecció de dades es pot complementar amb entrevistes o altres dades qualitatives, però no sempre es fa, i els resultats no poden generalitzar-se a altres contextos. A través d'aquest tipus d'immersió prolongada i profunda en el context de la investigació, l'investigador recull dades 'no estructurats naturalistes' (Flick, 2002), que més tard es codifiquen per tal de revelar els elements subjacents que componen el comportament i la cultura humana. La mateixa persona investigadora es converteix en un instrument en el procés d'interpretació de les dades, permetent les possibilitats que existeixi un biaix (Cohen i Manion, 1989).

De forma similar a l'etnografia, el mètode de MT presenta un conjunt de tècniques i estratègies per a la recopilació i l'anàlisi de dades amb la finalitat de comprendre els aspectes significatius del fenomen que s'investiga (Charmaz, 2006; Strauss i Corbin, 1998). En el MT, la persona investigadora és participant-observadora del fenomen en el seu ambient natural. Recull dades no estructurades 'naturalistes', que analitza a mesura que el procés de recollida avança, aïllant temes i verificant-ne contínuament la importància amb més dades dels participants. Com a mètode principalment basat en dades, el MT no es desenvolupa a partir d'hipòtesis preconcebudes, sinó de les mateixes dades, en què els participants indiquen què és important per comprendre el fenomen. Com el seu nom suggereix, l'objectiu del MT és desenvolupar una teoria d'abast mitjà per explicar la conducta i els processos humans (Charmaz, 2006). La persona investigadora realitza una extensa codificació per representar el fenomen que s'està investigant. Durant la codificació i categorització, pren notes per explicar i completar les categories codificades. Alhora, aquesta presa de notes vincula els processos de codificació de dades i l'escriptura dels primers esborranys de documents (Charmaz, 2006). El MT té com a objectiu proposar una teoria basada en dades. Per a això, cal seleccionar els esdeveniments d'un corpus més ampli que ajudin a desenvolupar explicacions i conceptes teòrics del fenomen (o fenòmens) que s'està investigant (Strauss i Corbin, 1998). Aquest procés s'anomena mostreig teòric o presa de mostres per a la construcció de teories. Una característica de l'enfocament del MT en la investigació qualitativa és que la persona investigadora endarrereix la revisió de la bibliografia per tal de no veure's influït a l'hora de llegir les dades. Això també marca una diferència important amb els estudis positivistes, on la revisió de la literatura és el primer pas en el disseny de la investigació i serveix com a base per establir els objectius i les metodologies d'investigació per arribar-hi.

5. Anàlisi del discurs

L'Anàlisi del Discurs (AD) és un enfocament general per a l'anàlisi de 'textos' escrits i verbals, per trobar una connexió entre aquests textos i els seus significats (Lemke, 2012). Prenent la llengua en ús o la parla-en-interacció com a l'eina simbòlica fonamental en el desenvolupament de la cognició, ens interessava especialment destriar les relacions entre discurs/llengua en ús i el desenvolupament de la cognició amb el temps, a través de persones i eines. Amb aquesta finalitat, vam utilitzar un enfocament d'anàlisi del discurs de l'antropologia lingüística de l'educació (Agha i Wortham, 2005; Wortham, 2006), que va tenir en compte la dimensió temporal i espacial de la interacció (cara a cara i en línia) per tal de conceptualitzar i identificar els recursos lingüístics i conceptuals que els estudiants-docents es trobaven, transferien i utilitzaven a través dels diferents espais en què estaven treballant, durant l'any acadèmic, així com el diferent posicionament associat a cada ús (Wortham, 2006). Aquest enfocament reestructura un tipus d'enfocament d'anàlisi de marcs (*frames* en anglès) (Tannen, 1993), que s'adapta a les necessitats del nostre context d'investigació i del procés de codificació, que va ser impulsat per les preguntes següents:

- Què fan els estudiants-docents en aquesta interacció i en quina disposició espacial? Quins coneixements/habilitats estan treballant?

- En quin moment del procés d'aprenentatge ho fan?

- Quins recursos utilitzen d'altres llocs, per exemple, dels continguts de les classes, de l'experiència al centre educatiu?

• Aquestes interaccions es relacionen amb els coneixements adquirits que els estudiants-docents demostren al final de l'any?

Codificar a partir d'aquestes idees ens va permetre traçar l'aprenentatge professional; és a dir, el desenvolupament del discurs del professor, i pensar en tots els espais en línia i cara a cara al llarg del temps. Ara descriurem les múltiples fonts d'evidència que hem utilitzat per interpretar, triangular, i recopilar dades i procediments analítics utilitzats per a la captura de l'*aprenentatge en procés*'.

6. La recollida de dades multimodal: els mètodes utilitzats i els tipus de dades recollides

6.1. Els qüestionaris i entrevistes a reunions de grup

Es van dur a terme grups de discussió amb els participants (vegeu Canals, en aquest volum) cara a cara just al començament del projecte de recerca per tal de fomentar una primera reunió entre els participants (estudiants-docents amb seu a Catalunya) i permetre que compartissin experiències i preocupacions d'aprenentatge sobre la col·laboració en línia. Els grups de discussió van permetre que els estudiants-docents recordessin, reflexionessin i sintetitzessin les experiències d'aprenentatge anteriors, aclarissin debilitats i objectius, i establissin les expectatives per al curs. Aquestes entrevistes grupals es van gravar, transcriure i incloure en l'anàlisi (vegeu el capítol de Moore i Llompart, en aquest volum). Quant a la investigació, es van utilitzar com a dades d'activitat orientades als processos, que marcaven l'etapa inicial del desenvolupament i que servien com a referència per comparar amb les millores d'aprenentatge a finals de l'any. Es van fer servir qüestionaris oberts (vegeu Canals, en aquest volum) per documentar els objectius i expectatives del curs. També es va demanar als estudiants-docents que classifiquessin les seves competències docents en una versió resumida del *European Portfolio of Student-Teacher of Languages* (Dossier d'Aprenentatge Europeu d'Estudiants-Docents) (Newby et al., 2007).

6.2. L'observació participant a l'aula i en línia

6.2.1. Observació a l'aula

Totes les sessions cara a cara a la universitat, 1r i 2n semestre, van gravar-se en vídeo i àudio setmanalment. Es pot considerar que, en aquesta investigació, la manera en què es va dur a terme l'observació participant a l'aula incloïa un nivell moderat de participació i hi havia una preocupació per mantenir un equilibri entre els papers de persona 'interna' i 'externa', el que permetia una bona combinació de compromís i distància necessaris per a ser objectiu (DeWalt i DeWalt, 2002; Schwartz i Schwartz, 1955). Es va deixar clar als participants que la investigadora no participava en l'avaluació del curs. Per tant, va ser capaç d'observar el procés que es va construir de forma natural entre la tutora universitària i els estudiants-docents. Amb el temps i a través de la interacció diària, es va desenvolupar una relació de confiança entre la investigadora i els participants. És especialment important desenvolupar una relació de confiança amb els participants, sobretot en contextos educatius. Tenint en compte la càrrega de treball que tenen els participants en aquests entorns, és imprescindible respectar les qüestions ètiques implicades i unir-se als participants en els seus interessos i activitats. En aquesta configuració, l'interès compartit era un veritable esforç cap a l'aprenentatge i la millora de la pràctica docent, fins i tot més enllà dels èxits acadèmics.

6.2.2. Observació en línia

En el primer semestre, els participants van dur a terme l'intercanvi en línia durant el seu temps fora de classe, sobretot a casa. L'observació participant, per tant, no podia dur-se a terme sense entrar en la privacitat dels participants. Tenint en compte la definició de l'EV com l'adaptació dels mètodes etnogràfics tradicionals, es va demanar als estudiants-docents que guardessin i enviessin per correu electrònic les seves interaccions en línia amb els seus companys dels Estats Units a la seva tutora i a la investigadora. Aquestes transcripcions es van adoptar com a 'protocols naturals' dels esforços dels estudiants per donar sentit i estructurar el seu entorn físic i social (Roth, 1996).

L'observació en línia es va dur a terme durant les reunions inicials de Second Life (plataforma utilitzada per a la telecol·laboració durant el segon semestre). Com que aquesta plataforma/eina era una 'localitat' completament nova per als estudiants-docents, l'observació en línia va proporcionar a la investigadora una visió d'estat emocional i la familiaritat dels estudiants amb diversos aspectes de la tecnologia, que eren, alhora, útils per traçar el desenvolupament digital al final del curs (això era rellevant per als objectius de la investigació). La investigadora, també present a Second Life, va documentar aspectes importants d'aquest procés en les notes de camp. Els participants també van documentar el seu punt de vista dels aspectes importants d'aquest procés en forma de narratives (descrites a continuació).

6.3. Entrevistes semiestructurades

Una vegada van començar a sorgir els temes de la lectura de les dades de la classe i en línia, la investigadora va seguir amb entrevistes semiestructurades amb els participants, per tal de corroborar el valor i, a més, investigar aquests temes (en línia amb la metodologia MT, com es va descriure anteriorment).

6.4. Narratives

Es va demanar als participants que escrivissin relats wiki en línia, que, posteriorment, la investigadora es va descarregar. Aquest tipus de dades va facilitar que els mateixos participants poguessin reconstruir els fets i va ajudar la investigadora a comprendre més profundament els temes d'interès, així com les descobertes de la triangulació dels resultats (Jangu, 2012).

- Les actes de les sessions de tutoria que documenten els principals successos i la rellevància per al procés d'aprenentatge. Aquestes notes es van contrastar amb les notes de camp de la investigadora, i es van utilitzar com a dades de triangulació que ofereixen una millor comprensió de les percepcions pròpies de l'experiència dels estudiants-docents.

- Els diaris de l'escola. Els estudiants-docents escrivien un diari de les seves experiències de pràctiques a centres d'educació primària, durant tot el procés de pràctiques. Aquestes documentacions proporcionaven dades sobre la interacció dels estudiants-docents amb l'entorn escolar i les formes en què associaven aquesta experiència d'ensenyament pràctic (coensenyament amb docents experts, observacions mentre fan classes) amb el que estaven aprenent a la universitat i en línia.

- Autoreflexions i avaluacions. Consistien en diversos textos wiki en què es duien a terme les activitats següents: (1) autoreflexions sobre la pròpia pràctica docent dels estudiants-docents, l'aplicació dels materials que havien creat en col·laboració amb la classe, i els companys virtuals i tutors; (2) les avaluacions dels estudiants sobre la seva experiència d'aprenentatge. En aquest últim cas, els estudiants-docents havien de reflexionar sobre les contribucions dels xats en línia i les sessions de formació del professorat a la universitat; (3) la reflexió sobre el desenvolupament de la competència docent, a partir d'una versió resumida del Dossier d'Aprenentatge Europeu d'Estudiants-Docents de Llengües, que es va entregar a l'inici de curs. Els estudiants-docents van escriure els textos del wiki des del principi fins al final del curs.

7. El mostreig de dades

Per a la investigació etnogràfica d'estudis de cas múltiples de qualitat cal seleccionar casos bons i rics en informació, la qual cosa s'anomena tècnica de mostreig orientada a la informació (Yin, 2003; vegeu també Dörnyei, 2007). La bibliografia proposa escollir subjectes que ofereixen informació molt valuosa, única o especialment reveladora sobre una sèrie de circumstàncies (Fenno, 1986), i no centrar-se en els casos típics que representen el fenomen que ens ocupa. En aquest projecte de recerca, es va optar per centrar-se en la trajectòria d'aprenentatge de tres dels set estudiants-docents que van participar en el curs. Amb aquesta selecció, volíem entendre com un nombre important d'agents amb diferents motivacions pel que fa a l'ensenyament i la CMO percep el potencial (*affordances*) d'aprenentatge de l'entorn de treball i aprenentatge, i l'utilitza per construir el coneixement. Aquesta polaritat entre els casos permet la generalització analítica (Yin, 2003) sobre el potencial d'aprenentatge d'aquest entorn híbrid, ja que proporciona evidència sobre les formes en què aquest entorn pot beneficiar persones de diferents nivells de competència i amb diverses motivacions. Disposàvem de dades completes per revelar i triangular les trajectòries i resultats d'aprenentatge d'aquests tres estudiants-docents i, per tant, dur a terme de forma fiable els objectius de la investigació.

En aquest projecte d'investigació, el cas clau va ser una estudiant-docent amb un rendiment i consistència exemplars al llarg del curs, que responia a les intencions i objectius de la tutora. Volíem, per tant, estudiar les circumstàncies relacionades amb aquesta actuació per tal d'extreure conclusions sobre els aspectes de telecol·laboració eficaç per a l'aprenentatge docent. El segon cas va considerar-se crític a causa de la barrera de llengua d'aquesta estudiant-professora. Es considerava una estudiant feble, amb poc domini de la llengua de destí, però era una estudiant amb bons coneixements de tecnologia i estava cada cop més motivada gràcies al suport constant que rebia en aquest ambient d'aprenentatge. El seu rendiment en els espais il·lustra processos d'aprenentatge únics, el desenvolupament de la identitat professional i habilitats a través de la imitació del discurs de la tutora i les pràctiques d'aprenentatge que va experimentar a l'aula i en línia. El tercer cas va ser particularment revelador sobre com la participació en aquest tipus d'entorn d'aprenentatge híbrid pot funcionar en circumstàncies estranyes. Aquesta estudiant-professora tenia un nivell limitat de competència digital, principalment a causa de l'aversió personal cap a la tecnologia. A més, el seu nivell d'anglès era baix i, al principi, es va sentir molt incòmoda participant en les activitats col·laboratives en línia.

A més de la selecció dels casos, el mostreig de dades també va incloure la distinció de dades focals i dades de triangulació. La triangulació implicava utilitzar les dades obtingudes de diferents fonts i mètodes 'superposats' (Guba i Lincoln, 1994), i contrastar-les amb els resultats de les dades focals per determinar-ne la validesa. La Figura 1 il·lustra la progressió i l'acumulació constant de dades al llarg dels escenaris multimodals. Com mostra aquesta figura, cada etapa de recol·lecció de dades genera, gradualment, més informació, el que va facilitar una comprensió seqüencial del procés d'aprenentatge dels docents.

Figura 1. Representació del procés de recollida de dades i els resultats

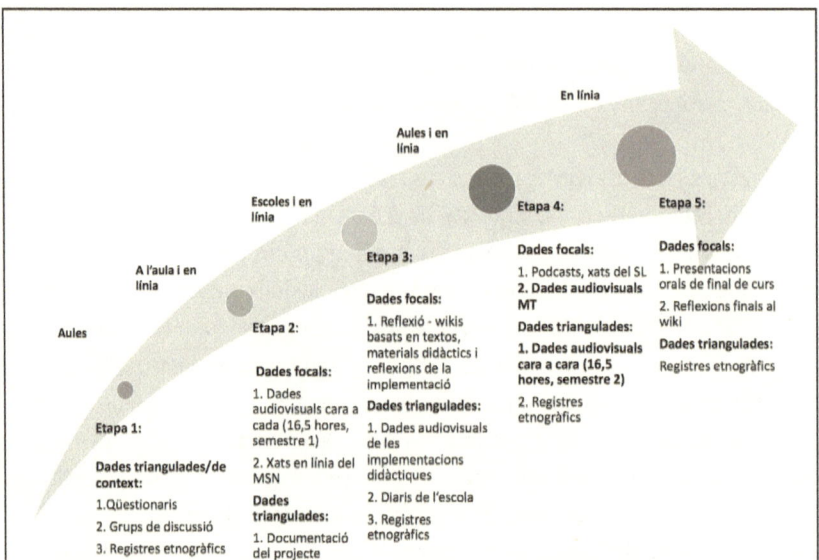

8. Anàlisi de les dades: gestió de dades, codificació i interpretació dels resultats amb assistència de NVIVO8

Totes les dades, focals i triangulades, es van emmagatzemar a la carpeta 'Elements interns' de NVIVO8 (Figura 2). Les referències bibliogràfiques, que vam fer servir per justificar teòricament aquesta investigació, es van vincular, enganxar o resumir a la carpeta 'Elements externs'. Els arxius originals es van emmagatzemar físicament a la carpeta de l'ordinador 'Documents' o estaven disponibles a llocs web fora de NVivo. En el cas d'articles de mida petita, es van importar com a arxius PDF a la carpeta 'Elements interns' (Figura 2).

Figura 2. Emmagatzematge de dades a NVIVO8

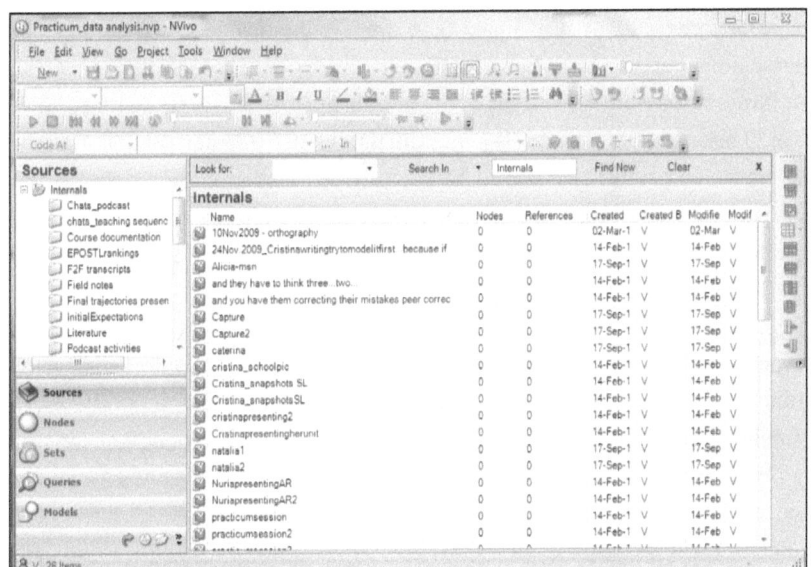

8.1. Anàlisi de dades

Amb les preguntes d'investigació al costat com a recordatori dels objectius d'investigació, vam començar el procés d'anàlisi de dades mitjançant la codificació de les dades focals, per exemple, les interaccions a l'aula i en línia, les reflexions sobre textos.

La codificació és el procés analític que facilita la categorització de grans quantitats de 'dades brutes/no estructurades' en bons esquemes de codificació que proporcionen a l'analista una 'trama' que permet contestar les preguntes de recerca (Strauss i Corbin, 1998). En aquesta investigació, la codificació va ajudar a revelar les relacions entre l'activitat d'aprenentatge a la universitat, en línia i a l'escola amb els resultats que els estudiants-docents van declarar al final del curs.

La nostra codificació estava orientada a un tema i tenia com a objectiu detectar totes les interaccions al voltant d'un mateix tema (per exemple, la planificació de classes, l'avaluació). A més, la investigadora va codificar les interaccions que van tenir lloc en diferents disposicions espacials i temporals. Era important assenyalar-ho als codis per als nostres objectius de recerca. Per això, la investigadora, en anglès, va utilitzar el sufix *-ing* per denotar el procés i el sufix *-ed* per als resultats. Un exemple de resultat codificat és *Learned terminology for setting linguistic objectives* (Terminologia apresa per establir objectius lingüístics), i un exemple de procés codificat és *Designing realistic objectives for 4 year-olds* (Dissenyar objectius realistes per a alumnat de 4 anys). Aquest mètode de codificació ha permès fer èmfasi en les relacions temporals entre els diferents extractes de dades, i també traçar les relacions temporals i temàtiques entre els codis per tal d'establir una xarxa d'episodis d'interacció a partir del qual els estudiants-docents visiblement van construir significat al voltant del tema/habilitat que aprenien (Barab, Hay, i Yagamata-Lynch, 2001; Roth, 1996).

Després de les etapes de codificació de la metodologia MT, l'anàlisi de dades va consistir en tres cicles de codificació; és a dir, oberta, axial i teòrica. Aquestes etapes de codificació tenen com a objectiu centrar gradualment l'anàlisi dels fragments rellevants de dades per respondre a les preguntes d'investigació. Els codis oberts són el resultat d'una lectura inicial de les dades, on els investigadors llegeixen i tornen a llegir les dades, i aïllen els aspectes interessants dels participants o paraules literals (Figura 3).

La codificació axial és la segona etapa dels codis de dades, que recull les relacions entre els codis i redueix el nombre de codis oberts fusionant codis similars. Juntament amb la codificació, es va elaborar i implementar un esquema de presa de notes que documentava els pensaments de la investigadora mentre codificava les dades, per respondre els coms i els perquès de la codificació i la categorització, i per ajudar a posar de manifest les relacions entre els codis durant l'etapa de codificació axial (Figura 4).

Figura 3. Nodes lliures – fase de codificació oberta

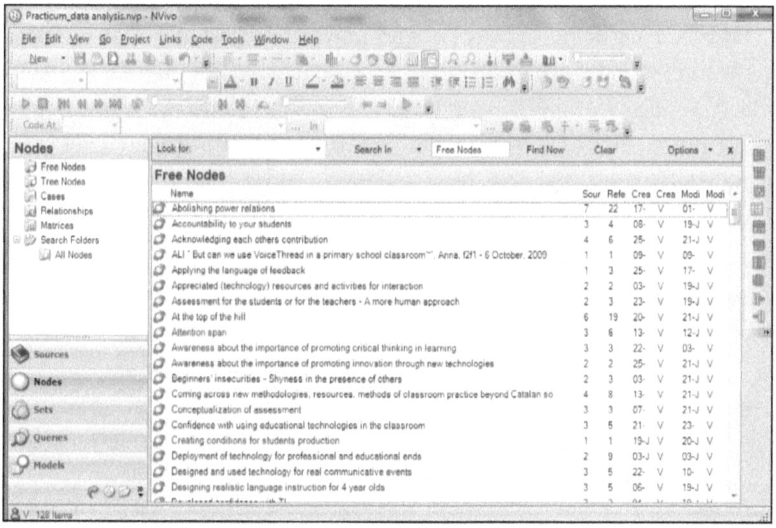

Figura 4. Arbre de nodes – etapa de codificació axial

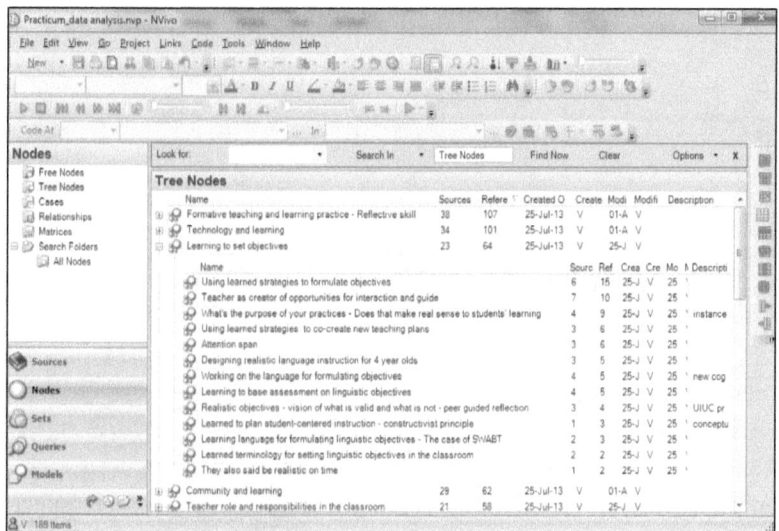

Capítol 7

Per a la tercera etapa de codificació, les persones investigadores revisen la literatura del marc teòric rellevant per explicar i/o interpretar les seves conclusions a partir de les dues etapes anteriors de codificació. En aquesta etapa, es creen categories més grans que relacionen les dades/codis amb la teoria. Aquest és l'últim bloc en la construcció de teories. La tercera i última etapa analítica estava formada per les vuit categories il·lustrades a la Figura 5, que indicaven el resultat d'aprenentatge, és a dir, el coneixement, la destresa i l'habilitat en diferents àrees de l'ensenyament, per exemple, el procés d'ensenyament i aprenentatge de la pràctica, la tecnologia i l'aprenentatge, i l'aprenentatge per establir objectius (planificació de les classes). Les referències bibliogràfiques donaven suport a aquestes categories finals i, a més, van ser reformulades d'acord amb les premisses teòriques que es van trobar a la literatura.

Figura 5. Categraritzacions finals a NVIVO – indicadors de rellevància

Tree Nodes		
Name	Sources	Referen
Formative teaching and learning practice - Reflective skill	38	107
Technology and learning	34	101
Learning to set objectives	23	64
Community and learning	29	62
Teacher role and responsibilities in the classroom	21	58
Developed confidence	15	44
Materializing CLT through concrete examples of classroom practice	20	40
Lifelong learning	7	9

9. Interpretació de les dades i resultats formals

Hem optat per centrar-nos en les tres categories més rellevants (segons els mesuraments quantitatius de NVIVO8), per tal de preservar el rigor analític. Les troballes van presentar-se com una història d''aprenentatge en procés' que va culminar en coneixements, habilitats i competències específics que els estudiants focals van declarar haver après al final de la pràctica.

L'anàlisi del discurs en profunditat, tal com es descriu a la secció introductòria de la metodologia anterior, ens va informar de la interpretació dels esdeveniments d'aprenentatge seqüencials que es van dur a terme a la universitat, en línia i en entorns escolars en diferents moments temporals, i van explicar la manera en què la interacció simètrica i asimètrica amb els companys virtuals i tutors, respectivament, sobre l'experiència d'aprenentatge de les pràctiques a l'escola i l'aplicació de l'ensenyament van ajudar als docents a aprendre, dins dels paràmetres formals de la formació del professorat contemporània (Antoniadou, 2013). Si s'observen de forma seqüencial, aquests episodis mostren que els estudiants-docents fan servir i combinen els recursos que tenen a la seva disposició a través de la interacció per construir nous coneixements i assolir nous resultats cognitius pel que fa a la planificació de la instrucció estratègica, les habilitats i els coneixements col·laboratius i digitals (Antoniadou, 2011, 2013; Dooly, 2011, 2013).

10. Conclusions

En aquest capítol, hem descrit un estudi d'EV. Hem il·lustrat els tipus i els processos de recollida de dades dins de l'EV i hem detallat com s'ha fet l'anàlisi de dades a través de múltiples espais educatius. Hem explicat com vam utilitzar aquesta informació per assolir els nostres objectius de recerca, amb l'esperança de proporcionar unes pautes de com fer-ho per a persones interessades a fer esforços etnogràfics en els ambients d'aprenentatge mediats per ordinador. Amb aquest enfocament, vam examinar l'aprenentatge com un procés, vam ser capaços de discernir episodis crítics d'interacció a través dels espais d'instrucció i il·lustrar els processos de construcció de significat seqüencials pel que fa a l'aprenentatge de l'ensenyament.

La investigació descrita en aquest capítol confirma que no hi ha una tipologia de procediments per a l'EV; sinó que l'aplicació de l'EV depèn necessàriament de les contingències contextuals i les rellevàncies de cada lloc en particular (Domínguez et al., 2007). Les especificitats institucionals i els desafiaments

Capítol 7

locals influeixen necessàriament en la forma de la investigació i requereixen ajustaments en la investigació etnogràfica tradicional.

Obres citades

Agha, A., i Wortham, S. (2005). Discourse across speech-events: intertextuality and interdiscursivity in social life. *Journal of Linguistic Anthropology, 15*(1), special issue.

Androutsopoulos, J. (2008). Potentials and limitations of discourse-centred online ethnography. *Language@internet, 5*. http://www.languageatinternet.org/articles/2008/1610

Antoniadou, V. (2011). Virtual collaboration, 'perezhivanie'and teacher learning: a socio-cultural-historical perspective. *Bellaterra Journal of Teaching & Learning Language & Literature, 4*(3), 53-70.

Antoniadou, V. (2013). *Expanding the socio-material spaces of teacher education programmes: a qualitative trace of teacher professionalization through blended pedagogy in Catalonia.* Tesi doctoral no publicada. Universitat Autònoma de Barcelona.

Antoniadou, V. (2017). Recoger, organizar y analizar corpus de datos multimodales: las contribuciones de los CAQDAS. A E. Moore i M. Dooly (Eds), *Enfocaments qualitatius per a la recerca en educació plurilingüe* (p. 451-467). Research-publishing.net. https://doi.org/10.14705/rpnet.2017.emmd2016.641

Barab, S. A, Hay, K. E., i Yagamata-Lynch, L. C. (2001). Constructing networks of action relevant episodes: an in-situ research methodology. *The Journal of the Learning Sciences, 10*(1 i 2), 63-112. https://doi.org/10.1207/S15327809JLS10-1-2_5

Beckmann, S., i Langer, R. (2005). Netnography: rich insights from online research. *Insights@ CBS, 14*(6). https://stosowana.files.wordpress.com/2010/10/670005_beckmann_langer_full_version.pdf

Bruner, J. S. (1986). *Actual minds, possible worlds*. Boston: Harvard University Press.

Canals, L. (2017). Instruments per a la recollida de dades. A E. Moore i M. Dooly (Eds), *Enfocaments qualitatius per a la recerca en educació plurilingüe* (p. 377-389). Research-publishing.net. https://doi.org/10.14705/rpnet.2017.emmd2016.636

Charmaz, K. (2006). *Constructing grounded theory: a practical guide through qualitative analysis*. Londres: Sage.

Cohen, L., i Manion, L. (1989). *Research methods in education* (3a edició). Londres: Routledge.

Corona, V. (2017). Un acercamiento etnográfico al estudio de las variedades lingüísticas de jóvenes latinoamericanos en Barcelona. A E. Moore i M. Dooly (Eds), *Enfocaments qualitatius per a la recerca en educació plurilingüe* (p. 151-169). Research-publishing. net. https://doi.org/10.14705/rpnet.2017.emmd2016.626

Darling, D. (2005). Improving minority student achievement by making cultural connections. *Middle Ground, 36*(5), 46-50. https://doi.org/10.1080/00940771.2005.11461505

DeWalt, K. M., i DeWalt, B. R. (2002). Participant observation: a guide for fieldworkers. Walnut Creek, CA: AltaMira Press.

Domínguez Figaredo, D., Beaulieu, A., Estalella, A., Gómez, E., Schnettler, B., i Read, R. (2007). Virtual ethnography. *FQS Forum: Qualitative Social Research, 8*(3). http://www.qualitative-research.net/index.php/fqs/article/view/274

Dooly, M. (2010). Empowering language minorities through technology: which way to Go? *eLearning Papers, 19*, 1-12. https://www.openeducationeuropa.eu/sites/default/files/legacy_files/old/6_1272021672.pdf

Dooly, M. (2011). Divergent perceptions of telecollaborative language learning tasks: task-as-workplan vs. task-as-process. *Language Learning & Technology, 15*(2), 69-91.

Dooly, M. (2013). Focusing on the social: research into the distributed knowledge of novice teachers in online exchange. A C. Meskill (Ed.), *Online teaching and learning: sociocultural perspectives. Advances in digital language learning and teachng* (p. 1-30). Londres/Nova York: Bloomsbury Academic.

Dooly, M. (2017). Una aproximació a dades multimodals amb l'anàlisi del discurs mediat. A E. Moore i M. Dooly (Eds), *Enfocaments qualitatius per a la recerca en educació plurilingüe* (p. 212-235). Research-publishing.net. https://doi.org/10.14705/rpnet.2017.emmd2016.629

Dooly, M., i Moore, E. (2017). Introducció: enfocaments qualitatius per a la recerca en educació plurilingüe. A E. Moore i M. Dooly (Eds), *Enfocaments qualitatius per a la recerca en educació plurilingüe* (p. 11-20). Research-publishing.net. https://doi.org/10.14705/rpnet.2017.emmd2016.619

Dooly, M., Moore, E., i Vallejo, C. (2017). Ética de la investigación. A E. Moore i M. Dooly (Eds), *Enfocaments qualitatius per a la recerca en educació plurilingüe* (p. 363-375). Research-publishing.net. https://doi.org/10.14705/rpnet.2017.emmd2016.635

Dörnyei, Z. (2007). *Research methods in applied linguistics: quantitative, qualitative and mixed methodologies*. Oxford: Oxford University Press.

Eisenhardt, K. M. (1989). Building theories from case study research. *Academy of Management Review, 14*(4), 532–550.

Elliot, R., i Jankel-Elliott, N. (2002). Using ethnography in strategic consumer research. *Qualitative Market Research: an International Journal, 6*(5), 215-223.

Erickson, F. (1973). What makes school ethnography 'ethnographic'? *Council on Anthropology and Education Newsletter, 4*(2), 10-19. https://doi.org/10.1525/aeq.1973.4.2.05x0129y

Fenno, R. (1986). Observation, context, and sequence in the study of politics. *American Political Science Review, 80*(1), 3-15. https://doi.org/10.2307/1957081

Flick, U. (2002). *An introduction to qualitative research* (2a edició). Thousand Oaks/Londres: Sage Publications.

Glaser, B. G., i Strauss, A. L. (1967). *The discovery of grounded theory: strategies for qualitative research.* Chicago: Aldine.

Green, J. L., Skukauskaite, A., i Baker, W. D. (2012). Ethnography as epistemology. A J. Arthur, M. Waring, R. Coe, i L.V. Hedges (Eds), *Research methods and nethodologies in education* (p. 309-321). Londres: Sage.

Greschke, H. M. (2007). Logging into the field—Methodological reflections on ethnographic research in a pluri-local and computer-mediated field. *FQS Forum: Qualitative Social Research, 8*(3). http://www.qualitative-research.net/index.php/fqs/article/view/279

Guba, E. G., i Lincoln, Y. S. (1994). Competing paradigms in qualitative research. A N. Denzin i Y. Lincoln (Eds), *Handbook of qualitative research* (p. 105-117). Londres: Sage.

Halaweh, M., Fidler, C., i McRobb, S. (2008). Integrating the grounded theory method and case study research methodology within IS Research: a possible 'road map'. *ICIS 2008 Proceedings.* Paper 165. http://aisel.aisnet.org/icis2008/165

Hefflin, B. R. (2002). Learning to develop culturally relevant pedagogy: a lesson about cornrowed lives. *Urban Review, 33*(2), 131-149.

Hines, C. (2000). *Virtual ethnography.* Londres/Nova Deli: Sage. https://doi.org/10.4135/9780857020277

Jangu, W. I. (2012). *Understanding the basics of qualitative research.* https://www.academia.edu/2321683/UNDERSTANDING_THE_BASICS_OF_QUALITATIVE_RESEARCH

Johnson, C. C. (2005). Making instruction relevant to language minority students at the middle level. *Middle School Journal, 37*(2), 10-14. https://doi.org/10.1080/00940771.2005.11461521

Kulavuz-Onal, D., i Vásquez, C. (2013). Reconceptualising fieldwork in a netnography of an online community of English language teachers. *Ethnography and Education, 8*(2), 224-238. https://doi.org/10.1080/17457823.2013.792511

Lemke, J. L. (2012). Multimedia and discourse analysis. A J. P. Gee i M. Handford (Eds), *Routledge handbook of discourse analysis* (p. 79-89). Nova York: Routledge.

Moore, E., i Llompart, J. (2017). Recoger, transcribir, analizar y presentar datos interaccionales plurilingües. A E. Moore i M. Dooly (Eds), *Enfocaments qualitatius per a la recerca en educació plurilingüe* (p. 418-433). Research-publishing.net. https://doi.org/10.14705/rpnet.2017.emmd2016.639

Newby, D., Allan, R., Fenner, A-B., Jones, B., Komorowska, H., i Soghikyan, K. (2007). *European portfolio for student teachers of languages. A reflection tool for language teacher education.* Graz: European Centre for Modern Languages.

Noblit, G. (1984). The prospects of an applied ethnography for education: a sociology of knowledge interpretation. *Educational Evaluation and Policy Analysis, 5*(1), 95-101. https://doi.org/10.3102/01623737006001095

Nussbaum, L. (2017). Investigar con docentes. A E. Moore i M. Dooly (Eds), *Enfocaments qualitatius per a la recerca en educació plurilingüe* (p. 23-45). Research-publishing.net. https://doi.org/10.14705/rpnet.2017.emmd2016.620

Robson, C. (1993). *Real world research: a resource for social scientists and practitioners-researchers.* Oxford: Blackwell.

Roth, W. M. (1996). Knowledge diffusion in a grade 4-5 classroom during a unit on civil engineering : an analysis of a classroom community in terms of its changing resources and practices. *Cognition and Instruction, 14*(2), 179-220. https://doi.org/10.1207/s1532690xci1402_2

Schwartz, M. S., i Schwartz, C. G. (1955). Problems in participant observation. *American Journal of Sociology, 60*(4), 343-353. https://doi.org/10.1086/221566

Strauss, A., i Corbin, J. (1998). *Basics of qualitative research: techniques and procedures for developing grounded theory.* Londres: SAGE.

Tannen, D. (Ed.). (1993). *Framing in discourse.* Oxford: Oxford University Press.

Taylor, S. J., i Bogdan, R. (2000). *Introducción a los métodos cualitativos* (3a edición). Barcelona: Paidós.

Unamuno, V., i Patiño, A. (2017). Producir conocimiento sobre el plurilingüismo junto a jóvenes estudiantes: un reto para la etnografía en colaboración. A E. Moore i M. Dooly (Eds), *Enfocaments qualitatius per a la recerca en educació plurilingüe* (p. 107-128). Research-publishing.net. https://doi.org/10.14705/rpnet.2017.emmd2016.624

Vygotsky, L. S. (1978). *Mind in society: the development of higher psychological processes.* Boston: Harvard University Press.

Wortham, S. (2006). *Learning identity: the joint emergence of social identification and academic learning.* Cambridge: Cambridge University Press.

Yin, R. K. (2003). Case study research: design and methods (3a edició). Thousand Oaks/Londres/Nova Deli: Sage.

Lectures recomanades

Falzon, M-A. (Ed.). (2009). *Multi-sited ethnography: theory, praxis and locality in contemporary research.* Surrey: Ashgate.

Herring, S. C. (2004). Computer-mediated discourse analysis: an approach to researching online behavior. A S. A. Barab, R. Kling, i J. Gray (Eds), *Designing for virtual communities in the service of learning* (p. 338-376). Cambridge/Nova York: Cambridge University Press.

8 L'anàlisi de la conversa al servei de la recerca en el camp de l'adquisició de segones llengües (CA-for-SLA)

Dolors Masats[1]

Conceptes clau: anàlisi de la conversa, CA-for-SLA, parla en interacció, aprenentatge situat.

1. Introducció

Aprendre una llengua en un context formal no és el mateix que aprendre una llengua en un àmbit natural, perquè una de les persones que participa en els esdeveniments comunicatius que es donen a l'aula, el/la docent, té l'objectiu d'ensenyar llengua i, per aquest motiu, la majoria de les accions que es realitzen van encaminades a aconseguir aquesta fita. Per això, observar i analitzar la interacció a l'aula esdevé un element clau per poder comprendre com s'aprèn. En aquest capítol presentarem la manera en què l'anàlisi de la conversa tracta d'aquesta qüestió.

L'anàlisi de la conversa estudia la parla en interacció, és a dir, té en compte els aspectes socials lligats a l'ús i a l'adquisició de la llengua. En el camp de l'aprenentatge de segones llengües, hi ha una tensió, àmpliament documentada, entorn de la relació entre aquests dos fenòmens. La recerca que es porta a terme des d'una perspectiva cognitivista, un dels corrents dominants, argumenta que l'estudi de l'ús de la llengua no aporta dades rellevants per comprendre el procés d'adquisició i, per això, es proposen estudis experimentals longitudinals. Per contra, la perspectiva sociocultural defensa la idea que l'aprenentatge se situa en la interacció i, per tant, per comprendre el procés d'adquisició d'una

---

1. Universitat Autònoma de Barcelona, Bellaterra, Catalunya/Espanya; dolors.masats@uab.cat

Per citar aquest capítol: Masats, D. (2017). L'anàlisi de la conversa al servei de la recerca en el camp de l'adquisició de segones llengües (CA-for-SLA). A E. Moore i M. Dooly (Eds), *Enfocaments qualitatius per a la recerca en educació plurilingüe* (p. 293-320). Research-publishing.net. https://doi.org/10.14705/rpnet.2017.emmd2016.632

llengua és necessari investigar com, a través de la llengua, els individus porten a terme accions socials en contextos concrets per assolir objectius específics. Per aconseguir-ho, es poden portar a terme estudis longitudinals o bé estudis de cas en què s'identifiquin i analitzin seqüències (de parla) en què els/les participants s'orienten cap a l'aprenentatge.

Si es parteix de la premissa que l'aprenentatge té lloc en la interacció i que qui aprèn adquireix coneixements i expertesa comunicativa participant en activitats socialment situades que es duen a terme en contextos d'ús concrets, és important estudiar els sistemes d'organització de la participació també de manera contextualitzada. Algunes formes de participació i de gestió dels recursos lingüístics que estan a l'abast dels/ de les participants són pròpies de les institucions educatives (per exemple, aixecar la mà per demanar el torn de paraula és una manera d'organitzar la participació en entorns escolars; emprar el català com a llengua vehicular de l'aprenentatge és un tret propi de les escoles catalanes i andorranes). D'altres són particulars de cada aula (per exemple, la participació s'organitza de manera diferent en aules en què l'alumnat treballa per projectes i en classes en què la interacció la controla qui ensenya).

Per últim, cal tenir present que l'aprenentatge de llengües és un procés complex i multimodal i, per tant, la recerca entorn de l'adquisició de llengües cal dur-la a terme amb d'una mirada interdisciplinària, des d'una perspectiva èmica (vegeu Nussbaum, en aquest volum), sobre dades d'ús real de la llengua, i observant processos en els quals la interacció, com a mitjà per portar a terme una activitat social, genera aprenentatge. Inspirant-se en camps com ara la pragmàtica, la teoria dels actes de parla, l'anàlisi de la variació, la sociolingüística interaccional, l'etnometodologia, l'etnografia de la comunicació, la teoria de la comunicació i la psicologia social, l'anàlisi de la conversa és la disciplina que compleix les premisses que hem esmentat.

En altres capítols d'aquest volum es justifica la validesa d'emprar procediments etnogràfics de recollida de dades i metodologies pròpies de l'anàlisi de la conversa per fer recerca a les aules des d'una perspectiva col·laborativa (vegeu, per exemple, Nussbaum, en aquest volum; Unamuno i Patiño, en aquest volum). En aquest capítol volem examinar amb detall què vol dir fer anàlisi de la conversa. Amb aquest fi, en primer lloc, revisarem l'origen d'aquesta disciplina; en segon lloc, descriurem els reptes a què han de fer front les persones que s'interessen per fer recerca des d'aquesta perspectiva i, per concloure, detallarem les premisses sobre les quals se sustenta aquesta proposta teòrica i metodològica i mostrarem, amb exemples, quin són els fenòmens pels quals s'interessa.

2. L'anàlisi de la conversa com a disciplina d'investigació

L'anàlisi de la conversa sorgeix a principis de la dècada de 1960 arran dels estudis de Sacks (1992, entre d'altres) sobre l'organització de la interacció social. L'autor parteix del treball de Garfinkel (1967, entre d'altres) des de l'etnometodologia i es proposa estudiar la parla mitjançant l'anàlisi d'enregistraments de converses ordinàries. En aquell moment, era una opció revolucionària, no només perquè els aparells d'enregistrar sons encara eren poc comuns, sinó principalment perquè els/les lingüistes de l'època no s'interessaven per l'estudi de la conversa ordinària.

Tanmateix, Sacks no s'interessa exclusivament per l'anàlisi de la conversa, sinó també per la interacció oral, la qual cosa vol dir que estudia tant el llenguatge verbal com el no verbal. El treball que realitza amb Schegloff i Jefferson (Sacks, Schegloff, i Jefferson, 1974; Schegloff, Jefferson, i Sacks, 1977) és especialment important per al desenvolupament de l'anàlisi de la conversa com a disciplina per a l'estudi de dades orals (vegeu una revisió sobre l'origen i el desenvolupament de l'anàlisi de la conversa a Goodwin i Heritage, 1990). Com hem assenyalat, a l'inici la disciplina s'interessava per la conversa ordinària, però posteriorment s'analitzarien altres gèneres discursius (entrevistes, discursos polítics, interrogatoris judicials, etc.) i avui l'objecte d'estudi és qualsevol forma d'interactuar que impliqui la realització d'activitats comunicatives tant verbals com no verbals.

En l'actualitat, l'anàlisi de la conversa és una disciplina consolidada en el camp de les ciències del llenguatge, però no sempre ha estat així. Per exemple, a principis del segle XXI, Seedhouse (2005) constata que el paper que té l'anàlisi de la conversa en el camp de la lingüística aplicada a l'ensenyament i aprenentatge de llengües no és el mateix que el que té, en aquell moment, en la recerca sobre l'adquisició de segones llengües. La lingüística aplicada no es qüestiona la validesa de l'anàlisi de la conversa com a metodologia de recerca, atès que els estudis que avalen aquesta disciplina fan aportacions rellevants per a l'ensenyament de llengües amb finalitats específiques (vegeu Wong i Waring, 2010, per conèixer-ne les propostes més recents), perquè ofereixen orientacions per al disseny de materials i llibres de text respecte als tipus de discursos que cal presentar per gestionar la interacció a l'aula o, entre d'altres elements, per comprendre com s'articula la conversa entre parlants nadius i no nadius o els canvis de codi en entorns bilingües o multilingües. No obstant això, com hem assenyalat, el mateix autor afirma que a principis del segle XXI l'anàlisi de la conversa en la recerca entorn de l'adquisició de segones llengües, la branca de la disciplina coneguda com a CA-for-SLA (Conversation Analysis for Second Language Acquisition), és objecte de debat. Per entendre aquesta afirmació cal tenir presents dos elements: d'una banda, l'anàlisi de la conversa ha estat un dels aparells teòrics i metodològics pels quals han optat els investigadors i les investigadores que se situen en la perspectiva sociocultural, però no ha interessat a qui se situa en el corrent cognitivista dominant. La discussió no està, doncs, relacionada amb la validesa de l'anàlisi de la conversa com a instrument per a la recerca, sinó en la mateixa conceptualització del procés d'aprenentatge que adopta qui investiga. D'altra banda, quan Seedhouse afirma que la recerca entorn de l'adquisició de llengües només s'interessa per l'anàlisi de la conversa a partir del període 2000-2004, és possible que només tingui en compte la recerca feta per lingüistes que explícitament s'han situat en la perspectiva sociocultural i han atacat els principis que defensa la perspectiva cognitiva. Existeix un gran nombre de treballs anteriors realitzats principalment a Suïssa, però també a França, Alemanya i Catalunya que se situen en el camp de la lingüística del contacte i de l'adquisició de llengües (de Pietro, Matthey, i Py, 1989; Lüdi, 1999; Lüdi i Py, 1986; Masats, 1999; Nussbaum, 1990; Pekarek Doehler, 1999; Py, 1997, entre d'altres) en els quals, a través de l'anàlisi de la conversa, es relacionen les pràctiques plurilingües amb el procés d'adquisició de segones llengües i llengües estrangeres.

Tots els estudis basats en l'anàlisi de la conversa tenen presents els tres principis bàsics que, segons Mondada (2003), ha de seguir la recerca que es proposa observar els fenòmens sobre el terreny: el principi d'observabilitat (els fenòmens que s'estudien s'han de poder observar i descriure), el principi de disponibilitat (per observar i descriure un fenomen observable s'ha de poder recollir) i el principi de simetria (la mirada que l'analista projecta sobre les dades que observa també és un fenomen que s'ha d'observar i descriure). Aquests conceptes s'han descrit en el capítol que Nussbaum (en aquest volum) dedica a la recerca col·laborativa. En la següent secció reflexionarem sobre els reptes que implica tenir-los presents.

3. El repte de documentar i descriure fenòmens observables

Un dels reptes clau per a qui fa recerca és decidir què investigar per tal de documentar l'aprenentatge. Hi ha consens que cal descriure la competència interactiva i analitzar com s'adquireix (vegeu Markee, 2000, 2008), però encara són escassos els estudis que expliquen com la interacció en les aules incideix en l'aprenentatge (Pekarek Doehler & Fasel Lauzon, 2015). En aquesta línia, per exemple, Unamuno i Nussbaum (2006) proposen estudiar aspectes com ara la manera en què els/les aprenents construeixen esquemes interactius, gestionen les activitats que duen a terme, participen amb un volum de conversa equilibrat, identifiquen i superen obstacles comunicatius, i adeqüen el seu repertori verbal en funció de l'activitat en curs i de la situació. Masats (2008), d'altra banda, recull aquests aspectes i els amplia quan es proposa estudiar l'aprenentatge de llengües estrangeres examinant la interacció entre parelles d'aprenents que duen a terme tasques comunicatives. El següent esquema (extret de Masats, 2008) il·lustra les macroactivitats discursives que es duen a terme a l'aula quan l'alumnat realitza una tasca. També mostra les accions que són observables en el seu discurs i que serveixen per caracteritzar la seva competència interactiva (Figura 1).

Figura 1. Accions observables en el marc de l'execució d'una tasca (Masats, 2008, p. 142)

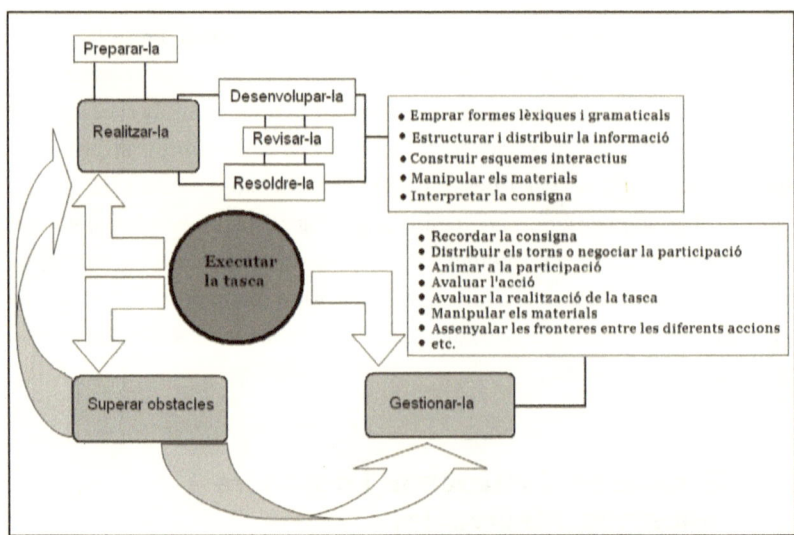

Per poder entendre com s'organitza la interacció quan els individus realitzen una activitat social concreta (per exemple, quan els/les aprenents resolen una tasca comunicativa) i com es construeix aquesta activitat social, cal tenir present que "la realitat i el sentit es construeixen en les interaccions socials i que és en la pròpia interacció on cal buscar les claus de la interpretació" (Nussbaum i Unamuno, 2006, p. 16). En primer lloc, això pressuposa analitzar els fets que són observables, com ara el comportament que els interlocutors exhibeixen quan interactuen, en comptes de teoritzar sobre fenòmens que no són observables, com el que els motiva a prendre-hi part. En segon lloc, és necessari formular les preguntes adequades per poder copsar el valor social dels fets que observem (vegeu com Moore i Llompart, en aquest volum, suggereixen tractar d'aquesta qüestió). En aquest sentit, Maynard (1989) proposa formular preguntes que impliquin observar com es comporten els/les participants en una interacció (com resolen entrebancs comunicatius, com gestionen els recursos lingüístics dels quals disposen, com coconstrueixen enunciats, etc.). No obstant això, no n'hi ha prou amb destriar els fets que són observables i amb plantejar preguntes pertinents, sinó que la necessitat de categoritzar allò que observem per tal de poder-ho descriure ens obliga a trobar les paraules adequades per fer-ho. Aquestes tres accions impliquen prendre decisions vinculades als processos de recollida, tractament i anàlisi de les dades. A continuació les examinarem breument.

4. La tria de les eines per recollir fenòmens observables

Com hem assenyalat, el principi de disponibilitat estableix que per poder descriure els fets observables primer cal recollir-los i després representar-los. A principis de la dècada de 1970, per exemple, Sacks va basar el seu treball en enregistraments sonors, però el matrimoni Goodwin, una dècada més tard, ja documentava les dades en vídeo. Sigui quina sigui l'eina que s'empra per enregistrar la interacció a l'aula (una càmera de vídeo, un dispositiu mòbil, una gravadora, etc.), en l'anàlisi no es pot tractar únicament com un instrument de recollida de dades, ja que la seva manipulació per part de l'alumnat també dona indicis sobre com es construeix interactivament el sentit de la tasca que duu a terme (vegeu les recomanacions que en aquest sentit fan Moore i Llompart, en aquest volum). Per exemple, si observem quines activitats discursives duu a terme una parella en el moment en què decideix aturar momentàniament la gravació i què és el que s'enregistra un cop es grava de nou, o quins enunciats es pronuncien en un to molt baix, o si s'adrecen a la càmera en alguna ocasió, podem determinar quin discurs es vol fer "públic" i quin no.

Atès que els elements no verbals presents en qualsevol interacció són significatius, és important poder documentar-los. En aquest sentit, enregistrar dades en vídeo és preferible a enregistrar dades en àudio (vegeu les observacions en aquest sentit de Moore i Llompart, en aquest volum). En cas que no sigui possible disposar de dades visuals (les famílies poden no donar autorització per enregistrar a l'aula), tampoc no hem de desestimar el valor de la comunicació no verbal. Per tant, les nostres transcripcions, igual que quan transcrivim dades visuals, han de contenir comentaris sobre els aspectes cinètics, gestuals o visuals que han deixat un rastre observable en la producció verbal. El repte, en aquest cas, té a veure amb la decisió de què és observable i què no ho és quan treballem només amb enregistraments d'àudio i no tenim el suport visual per entendre allò que passa (Mondada, 2003). El fragment 1, que és part d'una seqüència més llarga, ens serveix per il·lustrar aquesta idea.

Fragment 1

7.	Gemma:	{(P) ingredients of the—|}
8.	Jana:	cake |cake|[està escrivint]|**es que no sé cómo se escribe**|cake|
9.	Gemma	[crida a la mestra] María| com s'=escriu pastís=
CEIP Metropolità		
Execució d'una tasca de joc de rol		

En els torns 7 i 8, la Gemma i la Jana estan coconstruint un enunciat ("*ingredients of the cake*") que formarà part del diàleg fictici que les dues noies han d'elaborar. Tot seguit, la Jana (final del torn 8) verbalitza que no sap escriure una de les paraules que han proposat ("*cake*"). Llavors, la Gemma (torn 9) es dirigeix a la mestra per demanar-li-ho. En aquest cas, l'acció d'escriure queda registrada en el discurs d'aquesta parella perquè es topicalitza i origina un canvi de codi. És a dir, després de verbalitzar la paraula "*cake*", l'escriptura d'aquesta paraula esdevé l'objecte sobre el qual gira la interacció, que es realitza en una llengua diferent de la que empraven les noies en construir el diàleg inventat. La transcripció d'aquest fragment conté un comentari de qui fa la transcripció, fet que indica que en el moment de traduir les dades orals a dades escrites ha "visualitzat" l'existència d'aquesta acció cinètica i l'ha recollida, perquè l'ha categoritzat com a pertinent en la configuració de l'acció.

Complir el principi d'observabilitat implica reconèixer que sense una evidència observable en la parla interactiva que generen les dues noies de l'intercanvi que hem il·lustrat en el fragment 1 no podríem afirmar que, per resoldre la tasca que se'ls ha assignat, la Gemma i la Jana opten per escriure en un paper el diàleg que s'estan inventant i que és la Jana, concretament, qui s'encarrega de fer-ho.

5. La tria del sistema per representar fenòmens observables

Com hem apuntat en la secció anterior, per poder documentar els fenòmens observables és necessari representar-los un cop han estat recollits. Així doncs, l'anàlisi de la conversa obliga a treballar amb transcripcions, les quals actuen sovint com a mediadores entre la teoria i les dades. No obstant això, les transcripcions són parcials i selectives per natura, perquè redueixen la realitat social que es vol estudiar (Bucholtz, 2000; Ochs, 1979; Psathas i Anderson, 1990). Per a Haviland (1996), una transcripció representa la parla fora del context de producció. La voluntat de l'analista de "reconstruir" la situació en què es desenvolupa el discurs implica un procés de presa de decisions que repercutirà en l'anàlisi. Ochs (1979) afirma que qualsevol transcripció es construeix partint d'operacions de selecció (cal triar quins trets de la parla es fan 'visibles' i quins no, decidir si la transcripció serà fonètica o ortogràfica, seleccionar els símbols per representar la informació paralingüística i no verbal, escollir si la transcripció s'organitzarà en torns, unitats tonals, o en un altre sistema, etc.) i de simplificació (cal fer abstracció dels trets que se seleccionen). Per tant, tal com s'ha apuntat en els capítols de Nussbaum (en aquest volum) i de Moore i Llompart (en aquest volum), la transcripció s'ha d'entendre com una primera fase d'aquesta anàlisi (Ochs, 1979), com un punt de partida per a la reflexió (Mondada, 2002).

La tria del sistema de transcripció (vegeu els suggeriments que plantegen Moore i Llompart, en aquest volum) ve donada pels objectius de la recerca i l'objecte d'estudi. Això explica el motiu pel qual alguns lingüistes –com ara Auer (1998), quan analitza els canvis de codi– desenvolupen les seves pròpies convencions a l'hora de transcriure i analitzar dades. Alguns sistemes de transcripció de dades orals que gaudeixen d'acceptació en el camp de l'anàlisi de la interacció són els que han desenvolupat Atkinson i Heritage (1984), Jefferson (1985, 2004), du Bois (1991) o Gumperz i Berenz (1993). En aquest sentit, vegeu Moore i Llompart (en aquest volum) per a convencions per a la transcripció multimodal que s'han desenvolupat més recentment. Sovint, però, no hi ha consens sobre si les convencions que s'empren dificulten la lectura de les dades i porten a l'analista a fer feina innecessària, o si no és possible representar les dades orals mitjançant un sistema més simple com ara l'ortogràfic (vegeu el debat entre Potter i Hepburn, 2005a, 2005b; Smith, Hollway, i Mischler, 2005). Nosaltres creiem que el detall en la transcripció és necessari per reproduir amb la màxima fidelitat possible les dades i així poder-les analitzar detalladament i complir un dels quatre principis bàsics de l'anàlisi de la conversa. La simbologia de transcripció emprada en aquest capítol es basa en les convencions desenvolupades pel GREIP (vegeu Moore i Llompart, en aquest volum) i s'inclou en l'annex.

6. La tria de la terminologia per categoritzar fenòmens observables

El principi de simetria recomana observar amb els mateixos ulls tant qui informa com qui observa, fet que implica considerar que qui fa recerca també forma part de les dades que recull (Mondada, 1998) i que, per tant, també s'han d'observar i documentar les accions que duu a terme. En aquest sentit, el repte de descriure fets observables implica fer tries que tindran un impacte sobre la descripció i l'anàlisi de les dades, sobre el nostre posicionament com a investigadores vers aquestes dades i sobre la manera en què ens presentem dins la comunitat científica. Escriure un article o un treball de recerca és també una activitat social i una situació comunicativa (*encounter*): hi ha algú que explica 'una història convincent' (Silverman, 1989) i espera que algú altre la vulgui llegir.

Tanmateix, escollir els mots que descriuen els fenòmens observats en ocasions no és una tasca senzilla. En primer lloc, si es duu a terme una recerca qualitativa, la categorització no es pot crear abans d'analitzar les dades (Bryman, 1988), sinó que ha de ser el fruit de la seva anàlisi. En segon lloc, un cop s'ha observat un fenomen, s'ha de construir la categorització a partir d'una tria lèxica acurada que cal justificar, atès que sovint una mateixa paraula es fa servir per descriure fenòmens d'ordre divers o un mateix esdeveniment es descriu en termes diferents. En adreçar-nos a la nostra audiència com a investigadores fem unes tries lèxiques, perquè se'ns pugui relacionar amb un corrent de recerca determinat o amb una manera concreta de descriure la realitat que observem. Per exemple, el fet que optem pel terme *participant*, en comptes de *parlant* i *oient*, per referir-nos als individus que participen en una situació comunicativa implica que reconeixem que la interacció és una acció social, tal com defensa la perspectiva sociocultural de l'aprenentatge.

7. Els quatre principis bàsics de l'anàlisi de la conversa i els quatre elements clau que estudia

Per analitzar qualsevol interacció, l'anàlisi de la conversa parteix de quatre principis bàsics que es basen en els supòsits etnometodològics que defensa Garfinkel, qui, com hem assenyalat, és una de les fonts d'inspiració de Sacks. Aquestes quatre premisses guien el procés del tractament i l'anàlisi de les dades i es resumeixen de la següent manera:

- La interacció és una forma de discurs que té un ordre clar, i la feina de l'analista consisteix a esbrinar quina és la seva organització i seqüenciació.

- La interacció està lligada al context en què es produeix i, per tant, és imprescindible analitzar-la seqüencialment, per poder comprendre-la. Alhora, la interacció també crea el context, observable per la manera com se succeeixen les accions i com s'hi orienten els/les participants.

- Els detalls (els silencis, els canvis d'entonació o ritme, els murmuris, les pauses, etc.), per petits que siguin, no són mai insignificants. Per aquest motiu, és imprescindible que la interacció es transcrigui de manera acurada i detallada.

- L'anàlisi ha d'emergir de les dades. Les dades s'han d'observar des d'una perspectiva èmica, és a dir, cal analitzar cap on els/les participants s'orienten en el discurs i, per fer-ho, cal tenir en compte com interpreten allò que fan i hi donen sentit. Per exemple, un enunciat agramatical no és problemàtic si no es problematitza en la conversa. Els bagatges

Capítol 8

o els trets identitaris de les persones que hi participen tampoc no són rellevants, si no es posen en joc al llarg del discurs.

En el camp de l'anàlisi de la conversa, la descripció i explicació de l'ús del llenguatge com a acció social es focalitza en l'estudi dels quatre elements en què Sacks basa l'anàlisi de l'organització de la interacció: la construcció de parells adjacents, la noció preferència, la presa de torns i la reparació (vegeu una descripció detallada d'aquests elements a Schegloff et al., 2002; Seedhouse, 2004, 2005, entre d'altres).

8. Els parells adjacents i la noció de preferència

El constructe de parell adjacent es basa en el principi etnometodològic de la reflexivitat, el qual postula que els procediments que s'activen per a la producció d'una acció (o d'un enunciat) són els mateixos que s'activen a l'hora d'interpretar-la. Per exemple, una pregunta es genera per obtenir una resposta i així també ho interpreta la persona a qui va adreçada la pregunta. No obstant això, el sentit interactiu d'un torn només es pot interpretar en analitzar el següent torn. Els parells adjacents, doncs, serveixen per descriure l'ordre seqüencial en què s'organitza la interacció.

Tot i que en realitat només un nombre determinat d'accions es duen a terme a través de la construcció de parells adjacents, el raonament analític en què es basa aquest constructe és aplicable a altres maneres d'organitzar l'acció (Goodwin i Heritage, 1990). Tanmateix, el comportament dels individus a l'hora de seqüenciar i organitzar el discurs no s'analitza des d'un punt de vista normatiu, és a dir, els analistes de la conversa no s'interessen per explicar què és el que els/les parlants diuen, sinó per descriure cap on s'orienten o, el que és el mateix, quines preferències mostren a l'hora d'interactuar. Respondre a una salutació amb una altra salutació és una acció preferent, és la més habitual, però en interactuar les persones poden escollir no realitzar l'acció preferent. El fragment 2 il·lustra els conceptes de parell adjacent i de preferència.

Fragment 2

51	Héctor:	in my yes|in my picture the shop assistant_|| the hair is_| green\\| ay\\| is—<0> no\\| [riu] brown\\|
52	Josep:	eh| in_ |in my_| what colour_| what colour is| the shoes| of a woman?|
53	Héctor:	black\\|
54	Josep:	eh—| what colour is the hair_ [+jair+] ey ma_ of the woman?|
55	Héctor:	eh—| pink\\|
56	Josep:	eh—| what colour is the eyes [+eis+] the consumer?|
57	Héctor:	the customer/|| is green\\|
58	Josep:	eh um—|
59	Héctor:	{(DC) in a: basket}\ eh—|there are bananas\\| oranges\\| lettuce [+le'tuz+]\\| and milk \\|
60	Josep:	yes\\| um—| <1>
61	Hector:	in my picture there are two\ two cheese\\|
CEIP Metropolità		
Execució d'una tasca de trobar diferències		

El fragment 2 ens mostra part d'un intercanvi en la interacció entre dos aprenents de primària format per sis seqüències en què els nois intenten trobar diferències entre els dibuixos que té cadascú. Tres d'aquestes seqüències (els torns 51, 59-60 i 61) les inicia l'Héctor i les altres tres (els torns 52-53, 54-55 i 56-57), el seu company Josep. Com veiem, per resoldre aquesta tasca, el Josep empra un patró interactiu en el qual ell adopta la identitat discursiva d'indagador i atorga a l'Héctor la d'informant. Per aquest motiu, els dos nois construeixen seqüències basades en parells adjacents del tipus pregunta-resposta. L'ús consecutiu d'aquest tipus de patró interactiu serveix per indicar tàcitament que no hi ha cap diferència entre els dos dibuixos. És a dir, com que la resposta que el Josep rep per part del seu company no contradiu la informació que ell té en el seu dibuix, formula una nova pregunta per seguir indagant els dos dibuixos. En el torn 58, el Josep dubta abans de formular un nou enunciat, fet que aprofita l'Héctor per agafar-li el torn de parla i canviar d'esquema interactiu (torn 59).

Si observem les tres seqüències iniciades per l'Héctor, veurem com el noi mostra que la seva acció preferent és adoptar la identitat discursiva de descriptor. Per això, tant en el torn 51, com quan torna a agafar la paraula en el torns 59 i 61,

Capítol 8

el noi formula un enunciat que conté una descripció d'allò que es mostra en el seu dibuix. La seqüència formada pels torns 59 i 60 també és un exemple de parell adjacent (descripció-confirmació de la descripció), atès que el Josep pren la paraula per verbalitzar que el seu dibuix conté els mateixos elements que enumera el seu company. Les altres seqüències iniciades per l'Héctor estan formades per un únic torn, ja que l'obertura d'una nova seqüència per part del company (torn 52) serveix per confirmar que allò que l'Héctor ha descrit també es troba representat en el dibuix del Josep.

Com veiem, doncs, quatre de les seqüències d'aquest intercanvi que hem mostrat estan construïdes sobre la base de parells adjacents i dues no ho estan. Això és així perquè cada participant mostra preferència per un patró discursiu determinat.

9. La presa de torns

Els torns són les unitats mínimes de participació en què s'estructura la interacció. Com hem vist en el fragment anterior, els torns poden agrupar-se en unitats més grans, anomenades seqüències. Les seqüències poden estar formades per un únic torn (com en el cas dels torns 51 i 61 del fragment 2), per parells adjacents (com en el cas dels torns 52-53, 54-55, 56-57 i 59-60 del fragment 2), per seqüències IRF (*Initiation-Response-Follow up*) (com veurem en el fragment 3 a continuació) o per altres agrupaments més complexos que sorgeixen sobretot quan els aprenents intenten resoldre obstacles comunicatius (vegeu el fragment 4).

Fragment 3

3	María:	more or less/| do you understand this?|
4	Álex:	*que farem_ que farem una fitxa de diferències|*
5	María:	yes| that's it| that's it\\ alright|then— in order to spot the differences—| what you have to do is to describe your picture| right/ say—| for example| in my picture there's a:: dog| and the dog is brown|
CEIP Metropolità		
La mestra (María) dona les instruccions per realitzar una tasca de trobar diferències		

El fragment 3 mostra una seqüència de tres torns (iniciació-resposta-retroacció) coneguda amb la sigla anglesa IRF. Aquesta estructura discursiva és típica de la interacció en les aules en els moments en què el/la docent gestiona la participació (vegeu Nussbaum, 2016, per a una anàlisi més detallada d'aquest tipus de seqüència). El primer torn d'aquesta seqüència (torn 3), s'inicia (torn d'iniciació) amb una pregunta de la docent per comprovar si s'han entès les instruccions que acaba de donar. En el segon torn, un dels alumnes li respon (torn de resposta) afirmativament resumint en català el contingut de les instruccions donades. Per últim, en el torn 3, la docent valora (torn de retroacció o comentari avaluatiu) positivament la resposta de l'estudiant (*"yes, that's it, alright"*), abans d'emprendre un nou moviment d'iniciació per seguir donant instruccions en aquest mateix torn.

L'analista conversacional s'interessa tant pels mecanismes de la construcció de torns, que poden ser verbals o no verbals, com pels mecanismes que adopten els i les parlants per a la presa de torn. L'estudi dels torns i dels processos que hi estan relacionats (encavalcaments, pauses, interrupcions, silencis, gestos, etc.) és fonamental per poder entendre com es construeix i s'organitza la interacció i com es genera l'aprenentatge en interactuar. La pregunta bàsica que guia els estudis que s'emmarquen en la perspectiva de l'anàlisi de la conversa és la següent: Per què succeeix això d'aquesta manera en aquest precís moment? Per a Seedhouse (2004), aquesta pregunta resumeix l'essència dels principis de l'anàlisi de la conversa, atès que reflecteix que la interacció es conceptualitza com una acció (per què succeeix això?), que s'expressa a través d'unes formes lingüístiques concretes (per què s'expressa això d'aquesta manera?), inserides en el desenvolupament d'una seqüència (per què succeeix això, expressat així, en aquest precís moment?).

10. La reparació i els processos de resolució d'entrebancs comunicatius

Segons les perspectives interactivistes de l'aprenentatge de llengües, la realització de tasques de superació d'obstacles afavoreix l'adquisició d'expertesa comunicativa (Kasper, 2004; Hall, Cheng, i Carlson, 2006) per part de les persones que participen en un esdeveniment comunicatiu, en el sentit que són una font de pràctica de procediments o mètodes d'actuació social i no només una font d'accés a les formes de les llengües. Tradicionalment, l'anàlisi de la conversa s'ha interessat per la reparació, un dels mecanismes que empren els/les parlants per solucionar els entrebancs comunicatius que es troben, però no és l'únic. En aquest apartat, primer tractarem del concepte de reparació i a continuació esmentarem altres processos emprats per qui aprèn per mantenir el flux de la conversa, com ara els canvis de codi, la barreja de codis o l'ús de paràfrasis.

11. El concepte de reparació

A diferència d'altres mecanismes emprats pels individus que participen en un esdeveniment comunicatiu com a recurs per superar obstacles, les reparacions interrompen el flux de la comunicació. L'existència d'una reparació queda palesa discursivament pel fet que els/les parlants abandonen momentàniament l'acció que duien a terme i aquest entrebanc es resol dins una nova seqüència, anomenada lateral perquè es destina a focalitzar les formes de la llengua o a negociar el sentit de l'enunciat que ha interromput el flux comunicatiu. Un cop s'ha resolt (o s'ha abandonat l'intent de resoldre) l'entrebanc, es reprèn l'acció que havia quedat interrompuda.

Masats (1999) afirma que només és possible entendre el complex fenomen de la reparació si s'analitza des d'una perspectiva que tingui en compte tres eixos: la reparació en relació amb les accions que duen a terme els/les aprenents; la connexió entre l'objecte de la reparació i les identitats discursives que assumeixen els/les parlants en reparar, i els vincles entre la reparació i l'activitat metalingüística com a eines per afavorir l'aprenentatge. Pel que fa al primer eix, l'anàlisi de la conversa assenyala que es poden distingir quatre procediments per reparar el discurs, en funció de l'individu que assenyala l'obstacle comunicatiu i del que fa la proposta per resoldre'l:

- Autoreparació Autoiniciada (AA): la reparació la inicia i la clou l'interlocutor/a que ha trobat l'obstacle.

- Heteroreparació Heteroiniciada (HH): l'obstacle l'assenyala i el clou l'interlocutor/a que no ha produït l'enunciat en què es produeix.

- Heteroreparació Autoiniciada (HA): la reparació la inicia l'interlocutor/a que ha trobat l'obstacle, però la clou una altra persona.

- Autoreparació Heteroiniciada (AH): l'obstacle l'assenyala l'interlocutor/a que no ha produït l'enunciat en què es produeix, però la reparació la resol qui ha generat l'obstacle.

L'objecte de la reparació pot ser divers. Masats (1999) suggereix que per observar què és allò que es repara cal analitzar els tres eixos en què es mouen els/les aprenents: la resolució de problemes de codi, la negociació del sentit i la gestió de la tasca. Així mateix, reconeix el valor dels objectes que acompanyen l'acció (els materials de suport a la tasca) com a elements que configuren i reestructuren el posicionament de qui parla vers aquesta acció. La Taula 1 resumeix la proposta de l'autora.

Taula 1. L'objecte de les reparacions (Masats, 1999, p. 65)

REPARACIONS	Orientades cap AL CODI	REPARACIONS LÈXIQUES
		REPARACIONS SEMÀNTIQUES
		REPARACIONS MORFOSINTÀCTIQUES
		REPARACIONS FONÈTIQUES
	Orientades cap AL MISSATGE	REPARACIONS DE COHESIÓ
		REPARACIONS DE PRECISIÓ
		REPARACIONS D'AMBIGÜITAT
	Orientades cap a LA TASCA	
	Originades pels MATERIALS	FOCALITZACIÓ EN EL CODI
		FOCALITZACIÓ EN EL DISCURS
		FOCALITZACIÓ EN LA TASCA

Independentment de quin sigui l'objecte que es repara, quan es duu a terme una reparació sempre hi ha un/a participant que adopta la identitat discursiva de parlant inexpert/a i que atorga al company o companya la de parlant expert/a. Aquestes identitats no són fixes, sinó que canvien en funció de les accions discursives que es duen a terme. L'adopció indistintament de les identitats de parlant expert/a i inexpert/a entre els i les aprenents és un mecanisme que garanteix el desenvolupament de la competència interactiva i afavoreix l'aprenentatge, atès que els/les obliga a realitzar activitats metalingüístiques. Per aquest motiu, l'estudi de les seqüències laterals que s'obren quan hi ha una reparació és especialment interessant, perquè sovint es converteixen en seqüències potencials d'adquisició (de Pietro et al., 1989). Observem-ho en el fragment 4.

Fragment 4

85	Eli:	in my picture there are mm—| **cómo se llama?**| {(PP) XX}<14> {(PP) **la camisa**\}| <2>
86	Álex:	the shirt\ [+short+]| shirt\[+short+]|
87	María:	shirt\\|
88	Álex:	=shirt=
89	Eli:	=shirt=| in my picture there are shirt_ em—| shop assistant [+a'ssisten+] eh—| is red and blue\\|
90	Álex:	red and blue\\|
91	Eli:	yes\\| <1>
CEIP Metropolità **L'Eli i l'Álex duen a terme una tasca de trobar diferències**		

En el torn 85, l'Eli inicia una seqüència per descriure un element del seu dibuix, però es troba un entrebanc lèxic que no li permet concloure la descripció (torn 89) fins que no l'hagi resolt. Per fer-ho, la noia adopta la identitat discursiva de parlant inexperta, atorga al seu company la de parlant expert i inicia una seqüència lateral, inserida en el mateix torn 85. La construcció d'aquesta nova seqüència està precedida per un so que indica dubte ("*mm*"), està assenyalada amb un canvi de llengua i pren la forma d'una petició d'ajuda ("*¿cómo se llama la camisa?*") pronunciada en un to més baix. Atès que la participant que es troba l'entrebanc és la mateixa persona que l'assenyala, direm que la reparació és autoiniciada. En el torn següent, l'Álex respon a la seva companya, és a dir, heterorepara el seu discurs. En principi, la seqüència lateral d'aquesta reparació podria haver estat formada únicament per aquest parell adjacent (pregunta-resposta). No obstant això, la mestra, María, és prop d'aquesta parella i s'adona que l'Álex té problemes per pronunciar correctament el mot que vol oferir a l'Eli i decideix intervenir-hi. En fer-ho, ella s'autocategoritza com a parlant experta i assigna a l'Álex la identitat discursiva de parlant inexpert. El torn 87 és, doncs, una heteroreparació (la mestra corregeix l'Álex) heteroiniciada (la mestra assenyala a l'Álex que té un problema). El noi no ha demanat ajuda, però repeteix dues vegades la paraula. No obstant això, no podem saber si ho fa perquè no la sap pronunciar i simplement la diu dos cops, sense ser conscient que no la pronuncia correctament. Els torns 88 i 89 mostren com simultàniament l'Álex i l'Eli recullen la reparació de la mestra i, en el cas de la noia, la insereix en el seu discurs per completar l'enunciat que havia quedat interromput en el torn 85. En resum, el fragment 4 mostra un exemple d'heteroreparació autoiniciada entre l'Eli i l'Álex (torns 85 i 86) i un altre d'heteroreparació heteroiniciada de la mestra cap a l'enunciat de l'Álex (torns 86, 87 i 88). Tot i això, les troballes dels estudis entorn de la reparació –també les de l'estudi d'on procedeixen les dades que reproduïm (vegeu Masats, 2008)– mostren que els aprenents tenen preferència per les autoreparacions, ja siguin autoiniciades o heteroiniciades.

Per últim, és important assenyalar que analitzar les dades des d'una perspectiva èmica, un dels quatre principis que hem assenyalat que guien l'anàlisi de la conversa, implica observar-les des de la perspectiva de qui interactua. En el torn 89 del fragment 4, quan l'Eli reprèn la formulació del seu enunciat, observem que pronuncia malament la paraula "*shop assistant*". La transcripció recull aquesta informació (l'observa i la representa), però atès que és un fet que cap dels dos membres d'aquesta parella no tematitza, com a analistes del discurs no podem categoritzar aquesta desviació de la norma com un entrebanc que calgui ser reparat.

12. Altres procediments emprats per mantenir el flux de la conversa

Masats, Nussbaum, i Unamuno (2007) analitzen els reptes a què fan front els aprenents d'una manera més general, els quals transcendeixen el concepte de reparació. Les autores els categoritzen en funció d'allò que es tematitza: el format global de l'activitat (allò que s'ha de fer), els materials (com a objectes intermediaris de la interacció), la gestió global de la tasca (com s'ha de gestionar), o els recursos de què disposa l'alumnat per resoldre la tasca (si els tenen disponibles i/o els consideren pertinents per a la construcció local de l'activitat). En el fragment 5 podem observar alguns d'aquests procediments que, a diferència de les reparacions, no causen una interrupció en el flux de la conversa, sinó que el mantenen.

Fragment 5

75	Bawna:	it's a_ a_	a *deu mil* money|
76	Pau:	*deu mil* no| <2> *deu mil* moneys|
77	Bawna:	a ten_ <0>
78	Pau:	er_
79	Bawna>	ten thousand|
80	Pau:	ten thousand moneys|
81	Bawna:	XXXXX|
82	Pau:	yes yes **es que_ sube**| it's up\	it's up **navideit**|
83	Bawna:	=thank you\=
84	Pau:	=thank you\= bye bye|
85	Bawna:	=bye bye|=
CEIP BCN1 El Pau i la Bawna participen en un joc de rol		

En el fragment 5, el Pau i la Bawna es troben immersos en la coconstrucció d'un diàleg entre un botiguer i la seva clienta. La pauta que la mestra els ha donat per crear aquesta conversa fictícia els demana posar preu als productes que la clienta ha comprat. En aquest moment, el Pau i la Bawna abandonen els seus rols de venedor i compradora, respectivament, per solucionar conjuntament com a aprenents aquest repte comunicatiu. Així, en el torn 75, la Bawna proposa una quantitat. Com veiem, el seu enunciat és una forma híbrida que barreja dos codis: l'anglès (la llengua en què realitzen la tasca) i el català (la llengua que empra la noia per comunicar-se amb el seu company). L'observació d'allò que passa en els torns següents ens permet observar que l'ús d'aquest procediment no és fruit de la manca de domini de la noia sobre la llengua meta, sinó que és un recurs que li permet agafar el torn de paraula sense haver de pensar com construir la seva proposta. En el torn 76, el seu company li qüestiona la proposta i repara (incorrectament) la part de l'enunciat que la noia havia formulat en anglès. Aquesta interrupció permet la Bawna d'autocorregir el seu discurs (torns 77 i 79) i formular un enunciat íntegrament en anglès (torn 79) que no recull la proposta del Pau. El noi recull l'autoreparació de la companya i la complementa. En aquest moment, el Pau, qui en el joc de rol és el venedor, abandona l'activitat de reflexió metalingüística que duia a terme, adopta aquesta identitat discursiva i així la conversa prossegueix dins del joc de rol. És a dir, el venedor (el Pau) dona el preu dels productes que la clienta ha comprat (torn 81); la clienta (la Bawna) fa una observació inintel·ligible sobre aquest preu (torn 82); el venedor justifica el preu (torn 83) i la clienta l'accepta (torn 84); el venedor li ho agraeix i s'acomiada (torn 85), i la clienta respon a aquest comiat (torn 86).

La tasca que realitzen el Pau i la Bawna és complexa, perquè implica que en aquest esdeveniment comunicatiu han d'adoptar, a vegades simultàniament, identitats discursives diverses per intentar convertir la pauta que se'ls ha donat en un diàleg coherent dins del joc de rol (Masats i Unamuno, 2001). Activar tots els recursos lingüístics dels quals disposen els facilita aquesta tasca. Això explica també la raó per la qual, en un moment concret del diàleg fictici entre el venedor i la seva clienta (torn 82), el Pau construeix l'enunciat de la manera en què ho fa. En primer lloc, veiem com el noi i la seva companya estan interessats a mantenir el flux de la conversa dins del rol que assumeixen en el joc. Davant de la intervenció de la seva companya (qui possiblement es queixa del preu elevat de la fruita que ha comprat), li respon en castellà argumentant que el preus pugen. El canvi de codi, l'ús del castellà, li permet guanyar temps per pensar una manera d'expressar la idea de pujada en anglès (*"it's up"*) i de concloure la seva argumentació (els preus pugen perquè és Nadal –les dades es recullen la setmana prèvia a les vacances de Nadal) en aquest mateix torn 82 (*"it's up navideit"*). De nou, l'ús d'una forma híbrida (afegir un morfema que sona a anglès a una paraula mig formulada en castellà) és un procediment vàlid per a aquesta parella per aconseguir dur a terme la tasca que se li ha proposat.

13. Conclusions

En aquest capítol hem defensat que l'anàlisi de la conversa és la disciplina que ofereix a qui s'interessa pels processos d'adquisició de llengües des d'una perspectiva sociocultural de l'aprenentatge un marc teòric i metodològic adequat per estudiar la parla en interacció, atès que permet tenir en compte els aspectes socials lligats a l'ús i a l'adquisició de la llengua.

En primer lloc, hem resseguit l'origen d'aquesta disciplina. En segon lloc, hem revisat els postulats que defensa i, posteriorment, i a través de l'anàlisi de fragments de converses extretes d'aules de primària, hem mostrat els fenòmens pels quals s'interessa l'anàlisi de la conversa i la manera en què s'analitzen les dades des d'aquesta perspectiva.

Així, d'una banda, hem assenyalat que els estudis al voltant de l'adquisició de llengües en contextos formals demostren que alguns dels sistemes d'organització de la participació són propis de les institucions educatives, mentre que d'altres són particulars de cada aula. L'anàlisi de la conversa s'interessa per estudiar com en cada context es fan visibles aquests sistemes de participació i com contribueixen al fet que els/les aprenents gestionin els recursos lingüístics que estan al seu abast d'una manera concreta.

D'altra banda, també hem apuntat que l'anàlisi de la conversa defensa que per comprendre com s'aprèn una llengua cal descriure'n l'ús contextualitzat, i això només es pot fer mitjançant una anàlisi detallada partint d'una perspectiva èmica de la interacció que es genera en cada esdeveniment comunicatiu concret. Així doncs, el model d'anàlisi que planteja la disciplina sorgeix de les dades (*data-driven model*) i proposa d'estudiar, des de la perspectiva dels i de les participants, fenòmens d'ordre divers (la construcció de torns, l'organització de la participació, la formulació dels enunciats, els canvis de llengua, les reparacions, etc.).

Per últim, hem recalcat que qui s'interessa per descriure els processos d'adquisició de llengües des de la mirada que projecta l'anàlisi de la conversa parteix de la premissa que qui aprèn adquireix coneixements i expertesa comunicativa participant en activitats socialment situades en contextos d'ús concrets. Aquesta participació l'empeny a realitzar activitats de reflexió metalingüística i a posar en joc els recursos lingüístics dels quals disposa i així garantir que pot realitzar, en la llengua meta, les tasques comunicatives que se li plantegen. Des d'aquesta perspectiva, el desplegament de mecanismes diversos, com ara els canvis de llengua, l'ús de sinònims o perífrasis i de formes lèxiques mixtes, fa que el seu discurs sigui fluït i, alhora, ric i exploratori.

Obres citades

Atkinson, J. M., i Heritage, J. (Ed.). (1984). *Structures of social action: Studies in conversation analysis*. Cambridge: Cambridge University Press.

Auer, P. (Ed.). (1998). *Code switching in conversation: language, interaction and identity*. Londres: Routledge.

Bryman, A. (1988). *Quantity and quality in social research*. Londres: Unwin Hyman. https://doi.org/10.4324/9780203410028

Bucholtz, M. (2000). The politics of transcription. *Journal of Pragmatics, 32*(10), 1439-1465. https://doi.org/10.1016/S0378-2166(99)00094-6

De Pietro, J. F., Matthey, M., i Py, B. (1989). Acquisition et contrat didactique: les séquences potentiellement acquisitionnelles dans la conversation exolingue. A D. Weil i H. Fugier (Eds), *Actes du troisième colloque régional de linguistique* (p. 99-124). Estrasburg: Université des Sciences Humaines et Université Louis Pasteur.

Du Bois, J. W. (1991). Transcription design principles for spoken discourse research. *Pragmatics 1*(1), 71-106. https://doi.org/10.1075/prag.1.1.04boi

Garfinkel, H. (1967). *Studies in ethnomethodology*. Englewood Cliffs, NJ: Prentice-Hall.

Goodwin, C., y Heritage, J. (1990). Conversation analysis. *Annual Review of Anthropology, 19*, 283-307. https://doi.org/10.1146/annurev.an.19.100190.001435

Gumperz, J., i Berenz, N. (1993). Transcribing conversational exchanges. A J. A. Edwards i M. D. Lampert (Eds), *Talking language: transcription and coding in discourse research* (p. 91-122). Hillsdale, N. J.: Lawrence Erlbaum Associates.

Hall, J. K., Cheng, A., i Carlson, M. T. (2006). Reconceptualizing multicompetence as a theory of language knowledge. *Applied Linguistics, 27*(2), 220-240. https://doi.org/10.1093/applin/aml013

Haviland, J. B. (1996). Text from talk in Tzotzil. A M. Silverstein i G. Urban (Eds), *Natural histories of discourse* (p. 45-78). Chicago: University of Chicago Press.

Jefferson, G. (1985). An exercise in the transcription and analysis of laughter. A T. van Dijk (Ed.), *Handbook of discourse analysis, Vol. 3: discourse and dialogue* (p. 25-34). Londres: Academic Press.

Jefferson, G. (2004). Glossary of transcript symbols with an introduction. A G. H. Lerner (Ed.), *Conversation analysis: studies from the first generation* (p. 13-31). Amsterdam/Philadelphia: John Benjamins Publishing Company. https://doi.org/10.1075/pbns.125.02jef

Kasper, G. (2004). Participant orientations in German conversation-for-learning. *The Modern Language Journal, 88*(4), 551-67. https://doi.org/10.1111/j.0026-7902.2004.t01-18-.x

Lüdi, G. (1999). Alternance des langues et acquisition d'une langue seconde. A V. Castellotti i D. Moore (Eds), *Cahiers du Français contemporain numéro 5: alternances des langues et construction des savoirs* (p. 25-51). Fontenay/St-Cloud: E. N. S. Editions.

Lüdi, G., i Py, B. (1986). *Être bilingue*. Berna: Peter Lang.

Markee, N. (2000). *Conversation analysis*. Mahwah, Nova Jersey: Erlbaum.

Markee, N. (2008). Toward a learning behavior tracking methodology for CA-for-SLA. *Applied Linguistics, 29*, 404-427. https://doi.org/10.1093/applin/amm052

Masats, D. (1999). *La reparació en el discurs d'aprenents de llengües estrangeres*. Tesina inèdita. Universitat Autònoma de Barcelona.

Masats, D. (2008). *El discurs dels aprenents d'anglès com a llengua estrangera: una aproximació interactivista al procés de construcció de tasques comunicatives*. Tesi inèdita. Bellaterra: Universitat Autònoma de Barcelona.

Masats, D., Nussbaum, L., i Unamuno, V. (2007). When the activity shapes the repertoire of second language learners. A L. Roberts, A. Gürel, S. Tatar, i L. Martı (Eds), *EUROSLA Yearbook: Volume 7* (p. 121-147). Amsterdam: John Benjamins Publishing Company.

Masats, D., i Unamuno, V. (2001). Constructing social identities and discourse through repair activities. A S. Foster-Cohen i A. Nizegorodcew (Eds), *Eurosla Yearbook, Volume 1* (p. 239-254). Amsterdam: John Benjamins Publishing Company.

Maynard, D. (1989). On the ethnography and analysis of discourse in institutional settings. *Perspectives on Social Problems, 1*, 127-146.

Mondada, L. (1998). Technologies et interaction sur le terrain du linguiste. Actes du Colloque «Le travail du chercheur sur le terrain: questionner les pratiques, les méthodes, les techniques de l'enquête». *Cahiers de l'ILSL, 10*, 39-68.

Mondada, L. (2002). Pratiques de transcription et effets de catégorisation. *Cahiers de Praxématique, 39*, 45-75.

Mondada, L. (2003). Observer les activités de la classe dans leur diversité: Choix méthodologiques et enjeux théoriques. A J. Perera, L. Nussbaum i M. Milian (Eds), *L'educació lingüística en situacions multiculturals i multilingües* (p. 49-70). Barcelona: ICE de la Universitat de Barcelona.

Moore, E., i Llompart, J. (2017). Recoger, transcribir, analizar y presentar datos interaccionales plurilingües. A E. Moore i M. Dooly (Eds), *Enfocaments qualitatius per a la recerca en educació plurilingüe* (p. 418-433). Research-publishing.net. https://doi.org/10.14705/rpnet.2017.emmd2016.639

Nussbaum, L. (1990). Plurilingualism in foreign language classroom in Catalonia. A *Papers for the 3rd workshop on code-switching and language contact. Network on Code-Switching and Language Contact* (p. 141-163). Estrasburg: European Science Foundation.

Nussbaum, L. (2016). Estudio de la interacción en el aula de lengua extranjera. A D. Masats i L. Nussbaum (Eds), *Enseñanza y aprendizaje de las lenguas extranjeras en educación secundaria obligatoria* (p. 113-142). Madrid: Síntesis.

Nussbaum, L. (2017). Investigar con docentes. A E. Moore i M. Dooly (Eds), *Enfocaments qualitatius per a la recerca en educació plurilingüe* (p. 23-45). Research-publishing.net. https://doi.org/10.14705/rpnet.2017.emmd2016.620

Nussbaum, L., i Unamuno, V. (Ed.). (2006). *Usos i competències multilingües entre escolars d'origen immigrant*. Bellaterra: Servei de Publicacions de la Universitat Autònoma de Barcelona.

Ochs, E. (1979). Transcription as theory. A E. Ochs i B. B. Schieffelin (Eds), *Developmental pragmatics* (p. 43-72). Nova York: Academic Press.

Pekarek Doehler, S. (1999). *Leçons de conversation: dynamiques de l'interaction et acquisition de compétences discursives en classe de langue seconde*. Friburg: Editions Universitaires.

Pekarek Doehler, S., i Fasel Lauzon, V. (2015). Documenting change across time: longitudinal and cross-sectional CA studies of classroom interaction. A N. Markee (Ed.), *Handbook of classroom interaction.* (p. 409-424). Hoboken, Nova Jersey: Wiley-Blackwell.

Potter, J., i Hepburn, A. (2005a). Qualitative interviews in psychology: problems and possibilities. *Qualitative Research in Psychology, 2*(4), 281-307. https://doi.org/10.1191/1478088705qp045oa

Potter, J., i Hepburn, A. (2005b). Action, interaction and interviews: some responses to Smith, Hollway and Mischler. *Qualitative Research in Psychology, 2*(4), 319-325. http://dx.doi.org/10.1191/1478088705qp046cm

Psathas, G., y Anderson, T. (1990). The 'practices' of transcription in conversation analysis. *Semiotica, 78*, 75-99. https://doi.org/10.1515/semi.1990.78.1-2.75

Py, B. (1997). Pour une perspective bilingue sur l'enseignement et l'apprentissage des langues. *Études de Linguistique Appliquée, 108*, 495-503.

Sacks, H. (1992). *Lectures on conversation, volumes I and II*. Oxford: Basil Blackwell.

Sacks, H., Schegloff, E. A., y Jefferson, G. (1974). A simplest systematics for the organisation of turn-taking in conversation. *Language, 50*, 696-735. https://doi.org/10.1353/lan.1974.0010

Schegloff, E. A., Jefferson, G., y Sacks, H. (1977). The preference for self-correction in the organization of repair in conversation. *Language, 53*, 361-82. https://doi.org/10.1353/lan.1977.0041

Schegloff, E. A., Koshik, I., Jacoby, S., y Olsher, D. (2002). Conversation analysis and applied linguistics. *Annual Review of Applied Linguistics, 22*, 3-31. https://doi.org/10.1017/s0267190502000016

Seedhouse, P. (2004). *The interactional architecture of the language classroom: a conversation analysis perspective*. Malden, MA: Blackwell.

Seedhouse, P. (2005). Conversational analysis and language learning. *Language Teaching, 38*, 165-187. https://doi.org/10.1017/S0261444805003010

Silverman, D. (1989). Telling convincing stories: a plea for cautious positivism in case-studies. A B. Glassner i J. Moreno (Eds), *The qualitative-quantitative distinction in the social sciences* (p. 55-77). Dordrecht: Kluwer.

Smith, J. A., Hollway, W., i Mischler, E. G. (2005). Commentaries on Potter and Hepburn, 'Qualitative interviews in psychology: problems and possibilities'. *Qualitative Research in Psychology, 2*(4), 309-318. https://doi.org/10.1191/1478088705qp046cm

Unamuno, V., i Nussbaum, L. (2006). De la casa al aula: ámbitos y prácticas de transmisión y aprendizaje de lenguas. *Textos de Didáctica de la Lengua y de la Literatura, 42*, 43-51.

Unamuno, V., i Patiño, A. (2017). Producir conocimiento sobre el plurilingüismo junto a jóvenes estudiantes: un reto para la etnografía en colaboración. A E. Moore i M. Dooly (Eds), *Enfocaments qualitatius per a la recerca en educació plurilingüe* (p. 107-128). Research-publishing.net. https://doi.org/10.14705/rpnet.2017.emmd2016.624

Wong, J., i Waring, H. Z. (2010). *Conversational analysis and second Language pedagogy: a guide for ESL/ELF teachers*. Nova York: Routledge.

Lectures recomanades

Markee, N. (Ed.). (2015). *Handbook of classroom interaction*. Hoboken, Nova Jersey: Wiley-Blackwell.

Wong, J., i Waring, H. Z. (2010). *Conversational analysis and second Language pedagogy: a guide for ESL/ELF teachers*. Nova York: Routledge.

Apèndix

Adaptació de la simbologia de transcripció del GREIP (vegeu Moore i Llompart, en aquest volum)

Preguntes
    Preguntes sí/no /
    Preguntes amb interrogatiu (qui, què...) ?
Altres seqüències tonals
    Descendent \
    Sostingut —
Pauses
    Curta |
    Mitjana ||
    Llarga <nombre de segons>
Solapaments
    =Text del parlant A=
    =Text del parlant B=
Interrupcions: text_
Allargament sil·làbic: text:
Intensitat:
    piano {(P) text}
    forte {(F) tex}
Alternança de codi:

Capítol 8

Text en català
Text en castellà
Continuació d'un torn previ: Parlant>
Fragment incomprensible (nombre de segons): XXX | XXX XXX
Fragment dubtós: {(?) text}
Enunciats acompanyats de rialles: {(@) text}
Transcripció fonètica aproximada: [+text+]
Comentaris: [comentari]

8 Conversation analysis at the service of research in the field of second language acquisition (CA-for-SLA)

Dolors Masats[1]

Key concepts: conversation analysis, talk-in-interaction, CA-for-SLA, situated learning.

1. Introduction

Learning a language in a formal context is not the same as learning a language in a natural setting, in that the goal of one of the participants in the communicative events that occur in the classroom, the teacher, is to teach a language. For this reason, the majority of the actions undertaken by the participants are directed at achieving that goal. That is why observing and analyzing interaction in the classroom becomes a key element in understanding how we learn. In this chapter we set out how this issue is approached through conversation analysis.

Conversation analysis studies talk-in-interaction, which means taking into consideration the social aspects linked to the use and acquisition of language. In the field of second language acquisition, there is a widely documented tension surrounding the relationship between these two phenomena. Research undertaken from a cognitive perspective, one of the dominant approaches, argues that studying the use of language does not contribute relevant data for understanding the process of its acquisition and therefore proposes longitudinal experimental studies. Conversely, the sociocultural perspective supports the idea that learning occurs based on interaction and therefore, to understand the language acquisition process, it is necessary to investigate how, through language,

---

1. Universitat Autònoma de Barcelona, Bellaterra, Catalonia/Spain; dolors.masats@uab.cat

How to cite this chapter: Masats, D. (2017). Conversation analysis at the service of research in the field of second language acquisition (CA-for-SLA). In E. Moore & M. Dooly (Eds), *Qualitative approaches to research on plurilingual education* (pp. 321-347). Research-publishing.net. https://doi.org/10.14705/rpnet.2017.emmd2016.633

individuals complete social actions in specific contexts to attain concrete goals. To achieve this objective, one can either undertake longitudinal studies or else carry out case studies that identify and analyze sequences (of speech) in which the speakers orient to learning.

If we start from the premise that learning takes place through interaction and that learners acquire knowledge and communicative expertise through socially situated activities that take place in specific contexts of use, it is also important to study the organizational systems of participation in a contextualized way. Some forms of participation and the methods used to manage the linguistic resources available to participants are appropriate to educational institutions (for example, raising one's hand to ask for permission to speak is a method of organizing participation in a school environment; using Catalan as a vehicular language for learning is a characteristic typical of Catalan and Andorran schools, etc.), others are specific to each classroom (for example, participation is organized differently in classrooms where students are engaged in project work and classrooms in which interaction is controlled by the teacher).

Lastly, it should be remembered that learning languages is a complex and multimodal process and thus research into language acquisition must be carried out from an interdisciplinary perspective, using an emic approach (see Nussbaum, this volume) based on data relating to the real use of language and observing processes in which interaction, as a means of carrying out social action, generates learning. Conversation analysis is the discipline which, inspired by fields such as pragmatics, speech act theory, the analysis of variation, interactional sociolinguistics, ethnomethodology, the ethnography of communication, communication theory and social psychology, fulfills the premises we have set out.

There are other chapters in this handbook that justify the validity of using ethnographic procedures for gathering data and of using conversation analysis techniques to undertake classroom research from a collaborative perspective (see, for example, the chapters by Nussbaum, this volume; Unamuno & Patiño, this volume). In this chapter we want to undertake a detailed examination of what conversation analysis means. To this end, we will first review the origins of the discipline, secondly we will describe the challenges researchers interested in carrying out research from this perspective have to take on and, to conclude, we will set out the premises on which this theoretical and methodological proposal is based and we will show, giving examples, the phenomena it is most concerned with.

2. Conversation analysis as a research discipline

Conversation analysis emerged at the start of the 1960's as a result of the studies by Sacks (1992, among others) on the organization of social interaction. The author was inspired by the work of Garfinkel (1967, among others) based on ethnomethodology and proposed studying talk-in-interaction through analyzing recordings of everyday conversations. At that time, this was a revolutionary option, not only because sound recording equipment was a lot less common but mainly because linguistics in those days had no interest in studying ordinary conversation.

Sacks, however, was not interested in analyzing conversation exclusively, but rather oral interaction, which implies the study of both verbal and non-verbal communication. The work he carried out with Schegloff and Jefferson (Sacks, Schegloff, & Jefferson, 1974; Schegloff, Jefferson, & Sacks, 1977) is especially important for the evolution of conversation analysis as a discipline for studying oral data (see a review of its origins and development in Goodwin & Heritage, 1990). As we mentioned, at the beginning, the discipline was interested in ordinary conversation, but later on other varieties of discourse were analyzed (interviews, political speeches, legal interrogations, etc.) and nowadays the aim of the subject is to cover any type of interaction that implies performing both verbal and non-verbal activities.

These days, conversation analysis is a consolidated discipline in the language sciences, but this has not always been the case. For example, at the start of this century, Seedhouse (2005) noted that the role played by conversation analysis in the field of applied linguistics was not the same one as it had, at that

Chapter 8

time, in research undertaken into the acquisition of second languages. Applied linguistics does not question the validity of using conversation analysis as a research methodology and considers that studies based on this discipline make relevant contributions to teaching languages for specific purposes (see Wong & Waring, 2010, to discover more about the most recent proposals) as they provide guidance for (1) designing materials and text books based on the types of discourse that need to be presented, (2) managing interaction in the classroom or in other settings, and (3) understanding how conversations between natives and non-natives or codeswitching in bilingual or multilingual environments are structured. Notwithstanding all this, however, as we mentioned, the author himself states that at the beginning of the 21st century, conversation analysis in research into the acquisition of second languages, the branch of the discipline known as Conversation Analysis for Second Language Acquisition (CA-for-SLA), is the result of debate. Two things should be borne in mind in order to understand this statement: on the one hand, conversation analysis was one of the theoretical and methodological instruments adopted by researchers working from a sociocultural perspective, but held no interest for researchers from the dominant cognitive school of thought. The discussion is not, therefore, related to the validity of conversation analysis as a research tool, but instead depends on which concept of the learning process the researcher decides to adopt. On the other hand, when Seedhouse states that research into second language acquisition only took an interest in conversation analysis from the period 2000-2004, it is possible that he is only taking into account those researchers who explicitly adopted a sociocultural learning perspective and attacked the principles defended by supporters of the cognitive viewpoint. There are a great number of previous studies carried out mainly in Switzerland, but also in France, Germany and Catalonia that fall into the field of contact linguistics and language acquisition (de Pietro, Matthey, & Py, 1989; Lüdi, 1999; Lüdi & Py, 1986; Masats, 1999; Nussbaum, 1990; Pekarek Doehler, 1999; Py, 1997, among others) and in which, through conversation analysis, plurilingual practices are related to the process of acquiring second and foreign languages.

All studies based on conversation analysis contain three basic principles which, according to Mondada (2003), should feature in any research that proposes to observe phenomena on the ground: the principle of observability (the phenomena studied must be able to be observed and described), the principle of availability (in order to observe and describe a phenomenon it has to be collectable) and the principle of symmetry (the way a researcher projects his or her viewpoint on the data is also a phenomenon that must be observed and described). These concepts have been described in the chapter that Nussbaum (this volume) dedicates to collaborative research. In the next section we will consider the challenges they imply and that researchers should be aware of.

3. The challenge of documenting and describing observable phenomena

One of the key challenges for researchers is that of deciding what to investigate in order to document learning. There is a general consensus on the need to describe interactional competence and analyze how it is acquired (see Markee, 2000, 2008), but studies explaining how interaction in the classroom impacts on learning are still scarce (Pekarek Doehler & Fasel Lauzon, 2015). Along the same lines, Unamuno and Nussbaum (2006), for example, propose studying aspects such as how learners construct interactive scenarios, manage the activities they carry out, how they participate with a balanced level of conversation, how they identify and overcome communication barriers and how they adapt their verbal repertoire according to the activity they are involved in and the situation. Masats (2008), on the other hand, includes all of these aspects and expands them in the case of foreign language learning by exploring the interaction between pairs of learners carrying out communicative tasks. The following diagram (taken from Masats, 2008) illustrates the macro-discursive tasks that learners carry out when performing a task and shows the actions in their discourse which are observable and that serve to characterize their interactional competence.

To understand how interaction is organized when individuals perform a specific social activity (for example, when learners resolve a communicative task) and how that social activity is constructed, it must be remembered that "la realitat i el sentit es construeixen en les interaccions socials i que és en la pròpia interacció on cal

Chapter 8

buscar les claus de la interpretació" (Nussbaum & Unamuno, 2006, p. 16)[2]. Firstly, this presupposes an analysis of facts that are observable, such as the behavior that speakers exhibit when interacting, rather than theorizing over unobservable phenomena, such as their motivation for taking part in the interaction. Secondly, it is necessary to formulate the appropriate questions in order to grasp the social value of the facts being observed (see how Moore & Llompart, this volume, suggest approaching this topic in their chapter). In this respect, Maynard (1989) suggests formulating questions that involve observing how participants behave during an interaction (how to resolve barriers to communication, how to manage the linguistic resources at their disposal, how to co-construct statements, etc.). Nevertheless, it is not enough just to identify observable facts and pose pertinent questions; the need to categorize what we observe so that we can describe it obliges us to find the most appropriate vocabulary to do so. These three actions imply making decisions linked to the processes of data collection, treatment and analysis. We will take a brief look at these next (Figure 1).

Figure 1. Observable actions in the context of carrying out a task (Masats, 2008, p. 142)

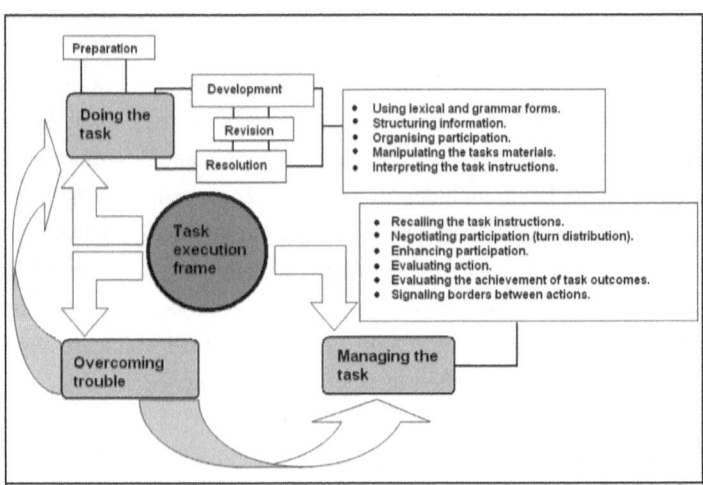

---

2. "reality and meaning are constructed out of social interactions and it is in the interaction itself that the keys to its interpretation can be found" (Translated from Nussbaum & Unamuno, 2006, p. 16)

4. The choice of tools to collect observable phenomena

As we have indicated, the principle of availability establishes that in order to describe observable facts it is first necessary to collect them and then represent them.

At the beginning of the 1970s, for example, Sacks based his work on sound recordings, but a decade later the Goodwins were already documenting their data on video. In terms of analysis, whichever tool is used to record interaction in the classroom (a video camera, a mobile device, a voice recorder, etc.), it cannot be viewed solely as a means of collecting data; the way the device is handled by students also gives pointers to how learners interactively construct the meaning of the task to be performed (see the recommendations regarding this made by Moore & Llompart, this volume). For example, we can determine which part of their discourse a pair of learners wish to make 'public' or otherwise by observing their discursive actions and paying attention to aspects such as the moment they decide to momentarily pause a recording, what they register when they restart a recording that was paused, what they whisper to each other, and when they address the camera directly, etc.

Given that the non-verbal elements in any interaction are significant, it is important to be able to document them. In this respect, recording data on video is preferable to audio-recorded data (see Moore & Llompart's comments on this subject in this handbook). If it is impossible to access to video data (there may be families that withhold permission for their children to be filmed), then the value of non-verbal communication should not be overlooked, which means that our transcripts, just in the same way as when we transcribe visual data, must contain comments on the kinetic, gestural and visual aspects that have left an observable trace in the verbal production. The challenge, in this case, is about deciding what is and what is not observable when working with audio recordings only without the visual support to understand what is happening (Mondada, 2003). Fragment 1, which is part of a longer sequence, serves to illustrate this issue.

Chapter 8

Fragment 1

7.	Gemma:	{(P) ingredients of the—|}
8.	Jana:	cake |cake|[she is writing]|**es que no sé cómo se escribe**|cake|
9.	Gemma	[calls out to the teacher] María| com s'=escriu pastís=
Metropolitan Infant and Primary School **Carrying out a role play task**		

In turns 7 and 8, Gemma and Jana are jointly putting together a script ("ingredients of the cake") that will form part of a fictitious dialogue the two girls have to develop. Suddenly, Jana (at the end of turn 8) verbalizes that she does not know how to spell one of the words that has come up ("cake"). Therefore, Gemma (turn 9) refers to the teacher to ask how to spell it. In this case, the action of writing is registered in the discourse of this dyad because one of the participants topicalizes it when she initiates a change of code. In other words, after verbalizing the word "cake", the spelling of that word becomes the subject around which the interaction turns, which is expressed in a different language to the one used by the girls when constructing the invented dialogue. The transcript of this fragment contains a comment by the transcriber, a fact that indicates that in the process of translating the oral data to written data, he or she 'visualized' the existence of that kinetic action and captured it because it was felt to be relevant to how the action was configured.

Fulfilling the principle of observability involves recognizing that, without observable evidence in the interactive speech generated by the two girls in the exchange illustrated in Fragment 1, we would not be able to confirm that, in order for Gemma and Jana to carry out the task they had been assigned, they decided to write the dialogue they were inventing down on paper and that it was Jana who took the responsibility for doing so.

5. The choice of a system to represent the observable phenomena

As we noted in the previous section, in order to document observable phenomena it is necessary to represent them once they have been collected. Therefore, conversation analysis obliges us to work with transcripts which often act as mediators between theory and data. By their very nature, however, transcripts are partial and selective because they restrict the social reality they wish to study (Bucholtz, 2000; Ochs, 1979; Psathas & Anderson, 1990). For Haviland (1996), a transcript represents talk-in-interaction out of the context of its production. The willingness of the researcher to 'reconstruct' the situation in which the discourse unfolds implies a process of decision-making that has an impact on the analysis. Ochs (1979) states that all transcriptions are built on the basis of applying selection processes (decisions need to be taken on which aspects of the conversation should be made 'visible' or not, whether to produce a phonetic or an orthographic transcript, the selection of symbols to represent the paralinguistic and non-verbal information, whether the transcription is organized into turns, tonal units or an alternative system, etc.) and simplification (abstracting from the aspects selected). Therefore, transcription, as noted in the chapters by Nussbaum (this volume) and that of Moore and Llompart (this volume), must be viewed as a first phase of this analysis (Ochs, 1979), and as a starting point for reflection (Mondada, 2002).

The act of choosing a transcription system (see the suggestions put forward by Moore & Llompart, this volume) is guided by the objectives of the research to be carried out and the subject of the study. This explains why some researchers (such as Auer, 1998, when analyzing codeswitching) develop their own conventions when it comes to transcribing and analyzing their own data. Some of the oral data transcription systems that have enjoyed widespread acceptance in the field of interactional analysis are those developed by Jefferson (1985, 2004), Atkinson and Heritage (1984), du Bois (1991) and Gumperz and Berenz (1993) (see Moore & Llompart, this volume, on more recent conventions for multimodal transcription that have been developed). Often, however, there is no consensus on whether the conventions adopted complicate the reading of the data and oblige the researcher to do unnecessary work or whether it would be possible to represent oral data through a simpler system such as the orthographic one (see the debate between Potter & Hepburn, 2005a, 2005b; Smith, Hollway, & Mischler, 2005). We believe that detail in the transcript is necessary for reproducing data as faithfully as possible, as that allows us to carry out a detailed analysis of it and thereby comply with one of the four basic principles of conversation analysis (see below). The transcription symbols used in this chapter are based on conventions developed by the GREIP group (see Moore & Llompart, this volume) and are included in the annex.

6. The choice of terminology to categorize observable phenomena

The principle of symmetry recommends viewing both informants and observers in the same way. This means that researchers should also be considered as forming part of the data collected (Mondada, 1998) and, therefore, their actions also need to be observed and made available. In this respect, the challenge of describing observable facts involves choices that will have an impact on the description and analysis of the data, on how we position ourselves as researchers in response to these data and on how we present ourselves to the scientific community. Writing an article or research study also constitutes a social activity and a communicative situation (encounter): someone relates 'a convincing story' (Silverman, 1989) in the hope that someone else might wish to read it.

However, choosing the words to describe observed phenomena is not always an easy task. Firstly, if a piece of qualitative research is undertaken, categorization cannot be created until the data have been analyzed (Bryman, 1988); categories emerge as the result of the analysis. Secondly, once a phenomenon has been observed, a categorization has to be constructed based on a careful lexical choice that must be fully justifiable since the same word can often be used to describe phenomena of a different nature or else the same event can be described using different terminology. By addressing our audience as researchers-writers, we make vocabulary choices that make it easier for readers to relate to a particular research tradition or to a specific way of describing the reality observed. For example, if we choose to make use of the term 'participant' rather than 'speaker' and 'listener' when referring to the individuals taking part in a communicative situation, it implies that we recognize their interaction as a social action, as defended from a sociocultural learning perspective.

7. The four basic principles of conversation analysis and the four key elements it studies

In order to analyze every interaction, conversation analysis is grounded on four basic principles rooted in the ethnomethodological suppositions defended by Garfinkel, who, as we said, was one of the sources of inspiration for Sacks. These four principles guide the process for treating and analyzing data and can be summarized as follows:

- Interaction is a form of discourse that has a clear order, and the job of the analyst is to work out how it is organized and sequenced.

- Interaction is linked to the context in which it occurs and therefore it is essential to analyze it sequentially in order to be able to understand it. At the same time, interaction also creates a context that is observable through the manner in which actions take place and how participants approach them.

- The details (silences, changes in intonation or rhythm, whispers, pauses, etc.) are never insignificant, no matter how small they might be. That is why it is essential that interaction be transcribed accurately and in detail.

- The analysis must be drawn from the data. Reviewing the data should be done from an emic perspective, i.e. analyzing what participants orient to in their discourse. To achieve this it is important to bear in mind how participants interpret and make sense of what they do. For example, an ungrammatical utterance is not a problem as long as the interlocutors do not make it one. Neither the background of the participants nor their identifying characteristics are relevant unless they are brought into play during the discourse.

In the field of conversation analysis, the description and explanation of the use of language as a social action is focused on the study of the four elements on which Sacks based his analysis of the organization of interaction: constructing adjacency pairs, the notion of preference, turn-taking and repair (see a detailed description of these elements in Schegloff, Koshik, Jacoby, & Olsher, 2002; Seedhouse, 2004, 2005, among others).

8. Adjacency pairs and the notion of preference

The construct of the adjacency pair is based on the ethnomethodological principle of reflexivity which states that procedures activated through the production of an action or utterance are the same as those activated when it comes to interpreting them. For example, a question is generated to elicit a response and that is also how the interlocutor to whom the question is directed interprets it. However, the interactive meaning of a turn can only be interpreted by analyzing the turn that follows. Adjacency pairs therefore, serve to describe the sequential order in which the interaction is organized.

Even though the reality is that only a set number of actions can be undertaken through constructing adjacency pairs, the analytical reasoning on which the construct is based is applicable to other ways of organizing action (Goodwin & Heritage, 1990). However, the behavior of interlocutors when it comes to the sequencing and organization of discourse is not analyzed from a regulatory perspective, i.e. conversation analysts are not interested in explaining what the speakers actually say, but rather their orientations or, in other words, what their preferences are when it comes to interacting. Responding to a greeting with another greeting is a preferred action and the most common one, but interlocutors may choose not to follow the preferred action. Fragment 2 serves to illustrate the adjacency pair concept and the notion of preference.

Fragment 2

51	Héctor:	in my yes|in my picture the shop assistant_|| the hair is_| green\\\| ay\\\| is—<0> no\\\| [laughs] brown\\\|
52	Josep:	eh| in_ |in my_| what colour_| what colour is| the shoes| of a woman?|

53	Héctor:	black|
54	Josep:	eh—| what colour is the hair_ [+jair+] ey ma_ of the woman?|
55	Héctor:	eh—| pink\\|
56	Josep:	eh—| what colour is the eyes [+eis+] the consumer?|
57	Héctor:	the customer/|| is green\\|
58	Josep:	eh um—|
59	Héctor:	{(DC) in a: basket}\ eh—|there are bananas\\| oranges\\| lettuce [+le'tuz+]\\| and milk \\|
60	Josep:	yes\\| um—| <1>
61	Hector:	in my picture there are two\ two cheese\\|
Metropolitan Infant and Primary School **Carrying out a task for identifying differences**		

Fragment 2 shows us part of an exchange in the interaction between two primary school learners comprising six sequences in which the boys try to find out what differences there are between the drawings each of them is holding. Three of these sequences (turns 51, 59-60 and 61) are initiated by Héctor and the other three (turns 52-53; 54-55 and 56-57) by his classmate, Josep. As we can see, Josep goes about this task by adopting an interactive pattern in which he takes on the discursive identity of the questioner and allocates the role of informant to Héctor. Thus, the two boys construct sequences based on adjacency pairs of the question-answer variety. The consecutive use of this type of pattern serves to tacitly indicate that there is no difference between the two drawings. That is to say, as the reply Josep receives from his classmate does not contradict the information that he has in his drawing, he formulates a new question to continue investigating the two drawings. In turn 58, Josep hesitates before formulating a new statement, which gives Héctor the chance to take his turn to speak, thus changing the interactional framework (turn 59).

If we look at the three sequences initiated by Héctor, we see how he shows that his preferred action is to take on the discursive identity of describer, for the following reason: both in turn 51 and when he picks up the conversation in turns 59 and 61, he formulates a statement containing a description of what is shown in his drawing. The sequence comprising turns 59 and 60 is also an example of an adjacency pair (description-confirmation of the description) in that Josep uses his turn to verbalize that his drawing contains the same elements listed by his classmate. The other sequences started by Héctor comprise just a single turn since the opening of a new sequence by his classmate (turn 52) serves to confirm that what Héctor has described also appears in Josep's drawing.

Thus, as we can see, four of the sequences that we have shown of this interchange are based on adjacency pairs and two are not; and that is because each participant shows a preference for a particular discursive pattern.

9. Turn-taking

Turns represent the minimum units of participation around which interaction can be structured. As we saw in the previous fragment, turns can be grouped together into bigger units called sequences. Sequences can be formed by just a single turn (as in the case of turns 51 and 61 in Fragment 2), by adjacency pairs (as in the case of turns 52-53, 54-55, 56-57 and 59-60 of Fragment 2), by Initiation-Response-Follow up (IRF) sequences (as we see in Fragment 3 which follows) or by other more complex groupings that arise, above all when learners are trying to resolve communication barriers (see Fragment 4).

Fragment 3

3	María:	more or less/| do you understand this?|
4	Álex:	*que farem_ que farem una fitxa de diferències\\|*
5	María:	yes\\| that's it\\| that's it|\\ alright\\|then— in order to spot the differences—| what you have to do is to describe your picture\\| right/ say—| for example\\| in my picture there's a:: dog\\| and the dog is brown\\|
Metropolitan Infant and Primary School **The teacher (María) gives instructions about how to perform a task about finding differences**		

Fragment 3 shows a sequence of three turns described by the abbreviation IRF. This discursive structure is typical of classroom interaction during the times when the teacher is managing class participation (see Nussbaum, 2016, for a more detailed analysis of this type of sequence). The first turn in this sequence (turn 3), begins (initiation turn) with a question from the teacher to establish whether the instructions she has just given have been understood. In the second turn, one of the students answers her (response turn) in the affirmative by summarizing in Catalan the content of the instructions given. Finally, in the third turn (follow up turn), the teacher gives a positive assessment of the student's answer ("yes, that's it, alright") before starting a new initiation move by continuing to give further instructions within the same turn.

Conversation analysts are just as interested in the mechanisms of turn construction, which could be verbal or non-verbal, as they are in the mechanisms speakers adopt for turn taking. The study of turns and the processes related to them (talking over, pauses, interruptions, silences, gestures, etc.) is essential for understanding how interaction is constructed and organized and how interaction generates learning. The basic question guiding studies undertaken from the conversation analysis perspective is the following: 'Why does that happen in that way at precisely that moment?' For Seedhouse (2004), this question summarizes the essence of the principles of conversation analysis, since it shows that interaction is conceptualized as an action (why does that happen?), expressed through specific linguistic forms (why is that being expressed in that way?), embedded into the development of a sequence (why does that happen, expressed in that way, at that precise moment?).

10. Repair and processes for avoiding communication breakdowns

According to proponents of interactive language learning, performing tasks to overcome barriers fosters participants' acquisition of communicative expertise (Hall, Cheng, & Carlson, 2006; Kasper, 2004) inasmuch as they provide practice in procedures and methods of social behavior and are not just a source of access to language forms. Traditionally, conversation analysis has been interested in repair, one of the mechanisms employed by interlocutors to solve any communication barriers they encounter, but not the only one. In this section we will first deal with the concept of repair and then move onto other processes used by learners, such as codeswitching, code-mixing or employing paraphrase to maintain the flow of the conversation.

11. The concept of repair

In contrast to other mechanisms employed by participants in a communicative event to overcome barriers, repair provokes interruptions in the flow of the conversation. Evidence of a repair may be seen discursively when interlocutors momentarily abandon the action they are engaged in and resolve the trouble within a new sequence. This is called a side sequence because its intention is to focus on language forms or negotiate the sense of the statement that has interrupted the flow of conversation. Once the barrier is resolved (or once the attempt at resolution is abandoned), the action that had been interrupted is resumed.

According to Masats (1999), it is impossible to understand the complex phenomenon of repair without analyzing it from a perspective that takes into account three core concepts: (1) repair in relation to the actions performed by the learners; (2) the connection between the object of the repair and the discursive identities assumed by the interlocutors during the repair sequence; and (3) the connection between repair and metalinguistic activity as tools to foster learning. Regarding the first factor, conversation analysis demonstrates that four procedures can be identified in order to repair conversation, depending on who flags up the communication barrier and who puts forward a proposal to solve it:

- Self-initiated Self-repair (SS): the repair is initiated and resolved by the speaker who encountered the trouble.

- Hetero-initiated Hetero-repair (HH): the trouble is identified and resolved by a speaker who did not utter the statement that caused it.

- Self-initiated Hetero-repair (SH): the repair is initiated by the speaker who encountered the trouble but resolved by another participant.

- Hetero-initiated Self-repair (HS): the barrier is identified by a speaker who did not utter the statement that caused it, but is resolved by the person who initiated the trouble.

A repair can serve a variety of purposes. Masats (1999) suggests that in order to observe what interlocutors are repairing, it is necessary to analyze the three areas in which the learners are operating: resolving problems related to code, negotiating meaning and managing the task, while recognizing the value of the objects that accompany the action (the support materials for the task) as a factor that shapes and restructures the approach of the speakers to that action. The following Table 1 summarizes her proposal.

Table 1. The object of repairs (Masats, 1999, p. 65)

REPAIRS	Directed at THE CODE	LEXICAL REPAIRS
		SEMANTIC REPAIRS
		MORPHOSYNTACTIC REPAIRS
		PHONETIC REPAIRS
	Directed at THE MESSAGE	COHESION REPAIRS
		PRECISION REPAIRS
		AMBIGUITY REPAIRS
	Directed at THE TASK	
	Directed at THE MATERIALS	FOCALIZATION ON THE CODE
		FOCALIZATION ON THE DISCOURSE
		FOCALIZATION ON THE TASK

Independently of the objective being repaired, when a repair is carried out there is always a participant that adopts the discursive identity of the non-expert speaker who thus bestows the identity of expert speaker on the other party. These identities are not fixed but change according to the discursive actions being performed. The indiscriminate adoption of expert and non-expert identities between learners is a mechanism that assures the development of their interactive abilities and encourages learning since it forces them to engage in metalinguistic activities. For this reason, the study of the side sequences that open up when a repair is made is especially interesting as they often become potential acquisition sequences (de Pietro et al., 1989). This can be observed in Fragment 4.

Fragment 4

85	Eli:	in my picture there are mm—| **cómo se llama?**| {(PP) XX}<14> {(PP) **la camisa**\}| <2>
86	Álex:	the shirt\ [+short+]| shirt\[+short+]|
87	María:	shirt\\|
88	Álex:	=shirt=
89	Eli:	=shirt=| in my picture there are shirt_ em—| shop assistant [+a'ssisten+] eh—| is red and blue\\||
90	Álex:	red and blue\\|
91	Eli:	yes\\| <1>
Metropolitan Infant and Primary School **Eli and Álex perform a task about finding differences**		

In turn 85, Eli initiates a sequence to describe something in her drawing but she encounters a lexical barrier that does not allow her to complete her description (turn 89) until it is resolved. To achieve this, she adopts the discursive identity of non-expert speaker, bestowing on her classmate the identity of expert speaker and initiates a side sequence, which she inserts into the same turn 85. The construction of this new sequence is preceded by a sound that indicates doubt ("mm"), is signaled by a change in language and takes the form of a request for help (*"cómo se llama la camisa?"*) uttered in a lower tone. Given that the participant who has encountered the barrier is the same as the one pointing it out, we categorize the repair as self-initiated. In the next turn, Álex replies to his classmate, which is to say he hetero-repairs her discourse. In principle, this repair's side sequence could have consisted entirely and exclusively in this adjacency pair (question-answer). However, the teacher, María, is near the children and notices that Álex has problems with correctly pronouncing the word he wishes to provide to Eli and so she decides to intervene. In doing so, she self-categorizes herself as an expert speaker and assigns Álex the discursive identity of non-expert speaker. Thus, turn 87 is a hetero-repair (the teacher corrects Álex) hetero-initiated (the teacher points out to Álex that he has a problem). The boy has not asked for help and repeats the word twice, but we cannot tell if he does that because he does not know how to pronounce it correctly or if he just says it twice without realizing that he is not pronouncing it correctly. Turns 88 and 89 show how, simultaneously, Álex and Eli assimilate the teacher's repair and, in the case of the girl, she inserts it into her discourse to complete the statement that had been interrupted in turn 85. To sum up, Fragment 4 shows an example of self-initiated hetero-repair between Eli and Álex (turns 85 and 86) and another hetero-repair by the teacher directed at Álex's utterance (turns 86, 87 and 88). Nevertheless, the findings of studies into repair, including the study which is the source of the data we are reproducing (see Masats, 2008), show that learners have a preference for self-repairs regardless of whether they are self-initiated or hetero-initiated.

Lastly, it is important to point out that analyzing data from an emic perspective, one of the four principles that we indicated as guiding conversation analysis, implies observing data from the viewpoint of the participants. In turn 89 of Fragment 4, when Eli returns to formulating her statement, we observe that she mispronounces the word "assistant". The transcription contains this information (observing and noting it) but as it is a fact that neither of the two participants in this exchange pick up on, we as researchers cannot categorize this deviation from the norm as a barrier in need of repair.

12. Procedures employed to maintain the conversational flow

Masats, Nussbaum, and Unamuno (2007) analyzed the problems that students come up against in a more general way, transcending the concept of repair, and categorized them according to the topics they fall under: the global format of the activity (what has to be done), the materials (as intermediary objects in the interaction), the global management of the task (how it should be managed), the resources available to the students in performing the task (if they have them available and/or consider them relevant to the local construction of the activity). In Fragment 5 we can observe some of these procedures that, unlike repairs, do not interrupt but rather maintain the conversational flow.

Chapter 8

Fragment 5

75	Bawna:	it's a_ a_ | a *deu mil* money|
76	Pau:	*deu mil* no| <2> *deu mil* moneys|
77	Bawna:	a ten_ <0>
78	Pau:	er_
79	Bawna>	ten thousand|
80	Pau:	ten thousand moneys|
81	Bawna:	XXXXX|
82	Pau:	yes yes **es que_ sube**| it's up\ | it's up **navideit**|
83	Bawna:	=thank you\=
84	Pau:	=thank you\= bye bye|
85	Bawna:	=bye bye|=
BCN1 Infant and Primary School **Pau and Bawna take part in a role play**		

In Fragment 5, Pau and Bawna find themselves immersed in co-constructing a dialogue between a shopkeeper and a customer. The scenario the teacher has given them on which to base this fictitious conversation involves giving the price for the products the customer has bought. The fragment shows the moment at which the learners abandon their roles as buyer and seller in order to find a joint solution to this communication challenge. Thus, in turn 75, Bawna proposes an amount. As we can see, her statement is in a hybrid form that mixes up two codes: English (the language the task is performed in) and Catalan (the language Bawna uses to communicate with her classmates). Observing what happens in the following turns allows us to appreciate that this procedure is not a product of the girl's lack of command of the target language but rather a resource that allows her to take her turn in the conversation without having to think about how to frame her proposal. In turn 76, her classmate questions her proposal and repairs (incorrectly) the part of the statement that the girl had formulated in English. This interruption allows Bawna to self-correct her discourse (turns 77 and 79) and formulate a statement entirely in English (turn 79) avoiding taking on board Pau's proposal. Pau assimilates his classmate's self-correction and supplements it. At this moment the boy, whose role in the role play is that of the shopkeeper, abandons the metalinguistic reflection activity he was engaged in and adopts this discursive identity and thus the conversation proceeds within the role play.

In other words, the shopkeeper (Pau) gives a price for the products the customer has bought (turn 81), the customer (Bawna) makes an unintelligible comment about the price (turn 82), the shopkeeper justifies the price (turn 83) and the customer accepts it (turn 84); the shopkeeper thanks her and says goodbye (turn 85) and the customer responds to this parting salutation (turn 86).

The task the learners are performing is complex in that it implies that the participants need to adopt, sometimes simultaneously, a variety of discursive identities in an attempt to turn the scenario they have been given into a coherent dialogue within the role play (Masats & Unamuno, 2001). Employing all the linguistic resources at their disposal makes this task easier for them. This also explains why, at a specific moment of the fictitious dialogue between the shopkeeper and his customer (turn 82), Pau constructs his statement in the way that he does. First we see how the boy and his classmate are interested in maintaining the flow of the conversation within the roles assumed for the role play. Faced with the intervention of his classmate (who is possibly complaining about the high price of the products she has purchased: fruit) he responds in Spanish, arguing that prices go up. The change of code, the use of Spanish, permits him to buy time to think of a way of expressing the idea of rising prices in English ("it's up") and to conclude his argument (prices go up because it's Christmas – the data were collected the week before the Christmas holidays) in the same turn 82 ("it's up navideit"). Once again, the use of a hybrid form (adding a morpheme that sounds like English to a half-formed word in Spanish) is a valid procedure for this dyad to succeed in completing the task assigned to them.

13. Concluding words

In this chapter, we have argued that conversation analysis is the discipline that provides a suitable theoretical and methodological framework for studying speech in interaction for those researchers interested in language acquisition processes from a sociocultural perspective of learning, in that it allows social aspects linked with acquiring languages to be taken into account.

Firstly, we re-examined the origins of this discipline. Secondly, we reviewed the principles it upholds and then, through analyzing fragments of conversation taken from primary school classrooms, we demonstrated some of the phenomena that are of interest to conversation analysis and how to analyze data from this perspective. Thus, on the one hand, we indicated that studies aimed at studying how languages are acquired in formal contexts show that some systems for organizing participation are dictated by educational institutions, while others are specific to each classroom. Conversation analysis is interested in studying how these participation systems are displayed in each context and how they contribute towards learners managing the linguistic resources they have at their disposal in a specific way.

On the other hand, we noted that conversation analysis argues that in order to understand how a language is learned, it is necessary to describe language use in its context, which can only be achieved through an emic and detailed analysis of the interaction generated in each particular conversational event. Thus, the analytical model set out by the discipline is based on data (data-driven model) and proposes to study, from the participants' perspective, a range of phenomena (turn-taking, how participation is organized, formulation of utterances, codeswitching, repair, etc.).

Lastly, we stressed that researchers interested in describing language acquisition processes from the viewpoint put forward by conversation analysis start from the premise that learners acquire communicative knowledge and expertise through participating in socially situated activities carried out in specific contexts of use. This participation encourages learners to engage in activities of metalinguistic reflection and call into play all of the linguistic resources at their disposal, thus guaranteeing that they can complete, in the target language, the communicative tasks given to them. From this perspective, it is the use of a variety of mechanisms such as codeswitching, using synonyms, paraphrasing or code-mixing that makes their discourse fluent and, at the same time, rich and exploratory.

Works cited

Atkinson, J. M., & Heritage, J. (Eds). (1984). *Structures of social action: studies in conversation analysis*. Cambridge: Cambridge University Press.

Auer, P. (Ed.). (1998). *Code switching in conversation: language, interaction and identity*. London: Routledge.

Bryman, A. (1988). *Quantity and quality in social research*. London: Unwin Hyman. https://doi.org/10.4324/9780203410028

Bucholtz, M. (2000). The politics of transcription. *Journal of Pragmatics, 32*(10), 1439-1465. https://doi.org/10.1016/S0378-2166(99)00094-6

De Pietro, J. F., Matthey, M., & Py, B. (1989). Acquisition et contrat didactique: les séquences potentiellement acquisitionnelles dans la conversation exolingue. In D. Weil & H. Fugier (Eds), *Actes du troisième colloque régional de linguistique* (pp. 99-124). Strasbourg: Université des Sciences Humaines et Université Louis Pasteur.

Du Bois, J. W. (1991). Transcription design principles for spoken discourse research. *Pragmatics 1*(1), 71-106. https://doi.org/10.1075/prag.1.1.04boi

Garfinkel, H. (1967). *Studies in ethnomethodology*. Englewood Cliffs, NJ: Prentice-Hall.

Goodwin, C., & Heritage, J. (1990). Conversation analysis. *Annual Review of Anthropology, 19*, 283-307. https://doi.org/10.1146/annurev.an.19.100190.001435

Gumperz, J., & Berenz, N. (1993). Transcribing conversational exchanges. In J. A. Edwards & M. D. Lampert (Eds), *Talking language: transcription and coding in discourse research* (pp. 91-122). Hillsdale, N.J.: Lawrence Erlbaum Associates.

Hall, J. K., Cheng, A., & Carlson, M. T. (2006). Reconceptualizing multicompetence as a theory of language knowledge. *Applied Linguistics, 27*(2), 220-240. https://doi.org/10.1093/applin/aml013

Haviland, J. B. (1996). Text from talk in Tzotzil. In M. Silverstein & G. Urban (Eds), *Natural histories of discourse* (pp. 45-78). Chicago: University of Chicago Press.

Jefferson, G. (1985). An exercise in the transcription and analysis of laughter. In T. van Dijk (Ed.), *Handbook of discourse analysis, Vol. 3: discourse and dialogue* (pp. 25-34). London, UK: Academic Press.

Jefferson, G. (2004). Glossary of transcript symbols with an introduction. In G. H. Lerner (Ed.), *Conversation analysis: studies from the first generation* (pp. 13-31). Amsterdam/Philadelphia: John Benjamins Publishing Company. https://doi.org/10.1075/pbns.125.02jef

Kasper, G. (2004). Participant orientations in German conversation-for-learning. *The Modern Language Journal, 88*(4), 551-67. https://doi.org/10.1111/j.0026-7902.2004.t01-18-.x

Lüdi, G. (1999). Alternance des langues et acquisition d'une langue seconde. In V. Castellotti & D. Moore (Eds), *Cahiers du Français contemporain numéro 5: alternances des langues et construction des savoirs* (pp. 25-51). Fontenay/ St-Cloud: E.N.S Editions.

Lüdi, G., & Py, B. (1986). *Être bilingue*. Bern: Peter Lang.

Markee, N. (2000). *Conversation analysis*. Mahwah, New Jersey: Erlbaum.

Markee, N. (2008). Toward a learning behavior tracking methodology for CA-for-SLA. *Applied Linguistics, 29*, 404-427. https://doi.org/10.1093/applin/amm052

Masats, D. (1999). *La reparació en el discurs d'aprenents de languages estrangeres*. Unpublished thesis. Universitat Autònoma de Barcelona.

Masats, D. (2008). El discurs dels aprenents d'anglès com a llengua estrangera: una aproximació interactivista al procés de construcció de tasques comunicatives. Unpublished thesis. Bellaterra: Universitat Autònoma de Barcelona.

Masats, D., Nussbaum, L., & Unamuno, V. (2007). When the activity shapes the repertoire of second language learners. In L. Roberts, A. Gürel, S. Tatar, & L. Martı (Eds), *EUROSLA Yearbook: Volume 7* (pp. 121-147). Amsterdam: John Benjamins Publishing Company.

Masats, D., & Unamuno, V. (2001). Constructing social identities and discourse through repair activities. In S. Foster-Cohen & A. Nizegorodcew (Eds), *Eurosla Yearbook, Volume 1* (pp. 239-254). Amsterdam: John Benjamins Publishing Company.

Maynard, D. (1989). On the ethnography and analysis of discourse in institutional settings. *Perspectives on Social Problems, 1*, 127-146.

Mondada, L. (1998). Technologies et interaction sur le terrain du linguiste. Actes du Colloque «Le travail du chercheur sur le terrain: questionner les pratiques, les méthodes, les techniques de l'enquête». *Cahiers de l'ILSL, 10*, 39-68.

Mondada, L. (2002). Pratiques de transcription et effets de catégorisation. *Cahiers de Praxématique, 39*, 45-75.

Mondada, L. (2003). Observer les activités de la classe dans leur diversité: choix méthodologiques et enjeux théoriques. In J. Perera, L. Nussbaum & M. Milian (Eds), *L'educació lingüística en situacions multiculturals i multilingües* (pp. 49-70). Barcelona: ICE de la Universitat de Barcelona.

Moore, E., & Llompart, J. (2017). Collecting, transcribing, analyzing and presenting plurilingual interactional data. In E. Moore & M. Dooly (Eds), *Qualitative approaches to research on plurilingual education* (pp. 403-417). Research-publishing.net. https://doi.org/10.14705/rpnet.2017.emmd2016.638

Nussbaum, L. (1990). Plurilingualism in foreign language classroom in Catalonia. In *Papers for the 3rd. workshop on code-switching and language contact. Network on Code-Switching and Language Contact* (pp. 141-163). Strasbourg: European Science Foundation.

Nussbaum, L. (2016). Estudio de la interacción en el aula de lengua extranjera. In D. Masats & L. Nussbaum (Eds), *Enseñanza y aprendizaje de las lenguas extranjeras en educación secundaria obligatoria* (pp. 113-142). Madrid: Síntesis.

Nussbaum, L. (2017). Doing research with teachers. In E. Moore & M. Dooly (Eds), *Qualitative approaches to research on plurilingual education* (pp. 46-67). Research-publishing.net. https://doi.org/10.14705/rpnet.2017.emmd2016.621

Nussbaum, L., & Unamuno, V. (Eds). (2006). *Usos i competències multilingües entre escolars d'origen immigrant*. Bellaterra: Servei de Publicacions de la Universitat Autònoma de Barcelona.

Ochs, E. (1979). Transcription as theory. In E. Ochs & B. B. Schieffelin (Eds), *Developmental pragmatics* (pp. 43-72). New York: Academic Press.

Pekarek Doehler, S. (1999). *Leçons de conversation: dynamiques de l'interaction et acquisition de compétences discursives en classe de langue seconde*. Fribourg, Switzerland: Editions Universitaires.

Pekarek Doehler, S., & Fasel Lauzon, V. (2015). Documenting change across time: longitudinal and cross-sectional CA studies of classroom interaction. In N. Markee (Ed.), *Handbook of classroom interaction*. (pp. 409-424). Hoboken, New Jersey: Wiley-Blackwell.

Potter, J., & Hepburn, A. (2005a). Qualitative interviews in psychology: problems and possibilities. *Qualitative Research in Psychology, 2*(4), 281-307. https://doi.org/10.1191/1478088705qp045oa

Potter, J., & Hepburn, A. (2005b). Action, interaction and interviews: some responses to Smith, Hollway and Mischler. *Qualitative Research in Psychology, 2*(4), 319-325. http://dx.doi.org/10.1191/1478088705qp046cm

Psathas, G., & Anderson, T. (1990). The 'practices' of transcription in conversation analysis. *Semiotica, 78*, 75-99. https://doi.org/10.1515/semi.1990.78.1-2.75

Py, B. (1997). Pour une perspective bilingue sur l'enseignement et l'apprentissage des langues. *Études de Linguistique Appliquée, 108*, 495-503.

Sacks, H. (1992). *Lectures on conversation, volumes I and II*. Edited by G. Jefferson with an introduction by E.A. Schegloff. Oxford: Basil Blackwell.

Sacks, H., Schegloff, E. A., & Jefferson, G. (1974). A simplest systematics for the organisation of turn-taking in conversation. *Language, 50*, 696-735. https://doi.org/10.1353/lan.1974.0010

Schegloff, E. A., Jefferson, G., & Sacks, H. (1977). The preference for self-correction in the organization of repair in conversation. *Language, 53*, 361-82. https://doi.org/10.1353/lan.1977.0041

Schegloff, E. A., Koshik, I., Jacoby, S., & Olsher, D. (2002). Conversation analysis and applied linguistics. *Annual Review of Applied Linguistics, 22*, 3-31. https://doi.org/10.1017/s0267190502000016

Seedhouse, P. (2004). *The interactional architecture of the language classroom: a conversation analysis perspective*. Malden, MA: Blackwell.

Seedhouse, P. (2005). Conversational analysis and language learning. *Language Teaching, 38*, 165-187. https://doi.org/10.1017/S0261444805003010

Silverman, D. (1989). Telling convincing stories: a plea for cautious positivism in case-studies. In B. Glassner & J. Moreno (Eds), *The qualitative-quantitative distinction in the social sciences* (p. 55-77). Dordrecht: Kluwer.

Smith, J. A., Hollway, W., & Mischler, E. G. (2005). Commentaries on Potter and Hepburn, 'Qualitative interviews in psychology: problems and possibilities'. *Qualitative Research in Psychology, 2*(4), 309-318. . https://doi.org/10.1191/1478088705qp046cm

Unamuno, V., & Nussbaum, L. (2006). De la casa al aula: ámbitos y prácticas de transmisión y aprendizaje de lenguas. *Textos de Didáctica de la Lengua y de la Literatura, 42*, 43-51.

Unamuno, V., & Patiño, A. (2017). Producing knowledge about plurilingualism with young students: a challenge for collaborative ethnography. In E. Moore & M. Dooly (Eds), *Qualitative approaches to research on plurilingual education* (pp. 129-149). Research-publishing.net. https://doi.org/10.14705/rpnet.2017.emmd2016.625

Wong, J., & Waring, H. Z. (2010). *Conversational analysis and second Language pedagogy: a guide for ESL/ELF teachers*. New York: Routledge.

Recommended reading

Markee, N. (Ed.). (2015). *Handbook of classroom interaction*. Hoboken, New Jersey: Wiley-Blackwell.

Wong, J., & Waring, H. Z. (2010). *Conversational analysis and second Language pedagogy: a guide for ESL/ELF teachers*. New York: Routledge.

Appendix

Adapted from GREIP transcription symbols (see Moore & Llompart, this volume):

Questions:
    Yes/no questions /
    Interrogative questions (who, what...) ?
Other tonal sequences:
    Descending \
    Sustained —
Pauses:
    Short |
    Medium ||
    Long <number of seconds>
Overlaps:
    =Speaker A text A=
    =Speaker B text B=
Interruptions: text_
Syllable lengthening: text :
Intensity:
    Piano {(P) text}
    Forte {(F) text}
Codeswitching:
    Text in Catalan
    Text in Spanish
Continuation of previous turn: Speaker>
Incomprehensible fragment (adjusted to length): XXX | XXX XXX
Uncertain fragment: {(?) text}
Utterances accompanied by laughter: {(@) text}
Approximate phonetic transcription: [+text+]
Comments: [comment]

Section 2

Secció 2

Sección 2

9 Research ethics

Melinda Dooly[1], Emilee Moore[2], and Claudia Vallejo[3]

Key concepts: informed consent, confidentiality, data collection, data storage, data presentation.

---

1. Introduction

Qualitative research, especially studies in educational contexts, often brings up questions of ethics because the study design involves human subjects, some of whom are under age (e.g. data collected in primary education classrooms). It is not always easy for young researchers to anticipate where ethical issues might emerge while designing their research project.

So what are some questions that a researcher might consider? A first premise for a researcher is to 'do no harm'. It is important for the researcher to try to think about any adverse effects the study could possibly have on any of the participants. Of course, even though the researcher may try to anticipate any potential ethical issues, unexpected adverse effects may occur, in which case, the study should be halted or modified.

Researchers should also take into consideration how they are going to ensure privacy and confidentiality of the participants. It is reasonable for anyone taking part in a study to expect a certain level of anonymity, although some participants may not feel this is too much of a concern for them (especially among the younger

---

1. Universitat Autònoma de Barcelona, Bellaterra, Catalonia/Spain; melindaann.dooly@uab.cat

2. Universitat Autònoma de Barcelona, Bellaterra, Catalonia/Spain; emilee.moore@uab.cat

3. Universitat Autònoma de Barcelona, Bellaterra, Catalonia/Spain; claudia.vallejo@uab.cat

How to cite this chapter: Dooly, M., Moore, E., & Vallejo, C. (2017). Research ethics. In E. Moore & M. Dooly (Eds), *Qualitative approaches to research on plurilingual education* (pp. 351-362). Research-publishing.net. https://doi.org/10.14705/rpnet.2017.emmd2016.634

generation of 'public-face' social media users). Whether or not identities will be revealed and how images and other identifying factors might be used must be carefully negotiated with the subjects of the study. This is, of course, directly linked to informed consent. Subjects in a study have a right to know enough about the study in order to decide whether they want to participate in the study. In the case of minors, parental permission (often through the schools) should be obtained.

Researchers should also try to be as ethical as possible when interpreting the study results. Researchers should do their best to not over-interpret or misinterpret the data and represent the possible conclusions as closely as possible. To do so, researchers can use triangulation techniques or corroborate their conclusions with the participants themselves through interviews and other techniques proposed in qualitative methodologies (see chapters in Section 1 of this volume for such procedures).

To help the young researcher, we include here the research ethic statement[4] drawn up by the GREIP research group as a guideline for setting up and carrying out qualitative research. We also provide an example of a signed consent form that can be adapted to the individual needs of each study.

2. GREIP research ethics protocol

(1) Before embarking on any research project, the researcher and/or research team will carefully consider whether the study can cause potential harm to anyone involved. If the researcher identifies any possible ill effects, the team will seek the best approach to minimize these effects.

(2) The researcher and/or research team will always provide sufficient information to reviewers, ethical board members and participants to fully comprehend the scope of any research project under the aegis of the research team. Participants will be fully informed of the purpose and approach of the

---

4. These protocols are based on the guidelines by the Comissió d'Ètica en Experimentació a la UAB [Universitat Autònoma Council on Research Ethics] and the European Ethics Documentation Centre.

research. Also, how the data will be collected and processed will be explained fully. The head researcher of the project will make their contact details available to all informants for any complaints or ethical issues that may arise during the period of research and these will be dealt with through the local ethics board. This procedure includes doctoral studies supervised by any research team member.

(3) The researcher and/or research team will always obtain informed consent from all parties involved in the research prior to implementing the research project. This will include full disclosure of any anticipated risks to the subjects, whether the respondents will be compensated in any way, the methodology to be used and data treatment. A compliance document between parties (researcher and/or research team and the informant) will be signed by the individuals who are responsible for each institution (e.g. head researcher, head of school). In the case of research carried out with children under the age of 18 and which is in collaboration with schools, the education center will provide parental consent for research to be carried out in the center. In the case of a research project carried out with informants outside of an institution, on a one-to-one basis, signed consent will be obtained by each informant prior to beginning the research. In the case of research carried out with children under the age of 18 and which is not in collaboration with schools, the head researcher will seek signed parental consent. These procedures include doctoral studies supervised by any research team member.

(4) Requests for consent will always include the possibility of opting out of the research. In cases where opting out carries ethical issues of an individual being unable to partake in educational activities, the individual will take part in the research activity but data will not be collected whenever possible. The filming of the whole group will avoid close-ups of these people. In cases where it is impossible to avoid up-close data recording of said persons, the data will be eliminated.

(5) The researcher and/or research team will ensure confidentiality of all research subjects, including data stemming from systematic reviews of

documents, which might be considered sensitive due to race, ethnicity, religion, politics, health, or sexual orientation.

(6) In the case of compilation of personal data from the informants, data will only be gathered to further the study and will not be used for any other purpose. No extra personal data will be gathered that is not immediately pertinent to the study. The personal data will be carefully organized and managed to ensure that no unauthorized use is made of them. This procedure includes doctoral studies supervised by any research team member.

(7) Participant schools or informants may request viewing of all data related to the research before data management begins. If data are considered objectionable by the participating school or individual informant they will be destroyed upon presentation of a justifiable argument for doing so.

(8) Access to raw data collected by the researcher or under the aegis of the research team will only be allowed to members of the immediate research team (in the case of locally, nationally and internationally funded research projects), to doctoral students and their supervisors (in the case of doctoral studies) and to collaborating researchers who are fully accredited (e.g. completion of an international ethics research exam; demonstrable research trajectory), following explicit permission by the research members involved in the data collection and full disclosure to the informants.

(9) The method of processing the data will be fully disclosed to the informants before beginning data compilation. These methods include anonymizing the names of individuals and institutions, blurring of faces in videos and images, and deleting information that can lead to recognition of participants such as locations, names of cities, etc.

(10) Processed data (anonymized, codified, etc.) may be used for academic or educational purposes such as publications, conferences, teaching materials and policy documents only if this has been included in the written consent form signed by the informants. Anyone who has not been directly involved in the

data compilation may only have access to processed data for such purposes (publications, teaching materials, etc.) after requesting explicit permission from those responsible for the data collection.

(11) In the case of international research collaboration in which the researcher or a member of the research team is the lead investigator, the Ethics Statements of all the countries involved in collecting and handling the data will be studied. Explicit protocols concerning collection and treatment of data as well as use of data for publications and other academic output will be elaborated to cover as many of the ethical requirements of the countries as possible. However, compliance to the ethical considerations concerning the collection and handling of data in each country will be the direct responsibility of the collaborating researcher in that country.

For researchers who are working with online or telecollaborative data (see chapters by Dooly, this volume, and Antoniadou & Dooly, this volume) there are other factors that need to be taken into consideration as there are now third parties involved in the interaction where the data are collected. Especially in the case of telecollaboration, researchers may find that they are dealing with data gathered from groups distributed across the globe, which inevitably means straddling numerous frontiers (national, cultural, geopolitical). And while practitioners and researchers often consider these borders as virtual, they can be all too real when it comes to legal issues. Here some examples of conceivable legal entanglements:

- What is considered lawful and permissible when dealing with data collected in the cyberworld in one country may not be allowed in the other countries where some of the study participants are located.

- The researcher doing 'virtual ethnography' (see chapter by Antoniadou & Dooly, this volume) may not be able to get explicit consent to gather data from all the individuals taking part in the virtual community. In the case where the community is not 'public' the legal rights to the data are unclear.

- Some legal cases have emerged concerning data that was gathered by one researcher in a country that does not have 'research ethic board exams'. This researcher was not allowed to use the data for publication in countries where these exams are required. In virtual environment research, 'new' issues such as this one will inevitably emerge and the researcher may need to seek legal advice.

- The researchers involved in collecting the data must think very carefully about who can have access to the data and how is this controlled? For instance, if the data are collected by two researchers in different countries, can these researchers provide access to the data to fellow colleagues who did not take part in the online interaction? Does this require written consent between all researchers?

- The researcher should find out if they need to have written consent from their collaborating partners in order to publish findings, even if the data set used in the publication only reflects local participants. This should be discussed prior to the data collection with all the telecollaborative partners (see previous point above).

These are just a few possible 'trouble' areas that should be taken into consideration when the data compilation process moves beyond the more traditional borders of local classrooms.

3. Example of written project information for participants

INFORMATION ABOUT THE RESEARCH PROJECT

[add the title of project – keep it simple]
[add the date of this document]
[adapt as necessary]

You (or a minor who you are parent or legal guardian of) are being invited to participate, on a voluntary basis, in a study about [complete]. This information sheet tells you about the study you (or the minor who you are legal guardian of) will be a part of provided you are willing to participate: what type of data will be collected, how the recordings will be carried out, how the data will be used and stored after the recordings are completed and how you can withdraw your consent if you decide to do so.

Please read the information and discuss it with the researcher before you sign informed consent to participate.

Who is the researcher?

[add in non-technical language – explain who you are, where you work and/or study, etc.]

What is the research about?

[add in non-technical language, especially if minors or other vulnerable populations are meant to read it]

What type of data will be collected?

[adapt as necessary]

The researcher will collect different data types to help answer the questions, including: written notes based on observations, audio or video recordings of interactions, audio or video recordings of interviews, photographs, written documents and records of online documents and interactions.

The procedure for audio and video recordings is very simple. The researcher will set up a number of microphones and one or more video cameras in the setting where you (or a minor who you are parent or legal guardian of) are carrying out normal activities which is to be recorded, and then you will simply be asked to go about your business as usual. The researcher will always check you are comfortable with recordings being made and you may ask for certain recordings to be deleted if you do not feel comfortable with them.

You (or the minor who you are parent or legal guardian of) might also be asked to participate in interviews, but the topics to be dealt with would be shared beforehand and can be negotiated.

You might also be asked to give the researcher access to online data (e.g. social networking site) or other face-to-face data (e.g. from home or with friends).

None of this is compulsory and each type of data that might be collected will be negotiated along the way with you in person or via phone or email.

How will be data be stored?

[adapt as necessary]

The data you (or the minor who you are parent or legal guardian of) participate in will be incorporated in a secure database. When you sign the consent form, you can decide how you are happy for the data to be used.

Whatever you choose, all material gathered during the study will be treated as confidential. Furthermore, data will be anonymized so people are not identifiable, unless you request otherwise. This means that in any use of the material names will be removed, images will be altered and, wherever relevant, information will be adjusted so that people cannot be identified.

Remember you are free to withdraw from the recordings at any time without having to give an explanation, by informing the researcher or her supervisor (see contact information below).

How will the data be presented?

[adapt as necessary]

It is common practice for researchers to present anonymized audio and visual data collected at research group meetings, conferences and in their university teaching, as well as to include images in academic publications. When you sign consent, you can decide exactly how you would like to give permission for the data to be used in academic contexts. Please note that research data will never be shown outside of these academic contexts. Throughout the study, the researcher will also consult you before presenting the data to make sure you are comfortable with how it is being used.

How can I withdraw from the study?

[adapt as necessary]

You can withdraw your consent to participate in the study at any time during data collection. You can also withdraw your consent to the use of your image in academic events and publications from the moment you communicate this wish onwards. To withdraw your consent, or to ask any questions in relation to the study at any time, please use the contact information at the end of this information sheet.

Will I find out the results?

[adapt as necessary]

If you would like to receive a summary of the project results at the end of the study, please include your email address on the consent form.

[include your contact details and those of your supervisor at the end of the document]

4. Example of a written informed consent form

INFORMED CONSENT
PARTICIPATION IN A RESEARCH PROJECT

Title of the project:

Researcher:

Supervisor:

Department:

I, Mr. / Ms.:

with ID/Passport number:

- Have read the attached written information about the study and have received a copy of it.

- Have received verbal information about the study.

- Have understood what has been explained to me, and the possible risks and benefits of participating in the study.

- Have been able to comment on the study and ask the researcher questions about it.

- Consent to taking part in the study and understand that my participation is entirely voluntary.

- Understand that audio and/or video data will be collected involving me, and I consent to (mark the options):

- The researcher, his/her supervisor and other members of the research project using the audio and/or video data in academic contexts (research group meetings, conferences, etc.).

- Other members of the research group using the audio and/or video data in academic contexts (research group meetings, conferences, etc.).

- The researcher, his/her supervisor and other members of the research project using images taken from the video data in academic publications (specialized journals, books, etc.).

- Other members of the research group using images taken from the video data in academic publications (specialized journals, books, etc.).

- The researcher, his/her supervisor and other members of the research project using fragments of audio, video and/or images in their university teaching.

- Other members of the research group using fragments of audio, video and/or images in their university teaching.

- Understand that I can withdraw from the study at any time during data collection.

- Understand that I can withdraw my consent to the use of my image in academic events and publications from the moment I communicate this wish onwards.

- Understand that I will receive a copy of this informed consent form.

By signing this informed consent form, I authorise the use of my personal data as described in this document, in accordance with the Law 15/1999, of 13 December, on the protection of personal data.

Participant's signature:

Date:

Researcher's signature:

Date:

If you would like to receive a copy of the results, please provide your email address:

Works cited

Antoniadou, V., & Dooly, M. (2017). Educational ethnography in blended learning environments. In E. Moore & M. Dooly (Eds), *Qualitative approaches to research on plurilingual education* (pp. 237-263). Research-publishing.net. https://doi.org/10.14705/rpnet.2017.emmd2016.630

Dooly, M. (2017). A Mediated Discourse Analysis (MDA) approach to multimodal data. In E. Moore & M. Dooly (Eds), *Qualitative approaches to research on plurilingual education* (pp. 189-211). Research-publishing.net. https://doi.org/10.14705/rpnet.2017.emmd2016.628

Websites with resources mentioned

Consent forms for downloading (GREIP model)

Consent form in English: http://grupsderecerca.uab.cat/greip/sites/grupsderecerca.uab.cat.greip/files/ConsentForm_Eng_WP_0.doc

Consent form in Catalan: http://grupsderecerca.uab.cat/greip/sites/grupsderecerca.uab.cat.greip/files/Consent_Cat_WP.doc

Consent form in Spanish: http://grupsderecerca.uab.cat/greip/sites/grupsderecerca.uab.cat.greip/files/Consent_Esp_WP.doc

9 Ética de la investigación

Melinda Dooly[1], Emilee Moore[2], y Claudia Vallejo[3]

Conceptos clave: consentimiento informado, confidencialidad, recogida de datos, almacenamiento de datos, presentación de datos.

1. Introducción

La investigación cualitativa, especialmente en los estudios en contextos educativos, plantea a menudo cuestiones éticas porque el diseño del estudio involucra a seres humanos, algunos de los cuales son menores de edad (por ejemplo, en el caso de datos recogidos en aulas de educación primaria). No siempre es fácil para quienes se inician en el campo de la investigación anticipar dónde pueden surgir problemas éticos al diseñar su proyecto de investigación.

Aquí, nos planteamos algunas preguntas que las personas investigadoras podrían considerar. Una primera premisa es 'no hacer daño'. Es importante intentar pensar en cualquier efecto adverso que el estudio pueda tener sobre cualquiera de las personas participantes. Por supuesto, aunque se pueda tratar de anticipar cualquier posible problema ético, pueden surgir efectos adversos inesperados, en cuyo caso, el estudio debe detenerse o modificarse.

También se debe tener en cuenta cómo se va a garantizar la privacidad y la confidencialidad de las personas participantes. Es razonable que cualquier persona que participe en un estudio espere un cierto nivel de anonimato,

---

1. Universitat Autònoma de Barcelona, Bellaterra, Cataluña/España; melindaann.dooly@uab.cat

2. Universitat Autònoma de Barcelona, Bellaterra, Cataluña/España; emilee.moore@uab.cat

3. Universitat Autònoma de Barcelona, Bellaterra, Cataluña/España; claudia.vallejo@uab.cat

Para citar este capítulo: Dooly, M., Moore, M., y Vallejo, C. (2017). Ética de la investigación. En E. Moore y M. Dooly (Eds), *Enfoques cualitativos para la investigación en educación plurilingüe* (pp. 363-375). Research-publishing.net. https://doi.org/10.14705/rpnet.2017.emmd2016.635

Capítulo 9

aunque esto no preocupe demasiado a quienes participen en la investigación (especialmente entre la generación más joven acostumbrada a usar redes sociales 'públicas'). Debe negociarse cuidadosamente con las personas sujeto de estudio si se revelarán o no sus identidades, y cómo se pueden usar las imágenes y otros factores de identificación. Por supuesto, esto está directamente relacionado con el consentimiento informado. Las personas sujeto de un estudio tienen derecho a saber lo suficiente sobre el estudio como para poder decidir si quieren participar. En el caso de menores, se debe obtener el permiso del padre, madre o persona responsable (a menudo a través de las escuelas).

Las personas investigadoras también deben ser éticas al interpretar los resultados del estudio. Deben esforzarse por no sobreinterpretar o malinterpretar los datos, y representar las conclusiones de la manera más fiel posible. Para ello, se pueden utilizar técnicas de triangulación o corroborar las conclusiones con las propias personas participantes, mediante entrevistas u otras técnicas propuestas en metodologías cualitativas (véanse los capítulos de la Parte 1 de este volumen para estos procedimientos).

Para ayudar a quienes se inician en el campo de la investigación, hemos incluido la declaración ética de investigación[4] elaborada por el grupo de investigación GREIP como directrices para crear y realizar investigaciones cualitativas. También proporcionamos un ejemplo de un formulario de consentimiento firmado, que puede adaptarse a las necesidades individuales de cada estudio.

2. Protocolo de ética de investigación del grupo GREIP

(1) Antes de emprender cualquier proyecto de investigación, el/la investigador/a y/o el equipo de investigación considerará cuidadosamente los posibles riesgos o daños que puedan surgir como resultado de la investigación. En el caso de

---

4. Estos protocolos se basan en las directrices de la Comisión de Ética en Experimentación de la UAB [Universitat Autònoma de Barcelona] y del Centro Europeo de Documentación sobre Ética.

riesgos potenciales, el equipo de investigación establecerá los medios para minimizar su probabilidad y el impacto de cualquier daño potencial que haya sido identificado.

(2) El/la investigador/a y/o el equipo de investigación siempre permitirán el acceso a la información a los revisores, comités de ética y a quienes participen en la investigación. La información que se presente será suficiente para comprender plenamente el alcance de cualquier proyecto de investigación en el que esté involucrado el equipo de investigación. Esto incluirá información clara sobre los objetivos, el fundamento y la justificación de la investigación; el diseño del estudio (incluyendo la metodología de recolección y análisis de datos), así como una justificación de todos los métodos de investigación que se utilizarán. La persona responsable del proyecto pondrá sus datos de contacto a disposición de todos los informantes para cualquier queja o cuestión ética que puedan surgir durante el período de investigación y que deban ser tratadas por el comité de ética local. Estos requerimientos afectan a los estudios de doctorado supervisados por cualquier miembro del equipo de investigación.

(3) El/la investigador/a y/o el equipo de investigación siempre obtendrán el consentimiento informado de todas las partes involucradas en la investigación antes del inicio del proyecto de investigación. Esto incluirá la divulgación completa de cualquier riesgo previsto para los sujetos, cómo se compensará a los participantes, y la metodología y el tratamiento de datos utilizados. Las personas responsables de cada institución (por ejemplo, la persona responsable del grupo de investigación, la dirección del centro de estudios) firmarán un documento de acuerdo entre las partes (investigador/a y/o equipo de investigación, y el informante). En el caso de que la investigación se realice con menores de 18 años y se lleve a cabo en colaboración con centros educativos, éstos proporcionarán el consentimiento de los progenitores o personas responsables para la investigación que se llevará a cabo en el centro. En el caso de un proyecto de investigación realizado con informantes fuera de una institución, se obtendrá el consentimiento firmado por cada informante antes de iniciar la investigación. En el caso de que la investigación involucre a menores de 18 años y que no se haga en colaboración con algún centro educativo, la

persona responsable de la investigación conseguirá el consentimiento firmado de los progenitores o personas responsables. Estos requerimientos afectan a los estudios de doctorado supervisados por cualquier miembro del equipo de investigación.

(4) Las solicitudes de consentimiento incluirán siempre la posibilidad de la exclusión voluntaria de la investigación. En los casos en que la exclusión plantee cuestiones éticas, como que una persona no pueda participar en actividades educativas, la persona en cuestión participará en las actividades, pero no se recopilarán datos cuando sea posible. Cuando se registre a todo el grupo, se evitarán los primeros planos de estas personas. En los casos en los que sea imposible evitarlos, los datos serán eliminados.

(5) El/la investigador/a y/o el equipo de investigación garantizarán la confidencialidad de todas las personas que participen en la investigación, incluidos aquellos datos, que podrían considerarse sensibles debido a factores como la raza, etnia, religión, política, salud u orientación sexual.

(6) Los datos personales se obtendrán únicamente para los fines específicos del estudio y no se utilizarán para ningún otro propósito. No se recopilarán datos personales adicionales que no sean directamente pertinentes para el estudio. Estos requerimientos afectan a los estudios de doctorado supervisados por cualquier miembro del equipo de investigación.

(7) Los centros de educación involucrados o las personas participantes en la investigación pueden solicitar visualizar todos los datos relacionados con la investigación antes de que empiece la gestión y el análisis de los mismos. Si algunos datos se consideran censurables, se destruirán, si se presenta una petición argumentada por parte de la institución o la persona participante.

(8) El acceso a los datos brutos recopilados por el/la investigador/a o bajo la égida del equipo de investigación sólo se permitirá a los miembros del equipo de investigación inmediato (en el caso de proyectos de investigación financiados

de forma local, nacional e internacional), a los/las estudiantes de doctorado y a quienes los supervisen (en el caso de los estudios de doctorado) y a las personas investigadoras colaboradoras que estén plenamente acreditadas (por ejemplo, que hayan aprobado un examen internacional de ética o tengan una trayectoria de investigación demostrable), después de conseguir autorización explícita de los miembros de la investigación que participan en la recopilación de datos y la divulgación completa a los/las informantes.

(9) Se dará información completa sobre el método de tratamiento de los datos a los/las informantes antes de comenzar la recopilación de datos. Estos métodos incluyen la referencia anónima a las personas y a las instituciones; la eliminación de las caras en los vídeos y las imágenes; la eliminación de información que pueda permitir el reconocimiento de los/las participantes, como lugares, nombres de ciudades, etc.

(10) Los datos procesados (anónimos, codificados, etc.) pueden utilizarse con fines académicos o educativos, como publicaciones, conferencias, material didáctico y documentos de política, sólo si así se ha indicado en el formulario de consentimiento por escrito firmado de los/las informantes. Cualquier persona que no haya participado directamente en la recopilación de datos sólo podrá acceder a los datos procesados para tales fines (publicaciones, material didáctico, etc.) después de solicitar el permiso explícito de las personas responsables de la recopilación de datos.

(11) En el caso de una investigación internacional en la que el/la investigador/a o un miembro del equipo de investigación sea la persona responsable de la investigación, se estudiarán los principios éticos de todos los países involucrados en la recolección y la gestión de datos. Se elaborarán protocolos explícitos sobre la recopilación y el tratamiento de datos, así como sobre el uso de datos para publicaciones y otros fines académicos, de manera que se incluya el mayor número posible de requisitos éticos de los países. Sin embargo, el cumplimiento de las consideraciones éticas relativas a la recopilación y gestión de datos en cada país será responsabilidad directa del equipo investigador colaborador en ese país.

Capítulo 9

Para investigadores e investigadoras que trabajan con datos en línea o telecolaborativos (véanse los capítulos de Dooly, en este volumen, y Antoniadou y Dooly, en este volumen), deben tenerse en cuenta otros factores, ya que en estos casos hay terceras personas involucradas en la interacción de la cual se recopilan los datos. Especialmente en el caso de la telecolaboración, se pueden haber recogido datos de grupos distribuidos por todo el mundo, lo que inevitablemente significa cruzar numerosas fronteras (nacionales, culturales, geopolíticas). Y aunque a menudo se considera que estas fronteras son virtuales, pueden ser muy reales cuando se trata de cuestiones legales. Aquí presentamos algunos ejemplos de problemas legales que podrían tener lugar:

- Lo que se considera lícito y permisible al tratar con los datos recogidos en el mundo cibernético en un país puede no estar permitido en los otros países donde se encuentren algunas de las personas participantes del estudio.

- En la 'etnografía virtual' (véase el capítulo de Antoniadou y Dooly, en este volumen) puede ser imposible obtener el consentimiento explícito para recopilar datos de todas las personas que participan en la comunidad virtual. En el caso de que la comunidad no sea 'pública', los derechos legales sobre los datos no están claros.

- Han aparecido algunos casos legales donde los datos fueron recogidos por una persona investigadora en un país que no tiene 'exámenes de ética de investigación'. A esta persona no se le permitió utilizar los datos para publicar en los países en los que se requieren estos exámenes.

- Investigadores e investigadoras que participan en la recolección de los datos deben pensar muy cuidadosamente quién puede acceder a los datos y cómo controlarlo. Por ejemplo, si dos investigadoras de diferentes países recogen datos, ¿pueden proporcionar el acceso a los datos a colegas que no participaron en la interacción en línea? ¿Requiere esta situación de un consentimiento por escrito entre todas las personas investigadoras?

- Se debe averiguar si se necesita del consentimiento por escrito de las personas colaboradoras para publicar los resultados, incluso si el conjunto de datos utilizado en la publicación sólo refleja datos de participantes locales. Esto debe discutirse antes de la recogida de datos con todas las personas participantes en la telecolaboración.

Éstas son sólo algunas de las posibles áreas 'problemáticas' que deben tenerse en cuenta cuando el proceso de recopilación de datos va más allá de las fronteras tradicionales de las aulas locales.

3. Ejemplo de información por escrito de un proyecto para los y las participantes

INFORMACIÓN SOBRE EL PROYECTO DE INVESTIGACIÓN

[Añadir el título del proyecto utilizando un lenguaje sencillo]

[Añadir la fecha del documento]

[Adaptar según sea necesario]

Usted (o un menor de edad de quien usted es padre, madre o responsable legal) ha sido invitado/a a participar, de forma voluntaria, en un estudio sobre [completar]. Esta hoja de información le proporcionará datos sobre el estudio en el que usted (o el menor de quien es responsable legal) formará parte, si está dispuesto/a a participar: qué tipo de datos se recogerán, cómo se llevarán a cabo las grabaciones, cómo se utilizarán y almacenarán los datos después de que se hayan completado las grabaciones y cómo puede retirar su consentimiento si decide hacerlo.

Por favor, lea la información y hable con el/la investigador/a antes de firmar el consentimiento informado para participar.

¿Quién es el/la investigador/a?

[Utilizando un lenguaje sencillo, explique quién es usted, dónde trabaja y/o estudia, etc.]

¿De qué trata la investigación?

[Escribir en un lenguaje sencillo, especialmente si esto se dirige a menores u otras poblaciones vulnerables.]

¿Qué tipo de datos se recogerán?

[Adaptar según sea necesario.]

El/la investigador/a recogerá diferentes tipos de datos para intentar responder las preguntas, que incluirán notas escritas basadas en observaciones, grabaciones de audio o vídeo de interacciones, grabaciones de audio o vídeo de entrevistas, fotografías, documentos escritos y registros de documentos e interacciones en línea.

El procedimiento para las grabaciones de audio y vídeo es muy sencillo. El/la investigador/a pondrá algunos micrófonos, y una o más cámaras de vídeo en el entorno en el que usted (o el menor de edad de quien es responsable) esté llevando a cabo las actividades normales que se van a registrar, y le pedirán que se comporte como de costumbre. El/la investigador/a siempre comprobará que se siente cómodo/a con las grabaciones que se están realizando y puede pedir que se eliminen ciertas grabaciones si no se siente cómodo/a con ellas.

Podría ser que se le invitara, a usted (o el menor de edad de quien es padre, madre o responsable legal), a participar en entrevistas, pero siempre se le indicarían los temas que se tratarán de antemano y pueden negociarse.

También se le puede pedir que dé acceso a datos en línea (por ejemplo, sitio de redes sociales) u otros datos cara a cara (por ejemplo, desde su casa o con amistades).

Nada de esto es obligatorio y a lo largo de la investigación se negociarán con usted en persona, o por teléfono o correo electrónico los diferentes tipos de datos que se pueden recoger.

¿Cómo se almacenarán los datos?

[Adaptar según sea necesario.]

Los datos en los que usted (o el menor de quien es padre, madre o responsable legal) participe se incorporarán en una base de datos segura. Al firmar el formulario de consentimiento, puede decidir cómo quiere que se utilicen los datos.

Sea cual sea su elección, todo el material recopilado durante el estudio se tratará como confidencial. Además, los datos serán anónimos para que las personas no sean identificables, a menos que solicite lo contrario. Esto significa que en cualquier uso del material, se eliminarán los nombres, se alterarán las imágenes y, donde sea relevante, se ajustará la información para que las personas no puedan ser identificadas.

Recuerde que es libre de retirarse de las grabaciones en cualquier momento sin tener que dar ninguna explicación, informando a la persona investigadora o a quien la supervise (véase la información de contacto a continuación).

¿Cómo se presentarán los datos?

[Adaptar según sea necesario.]

Es una práctica habitual que las personas investigadoras presenten datos audiovisuales que han recogido y anonimizado en reuniones del grupo de investigación, conferencias y en su enseñanza universitaria, así como para incluir imágenes en publicaciones académicas. Al firmar el consentimiento, puede decidir exactamente cómo le gustaría dar permiso para que los datos se utilicen en contextos académicos. Tenga en cuenta que los datos de investigación nunca se mostrarán fuera de estos contextos académicos. A lo largo del estudio, el/la investigador/a también le consultará antes de presentar los datos para asegurarse de que se siente cómodo/a con la forma en la que se están utilizando.

¿Cómo puedo retirarme del estudio?

[Adaptar según sea necesario.]

Puede retirar su consentimiento para participar en el estudio en cualquier momento durante la recogida de datos. También puede retirar su consentimiento para el uso de su imagen en eventos académicos y publicaciones a partir del momento en el que comunique este deseo. Para retirar su consentimiento o para hacer cualquier pregunta relacionada con el estudio en cualquier momento, utilice la información de contacto al final de esta hoja informativa.

¿Recibiré información de los resultados?

[Adaptar según sea necesario.]

Si desea recibir un resumen de los resultados del proyecto al final del estudio, incluya su dirección de correo electrónico en el formulario de consentimiento.

[Incluya sus datos de contacto y los de su supervisor/a al final del documento.]

Ejemplo de un formulario de consentimiento informado por escrito

CONSENTIMIENTO INFORMADO
PARTICIPACIÓN EN UN PROYECTO DE INVESTIGACIÓN

Título del proyecto:

Investigador/a:

Supervisor/a:

Departamento:

Yo, el Sr./la Sra.:

con DNI/pasaporte

- He leído la información escrita que se adjunta sobre el estudio, de la cual se me ha entregado una copia.

- He recibido información verbal sobre el estudio.

- He comprendido lo que se me ha explicado, y los posibles riesgos o beneficios por el hecho de participar en el estudio.

- He podido comentar el estudio y hacer preguntas a el/la investigador/a responsable.

- Doy mi consentimiento para tomar parte en el estudio y asumo que mi participación es totalmente voluntaria.

- Entiendo que se recogerán datos de audio y/o de vídeo en los cuales participo, y doy mi consentimiento para que (marque las opciones):

- El/la investigador/a abajo firmante, el/la supervisor/a y otros miembros del proyecto de investigación muestren los datos de audio y/o de vídeo en el ámbito académico (reuniones del grupo de investigación, conferencias, etc.).

- Otros miembros del grupo de investigación GREIP muestren los datos de audio y/o de vídeo en el ámbito académico (reuniones del grupo de investigación, conferencias, etc.).

- El/la investigador/a abajo firmante, el/la supervisor/a y otros miembros del proyecto de investigación reproduzcan imágenes de las grabaciones de vídeo en publicaciones académicas (revistas especializadas, libros, etc.).

- Otros miembros del grupo de investigación GREIP reproduzcan imágenes de las grabaciones de vídeo en publicaciones académicas (revistas especializadas, libros, etc.).

- El/la investigador/a abajo firmante, el/la supervisor/a y otros miembros del proyecto de investigación muestren fragmentos de audio, de vídeo y/o imágenes en sus actividades de docencia en la universidad.

- Otros miembros del grupo de investigación GREIP muestren fragmentos de audio, de vídeo y/o imágenes en sus actividades de docencia en la universidad.

- Entiendo que me podré retirar en cualquier momento durante la recogida de datos.

- También entiendo que podré retirar mi consentimiento para el uso de mi imagen en eventos o producciones académicas que se realizaran desde el momento en que comunico mi retirada en adelante.

- Entiendo que recibiré una copia de este formulario de consentimiento informado.

Mediante la firma de este formulario de consentimiento informado, doy mi consentimiento para que mis datos personales se puedan utilizar como se ha descrito, de acuerdo con lo que dispone la Ley orgánica 15/1999, de 13 de diciembre, de protección de datos de carácter personal.

Firma de el/la participante:

Fecha:

Firma del/de la investigador/a:

Fecha:

Si quiere recibir una copia de los resultados, indique su dirección de correo electrónico:

Obras citadas

Antoniadou, V., & Dooly, M. (2017). Etnografia educativa en contextos d'aprenentatge mixt. En E. Moore y M. Dooly (Eds), *Enfoques cualitativos para la investigación en educación plurilingüe* (pp. 264-292). Research-publishing.net. https://doi.org/10.14705/rpnet.2017.emmd2016.631

Dooly, M. (2017). Una aproximació a dades multimodals amb l'anàlisi del discurs mediat. En E. Moore y M. Dooly (Eds), *Enfoques cualitativos para la investigación en educación plurilingüe* (pp. 212-235). Research-publishing.net. https://doi.org/10.14705/rpnet.2017.emmd2016.629

Páginas web con recursos mencionados

Formularios de consentimiento para descargar (modelo del grupo GREIP)

Formulario de consentimiento en inglés: http://grupsderecerca.uab.cat/greip/sites/grupsderecerca.uab.cat.greip/files/ConsentForm_Eng_WP_0.doc

Formulario de consentimiento en catalán: http://grupsderecerca.uab.cat/greip/sites/grupsderecerca.uab.cat.greip/files/Consent_Cat_WP.doc

Formulario de consentimiento en español: http://grupsderecerca.uab.cat/greip/sites/grupsderecerca.uab.cat.greip/files/Consent_Esp_WP.doc

10 Instruments per a la recollida de dades

Laia Canals[1]

Conceptes clau: **tipus de dades, tasques d'aprenentatge, observació a l'aula, grups de discussió, debats, narratives i entrevistes, qüestionaris i enquestes.**

---

1. Introducció

En aquest capítol, es presenten alguns mètodes per obtenir dades rellevants sobre els usos lingüístics dels participants en una recerca. Aquests mètodes, que impliquen la interacció entre estudiants, docents i investigadors, són utilitzats en dissenys metodològics basats en la recerca acció, l'etnografia o l'anàlisi conversacional, com és el cas dels estudis presentats en la primera part d'aquest volum. En investigacions que segueixen aquestes metodologies, recollir dades sovint implica preparar situacions, tasques o activitats que permetin que la participació dels informants estigui encaminada a interactuar al voltant d'una temàtica concreta o mobilitzant unes destreses comunicatives determinades.

Els mètodes utilitzats per recollir dades, tal com s'ha explicat en d'altres capítols, estan determinats en gran mesura per les preguntes de recerca i els objectius de la investigació que es vol dur a terme. No obstant això, en la recerca qualitativa aquests elements es van modificant durant el procés. Generalment, en el camp de la didàctica de la llengua les dades es recullen en contextos que intenten reproduir situacions de comunicació reals, en les quals els participants fan aportacions orals o escrites útils per a la recerca i que resulten alhora també beneficioses per al seu aprenentatge.

---

1. Universitat Oberta de Catalunya, Barcelona, Catalunya/Espanya; ecanalsf@uoc.edu

Per citar aquest capítol: Canals, L. (2017). Instruments per a la recollida de dades. A E. Moore i M. Dooly (Eds), *Enfocaments qualitatius per a la recerca en educació plurilingüe* (p. 377-389). Research-publishing.net. https://doi.org/10.14705/rpnet.2017.emmd2016.636

Com s'exposarà al llarg de les pàgines següents, hi ha un ampli ventall de mètodes per fer-ho, que inclouen des dels més tradicionals, com les enquestes, els qüestionaris i les entrevistes, fins als més innovadors, és a dir, els projectes, les tasques o altres activitats a l'aula o els grups de discussió sobre un tema. Tal com explica Nussbaum (en aquest volum), és recomanable que la persona que investiga adopti també una posició activa com a participant compromès amb els processos d'ensenyament i aprenentatge i amb la innovació didàctica a l'hora de planificar la seva recerca.

2. Tipus de dades

Els objectius i les preguntes d'investigació d'una recerca concreta determinen si volem obtenir dades purament interaccionals o dades que ens informin també sobre el comportament interaccional dels nostres participants en el context que estudiem o en altres contextos. Al mateix temps, ens pot interessar obtenir dades que ens permetin indagar les identitats lingüístiques, les trajectòries d'aprenentatge, les actituds vers diferents llengües i altres aspectes no estrictament lingüístics, però que sovint són fonamentals en l'estudi de l'aprenentatge de llengües en situacions plurilingües.

Així doncs, en els següents apartats desxifrarem quin tipus de dades podem recollir en cada cas, per després examinar quins mètodes serien els més adequats. Les distincions que es proposen a continuació entre dades purament lingüístiques o interaccionals i dades que reflecteixen actituds, identitats i comportaments no són categories exclusives, sinó que més aviat estan pensades com a formes d'endreçar les dades. Aquesta distinció pot ser útil especialment a l'hora de plantejar-se els instruments o el tipus de preguntes i tasques que permeten obtenir un tipus de dades o un altre.

Amb els mètodes de recollida de dades descrits en aquest capítol normalment s'obtenen dades orals, les quals són enregistrades en àudio i/o vídeo per poder ser transcrites i analitzades posteriorment (vegeu Moore i Llompart, en aquest volum). Molts dels mètodes presentats poden servir-se d'eines digitals i dels procediments de tractament de les dades descrits en el capítol d'Antoniadou, en aquest volum.

2.1. Dades per estudiar allò que les persones plurilingües diuen que fan quan parlen

Les dades sobre els coneixements de llengües, les actituds, les identitats lingüístiques i els usos interaccionals dels informants en un context no observable (amb els amics, a casa, etc.), entre altres aspectes, sovint es poden obtenir de l'anàlisi d'interaccions a l'aula, d'entrevistes obertes, de grups de discussió i d'altres tipus de dades més naturals. De la mateixa manera, es poden elicitar dades similars mitjançant qüestionaris o enquestes en què sol·licitem dades personals amb preguntes tancades o semitancades, entre les quals hi pot haver informació sobre els coneixements, els usos, les filiacions i les actituds lingüístics dels participants.

El fet de preguntar, per exemple, la llengua que els participants fan servir amb els diferents membres de la família o amb els amics o els àmbits en què fan servir més una llengua que una altra ens pot permetre analitzar comportaments interaccionals o l'abast de l'ús d'una llengua o una altra. Aquesta informació es podria obtenir amb qüestionaris i enquestes amb preguntes tancades, però s'ha de preveure que hi pot haver respostes múltiples o que pot ser necessari afegir matisos en alguns casos. Cal tenir en compte que les llengües no sempre es fan servir de forma compartimentada, en àmbits diferents o per a propòsits distints. És, per tant, important considerar si l'instrument de recollida de dades permet descriure també els usos més híbrids (vegeu Nussbaum, en aquest volum, per una discussió sobre el plurilingüisme).

Pot ser interessant, sobretot si utilitzem qüestionaris o enquestes, fer una prova pilot per comprovar la funcionalitat de les preguntes. Sovint quan demanem respostes tancades, s'evidencia que les opcions de resposta no representen la realitat. Per exemple, s'ha de tenir en compte que en un estudi en què es pretén esbrinar la tria de llengua en persones bilingües en l'àmbit familiar, quan es pregunta sobre la llengua que fan servir els participants amb els seus germans el fet que l'informant només pugui donar com a resposta la llengua A o la llengua B pot no captar la realitat de la situació lingüística complexa que s'esdevé en un entorn bilingüe o plurilingüe. S'hi haurien d'incloure, per tant, opcions amb matisos del tipus: "parlo més A que B", "parlo més B que A", "parlo tant A com B", etc.

2.2. Dades per estudiar allò que les persones plurilingües fan quan parlen

Aquest tipus de dades es poden obtenir mitjançant projectes (vegeu els capítols de Nussbaum, en aquest volum; Unamuno i Patiño, en aquest volum), tasques (vegeu Masats, en aquest volum) o altres activitats que afavoreixen determinats tipus d'interacció. Els participants s'haurien de sentir lliures per expressar-se en un ambient relaxat. És difícil obtenir dades autèntiques en situacions de laboratori, ja que els parlants consideren aquest tipus d'activitats com a situacions extremadament formals en què se'ls demana un ús poc real de la llengua. El nerviosisme pot afectar la forma en la qual parlen o fer que s'expressin amb frases més curtes per la por a cometre errors.

El sociolingüista nord-americà William Labov (1972a) va evidenciar que si volem obtenir dades sobre la manera de parlar dels informants en àmbits informals haurem de recrear aquests ambients. Labov, que va fer servir el mètode d'entrevistes, només va aconseguir obtenir dades lingüístiques rellevants de la varietat d'anglès afroamericà en infants quan va poder recrear situacions sociolingüístiques òptimes amb els interlocutors adequats. Va propiciar un ambient informal per a les entrevistes (tothom estava assegut a terra amb una bossa de patates fregides) i les entrevistes les van realitzar interlocutors d'ètnia i edat similars als seus informants.

Si volem obtenir dades de l'ús de la llengua en situacions més quotidianes, com les classes de llengua a l'escola, quan dissenyem la nostra recerca hem de pensar com superar les inhibicions normals dels estudiants davant d'una càmera o enregistradora, la por a parlar i cometre errors, i també la diversitat de caràcters o personalitats dels informants.

En el següent apartat, es presenten alguns mètodes que han resultat útils en la recerca a l'aula. Posteriorment, es descriuen altres mètodes, com els grups de discussió, els debats i les entrevistes, que poden convertir-se en tasques d'aula o dur-se a terme fora de la classe. Finalment, es presenten els qüestionaris i les enquestes com una altra opció per obtenir dades, adoptades en estudis amb dissenys metodològics mixtos (vegeu, per exemple, el capítol de Pascual, en aquest volum).

3. Tasques d'aprenentatge

Mackey i Gass (2005) descriuen un bon nombre de tasques d'aprenentatge, que divideixen en tasques unidireccionals, en què la informació passa d'una persona a l'altra, o tasques bidireccionals, en què hi ha un intercanvi d'informació i cal cooperar per aconseguir acabar la tasca. Un exemple del primer tipus de tasques és la descripció d'un dibuix, mentre que el segon tipus de tasques incluouria exercicis amb buits d'informació diferents per a cada estudiant, de manera que cadascun té informació clau que ha de traslladar a l'altre per poder completar l'exercici.

Una altra forma de classificar les tasques seria pel tipus de producte final que s'espera obtenir-ne. Hi ha tasques tancades, en què es preveu una solució correcta o incorrecta, mentre que en les tasques obertes s'ha d'arribar a un acord o a conclusions comunes mitjançant una discussió o debat.

Cadascuna de les tasques següents permet obtenir diferents tipus de dades, sempre determinades pels interessos, els objectius i les preguntes de recerca del nostre estudi. Recordem que si volem enregistrar interaccions més naturals, cal triar tasques que ens permetin obtenir aquest tipus de llengua.

3.1. Descripcions de fotografies o imatges

Aquesta tasca pren com a punt de partida una imatge que motiva a recrear o descriure una història, per exemple, una situació còmica. A l'hora de triar les imatges, l'investigador ha de pensar si a ell mateix la imatge el motivaria a parlar. Si a nosaltres mateixos no se'ns acut res o poc a dir, serà ben difícil que la imatge sigui eficient a l'hora d'obtenir dades dels nostres participants.

3.2. Activitats de buscar les diferències

Aquesta activitat feta en parelles o grups de tres persones permet obtenir dades lingüístiques comparatives. Si bé és una tasca tancada, en què tots els informants tenen el mateix tipus d'informació, permet enregistrar força quantitat de parla, encara que no necessàriament interacció entre els diferents participants.

3.3. Exercicis amb buits d'informació diferents per a cada alumne.

Aquestes tasques s'acostumen a fer en parelles o grups de tres persones i els participants han de col·laborar i interactuar verbalment per aconseguir resoldre l'exercici. La tasca pot consistir, per exemple, en un mapa de la ciutat on cada persona ha de situar diferents botigues o edificis i esbrinar on són els dels altres. Així, s'obtenen dades d'interacció i també dades sobre elements lingüístics específics (l'ús dels adverbis de lloc, en aquest cas). És important que els participants no es mostrin els dibuixos entre ells perquè la tasca es resolgui de forma efectiva.

3.4. Activitats de reexplicar històries

Aquesta tasca es pot dur a terme usant vinyetes de còmic o petits vídeos (de dibuixos animats, per exemple) o fent que l'investigador expliqui de manera oral una història, en grups o a cada participant individualment. Els estudiants tenen un temps per llegir, visualitzar o escoltar la història i després han d'explicar en detall el que han llegit, sentit o vist. Depenent del tipus de dades que es vol obtenir en cada cas, es poden demanar aclariments o descripcions sobre els elements en els quals es vol centrar l'investigador.

3.5. Tasca de deduir regles

Aquesta tasca es pot fer en grups o individualment i es pot combinar amb fulls o fitxes on hi ha informació parcial del que es vol resoldre. En altres casos es poden donar frases correctes i incorrectes i es pot demanar als alumnes que en dedueixin les regles. Aquesta tasca permet obtenir dades metalingüístiques i interaccions entre els participants en què es formulen hipòtesis diverses. En classes de llengua de nivells inicials pot costar que els alumnes facin servir la llengua d'aprenentatge per resoldre les tasques. En aquest cas, pot ser interessant centrar-se en els coneixements lingüístics i metalingüístics o reflexionar-hi, independentment de la llengua que s'empri durant la tasca.

4. Observació a l'aula

Les observacions a classes en què l'investigador és també docent o un participant més són un dels mètodes més usats en la recerca en didàctica de la llengua. La persona que investiga pot fer servir guies d'observació que l'ajudaran a centrar-se en el que vol saber (vegeu el capítol de Pascual, en aquest volum). Aquestes guies són molt recomanables a l'hora de recollir dades si hi ha més d'un investigador, per garantir que tots recullen les dades de la mateixa manera.

5. Grups de discussió, debats, narratives i entrevistes

S'han separat els mètodes següents en un nou apartat, perquè encara que poden realitzar-se com a tasques d'aprenentatge a l'aula, sovint s'utilitzen també fora de la classe.

5.1. Grups de discussió

En els grups de discussió es convida els participants a parlar sobre les seves opinions, actituds o creences vers un tema, un concepte o una idea. S'hi poden incloure preguntes que guiïn els informants a parlar sobre els diferents aspectes que han de considerar per a cada tema o subtema. El tipus de dades que es pot obtenir són opinions, afirmacions sobre creences, expressions d'acord o desacord amb els altres participants, processos de construcció d'identitats individuals i col·lectives, etc.

5.2. Debats

Durant els debats es demana que cada persona es posicioni a favor o en contra d'un tema o idea. Es pot fer de forma aleatòria o assignant diferents rols als participants. Per exemple, una persona és l'alcalde d'una ciutat, una altra una mare amb dos fills adolescents, una altra el cap de la policia, una altra un adolescent i una altra un venedor de cerveses ambulant. Tots han de discutir sobre una nova proposta de llei que prohibeix el consum de begudes alcohòliques als espais públics. Aquestes tasques permeten obtenir dades sobre l'expressió d'opinions, d'argumentacions, de refutació d'arguments i de discussions que sovint es descontrolen. Convé que hi hagi la figura d'un moderador (el mestre, l'investigador o un participant, que s'imposi i controli els altres en cas que la tasca derivi cap a situacions conflictives).

5.3. Narracions personals

Aquestes tasques ens permeten obtenir produccions llargues dels participants. Les narracions solen ser explicacions d'esdeveniments en passat, ja que s'evoca la història personal de cada persona per recordar moments especials. Labov (1972b) proposa preguntar per moments en què els informants es van sentir en perill, mentre que Tannen (1984) demana una situació estranya o còmica viscuda. En ambdós casos, es tracta que l'informant se senti còmode i s'impliqui totalment a explicar una història, apel·lant a sentiments i emocions que el fan oblidar que està sent entrevistat, i es contribueixen a elicitar un llenguatge natural.

També existeix la possibilitat de fer escriure aquestes experiències als participants en lloc d'explicar-les oralment, per reduir l'ansietat i l'estrès, però aquesta decisió depèn del tipus de dades que vulguem obtenir. Tannen (1984) proposa alguns temes que poden generar narracions fluides: el primer dia en una nova escola o les primeres impressions en un país estranger o en una ciutat diferent. Salaberry i Comajoan (2013) suggereixen deixar escollir els informants entre diferents temes o mostrar-los diferents targetes o fotografies en què s'expressen emocions. Tot seguit es demanaria als participants que expliquessin una situació concreta on es van sentir especialment contents, tristos, enfadats, etc.

5.4. Entrevistes

Les entrevistes també poden ser activitats realitzades a l'aula entre els estudiants mateixos, que són susceptibles de convertir-se alhora en material de recerca i en material didàctic en tasques posteriors. Les entrevistes poden ser estructurades o semiestructurades. Les primeres es caracteritzen per seguir una pauta molt concreta en què les preguntes que es fan als participants i les condicions de l'entrevista són exactament les mateixes per garantir que hi hagi poca diferència entre una entrevista i una altra. D'aquesta manera, s'argumenta que són més comparables les unes amb les altres. Aquest tipus d'entrevistes també proporcionen dades d'orientació més quantitativa o que es poden quantificar millor.

En entrevistes semiestructurades l'entrevistador té més flexibilitat a l'hora d'afegir preguntes o demanar aclariments. Generalment, beneficien la recollida de dades personals, atès que el participant s'hi sent més còmode i relaxat, fent de l'entrevista una conversa més que no pas un torn calculat de preguntes i respostes. Aquestes entrevistes solen servir per recollir dades qualitatives, acostumen a tenir una durada més llarga i permeten que els entrevistadors aprofundeixin en les preguntes (vegeu el capítol de Corona, en aquest volum).

6. Qüestionaris i enquestes

Les dades es poden recollir també mitjançant qüestionaris o enquestes que alhora poden formar part d'entrevistes més extenses. Igual que en les entrevistes i altres mètodes semblants, el tipus de preguntes que incloem en els qüestionaris haurien de fer sentir còmodes als participants. Alhora, s'haurien de fer de forma no intrusiva perquè el participant no tingui la sensació que estem jutjant la seva forma de viure i de veure les llengües, ni els seus comportaments lingüístics. Atès que sovint les qüestions actitudinals vers les llengües i la forma d'autoidentificar-se lingüísticament poden ser preguntes delicades, és recomanable formular-les de manera indirecta o incorporar-les a converses més extenses.

A més de les dades actitudinals, hi ha altres informacions, com l'edat, el nivell d'estudis, la situació familiar, el país d'origen, el lloc de residència i el centre escolar, entre altres, que poden ser rellevants a l'hora d'analitzar les dades. Si més no, poden ser importants per definir el context de la recerca d'un grup de parlants o aprenents.

7. Informació que cal proporcionar als informants

Les qüestions relacionades amb la protecció de les dades que rebem dels participants en les recerques són de gran importància, especialment quan treballem amb infants i joves en situacions de desavantatge o socioeconòmicament complicades. Cal preveure i establir el consentiment dels participants o els seus tutors legals. Això es pot fer mitjançant una carta en què s'exposin clarament els objectius del projecte de recerca i els tipus de dades que s'obtindran dels participants. També és important explicar el tractament i l'abast de l'exposició pública que tindran les dades (vegeu el capítol de Dooly, Moore, i Vallejo, en aquest volum).

8. Altres consideracions

Molts dels possibles obstacles a l'hora de recollir dades es poden evitar si es fa una prova pilot amb les eines de recollida que farem servir administrades a un nombre reduït d'informants abans de la recollida final de dades. D'aquesta manera, es poden identificar ràpidament problemes imprevistos o preguntes o tasques que no han donat bon resultat i canviar-les per unes altres. El pilotatge es pot incloure en la memòria de la recerca com una part que permet treure conclusions ràpides dels possibles problemes de les eines o els mètodes de recollida de dades.

És important ser conscient del grup d'edat amb el qual es treballa, esbrinar què motiva els participants i què els pot motivar a parlar. També pot ser important posar-se físicament al seu nivell per no imposar-se com a autoritat, sinó com un participant més. En estudis de l'àmbit de les ciències socials es parla sovint de la paradoxa de l'investigador o observador, que consisteix que a l'hora d'observar un comportament o interacció la seva sola presència influeix en l'actitud i el comportament del què vol observar. És important ser conscient d'aquesta paradoxa i tractar-la explícitament quan s'analitzen les dades (vegeu els capítols de Moore i Llompart, en aquest volum; Nussbaum, en aquest volum).

Obres citades

Antoniadou, V. (2017). Recoger, organizar y analizar corpus de datos multimodales: las contribuciones de los CAQDAS. A E. Moore i M. Dooly (Eds), *Enfocaments qualitatius per a la recerca en educació plurilingüe* (p. 451-467). Research-publishing. net. https://doi.org/10.14705/rpnet.2017.emmd2016.641

Corona, V. (2017). Un acercamiento etnográfico al estudio de las variedades lingüísticas de jóvenes latinoamericanos en Barcelona. A E. Moore i M. Dooly (Eds), *Enfocaments qualitatius per a la recerca en educació plurilingüe* (p. 151-169). Research-publishing. net. https://doi.org/10.14705/rpnet.2017.emmd2016.626

Dooly, M., Moore, E., i Vallejo, C. (2017). Ética de la investigación. A E. Moore i M. Dooly (Eds), *Enfocaments qualitatius per a la recerca en educació plurilingüe* (p. 363-375). Research-publishing.net. https://doi.org/10.14705/rpnet.2017.emmd2016.635

Labov, W. (1972a). *Language in the inner city: studies in the Black English vernacular.* Filadèlfia: University of Pennsylvania Press.

Labov, W. (1972b). *Sociolingustic patterns.* Filadèlfia: University of Pennsylvania Press.

Mackey, A., i Gass, S. M. (2005). *Second language research: methodology and design.* Mahwah, Nova Jersey: Lawrence Erlbaum Associates.

Masats, D. (2017). L'anàlisi de la conversa al servei de la recerca en el camp de l'adquisició de segones llengües (CA-for-SLA). A E. Moore i M. Dooly (Eds), *Enfocaments qualitatius per a la recerca en educació plurilingüe* (p. 293-320). Research-publishing.net. https://doi.org/10.14705/rpnet.2017.emmd2016.632

Moore, E., i Llompart, J. (2017). Recoger, transcribir, analizar y presentar datos interaccionales plurilingües. A E. Moore i M. Dooly (Eds), *Enfocaments qualitatius per a la recerca en educació plurilingüe* (p. 418-433). Research-publishing.net. https://doi.org/10.14705/rpnet.2017.emmd2016.639

Nussbaum, L. (2017). Investigar con docentes. A E. Moore i M. Dooly (Eds), *Enfocaments qualitatius per a la recerca en educació plurilingüe* (p. 23-45). Research-publishing.net. https://doi.org/10.14705/rpnet.2017.emmd2016.620

Pascual, X. (2017). Investigar las propias prácticas docentes a través de la investigación-acción. A E. Moore i M. Dooly (Eds), *Enfocaments qualitatius per a la recerca en educació plurilingüe* (p. 69-87). Research-publishing.net. https://doi.org/10.14705/rpnet.2017.emmd2016.622

Salaberry, M. R., i Comajoan, L. (Eds). (2013). *Research design and methodology in studies on L2 tense and aspect*. Amsterdam, Filadèlfia: Walter de Gruyter. https://doi.org/10.1515/9781934078167

Tannen, D. (1984). *Conversational style: analyzing talk among friends*. Oxford University Press.

Unamuno, V., i Patiño, A. (2017). Producir conocimiento sobre el plurilingüismo junto a jóvenes estudiantes: un reto para la etnografía en colaboración. A E. Moore i M. Dooly (Eds), *Enfocaments qualitatius per a la recerca en educació plurilingüe* (p. 107-128). Research-publishing.net. https://doi.org/10.14705/rpnet.2017.emmd2016.624

Lectures recomanades

Gass, S. M., i Mackey, A. (2011). *Data elicitation for second and foreign language research*. Nova York i Londres: Routledge.

Nussbaum, L., i Unamuno, V. (Eds). (2006). *Usos i competències multilingües entre escolars d'origen immigrant*. Bellaterra: Servei de Publicacions de la UAB.

Pàgines web amb recursos mencionats

Tasques de recollida de dades i d'aprenentatge

Materials 'Biografies', en què es poden consultar exemples de com dur a terme narratives: http://biografiesgreip.blogspot.co.uk/

Materials del projecte 'La competència plurilingüe, audiovisual i digital com a vehicle per a la construcció de sabers en comunitats de pràctica multilingües i multiculturals (PADS)', en què s'aporten exemples de jocs de rols, entre d'altres tasques: http://pagines.uab.cat/pads/

Materials 'Històries viscudes, històries de vida', en què els estudiants han d'entrevistar altres persones com a part d'un projecte: http://grupsderecerca.uab.cat/greip/sites/grupsderecerca.uab.cat.greip/files/index_0.html

Materials 'Les parelles lingüístiques', en què es recullen tasques de diferents tipus: http://parellesling.blogspot.co.uk/

Materials 'Les tasques en parelles', en què es recullen tasques per realitzar en parelles: http://tasquesparelles.blogspot.co.uk//

10 Instruments for gathering data

Laia Canals[1]

Key concepts: data types, learning tasks, classroom observation, focus groups, debates, narratives and interviews, questionnaires and surveys.

---

1.   Introduction

This chapter sets out various methods for gathering important data on the language uses of participants in a research project. These methods imply interaction between students, teachers and researchers. They are used in the design of research projects based on action research, ethnography or conversational analysis, this being the case with the studies presented in the first section of this handbook. Gathering research data following these methodologies often implies preparing situations, tasks or activities that engage participants to interact around a specific theme or to mobilize certain communication skills.

The methods used to gather data, as explained in other chapters, are determined to a large extent by the research questions and objectives, although in qualitative research it should be borne in mind that these will change during the process. Generally speaking, data collection in the field of language education is done in situations that try to reproduce real-life communication scenarios in which the participants make oral or written contributions that are useful for research purposes and, at the same time, beneficial for their learning process.

As we shall see in the following pages, there is a broad spectrum of methods, including more traditional ones such as surveys, questionnaires and interviews,

---

1. Universitat Oberta de Catalunya, Barcelona, Catalonia/Spain; ecanalsf@uoc.edu

How to cite this chapter: Canals, L. (2017). Instruments for gathering data. In E. Moore & M. Dooly (Eds), *Qualitative approaches to research on plurilingual education* (pp. 390-401). Research-publishing.net. https://doi.org/10.14705/rpnet.2017.emmd2016.637

through to more innovative ones such as projects, tasks and other classroom-based activities or focus groups about a particular topic. As explained by Nussbaum (this volume), it is advisable that the researcher also takes on an active role as a committed participant in the learning and teaching processes, and includes educational innovation when planning his or her research.

2. Types of data to be collected

The research questions and objectives of a particular study will determine whether the aim is to obtain purely interactional data or data that also inform us about the interactional behavior of the participants in the context under study or in other contexts. At the same time, we might be interested in obtaining data that allow us to explore in greater depth the linguistic identities, learning pathways, attitudes towards different languages, and other aspects that may not be strictly language-related but are often essential to studying language learning in plurilingual situations.

Thus in the following sections we will examine what kinds of data we can gather in each case to subsequently clarify which methods will be the most appropriate. The distinctions suggested further on between purely linguistic or interactional data and those that reflect attitudes, identities and behavior are not exclusive categories, but rather are intended as ways of addressing the data. This distinction could be particularly useful when planning the tools or the types of questions and tasks that will enable us to obtain one type of data or another.

The data collection methods described in this chapter usually refer to oral data. These data are gathered by either audio or video recordings so they can be transcribed and analyzed later on (see Moore & Llompart, this volume). It is also worth mentioning that many of the methods presented herein can make use of the digital tools and data processing methods described in Antoniadou's chapter in the second part of this handbook.

2.1. Data that reveal how plurilingual people define their language use

Data on language knowledge, attitudes, linguistic identities and interactional uses of the informants in a non-observable context (with friends, at home, etc.), amongst other aspects, can often be deduced from an analysis of their interactions in the classroom, from open interviews, focus groups and other kinds of more naturalistic data. However, they can also be elicited from questionnaires or surveys that ask for personal details through closed-ended or semi-closed questions, which may include information on language knowledge, uses, affiliations and attitudes of the participants.

For example, asking participants what language they use with different members of their family or friends, or in which situations they tend to use one language over another, helps us to analyze interactional behavior or the scope of use of their languages. This information can be obtained with questionnaires and surveys using closed questions, but it should be taken into account that there may be multiple answers or a need to convey subtle nuances in certain cases. It should be borne in mind that languages are not always used in compartmentalized ways, in different surroundings or for different purposes. It is therefore important to consider whether the instrument for gathering data also allows more hybrid language usage to be described (see Nussbaum, this volume, for a discussion on plurilingualism).

It may be interesting, especially if questionnaires or surveys are used, to do a test run to check the suitability of the questions. When we ask closed-ended questions in a questionnaire, we often find out later on that the response options we gave do not help describe real language use. For example, in a study that aims to determine the choice of language by bilingual people in a family setting, when respondents are asked about what language they use with their siblings, it should be taken into account that only answering language A or language B does not allow the complex linguistic situations we can observe in bilingual or multilingual settings to be fully described. It would need to include options with distinctions such as: I speak more of language A than B, I use both A and B, I use language B more than A, and so on.

2.2. Data that reveal plurilingual people's language use

This kind of data can be obtained by projects (see Nussbaum, this volume; Unamuno & Patiño, this volume), tasks (see Masats, this volume), or other activities that facilitate certain types of interaction. The participants need to feel free to express themselves in a relaxed atmosphere. It is difficult to obtain true data in a laboratory setting, where the speakers see these kinds of activities as extremely formal situations in which they are expected to speak in ways that have little to do with their real-life use. Nerves can also affect the way people speak or can make them express themselves in shorter sentences out of fear of making mistakes.

North-American sociolinguist William Labov (1972a) showed that if we wish to obtain data on how the informants speak in informal situations, we need to recreate those same situations. Labov, who used the interview method, only managed to get relevant linguistic data on young speakers of African American Vernacular English when he was able to recreate the optimum sociolinguistic situations with the right interlocutors. He arranged an informal setting for the interviews (everyone sat on the floor with a bag of potato chips) that were conducted by interlocutors of a similar ethnicity and age as the informants.

If we want to obtain data from everyday situations of language use, such as language classes in school, we need to think of ways of overcoming the natural inhibitions of students in front of a camera or recording device, the fear of speaking and making mistakes, and take into account the personalities of the informants when planning the design of our research.

The following section presents some of the methods that have proved useful in classroom research. Later on, we describe other methods such as focus groups, debates and interviews, which can be used as a classroom task or as an independent instrument. Finally, we look at questionnaires and surveys as another way of obtaining data in mixed-methods research studies (see, for example, the chapter by Pascual, this volume).

3. Learning tasks

Mackey and Gass (2005) describe a good number of learning tasks divided into one-way tasks, where information is passed from one person to another, and two-way tasks, where there is an exchange of information between the participants who need to cooperate to complete the task. The first type of task could be, for instance, the description of a drawing, and the second type of task could be an information gap exercise, where each of the students has a piece of essential information that they need to share with the others in order to complete the exercise.

Another way of classifying tasks is based on the type of outcome expected from them. There are closed tasks, from which a correct or incorrect solution is expected, and open tasks, where participants have to reach a common agreement or extract conclusions after a discussion or debate.

Each one of the following tasks elicits different types of data which will be determined by our interests, objectives and research questions. When recording natural interactions it is worth remembering that the tasks should be chosen based on the type of language the research is set to obtain.

3.1. Descriptions of photos or images

This task takes as its starting point an image that might spark off a story or a descriptive narrative: for example, a comical situation. When it comes to choosing the images, the researcher needs to consider whether the image would motivate people to say something. If one cannot find anything interesting or appealing to talk about in the picture, it is highly unlikely that it will be effective for eliciting data from research participants.

3.2. Finding the differences

This activity, designed to be done in pairs or groups of three, elicits comparative linguistic data. While it is a closed task, whereby all the informants have the same type of information, it does facilitate the recording of a lot of speech, although not necessarily extensive interactions between the different participants.

3.3. Exercises in which each student has a piece of information missing

In these tasks, usually done in pairs or groups of three, the participants have to collaborate and interact verbally to solve the task. The task might consist of a city map on which each person has to position different shops or buildings and deduce where the other ones are. This helps to obtain data on interaction and also data on specific linguistic elements (the use of location adverbs in this particular case). For the task to be completed successfully, it is important that the participants do not show their drawings to one another.

3.4. Retelling stories

This task can be done using comic stories, short videos (cartoons, for example), or by verbally telling a story to groups or individuals. Students are given time to read, watch or listen to the story and then asked to give a detailed explanation of what they have read, seen or heard. Depending on the type of data elicited in each case, the researcher can ask for clarifications or more detailed descriptions of the elements on which the researcher would like to focus.

3.5. Deducing rules

This task can be done in groups or individually and can be combined with sheets or cards containing partial information on the final solution. In other cases, you might give the students correct and incorrect sentences and ask them to work out the rules. This task elicits metalinguistic data and interactions among participants when they formulate different hypotheses. In language classes, at the early stages, it might be difficult for students to use the target language to solve these tasks. In this case, it might be worth reflecting or focusing on linguistic and metalinguistic knowledge, regardless of the language actually used during the task.

4. Observation in the classroom

Observations in classrooms where the researcher is also the teacher, or a participant in a project, are one of the most widely-used methods for research in language education. Researchers can make use of observation guides that will help them focus on what they need to know (see the chapter by Pascual, this volume). This is highly recommended when more than one researcher is involved in gathering data as it ensures that everyone follows the same procedure.

5. Focus groups, debates, narratives and interviews

The following methods have been placed in a new section because although they can certainly be carried out as learning tasks in lessons, they are also often used outside the classroom.

5.1. Focus groups

In focus groups the participants are invited to talk about their views, attitudes and beliefs in relation to a particular subject, concept or idea. This might include questions to guide the informants on talking about certain aspects to be considered for each subject or sub-topic. The type of data that can be obtained in this way include opinions, assertions about beliefs, expressions of agreement or disagreement with other participants, and processes in which individual or group identities are built.

5.2. Debates

During a debate, each person is asked to take a stance either for or against a certain topic or idea. This can be done at random or by assigning different roles to the participants. For example, someone might be the city mayor, another a mother with two teenage children, a third might be the chief of police, a fourth a teenager, and someone else a beer hawker. Everyone needs to discuss the new draft law banning the consumption of alcoholic drinks in public spaces. These tasks help to elicit data such as the expression of opinions, arguments, rebuttals of arguments, and discussions that can often get out of control. It is advisable for there to be a moderator in charge (teacher, researcher or another participant who is charged with controlling the others if the task gives rise to disputes).

5.3. Personal narratives

These tasks enable us to obtain long interventions from the participants. The narratives tend to be explanations of past events as researchers ask the participants to look back on their personal life and remember special moments. Labov (1972b) suggests asking about a time when the informants felt in danger, while Tannen (1984) asks them to retell a strange or funny experience. In both cases, the idea is for the informant to feel comfortable and get completely involved in telling the story, arousing feelings and emotions that will make them forget they are being interviewed and elicit more natural speech.

There is also the possibility of getting the participants to write down these experiences instead of explaining them orally in order to reduce anxiety or stress, but this will depend on the type of data you want to obtain. Tannen (1984) suggests some topics that might generate good narratives: explaining their first day at a new school, their first impressions of a foreign country or a different city. Salaberry and Comajoan (2013) suggest letting the informants choose from a range of topics, or showing them different cards or photos that portray emotions. They can then be asked to explain a specific time when they felt particularly happy, sad, angry, etc.

5.4. Interviews

Interviews can be conducted in the classroom by the students themselves, and at the same time can be used as research and educational material for subsequent tasks. These interviews can be structured or semi-structured. The former follow a very specific pattern in which the questions posed to participants are exactly the same, or where the interview conditions are the same to minimize differences between interviews, which will make them comparable. This type of interview can also provide quantitative data, or data that can be better quantified.

In semi-structured interviews the interviewer has more flexibility when it comes to adding questions or asking for clarifications. Generally speaking, they facilitate the collection of personal data, given that the participant feels more comfortable and relaxed, making the interview more of a conversation than a calculated interrogation of questions and answers. These interviews tend to be used to gather qualitative data, usually last a little longer, and allow the interviewers to explore questions in greater depth (see the chapter by Corona, this volume).

6. Questionnaires and surveys

Data can also be collected using questionnaires and surveys which, at the same time, can become part of more extensive interviews. As in interviews and other similar methods, the type of questions we include in questionnaires should make the participants feel comfortable. They should also be posed in a non-intrusive way so participants do not get the feeling we are judging their lifestyle, beliefs about different languages or linguistic behavior. Given that questions about attitudes towards languages and the way people identify themselves linguistically are usually quite sensitive issues, it is advisable to pose them indirectly or include them in more extensive conversations.

In addition to data on attitudes, there are all kinds of other information such as age, educational level, family situation, country of origin, place of residence, school attended and many other additional details that might be relevant when it comes to the data analysis. This can be particularly important in defining the context of the research with a group of speakers or learners.

7. Information to be given to the informants

The issue of protecting participants' private data in research projects is very important, especially when working with children and young people in disadvantaged or socioeconomically complex situations. Provision needs to be made to obtain consent from all the participants and their legal guardians.

This can be done by sending an explanatory letter outlining the objectives of the research project and the type of data that will be collected from the participants. It is also important to explain how the data will be processed and the scope of their public disclosure (see the chapter by Dooly, Moore, & Vallejo, this volume).

8. Other considerations

Many of the possible obstacles when it comes to gathering data can be avoided by running a pilot with the data collection tools you intend to use with a small number of informants before you start the actual data collection process. This will help to quickly identify any unforeseen problems, and it will allow changing any questions or tasks that are unproductive. The test run can be included in the research report as an element that allows drawing conclusions on potential problems with the instruments or data collection methods.

It is important to be aware of the age group you are working with in order to find out what motivates your participants and what might encourage them to talk. It might also be important to put yourself on their level physically to avoid being regarded as an authoritative figure and to contribute to being regarded as another participant instead. In social science studies, we often talk about the paradox of the researcher or observer, which states that when it comes to observing a type of behavior or interaction, the presence of the observer influences the attitude and behavior of whoever is being observed. It is important to be aware of this paradox and address it explicitly when analyzing the data (see Moore & Llompart, this volume; Nussbaum, this volume).

Works cited

Antoniadou, V. (2017). Collecting, organizing and analyzing multimodal data sets: the contributions of CAQDAS. In E. Moore & M. Dooly (Eds), *Qualitative approaches to research on plurilingual education* (pp. 435-450). Research-publishing.net. https://doi.org/10.14705/rpnet.2017.emmd2016.640

Chapter 10

Corona, V. (2017). An ethnographic approach to the study of linguistic varieties used by young Latin Americans in Barcelona. In E. Moore & M. Dooly (Eds), *Qualitative approaches to research on plurilingual education* (pp. 170-188). Research-publishing.net. https://doi.org/10.14705/rpnet.2017.emmd2016.627

Dooly, M., Moore, E., & Vallejo, C. (2017). Research ethics. In E. Moore & M. Dooly (Eds), *Qualitative approaches to research on plurilingual education* (pp. 351-362). Research-publishing.net. https://doi.org/10.14705/rpnet.2017.emmd2016.634

Labov, W. (1972a). *Language in the inner city: studies in the Black English vernacular*. Philadelphia: University of Pennsylvania Press.

Labov, W. (1972b). *Sociolinguistic patterns*. Philadelphia: University of Pennsylvania Press.

Mackey, A., & Gass, S. M. (2005). *Second language research: methodology and design*. Mahwah, New Jersey: Lawrence Erlbaum Associates.

Masats, D. (2017). Conversation analysis at the service of research in the field of second language acquisition (CA-for-SLA). In E. Moore & M. Dooly (Eds), *Qualitative approaches to research on plurilingual education* (pp. 321-347). Research-publishing.net. https://doi.org/10.14705/rpnet.2017.emmd2016.633

Moore, E., & Llompart, J. (2017). Collecting, transcribing, analyzing and presenting plurilingual interactional data. In E. Moore & M. Dooly (Eds), *Qualitative approaches to research on plurilingual education* (pp. 403-417). Research-publishing.net. https://doi.org/10.14705/rpnet.2017.emmd2016.638

Nussbaum, L. (2017). Doing research with teachers. In E. Moore & M. Dooly (Eds), *Qualitative approaches to research on plurilingual education* (pp. 46-67). Research-publishing.net. https://doi.org/10.14705/rpnet.2017.emmd2016.621

Pascual, X. (2017). Investigating one's own teaching practices using action research. In E. Moore & M. Dooly (Eds), *Qualitative approaches to research on plurilingual education* (pp. 88-105). Research-publishing.net. https://doi.org/10.14705/rpnet.2017.emmd2016.623

Salaberry, M. R., & Comajoan, L. (Eds). (2013). *Research design and methodology in studies on L2 tense and aspect*. Amsterdam, Philadelphia: Walter de Gruyter. https://doi.org/10.1515/9781934078167

Tannen, D. (1984). *Conversational style: analyzing talk among friends*. Oxford University Press.

Unamuno, V., & Patiño, A. (2017). Producing knowledge about plurilingualism with young students: a challenge for collaborative ethnography. In E. Moore & M. Dooly (Eds), *Qualitative approaches to research on plurilingual education* (pp. 129-149). Research-publishing.net. https://doi.org/10.14705/rpnet.2017.emmd2016.625

Recommended reading

Gass, S. M., & Mackey, A. (2011). *Data elicitation for second and foreign language research.* New York and London: Routledge.

Nussbaum, L., & Unamuno, V. (Eds). (2006). *Usos i competències multilingües entre escolars d'origen immigrant.* Bellaterra: UAB Publication Service.

Websites with resources mentioned

Data collection and learning tasks

'Biographies' material, giving examples of how to conduct narratives: http://biografiesgreip.blogspot.co.uk/

'Language pair' material, featuring various types of tasks: http://parellesling.blogspot.co.uk/

'Living history, life stories' material, in which students have to interview other people as part of a project: http://grupsderecerca.uab.cat/greip/sites/grupsderecerca.uab.cat.greip/files/index_0.html

Material from the project 'Plurilingual, audiovisual and digital competence as a vehicle for constructing knowledge in multicultural and multilingual communities (PADS)', giving examples of role play, amongst other tasks: http://pagines.uab.cat/pads/

'Tasks in pairs' material, featuring tasks for doing as a pair: http://tasquesparelles.blogspot.co.uk/

11. Collecting, transcribing, analyzing and presenting plurilingual interactional data

Emilee Moore[1] and Júlia Llompart[2]

Key concepts: recording equipment, data preparation, transcription, ELAN, CLAN, data presentation.

1. Introduction

Is it enough if I just use audio? How many recorders do I need? Isn't there an automatic way of transcribing? Which program is best? What do all those symbols mean? Why do different researchers use different symbols? Can I show my data in public?

Do those questions sound familiar? Interactional data is often central to research in plurilingual learning environments. However, getting a grip on the processes of collecting, organizing, transcribing, analyzing and presenting audio and/or visual data is possibly the most exciting, but also one of the most challenging things about learning to do qualitative research. Although the entire process is interwoven with other aspects of research discussed elsewhere in this handbook (e.g. ethics, qualitative research design), in this chapter we will try to set out some basic recommendations to guide the reader through different stages of what Mortensen and Hazel (2012) have called the 'data cycle'.

---

1. Universitat Autònoma de Barcelona, Bellaterra, Catalonia/Spain; emilee.moore@uab.cat

2. Universitat Autònoma de Barcelona, Bellaterra, Catalonia/Spain; julia.llompart@uab.cat

How to cite this chapter: Moore, E., & Llompart, J. (2017). Collecting, transcribing, analyzing and presenting plurilingual interactional data. In E. Moore & M. Dooly (Eds), *Qualitative approaches to research on plurilingual education* (pp. 403-417). Research-publishing.net. https://doi.org/10.14705/rpnet.2017.emmd2016.638

2. Tools, resources and processes

This chapter starts out by dealing with some of the questions beginning researchers will most likely have before they even start recording (e.g. *what* to record, *why* and using *what instruments*). It will continue by discussing some aspects to be kept in mind when organizing a data corpus and selecting what needs to be transcribed and what does not. Some tips for producing both rough and fine transcriptions, as part of the analytical processes of the research, will then be given. Following that, some ideas for going further with the analysis will be introduced, although this aspect is mainly dealt with in the chapters in the first part of this handbook. Finally, we have included some hints for presenting interactional data publically, before closing with some of the issues that may be encountered during the research not mentioned elsewhere in the chapter.

Although we set out different stages of the data cycle, following from Mortensen and Hazel (2012), in a chronological sequence, obviously all of these processes are ones that we come back to time and time again throughout a research project. Rather than visualizing the stages as a simple, static flowchart, researchers should try to imagine something like a game of pinball, in which the researcher and the data roll back and forth, sometimes bumping into things and sometimes struggling, but this should not cause worry; if the process is thought through carefully, it is sure to be a fruitful game.

3. Before recording

3.1. What and why am I recording?

It is easy to assume that the process of analyzing comes after having collected the data; however, this is far from the reality. There are several considerations that are intimately linked to the analytical process that we have to take into account before we get into recording properly. Among them are the following:

- What initial questions do you want to set out to answer and what do you need to record in order to answer them?

- How important is fieldwork before starting recordings? That is to say, should you be using ethnography as a first or proto-analysis helping to shape your decisions on what and how to record, or are you just following your intuition?

Putting some thought into these two aspects before the technical aspects of recording can be considered – such as the number and quality of the device(s) to be used, or their position (see the next two sections below) – will enhance the quality of the data collection.

In terms of the first, the research questions will be basic in order to organize and give direction to the project, but also to help think about what kinds of data is needed to answer those questions (Silverman, 2003). Research questions have to be able to be answered; that is to say, they must be able to guide the researcher towards the kinds of data they will need. At the same time, this initial guidance must not lead to rigidity in the research process. As Silverman (2003) points out, astute researchers should always be willing to alter their focus as they continue to learn both from others and from their own data throughout the research process, and this is a feature of most qualitative research. Thus, the questions will change and be refined many times as data is gathered and the researcher becomes more familiar with what it is telling them, but the process does need to start from an initial focus of enquiry.

In terms of the latter, it is important to understand that the process of data collection in qualitative research (e.g. in the form of field notes) usually starts before audio and/or video recordings are gathered. Fieldwork for understanding the kind of activities people carry out at the site, and for understanding the broader ecology, is usually crucial for making decisions about how to record – such as the best conditions for setting up the camera(s) or voice recorders, or what visual field to cover (Mondada, 2012) – and often important for latter interpretations of the data. It is also essential for developing relationships of trust with research participants.

3.2. Should I record audio or video?

One of the decisions that most seems to worry beginning researchers when starting out on a project relates to the type of data to collect: audio and/or video? It is often tempting to record only audio as it can seem less intrusive for participants than filming with a video camera, and beginning researchers are often scared to make an impact on their site that would alter reality. Furthermore, in some sites, due to the sensitive nature of the activities taking place or the vulnerability of participants, it is not possible to gain permission to record video at all (see the chapter by Dooly, Moore, & Vallejo, this volume, on ethics and obtaining informed consent).

However, more and more researchers are interested not only in oral language, but also in multimodal aspects of interactions. As Mondada (2008) points out, using video recordings for the study of interaction is in fact not new at all, but goes back to the 1970's. The importance of aspects such as body position, gaze, facial expression, the manipulation of objects, spatial organization, etc., for understanding interaction is being taken more and more seriously in many streams of qualitative research, and might be essential to being able to fully answer the research questions asked.

For this reason, if video recordings are not a problem for participants, they are very highly recommended. Rather than worrying about not affecting participants' natural interaction by recording them, researchers should spend time considering how they might develop trust through fieldwork, and take the presence of themselves, the recording equipment and other factors explicitly into account when interpreting the data. It is important to be honest, transparent and reflexive in analyses, which also means analyzing the researcher and the recording equipment as participants in the activities being interpreted.

We recommend that novice researchers consult Mondada (2011) to decide what kind of device to use and to understand basic techniques of video recording for research purposes.

3.3. Recording equipment

Guidance from the research questions and the proto-analysis of the site will allow researchers to decide what kind of devices they might use (audio, video, both) and the quality of the devices they will need. Prior to recording, the complexity of the recording set-up will have to be determined, which might range from the simplest configuration consisting of a single audio recorder and/or a single camera, to a more complex set-up with several cameras (Mondada, 2012). In this regard, there are pros and cons that will have to be weighed up. By using a single camera some important events might be missed, but using a complex set of cameras can result in fragmentation of the event and some extra work in assembling and understanding the situation later on (e.g. in synchronizing the data, see below), as well as being overly intrusive in some sites.

Technology changes fast, so it is difficult for us to give specific recommendations on the latest recording equipment available. We recommend the TalkBank website (see reference below), which is maintained by experts in the study of multimodal interaction, for updated information about audio and video recording equipment that is useful for research purposes.

Depending on when and where recording is going to take place (e.g. how much environmental noise there is) and the detail needed to be picked up (e.g. if aspects such as voice pitch or intensity are important to the analysis, using a program such as Praat may be advisable), anything from a mobile phone with recording capabilities (the latest smartphones can collect some excellent data in the right environmental conditions) to professional video cameras will be needed. The basic recording equipment for a postgraduate or doctoral project would probably include two recorders, because it is always important to have a backup of the data (e.g. a mobile phone and a tablet, a video and an audio recorder). If recording will take place in a noisy environment, it is highly recommended to use good microphones linked to a video camera, or quality audio recorders, especially if the aim is to produce detailed transcriptions for the analysis (for example, if a conversation analysis approach is taken, or a program such as Praat is to be used). Quality audio data will also simply save time and energy when transcribing.

If two different recorders to capture the same interaction are used, as we have mentioned above, the media files will most likely need to be synchronized later (see the section on synchronizing audio and video below). A very simple tip, taken from Mortensen and Hazel (2012), will save researchers a lot of time later. When all the equipment is turned on and recording, it is a good idea to simply clap your hands once loudly. This sound will be much easier to locate in all the recordings as a synchronization point than any others.

4. Preparing to transcribe

4.1. Organize your data into a corpus

Computer-Assisted Qualitative Data Analysis Software (CAQDAS) packages, such as Nvivo or Atlas.ti (see chapter by Antoniadou, this volume), are probably the most sophisticated way of organizing all the data collected into a corpus. However, simply making folders that are coded (e.g. by date - 20152305) in the same way as the files put in them (e.g. Pepe_20152305.mp4, Marc_20152305.doc) on the computer hard drive, together with a spread-sheet listing all the data collected, may suffice for the project. Whichever way data is stored, it is imperative to keep it backed up, absolutely always!

4.2. Synchronizing audio and video

If a separate audio and a video recorder have been used, the sound quality from the audio recorder may be better than the sound from the video recorder. In this case, before transcribing, it is highly recommended that the better audio be added to the video file. If two video cameras have been used, it might also be a good idea to join them side-to-side so they play together, which can be done with most video editing programs. The online Tutorial for Transcribing Plurilingual and Multimodal Data (Moore, n.d., see reference below) explains some ways to synchronize data. It is important never to delete the original files! One never knows when they will be needed again.

The transcription programs listed below all include features for synchronizing different video sources if various cameras have been used, so if using one of them, data may not have to be synchronized previously. However, synchronization might be a good idea when preparing files to present in public, for example at a conference.

4.3. Deciding what to transcribe

The decision about what to transcribe is ultimately, like recording, linked to the questions being asked. Deciding what data to transcribe is therefore another important part of the analytical process. It is also one that will be returned to time and time again, given that as qualitative research advances, as we have already mentioned, questions tend to change, sending researchers back to the data corpus and to transcription. It is important to take into account that it is not always necessary to transcribe an entire corpus. If the data is stored well, it will always be there to come back to – and researchers should come back to it.

In deciding what to transcribe, although it might suit researchers to work through their audio or video files and take notes about interesting fragments using pen and paper, a word processor, etc., to later transcribe those fragments, it is recommendable to digitalize the process to help find the fragments easily later on. The online Tutorial for Transcribing Plurilingual and Multimodal Data (Moore, n.d., see reference below) explains how to do this using the program ELAN, although this can also be done with CAQDAS software (see chapter by Antoniadou, this volume).

4.4. What program should I use to transcribe?

Once decisions have been made about what to transcribe, media files should be prepared for transcription (e.g. by synchronizing as was discussed above, by making snippets of the fragments identified as interesting, and always keeping the original media files). The next question relates to the technicalities of producing the transcription. Although many researchers produce transcripts using just a media player and a word processor, there are several programs available for helping to transcribe audio-visual data. Of these, some commonly used programs are: CLAN (free), ELAN (free) and Transana (about USD60, with a free trial version). Other CAQDAS packages, such as Nvivo or Atlas.ti (see chapter by Antoniadou, this volume) also include transcription functions, although they also allow transcripts produced using other programs to be imported.

5. Transcribing

5.1. Rough transcription

As has been suggested already, once the data corpus has been organized and the researcher is familiar with it, at least some of the data will need to be transcribed in order to analyze it in depth and share it with others in a written dissertation, publications, etc. Transcription usually involves two stages: first of all, researchers usually carry out a rough transcription, meaning one without details of prosody, gesture, pauses, etc. Once more specific sections have been selected for in-depth analysis, researchers proceed to produce finer transcriptions.

The first rough transcription will be done by listening to and/or watching the selected data and writing out the verbal content of interactions, without any specific symbols. It is important to remember that even this rough transcription is also part of the analysis, as decisions are made about what is going on in the interactions, certain phenomena are noticed, etc. As the content of the interaction is worked through, certain utterances and actions will be assigned to certain participants, for whom pseudonyms should be used (see the chapter by

Dooly, Moore, & Vallejo, this volume, on ethics). It is important to decide what pseudonyms to use for each participant and to keep a record of that, especially when there are many participants in the data.

5.2. Fine transcription

After completing an initial, rough transcription, researchers usually go back and add symbols to best represent the multimodal features of the data they wish to analyze in depth (e.g. intonation, stress, rhythm, gesture, gaze) in text form. Conversation analysis is the field that has worked most on the development of transcription symbology, with the most standard conventions being those developed by Gail Jefferson (e.g. 2004). There is also the option of using the ICOR conventions developed by the team at the ICAR laboratory of the Université de Lyon 2, or those by Mondada (2014). Some authors in the volume use other conventions, including those developed by GREIP over the years following, on the one hand, those proposed by Jefferson and, on the other, those adopted by Payrató (1995), based on Du Bois (1991) (see Corona, this volume; Dooly, this volume; Masats, this volume; Nussbaum, 2006).

When adding symbols to a transcript, it is important to think carefully about the level of detail to include. The tutorials listed below by Antaki (2002) and Schegloff (n.d.), as well as the articles by Mondada (2008) and Nussbaum (2006), all listed in the reference section, should help make some decisions in this regard. A transcription including embodied actions and references to the material and spatial environment is what we call a multimodal transcription. If one considers that language, bodies, artifacts, etc. all take part in communication, multimodality really should be taken into account when transcribing data.

When it comes to detail, as a general rule, absolutely nothing should be discounted as irrelevant to a research at the outset, at the same time as data should be approached with absolutely no preconceptions or theories that might sway the decisions made when transcribing (e.g. researchers should only 'notice' and mark those instances when codeswitching has a pragmatic function – if at all – rather than immediately marking everything that looks like a change in language from a normative point of view). Researchers should try to understand what is relevant and what is not for their participants, as well as for the questions they are trying to answer. Therefore, if doing a multimodal transcription, it is not necessary to transcribe absolutely everything that the participants do (i.e. absolutely every micro eye or hand movement), only what seems to be relevant for the ongoing interaction to proceed and for the research. There is no doubt that these decisions require analysis from the researcher; as we have said, researchers are already interpreting their data as they transcribe it.

6. Analyzing interactional data

The process of qualitative analysis, especially in strongly interactionist traditions (e.g. conversation analysis), is basically manual, involving the researcher listening to and/or viewing their data over and over again, and being tuned into the phenomena that could be of interest for developing and responding to research questions. Furthermore, data sessions, in which data and transcriptions are presented to a group of researchers in order to triangulate analytical viewpoints, are a very useful way of ensuring the validity of interpretations and hearing others'. The basic organization of data sessions is explained in ten Have (2007, p. 140).

Some of the transcription programs also include some 'automatic' functions that can be run on completed transcripts that can complement a turn-by-turn, manual analysis of the data. The online Tutorial for Transcribing Plurilingual and Multimodal Data (Moore, n.d., see reference below) explains some very basic analyses that can be done using transcription programs such as CLAN. CAQDAS packages, such as Nvivo or Atlas.ti (see chapter by Antoniadou, this volume) include many more features in this regard.

In the reference section of this chapter, the link to Bezemer, Domingo, Jewitt, and Price's (n.d.) online workshop on Multimodal Methodologies For Researching Digital and Data Environments is of interest to anyone using multimodal data.

7. Presenting interactional data

When presenting data, besides practical issues, it is important to pay careful attention to research ethics (see the chapter by Dooly, Moore, & Vallejo, this volume). Every effort should be made to protect the real identity of the participants in the research by using pseudonyms in transcriptions, and ideally, by modifying audio-visual data when presenting it outside of one's research group (e.g. at conferences, in publications) and covering up faces. Common word processors and presentation programs include features to alter images using different artistic filters (e.g. to turn a photo into a sketch), or by adding solid shapes over faces when adding an image to a document or playing a video in public.

Another good idea when presenting video data in public is to add subtitles, to avoid having to refer to handouts that divert the audience's attention from the visual data. Most video editing software allow this to be done. The Tutorial for Transcribing Plurilingual and Multimodal Data (Moore, n.d., see reference below) explains how this can be done using some common programs.

8. Other considerations

These very important phases of research – collecting, transcribing, analyzing and presenting interactional data – can and probably will bring about certain problems, be they technical or otherwise. On the one hand, since researchers are working with technology, there is always the chance that something will not work (flat batteries, full memory cards, etc.). It is important to be ready to fix these problems on site and, therefore, a backup plan is needed (e.g. enough batteries to replace with, an extra memory card) in case something does not work.

On the other hand, and even though fieldwork will probably have been done to get to know the setting and the event before recording, there is always the possibility that something will have changed, or that participants will not react as expected. It is important to keep in mind that the process of recording is just another part of the research and needs to be documented as such. It involves continuous reflection and interpretation and will only work out well if researchers are flexible, resourceful and ready to make quick changes to the plan if necessary.

Finally, if dealing with plurilingual data, one of the problems that could be encountered once the data is gathered is that the participants use languages that the researcher might not know. The collection, transcription, analysis and presentation of this kind of data are very interesting, but very complex. In these situations especially, research should be collaborative. It is important to try to work with others who speak the languages of the participants or, even better, with the participants themselves in a process of collaborative research (e.g. Lassiter, 2005; Nussbaum, this volume; Unamuno & Patiño, this volume), thus enriching the process and the resulting quality of the investigation.

All of the chapters in this volume work with the collection, transcription, analysis and presentation of plurilingual data to some extent. They are a great place to start to get a feel for the complexities involved in the process and the different decisions taken by researchers for responding to their diverse enquiries by studying interaction.

Works cited

Antoniadou, V. (2017). Collecting, organizing and analyzing multimodal data sets: the contributions of CAQDAS. In E. Moore & M. Dooly (Eds), *Qualitative approaches to research on plurilingual education* (pp. 435-450). Research-publishing.net. https://doi.org/10.14705/rpnet.2017.emmd2016.640

Corona, V. (2017). An ethnographic approach to the study of linguistic varieties used by young Latin Americans in Barcelona. In E. Moore & M. Dooly (Eds), *Qualitative approaches to research on plurilingual education* (pp. 170-188). Research-publishing.net. https://doi.org/10.14705/rpnet.2017.emmd2016.627

Dooly, M. (2017). A Mediated Discourse Analysis (MDA) approach to multimodal data. In E. Moore & M. Dooly (Eds), *Qualitative approaches to research on plurilingual education* (pp. 189-211). Research-publishing.net. https://doi.org/10.14705/rpnet.2017.emmd2016.628

Dooly, M., Moore, E., & Vallejo, C. (2017). Research ethics. In E. Moore & M. Dooly (Eds), *Qualitative approaches to research on plurilingual education* (pp. 351-362). Research-publishing.net. https://doi.org/10.14705/rpnet.2017.emmd2016.634

Du Bois, J. W. (1991). Transcription design principles for spoken discourse research. *Pragmatics,* 1(1), 71-106. https://doi.org/10.1075/prag.1.1.04boi

Jefferson, G. (2004). Glossary of transcript symbols with an introduction. In G. H. Lerner (Ed.), *Conversation analysis: studies from the first generation* (pp. 13-23). Philadelphia: John Benjamins. https://doi.org/10.1075/pbns.125.02jef

Lassiter, L. E. (2005). *The Chicago guide to collaborative ethnography*. Chicago: University of Chicago Press. https://doi.org/10.7208/chicago/9780226467016.001.0001

Masats, D. (2017). Conversation analysis at the service of research in the field of second language acquisition (CA-for-SLA). In E. Moore & M. Dooly (Eds), *Qualitative approaches to research on plurilingual education* (pp. 321-347). Research-publishing.net. https://doi.org/10.14705/rpnet.2017.emmd2016.633

Mondada, L. (2008). Using video for a sequential and multimodal analysis of social interaction: videotaping institutional telephone calls. *Forum: Qualitative Social Research,* 9(3). http://www.qualitative-research.net/index.php/fqs/article/viewArticle/1161/2566

Mondada, L. (2011). *Exigences analytiques pour l'enregistrement de la parole-en-interaction (version 3.0.2). Protocole pour les enregistrements vidéo*. Lyon: Laboratoire ICAR.

Mondada, L. (2012). The conversation analytic approach to data collection. In J. Sidnell & T. Stivers (Eds), *Handbook of conversation analysis* (pp. 32-56). Chichester, UK: Blackwell-Wiley. https://doi.org/10.1002/9781118325001.ch3

Mondada, L. (2014). *Conventions for multimodal transcription*. https://franz.unibas.ch/fileadmin/franz/user_upload/redaktion/Mondada_conv_multimodality.pdf

Mortensen, J., & Hazel, S. (2012). The data cycle. In K. Ikeda & A. Brandt (Eds), *Kansai University International Symposium: challenges and new directions in the micro-analysis of social interaction* (pp. 22-29). Osaka: Kansai University.

Nussbaum, L. (2006). La transcripción de la interacción en contextos de contacto y de aprendizaje de lenguas. In Y. Bürki & E. de Steffani (Eds), *Transcribir la lengua: de la filología al análisis de la conversación* (pp. 195-218). Bern: Peter Lang.

Nussbaum, L. (2017). Doing research with teachers. In E. Moore & M. Dooly (Eds), *Qualitative approaches to research on plurilingual education* (pp. 46-67). Research-publishing.net. https://doi.org/10.14705/rpnet.2017.emmd2016.621

Payrató, L. (1995). La transcripción del discurso coloquial. In L. Cortés (Ed.), *El español coloquial* (pp. 45-70). Almería: Universidad de Almería.

Silverman, D. (2003). *Doing qualitative research: a practical handbook.* London, Thousand Oaks, New Delhi: SAGE Publications.

Ten Have, P. (2007). *Doing conversation analysis: a practical guide.* London: Sage.

Unamuno, V., & Patiño, A. (2017). Producing knowledge about plurilingualism with young students: a challenge for collaborative ethnography. In E. Moore & M. Dooly (Eds), *Qualitative approaches to research on plurilingual education* (pp. 129-149). Research-publishing.net. https://doi.org/10.14705/rpnet.2017.emmd2016.625

Recommended readings

Antaki, C., Billig, M., Edwards, D., & Potter, J. (2003). Discourse analysis means doing analysis: a critique of six analytic shortcomings. *Discourse analysis online.* http://extra.shu.ac.uk/daol/articles/v1/n1/a1/antaki2002002-paper.html

Copland, F., & Creese, A. (2015). *Linguistic ethnography: collecting, analysing and presenting data.* London: Sage. https://doi.org/10.4135/9781473910607

Mondada, L. (2012). The conversation analytic approach to data collection. In J. Sidnell & T. Stivers (Eds), *Handbook of conversation analysis* (pp. 32-56). Chichester, UK: Blackwell-Wiley. https://doi.org/10.1002/9781118325001.ch3

Mortensen, J., & Hazel, S. (2012). The data cycle. In K. Ikeda & A. Brandt (Eds), *Kansai University International Symposium: challenges and new directions in the micro-analysis of social interaction* (pp. 22-29). Osaka: Kansai University.

Psathas, G. (1995). *Conversation analysis: the study of talk-in-interaction.* California: Sage.

Ten Have, P. (2007). *Doing conversation analysis: a practical guide.* London: Sage.

Websites with resources mentioned

Programs for transcription

CLAN program and manual (Windows and Mac, free): http://childes.psy.cmu.edu/
ELAN program and manual (Windows and Mac, free): https://tla.mpi.nl/tools/tla-tools/elan/
Praat (for phonetic analyses): http://www.fon.hum.uva.nl/praat/

Transana program and manual (Windows and Mac, approximately EUR60): http://www.transana.org/

Online tutorials (transcription, multimodal analysis, etc.)

Antaki, C. (2002). *An introduction to conversation analysis*. http://ca-tutorials.lboro.ac.uk/sitemenu.htm

Bezemer, J., Domingo, M., Jewitt, C, & Price, S. (n.d.). *Multimodal methodologies for researching digital and data environments*. https://mode.ioe.ac.uk/training/

Moore, E. (n.d.). *Tutorial for transcribing plurilingual and multimodal data*. http://tutorialfortrans.blogspot.com.es/

Schegloff, E. A. (n.d.). *Transcript symbols for conversation analysis*. http://www.sscnet.ucla.edu/soc/faculty/schegloff/TranscriptionProject/index.html

Other useful resources

ICOR transcription conventions: http://icar.univ-lyon2.fr/projets/corinte/bandeau_droit/convention_icor.htm

TalkBank recommendations about digital audio recorders: http://talkbank.org/info/da.html

TalkBank recommendations about digital video recorders: http://talkbank.org/info/dv.html

11 Recoger, transcribir, analizar y presentar datos interaccionales plurilingües

Emilee Moore[1] y Júlia Llompart[2]

Conceptos clave: instrumentos de grabación, preparación de datos, transcripción, ELAN, CLAN, presentación de datos.

1. Introducción

¿Es suficiente usar sólo audios? ¿Cuántas grabadoras necesito? ¿Existe alguna forma de transcribir automática? ¿Cuál es el mejor programa? ¿Qué significan todos esos símbolos? ¿Por qué diferentes personas investigadoras usan símbolos distintos? ¿Puedo mostrar mis datos en público?

¿Algunas de las preguntas le resultan conocidas? Los datos interaccionales son a menudo básicos para la investigación en entornos de aprendizaje plurilingües. Controlar los procesos de recopilación, organización, transcripción, análisis y presentación de datos de audio y/o vídeo es posiblemente el aspecto más emocionante, pero también uno de los aspectos más difíciles de la investigación cualitativa. A pesar de que todo el proceso está relacionado con otros aspectos de la investigación discutidos en este manual (por ejemplo, la ética, el diseño de investigación cualitativa), en este capítulo trataremos de establecer algunas recomendaciones básicas para guiar a las personas lectoras a lo largo de diferentes etapas de lo que Mortensen y Hazel (2012) han llamado el 'ciclo de datos'.

---

1. Universitat Autònoma de Barcelona, Bellaterra, Cataluña/España; emilee.moore@uab.cat

2. Universitat Autònoma de Barcelona, Bellaterra, Cataluña/España; julia.llompart@uab.cat

Para citar este capítulo: Moore, E., y Llompart, J. (2017). Recoger, transcribir, analizar y presentar datos interaccionales plurilingües. En E. Moore y M. Dooly (Eds), *Enfoques cualitativos para la investigación en educación plurilingüe* (pp. 418-433). Research-publishing.net. https://doi.org/10.14705/rpnet.2017.emmd2016.639

2. Herramientas, recursos y procesos

Este capítulo empieza tratando algunas de las preguntas que investigadores e investigadoras principiantes probablemente se plantearán incluso antes de empezar a grabar (por ejemplo, *qué* grabar, *por qué* y con *qué* instrumentos). Después, se discutirán algunos aspectos que deben tenerse en cuenta al organizar un corpus de datos y seleccionar lo que hay que transcribir y lo que no. A continuación, se darán algunos consejos para producir transcripciones amplias y finas, como parte de los procesos analíticos de la investigación. Posteriormente, se introducirán algunas ideas para avanzar con el análisis, aunque este aspecto se trata principalmente en los capítulos de la primera parte de este manual. Finalmente, hemos incluido algunas sugerencias para presentar los datos interaccionales públicamente, antes de cerrar con algunas de las cuestiones que pueden surgir durante la investigación no mencionadas en otras partes del capítulo.

A pesar de que hemos establecido diferentes etapas del ciclo de datos, de acuerdo con Mortensen y Hazel (2012), en una secuencia cronológica, obviamente, tenemos que volver a todos estos procesos una y otra vez a lo largo de un proyecto de investigación. En vez de visualizar las etapas como un diagrama de flujo estático, se debe intentar imaginarlas como un juego de *pinball*, en el que la persona investigadora y los datos se mueven de un lado a otro, a veces chocando con cosas y, a veces, encontrándose con dificultades. Pero esto no debe causar preocupación; si el proceso se planea cuidadosamente, seguro que será un juego fructífero.

3. Antes de grabar

3.1. ¿Qué estoy grabando y por qué?

Es fácil asumir que el proceso de análisis viene después de haber recogido los datos. Sin embargo, esto no es así en la realidad. Hay varias consideraciones, que están íntimamente relacionadas al proceso analítico, que tenemos que tener en cuenta antes de empezar con la grabación adecuada. Entre estas cuestiones se encuentran las siguientes:

- ¿Qué preguntas iniciales se pretende responder y qué hay que grabar para poder hacerlo?

- ¿Cuál es la importancia del trabajo de campo antes de iniciar las grabaciones? Es decir, ¿debería estar utilizando la etnografía como un primer análisis o proto-análisis que ayude a dar forma a las decisiones sobre qué y cómo grabar, o simplemente está siguiendo su intuición?

Considerar estos dos aspectos antes de definir los detalles técnicos de la grabación —como el número de dispositivos que se van a utilizar y su calidad, o su posición (véanse las dos secciones siguientes)— mejorará la calidad de la recopilación de datos.

En cuanto a la primera cuestión, las preguntas de investigación serán básicas para organizar y dar dirección al proyecto, pero también para ayudar a saber qué tipo de datos se necesitan para responder a esas preguntas (Silverman, 2003). Las preguntas de investigación se deben poder contestar; es decir, deben guiarnos hacia los tipos de datos necesarios. Al mismo tiempo, esta orientación inicial no debe implicar una rigidez en el proceso de investigación. Como señala Silverman (2003), siempre debemos estar dispuestos a cambiar nuestro enfoque a medida que aprendemos de los demás y de nuestros propios datos durante el proceso de investigación, y esto es una característica necesaria para la mayoría de estudios de tipo cualitativo. Por lo tanto, muchas veces, las preguntas cambiarán y se refinarán a medida que se recopilan datos y nos familiarizamos con lo que nos están diciendo, pero el proceso necesita comenzar con un enfoque inicial de investigación.

En cuanto a la segunda consideración, es importante entender que el proceso de recopilación de datos en la investigación cualitativa (por ejemplo, en forma de notas de campo) suele comenzar antes de reunir las grabaciones de audio y/o vídeo. El trabajo de campo para comprender el tipo de actividades que las personas llevan a cabo en el sitio –y para comprender la ecología en general– normalmente es imprescindible para tomar decisiones sobre cómo grabar –es decir, cuáles son las mejores condiciones para configurar las cámaras o las grabadoras de voz o qué campo visual se debe cubrir (Mondada, 2012)– y es, a menudo, importante para las últimas interpretaciones de los datos. También es esencial para desarrollar relaciones de confianza con los participantes y las participantes de la investigación.

3.2. ¿Debo grabar audio o vídeo?

Una de las decisiones que más preocupa a investigadores e investigadoras noveles al iniciar un proyecto está relacionada con el tipo de datos que se deben recopilar: ¿audio y/o vídeo? Muchas veces es tentador grabar sólo audio, ya que puede parecer menos intrusivo que filmar con una cámara de vídeo, y a menudo se tiene miedo de causar un impacto en el sitio que alteraría la realidad. Además, en algunos casos, debido a la naturaleza delicada de las actividades que se llevan a cabo o a la vulnerabilidad de las personas participantes, es totalmente imposible obtener permiso para grabar vídeo (véase el capítulo de Dooly, Moore, y Vallejo, en este volumen, sobre la ética y cómo obtener el consentimiento informado).

Sin embargo, cada vez más personas se interesan no sólo por el lenguaje oral, sino también por los aspectos multimodales de las interacciones. Como señala Mondada (2008), el uso de grabaciones de vídeo para estudiar la interacción no es nuevo, sino que se remonta a los años setenta. La importancia de aspectos como la posición corporal, la mirada, la expresión facial, la manipulación de objetos, la organización espacial, etc., para comprender la interacción se toma cada vez más en serio en muchas corrientes de investigación cualitativa y puede ser esencial para poder responder plenamente a las preguntas de investigación.

Por esta razón, se recomiendan encarecidamente las grabaciones de vídeo si no representan un problema para las personas participantes. En lugar de preocuparse por no afectar la interacción natural de los participantes y las participantes al registrarlos, se debería dedicar tiempo a considerar cómo se puede desarrollar un ambiente de confianza a través del trabajo de campo, y tener en cuenta explícitamente su presencia, la del equipo de grabación y otros factores, al interpretar los datos. Es importante ser honesto, transparente y reflexivo en los análisis, lo que también significa analizar al investigador o la investigadora y al equipo de grabación como participantes en las actividades que se están interpretando.

Recomendamos la referencia de Mondada (2011) para ayudar a decidir qué tipo de dispositivo utilizar y comprender las técnicas básicas de grabación de vídeo con fines de investigación.

3.3. Equipo de grabación

Las preguntas de investigación y el análisis previo del sitio permitirán decidir qué tipo de dispositivos se debe utilizar (audio, vídeo, ambos) y la calidad de los dispositivos necesarios. Antes de registrar, habrá que determinar la complejidad de la configuración de la grabación, que puede ir desde una configuración más sencilla, con una sola grabadora de audio y/o una sola cámara, hasta una configuración compleja con varias cámaras (Mondada, 2012). En este sentido, hay ventajas y desventajas que tendrán que sopesarse. Si se utiliza una sola cámara, pueden perderse algunos eventos importantes, pero el uso de un conjunto complejo de cámaras puede fragmentar el evento e implicará más trabajo para juntar y entender la situación más adelante (por ejemplo, en la sincronización de los datos, como veremos más adelante), así como ser excesivamente intrusivo en algunos casos.

La tecnología cambia rápidamente, por lo que es difícil dar recomendaciones específicas sobre los últimos equipos de grabación disponibles. Recomendamos el sitio web de TalkBank (véase la referencia más abajo), creado por expertos en el estudio de la interacción multimodal, para obtener información actualizada sobre el equipo de grabación de audio y vídeo más útil para fines de investigación.

Dependiendo de cuándo y dónde se realice la grabación (por ejemplo, si hay ruido ambiental) y el detalle necesario que deba recogerse (por ejemplo, si son importantes para el análisis aspectos como el tono de la voz o la intensidad, o si se va a utilizar un programa como Praat), se puede usar cualquier cosa para grabar: desde un teléfono móvil (los últimos teléfonos inteligentes pueden recoger algunos datos excelentes en condiciones ambientales adecuadas) a cámaras de vídeo profesionales. El equipo de grabación básico para un proyecto de posgrado o doctorado probablemente debería incluir dos grabadoras/cámaras, ya que siempre es importante tener una copia de seguridad de los datos (por ejemplo, un teléfono móvil y una tableta, una cámara de vídeo y una grabadora de audio). Si la grabación se lleva a cabo en un entorno ruidoso, se recomienda utilizar buenos micrófonos conectados a una videocámara o grabadoras de audio de calidad, especialmente si el objetivo es producir transcripciones detalladas para el análisis (por ejemplo, si debe usarse un enfoque de análisis de la conversación o un programa como Praat). La calidad de los datos de audio también ahorrará tiempo y energía en la transcripción.

Si se usan dos grabadoras diferentes para capturar la misma interacción, como se mencionó anteriormente, es muy probable que los archivos multimedia deban sincronizarse más tarde (véase la sección sobre sincronización de audio y vídeo a continuación). Ofrecemos un consejo muy simple, tomado de Mortensen y Hazel (2012), que ahorrará mucho tiempo. Cuando todo el equipo esté encendido y grabando, es una buena idea simplemente dar una palmada fuerte. Este sonido será mucho más fácil de localizar que cualquier otro en todas las grabaciones y servirá como punto de sincronización.

4. Prepararse para transcribir

4.1. Organizar los datos en un corpus

Los paquetes de software de análisis de datos cualitativos asistido por ordenador (*Computer-Assisted Qualitative Data Analysis Software*, CAQDAS, en inglés), como Nvivo o Atlas.ti (véase el capítulo de Antoniadou, en este volumen), son probablemente la forma más sofisticada de organizar todos los datos recopilados en un corpus. Sin embargo, dependiendo del proyecto, puede ser suficiente simplemente crear carpetas que estén codificadas (por ejemplo, por fecha, 20152305) de la misma manera que los archivos que contengan (por ejemplo, Pepe_20152305.mp4, Marc_20152305.doc) en el disco duro del ordenador, junto con una hoja de cálculo que liste todos los datos recogidos. Independientemente de la manera en la que se almacenen los datos, es imprescindible hacer siempre una copia de seguridad.

4.2. Sincronizar el audio y el vídeo

Si se ha utilizado una grabadora de audio y una cámara de vídeo independientemente, puede ser que la calidad del sonido de la grabadora de audio sea mejor que el sonido de la cámara de vídeo. En este caso, antes de transcribir, se recomienda agregar el mejor audio al archivo de vídeo. Si se han utilizado dos cámaras de vídeo, también podría ser una buena idea unirlas lado a lado para reproducirlas juntas; esto se puede hacer con la mayoría de programas de edición de vídeo. El Tutorial for Transcribing Plurilingual and Multimodal Data (*Tutorial para la transcripción de datos plurilingües y multimodales*) (Moore, n.d., véase la referencia más abajo), en línea, explica algunas maneras de sincronizar datos. ¡Es importante no borrar nunca los archivos originales! Nunca se sabe cuándo se necesitarán de nuevo.

Los programas de transcripción que se enumeran a continuación incluyen funciones para sincronizar diferentes fuentes de vídeo si se han utilizado varias cámaras, por lo que si se utiliza uno de ellos, es posible que los datos no tengan que sincronizarse previamente. Sin embargo, la sincronización podría ser una buena idea al preparar los archivos para presentar en público, por ejemplo en una conferencia.

4.3. Decidir qué transcribir

La decisión sobre qué transcribir, en última instancia, igual que la grabación, está vinculada a las preguntas que se hacen. Por lo tanto, decidir qué datos transcribir es otra parte importante del proceso analítico. Es también una cuestión a la que volverá una y otra vez, dado que a medida que la investigación cualitativa avanza, como ya hemos mencionado, las preguntas tienden a cambiar, lo que implica que se debe volver al corpus de datos y a la transcripción. Es importante tener en cuenta que no siempre es necesario transcribir un corpus completo. Si los datos se almacenan bien, siempre estarán allí para recuperarlos.

Al decidir qué transcribir, aunque algunas personas prefieran escuchar sus archivos de audio o vídeo y tomar notas sobre fragmentos interesantes con papel y lápiz, un procesador de textos, etc., para luego transcribirlos, es recomendable digitalizar el proceso para facilitar la búsqueda más adelante. El tutorial en línea para la transcripción de datos plurilingües y multimodales (Moore, n.d., véase la referencia a continuación) explica cómo hacerlo utilizando el programa ELAN, aunque también puede hacerse con software CAQDAS (véase el capítulo de Antoniadou, en este volumen).

4.4. Programas para la transcripción

Una vez que se han tomado decisiones sobre qué transcribir, los archivos multimedia deben prepararse para la transcripción (por ejemplo, sincronizarse como se discutió anteriormente, haciendo trozos de los fragmentos identificados como interesantes, manteniendo siempre los archivos multimedia originales). La siguiente pregunta se refiere a los detalles técnicos de la producción de la transcripción. Aunque muchas personas transcriben usando sólo un reproductor multimedia y un procesador de textos, hay varios programas disponibles para ayudar a transcribir datos audiovisuales. A continuación, citamos algunos de estos programas de uso común: CLAN (gratuito), ELAN (gratuito) y Transana (alrededor de 60 EUR, con una versión de prueba gratuita). Otros paquetes de software de análisis de datos cualitativos asistido por ordenador (CAQDAS), como Nvivo o Atlas.ti (véase el capítulo de Antoniadou, en este volumen), incluyen funciones de transcripción, aunque también permiten importar transcripciones producidas con otros programas.

5. Transcribir

5.1. Transcripción amplia

Como ya se ha sugerido, cuando se haya organizado el corpus de datos y el investigador se haya familiarizado con él, deberán transcribirse al menos algunos de los datos para poderlos analizar en profundidad y compartirlos con otros en una disertación escrita, publicaciones, etc. La transcripción suele implicar dos etapas: en primer lugar, se suele realizar una transcripción aproximada, es decir, sin detalles de prosodia, gestos, pausas, etc. Cuando se han seleccionado secciones más específicas para un análisis en profundidad, se llevan a cabo transcripciones más finas.

La primera transcripción amplia se realiza escuchando y/o viendo los datos seleccionados y escribiendo el contenido verbal de las interacciones, sin símbolos específicos. Es importante recordar que incluso esta transcripción aproximada es también parte del análisis, puesto que a medida que se toman decisiones sobre lo que está pasando en las interacciones, se notan ciertos fenómenos, etc. Mientras se trabaja el contenido de la interacción, se asignan ciertas expresiones y acciones a determinados participantes, para quienes se deben usar seudónimos (véase el capítulo de Dooly, Moore, y Vallejo, en este volumen sobre ética). Es importante decidir qué seudónimos utilizar para cada participante y mantener un registro de eso, especialmente cuando hay muchas personas participantes en los datos.

5.2. Transcripción fina

Después de ultimar una transcripción inicial, amplia, se suele retroceder y agregar símbolos para representar mejor las características multimodales de los datos que desean analizar en profundidad (por ejemplo, entonación, énfasis, ritmo, gestos, miradas) en forma de texto. El análisis de la conversación es el campo que más ha trabajado en el desarrollo de la simbología de la transcripción y los símbolos más convencionales fueron los desarrollados por Gail Jefferson (por ejemplo, 2004).

También se pueden utilizar las convenciones ICOR, desarrolladas por el equipo del laboratorio ICAR de la Université de Lyon 2, o las de Mondada (2014). Algunos autores del volumen utilizan otras convenciones, entre ellas las desarrolladas por el GREIP a lo largo de los años siguiendo, por una parte, las propuestas de Jefferson y, por otra, las adoptadas por Payrató (1995), basadas en Du Bois (1991) (véanse Corona, en este volumen; Dooly, en este volumen; Masats, en este volumen; Nussbaum, 2006).

Al agregar símbolos en una transcripción, es importante pensar cuidadosamente en el nivel de detalle que se debe incluir. Los tutoriales listados a continuación, de Antaki (2002) y Schegloff (n.d.), así como los artículos de Mondada (2008) y Nussbaum (2006), todos ellos listados en la sección de referencias, deberían ayudar a tomar decisiones al respecto. Una transcripción que incluye acciones y referencias al entorno material y espacial se llama transcripción multimodal. Si se considera que el lenguaje, los cuerpos, los artefactos, etc., participan en la comunicación, realmente debe tenerse en cuenta la multimodalidad al transcribir los datos.

Cuando se trata de los detalles, como regla general, absolutamente nada debe considerarse como irrelevante para una investigación desde el principio; asimismo, los datos deben abordarse sin ninguna preconcepción o teoría que puedan influir en las decisiones tomadas al transcribir (por ejemplo, sólo se debe 'notar' y marcar aquellos casos en los que el cambio de código tiene una función pragmática –si es que la tiene– en lugar de marcar inmediatamente todo lo que parece un cambio de lengua desde un punto de vista normativo). Se debe intentar entender lo que es relevante y lo que no lo es para los participantes, así como para las preguntas que están tratando de responder. Por lo tanto, si se hace una transcripción multimodal, no es necesario transcribir absolutamente todo lo que hacen los participantes y las participantes (es decir, completamente todos los detalles de los movimientos de ojos y manos), sólo lo que parece relevante para que proceda la interacción y para la investigación. No hay duda de que estas decisiones requieren un análisis. Como ya hemos dicho, ya se está interpretando los datos a medida que se transcriben.

6. Analizar datos interaccionales

El proceso del análisis cualitativo, especialmente en las tradiciones principalmente interaccionistas (por ejemplo, el análisis de la conversación), es básicamente manual: la persona investigadora escucha y/o ve sus datos una y otra vez, y se familiariza con los fenómenos que podrían ser interesantes para desarrollar y responder las preguntas de investigación. Además, las sesiones de datos, en las que se presentan los datos y las transcripciones a un grupo de personas investigadoras con el fin de triangular puntos de vista analíticos, son una forma muy útil de garantizar la validez de las interpretaciones y escuchar a los demás. La organización básica de las sesiones de datos se explica en ten Have (2007, p. 140).

Algunos de los programas de transcripción también incluyen algunas funciones 'automáticas' que se pueden ejecutar en transcripciones completadas para complementar un análisis manual paso a paso de los datos. El tutorial en línea para la transcripción de datos plurilingües y multimodales (Moore, n.d., véase la referencia a continuación) explica algunos análisis muy básicos que se pueden hacer utilizando programas de transcripción como CLAN. Los paquetes de software de análisis de datos cualitativos asistido por ordenador (CAQDAS), como Nvivo o Atlas.ti (véase el capítulo de Antoniadou, en este volumen) incluyen muchas más características con esta finalidad.

En la sección de referencias de este capítulo, hay un enlace al taller en línea de Bezemer, Domingo, Jewitt, y Price (n.d.) sobre metodologías multimodales, que puede resultar interesante para cualquiera que utilice datos multimodales.

7. Presentar los datos interaccionales

Cuando se presentan datos, a parte de cuestiones prácticas, es importante prestar mucha atención a la ética de la investigación (véase el capítulo de Dooly, Moore, y Vallejo, en este volumen). Se debe hacer todo lo posible para proteger la identidad real de las personas participantes en la investigación mediante el uso de seudónimos en las transcripciones e, idealmente, mediante la modificación de los datos audiovisuales para tapar las caras al presentarlos fuera del grupo de investigación (por ejemplo, en una conferencia, en publicaciones). Los procesadores de texto y los programas de presentación más habituales incluyen funciones para alterar imágenes utilizando diferentes filtros artísticos (por ejemplo, para convertir una foto en un boceto) o añadiendo formas sólidas sobre caras al agregar una imagen en un documento o reproducir un vídeo en público.

Otra buena idea al presentar los datos de vídeo en público es agregar subtítulos, para evitar tener que hacer referencia a los *handouts* que desvían la atención del público de los datos visuales. La mayoría de software de edición de vídeo permite hacerlo. El Tutorial for Transcribing Plurilingual and Multimodal Data (Moore, n.d., véase la referencia a continuación) explica cómo se pueden crear subtítulos usando algunos programas comunes.

8. Otras consideraciones

Estas fases –recoger, transcribir, analizar y presentar datos interaccionales– son muy importantes en la investigación, y pueden ocasionar ciertos problemas, ya sean técnicos o de otro tipo. Por un lado, si se trabaja con tecnología, siempre existe la posibilidad de que algo no funcione (baterías descargadas, tarjetas de memoria llenas, etc.). Es importante estar preparado para solucionar estos problemas al momento y, por lo tanto, se necesita un plan B (por ejemplo, llevar baterías suficientes para cambiarlas, tener una tarjeta de memoria extra) en caso de que algo no funcione.

Por otro lado, y aunque el trabajo de campo probablemente se haya hecho para conocer el entorno y el evento antes de grabar, siempre existe la posibilidad de que algo haya cambiado o que los participantes y las participantes no reaccionen como se esperaba. Es importante tener en cuenta que el proceso de grabación es sólo otra parte de la investigación y debe documentarse como tal. Este proceso implica la reflexión y la interpretación continuas, y funcionará bien únicamente si somos flexibles, ingeniosos y listos para adaptar rápidamente el plan, si es necesario.

Por último, si se trata de datos plurilingües, uno de los problemas que puede haber una vez recopilados los datos es que las personas participantes usen lenguas que el equipo investigador no conoce. La recopilación, transcripción, análisis y presentación de este tipo de datos son procesos muy interesantes, pero muy complejos. En estas situaciones concretas, la investigación debe ser colaborativa. Es importante intentar trabajar con otros que hablan los idiomas de los participantes y las participantes o, mejor aún, con los propios participantes en un proceso de investigación colaborativa (por ejemplo, Lassiter, 2005; Nussbaum, en este volumen; Unamuno y Patiño, en este volumen), enriqueciendo el proceso y la calidad resultante de la investigación.

Todos los capítulos de este volumen trabajan con la recogida, transcripción, análisis y presentación de datos plurilingües hasta cierto punto. Son una buena manera para empezar a tener una idea de las complejidades involucradas en el proceso y las diferentes decisiones que se toman para responder a preguntas varias mediante el estudio de la interacción.

Obras citadas

Antoniadou, V. (2017). Recoger, organizar y analizar corpus de datos multimodales: las contribuciones de los CAQDAS. En E. Moore y M. Dooly (Eds), *Enfoques cualitativos para la investigación en educación plurilingüe* (pp. 451-467). Research-publishing.net. https://doi.org/10.14705/rpnet.2017.emmd2016.641

Corona, V. (2017). Un acercamiento etnográfico al estudio de las variedades lingüísticas de jóvenes latinoamericanos en Barcelona. En E. Moore y M. Dooly (Eds), *Enfoques cualitativos para la investigación en educación plurilingüe* (pp. 151-169). Research-publishing.net. https://doi.org/10.14705/rpnet.2017.emmd2016.626

Dooly, M. (2017). Una aproximació a dades multimodals amb l'anàlisi del discurs mediat. En E. Moore y M. Dooly (Eds), *Enfoques cualitativos para la investigación en educación plurilingüe* (pp. 212-235). Research-publishing.net. https://doi.org/10.14705/rpnet.2017.emmd2016.629

Dooly, M., Moore, E., y Vallejo, C. (2017). Ética de la investigación. En E. Moore y M. Dooly (Eds), *Enfoques cualitativos para la investigación en educación plurilingüe* (pp. 363-375). Research-publishing.net. https://doi.org/10.14705/rpnet.2017.emmd2016.635

Du Bois, J. W. (1991). Transcription design principles for spoken discourse research. *Pragmatics,* 1(1), 71-106. https://doi.org/10.1075/prag.1.1.04boi

Jefferson, G. (2004). Glossary of transcript symbols with an introduction. En G. H. Lerner (Ed.), *Conversation analysis: studies from the first generation* (pp. 13-23). Filadelfia: John Benjamins. https://doi.org/10.1075/pbns.125.02jef

Lassiter, L. E. (2005). *The Chicago guide to collaborative ethnography.* Chicago: University of Chicago Press. https://doi.org/10.7208/chicago/9780226467016.001.0001

Masats, D. (2017). L'anàlisi de la conversa al servei de la recerca en el camp de l'adquisició de segones llengües (CA-for-SLA). En E. Moore y M. Dooly (Eds), *Enfoques cualitativos para la investigación en educación plurilingüe* (pp. 293-320). Research-publishing.net. https://doi.org/10.14705/rpnet.2017.emmd2016.632

Mondada, L. (2008). Using video for a sequential and multimodal analysis of social interaction: videotaping institutional telephone calls. *Forum: Qualitative Social Research, 9*(3). http://www.qualitative-research.net/index.php/fqs/article/viewArticle/1161/2566

Mondada, L. (2011). *Exigences analytiques pour l'enregistrement de la parole-en- interaction (version 3.0.2). Protocole pour les enregistrements vidéo.* Lyon: Laboratoire ICAR.

Mondada, L. (2012). The conversation analytic approach to data collection. En J. Sidnell y T. Stivers (Eds), *Handbook of conversation analysis* (pp. 32-56). Chichester, Reino Unido: Blackwell-Wiley. https://doi.org/10.1002/9781118325001.ch3

Mondada, L. (2014). *Conventions for multimodal transcription.* https://franz.unibas.ch/fileadmin/franz/user_upload/redaktion/Mondada_conv_multimodality.pdf

Mortensen, J., y Hazel, S. (2012). The data cycle. En K. Ikeda y A. Brandt (Eds), *Kansai University International Symposium: challenges and new directions in the micro-analysis of social interaction* (pp. 22-29). Osaka: Kansai University.

Nussbaum, L. (2006). La transcripción de la interacción en contextos de contacto y de aprendizaje de lenguas. In Y. Bürki y E. de Steffani (Eds), *Transcribir la lengua: de la filología al análisis de la conversación* (pp. 195-218). Bern: Peter Lang.

Nussbaum, L. (2017). Investigar con docentes. En E. Moore y M. Dooly (Eds), *Enfoques cualitativos para la investigación en educación plurilingüe* (pp. 23-45). Research-publishing.net. https://doi.org/10.14705/rpnet.2017.emmd2016.620

Payrató, L. (1995). La transcripción del discurso coloquial. In L. Cortés (Ed.), *El español coloquial* (pp. 45-70). Almería: Universidad de Almería.

Silverman, D. (2003). *Doing qualitative research: a practical handbook.* Londres, Thousand Oaks, Nueva Delhi: SAGE Publications.

Ten Have, P. (2007). *Doing conversation analysis: a practical guide*. Londres: Sage.

Unamuno, V., y Patiño, A. (2017). Producir conocimiento sobre el plurilingüismo junto a jóvenes estudiantes: un reto para la etnografía en colaboración. En E. Moore y M. Dooly (Eds), *Enfoques cualitativos para la investigación en educación plurilingüe* (pp. 107-128). Research-publishing.net. https://doi.org/10.14705/rpnet.2017.emmd2016.624

Lecturas recomendadas

Antaki, C., Billig, M., Edwards, D., y Potter, J. (2003). Discourse analysis means doing analysis: a critique of six analytic shortcomings. *Discourse analysis online*. http://extra.shu.ac.uk/daol/articles/v1/n1/a1/antaki2002002-paper.html

Copland, F., y Creese, A. (2015). *Linguistic ethnography: collecting, analysing and presenting data*. Londres: Sage. https://doi.org/10.4135/9781473910607

Mondada, L. (2012). The conversation analytic approach to data collection. En J. Sidnell y T. Stivers (Eds), *Handbook of conversation analysis* (pp. 32-56). Chichester, Reino Unido: Blackwell-Wiley. https://doi.org/10.1002/9781118325001.ch3

Mortensen, J., y Hazel, S. (2012). The data cycle. En K. Ikeda y A. Brandt (Eds), *Kansai University International Symposium: challenges and new directions in the micro-analysis of social interaction* (pp. 22-29). Osaka: Kansai University.

Psathas, G. (1995). *Conversation analysis: the study of talk-in-interaction*. California: Sage. https://doi.org/10.4135/9781412983792

Ten Have, P. (2007). *Doing conversation analysis: a practical guide*. Londres: Sage.

Páginas web con recursos mencionados

Programas para transcribir

Programa y manual de CLAN (Windows y Mac, gratuito): http://childes.psy.cmu.edu/
Programa y manual de ELAN (Windows y Mac, gratuito): https://tla.mpi.nl/tools/tla-tools/elan/
Praat (para análisis fonéticos): http://www.fon.hum.uva.nl/praat/
Programa y manual de Transana (Windows y Mac, unos 60 EUR): http://www.transana.org/

Tutoriales en línea (transcripciones, análisis multimodales, etc.)

Antaki, C. (2002). *An introduction to conversation analysis.* http://ca-tutorials.lboro.ac.uk/sitemenu.htm

Bezemer, J., Domingo, M., Jewitt, C, y Price, S. (n.d.). *Multimodal methodologies for researching digital and data environments.* https://mode.ioe.ac.uk/training/

Moore, E. (n.d.). Tutorial for transcribing plurilingual and multimodal data. http://tutorialfortrans.blogspot.com.es/

Schegloff, E. A. (n.d.). *Transcript symbols for conversation analysis.* http://www.sscnet.ucla.edu/soc/faculty/schegloff/TranscriptionProject/index.html

Otros recursos útiles

Convenciones de transcripción ICOR: http://icar.univ-lyon2.fr/projets/corinte/bandeau_droit/convention_icor.htm

Recomendaciones de cámaras de vídeo digitales en Talk Bank: http://talkbank.org/info/dv.html

Recomendaciones de grabadoras en Talk Bank: http://talkbank.org/info/da.html

12. Collecting, organizing and analyzing multimodal data sets: the contributions of CAQDAS

Victoria Antoniadou[1]

Key concepts: multimodal data, data sampling, CAQDAS, Transana, Altas.ti, NVIVO.

1. Introduction

Reflecting the inter-connected reality of today's world, contemporary education is striving to keep up with the exponentially rapid changes that individuals around the globe are facing. Innovative educational proposals carry labels such as connective learning (Downes, 2006), e-learning 2.0 (Downes, 2005), education 2.0 (Carr et al., 2008), or social learning 2.0 (Dron & Anderson, 2007). Such transformations embody new theoretical premises which postulate that human learning and development are prompted in interaction and distributed across people, tools, time and space (Mercer, 2000, 2004; Mercer & Howe, 2012). Researchers should try to investigate learning processes holistically in order to fully understand the complexity of socially-distributed learning processes (Sfard, 1998). A holistic approach to research in teaching and learning seeks to capture and document learning 'in the making' (Barab, Hay, & Yagamata-Lynch, 2001) and the relationship between processes and outcomes that cross modes and modalities (Antoniadou, 2011, 2013; Dooly, 2011).

Along these lines, this chapter defines multimodality and discusses processes involved in multimodal data collection and analysis, as well as their bearing on scientifically sound qualitative research, endeavoring to embody the aforementioned holistic approach. The term multimodality is used in this chapter

---

1. Independent scholar, Nicosia, Cyprus; vicky.antoniadou@gmail.com

How to cite this chapter: Antoniadou, V. (2017). Collecting, organizing and analyzing multimodal data sets: the contributions of CAQDAS. In E. Moore & M. Dooly (Eds), *Qualitative approaches to research on plurilingual education* (pp. 435-450). Research-publishing.net. https://doi.org/10.14705/rpnet.2017.emmd2016.640

to describe research in which interaction takes place entirely or partially online. To tackle the practicalities involved in multimodal data collection and analysis, this chapter describes software packages for efficiently managing multimodal data corpora. Concretely, the readers of this chapter will find a description of Computer-Assisted Qualitative Data Analysis Software (CAQDAS), namely the Transana, Atlas.ti, and NVIVO software packages, their main features, and ways in which they can support efficient storage, management and analysis of vast multimodal datasets. The chapter finishes with some recommendations to guide young researchers in choosing the right software package for their research purposes.

2. Defining multimodal datasets while marking collection processes and complexities

Multiple modalities refer to the diverse modes and tools people use to communicate beyond language. In education, the role that these modalities play in mediating contemporary meaning-making processes, underlying learning and cognitive development acquire particular interest.

Modalities may include image, sound, music, gestures, posture, even the use of space, which is nowadays virtual or blended. Meaning is multimodal, conveyed by image, text, interaction, sound, and music in unique and complementary ways, each adding a particular value to the whole; this added value cannot be deduced or obtained from any of the other modalities. Another example is online communication, be it synchronous or asynchronous and taking place via chat or webcam, while googling information and images in regards to the topic. Meaning, in such cases, is made through the contributions of all these modes and thus needs to be investigated holistically.

Discussing the theoretical assumptions underlying multimodal research, Bezemer and Mavers (2011) point out: (1) the complementarity of modes/resources in meaning-making processes; (2) the ways the mode frames and/or conditions interaction and meaning, which needs to be taken into account for understanding the deriving meaning-making processes; and (3) the organizing principles underlying the communication and representation in each mode. Multimodal research can shed light on the ways different modes in text and oral interaction come together to afford higher order thinking. Of interest to researchers studying multimodality are the ways the participants in the research context are making use of the symbolic and physical resources available to construct meaning, and how the use of these resources changes over time to become part of the normal cultural practice (Bezemer & Mavers, 2011).

In this light, educational researchers interested in studying multimodality are called to adjust and refine their methods and techniques in order to adequately and sufficiently represent this current reality of human-computer interaction and the intellectual benefit that stems out of it. Video recordings have been widely used in mainstream qualitative research as rich forms of representation of multimodality in classrooms and other settings; the researcher can use video to capture and discern the pedagogical value of these multiple modes in promoting meaning-making and higher order thinking (Hackling, Murcia, Ibrahim-Didi, & Hill, 2014). In mainstream ethnography, audiovisual recordings of face-to-face interactions have been primary resources, and unquestionably useful for providing "fine-grained information on the moment-to-moment conduct of people in social interaction" (Erickson, 2006, p. 177). To overcome the degree of bias associated with the presence of a camera during an interaction – known as the observer's effect (Labov, 1972) – qualitative researchers have argued that, with time, the effect of the camera and other recording devices gradually disappears, as the participants gradually come to perceive and accept the observation equipment. That is, they eventually consider the camera and audio recorders as part of the setting and not as threats, and maybe even as motivating elements (see Antoniadou, 2013; Moore & Llompart, this volume).

With the rise of virtuality and online interaction, and the increasingly multimodal research milieu, García, Standlee, Bechkoff, and Yan Cui (2009) emphasize that researchers need to refine their skills in order to be able to collect, analyze and interpret complex textual and audiovisual material. In virtual ethnography,

Chapter 12

the setting and data collection practices, e.g. participant observation, have become necessarily mediated. The researcher may no longer be physically (directly) present in the online field, but observes the happenings indirectly (García et al., 2009; see also Antoniadou & Dooly, this volume). Social media tools serve as online repositories of data and thus facilitate the data collection process (Onwuegbuzie, Leech, & Collins, 2010). The qualitative researcher/ ethnographer can download data without necessarily participating in the interactions that generated this data. On the one hand, this may mean that online data are easier to collect. Nevertheless, other considerations must be made, e.g. new ethics that may apply to online settings (see Dooly, Moore, & Vallejo, this volume), using participants as a resource in the data collection process, and finding ways of receiving and storing large data files. Collecting online data is challenging from a technological point of view. This is not a petty concern, since technological breakdowns (in the case of synchronous tele-collaboration for example) can jeopardize the process, the quality of collected data and therefore the research itself. It is also important to bear in mind that online ethnographies have tended to favor text data over audiovisual recordings that would also require transcription (García et al., 2009). Participants themselves can be of valuable help in overcoming this challenge. Instructing participants to save data, e.g. using online recorders to record synchronous video interactions, save chat interactions, along with time stamped screenshots, will ensure the quality of data collected (Antoniadou, 2013). Hackling et al. (2014) discuss the needs and challenges of comprehensive transcription methods for multimodal data, and offer examples of multimodal transcripts that include contextual information, timestamps, transcripts of discourse, and descriptions of semiotic resources such as gestures, role plays, manipulations of equipment, and images as well as short video clips. With this type of transcript, researchers can gather and examine the relationships between the multiple modes used to convey instructional content and the pedagogical value that these modes carry for intellectual development, as mentioned above.

With the vast data corpora that typically characterize qualitative and ethnographic research, it is very important to keep track of people, roles and tools in what has been called an 'audit trail' of the data collection and analytical and interpretative process. This audit trail serves to enhance dependability and confirmability of results, and transferability of methods and techniques as basis for further empirical work (Dörnyei, 2007; Lincoln & Guba, 1985; for an example see also Antoniadou & Dooly, this volume).

3. Purposeful data sampling in qualitative research involving multimodal datasets

In order to efficiently and effectively manage the data, the researcher is required to define purposeful sampling schemes for identifying and selecting focal datasets. Purposeful sampling, in qualitative research, is referred to as a technique for identifying and selecting information-rich cases in order to make the most effective use of limited resources (Patton, 2002). The criteria for this selection should align with the research objectives and be clearly stated in the methodology section of the research output (see Dörnyei, 2007 for a thorough account of how to draft purposeful sampling schemes in mixed-method research projects). Briefly, there are various strategies that can be used for purposeful data sampling in qualitative research. These strategies may involve theoretical sampling, criterion-based sampling, maximum variation sampling, snowball sampling, and sampling contrasting cases (Palinkas et al., 2013). Theoretical sampling involves finding manifestations of a theoretical construct and using them to elaborate on the construct and examine its variations. According to Patton (2001), criterion sampling involves selecting, reviewing and studying "all cases that meet some predetermined criterion of importance" (p. 238), previously set by the researcher. Purposeful sampling may also be the selection of cases of maximum variation, which, as its name denotes, serves the purpose of documenting unique or diverse variations that resulted from adapting to diverse conditions. It is useful for discerning common patterns across variations. In snowball sampling, the researcher locates and identifies cases of interest from sampling people through other people that have similar characteristics. The strategy of sampling contrasting cases involves focusing on both exemplary and deviant cases, and shedding light on the characteristics of each case (Palinkas et al., 2013; see also Antoniadou & Dooly, this volume for an application of data sampling in virtual ethnographic multiple-case study research in blended learning environments).

The following sections describe how three different types of CAQDAS can be used to manage the complexity of qualitative research and assist the analysis of multimodal data, as well as purposeful data sampling, as described above.

4. CAQDAS: tools and processes for efficiently managing qualitative research

CAQDAS, or Qualitative Data Analysis Software (QDAS), are packages of multiple tools that are designed to provide valuable practical support to an otherwise, complex, messy and time-consuming qualitative research process. These software packages enable researchers to store and code text, graphic, audio and/or video data, search content, locate and explore relationships between codes, and link visual to audio and text data.

Through CAQDAS, the researcher can store all data in one single repository so that s/he can access, at any time, the context of what s/he is focusing on in order to discover and establish meaningful relationships in the data and create themes and categories (Bazeley, 2009). Latest versions of this software also allows researchers to collaborate in real time with colleagues at geographical proximity or over distance.

The following sections present and discuss Transana, Atlas.ti, and NVIVO in order to introduce researchers into the world of CAQDAS. Transana is often preferred by qualitative researchers who want to focus on the analysis of audiovisual data (ELAN and CLAN might also serve this purpose, see Moore & Llompart, this volume). NVIVO and Atlas.ti provide additional functions; they allow researchers to organize and code the literature review, during all phases of the research pre- and post- analysis and they may also incorporate quantitative (numeric) data and take quantitative approaches to qualitative data, assisting the purposeful data sampling scheme, explained above.

These three software packages are only a few of the software packages currently available in the market, and are amongst the most popular ones used by qualitative researchers. Readers can read up on CAQDAS at: http://www.surrey.ac.uk/sociology/research/researchcentres/caqdas/support/choosing/.

4.1. The Transana software

Transana offers multimedia integration and tools for transcription and analysis of audiovisual data. It is distinguished from other software packages that tend to favor textual analysis (https://www.transana.com/).

With Transana, researchers can isolate analytically interesting portions of audio and video files (their raw data collected on-site), transcribe them and create clips, i.e. episodes of their overall data, which they can use as their analytic units. Researchers can also compare clips and codes across episodes and can assign keywords to these clips, code them, and categorize them under themes. They can also arrange them in the order that they deem appropriate to their research objectives. For better visualization, researchers can also take screenshots from these videos and add them to their analysis, including still images taken on-site. These still images can also be coded and analyzed as part of larger media files and/or standalone, and added to the final research output.

The standard version limits the analytical process to single file processing (one document/media file at a time, i.e. videos, audios, transcripts, and still images) while the professional version supports multiple-file and multiple user simultaneous analysis (supports overlapping documents during analysis e.g. 2+ transcripts, 2+ videos, 2+ audios). There is also a Transana multi-user version that enables real-time collaboration between multiple researchers, working on the same project from a distance or in physical proximity.

4.2. Atlas.ti

Atlas.ti (similarly to NVIVO below) supports large volumes of data sources in multiple formats, including websites and social media. This support of multiple formats means that researchers do not need to transform the format of their primary data, should they be word documents, PDF documents, or websites. This saves time and keeps the research practical, while the data remain intact for the analysis phase. The researchers work with primary data as they were collected from the field, without alterations in terms of format or layout. Atlas.ti tools and functions include transcription, codification of text, image, audio and video materials. Cloud views (see http://atlasti.com/product/features/) are particularly useful for visualizing most-recurrent codes and keywords and re-arranging relationships as appropriate; the codes can be arranged or re-arranged alphabetically or according to frequency, or for whatever research objective, and can then be exported to Excel.

Network views are also available, which allow the researcher to visualize relationships between codes, which, in turn, help break down complex concepts in simpler chunks of information, thus facilitating understanding and interpretation.

The researcher can then manipulate and present the relationships on the networks as s/he deems appropriate for better serving their research and objectives. Such functions facilitate analytical processes such as comparison and contrast between data sources, e.g. interview transcripts, web content and other supported formats, thus supporting interpretative processes and reporting of the findings.

Very importantly, researchers can also use Atlas.ti to organize, code and add annotations to literature reviewed prior to engaging in data analysis. They can later link literature codes and annotations to the data codes. Atlas.ti also supports geographical data from Google Earth so that researchers can connect to Google Earth from Atlas.ti, take snapshots, code them, add comments and annotations, and use them as primary research data.

4.3. NVIVO

The NVIVO database can be deployed easily and very intuitively, given its resemblance to the Word interface. Researchers can use NVIVO to process multimodal data e.g. transcribe audiovisual data, format interviews and discussion groups, download data from the Internet, create projects, import sources, and link data to external sources and analyze images. NVIVO also supports diverse formats of data i.e. text, multimedia, PDFs, images, Excel surveys, notes, websites and social media such as Facebook, LinkedIn, Twitter, YouTube videos and Survey Monkey. These documents can be stored and organized in different folders in the software itself (and not another file on the computer, which is the case in Atlas.ti).

An NVIVO project can also be linked to external information such as websites or other files saved on the computer, and used to make cross-references across documents in order to facilitate access to them, and to compare, analyze and annotate them. For example, researchers can use this software to code literature references (also provided by Atlas.ti). NVIVO query and annotation tools can be used to identify and code key themes and concepts in the literature; this way researchers can develop an analytical framework and document their own thoughts about how these themes relate to their own research. They can compare and critically evaluate the work of various authors on a specific topic and identify gaps that their research can breach. Through this process, the researchers can refine their research questions.

Researchers can use NVIVO to code and categorize data in line with the 3-cycles proposed in grounded theory methodology (Charmaz, 2006). They include free nodes (for open and verbatim coding for making sense of the setting) and tree nodes (for axial and theoretical coding for focusing research). Other facilities allow researchers to create cases. This is compatible with single and multiple case study methodology (Yin, 2003) and with assigning attributes for further classification.

Search tools are also available in order to manage large volumes of data and also frequency measures that researchers can use to locate keywords in the data and produce cloud visualizations. NVIVO models, tables and networks help researchers present an overall visualization of the research design, analysis, relationships and findings (Figure 1 and Figure 2).

Chapter 12

Figure 1. Analytical tools on the NVIVO interface (sources, nodes, cases, sets) – data from the thesis of Antoniadou (2013)

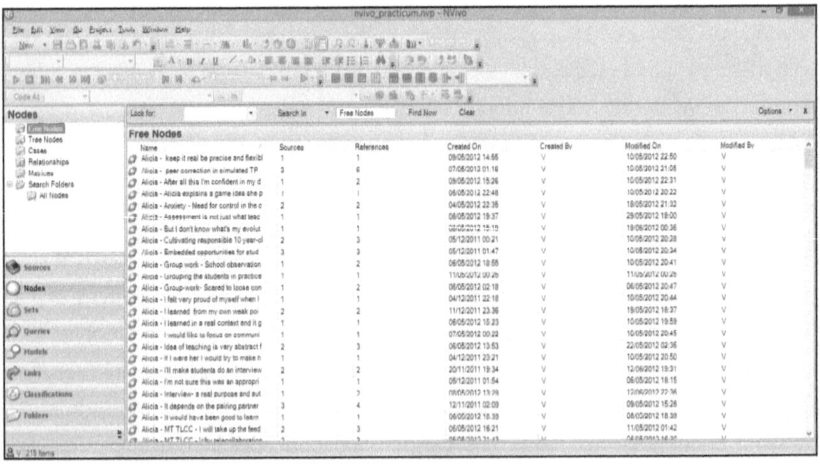

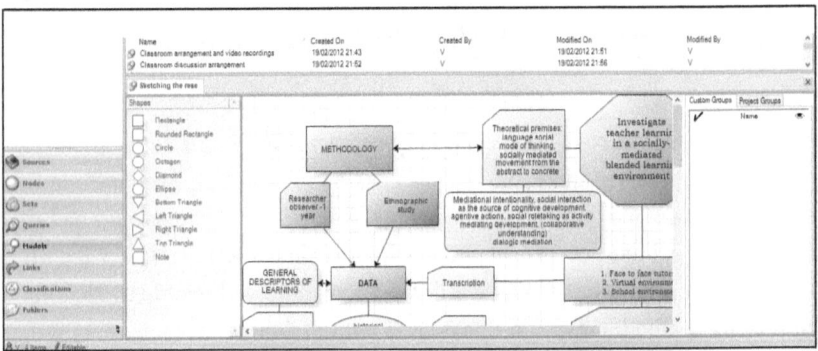

Figure 2. Models in NVIVO – data from the thesis of Antoniadou (2013)

Tools for note- and memo-taking support researchers in keeping an "audit trail" of the analytical process (Dörnyei, 2007, p. 62), allowing researchers to take notes documenting their thoughts and decisions during coding. This, in turn facilitates the interpretive process, and guides researchers into creating a storyline of the experience (Charmaz, 2006; Glaser & Strauss, 1967; Lincoln & Guba, 1985).

5. Selection criteria for choosing the right package for you and your research

Weitzman (2000, pp. 810-815) proposes that the researcher answer the following questions when in the process of choosing software packages: (1) What kind of computer user am I?, (2) Am I choosing for one project or for numerous projects over the next few years?, (3) What kind of project(s) and database(s) will I be working on?, and (4) What kinds of analyses am I planning to do?

Evidently, the choice of software will primarily depend on the research project, the type and format of data used, objectives and ambitions and to the extent to which the software package can efficiently address them. At the same time, selection criteria may adhere to subjective criteria such as software price and research budget, on-campus accessibility of software, available training for each software package, or mere individual preference. For packages that offer similar tools, facilitate comparable tasks and account for similar results such as the NVIVO and Atlas.ti, the choice might come down to a matter of personal preference and the interface the researchers find themselves more comfortable with.

The amount of collaboration required in order to effectively carry out the project's objectives would also be a factor to consider. Standard and professional versions are available for each software package. There are also versions that do or do not support collaboration between multiple users and can therefore be used by individuals or by teams. These functionalities carry significant price differences.

Either way, it is essential for the researchers to receive training in order to take full advantage of the affordances of the software. Researchers can find their way through the above-mentioned software packages using freely available online resources such as tutorials, video manuals and forum discussions. There are also formal workshops that offer tours around the features and affordances of each of these software packages, as well as hands-on experience under the guidance of expert researchers.

6. Data analysis: transcription conventions

As a final note, when audiovisual data is included in an online ethnography, the transcription of that data should be based on a transcription key (see Moore & Llompart, this volume), examples of which can be found in books or online (Agha & Wortham, 2005; Hutchby & Wooffitt, 2008; Sacks, Schegloff, & Jefferson, 1974).

7. Other considerations

The era of increased inter-connectedness and media convergence calls for qualitative research that draws from multiple and diverse data sources in order to accurately investigate and represent reality. CAQDAS help to efficiently manage large volumes of multimodal data timely and effectively. Authors highlight that modern CAQDAS allow not only an easy access but also a systematic exploration of the corpus, and, very importantly, a tidy printable output of coded data to facilitate interpretation. Nevertheless, and this has been multiply and repeatedly highlighted, the computer cannot replace the human mind in detecting and interpreting meanings and relationships in the data.

It is also very important to keep in mind that the package itself might pose limitations to researchers' plans and ambitions (García-Horta & Guerra-Ramos, 2008). It is useful for researchers to remain aware of these constraints throughout the research, and to detect and document them in their written project. Good old traditional paper can still be a useful support tool during computer-assisted data analysis. Keeping and referring back to supporting tools such as the research questions or keywords of the research being conducted, written down on paper and kept on the side throughout the process of codification and analysis, will help researchers/analysts to maintain focus on the aims and objectives of the research, which can easily get lost in large-scale, multimodal research projects.

Last but not least, training for the skills needed to design qualitative investigations and take advantage of the analytical possibilities of qualitative software packages is highly recommended. Researchers may find that a literature review of the philosophical, epistemological and methodological traditions prior to embarking on research (Guba & Lincoln, 1994), as well as specific case studies in education, can also lend valuable support to their methodological decisions (see for example Antoniadou & Dooly, this volume).

Works cited

Agha, A., & Wortham, S. (2005). Discourse across speech-events: intertextuality and interdiscursivity in social life. *Special Issue of the Journal of Linguistic Anthropology*, 15(1).

Antoniadou, V. (2011). Virtual collaboration, perezhivanie and teacher learning: a socio-cultural-historical perspective. *Bellaterra Journal of Teaching & Learning Language & Literature*, 4(3), 53-70.

Antoniadou, V. (2013). *Expanding the socio-material spaces of teacher education programmes: a qualitative trace of teacher professionalization through blended pedagogy in Catalonia*. Unpublished PhD dissertation. Universitat Autònoma de Barcelona.

Antoniadou, V., & Dooly, M. (2017). Educational ethnography in blended learning environments. In E. Moore & M. Dooly (Eds), *Qualitative approaches to research on plurilingual education* (pp. 237-263). Research-publishing.net. https://doi.org/10.14705/rpnet.2017.emmd2016.630

Barab, S. A, Hay, K. E., & Yagamata-Lynch, L. C. (2001). Constructing networks of action relevant episodes: an in-situ research methodology. *The Journal of the Learning Sciences*, 10 (1&2), 63-112. https://doi.org/10.1207/S15327809JLS10-1-2_5

Bazeley, P. (2009). Integrating data analysis in mixed methods research. *Journal of Mixed Methods Research*, 3(3), 203-207.

Bezemer, J., & Mavers, D. (2011). Multimodal transcription as academic practice. *International Journal of Social Research Methodology*, 14(3), 191-206. https://doi.org/10.1080/13645 579.2011.563616

Carr, D., Crook, C., Noss, R., Carmichael, P., & Selwyn, N. (2008). *Education 2.0? Designing the web for teaching and learning: a commentary by the technology enhanced learning phase of the teaching and learning research programme*. London: Teaching and Learning Research Programme, Institute of Education, University of london.

Charmaz, K. (2006). *Constructing grounded theory: a practical guide through qualitative analysis*. London: Sage.

Dooly, M. (2011). Divergent perceptions of telecollaborative language learning tasks: task-as-workplan vs. task-as-process. *Language Learning & Technology*, 15(2), 69-91.

Dooly, M., Moore, E., & Vallejo, C. (2017). Research ethics. In E. Moore & M. Dooly (Eds), *Qualitative approaches to research on plurilingual education* (pp. 351-362). Research-publishing.net. https://doi.org/10.14705/rpnet.2017.emmd2016.634

Dörnyei, Z. (2007). *Research methods in applied linguistics: quantitative qualitative and mixed methodologies*. Oxford: Oxford University Press.

Downes, S. (2005). *E-Learning 2.0*. https://doi.org/10.19173/irrodl.v6i2.284

Downes, S. (2006). *Learning networks and connective knowledge*. http://philpapers.org/archive/DOWLNA.1.pdf

Dron, J., & Anderson, T. (2007). Collectives, networks and groups in social software for e-learning. In T. T. Bastiaens & S. Carliner (Eds), *Proceedings of world conference on e-learning in corporate, government, healthcare, and higher education* (pp. 2460-2467). Chesapeake, VA: Association for the Advancement of Computing in Education (AACE).

Erickson, F. (2006). Definition and analysis of data from videotape: some research procedures and their rationales. In J. L. Green, G. Camilli, P. B. Elmore, A. Skukauskaiti & E. Grace (Eds), *Handbook of complementary methods in education research* (pp. 177-192). American Education Research Association: Lawrence Erlbaum.

García, A. C., Standlee, A. I., Bechkoff, J., & Yan Cui. (2009). Ethnographic approaches to the Internet and computer-mediated communication. *Journal of Contemporary Ethnography*, 38(1), 52-84. https://doi.org/10.1177/0891241607310839

García-Horta, J. B., & Guerra-Ramos, M. T. (2008). The use of CAQDAS in educational research: some advantages, limitations and potential risks. *International Journal of Research & Method in Education*, 32(2), 151-165. https://doi.org/10.1080/17437270902946686

Glaser, B., & Strauss, A. (1967). *The discovery of grounded theory: strategies for qualitative research*. Chicago: Aldine.

Guba, E. G., & Lincoln, Y. S. (1994). Competing paradigms in qualitative research. In N. Denzin & Y. Lincoln (Eds), *Handbook of qualitative research* (pp. 105-117). Thousand Oaks/London/New Delhi: Sage.

Hackling, M., Murcia, K., Ibrahim-Didi, K., & Hill, S. (2014). *Methods for multimodal analysis and representation of teaching-learning interactions in primary science lessons captured on video*. https://www.esera.org/media/esera2013/Mark_Hackling_04Feb2014.pdf

Hutchby, I., & Wooffitt, R. (2008). *Conversation analysis* (2nd ed.). Chichester, U.K.: Polity Press.

Labov, W. (1972). *Sociolinguistic patterns*. Oxford: Blackwell.

Lincoln, Y. S., & Guba, E. G. (1985). *Naturalistic inquiry*. Thousand Oaks/London/New Delhi: Sage.

Mercer, N. (2000). *Words & Minds: how we use language to think together*. London/New York: Routledge. https://doi.org/10.4324/9780203464984

Mercer, N. (2004). Sociocultural discourse analysis: analysing classroom talk as a social mode of thinking. *Journal of Applied Linguistics*, 1(2), 137-168. https://doi.org/10.1558/japl.2004.1.2.137

Mercer, N., & Howe, C. (2012). Explaining the dialogic processes of teaching and learning: the value and potential of sociocultural theory. *Learning, Culture and Social Interaction*, 1(1), 12-21. https://doi.org/10.1016/j.lcsi.2012.03.001

Moore, E., & Llompart, J. (2017). Collecting, transcribing, analyzing and presenting plurilingual interactional data. In E. Moore & M. Dooly (Eds), *Qualitative approaches to research on plurilingual education* (pp. 403-417). Research-publishing.net. https://doi.org/10.14705/rpnet.2017.emmd2016.638

Onwuegbuzie, A., Leech, N., & Collins, K. M. (2010). Innovative data collection strategies in qualitative research. *Qualitative Report*, 15(3), 696-726.

Palinkas, L. A., Horwitz, S. M., Green, C. A., Wisdom, J. P., Duan, N., & Hoagwood, K. (2013). Purposeful sampling for qualitative data collection and analysis in mixed method implementation research. *Administration and Policy in Mental Health and Mental Health Services Research*, 42(5), 533-544. https://doi.org/10.1007/s10488-013-0528-y

Patton, M. Q. (2001). *Qualitative research and evaluation methods* (2nd Ed.). Thousand Oaks, CA: Sage Publications.

Patton, M. Q. (2002). *Qualitative research and evaluation methods* (3rd ed.). Thousand Oaks, CA: Sage.

Sacks, H., Schegloff, E. A., & Jefferson, G. (1974). A simplest systematics for the organization of turn-taking for conversation. *Language*, 50(4), 696-735. https://doi.org/10.1353/lan.1974.0010

Sfard, A. (1998). On two metaphors for learning and the dangers of choosing just one. *Educational Researcher*, 27(2), 4-13. https://doi.org/10.3102/0013189X027002004

Weitzman, E. (2000). Software and qualitative research. In N. K. Denzin & Y. S. Lincoln (Eds), *Handbook of qualitative research* (2nd ed.) (pp. 803-820). Thousand Oaks/London/New Delhi: Sage.

Yin, R. K. (2003). *Case study research: design and methods* (3rd ed.). Thousand Oaks/London/New Delhi: Sage.

Recommended reading

Bazeley, P. (2009). Integrating data analysis in mixed methods research. *Journal of Mixed Methods Research, 3*(3), 203-207. https://doi.org/10.1177/1558689809334443

Charmaz, K. (2006). Constructing grounded theory: a practical guide through qualitative analysis (1st ed.). London: Sage.

Dörnyei, Z. (2007). *Research methods in applied linguistics: quantitative, qualitative and mixed methodologies*. Oxford: Oxford University Press.

Saldaña, J. (2009). *The coding manual for qualitative researchers*. London: Sage.

Websites with resources mentioned

Altas.ti (Windows, Mac, iPad, Android, need to purchase a license, free trial available): http://atlasti.com/

NVIVO (Windows and Mac, need to purchase a license, free trial available): http://www.qsrinternational.com/

Transana (Windows and Mac, need to purchase a license, free trial available): http://www.transana.org/

12. Recoger, organizar y analizar corpus de datos multimodales: las contribuciones de los CAQDAS

Victoria Antoniadou[1]

Conceptos clave: datos multimodales, muestreo intencional, CAQDAS, Transana, Altas.ti, NVIVO.

1. Introducción

Reflejando la realidad interconectada del mundo de hoy, la educación contemporánea está esforzándose por estar al día de los cambios exponencialmente rápidos con los que las personas en todo el mundo se enfrentan. Las propuestas educativas innovadoras llevan etiquetas como aprendizaje conectivista (Downes, 2006), e-learning 2.0 (Downes, 2005), aprendizaje 2.0 (Carr et al., 2008), o aprendizaje social 2.0 (Dron y Anderson, 2007). Estas transformaciones encarnan las premisas teóricas que entienden que el aprendizaje y el desarrollo humanos se impulsan en la interacción y se distribuyen a través de las personas, las herramientas, el tiempo y el espacio (Mercer, 2000, 2004; Mercer y Howe, 2012). Las personas investigadoras deben proponerse estudiar el aprendizaje de manera holística para comprender plenamente la complejidad del aprendizaje distribuido socialmente (Sfard, 1998). Un enfoque holístico pretende captar y documentar el aprendizaje en proceso (Barab, Hay, y Yagamata-Lynch, 2001) y la relación entre los procesos y los resultados que combinan modos y modalidades (Antoniadou, 2011, 2013; Dooly, 2011).

---

1. Investigadora independiente, Nicosia, Chipre; vicky.antoniadou@gmail.com

Para citar este capítulo: Antoniadou, V. (2017). Recoger, organizar y analizar corpus de datos multimodales: las contribuciones de los CAQDAS. En E. Moore y M. Dooly (Eds), *Enfoques cualitativos para la investigación en educación plurilingüe* (pp. 451-467). Research-publishing.net. https://doi.org/10.14705/rpnet.2017.emmd2016.641

Capítulo 12

En este sentido, este capítulo define la multimodalidad y analiza los procesos involucrados en la recolección y análisis de datos multimodales, así como su relación con la investigación cualitativa científicamente sólida, que incorpora el enfoque holístico antes mencionado. El término 'multimodalidad' se utiliza en este capítulo para describir la investigación en la que la interacción tiene lugar total o parcialmente en línea. Para abordar los aspectos prácticos de la recopilación y el análisis de datos multimodales, en el capítulo se describen los paquetes de software para la gestión eficiente de los corpus de datos multimodales. Concretamente, en este capítulo se describirán algunos CAQDAS (software de análisis de datos cualitativos) –Transana, Atlas.ti y NVIVO–, sus principales características y cómo pueden ayudar en el almacenamiento, la gestión y el análisis eficientes de grandes corpus de datos multimodales. El capítulo termina con algunas recomendaciones para guiar a quienes se inician en el campo de la investigación a elegir el paquete de software adecuado para sus propósitos de investigación.

2. Definir los corpus de datos multimodales, y señalar los procesos de recolección de datos y sus problemas

Las modalidades múltiples hacen referencia a las diversas vías y herramientas que las personas usan para comunicarse, más allá del lenguaje. En educación, es de especial interés el papel que desempeñan estas modalidades en la mediación de los procesos de creación de significado contemporáneos, el aprendizaje subyacente y el desarrollo cognitivo.

Las modalidades pueden incluir imágenes, sonido, música, gestos, posturas, e incluso el uso del espacio, que hoy en día puede ser virtual o mixto. El significado es multimodal, se transmite a través de la imagen, el texto, la interacción, el sonido, la música, de maneras únicas y complementarias, y cada una agrega un valor particular al todo. Este valor añadido no puede deducirse ni obtenerse a través de ninguna de las otras modalidades. Un ejemplo es la comunicación en línea, ya sea sincrónica o asincrónica, que tiene lugar a través de chat o webcam, mientras se buscan en Google imágenes y otra información en relación con el tema. El significado, en tales casos, se construye a través de las contribuciones de todos estos modos y, por lo tanto, debe investigarse holísticamente.

Al discutir los supuestos teóricos subyacentes a la investigación multimodal, Bezemer y Mavers (2011) señalan: (1) la complementariedad de los modos/recursos en los procesos de creación de significado; (2) las formas en las que el modo enmarca y/o condiciona la interacción y el significado, que deben tenerse en cuenta para comprender los procesos derivados del significado y (3) los principios organizativos subyacentes a la comunicación y representación en cada modo. La investigación multimodal puede ayudar a comprender las formas en las que los diferentes modos se unen en el texto y la interacción oral para permitir un pensamiento más complejo. Pueden resultar interesantes las formas en las que los participantes en el contexto de la investigación usan los recursos simbólicos y físicos disponibles para construir significado o cómo el uso de estos recursos cambia con el tiempo para convertirse en parte de la práctica cultural normal (Bezemer y Mavers, 2011).

En este sentido, los investigadores educativos interesados en estudiar la multimodalidad deben ajustar y refinar sus métodos y técnicas para representar de forma adecuada y suficiente esta realidad actual de la interacción entre las personas y los ordenador, y el beneficio intelectual que se deriva de ella. Las grabaciones de vídeo se han utilizado ampliamente en la investigación cualitativa tradicional, como formas ricas de representación de la multimodalidad en el aula y otros entornos. Las personas investigadoras pueden usar el vídeo para capturar y discernir el valor pedagógico de varios modos para promover la creación de sentido y el pensamiento más complejo (Hackling, Murcia, Ibrahim-Didi, y Hill, 2014). La tendencia general en la etnografía es usar las grabaciones audiovisuales de las interacciones cara a cara como recursos primarios e incuestionablemente útiles para proporcionar "fine-grained information on the moment-to-moment conduct of people in social interaction" (Erickson, 2006, p. 177)[2]. En relación

---

2. "información detallada sobre la conducta a cada instante de las personas en la interacción social".

Capítulo 12

con el grado de influencia asociado a la presencia de una cámara durante una interacción –conocido como la paradoja del observador (Labov, 1972)– se ha argumentado que, con el tiempo, el efecto de la cámara y otros dispositivos de grabación gradualmente desaparecen; los participantes acaban aceptando el equipo de observación. Es decir, acaban considerando la cámara y las grabadoras de audio como parte del escenario y no como amenazas, y tal vez como aspectos motivadores de la experiencia (véanse Antoniadou, 2013; Moore y Llompart, en este volumen).

Con el auge de la virtualidad y la interacción en línea, y teniendo en cuenta que el campo de investigación es cada vez más multimodal, García, Standlee, Bechkoff, y Yan Cui (2009) destacan que las personas investigadoras necesitan afinar sus habilidades para poder recopilar, analizar e interpretar material textual y audiovisual complejo. En la etnografía virtual, el escenario y las prácticas de recogida de datos (por ejemplo, la observación participante) deben ser necesariamente mediados. La persona investigadora puede no estar físicamente (directamente) presente en el campo en línea, pero puede observar los sucesos indirectamente (García et al., 2009; véanse también Antoniadou y Dooly, en este volumen). Las herramientas de los medios sociales sirven como repositorios en línea de datos y facilitan el proceso de recopilación de datos (Onwuegbuzie, Leech, y Collins, 2010). Es posible descargar datos sin participar necesariamente en las interacciones que los generan. Por un lado, esto puede significar que los datos en línea son más fáciles de recopilar. Por otro lado, deben tenerse en cuenta otras consideraciones; por ejemplo, que se pueden aplicar nuevas consideraciones éticas a los contextos en línea (véanse Dooly, Moore, y Vallejo, en este volumen), que se pueden usar a los participantes como un recurso en el proceso de recolección de datos, y que se deben encontrar maneras de recibir y almacenar archivos de datos grandes. La recopilación de datos en línea es un desafío desde el punto de vista tecnológico. Esto no es una preocupación menor, ya que los problemas tecnológicos (en el caso de la telecolaboración síncrona, por ejemplo) pueden poner en peligro el proceso, la calidad de los datos recopilados y, por lo tanto, la propia investigación. También es importante tener en cuenta que las etnografías en línea normalmente han favorecido los datos de texto sobre las grabaciones audiovisuales, que también requieren transcripción (García et al., 2009). Los propios participantes pueden ser un elemento clave para ayudarnos a superar este desafío. Se puede pedir a los participantes colaboración para guardar datos; por ejemplo, si graban sus interacciones de vídeo sincrónicas, guardan sus interacciones de chat, junto con capturas de pantalla con la hora, etc., esto nos garantizará la calidad de los datos recogidos (Antoniadou, 2013). Hackling et al. (2014) se plantean las necesidades y retos de los métodos de transcripción para los datos multimodales y ofrecen ejemplos de transcripciones multimodales que incluyen información contextual, marcas de tiempo, transcripciones del discurso, y descripciones de recursos semióticos como gestos, juegos de rol, manipulaciones de equipos, imágenes, así como clips de vídeo cortos. Con este tipo de transcripción, las personas investigadoras pueden recoger y examinar las relaciones entre los múltiples modos utilizados para transmitir el contenido académico y el valor didáctico que estos modos tienen para el desarrollo cognitivo, como se mencionó anteriormente.

Con los corpus de datos grandes, típicos de la investigación cualitativa y la etnográfica, es muy importante hacer un seguimiento de las personas, los roles y las herramientas, lo que se llama un 'registro de auditoría' del proceso de recogida de datos, análisis e interpretación. Este registro de auditoría sirve para mejorar la fiabilidad y la confirmación de los resultados, y la transferibilidad de los métodos y técnicas como base para trabajos empíricos adicionales (Dörnyei, 2007; Lincoln y Guba, 1985; véanse también Antoniadou y Dooly, este volumen).

3. El muestreo intencional en la investigación cualitativa con datos multimodales

Con el fin de administrar los datos de manera eficiente y eficaz, la persona investigadora está obligada a definir esquemas de muestreo para identificar y seleccionar conjuntos de datos focales. El muestreo intencional, en la investigación cualitativa, es una técnica para identificar y seleccionar casos con información rica para usar de forma efectiva unos recursos limitados (Patton, 2002). Los criterios para esta selección deben ajustarse a los objetivos de la investigación y explicarse claramente en la sección de metodología de los trabajos de investigación (véase Dörnyei, 2007 para una explicación exhaustiva sobre cómo crear esquemas de muestreo intencional en proyectos de investigación con métodos mixtos). En pocas palabras, existen varias estrategias que pueden utilizarse para el muestreo de datos en la investigación cualitativa; estas estrategias pueden incluir el muestreo teórico, muestreo basado en criterios, muestreo de variación máxima, muestreo de bola de nieve y muestreo de casos contrastantes (Palinkas et al., 2013). El muestreo teórico implica encontrar manifestaciones de un constructo teórico y utilizarlas para elaborar el constructo y examinar sus variaciones. Según Patton (2001, p. 238), el muestreo basado en criterios consiste en seleccionar casos que cumplan o no un criterio importante predeterminado, establecido por el investigador. El muestreo intencional también puede consistir en la selección de casos de variación máxima que, como su nombre indica, sirven para documentar variaciones únicas o diversas que resultaron de la adaptación a diversas condiciones. Es útil para discernir patrones comunes a través de variaciones. En el muestreo de la bola de nieve, la persona investigadora localiza e identifica los casos de interés a través de otras personas con características similares. La estrategia de muestreo de casos contrastantes se centra tanto en los casos ejemplares como en los que se desvían de la norma, para destacar las características de cada caso (Palinkas et al., 2013; véanse también Antoniadou y Dooly, en este volumen para una aplicación de muestreo de datos).

Las siguientes secciones describen cómo pueden usarse tres tipos diferentes de software de análisis de datos cualitativos asistido por ordenador (CAQDAS[3]) para gestionar la complejidad de la investigación cualitativa y como estos programas ayudan en el análisis de datos multimodales y el muestreo intencional de datos descrito anteriormente.

---

3. Computer-Assisted Qualitative Data Analysis Software

4. CAQDAS: herramientas y procesos para gestionar la investigación cualitativa

Los CAQDAS o QDAS[4] (software de análisis de datos cualitativos) son paquetes con múltiples herramientas diseñadas para proporcionar apoyo práctico a un proceso de investigación cualitativa que, de otra manera, es un proceso complejo, desordenado y que consume mucho tiempo. Estos paquetes de software permiten: almacenar y codificar datos de texto, gráficos, de audio y/o vídeo; buscar contenido; localizar y explorar relaciones entre códigos y vincular visualmente datos de audio y texto.

Con el CAQDAS, la persona investigadora puede almacenar todos los datos en un solo repositorio para acceder al contexto de lo que le interesa en cualquier momento y, así, descubrir y establecer relaciones significativas en los datos para crear temas y categorías (Bazeley, 2009). Las últimas versiones de estos programas también permiten que las personas investigadoras colaboren en tiempo real con colegas que trabajen cerca o a distancia.

Las siguientes secciones presentan y discuten Transana, Atlas.ti y NVIVO con el fin de ofrecer una introducción al mundo de los CAQDAS. Transana es, a menudo, la opción preferida de las personas que quieren centrarse en el análisis de datos audiovisuales (ELAN y CLAN también podrían usarse con este propósito, véanse Moore y Llompart, en este volumen). NVIVO y Atlas.ti proporcionan funciones adicionales; permiten organizar y codificar la bibliografía, durante todas las fases de la investigación, antes y después del análisis, y también permiten incorporar datos cuantitativos (numéricos) y dar enfoques cuantitativos a los datos cualitativos. Estos tres paquetes de software son sólo algunos de los que están disponibles actualmente en el mercado, y son algunos de los más populares entre los investigadores cualitativos. Se puede encontrar más información sobre los CAQDAS en: http://www.surrey.ac.uk/sociology/research/researchcentres/caqdas/support/choosing/.

---

4. Qualitative Data Analysis Software

Capítulo 12

4.1. El software Transana

Transana ofrece integración multimedia y herramientas para transcribir y analizar datos audiovisuales. Se distingue de otros paquetes de software que tienden a favorecer el análisis textual (https://www.transana.com/).

Con Transana, las personas investigadoras pueden aislar trozos de archivos de audio y vídeo que resulten analíticamente interesantes (sus datos en bruto recolectados en el sitio), transcribirlos y crear clips; es decir, episodios con sus datos generales, que pueden usar como unidades analíticas. También pueden comparar clips y códigos a través de episodios y les pueden asignar palabras clave, codificarlos y categorizarlos por temas. Otra opción que ofrece este software es organizar los clips en el orden que se considere adecuado de acuerdo con los objetivos de investigación. Para una mejor visualización, existe la opción de tomar capturas de pantalla de estos vídeos y añadirlos al análisis, incluyendo imágenes fijas tomadas en el sitio. Estas imágenes fijas también se pueden codificar y analizar como parte de archivos multimedia más grandes y/o independientes, y agregarlos a los resultados finales de la investigación.

La versión estándar limita el proceso analítico y sólo permite procesar un archivo (un documento/archivo multimedia a la vez; es decir, videos, audios, transcripciones, transcripción de imágenes fijas), mientras que la versión profesional admite trabajar con múltiples archivos y que varias personas los analicen simultáneamente (permite la superposición de documentos por ejemplo, 2+ transcripciones, 2+ videos, 2+ audios). También hay una versión multiusuario de Transana, que permite la colaboración en tiempo real entre múltiples personas, que trabajan en el mismo proyecto a distancia o en proximidad física.

4.2. Atlas.ti

Atlas.ti (de forma similar a NVIVO, explicado a continuación) soporta grandes volúmenes de fuentes de datos en múltiples formatos, incluyendo sitios web y medios sociales. El hecho de poder usar varios formatos significa que no se necesita cambiar el formato de los datos primarios, si son documentos de Word, documentos PDF o sitios web. Esto ahorra tiempo y facilita la investigación, al mismo tiempo que los datos permanecen intactos para la fase de análisis. Se trabaja con datos primarios como se recogieron en el trabajo de campo, sin alteraciones en términos de formato o diseño. Las herramientas y funciones de Atlas.ti incluyen la transcripción, la codificación de textos, las imágenes, los materiales de audio y vídeo. Las vistas en nube (véase http://atlasti.com/product/features/) son especialmente útiles para visualizar los códigos y palabras clave más recurrentes, y reorganizar relaciones según convenga. Los códigos pueden ordenarse o reordenarse alfabéticamente o según la frecuencia, o según cualquier objetivo de investigación, y pueden exportarse a Excel.

También se dispone de vistas de red, que permiten ver las relaciones entre los códigos. Esto ayuda a dividir conceptos complejos en partes más simples de información, facilitando así la comprensión y la interpretación.

La persona investigadora puede manipular y presentar las relaciones en las redes que considere apropiadas para mejorar sus objetivos de investigación. Estas funciones facilitan procesos analíticos como la comparación y el contraste entre fuentes de datos, por ejemplo, transcripciones de entrevistas, contenido web y otros formatos soportados, y facilita los procesos interpretativos e informes de los hallazgos.

Una de las características más relevantes de Atlas.ti es que permite organizar, codificar y agregar anotaciones a la bibliografía revisada antes de empezar el análisis de datos. Posteriormente, se pueden vincular los códigos de la bibliografía y las anotaciones con los códigos de datos. Atlas.ti también admite datos geográficos de Google Earth para que las personas investigadoras puedan conectarse a Google Earth desde el mismo software, tomar capturas de pantallas, codificarlas, agregar comentarios y anotaciones, y utilizarlas como datos de investigación primarios.

4.3. NVIVO

La base de datos NVIVO se puede usar fácilmente y de forma muy intuitiva, ya que se parece a la interfaz del Word. Se puede utilizar NVIVO para procesar datos multimodales; por ejemplo, transcribir datos audiovisuales, dar formato a entrevistas y grupos de discusión, descargar datos de Internet, crear proyectos, importar fuentes, vincular datos a fuentes externas y analizar imágenes. NVIVO también puede usarse con diversos formatos de datos, como texto; multimedia; PDF; imágenes; encuestas de Excel; notas; sitios web y redes sociales, como Facebook, LinkedIn, Twitter, vídeos de YouTube y Survey Monkey. Estos documentos pueden almacenarse y organizarse en diferentes carpetas en el propio software (y no en otro archivo del ordenador, como ocurre en Atlas.ti).

Un proyecto NVIVO también se puede vincular a información externa, como sitios web u otros archivos guardados en el equipo, y se puede utilizar para hacer referencias cruzadas entre documentos con el fin de facilitar el acceso y comparar los documentos, analizarlos y anotarlos. Por ejemplo, este software permite codificar referencias bibliográficas (opción también disponible por Atlas.ti). Las herramientas de consulta y anotación de NVIVO pueden usarse para identificar y codificar temas y conceptos clave en la bibliografía; de esta manera, las personas investigadoras pueden desarrollar un marco analítico y documentar sus propias reflexiones sobre cómo se relacionan estos temas con su propia investigación. Pueden comparar y evaluar críticamente el trabajo de varios autores sobre un tema específico e identificar aspectos en los que falta información, que su investigación puede cumplimentar. A través de este proceso, se pueden refinar las preguntas de investigación.

Puede usarse NVIVO para codificar y categorizar datos de acuerdo con los tres ciclos que propone la metodología del muestreo teórico y la teoría fundamentada (Charmaz, 2006). Incluyen nodos libres (para la codificación abierta y textual para dar sentido a la configuración) y nodos de árbol (para la codificación axial y teórica para la investigación). Otros servicios permiten crear casos. Esto es compatible con una metodología de estudio de caso único y múltiple (Yin, 2003), y con la asignación de atributos para una clasificación posterior.

Las herramientas de búsqueda también pueden gestionar grandes volúmenes de datos y medir frecuencias para que se puedan localizar palabras clave en los datos y producir visualizaciones en forma de nube. Los modelos, tablas y redes NVIVO ayudan a presentar una visualización general del diseño, análisis, relaciones y hallazgos de la investigación (Figura 1 y Figura 2).

Las herramientas para tomar de notas ayudan a mantener un 'registro de auditoría' del proceso analítico (Dörnyei, 2007, p. 62), y documentar los pensamientos y decisiones tomadas durante la codificación. Esto, a su vez, facilita el proceso interpretativo y orienta a las personas investigadoras al crear una historia de la experiencia (Charmaz, 2006; Glaser y Strauss, 1967; Lincoln y Guba, 1985).

Figura 1. Herramientas analíticas en la interfaz NVIVO (redes, nodos, casos, conjuntos) – datos de la tesis de Antoniadou (2013)

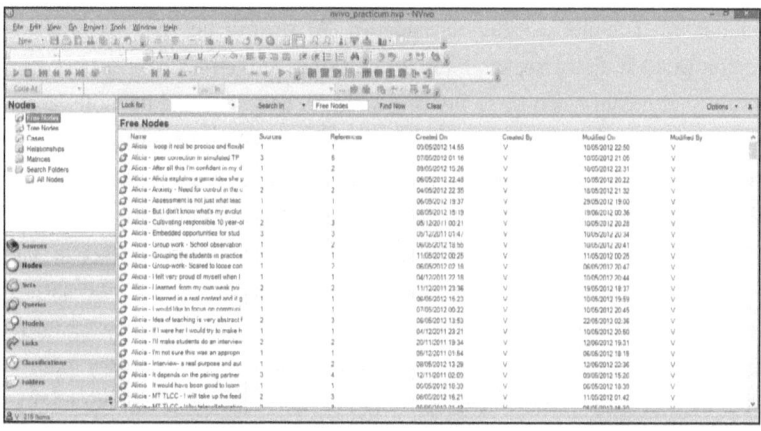

Figura 2. Modelos en NVIVO – datos de la tesis de Antoniadou (2013)

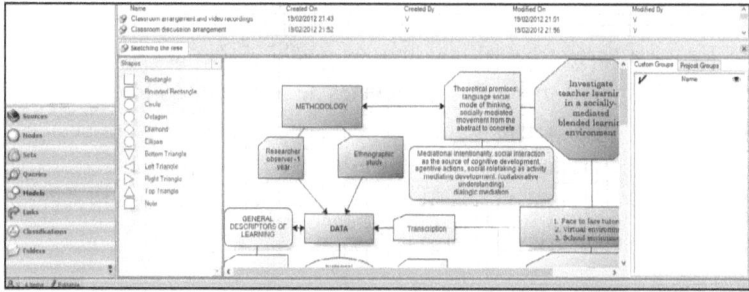

5. Criterios de selección para elegir el paquete correcto

Weitzman (2000, pp. 810-815) propone responder a las siguientes preguntas para elegir paquetes de software: (1) ¿Qué tipo de usuario/a de ordenador soy?, (2) ¿Estoy eligiendo para un proyecto o para varios proyectos en los próximos años?, (3) ¿Con qué tipo de proyecto(s) y base de datos(s) trabajaré?, y (4) ¿Qué tipo de análisis quiero hacer?

Evidentemente, la elección del software dependerá principalmente del proyecto de investigación, del tipo y el formato de los datos utilizados, de los objetivos y de las ambiciones, y en la medida en la que el paquete de software pueda responder eficazmente a estas necesidades. Al mismo tiempo, los criterios de selección pueden ajustarse, también, a cuestiones subjetivas, como el precio del software y el presupuesto de la investigación, la accesibilidad del software en el campus, la formación disponible para cada paquete de software o, simplemente, la preferencia individual. Para los paquetes que ofrecen herramientas similares, facilitan tareas comparables y dan cuenta de resultados similares, como NVIVO y Atlas.ti, la elección puede ser una cuestión de preferencia personal y la interfaz con la que la persona se siente más cómoda. La colaboración necesaria para llevar a cabo eficazmente los objetivos del proyecto también debería ser un factor considerado. Están disponibles versiones estándar y profesionales para cada paquete de software. También existen versiones que admiten la colaboración entre múltiples usuarios y, por lo tanto, pueden utilizarlas múltiples personas o equipos. Estas funcionalidades están relacionadas con diferencias significativas de precios.

De cualquier manera, es imprescindible que las personas investigadoras reciban formación para aprovechar al máximo las posibilidades del software. Pueden encontrar su camino a través de los paquetes de software con los recursos libres disponibles en línea, como tutoriales, manuales de vídeo y discusiones de foro. También hay talleres que ofrecen información sobre las características y posibilidades de cada uno de estos paquetes de software, así como la experiencia práctica con la supervisión de personas expertas.

6. Análisis de datos: convenciones de transcripción

Cuando se incluyen datos audiovisuales en una etnografía en línea, la transcripción de esos datos debe basarse en una clave de transcripción (véanse Moore y Llompart, este volumen), de las que se pueden encontrar ejemplos en libros o en línea (Agha y Wortham, 2005; Hutchby y Wooffitt, 2008; Sacks, Schegloff, y Jefferson, 1974).

7. Otras consideraciones

El aumento de la interconexión y la convergencia de los medios actual exige una investigación cualitativa basada en fuentes de datos múltiples y diversas para investigar con precisión y representar la realidad. Los CAQDAS ayudan, precisamente, a gestionar eficientemente grandes volúmenes de datos multimodales de manera oportuna y efectiva. Los CAQDAS modernos permiten no sólo un acceso fácil al corpus, sino también una exploración sistemática y, muy importante, una salida imprimible y ordenada de los datos codificados para facilitar la interpretación. Sin embargo, y esto se ha destacado repetidamente, el ordenador no puede reemplazar la mente humana en la detección e interpretación del significado y las relaciones de los datos.

También es muy importante tener en cuenta que el paquete se software puede suponer limitaciones para nuestros planes y ambiciones (García-Horta y Guerra-Ramos, 2008). Es útil que las personas investigadoras sean conscientes de estas limitaciones a lo largo de la investigación, y que las detecten y documenten en su proyecto escrito. El lápiz y el papel tradicionales todavía pueden ser herramientas muy útiles durante el análisis de datos asistido por ordenador. Mantener y hacer referencia a las herramientas de apoyo, a las preguntas de investigación o palabras clave de la investigación que se está llevando a cabo, anotarlas en un papel y dejarlas a la vista durante todo el proceso de codificación y análisis, ayudará a mantener la atención en los objetivos de la investigación, que pueden olvidarse fácilmente en grandes proyectos de investigación multimodal.

Por último, se recomienda encarecidamente formarse en las habilidades necesarias para diseñar investigaciones cualitativas y aprovechar las posibilidades analíticas de los paquetes de software cualitativos. Hacer una revisión bibliográfica de las tradiciones filosóficas, epistemológicas y metodológicas antes de embarcarse en la investigación (Guba y Lincoln, 1994), igual que revisar estudios de casos concretos en educación, pueden ser un gran apoyo para tomar decisiones metodológicas (véanse por ejemplo Antoniadou y Dooly, este volumen).

Obras citadas

Agha, A., y Wortham, S. (2005). Discourse across speech-events: intertextuality and interdiscursivity in social life. *Special Issue of the Journal of Linguistic Anthropology*, 15(1).

Antoniadou, V. (2011). Virtual collaboration, perezhivanie and teacher learning: a socio-cultural-historical perspective. *Bellaterra Journal of Teaching & Learning Language & Literature*, 4(3), 53-70.

Antoniadou, V. (2013). *Expanding the socio-material spaces of teacher education programmes: a qualitative trace of teacher professionalization through blended pedagogy in Catalonia*. Tesis de doctorado no publicada. Universitat Autònoma de Barcelona.

Antoniadou, V., y Dooly, M. (2017). Etnografia educativa en contextos d'aprenentatge mixt. En E. Moore y M. Dooly (Eds), *Enfoques cualitativos para la investigación en educación plurilingüe* (pp. 264-292). Research-publishing.net. https://doi.org/10.14705/rpnet.2017.emmd2016.631

Barab, S. A, Hay, K. E., y Yagamata-Lynch, L. C. (2001). Constructing networks of action relevant episodes: an in-situ research methodology. *The Journal of the Learning Sciences*, 10 (1y2), 63-112. https://doi.org/10.1207/S15327809JLS10-1-2_5

Bazeley, P. (2009). Integrating data analysis in mixed methods research. *Journal of Mixed Methods Research*, 3(3), 203-207.

Bezemer, J., y Mavers, D. (2011). Multimodal transcription as academic practice. *International Journal of Social Research Methodology*, 14(3), 191-206. https://doi.org/10.1080/13645579.2011.563616

Carr, D., Crook, C., Noss, R., Carmichael, P., y Selwyn, N. (2008). *Education 2.0? Designing the web for teaching and learning: a commentary by the technology enhanced learning phase of the teaching and learning research programme*. Londres: Teaching and Learning Research Programme, Institute of Education, University of london.

Charmaz, K. (2006). *Constructing grounded theory: a practical guide through qualitative analysis*. Londres: Sage.

Dooly, M. (2011). Divergent perceptions of telecollaborative language learning tasks: task-as-workplan vs. task-as-process. *Language Learning & Technology*, 15(2), 69-91.

Dooly, M., Moore, E., y Vallejo, C. (2017). Ética de la investigación. En E. Moore y M. Dooly (Eds), *Enfoques cualitativos para la investigación en educación plurilingüe* (pp. 363-375). Research-publishing.net. https://doi.org/10.14705/rpnet.2017.emmd2016.635

Dörnyei, Z. (2007). *Research methods in applied linguistics: quantitative qualitative and mixed methodologies*. Oxford: Oxford University Press.

Downes, S. (2005). *E-Learning 2.0*. https://doi.org/10.19173/irrodl.v6i2.284

Downes, S. (2006). *Learning networks and connective knowledge*. http://philpapers.org/archive/DOWLNA.1.pdf

Dron, J., y Anderson, T. (2007). Collectives, networks and groups in social software for e-learning. En T. T. Bastiaens y S. Carliner (Eds), *Proceedings of world conference on e-learning in corporate, government, healthcare, and higher education* (pp. 2460-2467). Chesapeake, VA: Association for the Advancement of Computing in Education (AACE).

Erickson, F. (2006). Definition and analysis of data from videotape: some research procedures and their rationales. En J. L. Green, G. Camilli, P. B. Elmore, A. Skukauskaiti y E. Grace (Eds), *Handbook of complementary methods in education research* (pp. 177-192). American Education Research Association: Lawrence Erlbaum.

García, A. C., Standlee, A. I., Bechkoff, J., y Yan Cui. (2009). Ethnographic approaches to the Internet and computer-mediated communication. *Journal of Contemporary Ethnography*, 38(1), 52-84. https://doi.org/10.1177/0891241607310839

García-Horta, J. B., y Guerra-Ramos, M. T. (2008). The use of CAQDAS in educational research: some advantages, limitations and potential risks. *International Journal of Research & Method in Education*, 32(2), 151-165. https://doi.org/10.1080/17437270902946686

Glaser, B., y Strauss, A. (1967). *The discovery of grounded theory: strategies for qualitative research*. Chicago: Aldine.

Guba, E. G., y Lincoln, Y. S. (1994). Competing paradigms in qualitative research. En N. Denzin y Y. Lincoln (Eds), *Handbook of qualitative research* (pp. 105-117). Thousand Oaks/Londres/Nueva Delhi: Sage.

Hackling, M., Murcia, K., Ibrahim-Didi, K., y Hill, S. (2014). *Methods for multimodal analysis and representation of teaching-learning interactions in primary science lessons captured on video.* https://www.esera.org/media/esera2013/Mark_Hackling_04Feb2014.pdf

Hutchby, I., y Wooffitt, R. (2008). *Conversation analysis* (2nd ed.). Chichester, U.K.: Polity Press.

Labov, W. (1972). *Sociolinguistic patterns*. Oxford: Blackwell.

Lincoln, Y. S., y Guba, E. G. (1985). *Naturalistic inquiry*. Thousand Oaks/Londres/Nueva Delhi: Sage.

Mercer, N. (2000). *Words & Minds: how we use language to think together*. Londres/Nueva York: Routledge. https://doi.org/10.4324/9780203464984

Mercer, N. (2004). Sociocultural discourse analysis: analysing classroom talk as a social mode of thinking. *Journal of Applied Linguistics*, 1(2), 137-168. https://doi.org/10.1558/japl.2004.1.2.137

Mercer, N., y Howe, C. (2012). Explaining the dialogic processes of teaching and learning: the value and potential of sociocultural theory. *Learning, Culture and Social Interaction*, 1(1), 12-21. https://doi.org/10.1016/j.lcsi.2012.03.001

Moore, E., y Llompart, J. (2017). Recoger, transcribir, analizar y presentar datos interaccionales plurilingües. En E. Moore y M. Dooly (Eds), *Enfoques cualitativos para la investigación en educación plurilingüe* (pp. 418-433). Research-publishing.net. https://doi.org/10.14705/rpnet.2017.emmd2016.639

Onwuegbuzie, A., Leech, N., y Collins, K. M. (2010). Innovative data collection strategies in qualitative research. *Qualitative Report*, 15(3), 696-726.

Palinkas, L. A., Horwitz, S. M., Green, C. A., Wisdom, J. P., Duan, N., y Hoagwood, K. (2013). Purposeful sampling for qualitative data collection and analysis in mixed method implementation research. *Administration and Policy in Mental Health and Mental Health Services Research*, 42(5), 533-544. https://doi.org/10.1007/s10488-013-0528-y

Patton, M. Q. (2001). *Qualitative research and evaluation methods* (2ª Ed.). Thousand Oaks, CA: Sage Publications.

Patton, M. Q. (2002). *Qualitative research and evaluation methods* (3rd ed.). Thousand Oaks, CA: Sage.

Sacks, H., Schegloff, E. A., y Jefferson, G. (1974). A simplest systematics for the organization of turn-taking for conversation. *Language*, 50(4), 696-735. https://doi.org/10.1353/lan.1974.0010

Sfard, A. (1998). On two metaphors for learning and the dangers of choosing just one. *Educational Researcher*, 27(2), 4-13. https://doi.org/10.3102/0013189X027002004

Weitzman, E. (2000). Software and qualitative research. En N. K. Denzin y Y. S. Lincoln (Eds), *Handbook of qualitative research* (2nd ed.) (pp. 803-820). Thousand Oaks/Londres/Nueva Delhi: Sage.

Yin, R. K. (2003). *Case study research: design and methods* (3rd ed.). Thousand Oaks/Londres/Nueva Delhi: Sage.

Lecturas recomendadas

Bazeley, P. (2009). Integrating data analysis in mixed methods research. *Journal of Mixed Methods Research*, 3(3), 203-207. https://doi.org/10.1177/1558689809334443

Charmaz, K. (2006). *Constructing grounded theory: a practical guide through qualitative analysis* (1st ed.). Londres: Sage.

Dörnyei, Z. (2007). *Research methods in applied linguistics: quantitative, qualitative and mixed methodologies*. Oxford: Oxford University Press.

Saldaña, J. (2009). *The coding manual for qualitative researchers*. Londres: Sage.

Páginas web con recursos mencionados

Altas.ti (Windows, Mac, iPad, Android, debe comprarse una licencia, prueba gratuita disponible): http://atlasti.com/

NVIVO (Windows y Mac, debe comprarse una licencia, prueba gratuita disponible): http://www.qsrinternational.com/

Transana (Windows y Mac, debe comprarse una licencia, prueba gratuita disponible): http://www.transana.org/

13 Com s'escriu un text de recerca?

Eulàlia Borràs[1]

Conceptes clau: tipus de text, redacció, revisió, bibliografia, estil APA.

---

1. Introducció

En general, quan escrivim sobre la nostra recerca fem una contribució a la comunitat científica i disseminem els resultats dels nostres estudis en articles científics. D'aquesta manera, altres persones investigadores tindran accés a la recerca que produïm i podran aprofundir en els temes que plantegem per avançar en el coneixement científic.

Així mateix, podem concebre la disseminació de la recerca com una oportunitat més de col·laborar amb les persones amb les quals hem dut a terme la investigació, fent de coautors amb docents, estudiants i altres agents que han estat importants en el procés de recollida i d'interpretació de les dades. També la podem considerar com una manera d'establir diàlegs amb la comunitat educativa, publicant textos més divulgatius en revistes que llegeixen docents, personal de l'Administració pública, professorat en formació, etc.

Finalment, podem entendre la disseminació de la recerca com un deure que tenim amb la societat que ens la finança (fent universitats públiques, aportant diners per a projectes i beques). Cada cop és més comú que s'expliquin els resultats de la recerca en articles de premsa i en altres mitjans d'accés obert. Algunes revistes científiques ofereixen aquesta opció, i cada cop més persones publiquen els

---

1. Escola d'Enginyeria d'Igualada (UPC), Igualada, Catalunya/Espanya; eulalia.borras@eei.upc.edu

Per citar aquest capítol: Borràs, E. (2017). Com s'escriu un text de recerca? A E. Moore i M. Dooly (Eds), *Enfocaments qualitatius per a la recerca en educació plurilingüe* (p. 469-482). Research-publishing.net. https://doi.org/10.14705/rpnet.2017.emmd2016.642

manuscrits de la seva recerca (és a dir, versions prèvies a l'acceptació, segons la normativa de cada editorial) en xarxes socials acadèmiques, com ara Academia.edu o Researchgate.net.

En aquest capítol, parlarem del format dels textos més estrictament de recerca. L'estructura concreta del text vindrà determinada pel tipus de text que hem de produir: un treball de fi de màster, una tesi doctoral, un capítol d'un llibre especialitzat o un article per a una revista científica. En el cas de la recerca qualitativa, cal que el text tingui en compte un seguit de processos que s'han explicat en aquest volum, com ara:

- la justificació de la recerca en termes teòrics i de l'interès social i educatiu;

- la recollida d'informació o de dades;

- el tractament i l'organització de les dades;

- l'adopció d'un marc teòric i metodològic;

- l'anàlisi de les dades;

- la interpretació de les dades de manera original i/o creativa i l'obtenció de resultats;

- el plantejament d'una discussió sobre la rellevància dels resultats;

- el plantejament d'unes conclusions.

2. Diferències entre el treball de fi de màster i la tesi

Probablement, moltes de les persones que llegeixen aquest volum estan en procés d'escriure un treball de fi de màster o una tesi doctoral. En ambdós casos es duu a terme una recerca acadèmica per assolir una titulació. La tesi doctoral, tanmateix, té un abast més extens i un caràcter més profund que el treball de màster. Igualment, la metodologia de recerca és més rigorosa en el cas de la tesi.

Les tesis doctorals han d'exposar el propòsit de la recerca, el marc teòric al voltant del qual gira el nostre tema d'estudi, la metodologia utilitzada, els resultats de la recerca, les discussions i les conclusions. Normalment el contingut s'estructura en diversos capítols, que en els treballs qualitatius hauran d'incloure la informació següent:

- *Títol:* té la funció de captar l'atenció del lector i proporcionar prou informació sobre el contingut del text. Els títols no haurien d'excedir les 10 paraules.

- *Resum o abstract:* és una síntesi del treball perquè el lector pugui decidir d'antuvi si li interessa llegir tot el text.

- *Paraules clau:* normalment, es demanen al voltant de cinc paraules que ajuden a identificar el tema, el context, la metodologia i els conceptes teòrics clau de la recerca.

- *Introducció:* presenta el tema o problema de la recerca, la rellevància i l'abast del tema, la posició de la persona investigadora en el context estudiat (per exemple, si és també el docent), la seva motivació personal cap a la recerca, etc.

- *Objectius i preguntes de recerca*: han de ser el més clar possible. Convé presentar-los en format de llista.

- *Marc teòric:* revisa les bases teòriques de la recerca. En aquest capítol informem el lector sobre la recerca prèvia en què fonamentem el treball, l'estat de la qüestió, i el nostre enfocament científic.

- *Metodologia:* exposa el disseny de la recerca i els mètodes de recollida i d'anàlisi de les dades. Expliquem com hem portat a terme la recerca, quines eines hem utilitzat per assolir els objectius de la investigació (vegeu el capítol de Canals, aquest volum), quines dades hem recollit i com les hem gestionat (tipus d'anàlisi, transcripcions, etc.). També donem compte dels procediments seguits per assegurar la validesa interna de la recerca, com triangulació, sessions de dades, etc. (vegeu Antoniadou, aquest volum; Moore i Llompart, aquest volum).

- *Resultats de la recerca:* analitza les dades seguint el procediment descrit en la metodologia i amb referència al marc teòric establert. Les dades s'hi inclouen en format de transcripció, amb imatges, etc.

- *Discussió dels resultats:* posa en relleu els resultats més rellevants i els contextualitza en els marcs teòrics i metodològics escollits. Tracta de respondre a les preguntes: com contribueix la nostra recerca a la comunitat científica i educativa? Què assenyalen els resultats? Quines bases deixem per a recerques posteriors?

- *Conclusions:* en aquest capítol es resumeixen les aportacions i les limitacions de l'estudi, i es recomanen recerques futures.

Generalment no hi ha limitacions d'extensió, però es recomana escriure al voltant de 250-350 pàgines DIN A4, a 1,5 espais.

Actualment, la tesi doctoral pot estar formada per un compendi d'articles de recerca publicats, alguns en revistes d'alt impacte. Cal consultar la normativa de cada universitat per comprovar les condicions d'aquesta modalitat.

Els treballs de fi de màster, tot i ser projectes de recerca avançada, tenen un abast més limitat i una extensió més reduïda. Per fer-nos-en una idea, poden tenir entre 50 i 150 pàgines, amb un espaiat d'1,5 en paper DIN A4, segons els requisits de cada universitat. Els treballs de màster han de forjar un argument sòlid, coherent i amb unitat interna que recolzi la recerca de manera convincent. Igualment, s'hi ha de demostrar que es coneixen les eines de recerca i que se saben aplicar en una situació determinada. Els apartats de les tesis de màster són els mateixos que els de les tesis doctorals.

3. Diferències entre els articles de revistes científiques i els capítols de llibre

Les revistes amb més prestigi i que compten més a l'hora d'avaluar la capacitat acadèmica són les que segueixen un procés d'avaluació d'experts pel mètode de cegament (*blind peer-reviewed*), en què altres persones investigadores revisen el treball de manera anònima i n'estimen o desestimen la publicació. Entre aquestes revistes, n'hi ha que tenen un índex d'impacte més alt. Això vol dir que els articles que s'hi han publicat s'han citat més cops en altres publicacions. Els índexs més reconeguts són el Social Sciences Citation Index (Thomson Reuters, Journal Citation Reports) i el SCImago Journal & Country Rank (Scopus). En l'àmbit català, també hi ha l'índex Carhus Plus+ (AGAUR). Les biblioteques de les universitats sovint organitzen cursos per entendre com funcionen aquests índexs i com hem d'interpretar la informació que ens proporcionen.

Per publicar en un llibre, normalment els editors inviten els autors a proposar un capítol segons la seva àrea d'expertesa, en convocatòries obertes o tancades, i els capítols normalment són revisats per experts externs.

Els articles científics generalment consten de les mateixes parts que una tesi doctoral o de màster, però se centren en un aspecte concret de l'estudi. Es pot escriure sobre una qüestió metodològica determinada, un concepte teòric que l'estudi fa avançar, unes dades específiques, un fenomen o context poc descrit en altres recerques, etc.

Cal destacar que els capítols de llibre no segueixen necessàriament l'estructura dels articles de recerca. Si són de divulgació entre un públic més general, tendeixen a aprofundir en les seccions de resultats, en la discussió i en les conclusions, les més vinculades a la part pràctica de la recerca. Així, els capítols no s'endinsen excessivament en el marc teòric i en la metodologia, sinó que aquestes seccions principalment contribueixen a la contextualització de les dades i a la interpretació dels resultats de les anàlisis.

La base de dades Scholarly Publishing Indicators (SPI) in Humanities and Social Sciences elabora un rànquing del prestigi de les editorials espanyoles i internacionals que ens pot donar indicacions sobre la qualitat dels llibres.

4. Per on es comença a escriure?

4.1. Les dades com a base de l'escriptura

És important tenir en compte que les idees es van organitzant a mesura que escrivim. Per aquesta raó, és recomanable posar-nos a escriure per poder explorar idees o pensaments inconnexos, més que no pas esperar a tenir totes les idees clares abans de disposar-nos a emplenar el full en blanc. Per exemple, suposem que mentre transcrivim ens adonem que es poden establir connexions entre certs tipus d'interaccions, o bé mentre analitzem una transcripció se'ns acut una idea que estableix una connexió sòlida amb els objectius que estem explorant en el treball. Aleshores, encara que no tinguem clarament definits els objectius de la recerca ni les nostres preguntes, és important escriure ja una primera anàlisi que es pot anar redefinint com a capítol. És en aquests moments valuosos i plens de lucidesa quan anem forjant els objectius i les preguntes finals de la recerca.

Així, a més, aconseguirem que la selecció i l'anàlisi de les dades estiguin ben connectades amb els objectius i amb la redacció. D'aquesta manera, aquests tres elements es tracten de manera quasi simultània i s'articulen conjuntament des del principi. Si, per contra, primer seleccionem les dades i les analitzem, al cap d'un temps busquem els objectius del treball i finalment escrivim la connexió entre aquests processos, correm el risc que la redacció del producte final (la tesi, en definitiva) esdevingui inconnexa.

No obstant això, aquesta connexió no té lloc només en l'estructura de la redacció. Especialment en la recerca etnogràfica, hi ha una relació molt estreta entre la recollida de dades, la seva anàlisi i la manera de plasmar-ho tot plegat en l'escriptura, i això ens ajuda a centrar el treball. Així, com ja hem apuntat, hem d'anar analitzant les dades a mesura que les recollim (Wolcott, 1999), per determinar si emergeixen idees d'interès i anar focalitzant la recollida de dades en aquella direcció. Això és crucial, perquè a mesura que analitzem dades (ja siguin entrevistes, enregistraments de classe o documents textuals) hauríem d'anar redactant les anàlisis inicials, que ens serviran per anar donant cos a la recerca. Es tracta d'un procés que es retroalimenta i que anirà centrant l'orientació de la recerca (vegeu els capítols de la primera part d'aquest volum).

És aconsellable, doncs, aprofundir primer en les dades, posant per escrit les anàlisis que anem portant a terme. Tant és així que en els enfocaments de baix a dalt (*bottom-up approaches*) que es practiquen en les orientacions etnometodològiques (Garfinkel, 1967; Heritage, 1984; vegeu Masats, aquest volum; Moore i Llompart, aquest volum; Nussbaum, aquest volum) les dades assenyalen els temes que cal explorar i ens conduiran als objectius de la recerca en un context de recerca basada en les dades (*data-driven research*). Aquesta és també la manera d'actuar en recerques que utilitzen el mostreig teòric o *grounded theory* (vegeu Antoniadou, aquest volum). En altres paraules, a partir de la recerca duta a terme per a les dades (i la seva escriptura) sorgiran preguntes més concretes que ens ajudaran a perfilar els objectius i possiblement planificar noves recollides de dades.

4.2. L'escriptura com a procés no lineal

Disposar d'un índex preliminar del treball ens permetrà anar omplint apartats i ens ajudarà, d'una banda, a tenir la sensació que anem progressant i, de l'altra, a explorar les idees que estem gestant. Es tracta d'anar completant l'índex amb les idees (petits textos que hem anat generant) de manera no lineal i a la vegada tenint present que l'índex s'haurà d'anar modificant a mesura que avança el procés de recerca i d'escriptura. Ens pot ajudar tenir una carpeta a l'ordinador per a cada apartat de l'índex, per anar-hi posant els apunts que anem escrivint, bibliografia interessant, fragments de dades, etc.

Així, després d'analitzar les dades i escriure els capítols dels resultats podem, posem per cas, escriure la introducció o els capítols sobre el marc teòric i la metodologia. Escrivint de manera no lineal vetllem, doncs, perquè el marc teòric estigui articulat de manera coherent dins l'estructura del treball amb referències a elements que seran analitzats posteriorment en el mateix treball. Així, anirem advertint el lector dels fonaments teòrics que trobarà després i anirem establint la coherència interna, fonamental per a l'estructura unitària del treball.

Considerem que pot ser útil escriure els capítols de la introducció i de les conclusions cap al final del procés, per disposar d'una visió general de tots els capítols i així establir relacions entre els objectius i els resultats. Les preguntes de recerca que normalment figuren al principi del treball, en el capítol d'objectius o en la introducció, han de ser subjacents a tot el treball de recerca. És per això que també pot ésser recomanable incloure en el capítol introductori un esquema transversal que relacioni les preguntes de recerca, les dades, els resultats i els capítols. Això pot facilitar la feina d'organització a qui escriu, servir de referència al lector i, en definitiva, esdevenir una eina que deixi ben travada l'estructura unitària del treball.

Cal tenir també en compte que quan escrivim un article o un capítol pot ser útil revisar el text periòdicament per extreure la idea principal de cada paràgraf (*topic sentence*) i així comprovar la fluïdesa i la coherència interna del capítol o de l'article. En el cas d'un text llarg, doncs, es recomana combinar aquestes idees principals extretes de cada paràgraf per construir un paràgraf al final de cada capítol (o al final de l'article) que resumeixi tot el text. Això contribueix que les idees flueixin amb coherència i ens pot ajudar a detectar idees inconnexes que haurem d'esmenar.

4.3. Les revisions

El procés d'escriptura implica la producció de diversos esborranys que després hauran de ser revisats i editats (*proof-reading*). Això vol dir que hem de gestionar acuradament el temps per poder lliurar la feina dins la data límit.

La constància és crucial en el procés d'escriptura. És important, doncs, que el procés d'escriptura comenci al més aviat possible per poder tenir la sensació que 'ja estem escrivint', que ja estem produint alguna cosa, i fer que les idees, indefectiblement, vagin madurant. Ara ja sabem que la revisió (la reescriptura) forma part del procés d'escriptura.

De fet, un cop lliurada la primera versió del nostre treball encara cal esperar diverses interaccions amb correccions. Aquestes correccions poden ser de diferents tipus: les que assenyalen la conveniència d'una reorganització general del contingut o les que proposen reorganitzacions parcials. Sovint hi ha suggeriments d'ajustos en el contingut o es poden detectar errors factuals. Algunes revisions poden esmentar qüestions estilístiques o ortogràfiques.

Les interaccions amb el tutor o editor (normalment en el cas dels capítols de llibre) de l'estudi són fonamentals, sobretot en els primers estadis de l'escriptura, quan encara es treballa en esborranys. És una llàstima que l'estudiant hagi elaborat molt a fons una línia de recerca que no hagi estat ben consensuada prèviament o bé que hagi esmerçat molts esforços en elements que, al final, en el procés de revisió es deixen de banda i s'eliminen. Ara bé, això és escriure un treball de recerca: un procés d'anar tres passes endavant i dues endarrere.

5. Com se cita?

5.1. Què és la citació?

En el treball, si l'autor utilitza material que no sigui propi l'ha d'identificar clarament en el cos del text o bé en notes a peu de pàgina o en notes finals. Aquesta identificació permetrà que el lector pugui accedir a la descripció completa de la font i consultar-la si així ho desitja.

És essencial citar totes les fonts utilitzades, perquè altrament es podria incórrer en plagi. El plagi consisteix a utilitzar material d'altri sense identificar-ne l'origen, de manera que el lector podria inferir que aquest material és original i ha estat creat pel mateix autor. Així, si utilitzem continguts d'altri per portar a terme la nostra recerca hem de justificar d'on provenen i donar crèdit a l'autor. Per fer-ho, cal que mentre redactem el treball alhora incorporem les citacions i les referències bibliogràfiques en un nou document per ser més eficients.

La citació pot ser literal o bé a partir d'una paràfrasi (utilitzant les nostres paraules per explicar el contingut d'un material d'altri). Així, si el nostre treball cita directament una font i reprodueix de manera literal un altre text sempre se n'ha d'indicar l'autor, l'any de publicació i les pàgines citades. Si aquesta citació no arriba a les 40 paraules, normalment s'incorpora en el text entre cometes. Ara bé, si el text citat excedeix les 40 paraules, normalment l'hem de sagnar en un paràgraf a part. Igualment, si en lloc de citar literalment parafrasegem el material al qual ens referim, se n'han d'especificar l'autor i la data, però no caldrà incloure-hi les pàgines. En ambdós casos, les crides al document original ens permetran localitzar-lo en l'apartat de referències bibliogràfiques.

5.2. Els sistemes de gestió de citacions i referències bibliogràfiques

Encara que les citacions i les referències bibliogràfiques es poden gestionar manualment de la manera que hem descrit, els sistemes de gestió de la recerca, com ara Mendeley o EndNote, són cada vegada més populars perquè permeten trobar, emmagatzemar i compartir informació amb molta eficàcia. A més, les citacions i les bibliografies es generen automàticament segons l'estil de citació que preferim i això ens permet incorporar canvis fàcilment. L'editor de referències de Microsoft Word és també una eina útil per a la gestió de la bibliografia.

La majoria de les biblioteques universitàries imparteixen cursos sobre gestors de referències, tot i que també podem trobar tutorials a Internet. Si bé al principi l'adaptació a aquest sistema pot ser dificultós, l'esforç es veu recompensat amb escreix amb l'automatització de les referències.

5.3. L'estil APA

Hi ha diversos estils de citació, American Psychological Association (APA), Chicago Manual of Style (CMS), Modern Language Association (MLA), tot i que en el camp de les ciències socials s'acostuma a emprar el de l'APA. En l'apartat de recursos a la xarxa d'aquest capítol, s'hi inclouen algunes pàgines on es presenta aquest format. S'hi poden trobar resums que ajuden a entendre millor les normes generals d'aquest estil, així com seccions exhaustives que aclareixen situacions particulars. A continuació, esbossem els trets generals de l'estil APA. Tanmateix, us animem a donar un cop d'ull als llocs web que hem esmentat.

Per a les citacions dins del text en l'estil APA utilitzem parèntesis amb el cognom de l'autor i l'any de publicació. Com s'ha esmentat, inclourem les pàgines en els parèntesis si ens referim a unes pàgines en particular i no a tota l'obra en general. Aquestes normes generals es modifiquen lleugerament si l'autor ja ha estat anomenat prèviament i llavors en els parèntesis només apareix l'any. Un altre detall important és que si citem un treball amb múltiples autors, la primera vegada que se citi s'especificaran els cognoms de tots els autors (fins a cinc). Les altres vegades que se citi aquell treball en el text ja només s'hi inclourà el primer autor seguit de l'abreviació *et al.*

La llista de referències s'inclou al final del treball, a doble espai i en ordre alfabètic. En aquesta llista hi han de figurar totes les referències de les publicacions citades en el treball i a la inversa; és a dir totes les referències d'aquesta llista han d'estar citades en el text. És important creuar les dades per detectar possibles omissions o redundàncies.

Hem de seguir la guia que escollim (APA, en aquest cas) al peu de la lletra (punts, comes, espais, etc.) i sobretot ser coherents al llarg de tot el text. Els treballs citats es referencien de manera diferent segons la seva naturalesa: llibres sencers, capítols en llibres editats per un o diversos autors, articles en publicacions periòdiques, audiovisuals i fonts electròniques. Cal que estiguem atents a les petites diferències de format de cadascuna de les modalitats.

De la mateixa manera, cal tenir en compte que les fonts electròniques han d'incloure l'URL (l'adreça de la pàgina d'Internet), així com la data de consulta.

6. Altres consideracions

Molt sovint els articles de recerca, sobretot en les revistes d'alt impacte, no són acceptats en el primer intent de publicació. És important rebre els consells dels experts de manera positiva i sense desanimar-se. Intercanviar els esborranys amb els companys és una bona manera de practicar l'art de donar i rebre avaluacions sobre allò que llegim i escrivim com a investigadors i investigadores.

Obres citades

Antoniadou, V. (2017). Recoger, organizar y analizar corpus de datos multimodales: las contribuciones de los CAQDAS. A E. Moore i M. Dooly (Eds), *Enfocaments qualitatius per a la recerca en educació plurilingüe* (p. 451-467). Research-publishing.net. https://doi.org/10.14705/rpnet.2017.emmd2016.641

Canals, L. (2017). Instruments per a la recollida de dades. A E. Moore i M. Dooly (Eds), *Enfocaments qualitatius per a la recerca en educació plurilingüe* (p. 377-389). Research-publishing.net. https://doi.org/10.14705/rpnet.2017.emmd2016.636

Garfinkel, H. (1967). *Studies in ethnomethodology*. Englewood Cliffs, NJ: Prentice-Hall.

Heritage, J. (1984). *Garfinkel and ethnomethodology*. Cambridge: Polity Press.

Masats, D. (2017). L'anàlisi de la conversa al servei de la recerca en el camp de l'adquisició de segones llengües (CA-for-SLA). A E. Moore i M. Dooly (Eds), *Enfocaments qualitatius per a la recerca en educació plurilingüe* (p. 293-320). Research-publishing.net. https://doi.org/10.14705/rpnet.2017.emmd2016.632

Moore, E., i Llompart, J. (2017). Recoger, transcribir, analizar y presentar datos interaccionales plurilingües. A E. Moore i M. Dooly (Eds), *Enfocaments qualitatius per a la recerca en educació plurilingüe* (p. 418-433). Research-publishing.net. https://doi.org/10.14705/rpnet.2017.emmd2016.639

Nussbaum, L. (2017). Investigar con docentes. A E. Moore i M. Dooly (Eds), *Enfocaments qualitatius per a la recerca en educació plurilingüe* (p. 23-45). Research-publishing.net. https://doi.org/10.14705/rpnet.2017.emmd2016.620

Wolcott, H. (1999). *Ethnography: a way of seeing*. Oregon: Altamira Press.

Lectures recomanades

Joyner, R. L., Rouse W. A., i Glatthorn, A. A. (2013). *Writing the winning thesis or dissertation: a step-by-step guide* (3a ed.). Thousand Oaks, CA.: Sage.

Lester, J. D. (1976). *Writing research papers: a complete guide* (2a ed.). Glenview, IL.: Scott, Foresman and Company.

Rigo, A., i Genescà, G. (2002). *Tesis i treballs. Aspectes formals*. Vic: Eumo Editorial.

Soriano, R. (2008). *Cómo se escribe una tesis. Guía práctica para estudiantes e investigadores*. Córdoba: Berenice Manuales.

Pàgines web amb recursos mencionats

Pàgines amb consells sobre la redacció de treballs de recerca

Escola de doctorat de la UAB: http://www.uab.cat/web/doctorats/que-em-cal-saber-de-la-tesi-doctoral-1224656373657.html

Programes

EndNote (Windows i Mac, de pagament, llicència de prova gratuïta): http://endnote.com/
Mendeley (Windows i Mac, gratuït): http://www.mendeley.com/

Índexs de qualitat de les publicacions

Carhus Plus+ (AGAUR): http://agaur.gencat.cat/ca/avaluacio/carhus/carhus-plus-2014/
Scholarly Publishing Indicators in Humanities and Social Sciences (SPI): http://ilia.cchs.csic.es/SPI/index.html
SCImago Journal & Country Rank (Scopus): http://www.scimagojr.com/

Social Sciences Citation Index (Thomson Reuters, Journal Citation Reports, normalment cal accedir-hi des de la biblioteca de la universitat): http://login.webofknowledge.com/

Informació sobre l'estil APA

Biblioteca de la Universitat de Girona: http://www.udg.edu/LaBibliotecaforma/Comcitar documents/EstilAPAencatala/tabid/11972/language/ca-ES/Default.aspx
Owl Purdue Online Writing Lab: https://owl.english.purdue.edu/owl/resource/560/01/
Servei de Biblioteques de la UAB: http://www.uab.cat/web/recursos-d-informacio/citacions-i-bibliografia-1326267851837.html
Web de l'American Psychologial Association: http://www.apastyle.org/

13 How to write a research paper

Eulàlia Borràs[1]

Key concepts: text types, composition, revision, bibliography, APA style.

---

1. Introduction

Generally speaking, when we write about our research, we are making a contribution to the scientific community and disseminating the results of our findings in scientific articles. This means that other researchers have access to the research we produce and can examine the subjects raised in greater depth to advance scientific knowledge.

At the same time, we can see the dissemination of this research as another opportunity to collaborate with the people with whom we have undertaken the research, giving the status of co-authors to the teachers, students and other people who played an important role in the process of gathering and interpreting the data. We might also consider it as a way of establishing a dialogue with the educational community by publishing texts in a more accessible style in journals or magazines read by teachers, people in public administration, trainee teachers, etc.

Finally, we might see the dissemination of research as a responsibility towards the society that funds our work (providing public universities, and money for projects and scholarships). It is more and more common for researchers to explain the results of their work in press articles and other open-access forums. Some scientific journals offer this option and increasing numbers of people are publishing the manuscripts of their research (i.e. the pre-acceptance versions,

---

1. Igualada School of Engineering (UPC), Igualada, Catalonia/Spain; eulalia.borras@eei.upc.edu

How to cite this chapter: Borràs, E. (2017). How to write a research paper. In E. Moore & M. Dooly (Eds), *Qualitative approaches to research on plurilingual education* (pp. 483-496). Research-publishing.net. https://doi.org/10.14705/rpnet.2017.emmd2016.643

depending on the regulations of each publishing house) on academic networks such as Academia.edu and Researchgate.net.

In this chapter, we will discuss the format of papers that are strictly academic. The specific structure of the text will be determined by whether it is for a master's dissertation, a doctoral thesis, a chapter of a specialist book or an article for a scientific journal. In the case of qualitative research, it is necessary, when writing the text, to bear in mind a series of processes that will be explained in this handbook, such as:

- the justification for the research in terms of its social and educational interest, and in theoretical terms;

- the gathering of information or data;

- the treatment and organization of the data;

- the adoption of a theoretical and methodological framework;

- data analysis;

- the interpretation of data in an original and/or creative way, and obtaining the findings;

- setting out a discussion on the relevance of the results;

- setting out the conclusions.

2. Differences between a master's dissertation and a thesis

Many of the people who read this handbook will be in the process of writing their master's or doctoral dissertation. In both cases, academic research is undertaken with a view of achieving the degree. At the same time, work on doctoral dissertations has a wider scope and a more in-depth approach than a master's thesis. Similarly, the research methodology is more rigorous in the case of the doctoral dissertation.

Doctoral dissertations have to explain the purpose of the research, the theoretical framework within which the subject matter sits, the methodology used, the results of the research, and final discussions and conclusions. Normally, the content is structured into various chapters which in qualitative research must include the following information:

- *Title:* the purpose of the title is to capture the reader's attention and provide concise information about the content of the text. Titles should not exceed ten words.

- *Abstract:* this should contain a brief summary of the paper so the reader can decide in advance if they are interested in reading the full text.

- *Keywords:* around five keywords are usually expected, which help to identify the subject, the context, the methodology and the key theoretical concepts of the research.

- *Introduction:* this presents the research subject/problem, the relevance and scope of the subject, the position of the researcher within the context being studied (for example, if he/she is also the teacher), their personal justification for conducting the research, etc.

- *The objectives and questions of the research*: these must be as clear as possible. They should be presented in the form of a list.

- *The theoretical framework:* this covers the theoretical basis of your research, informing the reader about any previous research upon which this work is based, the state of the art, and your scientific approach.

- *Methodology:* this explains the design of the research and the methods of gathering and analyzing data. It should explain how the research has been conducted, which tools were used to achieve the research objectives (see the chapter by Canals, this volume), which data have been gathered and how they have been managed (types of analysis, transcriptions, etc.). It also explains the procedures followed to ensure the internal validity of the research (triangulation, data sessions, etc.; see the chapters by Antoniadou, this volume; Moore & Llompart, this volume).

- *The results of the research:* in other words, the analysis of the data following the procedure described in the section on methodology, with reference to the established theoretical framework. The data are included in a transcription format, with images, etc.

- *Discussion of the results:* this puts an emphasis on the most important results, contextualizing them within the chosen theoretical and methodological frameworks. How does our research contribute to the scientific and educational community? What do the results show? What foundations are we leaving for subsequent research?

- *Conclusions:* this chapter should sum up the contributions of the study, its limitations, and recommendations for future research.

As a rule there is no limit on the length of the text, but the generally accepted recommendation for a doctoral dissertation is 250-350 pages in 1.5 spacing on A4 paper.

It should be borne in mind that doctoral dissertations nowadays can comprise a compendium of published research papers, some of them in high-profile journals. The regulations of each university should be referred to with regard to the conditions of this format.

Master's theses, even while being advanced research projects, are shorter and more limited in scope. To give you an idea, they might comprise 50-150 pages of 1.5 spacing on A4 paper, depending on the requirements of each individual university. Master's theses should put forward a solid and coherent argument with an internal unity that supports the research in a convincing manner. In addition, the author must demonstrate that they are familiar with the research tools and know how to use them in a specific situation. The sections in a master's dissertation are the same as those of a doctoral thesis.

3. Differences between articles in scientific journals and chapters of a book

The most prestigious journals and the most widely respected when it comes to evaluating academic competence are known as blind peer-reviewed journals (whereby other researchers check the work anonymously and either approve or recommend against its publication). These include journals with the highest impact factor; in other words, the articles published in them are most often quoted in other publications. The most respected indexes are the Social Sciences Citation Index (Thomson Reuters, Journal Citation Reports) and the SCImago Journal & Country Rank (Scopus). In Catalonia, there is also the Carhus Plus+ index (AGAUR). University libraries often organize courses on understanding how these indexes work and how to interpret the information they provide.

The usual process for book publishing is for editors to invite authors to propose a chapter according to their area of expertise, by means of open or closed calls, these chapters usually being reviewed by external experts.

Scientific articles generally consist of the same sections as a master's or doctoral dissertation but focus on a specific aspect of the study. You can write about a particular methodological issue, a theoretical concept that the study takes further, specific data, a phenomenon or context that has not been covered fully in other research, etc.

It is worth remembering that the chapters of a book do not necessarily follow the structure of the research articles. If they are for reading by a more general audience, they tend to concentrate on the sections relating to results, discussions and conclusions, which are linked more to the practical part of the research. Thus, the chapters do not explore the theoretical framework and methodology too deeply but instead the main contribution of these sections is to contextualize the data and the interpretations of the results of the analysis.

The database of Scholarly Publishing Indicators (SPI) in Humanities and Social Sciences provides a ranking of the importance of Spanish and international publishers that can provide useful information on the quality of books.

4. How do you go about starting to write?

4.1. Data as a basis for writing

It is important to remember that ideas tend to organize themselves as you write. For this reason, it is advisable to get writing in order to explore ideas or unconnected thoughts rather than expect to have all your ideas completely clear in your head prior to sitting down before a blank page. For example, let us imagine that while you are writing you realize that it might be possible to make a connection between certain types of interactions, or while analyzing a transcription an idea suddenly occurs to you that establishes a solid connection with the objectives you are exploring in that particular work. Thus, even if you have not yet clearly defined the objectives of your research or your questions, it is important to get writing as an initial analysis which could later redefine itself into a chapter. It is at these valuable moments when you are fully lucid that you start shaping the final objectives and questions of the research.

Furthermore, you will manage to ensure that (1) the selection of the data and their analysis are fully consistent with (2) the objectives, and (3) how they are written up. In this way, these three elements are dealt with almost simultaneously, and articulated as a whole right from the start of the process. If, on the other hand, (1) you first select the data and analyze them, and (2) after a time peruse the objectives of the work, and (3) finally record the connection between these processes in the end product (i.e. the thesis or dissertation), you run the risk that the narrative of the thesis will appear disjointed.

But this connection is not only found at the level of structuring the writing. In ethnographic research in particular, the relationship between (1) data collection, (2) its analysis, and (3) putting it down in writing is very close and this helps us to focus the work. Thus, as noted earlier, we need to be analyzing the data as and when they are collected (Wolcott, 1999) to determine whether any interesting ideas emerge and thus steer the data collection in this direction. This is crucial because as the data are analyzed (whether these are from interviews, recordings in class or text documents) we need to be writing down the initial analyses so they can be used to give body to the research. This is a self-sustaining process that will help to focus the orientation of the research (see the chapters in the first section of this handbook).

It is therefore advisable to first concentrate on the data, writing down all the analyses you undertake. So much so, that in bottom-up approaches, which are practiced in ethnomethodological approaches (Garfinkel, 1967; Heritage, 1984; see also Masats, this volume; Moore & Llompart, this volume; Nussbaum, this volume), the data will show us which topics to explore and steer us towards the research objectives in a context of *data-driven research*. This is also the mode of action in research that uses a *grounded theory* (see Antoniadou, this volume). In other words, based on the research carried out on the data (and the writing process) more specific questions will emerge that will help you to outline the objectives and possibly even plan new data collection sessions.

4.2. Writing as a nonlinear process

Having a preliminary working index helps you to complete the sections and gives the feeling that you are on the one hand making progress and on the other exploring the ideas you have gestated. The plan is to fill out the index with your ideas (short texts that have been produced along the way) in a nonlinear way, while at the same time being aware that the index will need to be modified as

Chapter 13

you progress in the research and writing process. It may be useful to have a separate folder on your computer for each section of the index so you can add any notes as and when you make them, useful bibliographical references, data excerpts, etc.

Thus after analyzing the data and writing the chapters of the results, we can, for example, write the introduction or the chapters on the theoretical framework and methodology. Writing in a nonlinear fashion allows, therefore, for the theoretical framework to be articulated in a coherent way within the structure of the work, with references to elements that will be analyzed subsequently in the same work. This forewarns the reader about the theoretical foundations of what they will find later on, and establishes the fundamental internal consistency for the unitary structure of the work.

We believe it can be useful to write the introductory chapter and the conclusions towards the end of the process, by which time you will have a more general vision of all the chapters and thus be able to establish relations between the objectives and the results. The research questions that normally appear at the beginning of the work in the chapter on objectives or in the introduction should be underlying the entire research paper. It is for this reason that it might also be advisable to include a cross-cutting outline in the introductory chapter that lists the research questions, data, results and chapters. This can help the person writing it to organize their tasks, serve as a reference for readers and, in short, provide a tool that leaves the overall structure of the work well supported.

It is also worth bearing in mind that, when writing an article or a chapter, it might be useful to review the text regularly to extract the main topic sentence from each paragraph and thus check the fluency and internal consistency of the chapter or the article. In the case of a long text, therefore, we recommend combining these key ideas, extracted from each paragraph, to construct a section at the end of each chapter (or at the end of the article) to provide a summary of the whole text. This helps ideas to flow together consistently and can also help to identify non-connecting ideas that need to be amended.

4.3. Revisions

The process of writing entails the production of various drafts which later need to be proof-read and edited. This means managing your time sensibly in order to deliver the project within the deadline. Consistency is crucial in the writing process. It is therefore important that the writing process starts as soon as possible so you have the feeling of 'putting it down on paper', that you are producing something, and that your ideas are inexorably maturing. We now know that revision (or rewriting) is a key part of the writing process.

Indeed, once you have handed in the first version of your work, you should still expect various interactions with their subsequent corrections. These corrections may be of different types: those that point to the desirability of a general reorganization of the content, or else to partial reorganizations. There are often suggestions for adjusting the content, or factual errors might have been detected. Some revisions might mention stylistic or orthographical points.

Interactions with the tutor or editor (usually in the case of book chapters) of the work are essential, especially in the early stages of writing, when the work is still in draft form. It is a real shame when students have pursued a line of work in great depth that has not been properly agreed in advance, or put a lot of effort into certain areas which finally, during the revision process, are left out. Having said that, this is what writing a research paper is all about: a process of three steps forward and two steps back.

5. How do you cite?

5.1. What is a citation?

If, in his or her work the author uses material that is not his or her own, this must be clearly identified in the text, either by footnotes or in final notes. This identification allows the reader to access the full description of the source for further consultation if they wish.

It is essential to cite all the sources used as otherwise you could be accused of plagiarism. Plagiarism consists of using someone else's material without identifying the source so the reader might infer that this material is original and written by the author themself. Thus if you use someone else's content to carry out your research, you must justify where this information came from and give credit to the author. To do so, you need to include these citations and bibliographic references while writing the work in a new document for greater efficiency.

The citation might be literal or paraphrased (using your own words to explain the content of someone else's material). If your work makes a direct quotation from a source and reproduces it literally, you must always cite the author, the year of publication and the pages cited. If the quotation is under 40 words, it is normally included in the text within inverted commas. However, if the text contains more than 40 words, the norm is to indent it in a separate paragraph. Similarly, if instead of using a literal quote you choose to paraphrase the material you are referring to, you must specify the author and the date of the material in question but there is no need to include page numbers. In both cases, the mentions of the original document will allow us to locate it in the bibliographical references section.

5.2. Management systems for citations and bibliographical references

Although citations and bibliographical references can be managed manually as described above, research management systems such as Mendeley or EndNote are becoming increasingly popular because they enable you to find, save and share information very efficiently. In addition, citations and bibliographies are generated automatically according to your preferred citation style which lets you make changes easily. The Microsoft Word editor is also a useful tool for managing bibliographies.

Most university libraries give courses on data managers, though you can also find tutorials on the internet. While it may be difficult to adapt to this system at the beginning, your efforts will be amply rewarded with the automation of references.

5.3. The APA style

There are various citation styles, e.g. American Psychological Association (APA), Chicago Manual of Style (CMS), Modern Language Association (MLA), though in the field of social sciences the most widely used system is that of the APA. In the section on online resources in this chapter there are a few pages on presenting in this format. You can find summaries which help to give a better understanding of the general rules of this style, as well as exhaustive sections to clarify specific situations. We have outlined below the general features of the APA style while encouraging you to take a look at the websites we have mentioned.

For citations in a text in the APA style, we use brackets with the author's surname and the year of publication. As mentioned earlier, we include the page number in brackets if referring to one or more pages in particular and not the whole work in general. These general rules change slightly if the author has already been mentioned previously, in which case only the year appears in brackets. Another important detail is that if you are citing a work with multiple authors, the first time you mention it you must give the surnames of all the authors (up to a maximum of five). On further mentions of this work in the text, you only need to include the first author followed by the abbreviation 'et al.'.

The list of references is included at the end of the text in double spacing and alphabetical order. This list should show all the references to the publications cited in the work and vice versa; in other words, all the references given in the list must be cited in the text. It is important to cross-check the details for any omissions or redundancies.

You should follow the chosen style guide (the APA in this case) to the letter (full stops, commas, spaces, etc.) and ensure the whole text is consistent. The works cited are referenced differently depending on their type: full books, chapters in books published by one or several authors, articles in periodicals, audiovisual and electronic sources. It is important to be alert to the tiny differences in format of each of these media. Similarly, you need to bear in mind that electronic sources must include the URL (the internet page address) and the date of the consultation.

6. Other considerations

Very often, research articles are not accepted at the first attempt at publication, especially by high-profile journals. It is important to take the advice from experts in a positive way and not get discouraged. Sharing drafts with colleagues is a good way of practicing the art of giving and receiving appraisals of what we read and write as researchers.

Works cited

Antoniadou, V. (2017). Collecting, organizing and analyzing multimodal data sets: the contributions of CAQDAS. In E. Moore & M. Dooly (Eds), *Qualitative approaches to research on plurilingual education* (pp. 435-450). Research-publishing.net. https://doi.org/10.14705/rpnet.2017.emmd2016.640

Canals, L. (2017). Instruments for gathering data. In E. Moore & M. Dooly (Eds), *Qualitative approaches to research on plurilingual education* (pp. 390-401). Research-publishing.net. https://doi.org/10.14705/rpnet.2017.emmd2016.637

Garfinkel, H. (1967). Studies in ethnomethodology. Englewood Cliffs, NJ: Prentice-Hall.

Heritage, J. (1984). Garfinkel and ethnomethodology. Cambridge: Polity Press.

Masats, D. (2017). Conversation analysis at the service of research in the field of second language acquisition (CA-for-SLA). In E. Moore & M. Dooly (Eds), *Qualitative approaches to research on plurilingual education* (pp. 321-347). Research-publishing.net. https://doi.org/10.14705/rpnet.2017.emmd2016.633

Moore, E., & Llompart, J. (2017). Collecting, transcribing, analyzing and presenting plurilingual interactional data. In E. Moore & M. Dooly (Eds), *Qualitative approaches to research on plurilingual education* (pp. 403-417). Research-publishing.net. https://doi.org/10.14705/rpnet.2017.emmd2016.638

Nussbaum, L. (2017). Doing research with teachers. In E. Moore & M. Dooly (Eds), *Qualitative approaches to research on plurilingual education* (pp. 46-67). Research-publishing.net. https://doi.org/10.14705/rpnet.2017.emmd2016.621

Wolcott, H. (1999). *Ethnography: a way of seeing*. Oregon: Altamira Press.

Recommended reading

Joyner, R. L., Rouse W. A., & Glatthorn, A. A. (2013). *Writing the winning thesis or dissertation: a step-by-step guide* (3rd ed.). Thousand Oaks, CA.: Sage.

Lester, J. D. (1976). *Writing research papers: a complete guide* (2nd ed.). Glenview, IL.: Scott, Foresman and Company.

Rigo, A., & Genescà, G. (2002). *Tesis i treballs. Aspectes formals*. Vic: Eumo Editorial.

Soriano, R. (2008). *Cómo se escribe una tesis. Guia práctica para estudiantes e investigadores*. Córdoba: Berenice Manuales.

Websites with resources mentioned

Sites with advice on writing research papers

UAB doctorate school: http://www.uab.cat/web/doctorats/que-em-cal-saber-de-la-tesi-doctoral-1224656373657.html

Programs

EndNote (Windows and Mac, paying, free test license): http://endnote.com/
Mendeley (Windows and Mac, free): http://www.mendeley.com/

Quality indexes of publications

Carhus Plus+ (AGAUR): http://agaur.gencat.cat/ca/avaluacio/carhus/carhus-plus-2014/
Scholarly Publishing Indicators in Humanities and Social Sciences (SPI): http://ilia.cchs.csic.es/SPI/index.html
SCImago Journal & Country Rank (Scopus): http://www.scimagojr.com/

Chapter 13

Social Sciences Citation Index (Thomson Reuters, Journal Citation Reports – normally accessed via your university's library): http://login.webofknowledge.com/

Information on the APA style

Owl Purdue Online Writing Lab: https://owl.english.purdue.edu/owl/resource/560/01/
UAB Library Service: http://www.uab.cat/web/recursos-d-informacio/citacions-i-bibliografia-1326267851837.html
University of Girona Library: http://www.udg.edu/LaBibliotecaforma/Comcitardocuments/EstilAPAencatala/tabid/11972/language/ca-ES/Default.aspx
Website of the American Psychological Association: http://www.apastyle.org/

Epíleg

Artur Noguerol[1]

Benvolguda lectora o lector,

Has arribat al final del manual, suposant que hagis seguit l'ordre d'edició. La seva lectura ha estat una aventura compartida amb els membres del grup de recerca GREIP. Esperem, però, que això sigui l'inici d'un nou procés, també compartit, de creació de noves pràctiques educatives inspirades i potenciades per tot el que has llegit en aquestes pàgines. Aquí, hi has trobat moltes eines i recursos per a la recerca sobre l'educació plurilingüe i intercultural. Amb la seva lectura, però, no acaba res, sinó que s'obre la possibilitat d'actuar a partir del llegit, d'iniciar nous projectes que porten a un millor aprenentatge de la diversitat de llengües i cultures. A més de ser el punt de partida, aquest llibre pot i ha d'esdevenir un acompanyant fidel, i alhora crític, del camí que emprenguis, una nova empenta en la teva professió, perquè un bon docent és qui es fa preguntes i cerca respostes sobre allò que fa i el que cal fer per millorar.

Aquest text, atès que és un manual, ha estat concebut, en primer lloc, com a guia per a les persones investigadores de doctorat que volen fer recerca en els diferents camps de l'educació plurilingüe i intercultural, objectiu central del GREIP. És un molt bon instrument perquè, en aquestes pàgines, hi ha molt variades propostes de recerca, s'hi aporten eines i recursos concrets per a realitzar-les, i fins i tot es donen claus per a l'escriptura d'articles per comunicar les recerques i els seus resultats, base per socialitzar i donar visibilitat a les feines de l'escola. Evidentment, per als estudiants universitaris és una font de múltiples idees i recursos per a la realització dels treballs universitaris. L'interessant, a més, és que aquestes eines i recursos es presenten en relació a recerques concretes i amb una mirada, la de l'etnografia i l'anàlisi de la conversa, que dona sentit i unitat a tot plegat. D'aquesta manera es mostra que, per a ser rigorós en l'ús del que es

---

1. Universitat Autònoma de Barcelona, Bellaterra, Catalunya/Espanya; artur.noguerol@uab.cat

Per citar: Noguerol, A. (2017). Epíleg. A E. Moore i M. Dooly (Eds), *Enfocaments qualitatius per a la recerca en educació plurilingüe* (p. 497-500). Research-publishing.net. https://doi.org/10.14705/rpnet.2017.emmd2016.644

Epíleg

proposa al manual, s'ha de saber adaptar a la situació concreta en què s'empra, l'escola i les aules.

Al llibre es plantegen també perspectives que van més enllà de les recerques i estudis universitaris, ja que trenca amb la tradicional manera de veure el treball universitari, tancat en la mateixa universitat. Això ho fa a partir d'un nou enfocament de la recerca en didàctica de les llengües: l'educació plurilingüe i intercultural. Aquest manual recull, des de molts punts de vista, la història del GREIP que, essent un grup universitari, ha sentit la necessitat de ser una porta oberta per on han entrat els professionals de l'ensenyament de llengües i les seves pràctiques escolars que han esdevingut un dels eixos centrals del seu quefer universitari. D'aquesta manera, el GREIP trenca els límits entre la producció de coneixement i les pràctiques docents: teoria i pràctica es construeixen recíprocament.

Com recomanen diverses autores del manual, l'ideal de la recerca és que, en el seu disseny, qui investiga adopti una posició activa com a participant compromès en la millora dels processos de l'educació plurilingüe i intercultural. Cal viure les pràctiques docents per poder fer recerca, observació participant, recerca acció... En definitiva, fer recerca ha d'ajudar a intervenir críticament en els processos d'ensenyament per millorar-los. I en les propostes del manual, els estudiants universitaris, el seu professorat, i els docents no universitaris trobaran vies per a la seva millora professional. Perquè com es diu al llibre, l'objectiu del GREIP és fer recerca tots plegats per trobar noves formes d'ensenyar les llengües de manera integrada; proposar noves formes que atenguin la diversitat de contextos que es donen en la societat multilingüe que ens ha tocat viure, i així aconseguir que els i les aprenents esdevinguin persones plurilingües sensibles a la diversitat lingüística del seu entorn i de tot el món.

La nostra societat està vivint uns canvis molt profunds i ràpids que fan que, en l'ensenyament de llengües, moltes de les propostes didàctiques, que eren de referència, hagin esdevingut un fre per donar respostes viables i eficaces a les noves situacions. Al manual es revisen moltes concepcions d'aquesta realitat plural i diversa, així com de la manera d'ensenyar llengües. En diferents capítols, es va primfilant el significat de la competència plurilingüe i intercultural, i també el que suposa en la creació d'activitats docents per al seu desenvolupament, la qual cosa suposa una coordinació i integració entre les diferents llengües de l'escola, alhora que també es consideren les llengües de l'alumnat, les de l'entorn i altres llengües amb què es puguin relacionar els nois i noies de l'escola. A més, com que al manual es reconeix que l'aprenentatge de llengües és una activitat social que es realitza en interacció amb altres persones, sigui directament o a través de documents escrits o multimodals, i amb la mediació de les tecnologies, les propostes obren el camp de la recerca a la telecol·laboració i a altres formes de comunicació de la societat actual. Ensenyar llengua pren en el manual una dimensió global que té en compte totes les variacions que es donen segons la diversitat de textos, d'àmbits d'ús, de canals i de suports en què es vehiculen, de formats, de modes d'organització textual, de llengües... En definitiva, la llengua es tracta com allò que veritablement és: un mitjà complex de construcció del pensament, de les emocions, de les identitats personals i socials...

Una de les particularitats del manual és que, en ell, hi és present la vida d'un grup de recerca i d'unes companyes i companys de viatge, i aquest relat més personal pot servir com a model per a una veritable millora de l'ensenyament de llengües. El GREIP promociona la reflexió cooperativa amb docents, estudiants en pràctiques i persones investigadores en formació, centrada en l'observació i l'estudi de les competències de partida de l'alumnat, de les seves pràctiques socials habituals i del paper de l'escola en la seva educació plurilingüe i intercultural. Aquest treball, fet braç a braç amb el professorat, apareix al manual com un punt de partida que és imprescindible tenir en compte. Ja s'ha dit abans que el manual vol ser un company del camí, i un bon camí cal no emprendre'l sol perquè el treball en equip és la clau del progrés i professionalització dels que es dediquen a l'ensenyament de llengües. La investigació col·laborativa té una doble vessant: d'una banda planteja la necessitat, que apareix en tots els capítols, de recolzar-se en el treball cooperatiu, d'obrir-se al grup de treball i no quedar-se en la recerca personal; d'una altra banda planteja la necessitat d'implicar-se amb el professorat de les aules en l'esdevenir de les pràctiques docents i en la millora de la didàctica de la llengua, de les llengües.

Epíleg

I ara, anem per feina!

Ara sí que han acabat les pàgines del llibre. Antigament, un cop el llibre sortia de la llibreria o la biblioteca, es feia difícil conèixer la vida que seguia. Ara, però, la situació ha canviat i el web del GREIP pot potenciar la relació amb els lectors i lectores. El manual, com a *opera aperta* que és, espera conèixer les vostres pràctiques per poder ser l'acompanyant fidel i crític que us ajudi a reescriure les seves pàgines.

Epilogue

Artur Noguerol[1]

Dear reader,

You have now arrived at the end of this handbook, assuming you have followed the order of the contributions. This reading has been an adventure shared with members of the GREIP research group. Let us hope that it will also be the beginning of a new, shared process of creating new educational practices, inspired and strengthened by these pages. In them, you will have found many tools and resources for research on plurilingual and intercultural education. Having come to the end of the handbook, however, does not mean an end at all, but rather the opening up of possibilities for action based on what you have read, and the beginning of new projects aimed at improving language and cultural learning in contexts of diversity. In addition to being a starting point, this handbook should be a faithful, yet critical companion for the journey that you embark on, as you take on new professional commitments, and you ask questions and seek answers.

This handbook is designed primarily as a guide for graduate students who want to conduct research on different aspects of plurilingual and intercultural education, which have been the main focus of GREIP's work. The handbook will prove to be a very useful instrument, as, throughout its pages, readers will encounter a variety of research proposals, practical tools and resources, and even clues for writing texts to communicate the results of research, and to give visibility to the work carried out in educational settings. For university students, the handbook offers guidance for the completion of research projects. Tools and resources are presented in relation to specific investigations, mostly with an ethnographic and conversation analytic approach, that give meaning and unity to the volume. These studies help show how, in order to be rigorous in the application of the

---

1. Universitat Autònoma de Barcelona, Bellaterra, Catalonia/Spain; artur.noguerol@uab.cat

How to cite: Noguerol, A. (2017). Epilogue. In E. Moore & M. Dooly (Eds), *Qualitative approaches to research on plurilingual education* (pp. 501-504). Research-publishing.net. https://doi.org/10.14705/rpnet.2017.emmd2016.645

Epilogue

proposals put forward in the handbook, one must be able to adapt to the specific circumstances of schools, classrooms and other educational settings.

The book also raises prospects that go beyond university-based studies and research, as it breaks with the traditional way of viewing the work of scholars, enclosed within institutions. It does this by tacking a relatively new approach to research in language teaching and learning, being that of plurilingual and intercultural education. This handbook encompasses, through different voices, the history of GREIP, a group based at a university that has always opened its doors to professional teachers and their educational practices, as central participants and objects of university research and teaching. GREIP breaks the boundaries between knowledge production and teaching practices: theory and practice are built reciprocally.

As several authors recommend in the handbook, active participation by the researcher and commitment to improving the processes of plurilingual and intercultural education must be embedded in research design. Teaching practices must be lived in order for research to be done on them, through participant observation or action research, among other approaches. In short, research should help critically mediate teaching processes in order to improve them. In the proposals found in this handbook, university students, university researchers and teachers engage on paths towards professional development. As the authors make clear, the goal of GREIP is to research collaboratively in order to find new ways of teaching languages in an integrated manner, to propose new ways of addressing the diversity of educational contexts in the multilingual societies we live in, and to ensure that plurilingual learners become adults who are sensitive to the linguistic diversity of their environment and the world.

Our society is undergoing profound and rapid changes that mean that, in language teaching, many key educational proposals have become a handicap to offering viable and effective responses to new situations. In this handbook, different conceptions of this plural and diverse reality, as well as how to teach languages, are touched on. In the different chapters, plurilingual and intercultural competence are referred to, as well as what it means to create educational activities for their development. This involves coordination and integration between different taught languages, while also considering students' languages, languages of the environment, and other languages with which learners interact. In addition, the handbook recognizes that language learning is a social activity that takes place in interaction with other people, either directly or through written or multimodal texts, and through the mediation of technology. This includes the research presented in the handbook on telecollaboration, among other emergent forms of communication in today's society. In the handbook, language teaching takes a global dimension that accounts for variations depending on the variety of texts, areas of use, channels, media, formats, modes of textual organization, languages, etc. In short, language is treated as what it truly is: a means for the construction of complex thought, emotions, and personal and social identities.

One of the particularities of the handbook is that it represents the life of a research group, whose members have become traveling companions. This more personal story can serve as a model for real improvements in language education. GREIP promotes cooperative reflection with teachers, researchers and teachers in training, focusing on the observation and study of students' competences, their common social practices, and the role of educational institutions in plurilingual and intercultural education. Working side by side with teachers is foregrounded in the handbook as an essential starting point. I have already said that the handbook could be a faithful companion, and a good journey should never be embarked on alone, as teamwork is the key to the development and professionalization of those engaged in language teaching. Two aspects of collaborative research must be kept in mind: firstly, the need, which emerges in all the chapters, to rely on teamwork, to be open to working as a group and to avoid becoming fixed on personal research goals; on the other hand, the need to engage with educators on the development of educational practices that improve the teaching of language, and of languages.

And now, let's get to work!

Now you really have finished reading. Previously, once a book left the library or the bookshop, it was difficult to know what life it had afterwards. The situation

Epilogue

has now changed and the GREIP website might serve to strengthen the group's relationships with readers. The authors of this handbook, as an *opera aperta*, also hope to hear about your own research practices, as critical and faithful companions, in order to rewrite these pages with your own experiences.

Author index
Índex d'autores i autors
Índice de autoras y autores

A
Antoniadou, Victoria vii, 237, 264, 435, 451

B
Borràs, Eulàlia vii, 469, 483

C
Canals, Laia vii, 377, 390
Corona, Víctor viii, 151, 170

D
Dooly, Melinda vi, 1, 11, 189, 212, 237, 264, 351, 363

L
Llompart, Júlia viii, 403, 418

M
Masats, Dolors viii, 293, 321
Moore, Emilee vi, 1, 11, 351, 363, 403, 418

N
Noguerol, Artur ix, xiii, 497, 501
Nussbaum, Luci ix, 23, 46

P
Pascual, Xavier x, 69, 88

Patiño, Adriana x, 107, 129

T
Tusón Valls, Amparo x, xiii, xiv, xviii

U
Unamuno, Virginia xi, 107, 129

V
Vallejo, Claudia xi, 351, 363

www.ingramcontent.com/pod-product-compliance
Lightning Source LLC
Chambersburg PA
CBHW021812300426
44114CB00009BA/145